The Politics of Justice in European Private Law

The Politics of Justice in European Private Law intends to highlight the differences between the Member States' concepts of social justice, which have developed historically, and the distinct European concept of access justice. Contrary to the emerging critique of Europe's justice deficit in the aftermath of the Eurozone crisis, this book argues that beneath the larger picture of the Monetary Union, a more positive and more promising European concept of justice is developing. European access justice is thinner than national social justice, but access justice represents a distinct conception of justice nevertheless. Member States or nation-states remain free to complement European access justice and bring to bear their own pattern of social justice.

Hans-W. Micklitz is Professor of Economic Law at the European University Institute in Florence, Italy. He is Finland Distinguished Professor at the University of Helsinki, 2015-2020, and Head of the Institute of European and Consumer Law (VIEW) in Bamberg. He has also been a consultant for the OECD, UNEP and CI (Consumers International), a visiting professor at the University of Michigan-Ann Arbor and at Columbia University, and a Visiting Fellow at Somerville College, University of Oxford.

Hans Micklitz's new book explores and illuminates the social and economic transformations leading to the emergence of European private law. It furthermore elucidates the concept of access justice on which European private law relies, and provides a spirited defense of the legal order it constitutes. *The Politics of Justice in European Private Law* is a major contribution to private law theory, and an essential reading for anyone serious about private law beyond the nation state.

    Hanoch Dagan, Stewart and Judy Colton Professor of Legal Theory and Innovation, Tel-Aviv University

Hans Micklitz's unerring pursuit of social justice through private law provides us here with an inspiring vision of societally responsible regulation in a post-State era. His reflections on the emergence of a specifically European legal consciousness are both a thoughtful response to the justice deficit critique frequently addressed to EU law in general, and a profound reflexion on the social values that lie somewhere beneath the surface of private law.

    Horatia Muir Watt, Professor, Sciences-Po Law School, Paris

'This new book by one of the leading voices in the debate on European private law and its politics, invites us to understand a wide range of seemingly incoherent interventions by EU law into the private laws of the member states, in the light of one single, powerful idea: access justice. The argument is lucid, though-provoking and impassioned at times. A must-read for anyone interested in the justice of European private law.'

    Martijn W Hesselink, Professor of Law, University of Amsterdam

Cambridge Studies in European Law and Policy

This series aims to produce original works which contain a critical analysis of the state of the law in particular areas of European law and to set out different perspectives and suggestions for its future development. It also aims to encourage a range of work on law, legal institutions and legal phenomena in Europe, including 'law in context' approaches. The titles in the series will be of interest to academics; policymakers, especially those who are interested in European legal, commercial and political affairs; practising lawyers, including the judiciary; and advanced law students and researchers.

Joint Editors

Professor Dr Laurence Gormley
University of Groningen
Professor Jo Shaw
University of Edinburgh

Editorial Advisory Board

Professor Kenneth Armstrong, *University of Cambridge*
Professor Catherine Barnard, *University of Cambridge*
Professor Richard Bellamy, *University College London*
Professor Marise Cremona, *European University Institute, Florence*
Professor Michael Dougan, *University of Liverpool*
Professor Dr Jacqueline Dutheil de la Rochère, *University of Paris II Pantheon-Assas, Director of the Centre for European Law, Paris*
Professor Daniel Halberstam, *University of Michigan*
Professor Dora Kostakopoulou, *University of Warwick*
Professor Dr Ingolf Pernice, *Director of the Walter Hallstein Institute, Humboldt University of Berlin*
Judge Sinisa Rodin, *Court of Justice of the European Union*
Professor Eleanor Spaventa, *Durham University*
Professor Neil Walker, *University of Edinburgh*
Professor Stephen Weatherill, *University of Oxford*

Books in the Series

The Politics of Justice in European Private Law
Hans-W. Micklitz

The Transformation of EU Treaty Making: The Rise of Parliaments, Referendums and Courts Since 1950
Dermot Hodson and Imelda Maher

Redefining European Economic Integration
Dariusz Adamski

Human Rights in the Council of Europe and the European Union
Steven Greer, Janneke Gerards and Rosie Slowe

Core Socio-Economic Rights and the European Court of Human Rights
Ingrid Leijten

Green Trade and Fair Trade in and with the EU: Process-Based Measures within the EU Legal Order
Laurens Ankersmit

New Labour Laws in Old Member States
Rebecca Zahn

The Governance of EU Fundamental Rights
Mark Dawson

The International Responsibility of the European Union: From Competence to Normative Control
Andrés Delgado Casteleiro

Frontex and Non-Refoulement: The International Responsibility of the EU
Roberta Mungianu

Gendering European Working Time Regimes: The Working Time Directive and the Case of Poland
Ania Zbyszewska

EU Renewable Electricity Law and Policy: From National Targets to a Common Market
Tim Maxian Rusche

European Constitutionalism
Kaarlo Tuori

Brokering Europe: Euro-Lawyers and the Making of a Transnational Polity
Antoine Vauchez

Services Liberalization in the EU and the WTO: Concepts, Standards and Regulatory Approaches
Marcus Klamert

Referendums and the European Union: A Comparative Enquiry
Fernando Mendez, Mario Mendez and Vasiliki Triga

The Allocation of Regulatory Competence in the EU Emissions Trading Scheme
Jospehine Van Zeben

The Eurozone Crisis Kaarlo Tuori and
Klaus Tuori

International Trade Disputes and EU Liability
Anne Thies

The Limits of Legal Reasoning and the European Court of Justice
Gerard Conway

New Governance and the Transformation of European Law: Coordinating EU Social Law and Policy
Mark Dawson

The Lisbon Treaty: A Legal and Political Analysis
Jean-Claude Piris

The European Union's Fight against Corruption: The Evolving Policy towards Member States and Candidate Countries
Patrycja Szarek-Mason

The Ethos of Europe: Values, Law and Justice in the EU
Andrew Williams

State and Market in European Union Law: The Public and Private Spheres of the Internal Market before the EU Courts
Wolf Sauter and Harm Schepel

The European Civil Code: The Way Forward
Hugh Collins

Ethical Dimensions of the Foreign Policy of the European Union: A Legal Appraisal
Urfan Khaliq

Implementing EU Pollution Control: Law and Integration
Bettina Lange

European Broadcasting Law and Policy
Jackie Harrison and Lorna Woods

The Transformation of Citizenship in the European Union: Electoral Rights and the Restructuring of Political Space
Jo Shaw

The Constitution for Europe: A Legal Analysis
Jean-Claude Piris

The European Convention on Human Rights: Achievements, Problems and Prospects
Steven Greer

Social Rights and Market Freedom in the European Constitution: A Labour Law Perspective
Stefano Giubboni

EU Enlargement and the Constitutions of Central and Eastern Europe
Anneli Albi

The Politics of Justice in European Private Law

Hans-W. Micklitz
European University Institute

CAMBRIDGE
UNIVERSITY PRESS

University Printing House, Cambridge CB2 8BS, United Kingdom

One Liberty Plaza, 20th Floor, New York, NY 10006, USA

477 Williamstown Road, Port Melbourne, VIC 3207, Australia

314-321, 3rd Floor, Plot 3, Splendor Forum, Jasola District Centre, New Delhi - 110025, India

79 Anson Road, #06-04/06, Singapore 079906

Cambridge University Press is part of the University of Cambridge.

It furthers the University's mission by disseminating knowledge in the pursuit of education, learning and research at the highest international levels of excellence.

www.cambridge.org
Information on this title: www.cambridge.org/9781108439374
DOI: 10.1017/9781108539777

© Hans-W. Micklitz 2018

This publication is in copyright. Subject to statutory exception and to the provisions of relevant collective licensing agreements, no reproduction of any part may take place without the written permission of Cambridge University Press.

First published 2018
First paperback edition 2020

A catalogue record for this publication is available from the British Library

Library of Congress Cataloging in Publication data
Names: Micklitz, Hans-W., author.
Title: The politics of justice in European private law / Hans-W Micklitz, European University Institute, Florence.
Description: Cambridge [UK] ; New York, NY : Cambridge University Press, [2018] | Series: Cambridge studies in European law and policy
Identifiers: LCCN 2018024668 | ISBN 9781108424127
Subjects: LCSH: Justice, Administration of – Political aspects – European Union countries. | Civil law – European Union countries. | Monetary unions – European Union countries. | Monetary policy – European Union countries. | European Union countries – Economic policy. | Financial crises – European Union countries | Social justice – European Union countries.
Classification: LCC KJE3655 .M53 2018 | DDC 346.4–dc23
LC record available at https://lccn.loc.gov/2018024668

ISBN 978-1-108-42412-7 Hardback
ISBN 978-1-108-43937-4 Paperback

Cambridge University Press has no responsibility for the persistence or accuracy of URLs for external or third-party internet websites referred to in this publication, and does not guarantee that any content on such websites is, or will remain, accurate or appropriate.

Contents

Preface	*page* xv
Series Editors' Preface	xix
Table of Cases	xxii

Introduction   1
The Argument   2
Introduction: Justice, State/the EU and Private Law   3
   1   The Transformation of Private Law, the Nation-State
       and Social Justice   4
      1.1   The Transformation to the Law of the Labour
            and Consumer Market Society   7
      1.2   The Transformation of the Nation-State
            and the European Experiment   10
      1.3   The Transformation of National Social Justice
            and European Access Justice   12
   2   The Theoretical Localisation of Access Justice   18
      2.1   Social Distributive, Allocative Libertarian
            and Access Justice   19
      2.2   Critique: Equal Opportunity and Market Justice   24
      2.3   Access Justice and Social Justice in Tandem   27
   3   Preconceptions and Methodology   30
      3.1   Ideological Criticism   31
      3.2   The Post-Classical Move   35
      3.3   Intellectual History and Legal Consciousness   38
   4   How to Read the Book   41

Part I The Awakening of the Social and Its Transformation in England, France and Germany — 45

1 Socioeconomic and Political Background of Social Justice in France, Germany and England — 47
- 1.1 A Chart towards Orientation — 48
- 1.2 The English Model: A Liberal and Pragmatic Design Fit for Commercial Use — 50
  - 1.2.1 English Pragmatism and English Personalism — 50
  - 1.2.2 Origins of Utilitarian Thinking — 54
  - 1.2.3 Societal Continuity and Economic Success — 57
  - 1.2.4 Intrusion of Social Justice into Labour Law — 58
  - 1.2.5 Intrusion of Social Justice into Consumer Law — 64
- 1.3 The French Model: An Intellectual Political Design of a (Just) Society — 67
  - 1.3.1 French Intellectualism — 68
  - 1.3.2 Origins of the Intellectual and Political Conception — 73
  - 1.3.3 Constitution and Code beyond National Boundaries — 76
  - 1.3.4 The Rise of 'The Social' via Self- and State Help — 79
  - 1.3.5 Politicising Private Law as Social Law — 83
- 1.4 The German Model: A Paternalistic Market Design — 89
  - 1.4.1 The Axiomatic Role of Law — 92
  - 1.4.2 Paternalistic Market Pragmatism and Idealistic Societal Visions — 97
  - 1.4.3 From Authoritarian to (Ordo-)Liberalism — 100
  - 1.4.4 Turmoil and Continuity — 103
  - 1.4.5 The German Civil Code and *Sonderprivatrecht* — 106
- 1.5 Conceptions of Social Justice in Comparison — 111
  - 1.5.1 Perceived Patterns of Justice — 111

		1.5.2	Perceived Function of the Role of Law in Remedying Social Justice Deficits	113
		1.5.3	Interaction between Market Order, Society and the Social	115
		1.5.4	Social Expectations, Relationship between State and Individuals	117

2 Success and Failure of Social Justice through Private Law — 119

2.1 The 'Social' Effective, Desirable, Affordable and Efficient — 119

2.2 Measuring the Distributive (Collective) Effectiveness of Private Law — 124
  2.2.1 A Blind Eye on Facts — 125
  2.2.2 Expert Statements — 128
  2.2.3 Collective Control of Standard Contract Terms — 130

2.3 Measuring the Social (Individual) Effectiveness in Private Law — 134
  2.3.1 Imbalance of Power — 135
  2.3.2 Status — 137
  2.3.3 Access to Justice — 140

2.4 Social Effectiveness vs. Economic Efficiency — 145
  2.4.1 Relaxed Attention: Socially Achieved? — 146
  2.4.2 Efficiency and Society — 148

3 Path Dependency, Irritations: The Post-Classical Move? — 152

3.1 Irritations at the Foundational Level of the Three Models — 153

3.2 Irritations at the Surface Level of Labour and Consumer Law — 156

Part II Justice beyond the Nation-State: The European Experiment — 161

1 Socioeconomic and Political Background of Social Justice in the EU — 163

1.1 A Chart towards Orientation — 164

1.2 The First Thirty Years Built on the Common
    Intellectual History   166
    1.2.1 The First Thirty Years, 1957–1986   166
    1.2.2 The Common Heritage   168
1.3 The Heyday of the Social, 1986 until 2000
    and Beyond   172
    1.3.1 The Second Phase   173
    1.3.2 The Limits of the Common Heritage   176
1.4 The Post-Classical Move in the European
    Integration   180
    1.4.1 The Lisbon Council, Economic Efficiency
          and Social Inclusion   181
    1.4.2 Constitutional Standstill and Political
          Move to Financial Inclusion   186
    1.4.3 The Post-Classical Foundations   191

2 **The Impact of EU Law on Employment,
   Non-Discrimination and Consumer Law**   196
   2.1 A Chart for an Overview of Primary and
       Secondary EU Law   196
   2.2 The Impact of the Determinants on Labour
       and Non-Discrimination Law   201
       2.2.1 Establishing the Free Movement of
             Workers   203
       2.2.2 Building Social Europe after 1986   207
       2.2.3 From Labour to Non-Discrimination
             Law after Lisbon 2000   211
       2.2.4 The Post-Classical EU Labour and
             Non-Discrimination Law   215
   2.3 The Impact of the Determinants on
       Consumer Law   222
       2.3.1 Establishing the Consumer Protection
             Paradigm   225
       2.3.2 Building European Consumer Law
             after 1986   228
       2.3.3 From Consumer Protection Law to
             Consumer Law and Back   233
       2.3.4 The Post-Classical Consumer Law   239

3	**Post-Classical European Private Law in Outline**	246
	3.1 General Features of Post-Classical Private Law	246
	3.2 General Features of the Private Law Laboratory	251
4	**The Way Ahead: Rationality Test, Shared Responsibilities, Fragmented Status**	257
	4.1 The Power and Reach of the Rationality Test	258
	4.2 Shared Public-Private Competences and Shared Public-Private Responsibilities	265
	4.3 Fragmented Status, Fragmented Justice and Legal Consciousness	270
5	**Summary: Social, Access and Societal Justice**	276

Part III Considerations on the Post-Classical Private Law 281

1	**The Basic Elements of the Tripartite Private Law Order**	283
2	**Universal Service Obligations (USOs)**	288
	2.1 The Vulnerable	291
	2.2 Access and Substance	295
	2.3 Rights, Remedies and Procedures	302
	2.4 Balancing of USOs and Residence Rights	307
	2.5 Order of Competence and Responsibilities	310
3	**The Law of the Labour and Consumer Market Society**	316
	3.1 The Vulnerable, the Weak and the Confident	318
	3.2 Access and Substance	325
	3.3 Rights, Remedies and Procedures	334
	3.4 Balancing of Rights, Expectations and Needs	344
	3.5 Order of Competence and Responsibilities	352
4	**The 'Societal' Private Law**	358
	4.1 The Self and the Societally Responsible	360
	4.2 Substance Shaping	364
	4.3 Rights, Remedies and Procedures	368
	4.4 Balancing of Legitimate Expectations beyond the State	373
	4.5 Order of Competence and Responsibilities	377
5	**Summary**	383

Conclusions and Outlook — 385
1 Path Dependency of National (Social) Legal Consciousness — 386
2 European (Social) Legal Consciousness — 388
3 Hybridisation of Legal Consciousness — 389
4 European Access Justice and European Societal Justice — 390
5 The Tripartite European Private Legal Order — 392
6 Shared Competences, Shared Responsibilities of the EU, MS and PPs — 393
7 Drivers behind the Transformations — 395
8 Rationality Test — 396
9 European Laboratory — 398
10 Brexit, the Social and European Legal Consciousness — 400
11 Interaction between European and National Private Law — 402
12 'Geometric' and 'Relative' State — 404

Bibliography — 406
Index — 451

Preface

The idea of the book has preoccupied me since I accepted Thomas Wilhelmsson's invitation to speak at the University of Helsinki in 1993 on the subject of social justice in European private law. It is there I developed the concept of 'legitimate expectations' as a European model of justice. The second trigger was an invitation by Horatia Muir Watt and Ruth Sefton-Green at the French *Cour de Cassation* in 2007 to speak about social justice. How does the European concept of legitimate expectations fit into the nation-state's understanding of social justice in private law? The French Revolution, the elaboration of the Code Civil and its transformation were the 'natural' starting points for such a research question, complemented by England/the United Kindom and Germany. However, Germany was 100 years behind in nation-state building and private law building. The comparative analysis encouraged me to dive into the intellectual history of the three countries. The book project took shape when I joined the European University Institute in 2007. It led, in a first step, to the edited volume *The Many Concepts of Social Justice in Private Law,* published in 2011. The different contributions combine three strands of discussions: the legal philosophical debate on social justice, the path dependence of social justice in nation-states, and the development of social justice beyond the nation-state through the European Union (EU) and through international institutions.

My European Research Council (ERC) project on European Regulatory Private Law (2011–2016)[1] enabled me to give shape to the European

---

[1] The research leading to these results has received funding from the European Research Council under the European Union's Seventh Framework Programme (FP/2007–2013) / ERC Grant Agreement no. [269722].

regulatory private law and its patterns of justice. The present book bears a comparative dimension on the path dependency of national private law orders, on the rise and decline of social justice in private law during the twentieth century and on the genuinely European dimension that started by and large with the adoption of the Single European Act in 1986, which paved the way for the EU to engage in social regulation. In the aftermath of the now uncertain future of the EU, it is a book on risks and opportunities, on if and how social justice in European private law appears and how it may look in the post-nation-state area. In that sense, it will not lose its importance even if the EU collapses. It informs about the opportunities and the limits of transnational justice and the remaining responsibility of the nation-state.

Ten years of thinking and writing were also ten years of discussion, of feedback, and of rewriting. I presented earlier versions of the argument at the universities of Amsterdam, Bigli Istanbul, Helsinki, Oxford and Tel Aviv. I would like to thank G. Alpa, O. Ben Shahar, R. Brownsword, F. Cafaggi, H. Collins, G. Comandé, H. Dagan, M. Freedland, F. Gomez, R. van Gestel, L. Gormley, S. Grundmann, A. Hartkamp, A. Héritier, M. Hesselink, C. Hodges, A. Höland, E. Hondius, G. Howells, P. Letto-Vanamo, M. Loos, C. Mak, G. Miller, M.-A. Moreau, F. Möslein, H. Muir Watt, L. Niglia, K. Nuoti, A. Potocki, K. Riesenhuber, T. Roethe, P. Rott, C. Sabel, M. Safjan, R. Sefton-Green, C. Sieburg, J. Smits, A. Somma, J. Stuyck, K. Tonner, C. Torp, Tuori, S. Weatherill, T. Wilhelmsson, C. Willett and B. de Witte for their critique and their enduring scepticism over so many years. Three of my colleagues deserve more than just a general expression of gratitude. N. Reich, my mentor, colleague and friend, accompanied me through the early years of formation and thinking. He could not share the final version with me, but his written comments allowed me to engage into a spiritual dialogue. The German words of my colleague and friend Dennis Patterson spoken in his wonderful American accent will ring in my ears forever: Hans, *Du musst Dein Buch schreiben* ('Hans, you must write your book'), as did his lasting challenge 'What is your argument? I do not see your argument'. Thomas Roethe and I have conducted an endless number of projects. We discussed the deeper questions behind the book in all variations without coming even close to agreement. He does not share my optimism:

Nothing, neither access justice nor the experimental character of the EU, will ever work. The municipal reality in the Land of Lower Saxony [where he lives] is identical. The EU has erroneously safeguarded universal instead of particular (EU fortress) rights. The EU leaves alone all those citizens who are the true Europeans between Niebüll (Northern Germany) and Salzburg (Austria) and who still know how everything fits together.

Over the last ten years, I have continuously asked young researchers for their input, critique and advice. My wholehearted thanks go to L. de Almeida, M. Cantero Gamito, K. Carr, G. Comparato, R. Condon, E. Deutscher, L. Diez-Sanchez, I. Domurath, J. Habib, B. Kas, B. v. Leeuwen, H. Marjosola, F. della Negra, P. Palka, K. Purnhagen, H. Schebesta, B. Schüller, Y. Svetiev, R. Vallejo, R. Xenidis and J. Zglinski. You raised endless questions that challenged my argument and allowed me to sharpen my ideas. Rónán Condon became my interlocutor on the theoretical dimension of access justice; Yane Svetiev on the implications of the turn to experimentalist governance and its theoretical implications for European private law; and Guido Comparato sharpened my awareness on nationalism in private law and on financialisation. Rónán Condon brought the book written in my best 'Germish' into better English, giving it hopefully an Irish flavor. Dawn Wade offered additional editing help. Betül Kas supported me patiently in formatting footnotes and producing a bibliography. Without you this book would not exist and certainly not in the current form! I owe you more than you might think. Last but certainly not least, I bow to my wife, Alexandra, for her patience, for her encouragement over so many years and for the uncountable hours she saw me sitting at my computer and supplied me with tea, juice, fruits and vegetables. And not only this: my wife, as well as my daughter Maxie, were so empathic with my research that, though both are non-lawyers, they discovered two foundational books that influenced the overall argument.

Series Editors' Preface

The European Union's aim, expressed in Article 3(1) TEU, is 'to promote peace, its values and the well-being of its peoples'. Unsurprisingly, it is to work for, inter alia, 'a highly competitive social market economy, aiming at full employment and social progress (Article 3(3) TEU), and is to promote, inter alia, 'social justice and protection'. The values on which the Union is founded include the rule of law, and Article 47 of the Charter of Fundamental Rights of the Union emphasizes the right to an effective remedy and a fair trial. Access to justice becomes an element of access justice, which is at the heart of the various rights guaranteed to European citizens and market participants. It is also at the heart of the duties to ensure those rights imposed by the TEU and the TFEU on the Member States and on the Union institutions.

Access justice moves beyond national social justice, becoming transformed into societal justice through participation in the development of the Union and the achievement of its objectives. In this European transnational context, in which European citizens and market participants perceive familiar private law rights and duties balanced and rebalanced in the light of wider objectives, the wider horizons afforded by European societal private law are not always welcomed by those concerned with protecting their cosy cartels or their local petty protectionist practices. Yet the European Union Treaties, like the American Constitution, are founded on the basis that we all sink or swim together, and that European society is broader than life in the local hamlet. The European Union project makes an appeal to greatness of soul, not pettiness of mind: the village next door is not the limit of the neighbourhood, and my neighbour may well be a European market participant, not necessarily a European citizen. While the European vision does not displace national conceptions, it complements and at the same time challenges them by affording new dimensions. It seeks to enrich minds rather than to close them.

This book seeks to counter the arguments about a perceived justice deficit, which are frequently raised in the literature. Micklitz rightly observes that 'What is missing in the debate is the post-nation-state dimension that is enshrined in the European integration project. Most of the time, more implicitly than explicitly, the benchmark for measuring the EU is an idealised version of the old national welfare state. In the transnational society beyond the nation-state, the responsible consumer-citizen has more freedom but also more responsibilities towards society' (p. 363).

This work is a remarkable and thought-provoking contribution to the literature on European law and policy, and it forces its readers to look at the dimensions of the European project, in particular its private law aspects, through wider, yet more clearly focused eyes. Micklitz recognises that 'Access and societal justice are the result of a dynamic interactive process where the Member States, the EU and private parties are involved' (p. 391). Normatively, he sees access justice as requiring the breaking down of barriers limiting participation and access, strengthening the position of workers and consumers in enforcing their rights in a multi-governance legal order, and establishing an institutional design capable of coping with the move from social protection laws to laws on the consumer and labour market. Societal justice requires in his vision a further step, an overarching element opening up private law relationships to take account of third parties affected by interpersonal agreements. It embraces the people, the workers, the consumers, the employers, and suppliers in a European society. This society is market-biased, but is not limited to the market, as Micklitz well demonstrates. Moving away from the focus on classical legal categories into a new understanding or a new perception is fundamental to the understanding of the challenges and perspectives opened up by the European societal order.

Micklitz's book challenges established ideas and confronts them with their limitations. It presents a vision and understanding that sees a clear path. There is clearly a way to go, and Micklitz does not shy away from the problems, but this important work will broaden the horizons of scholars, policymakers, and the judiciary, and stimulate researchers to plough new furrows and broaden their horizons. This impressive work is the product of mature reflection by a distinguished scholar, and we are very pleased indeed to welcome it in the *Cambridge Studies in Law and Policy* series.

Laurence Gormley
Jo Shaw

Table of Cases

ECJ Case Law

Case 8/74, *Dassonville* [1974] ECR 837.
Case 36/74, *Walrave and Koch* v. *Association Union Cycliste Internationale and Others* [1974] ECR 1405.
Case 43/75, *Defrenne v. Sabena* [1976] ECR 455.
Case 120/78, *Rewe-Zentral AG v. Bundesmonopolverwaltung für Branntwein* [1979] ECR I-649.
Case 14/83, *Von Colson and Kamann v. Land Nordrhein-Westfalen* [1984] ECR I-1891.
Case C- 143/83 *Commission v. Kingdom of Denmark* [1985] ECR 427
Case 178/84, *Commission v. Germany* [1987] ECR I-1227.
Case 103/88, *Fratelli Costanzo v. Comune di Milano* [1989] ECR I-1839.
Case C-262/88, *Barber v. Guardian Royal Exchange Assurance Group* [1990] ECR I-1889.
Case C-339/89, *Alsthom Atlantique* [1991] ECR I-107.
Joined cases C-6/90 and C-9/90, *Francovich and Bonifaci v. Italy* [1991] ECR I-5357.
Joined cases C-241/91 P and C-242/91 P, *RTE and ITP v. Commission* [1995] ECR I-743.
Case C-93/92, *CMC Motorradcenter v. Baskiciogullari* [1993] ECR I-5009.
Case C-127/92, *Enderby v. Frenchay Health Authority and Secretary of State for Health* [1993] ECR I-5535.
Case C-392/92, *Schmidt v. Spar- und Leihkasse der früheren Ämter Bordesholm, Kiel und Cronshagen* [1994] ECR I-1311.
Case C-408/92, *Smith and Others v. Avdel Systems* [1994] ECR I-4435.

Joined cases C-46/93 and C-48/93, *Brasserie du pêcheur* v. *Bundesrepublik Deutschland and The Queen / Secretary of State for Transport, ex parte Factortame and Others* [1996] ECR I-1029.
Case C-415/93, *Union royale belge des sociétés de football association and Others* v. *Bosman and Others* [1995] ECR I-4921.
Case C-192/94, *El Corte Inglés* v. *Blázquez Rivero* [1996] ECR I-1281.
Case C-233/94, *Germany* v. *Parliament and Council* [1997] ECR I-2405.
Case C-265/95, *Commission* v. *France* [1997] I-6959.
Case C-269/95, *Benincasa* v. *Dentalkit* [1997] ECR I-3767.
Case C-67/96, *Albany* [1999] ECR I-5751.
Case C-85/96, *Martínez Sala* v. *Freistaat Bayern* [1998] ECR I-2691.
Case C-220/98, *Estée Lauder* [2000] ECR I-117.
Case C-240/98, *Océano Grupo Editorial and Salvat Editore* [2000] ECR I-4941.
Case C-281/98, *Angonese* [2000] ECR I-4139.
Case C-376/98, *Germany* v. *Parliament and Council* [2000] ECR I-8419.
Case C-381/98, *Ingmar GB* [2000] ECR I-9305.
Case C-309/99, *Wouters and Others* [2000] ECR I-1577.
Case C-453/99, *Courage and Crehan* [2001] ECR I-06297.
Case C-481/99, *Heininger* [2001] I-9945.
Case C-541/99, *Cape and Idealservice MN RE* [2001] ECR I-9094.
Case C-96/00, *Gabriel* [2002] ECR I-6367.
Case C-183/00, *González Sánchez* [2002] ECR I-3901.
Case C-473/00, *Cofidis* [2002] ERC I-10875.
Joined cases C-397/01 to C-403/01, *Pfeiffer and Other* [2004] ECR I-8835.
Case C-147/03, *Commission* v. *Austria* [2005] ECR I-5969.
Case T-289/03, *BUPA and Others* v. *Commission* [2008] ECR II-81.
Case C-436/03, *Parliament* v. *Council* [2006] ECR I-3733.
Case C-27/04, *Commission* v. *Council* [2004] I-6649.
Case C-144/04, *Mangold* [2005] ECR I-9981.
Case C-295/04, *Manfredi* [2006] ECR I-06619.
Case C-13/05, *Chacón Navas* [2006] ECR I-6467.
Case C-127/05, *Commission* v. *United Kingdom* [2007] ECR I-4619.
Case C-168/05, *Mostaza Claro* [2006] ECR I-10421.
Case C-341/05, *Laval un Partneri* [2007] ECR I-11767.
Case C-411/05, *Palacios de la Villa* [2007] I-8531.
Case C-429/05, *Rampion and Godard* [2007] ECR I-8017.
Case C-432/05, *Unibet* [2007] ECR I-2271.
Case C-438/05, *The International Transport Workers' Federation and The Finnish Seamen's Union* [2007] ECR I-10779.

Case C-64/06, *Telefónica 02 Czech Republic* [2007] ECR I-4887.
Case C-243/08, *Pannon GSM* [2009] ECR I-04713.
Case C-404/06, *Quelle* [2008] ECR I-02685.
Case C-445/06, *Danske Slagterier* [2009] ECR I-2119.
Case C-501/06 P, *GlaxoSmithKline Services and Others v. Commission and Others* [2009] ECR I-9291.
Case C-54/07, *Feryn* [2008] ECR I-5187.
Case C-205/07, *Gysbrechts and Santurel Inter* [2008] ECR I-9947.
Case C-227/08, *Martín Martín* [2009] ECR I-11939.
Case C-237/07, *Janecek* [2008] I-06221.
Case C-239/07, *Sabatauskas and Others* [2008] ECR I-7523.
Case C-555/07, *Kücükdeveci* [2010] ECR I-00365.
Case C-40/08, *Asturcom Telecomunicaciones* [2009] ECR I-9579.
Case C-58/08, *Vodafone and Others* [2010] ECR I-4999.
Case C-137/08, *VB Pénzügyi Lízing* [2010] ECR I-10847.
Case C-147/08, *Römer* [2011] ECR I-3591.
Case C-265/08, *Federutility and Others* [2010] ECR I-3377.
Case C-310/08, *Ibrahim und Secretary of State for the Home Department* [2010] ECR I-1065.
Case C-317/08, *Alassini and Others* [2010] ECR I-2213.
Case C-325/08 *Olympique Lyonnais* [2010] ECR I-02177.
Case C-480/08, *Teixeira* [2010] ECR I-1107.
Case C-484/08, *Caja de Ahorros y Monte de Piedad de Madrid* [2010] ECR I-4785.
Case C-34/09, *Ruiz Zambrano* [2011] ECR I-1177.
Case C-45/09, *Rosenbladt* [2010] ECR I-9391.
Case C-65/09, *Gebr. Weber und Putz* [2011] ECR I-5257.
Case C-208/09, *Sayn-Wittgenstein* [2010] ECR I-13693.
Case C-236/09, *Association Belge des Consommateurs Test-Achats and Others* [2011] ECR I-773.
Case C-250/09, *Georgiev* [2010] ECR I-11869.
Case C-391/09, *Runevič-Vardyn and Wardyn* [2011] ECR I-3787.
Case C-70/10, *Scarlet Extended* [2011] ERC I-11959.
Case C-76/10, *Pohotovost'* [2010] ECR I-11557.
Case C-453/10, *Pereničová and Perenič* [2012] ECR I-000.
Case C-472/10, *Invitel* [2012] ECR I-000.
Case C-618/10, *Banco Español de Crédito* [2012] ECR I-000.
Case C-12/11, *McDonagh* [2013] ECR I-000.
Case C-92/11, *RWE Vertrieb* [2013] ECR I-000.
Joined Cases C-335/11 and C-337/11, *HK Danmark* [2013] I-000

Case C-171/11, *Fra.bo* [2012] ECR I-000.
Case C-202/11, *Las* [2013] ECR I-000.
Case C-283/11, *Sky Österreich* [2013] ECR I-000.
Case C-394/11, *Belov* [2013] ECR I-000 000.
Case C-399/11, *Melloni* [2013] ECR I-000.
Case C-415/11, *Aziz* [2013] ECR I-000.
Case C-426/11, *Alemo-Herron and Others* [2013] ECR I-000.
Case C-472/11, *Banif Plus Bank* [2013] ECR I-000.
Case C-604/11, *Genil 48 und Comercial Hostelera de Grandes Vinos* [2013] ECR I-000.
Case C-32/12, *Duarte Hueros* [2013] ECR I-000.
Case C-174/12, *Hirmann* [2013] ECR I-00.
Case C-270/12, *United Kingdom v. Parliament and Council* [2014] ECR I-00.
Case C-222/13, *TDC* [2014] ECR I-00.
Case C-333/13, *Dano* [2014] ECR I-00.
Case C-370/12, *Pringle* [2012] I-00.
Case C-497/13, *Faber* [2015] ECR I-00.
Case C-1/14, *Base Company und Mobistar* [2015] ECR I-00.
Case C-36/14, *Commission v. Poland* [2015] ECR I-00.
Case C-83/14, *CHEZ Razpredelenie Bulgaria* [2015] ECR I-00.
Case C-169/14, *Sánchez Morcillo and Abril García* [2014] ECR I-00.
Joined Cases C-381/14 and C-385/14, *Sales Sinués* [2016] ECR I-00.
Case C-508/14, *T-Mobile Czech Republic and Vodafone Czech Republic* [2015] ECR I-00.
Case C-613/14, *James Elliott Construction* [2016] ECR I-00.
Case C-105/15 P, *Mallis and Malli v. Commission and the ECB* [2016] ECR I-00.
Case C-119/15, *Biuro podróży Partner* [2016] ECR I-00.
Case C-121/15, *ANODE* [2016] ECR I-00.
Joined cases C-154/15, C-307/15 and C-308/15, *Gutiérrez Naranjo* [2016] ECR I-00.
Case C-191/15, *Verein für Konsumenteninformation* [2016] ECR I-00.
Case C-201/15, *AGET Iraklis* [2016] ECR I-00.
Case C-219/15, *Schmitt* [2017] ECR I-00.
Case C-75/16, *Menini and Rampanelli* [2017] ECR I-00.
ECJ Opinion 2/13, *Adhésion de l'Union à la CEDH*.

UK Case Law

High Court, Ford Motor Co v. Amalgamated Union Of Engineering And Foundry Workers (A.U.E.W.) [1969] 2 QB 303.

Supreme Court, Liverpool v. Irwin [1977] AC 239.
High Court, Customs and Excise Commissioners v. ApS Samex [1983] 1 All ER 1042, 3 CMLR 194.
Supreme Court, James v. Eastleigh Borough Council [1990] 2 AC 751 HL.
Supreme Court, Office of Fair Trading v. Abbey National plc & Others [2009] UKSC 6.
Supreme Court, Cavendish v. Makdessi; ParkingEye v. Beavis [2015] UKSC 67.

German Case Law

Bundesverfassungsgericht, *Lüth* [1958] 1 BvR 400/51.
Bundesarbeitsgericht, *Friedenspflicht – Schlichtungsvereinbarung der IG Metall* [1958] 1 AZR 632/57.
Bundesverfassungsgericht, *Bürgschaftsverträge* [1993] 1 BvR 567/89, 1 BvR 1044/89.
Bundesverfassungsgericht, *Vertrag von Lissabon* [2009] 2 BvE 2/08, 2 BvE 5/08, 2 BvR 1010/08, 2 BvR 1022/08, 2 BvR 1259/08, 2 BvR 182/09.

French Case Law

Cour de Cassation, *Bancherau* v. *Chronopost*, D. 1997, Jur., p. 121.

Others

High Court of Australia, *Hollis* v. *Vabu* [2001] HCA 44.
Appeal Court of Brussels, *D. Duchesne* v. *Office of Fair Trading* [2005].
ECHR, *Grainger* v. *the UK* [2012] No. 34940/10.
Spanish Supreme Court, [2013] No. 241/2013 (ES:TS:2013:1916) and [2015] No. 139/2015 (ES:TS:2015:1280).

Introduction

The 'Politics of Justice in Private Law' intends to highlight the differences between the Member States' concepts of social justice, which have developed historically, and the distinct European concept of access justice. Contrary to the emerging critique of Europe's justice deficit in the aftermath of the Eurozone crisis, I argue that beneath the larger picture of the Monetary Union, a more positive and more promising European concept of justice is developing. European access justice is thinner than national social justice, but access justice represents a distinct conception of justice nevertheless. It is both descriptive and normative.[1] I will neither defend national cultures and traditions[2] nor proclaim European access justice as a substitute for national social justice. Member States/nation-states remain free to complement European access justice and bring to bear their own pattern of social justice. However, the ongoing economic and societal transformations force us in light of 'intuitively felt cracks'[3] to rethink national patterns of social justice and their compatibility with the European concept of justice. This book defends the European experiment as good and useful. The European legal order and European society yield genuine social

---

[1] J. Neyer, 'Justice and the Right to Justification: Conceptual Reflections', discusses justice in the EU as a substitute for democracy; R. Forst, 'Justice, Democracy and the Right to Justification: Reflections on Jürgen Neyer's Normative Theory of the European Union', claims that a just political order can only be a democratic order, in D. Kochenov, G. de Búrca and A. Williams (eds.), *Europe's Justice Deficit?* (Oxford: Hart Publishing, 2015), pp. 211-226; pp. 227-234, respectively.
[2] U. Mattei and A. di Robilant, 'The Art and Science of Critical Scholarship. Post-Modernism and International Style in the Legal Architecture of Europe' (2002) 10 *European Review of Private Law* 29-59.
[3] H. J. Berman, *Recht und Revolution. Die Bildung der westlichen Rechtstradition* (Frankfurt a.M.: Suhrkamp, 1991), at pp. 47, 65.

values. Nostalgia for the national welfare state of the 1970s or the sovereign nation-state is not likely to be an adequate answer to the societal and economic transformations which arose at the beginning of the twenty-first century.

The Argument

The clarion call for justice in private law, which first emerged in the late nineteenth century, places the nation-state in a prominent position. Today, the nation-state is subject to deeply penetrating transformation processes that affect its ability to deliver its preferred option of justice.[4] The European experiment – the building of a transnational quasi-statutory entity through law with all its turbulence – allows us to study the effects of these transformation processes on private law, on the nation-state and on patterns of justice. Peering through a looking glass, EU private law mirrors the limits of the national welfare state, but also allows us to study the potential for building a concept of justice beyond the nation-state in a regulated economy through private law – access justice. Long-standing national legal traditions and legal cultures clash with the transformative power of the EU that challenges entitlements held dear but offers opportunities for rethinking justice through private law. Here is a tentative definition:

Access justice materialises the *theoretical chance* of EU citizens to participate in the market so as to make it a *realistic opportunity*. Access justice lays down *procedural* requirements for proper enforcement of EU private law. Access justice provides for an *institutional* design that allows for the participation of EU citizens in civil society. Access justice distributes and redistributes opportunities. Therefore, access justice should be understood as a thin version of social distributive justice. However, in its participatory form it turns into societal justice.

The following introduction highlights the transformation of private law, of the nation-state and of social justice. It provides guidance to the theoretical localisation of access justice and the methodology used. The overall argument of the book is then unfolded in three consecutive steps. The first part analyses the transformation process of social justice in the private legal orders of France, Germany and the United Kingdom.

---

[4] H.-W. Micklitz and D. Patterson, 'From the Nation-state to the Market: The Evolution of EU Private Law as Regulation of the Economy beyond the Boundaries of the Union?', in B. van Vooren, S. Blockmans and J. Wouters (eds.), *The EU's Role in Global Governance. The Legal Dimension* (Oxford: Oxford University Press, 2013), pp. 59–78.

Despite all the alterations, the three legal orders demonstrate intellectual path dependency, which, however, was severely shattered only after the Second World War through the European integration process. How the EU is interfering in the foundations of private law and the patterns of justice is the theme of the Part II. It goes to show that the EU is developing a genuine model of access justice that sits uncomfortably with national patterns of justice and provokes strong political and ideological reactions.[5] The third part is devoted to identifying the shape of the new private law beyond the nation-state, which is already in the making. All three parts lead to a single conclusion: Access justice is claimed to be the paradigm for the emergent private law order beyond the nation-state.

Introduction: Justice, State/the EU and Private Law

The history of the transformations of private law, the nation-state and social justice needs to be structured. D. Kennedy's[6] distinction between the three waves of globalisation of legal thought, from classical legal thought to the Social and from there to neoformalism helps explain the three transformations. The three waves are used as labels that capture a set of common features in each of the three epochs, but they leave space for contingency in the evolution of scenarios. At the apogee of classical legal thought, the 'state' is governed through formal law expressing norms of corrective justice. During the second wave of globalisation of legal thought, 'the Social' arises as a general pattern in social welfare states that comes to dominate private law. The third wave of globalisation is characterised by Kennedy's concept of neoformalism.[7] Private law thinking intrudes into the formerly public sector, the different policies and institutions, shattering established patterns of social justice. The nation-states have new challenges to master, in which social and distributive justice appear in a new light,

---

[5] In a similar direction though not discussing private law, F. de Witte distinguishes between market, communitarian and aspirational solidarity in *Justice in the EU. The Emergence of Transnational Solidarity* (Oxford: Oxford University Press, 2015).
[6] D. Kennedy, 'Three Globalizations of Law and Legal Thought: 1850–2000', in D. M. Trubek and A. Santos (eds.), *The New Law and Economic Development. A Critical Appraisal* (Cambridge; New York: Cambridge University Press, 2006), pp. 19–73.
[7] D. Kennedy uses neoformalism, in particular through his claim of 'managing difference'. The critique that he forgets about the role and function of the 'market' seems to be overstated, J. Desautels-Stein and D. Kennedy, 'Foreword: Theorizing Contemporary Legal Thought' (2015) 78 *Law and Contemporary Problems* i–x.

no longer as a matter of the nation-state alone, but as one that affects the overall position of each nation-state vis-à-vis the global economy.[8]

The next step is to delineate access justice from pure market justice[9] and to clarify the relationship between the European model of access justice and national patterns of social justice. The substantive part of this Introduction concludes with a clarification on the chosen three-layered methodology which underpins the overall argument. First and foremost, there is ideological criticism on the over-instrumentalisation of the law as a means to build a social market and a more just society. The European experiment contributes to dismantle blind spots[10] in the national welfare state *and* to provide a forum for the suggested post-classical move that lays bare the architecture of post-national private law. Legal consciousness and intellectual history constitute the third layer and serve as the tool through which the transformation process of the last 200 years can be reconstructed, explained and made comprehensible. In what comes I will first analyse the transformations, then locate access justice before I turn to the preconceptions and the methodology.

1 The Transformation of Private Law, the Nation-State and Social Justice

The Member States of the European Union developed over the twentieth century their own model of social justice in private law. For the purposes of this book, private law is understood as economic law. It covers contract and tort as well as labour law, non-discrimination law and consumer law.[11] Each model of social justice is inherently linked to the specificities of the particular country, its economic and social conditions, and the national culture and tradition. However, all

---

[8] D. Patterson and A. Afilalo, *The New Global Trading Order: The Evolving State and the Future of Trade* (Cambridge; New York: Cambridge University Press, 2008); P. Bobbitt, *The Shield of Achilles: War, Peace, and the Course of History* (New York: Anchor Books, 2003).
[9] J. N. Adams and R. Brownsword, 'The Ideologies of Contract' (1987) 7 *Legal Studies* 205-223.
[10] C. Joerges, 'On the Legitimacy of Europeanising Private Law: Considerations on a Law of Justi(ce)-fication (justum facere) for the EU Multi-Level System', in A. Hartkamp, M. W. Hesselink, E. Hondius, C. Joustra, E. du Perron and M. Veldman (eds.), *Towards a European Civil Code*, 3rd ed. (Alphen aan den Rijn: Kluwer Law International; Nijmegen: Ars Aequi Libri, 2004), pp. 159-190.
[11] H. D. Assmann, G. Brüggemeier, D. Hart and C. Joerges (eds.), *Wirtschaftsrecht als Kritik des Privatrechts* (Königstein/Ts.: Athenäum, 1980).

models have in common that sooner or later it is for the (nation) state[12] to use the law as a means to protect the weaker party against the stronger party, the employee against the employer, the tenant against the landlord,[13] and the consumer against the supplier. Therefore, social justice is bound to the idea of redistribution of wealth and loss shifting from the richer to the poorer part of the society, individually and collectively. That is where the idea of the social welfare state is located and that is where the rhetoric of social distributive justice via the (nation) state is rooted.

The integration of social justice into private law and the rise of the welfare state in the twentieth century were made possible through the economic, social, political and technological developments that shook Europe between the seventeenth and nineteenth century and that freed private law from feudal and corporative (*ständische*) barriers.[14] Social justice itself is a product of the late nineteenth and early twentieth centuries, a result of the socialist labour movement. States responded to the rise of the labour movement in various ways, mostly by transforming their private law systems through the '*protective*' welfare state in the late nineteenth and early twentieth centuries. The second wave of social justice started after World War II with the rise of the consumer society.[15] Again states' private law systems were confronted with the call for social justice. This time the response came from the 'regulatory' welfare state. Labour law became a subject of its own and emigrated from the private law system, becoming a separate area of law. A similar development can be observed in consumer law, which is

---

[12] B. Hepple, 'Welfare Legislation and Wage-Labour', in B. Hepple (ed.), *The Making of Labour Law in Europe: A Comparative Study of Nine Countries up to 1945* (London: Mansell Publishing, 1986), pp. 114–153, p. 122 'very uneven development'.

[13] 'TENLAW: Tenancy Law and Housing Policy in Multi-level Europe' directed by Christoph Schmid, Centre of European Law and Politics at the University of Bremen, www.tenlaw.uni-bremen.de/.

[14] J.-W. Hedemann, *Die Fortschritte des Zivilrechts im XIX. Jahrhundert. Ein Überblick über die Entfaltung des Privatrechts in Deutschland, Österreich, Frankreich und der Schweiz. Erster Teil. Die Neuordnung des Verkehrslebens*, Vol. I (Berlin: Heymann, 1910). Hedemann was later involved in the Nazi regime and in the development of the so-called Volksgesetzbuch (the attempt of Third Reich jurists in the Akademie für Deutsches Recht to replace the Bürgerliche Gesetzbuch by a civil law code aligned with the principles of National Socialism).

[15] On the much longer history of consumption, F. Trentmann, *Empire of Things: How We Became a World of Consumers, from the Fifteenth Century to the Twenty-First* (London: Penguin Books, 2016); on the rise of the consumer society after World War II, p. 272.

about to segregate from private law independent of its form, whether it is part of a national civil code or not.[16]

The European Economic Community (EEC) as originally envisaged in the 1950s, in contrast, was to be built on a clear separation of responsibilities, between the EEC – to establish the Common Market – and the Member States that remained responsible for social policy.[17] The constitutional construction of the EEC changed considerably over time. Since the adoption of the Single European Act in 1986, the European Union bears a 'social outlook', which gradually developed over time and has now taken shape in the Lisbon Treaty and the Charter of Fundamental Rights. There was even an ongoing discussion on an existing or emerging European Social Model,[18] which is currently being superseded by debates about the injustice resulting from the Eurozone crisis and the way it is managed through the EU, Member States and the IMF.[19] The democratic and social deficit critiques are not new. They have accompanied the EU from its beginning and gained pace after the Single European Act in 1986, which granted the EU powers in social regulation. However, the Eurozone crisis has added a new layer to the debate about the justice deficit and its proclaimed neoliberal outlook,[20] which has placed the blame for undermining national democracies firmly at the door of the EU. This debate somewhat overshadows that the EU is not the cause of the transformation process and that its role and function needs a much

---

[16] H.-W. Micklitz, 'Do Consumers and Businesses Need a New Architecture for Consumer Law? A Thought Provoking Impulse' (2013) 32 *Yearbook of European Law* 266-367; against a separate codification, M. W. Hesselink, 'Post-Private Law?' and E. Hondius, 'Against a New Architecture of Consumer Law – A Traditional View', in K. Purnhagen and P. Rott (eds.), *Varieties of European Economic Law and Regulation: Liber Amicorum for Hans Micklitz* (New York: Springer International Publishing, 2014), pp. 31-42 and pp. 599-610, respectively.

[17] Intergovernmental Committee on European Integration, *The Brussels Report on the General Common Market* (hereafter referred to as 'Spaak Report'), June 1956, available at: http://aei.pitt.edu/995/1/Spaak_report.pdf.

[18] F. Rödl, 'Labour Constitution', in A. v. Bogdandy and J. Bast (eds.), *Principles of European Constitutional Law*, 2nd ed. (Oxford: Hart Publishing, 2009), pp. 623-658; N. Countouris, 'European Social Law as an Autonomous Legal Discipline' (2009) 28 *Yearbook of European Law* 95-122; B. P. T. Haar and P. Copeland, 'What Are the Future Prospects for the European Social Model? An Analysis of EU Equal Opportunities and Employment Policy' (2010) 16 *European Law Journal* 273-291.

[19] F. W. Scharpf, 'Monetary Union, Fiscal Crisis and the Pre-Emption of Democracy' (2011) 9 *Zeitschrift für Staats- und Europawissenschaften / Journal for Comparative Government and European Policy* 163-198.

[20] W. Streeck, *How Will Capitalism End?* (London: Verso, 2016).

more sophisticated understanding here enshrined in the model of shared responsibilities.[21]

1.1 The Transformation to the Law of the Labour and Consumer Market Society

Member States developed their national labour laws long before the European Union turned into a political, economic and social actor. Where the European Union succeeded in gaining competence through various treaty amendments, the matters were either genuinely European in that they concerned cross-border issues within the EU or the competence transfer was to serve, in tacit agreement with the majority of the Member States, the 'modernising'[22] of national economies so as to make them fit for competing in ever more globalised markets. The 'erosion' of the welfare state and the 'decline' of the Social lie at the heart of social justice critiques of the EU.[23]

'Modernisation' does not take on the same contours in the three Member States under scrutiny. One might wonder, therefore, who is modernising whom – is the EU modernising the Member States, or are the Member States modernising the EU? It will be shown that UK labour law precedes labour law developments via the EU. Therefore, UK labour law might be the driver behind the EU approach on labour law, with some modifications through the promotion of social rights. In consumer law, Member States left the field to the EU, which is about to develop a second generation of consumer law that reaches beyond national welfarist thinking.[24] In reaction to the Eurozone crisis, the EU legislator is gradually developing a genuine approach with regard to investor protection and debtor protection, though it seems

---

[21] Y. Svetiev, 'The EU's Private Law in the Regulated Sectors: Competitive Market Handmaiden or Institutional Platform?' (2016) 22 *European Law Journal* 659-680, at 679-680; also see in more detail in Part II. 4.2, this volume.

[22] B. Eichengreen, *The European Economy since 1945: Coordinated Capitalism and Beyond* (Princeton: Princeton University Press, 2008), pp. 335-341; S. Weatherill, 'Competence and Legitimacy', in C. Barnard and O. Odudu (eds.), *The Outer Limits of European Union Law* (Oxford: Hart Publishing, 2009), pp. 17-34, stresses the potential of EU law to overcome nationalism and protectionism in Member States.

[23] C. Crouch, *The Strange Non-Death of Neo-Liberalism* (Cambridge: Polity Press, 2011); A. Somek, *The Cosmopolitan Constitution* (Oxford: Oxford University Press, 2014).

[24] Report of the Advisory Council for Consumer Affairs at the Federal Ministry of Justice and Consumer Protection, 'Consumer Rights 2.0: Consumers in the Digital World', available at: www.svr-verbraucherfragen.de/en/wp-content/uploads/sites/2/Report-1.pdf.

as if the European Court of Justice (ECJ), rather than the EU legislator, is the driving force.[25]

The functional transfer of regulatory powers from Member States to the European Union since the adoption of the White Paper on the Completion of the Single European Market in 1985[26] has triggered a fierce debate; first, on Europe's *social deficit* in the aftermath of *Viking* and *Laval*[27] and, second, on Europe's *justice deficit*. Scholars ask why Member States were not ready to grant the EU more comprehensive powers to shape and elaborate the Social? A rather simple explanation is the unwillingness of the Member States to build the 'United States of Europe' after 1989 with a common social, economic and fiscal policy. This suggests that the Social could have been preserved in a fully federalised European Union. The subtler explanation is that the Member States needed the EU to prepare their citizens for the much more competitive economic, political and social environment. Therefore, the 'debate on deficits' – social deficit, democratic deficit, justice deficit – could be explained as a tension between models of the national welfare state and the fact that there may be limits to the Social in a globalised economy.

The EU's limited competences did not allow for deeper intervention into labour law, at least if one understands labour law as reaching beyond personal employment law. A holistic view demonstrates the EU's limited impact on industrial relations, social security, collective bargaining, minimum wages and unemployment policy,[28] and commercial and company law.[29] The two most visible developments notwithstanding the EU's restricted competence relate to the much debated approach taken to the role and function of trade unions in the making and enforcement of self-standing rules (*Viking* and *Laval*) and, secondly, the individualisation of the employees through subjective enforceable 'rights'.

---

[25] G. Comparato, *The Financialisation of the Citizen* (Oxford: Hart Publishing, forthcoming 2018).

[26] COM (85) 310 final, 14.6.1985

[27] Case C-438/05, *The International Transport Workers' Federation und The Finnish Seamen's Union* [2007] ECR I-10779; Case C-341/05, *Laval un Partneri* [2007] ECR I-11767.

[28] B. Hepple and B. Veneziani, 'Introduction', in B. Hepple and B. Veneziani (eds.), *The Transformation of Labour Law in Europe. A Comparative Study of 15 Countries 1945–2004* (Oxford: Hart Publishing, 2009), pp. 1–29, at p. 3.

[29] S. Deakin and F. Wilkinson, *The Law of the Labour Market. Industrialization, Employment and Legal Evolution* (Oxford: Oxford University Press, 2005), p. 2, covers social security, active market policy, and even elements of commercial, competition and company law.

National consumer law, in contrast, was not at rest yet in Member States when the European Union took on a leading policy role.[30] The European Union 'saved' consumer law from its decline in the Member States, transforming it into an instrument of Internal Market-building and, later, for the management of the Eurozone crisis.[31] That is why consumer law *with* or *without* protection[32] is of particular interest for the concept of justice. In national law, van der Heijden characterises regulatory intervention as 'inequality compensation'[33]: 'the legislator has considered it useful and necessary to compensate the economic imbalance between employer and employee through law'. At an EU level, however, new language is required that combines EU market and European society building. It might be more appropriate to speak of the European 'law of the labour market society' and the European 'law of the consumer market society'. Only such a label combines the two perspectives, the market and the society.[34]

The EU has introduced a third dimension into the debate on the Social, a dimension which is crucial for understanding the European social morals and for conceptualising the European model of justice. Art. 119 ECC Treaty of Rome introduced 'Equal Pay of Men and Women' (now Art. 141 TFEU). The various treaty amendments broadened the scope of equal pay in Art. 141 TFEU and expanded the recognised forms of discrimination. The EU legislature extended the reach of the anti-discrimination principle to transgender, race, age, disability and religion. Today EU anti-discrimination law has expanded into ever wider fields of the economy and society. Member States with a colonial past had adopted race discrimination laws long before. The change in language from anti- to non-discrimination changes the

---

[30] H.-W. Micklitz, 'The Visible Hand of European Regulatory Private Law: The Transformation of European Private Law from Autonomy to Functionalism in Competition and Regulation' (2009) 28 *Yearbook of European Law* 3-59.

[31] F. Della Negra, *Private Law and Private Enforcement in the Post-Crisis EU Retail Financial Regulation*, PhD thesis, European University Institute (2017).

[32] H.-W. Micklitz, 'The Expulsion of the Concept of Protection from the Consumer Law and the Return of Social Elements in the Civil Law: A Bittersweet Polemic' (2012) 35 *Journal of Consumer Policy* 283-296.

[33] P. van der Heijden, 'Post-industrial Labour Law and Industrial Relations in The Netherlands', in Lord Wedderburn, M. Rood, G. Lyon-Caen, W. Däubler and P. van der Heijden (eds.), *Labour Law in the Post-Industrial Era: Essays in Honour of Hugo Sinzheimer* (Aldershot: Dartmouth, 1994), pp. 133-148, 135-136; R. Dukes, *The Labour Constitution: The Enduring Idea of Labour Law* (Oxford: Oxford University Press, 2014).

[34] R. Münch, 'Constructing a European Society by Jurisdiction' (2008) 14 *European Law Journal* 519-541, analyses the role of the ECJ in the making of transnational society.

focus. Non-discrimination is positive, namely an obligation to find discrimination, whereas anti-discrimination is negative, it limits discrimination where it is found and brought to the public (judicial) attention.[35] The ethics of non-discrimination as an overarching principle is directly connected to what D. Kennedy termed the third wave of globalisation of legal thought.[36]

Since the White Paper on the Completion of the Internal Market[37] the EU has adopted a large amount of secondary legislation. The regulations and directives influence private law matters either directly (consumer, labour, non-discrimination, commercial and company law directives) or indirectly (directives meant to liberalise markets, e.g. telecommunication, postal services, energy or electricity, gas, transport, health care and financial services). The first set of rules mimic the design of *protective* legislation in line with national social welfare thinking. The second set of rules move away from protective regulation to social market regulation, from social distributive justice to European access justice. The European rules on labour, non-discrimination and consumer law are governed by a different philosophy, which cannot be brought in line with the social welfare understanding of justice. These three areas of European regulatory private law form the core of the analysis in the Member States (Part I), the EU (Part II) and in the tripartite private legal order beyond the nation-state (Part III).

1.2 The Transformation of the Nation-State and the European Experiment

European integration, the building of a genuine European legal order in the words of the ECJ, and what others refer to as the European 'constitutional charter' cannot be compared with the twentieth-century social welfare state. The European legal order represents a unique constitutional construct, which is neither a nation-state in the European sense nor a federation of states in the American understanding. There is strong support for the uniqueness of the European legal order and for the opportunities it offers in the post-nation-state era;[38] however, there

---

[35] Part II. 2.2.
[36] Kennedy, 'Three Globalizations of Law and Legal Thought'.
[37] COM (85) 310 final, 14.6.1985.
[38] L. Azoulai, 'The Court of Justice and the Social Market Economy: The Emergence of an Ideal and the Conditions for its Realisation' (2008) 45 *Common Market Law Review* 1335–1355; Svetiev, 'The EU's Private Law in the Regulated Sectors'; C. F. Sabel and J. Zeitlin, 'Learning from Difference. The New Architecture of Experimentalist

is equally strong and growing critique.³⁹ Insisting on the particularities of the European legal order is claimed to be 'unhelpful' and 'dogmatic' when it comes to discussing 'justice'.⁴⁰ The political basis of the self-legitimating European integration process seems to be exhausted. Defending the EU is demanding. Much ink has been spilt on the open constitutional design of the EU. In 2017, the EU appeared more than ever to be an experiment with an open outcome. The common heritage that guided European nation-states to overcome the legacy of two world wars did not help to manage the political challenges after the fall of the Berlin Wall and the economic challenges of increased globalisation.⁴¹

There is no doubt that European integration is challenging national social welfare state models and with it the Social. This lay behind the understanding of the EU as a market state and of the EU as the driver of the transformation process.⁴² However, the Eurozone crisis and its impact on the European periphery⁴³ have made leftist dreams of a 'social Europe' implausible. The European version of the 1970s welfare state could not compensate for the decline of the national social welfare state in the 1980s. Redistribution requires rich states to support poor states. Europe is about to move into the opposite direction by introducing a kind of fair return principle where Member States assume that contributions to the

---

Governance in the EU' (2008) 14 *European Law Journal* 271-327; C. F. Sabel and O. Gerstenberg, 'Constitutionalising an Overlapping Consensus: The ECJ and the Emergence of a Coordinate Constitutional Order' (2010) 16 *European Law Journal* 511-550.

³⁹ The different contributions in D. Kochenov, G. de Búrca and A. Williams (eds.), *Europe's Justice Deficit?* (Oxford: Hart Publishing, 2015) can be grouped around two camps, those who focus on the downside and those who see potential. Here is a rough overview on the argument: Nagel under reference to Rawls: no background justice beyond the state (p. 4); Forst: a just political order is a democratic order (p. 10); Somek: human rights and fundamental rights no substitute (p. 13); Williams: justice and rights are different (p. 33); Menendez: no justice without democratic politics (pp. 145-146); Menéndez: the EU legal order is taking politics away from democracy (p. 139); Wilkinson: European integration has eroded the Keynesian Westphalian compromise (p. 123); Davies: politicization no panacea (p. 11). At the other end are those who rely on the potential, Gerstenberg and Viehoff/Nicolaïdis: fertile testing ground for hybrid theories of justice (p. 12); Wilkinson: no reason why the EU cannot be treated as offering a form of community or society (pp. 117-118).

⁴⁰ D. Kochenov, 'The Ought of Justice', in D. Kochenov, G. de Búrca and A. Williams (eds.), *Europe's Justice Deficit?* (Oxford: Hart Publishing, 2015), pp. 21-33.

⁴¹ C. Glinki and C. Joerges, 'European Unity in Diversity?! A Conflicts-Law Reconstruction of Controversial Current Developments', in K. Purnhagen/P. Rott (eds.), *Varieties of European Economic Law and Regulation: Liber Amicorum for Hans Micklitz*, pp. 285-314, p. 289, frame the question in terms of the 'exhaustion of the legal integration theory'.

⁴² Micklitz and Patterson, 'From the Nation-State to the Market'.

⁴³ D. Kukovec, 'Law and the Periphery' (2015) 21 *European Law Journal* 406-428.

EU budget should result in roughly equivalent returns from the EU.[44] The zero-interest policy of the European Central Bank (ECB), to the contrary, might regressively redistribute wealth, and not only to the detriment of the citizens in the crisis states.[45] The focus of this book is not on macro level ECB policy, but on the micro level of private law. The 'justice deficit' of the EU when measured against national welfare state standards should not overshadow the social and societal dimension of the EU and the EU private law order. Against Rawls' statement that there cannot be justice 'beyond the state'[46], the EU succeeds in doing justice in a supranational legal order and for a transnational European society. In a complex division of competences, the quasi-statutory character of the EU leaves room for Member States to maintain their level of social justice, according to their available resources and the willingness of Member States' citizens to pay through higher taxes.[47] Access justice is not meant to substitute national patterns of justice.

1.3 The Transformation of National Social Justice and European Access Justice

From Aristotle to Rawls, justice has been regarded as the elemental part of social morals, whose recognition human beings owe each other.[48] Social justice bears a *collective* element, the protection not of individuals alone but of individuals who form particular groups within society. Social justice is not at the core of classical (philosophical) theories of justice. Social justice emerges in Marxist and socialist theories.[49] Two lines of

---

[44] A. J. Menéndez, 'Whose Justice? Which Europe?', in D. Kochenov, G. de Búrca and A. Williams (eds.), *Europe's Justice Deficit?* (Oxford: Hart Publishing, 2015), pp. 137–152, p. 149 with a deeper analysis of those parts of the society within the Member States who benefit from the return.

[45] P. Triana, 'Debt That Costs Less Than Nothing: Greece's Unique Opportunity' (2017), available at: https://papers.ssrn.com/sol3/papers.cfm?abstract_id=2941023.

[46] J. Rawls, *The Law of Peoples* (Cambridge, MA: Harvard University Press, 1999).

[47] S. Steinmo, *The Evolution of Modern States. Sweden, Japan, and the United States* (New York: Cambridge University Press, 2010).

[48] O. Höffe, *Gerechtigkeit. Eine philosophische Einführung* (München: C. H. Beck, 2001) and O. Höffe, 'Soziale Gerechtigkeit. Über die Bedingungen realer Freiheit', short version, (2005) *Neue Zürcher Zeitung* 67.

[49] K. Marx, 'On the Jewish Question', in J. O'Malley and R. A. Davies (eds.), *Marx. Early Political Writings* (Cambridge: Cambridge University Press, 1994), pp. 28–56;
E. Paschukanis, *Allgemeine Rechtslehre und Marxismus*, 3rd ed. (Frankfurt a.M.: Verlag Neue Kritik, 1970), p. 33; Paschukanis, one of the leading Marxist legal theorists, developed the idea from the withering of the law in a socialist society (Absterben des Rechts). Already Lenin underlined the role of law as a means to realise Marxism-Leninism; see E. Bloch, *Naturrecht und menschliche Würde* (Frankfurt a.M.: Suhrkamp, 1961), p. 252.

arguments have to be kept distinct in the discourse: first, the idea of social justice as distributive justice where it remains for the state to redistribute wealth between citizens so as to achieve a fairer balance between the rich and the poor; second as a principle of political action to create a better and more just society. In the words of A. Sen[50]: 'a theory of justice that can serve as the basis of practical reason must include ways of judging how to reduce injustice and advance justice rather than aiming only at the characterisation of perfectly just societies.'

The analysis focuses on the ways in which matters of justice found their way into the protective welfare state and later into the EU, its historical origins, its rise in the three nation-states, and later its transformation through the EU. In Germany, Christian social ethics, namely catholic social theory, played a crucial role in the transformation of a socialist movement which grew outside the political order into a democratic movement inside the political order.[51] In the United Kingdom, a similar story can be told regarding the trade union movement/formation of the Labour party and, in their case, Methodists.[52] Pope Leo VIII's encyclical *Rerum Novarum* (*New Things*; 1891) gave rise to a 'new vision' of a state, which had to compensate for the missing social structures (rural families, guilds) of the Industrial Age. It even paved the way for internationally recognising that *labour is not a commodity*, but encompasses a *societal dimension*. The Social was introduced in the Treaty of Versailles 1919, then reiterated in the Declaration of Philadelphia adopted by the International Labour Organisation in 1944:[53] 'All human

---

[50] A. Sen, *The Idea of Justice* (Cambridge, MA: Harvard University Press, 2009) as quoted by S. Douglas-Scott, 'Justice, Injustice and the Rule of Law in the EU', in D. Kochenov, G. de Búrca and A. Williams (eds.), *Europe's Justice Deficit?* (Oxford: Hart Publishing, 2015), pp. 51–66, at p. 63.

[51] F. Wieacker, *A History of Private Law in Europe*, translated by T. Weir (Oxford: Clarendon Press, 1995), p. 470; F. Wieacker, *Privatrechtsgeschichte der Neuzeit unter besonderer Berücksichtigung der deutschen Entwicklung*, 2nd rev. ed. (Göttingen: Vandenhoeck & Ruprecht, 1967), p. 600.

[52] 'The English Labour Movement was not in itself explicitly religious but it was nevertheless permeated by religion both in its origin and in its subsequent development. Its roots lay in three areas in particular: the French revolutionary spirit of 'liberty, fraternity and equality', early Owenite socialism and John Wesley's Methodist religion of the poor', N. Scotland, 'Methodism and the English Labour Movement 1800–1906' (1997) 14 *Anvil* 36–48, available for free via Google.

[53] Hepple and Veneziani, 'Introduction', p. 5; T. Ramm, 'Epilogue: The New Ordering of Labour Law 1918–45', in B. Hepple (ed.), *The Making of Labour Law in Europe. A Comparative Study of Nine Countries up to 1945* (London; New York: Mansell, 1986), pp. 277–300, at p. 298 claiming that the ILO declaration was inspired through Roosevelt's essential freedoms.

beings irrespective of race, creed or sex, have the right to pursue both their material well-being and their spiritual development in conditions of freedom, dignity, of economic security and equal opportunity.' The distributive dimension of the social justice paradigm – something that will have to be demonstrated – opened the door for economic consideration. Today social distributive justice is under pressure through economic efficiency.[54]

It is clear that social changes led to the rise of labour law in the late nineteenth century, later consumer law[55] in the twentieth century, at least in industrialised Western democracies. The process of societal differentiation (*Ausdifferenzierung der Gesellschaft*)[56] has yielded different fields of law – not withstanding their common origin – private law relations, have ended up in segmentation. Labour law and land law (tenancy law), laws which are only loosely tied to the bigger world of private law, became a matter for specialists. 'Yielding' is certainly a debatable circumscription of what in societal reality was the result of a century-long fight and fierce conflict.[57] The highly conflictual dimension behind justice in labour law is highlighted in Jhering's famous book *Kampf ums Recht* (*The Struggle for Law*) which alludes to Darwin's 'struggle for life' concept.[58]

Historically, there is a strong connection between labour law and non-discrimination law, both with regard to gender and to race. Women were not only excluded from the political process until the early twentieth century, but they were also barred from participating in the labour market. Where they were granted access to the labour market, they suffered from many forms of discrimination. In that sense, equal treatment of men and women bears a strong moral connotation. The position of women within the family – the famous three Ks, *Kinder, Küche und Kirche* (children, kitchen and church)[59] – remained untouched

---

[54] Part I. 2.4.
[55] The early origins of consumer protection have long been neglected, but now K. Soper and F. Trentmann (eds.), *Citizenship and Consumption* (Basingstoke, England; New York: Palgrave Macmillan, 2008); H.-G. Haupt and C. Torp (eds.),
Die Konsumgesellschaft in Deutschland 1890–1990. Ein Handbuch (Frankfurt; New York: Campus Verlag, 2009).
[56] N. Luhmann, *Soziale Systeme. Grundriss einer allgemeinen Theorie* (Frankfurt a.M.: Suhrkamp, 1984).
[57] The description of the strikes in the British Mining Industry 1921/1926, Ramm, 'Epilogue', p. 277; Hepple and Veneziani, 'Introduction', pp. 1–3, 25–26.
[58] Wieacker, *A History of Private Law*, p. 447.
[59] S. Paletschek, 'Kinder, Küche, Kirche', in É. François and H. Schulze (eds.), *Deutsche Erinnerungsorte*, Vol. 2 (München: C.H. Beck, 2001), pp. 419–433; R. Bridenthal, 'Beyond Kinder, Küche, Kirche. Weimar Women at Work' (1973) 6 *Central European History* 148–166.

for a long time despite their integration into the labour market. The second strand of development comes from race discrimination.[60] The former colonial countries were supposed to integrate citizens of the colonies into their national labour market. It took international institutions and later the European Union to turn non-discrimination into a genuine European legal principle,[61] covering all forms of discrimination and reaching far beyond the labour market deeply into society. Today, non-discrimination law is about to separate from labour law and become a self-standing discipline.[62] This is the new political and juridical battlefield that divides national societies, legal systems and courts.

What remains is consumer law. Consumer law is certainly not the result of a 'fight' between two conflicting parties, perhaps with the exception of France.[63] Even in the heyday of national consumer policy in the 1960s and 1970s, such a material language would not correctly capture the character of the conflict, which was much more located in the political fora than in civil society. Health and safety issues (the thalidomide catastrophe and later Bhopal)[64] and the eviction of over-indebted house owners were rare occasions that raised political and societal awareness.[65] In consumer law the linkages to traditional private law are still close, although consumer law drives the ongoing materialisation of private law.[66] This finding holds true whether

---

[60] B. Hepple, 'Equality at Work', in B. Hepple and B. Veneziani (eds.), *The Transformation of Labour Law in Europe. A Comparative Study of 15 Countries 1945–2004* (Oxford: Hart Publishing, 2009), pp. 129–164, at pp. 133–134.

[61] The literature is abundant with regard to private law; N. Reich, *General Principles of EU Civil Law* (Cambridge: Intersentia, 2014), Chapter 3, pp. 59–88.

[62] D. Schiek, 'Zwischenruf: Den Pudding an die Wand nageln? Überlegungen zu einer progressiven Agenda für das EU-Anti-Diskriminierungsrecht' (2014) 47 *Kritische Justiz* 396–402; D. Schiek, L. Waddington and M. Bell (eds.), *Cases, Materials and Text on National, Supranational and International Non-Discrimination Law* (Oxford: Hart Publishing, 2007); M. Bell, *Anti-Discrimination Law and the European Union* (Oxford; New York: Oxford University Press, 2002).

[63] It is a pity that Trentmann's fascinating history of consumption (*Empire of Things*) does not engage with countries where the rise of consumer law bears a very strong political dimension, such as Spain or Brazil.

[64] For the thalidomide catastrophe, see, e.g. P. Derleder and G. Winter, 'Die Entschädigung für Contergan' (1976) *Demokratie und Recht* 260–304.

[65] H.-W. Micklitz and I. Domurath (eds.), *Consumer Debt and Social Exclusion in Europe* (Farnham; Burlington: Ashgate, 2015).

[66] C.-W. Canaris, 'Wandlungen des Schuldvertragsrechts – Tendenzen zu seiner "Materialisierung"' (2000) 200 *Archiv für die civilistische Praxis* 273–364, at least as long 'materialisation' is equated with contractual justice as it is done here; pp. 282–292, where he distinguishes between three forms of materialisation (materialisation of

consumer law forms an integral part of civil codes or whether it is separated from the civil code and compiled in a separate body of law. The deeper reason for the separation of labour and consumer law might be their greater permeability to social concerns. Societally the conflicts to be solved quite often cut across the two fields of law.[67]

The EU's takeover of the Social results from a political decision by the Member States to enshrine social elements in the Single European Act. It accelerated the transformation of the Social and the EU, which manifested itself in the changing face of social law and of the conception of justice that lies behind it. In the place of social distributive justice, a genuinely European concept of access justice is emerging. European access justice responds to the transformation of the state through globalisation, the decline of the Social and changes in society. Social justice presupposes the existence of a 'well-ordered society' (Rawls) whose citizens are able and willing to take the necessary redistributive steps. Access justice transcends nation-state thinking and takes matters of justice beyond the nation-state. Access justice involves not only the multi-level dimension in the EU and the shared competences between the EU and the Member States, but it also provides the deeper foundations as to why private actors have to accept political and social responsibilities. Access justice gains a thicker relational dimension in that not only the state but also companies and private individuals bear a legal responsibility towards and beyond the contracting parties. This is not to claim that the European legal order has already recognised the deep change in the private legal order. Such a consequence is in the offing ever since *Viking* and *Laval*[68] and the 'reverse' rationalisation logic which follows from the *Cassis de Dijon* doctrine.[69] The result is a shared responsibility for access which is shared between the political branches of the EU and Member States, as well as private parties.

Invoking access to the Internal Market and barring access to European society cannot be dismissed as an instance of instrumentalisation for the market alone. It is, rather, a genuine and emerging concept of post-national justice that enshrines a substantive and an

---

private autonomy, materialisation of contractual justice and of the politics behind materialisation); and pp. 320–364, where he analyses consumer law.

[67] H. Collins, *Regulating Contracts* (Oxford; New York: Oxford University Press, 1999), pp. 70–74 discussing *Liverpool v Irwin* [1977] A.C. 239.

[68] Azoulai, 'The Court of Justice and the Social Market Economy'.

[69] Case 120/78, *Rewe-Zentral AG v Bundesmonopolverwaltung für Branntwein* [1979] ECR I-649; see also Part II. 4.1.

institutional procedural dimension; it guarantees materialised access and involves trade unions and civil society organisations.

The substantive dimension is most outspoken in the non-discrimination principle. The latter mutated from gender discrimination to a kind of catch-all rule for discrimination on the basis of nationality, sexual orientation, race/ethnicity, age, disability and religion, migrating ever more broadly and deeply from the economic into the societal environment. Whilst this strand of development focuses on social discrimination through unequal treatment, there is a second strand of development that emphasises the consequences of economic discrimination through price discrimination and/or through unaffordable prices in universal services.[70] Another way to capture the overall importance of the non-discrimination principle is to stress the move from social to financial inclusion. One might go as far as to argue that the non-discrimination principle in its two strands constitutes the European contribution to a distinct moral system in private law and maybe even in European society. European access justice guarantees the people of Europe the right to discrimination-free access to the market, as workers and as consumers, but also access to society, where participation depends on access to basic services.

Access justice reaches beyond individually enforceable rights. Access justice invokes an institutional procedural dimension. Historically trade unions claimed the right to negotiate and to monitor the relationship between workers and employers. It will have to be shown that in line with the rise of the welfare state thinking, nation-states were getting ever more deeply involved in the shaping of industrial relations. Art. 118 b) SEA (now Art. 155 TFEU) introduced 'Social Dialogue' as a means to promote collective labour agreements at the EU level. The expectations set into the mechanism were never realised, though.[71] In light of *Viking* and *Laval*, justice through collective agreements has turned into a particularly sensitive political issue, where the EU is all too often seen as the mere cause of social decline. A fairer account seems to be that the EU and the ECJ are accelerating a process

---

[70] However, the different classes of consumers allow for 'discrimination'; see Part III. 2.1, 3.1, 4.1.

[71] As to possible parallels with Weimar-era corporatism and its blatant failure, C. Thornhill, 'The Constitutionalization of Labour Law and the Crisis of National Democracy', in P. F. Kjaer and N. Olsen (eds.), *Critical Theories of Crisis in Europe. From Weimar to the Euro* (London: Rowman & Littlefield, 2016), pp. 89–105.

that has its origin in the transformation of the economy and the society. Collective agreements outside the labour market never reached a similar level of legal and political awareness at EU level, although the transformation of labour and consumer law to the law of the labour and consumer market *society* leaves ample space for the participation of non-governmental organisations in the making and enforcement of collective agreements. With regard to labour law, Hugh Collins has characterised what is at stake. His findings can be read in conjunction with consumer law:[72]

> Workers and employers [consumers and suppliers] are not merely private actors in the labour market [the consumer market], but also participants in the process of governance that reconcile the needs of social cohesion and a broad notion on citizenship with the pressing requirements constantly to improve the competitiveness of the relations of production [consumption HM].

Emphasis should be placed on the move from private actors in the market to participants in transnational European society, from mere economic to political actors, from workers and consumers in private bilateral relations, to worker citizens and consumer citizens in a political order that surpasses the national, i.e. nation-state, boundaries. Access justice through collective agreements breaks down individualisation and enables a collective justice management through the involvement of societal organisations and associations in the making and the monitoring of contractual relations far beyond individual discrimination and individual exclusion. The potential will have to be demonstrated throughout the analysis of the tripartite legal order beyond the nation-state.[73]

2 The Theoretical Localisation of Access Justice

What remains to be done is to locate access justice within the justice discourse. European private law, this is my argument, escapes the economic, social and political polarisation between *social distributive justice* and *allocative (libertarian) justice*. This results from the particularities of the European experiment. The EU remains a quasi-statutory entity that regulates the economy and society beyond the nation-state. It is here where *access justice* crystallises. But what then is access justice, positively

---

[72] H. Collins, *Employment Law*, 2nd ed. (Oxford: Oxford University Press, 2010), p. 259.
[73] Part III. 2.5; 3.5; 4.5.

speaking? Where can it be located?[74] Is access justice *more* than allocative libertarian justice but *less* than social distributive justice, standing in the middle between the two? Or must it be regarded as a new category of justice?[75] I will first delineate access justice from social justice and allocative libertarian justice, before I engage into the critique that access justice is no more than market justice and that it challenges more far-reaching normative standards of justice. The localisation exercise requires clarification of treaty competences and societal responsibilities of the Member States and the EU. European access justice, this is my claim, is normative and descriptive. It reaches beyond the market. It does not replace national patterns of justice but stands side-by-side with national patterns of social justice, legally and societally.

2.1 Social Distributive, Allocative Libertarian and Access Justice

The theoretical localisation is developed in three steps: first, access justice is distinguished from social redistributive justice; second, it is distinguished from allocative libertarian justice before, third, the concept of access justice is positively elaborated.

First, access justice differs from national protective concepts in that it does not primarily aim at social protection in a redistributive perspective. The addressees of EU labour law and first-generation consumer law are not the 'poor who pay more' – to allude to Caplovitz's[76] famous study. These are the dynamic, open-minded, flexible, well-informed, self-standing and self-conscious mobile workers who travel around Europe and would accept a job anywhere. It is the consumer who seeks the best value on the market of consumer goods and services to reap the benefits of the Internal Market.[77] The normative *leitbild*, which dominates EU

---

[74] S. Robin-Olivier, (2012) 48(4) *Revue Trimestrielle de Droit European* LXXVI-LXXIX and N. Reich, (2013) 50 *Common Market Law Review* 1523-1525 in their review of H.-W. Micklitz (ed.), *The Many Concepts of Social Justice in European Private Law* (Cheltenham: Edward Elgar, 2011).

[75] H. Dagan, 'Between Regulatory and Autonomy-Based Private Law' (2016) 22 *European Law Journal* 644-658 and M. W. Hesselink, 'Private Law, Regulation and Justice' (2016) 22 *European Law Journal* 681-695; L. Niglia, Law or Economics – Some Thoughts on Transnational Private Law, in K. Purnhagen/P. Rott (eds.), *Varieties of European Economic Law and Regulation: Liber Amicorum for Hans Micklitz*, pp. 93-104; H. Dagan and M. Heller, *The Choice Theory of Contracts* (Cambridge; New York: Cambridge University Press, 2017).

[76] D. Caplovitz, *The Poor Pay More: Consumer Practices of Low Income Families* (New York: The Free Press, 1967); I. Ayres, 'Fair Driving: Gender and Race Discrimination in Retail Car Negotiations' (1991) 104 *Harvard Law Review* 817-872.

[77] Commission of the European Communities, Proposal for a directive of the European Parliament and of the Council on consumer rights, COM (2008) 614 final, 8.10.2008, p. 2.

labour and consumer law-making, requires this omnipresent market citizen for the completion of the Internal Market and for aligning the EU with the Lisbon 2000 agenda:[78] that is, to make Europe the most competitive economy in the world. This category of worker and consumer is much coveted by employers and suppliers. The problem then is not so much access, per se, but access to the market under 'fair conditions'. This is exactly what EU secondary law adopted in the heyday of the Social focused on: private law as a tool to institute *fair access* to the market, by compensating for information asymmetries and by clearing the market from unfair conditions, terms and procedures that block access. Fairness is not so much a form of substantive but of procedural justice.

Whilst the EU has to some extent absorbed and transformed the protective outlook of early national welfare-state legislations, the EU non-discrimination directives and the EU directives and regulations on regulated markets have set a new tone in the debate. The regulation of vulnerability – resulting from social discrimination (subject-/group-related) and economic discrimination (object-related) – gained ground. Access read in conjunction with vulnerability sets different priorities. The addressees are not those customers that business is looking after. The vulnerable usually have no access to the market. No access means exclusion from the labour market and exclusion from the consumer market. By emphasising access justice, a new horizon opens. There is no choice between access to unfair conditions or no access; the vulnerable consumer is socially and financially excluded. As early as 1995 in *Magill*, the ECJ used Art. 86 EC (today Art. 102 TFEU) to open up the market for new competitors against incumbents, who were defending their monopoly by reference to intellectual property rights.[79] Far beyond the specific context of the case, there is a much broader animating idea. Directives and regulations on regulated markets are not only instrumentalised to grant access to new competitors, but to ensure access to those who are at risk of exclusion from 'essential facilities'. These workers and consumers are constitutive not only for participation in the market, but also for participating in civil society.[80]

The rise of the social exclusion/inclusion rhetoric coincides with the refusal of the Member States to grant the EU comprehensive competences in labour and social policies. The so-called Open Method of

---

[78] The Lisbon Strategy of 2000 (Lisbon European Council 23–24 March 2000, Presidency conclusions), available at: www.europarl.europa.eu/summits/lis1_en.htm.
[79] Joined cases C-241/91 P and C-242/91 P, *RTE and ITP v. Commission* [1995] ECR I-743.
[80] This will be developed in Part III. 4.

Coordination (OMC) was developed in the 1990s as an integral part of the employment policy. Since 2003 OMC is anchored in the treaty, now Art 153 TFEU. It empowers the European Commission in non-harmonised areas of EU labour law, to foster social inclusion of those workers who are not able to keep up with the pace of the changing labour market. The OMC is regarded as the epitome of the 'new modes of governance' favoured by the European Commission since the adoption of the White Paper on European Governance in 2001.[81] Governance crosses the borders between public and private, between administrative action and contract, between law-making and rule enforcement within or outside the competence boundaries.[82] 'New modes of governance' in different shades and forms have reached or are about to reach non-discrimination, consumer policy and universal services. The Fundamental Rights Agency manages social discrimination via the charter; the European Commission uses new modes of governance outside its treaty competences to enforce unfair commercial practices law. Hand in hand with the economic and the Eurozone crises, 'financial inclusion' turned into policy objective. Again new modes of governance are regarded as an appropriate tool of implementation. The OMC in particular seems suitable so as to monitor and manage the Member States' differences in implementing universal services obligations.[83] The OMC could, in theory, approximate the different policies of Member States and define best practices for the protection of the vulnerable. In order to avoid economisation of vulnerability as a form of market rationality, the vulnerable should have certain entitlements. The language of vulnerability is social. Extending the language is a political question.[84]

---

[81] COM (2001) 428 final, 25.7.2001.
[82] For a clarification on governance, see Introduction 3.2.
[83] There is a world of discussion on services of general economic interests, services of general interest and services of non-economic interests. W. Sauter, *Public Services in EU Law* (Cambridge: Cambridge University Press, 2015); and with regard to consumer law, A. Johnston, 'Seeking the EU 'Consumer' in Services of General Economic Interest', in D. Leczykiewicz and S. Weatherill (eds.), *The Images of the Consumer in EU Law. Legislation, Free Movement and Competition Law* (Oxford: Hart Publishing, 2016), pp. 93–138.
[84] For a critical assessment, see M. Bartl, 'The Affordability of Energy: How Much Protection for the Vulnerable Consumer?' (2010) 33 *Journal of Consumer Policy* 225–245; for a nuanced account, see the contributions in U. Neergaard, E. Szyszczak, J. W. van de Gronden and M. Krajewski (eds.), *Social Services of General Interest in the EU* (The Hague: T.M.C. Asser Press, 2013), particularly the joint conclusions written by the editors, p. 595, also E. Szyszczak, J. Davies, M. Andenas and T. Bekkedal (eds.), *Developments in Services of General Interest* (The Hague: T.M.C. Asser Press, 2011).

Second, the EU concept of justice differs from allocative libertarian concepts of justice, as EU labour, non-discrimination and consumer law is, in substance, regulatory law, which restricts not only the exercise of the market freedoms but also the private autonomy of parties to a labour and a consumer contract. None of the treaty amendments and none of the secondary rules are inspired and guided by the idea that it is a prominent task for the European Union to establish and to ensure a European principle of freedom of contract and private autonomy. While the ECJ has read such a principle into the four market freedoms,[85] it has also broadened the concept so as to integrate third-party interests.[86] The concept of regulatory law forms the legal paradigm of EU law-making via the treaty and via secondary law. Broadening the freedom of contract and setting boundaries to the enlarged freedoms goes hand in hand. The EU is transforming private law rules 'from autonomy to functionalism in competition and regulation'. Private autonomy turns into 'regulated autonomy'.[87]

EU regulatory private law uses mandatory contract law rules as a device to achieve particular policy purposes, which might be sector related or, as it is the case in labour, non-discrimination and consumer law, subject and sector related. The mandatory EU rules on labour, non-discrimination and consumer law are guided by the same philosophy. They are meant to bring the consumer and the worker into a legal position where she or he is equipped with the necessary set of rights to participate in the Internal Market. EU regulatory law starts from the premise that the European legal order, based on the four market

---

[85] C. Müller-Graff, *Privatrecht und Europäisches Gemeinschaftsrecht. Gemeinschaftsprivatrecht* (Baden-Baden: Nomos, 1989); G. Rühl, 'Extending Ingmar to Jurisdiction and Arbitration Clauses: The End of Party Autonomy in Contracts with Commercial Agents?' (2007) 15 *European Review of Private Law* 891–903; G. Rühl, 'Party Autonomy in the Private International Law of Contracts: Transatlantic Convergence and Economic Efficiency', in E. Gottschalk, R. Michaels, G. Rühl and J. von Hein (eds.), *Conflict of Laws in a Globalized World* (Cambridge: Cambridge University Press, 2007), pp. 153–183.
[86] F. Cafaggi and H. Muir-Watt (eds.), *Making European Private Law. Governance Design* (Cheltenham: Edward Elgar, 2008); H.-W. Micklitz and C. Sieburgh (eds.), *Primary EU law and Private Law Concepts* (Cambridge; Antwerp: Intersentia, 2017).
[87] Special section 'European Regulatory Private Law' in the *European Law Journal* with contributions from G. Comparato, H. Dagan, M. W. Hesselink, Y. Svetiev and H.-W. Micklitz, 22(5) (2016), 621–695; G. Comparato and H.-W. Micklitz, 'Regulated Autonomy between Market Freedoms and Fundamental Rights in the Case Law of the CJEU', in U. Bernitz, X. Groussot and F. Schulyok (eds.), *General Principles of EU Law and European Private Law* (Aldershot: Ashgate 2013), pp. 121–154.

freedoms, and competition law does not produce these results by itself. Additional tools are needed to guarantee *access* to the market, whether for the well-informed or for the vulnerable consumer. This is exactly what the Lisbon Council and the various documents of the European Commission mean when they constantly reiterate the formula of 'reaping the benefits of the internal market'. Everybody must be on board to get the system going – even the vulnerable – so that the EU is legitimated. Whilst this catches the spirit of the agenda, it should not be overlooked that the Lisbon Declaration directs attention to the 'underdogs' or the 'losers' of globalisation.

Third, provided the EU model of justice cannot be equated with social justice or with a libertarian concept of justice. What does access justice mean positively speaking? In German, the concept would be *Zugangsgerechtigkeit*, which literally means 'access justice'. The term is used in a document of the German Catholic Church which was prepared at the beginning of the new millennium by eminent German academics as a response to the plea to reform the German welfare state.[88] Access justice contains three elements: first, it seeks to break down the barriers which limit participation and access; second, it aims to strengthen the position of consumer and workers to enforce their rights in a multi-governance legal order; and third, to develop an institutional design that is necessary to cope with the move from protection laws to the laws on the labour and consumer market society. With regard to the first category, access justice requires that all market participants, including consumers, must have a fair and realistic chance to enter the market, avail themselves of its products and services, and partake in the benefits of the market. Access justice in the second sense relates to the degree of justice the individual might gain after he or she has been granted access. Rights are useless if they cannot be enforced. But against whom? Member States, the EU or even the parties directly? The ECJ strongly

---

[88] Die deutschen Bischöfe, Kommission für gesellschaftliche und soziale Fragen, 'Das Soziale neu denken. Für eine langfristig angelegte Reformpolitik', Nr. 28, 12. Dezember 2003, available at: www.dbk.de/fileadmin/redaktion/veroeffentlichungen/kommissionen/Ko_28 .pdf, at p. 16: 'Heute erscheint nicht mehr vorrangig die Verteilungsgerechtigkeit als das Hauptproblem. Vielmehr müssen auch Wege eröffnet werden, um die Beteiligungsgerechtigkeit für alle zu stärken'. ('Today distributional justice no longer appears as the main problem. Rather, ways must also be opened to strengthen participation equity for all'.) One may wonder whether there is something catholic about access justice versus protestant in allocative or libertarian justice; See on the link between the common law (meaning liberal common law), nineteenth century and Puritanism, Roscoe Pound, *The Spirit of the Common Law*, College of Law, Faculty Publications (Francestown, New Hampshire: Marshall Jones Company, 1921), p. 32.

advocates for judicial protection as now enshrined in Art. 47 of the Charter of Fundamental Rights. Mediation and dispute settlement outside courts is gaining ground. Last but not least, an institutional design is needed that involves trade unions, consumer associations and more broadly civil society in the making of the rules that underpin modern private law relations and their enforcement. This is the private law of networks where the second generation of consumer law may benefit from the experience of the labour movement in collective bargaining. Access justice then reaches beyond the market and gains a particular societal relational dimension. It connects the people, the workers, the consumers, the employers and the suppliers in a society beyond the nation-state. Private law relations here gain a new outlook, one which is to be associated with a new societal private law order.[89]

In sum: access justice means more than a formal guarantee to workers and consumers that they may have a theoretical chance in participating in the market and reaping the benefits of the market. Access justice *materialises* (Max Weber) the *theoretical* chance into a *realistic* opportunity, lays down *procedural* requirements for proper law enforcement and provides for an *institutional* design that allows for the participation of civil society. Therefore, access justice should be understood as a thin version of social distributive justice. However, in its participatory form it turns into societal justice.

2.2 Critique: Equal Opportunity and Market Justice

When I presented my outline of access justice in 2005 at the French Cour de Cassation in Paris, I saw myself confronted with a critique that runs through the last decade as a red thread: (1) is access justice a *descriptive* or a *normative* model; (2) does access justice boil down to *market justice,* setting aside the political societal dimension of justice, complying nicely with the rise of the *market state* via the EU with *social inclusion* instead of social justice; (3) does access justice in its insistence on substantive equality *sacrifice individual autonomy* to the promotion of public goods? (4) from where does the EU obtain its *legitimacy* to initiate such a far-reaching transformation?

Access justice is *descriptive* and *normative*. The factual background to access justice is taken from lifelong empirical research investigating how and why the EU took over major fields of social regulation. Whilst labour law, consumer law and, to some extent, non-discrimination law

---

[89] This societal private law is developed in Part III.4.

have been extensively debated mostly in a normative perspective, the descriptive side has attracted less attention. N. Jansen identifies the strength of European regulatory private law in its explanatory power.[90] What Europe 'achieved' is to reinvigorate the deep relationship between the economic and the Social in a market society. *The Social cannot be disconnected from the market*. Political and theoretical claims for the institutional independence of the Social and of social private law from economics and economic law that dominated the legal discourse in the second half of the twentieth century did not provide enough intellectual attention to 'who pays' for the social achievements and who provides the state with the necessary resources.[91]

Justice in whichever form necessarily implies a *normative* dimension. The policy objectives enshrined in labour law, non-discrimination law and consumer law cannot be pursued without having at least implicitly a vision of the degree and type of justice that could and should be achieved. By taking over social regulation, the EU accepts a moral and a legal responsibility to ensure justice in the internal market.[92] The EU market state is criticised for reducing justice to market justice, to the realisation of equal opportunities. It will have to be shown throughout the analysis of the European social law that access justice not only materialises 'equal opportunity' but that access justice reaches beyond the market into society. The EU market state paradigm is complemented by the claim for social inclusion.[93] It enshrines the moral

---

[90] Paper presented at the European University Press post-ERC-ERPL conference 'Forms of Interaction between European and National Private Law', organised by G. Comparato, H.-W. Micklitz and Y. Svetiev, 2–3 March 2017, paper on file with the author.
[91] Contributions in A. Bogg, C. Costello, A. C. L. Davies, and J. Prassl (eds.), *The Autonomy of Labour Law* (Oxford: Hart Publishing, 2015); more particularly M. Freedland's 'Otto Kahn-Freund, the Contract of Employment and the Autonomy of Labour Law', in that book on pp. 29–44, at p. 43, where he concludes that Kahn-Freund 'always preferred to suggest positive paths for the doctrinal development of labour law from within the general law than to demand a declaration of independence from it.' Much more in the other direction, see M. Bell, 'The Principle of Equal Treatment: Widening and Deepening', in G. de Búrca and P. Craig (eds.), *The Evolution of EU law*, 2nd ed. (Oxford: Oxford University Press, 2011), pp. 611–639; and M. W. Hesselink, 'Unjust Conduct in the Internal Market: On the Role of European Private Law in the Division of Moral Responsibility between the EU, Its Member States and Their Citizens' (2016) 35 *Yearbook of European Law* 410–452.
[92] Hesselink, 'Unjust Conduct in the Internal Market'.
[93] EU financial regulation offers strange indications of how training and education should steer the correct behaviour, when non-compliance with voluntary training programmes for financial inclusion are indirectly sanctioned: Comparato, *The Financialisation of the Citizen*.

responsibility of all relevant actors, the European Union, Member States, businesses and their economic counterparts, EU citizens. The rationality test rooted in *Cassis de Dijon* is to be interpreted as a tool to submit not only Member States social regulation but also EU social regulation and even the activities of private parties to a rationality test.[94]

In a private law context, the potential impact of this responsibility is not limited to the EU and the Member States as regulators; it affects the autonomy and responsibility of private parties. Individual autonomy of the private parties is societally embedded. This does not mean that the collective purpose behind social regulation automatically prevails over individual autonomy. Seen through the eyes of the individual, social inclusion is an option not an obligation. The individual must have the choice to opt out and to decide that being excluded is better than being commandeered to pursue an over-individualised public purpose. The increased space for autonomy beyond the state implies increased responsibilities of private parties, workers/consumers and companies. Not only is business about to become the direct addressee of social rights if not of the holders of the public good, but workers, consumers and civil society associations might also have to bear a greater responsibility for the public good. The subsequent tension between the autonomy-based foundation of access justice and the collective dimension of access justice is obvious[95] and will be discussed in the procedural and institutional design of European access justice.[96]

It is not the purpose of this book to deepen the relationship between the regulatory power of the EU and its legitimacy. The increasing powers of the EU through various treaty amendments in the 1980s and 1990 triggered a debate on whether alternative models of legitimacy can compensate the apparent democratic deficit. Fritz W. Scharpf[97] draws the catchy distinction between input and output legitimacy; N. Walker[98] insists on the need of polity legitimation to increase Europe's constitutional momentum. The EU is criticised for its bureaucratic Eurozone-crisis management that is claimed to

---

[94] Part II. 4.1.
[95] This is the key critique of Dagan, 'Between Regulatory and Autonomy-Based Private Law'.
[96] Part III. 2.5, 3.5, 4.5.
[97] F. W. Scharpf, *Governing in Europe: Effective and Democratic?* (Oxford; New York: Oxford University Press, 1999).
[98] N. Walker, 'Europe's constitutional momentum and the search for polity legitimacy' (2005) 3 *International Journal of Constitutional law* 211–238.

undermine national democracies through undemocratic decision-making in the hands of Eurocrats.[99] Justice, this seems to be the consequence, can only be achieved within a national democracy. There is an undeniable deeper link between standards of justice and the legitimacy of the authority which stands behind distributive policies. Not enough attention, however, has been given to the hidden role that Member States are playing in using the EU to modernise – or to dismantle, as the critics would say – the social welfare state, social standards and a vision of a just society; nor has the increasing responsibility of private parties within the EU legal order attracted the degree of attention it deserves.[100]

2.3. Access Justice and Social Justice in Tandem

There are two arguments why European access justice cannot replace national patterns of social justice: the first results from the non-existence of a European polity; the second from the limited competences of the EU. Whilst the first has already been touched upon,[101] the limits of the Order of Competence in regulating justice have to be clarified.[102]

The basic structure of the European Order of Competence has remained largely the same since 1957, with two exceptions: Art. 114 TFEU in the SEA and Art. 81 TFEU on international private law issues. The functional market-driven logic enabled the EU to adopt labour law, non-discrimination law and consumer law, mostly through minimum

---

[99] D. Chalmers, M. Jachtenfuchs, C. Joerges (eds.), *The End of the Eurocrats' Dream. Adjusting to European Diversity* (Cambridge: Cambridge University Press, 2016), in particular the introductory chapter 'The Retransformation of Europe' written by the editors, 1–28.

[100] Contrary to the strong focus on the responsibilities of multinationals in transnational private law in particular, special issue 'Les Grandes Théories du Droit Transnational', with contributions by K. Tuori; B. Kingsbury, N. Krisch and R. B. Stewart; H. Muir-Watt; C. Joerges and F. Rödl; F. Cafaggi; R. Zimmermann; G.-P. Calliess and M. Renner; A. Fischer-Lescano and G. Teubner; and P. Schiff Berman, in (2013) *Revue Internationale de Droit Economique*, 1–256.

[101] D. Chalmers and S. Trotter, 'Fundamental Rights and Legal Wrongs: The Two Sides of the Same EU Coin' (2016) 22 *European Law Journal* 9–39; D. Chalmers and L. Barroso, 'What Van Gend en Loos Stands For' (2014) 12 *International Journal of Constitutional Law* 105–134.

[102] Updated version of my contribution, 'The EU as a Federal Order of Competences and the Private Law', in L. Azoulai (ed.), *The Question of Competence in the European Union* (Oxford: Oxford University Press, 2014), pp. 125–152; on the need for clarification, J. Smits, 'Who Does What? On The Distribution of Competences Among the European Union and the Member States', in K. Purnhagen/P. Rott (eds.), *Varieties of European Economic Law and Regulation: Liber Amicorum for Hans Micklitz*, pp. 343–357.

harmonisation but increasingly through maximum standards.[103] In the harmonised field of European regulatory private law, the ECJ tends to broaden the scope and reach of EU law: reading full harmonisation *contra legem* into directives which remain silent on the degree of harmonisation,[104] giving a broad reading to directives which provide for full harmonisation[105] or submitting national legislation that reaches beyond the European minimum to a proportionality test.[106] The much-debated *Tobacco* judgment[107] and its aftermath seems to have slowed but not halted the expansion of the EU legislator's competence in key areas of traditional private law.[108] In its judgment on the annulment of Regulation (EC) No 1435/2003 (European Cooperative Society (SCE)),[109] the ECJ held that Art. 352 TFEU is the correct legal basis which requires unanimity.[110] That is why one might argue that if any, a European Civil Code or European Sales Law could only be adopted provided Member States unanimously agree on the harmonisation of civil law and on the level of 'social' justice or 'access' justice. Art. 169 TFEU, on the other hand, allows for the adoption of a European regulation on consumer law but only in the form of minimum standards.[111]

The Lisbon Treaty is said to have changed the functional logic of market-driven EU private law. Art. 3 (1) TEU is making the values laid down in Art. 2 TEU (inter alia Justice) one of the three aims of the EU (the

---

[103] For an early analysis on the consequences, E. Steindorff, *EG-Vertrag und Privatrecht* (Baden-Baden: Nomos, 1996).
[104] Case C-183/00, González Sánchez [2002] ECR I-3901; see also Part II. 4.2.
[105] J. Stuyck, 'The Court of Justice and the Unfair Commercial Practices Directive' (2015) 52 *Common Market Law Review* 721-752. On the differences between the product liability directive and the Directive on Unfair Commercial Practices, V. Mak, 'Full Harmonization in European Private Law: A Two-Track Concept' (2012) 20 *European Review of Private Law* 213-235.
[106] Case C-205/07, *Gysbrechts and Santurel Inter* [2008] ECR I-9947.
[107] Case C-376/98, *Germany v. Parliament and Council* [2000] ECR I-8419
[108] K. Gutman, 'The Commission's 2010 Green Paper on European Contract Law: Reflections on Union Competence in Light of the Proposed Options' (2011) 7 *European Review of Contract Law* 151-172, at 155; S. Weatherill, 'The Consumer Rights Directive: How and Why a Quest for 'Coherence' Has (Largely) Failed' (2012) 49 *Common Market Law Review* 1279-1317, at 1317, under 6; now more fully from the same author, S. Weatherill, *Contract Law of the Internal Market* (Cambridge: Intersentia, 2016). The bottom line of a rather lenient approach of the ECJ is Case C-58/08, *Vodafone and Others* [2010] ECR I-4999.
[109] Council Regulation (EC) No 1435/2003 of 22 July 2003 on the Statute for a European Cooperative Society (SCE), OJ No. L 207, 18.8.2003, p. 1.
[110] C-436/03, *Parliament v. Council* [2006] ECR I-3733.
[111] N. Reich, 'A European Contract Law, or an EU Contract Law Regulation for Consumers?' (2005) 28 *Journal of Consumer Policy* 383-407.

other two being the peace and well-being of people). Art. 3 (3) TEU establishes 'a highly competitive social market economy'. The vague reference to 'justice' can hardly pave the way for a fully harmonised private law.[112] This is all the more evident because, as the ECJ confirmed in *Glaxo Smith*,[113] the Lisbon Treaty did not change the character of the EU market economy. Many advocates of the Social understand fundamental and human rights as a tool for a better society and for a more social private law, against which private law rules are to be measured.[114] However, it seems excessive to understand the charter as a value system that legitimates the full harmonisation of standards of justice in private law matters.

The strongest argument for shared responsibilities that leaves room for European access justice and national social justice can be taken from the subsidiarity principle (Art 5 (1) TEU). The first time the subsidiarity principle played a crucial rule in private law-making, occurred in the discussion on the legal basis for Common European Sales Law (CESL) (not on the values enshrined in the CESL), where four Member States, Austria, Belgium, Germany and the United Kingdom,[115] raised the newly introduced subsidiarity claim, but did not achieve the quorum set out in Art. 7 of Protocol 2. Art 4 (2), which requires respect for

---

[112] On the misleading parallel between (German) social market economy (*sozialer Marktwirtschaft*) and the treaty revision, C. Joerges, 'A Renaissance of the European Economic Constitution', in U. Neergaard, R. Nielsen, L. M. Roseberry (eds.), *Integrating Welfare Functions into EU Law. From Rome to Lisbon* (Copenhagen: Djøf Publishing, 2009), pp. 42–52.

[113] Case C-501/06 P, *GlaxoSmithKline Services and Others v Commission and Others* [2009] ECR I-9291, para. 63; J. Drexl, 'La Constitution économique européenne—L'actualité du modèle ordolibéral' (2011) *Revue internationale de droit économique* 419–454.

[114] In favour, D. Caruso, 'Fairness at a Time of Perplexity: The Civil Law Principle of Fairness in the Court of Justice of the European Union', in S. Vogenauer and S. Weatherill (eds.), *General Principles of Law. European and Comparative Perspectives* (Oxford: Hart Publishing, 2017), pp. 329–354; the critical Lord Hoffmann, 'The Universality of Human Rights', Judicial Studies Board Annual Lecture, 19 March 2009, available at: www.judiciary.gov.uk/announcements/speech-by-lord-hoffmann-the-universality-of-human-rights/; nuanced with regard to the position of the ECJ, S. Weatherill, 'The Empowerment is not the only fruit', in D. Leczykiewicz and S. Weatherill (eds.), *The Images of the Consumer in EU Law. Legislation, Free Movement and Competition Law* (Oxford: Hart Publishing, 2016), pp. 203–222; H. Collins, 'The Constitutionalization of European Private Law as a Path to Social Justice', in H.-W. Micklitz (ed.), *The Many Concepts of Social Justice in European Private Law* (Cheltenham: Edward Elgar, 2011), pp. 133–166.

[115] On file with the author, not all are publicly available, for the UK Council Doc. 18547/11 of 14 December 2011, for Germany BT-Drucksache 17/800, for Austria 8609 Beilagen zu den stenographischen Protokollen des Bundesrates. Another three Member States have provided critical statements.

national identities and for essential state functions. The ECJ has referred to Art. 4 (2) on three occasions. In *Sayn-Wittgenstein*,[116] the ECJ accepted that the republican government may form part of the national identities of Member States. In *Runevič-Vardyn* and *Anton Las*, the court held that the protection of official language(s) is a facet of national identity.[117] The German Constitutional Court (GCC) regards social security as part of German identity.[118] The reference to 'essential state function' and 'national identity' strikes down *full harmonisation* of private law as a constitutional means of completing the Internal Market. Shared competence in respect of the subsidiarity principle is calling for a common European platform for which both the EU and the Member States accept responsibility.[119] D. Chalmers' proposal to grant Art. 4 (2) horizontal direct effect would allow for making the different responsibilities for the common platform and for national standards beyond the platform much more transparent.[120] Therefore the rules of the treaty do not enable the EU to replace the variety of national patterns of social justice through European access justice. The EU and the Member States are tied together, each of them promoting its own pattern of justice.

3 Preconceptions and Methodology

The reconstruction of the achievements of the Social in the Member States, and how and why the EU complements it, requires clarification

[116] Case C-208/09, *Sayn-Wittgenstein* [2010] ECR I-13693, paras. 88, 92.
[117] Case C-391/09, *Runevič-Vardyn und Wardyn* [2011] ECR I-3787 and Case C-202/11, *Las* [2013] ECR I-000.
[118] German Constitutional Court, 2 BvE 2/08, 30.6.2009, the judgment is available in English at: www.bundesverfassungsgericht.de/SharedDocs/Entscheidungen/EN/2009/06/es20090630_2bve000208en.html, at para 258: ' pursuant to Article 23.1 first sentence of the Basic Law, Germany's participation in the process of integration depends, inter alia, on the European Union's commitment to social principles. Accordingly the Basic Law ... aims at committing the European public authority to social responsibility in the spectrum of tasks transferred to it (Heinig, Der Sozialstaat im Dienst der Freiheit, 2008, pp. 531 et seq.). But the social state necessarily requires political and legal concretisation in order for it to have an effect.'; F. de Witte, *Justice in the EU*, pp. 55, 59; H.-W. Micklitz, 'German Constitutional Court (Bundesverfassungsgericht BVerfG) 2 BvE 2/08, 30.6.2009—Organstreit proceedings between members of the German Parliament and the Federal Government' (2011) 7 *European Review of Contract Law* 528–546.
[119] Invoking subsidiarity implies responsibility, H.-W. Micklitz, 'The Maastricht Treaty, the Principle of Subsidiarity and the Theory of Integration' (1993) 4 *LAKIMIES Special Issue on European Integration* (periodical of the Association of Finnish lawyers) 508–539.
[120] Chalmers and Barroso, 'What Van Gend en Loos Stands For'; and in this volume, Part III. 2.5, 3.5, 4.5 on the need to allocate responsibilities to the different levels of justice.

on two basic preconceptions and on the concrete methodology used. The first preconception is the critical undertone that guides the use of law in the political design of justice in private law through nation-states and the EU. The focal point is an *ideological criticism* of the instrumentalisation[121] of law for societal and political purposes. The second preconception is the understanding of the European integration process as an *experiment*. Herein lies the connection to debates on the constitutionalisation process of the EU, on the EU experiment as a discovery process, and on the EU as the epitome of governmental experimentalism or as a political and societal laboratory. The label that holds all these debates together is the post-classical move at the times of the third globalisation. The methodology used to describe and analyse the transformation processes is a combination of intellectual history and 'legal consciousness'.[122] The latter is understood as the set of deeper assumptions laypersons share about their own legal systems based on the expectations they have in the functioning of legislatures, courts, the executive and of society. Historical path dependencies develop in accordance with a logic that is displayed in various parts of the regulated economy.

3.1 Ideological Criticism

The concept of social justice to be realised by the nation-state is based on deep-rooted assumptions. The market cannot produce appropriate results – in particular it cannot produce social justice (market failure). Neither the individual nor self-organisation via trade unions, consumer and tenant associations are in a position to compensate for these market failures (corporatist failure). Therefore, the state enjoys a twofold task; via its (democratic) powers, the state becomes and then is responsible for the protection of the weaker party and for the *redistribution of wealth*. This is the *economic* dimension of social justice. The *political* dimension of social justice points to the society the citizens live in and therewith the different societal role the citizens have to play in a democratic society.[123]

The rise of the Social implies that the nation-state is in a position to meet such self-imposed tasks. The state has to *define the weaker parties*,

---

[121] Instrumentalism and functionalism are used as interchangeable terms throughout the text.
[122] For a fuller analysis, H.-W. Micklitz, 'On the Intellectual History of Freedom of Contract and Regulation' (2015) 4 *Penn State Journal of Law & International Affairs* 1–32.
[123] For the deeper tensions between democracy and a Keynesian market capitalism, Streeck, *How Will Capitalism End?*

which over time resulted in ever more sophisticated status-related rules.[124] The state has to *define the interests of the weaker parties*, which contradicts individual and collective autonomy.[125] The welfare state and the regulatory state differ from the authoritarian state (John Stuart Mill), against which the individual seeks protection. The welfare state interferes into society and regulates autonomy. C. Sunstein and E. Thaler do not understand libertarian paternalism as an oxymoron. The state is claimed to be able to combine liberal and paternalist/welfarist instruments.[126] The state has *to define (and know) the yardstick* of what shall be distributed to whom and under what conditions. Insights on the economic consequences of the intended redistribution have to be merged with political considerations on societal acceptability. The state has to *clarify the political role of private parties, business, workers and consumers in a democratic society* beyond the formal election procedures through modes of participation in law-making and law enforcement. This overall move towards a more just society creates expectations. The political promises become subject to a validity test.

The decision of the Member States to grant the European Union ever more powers, with or without treaty amendments in the relevant fields of social interests, is equally based on a whole series of courageous assumptions which draw their inspiration from the Member States. The EU started to regulate labour, consumer and non-discrimination law at a time when the Social began to lose impetus in the Member States. This coincidence explains why social expectations, which were nourished and generated over decades in the Member States, were transposed more or less directly to the European Union. Consequently, and somewhat overstatedly, the European Union is then expected to develop distributive standards of justice for an Internal Market and societal standards for a just European society. The European Union is implicitly seen as competent and able to define these social standards at the minimum or even at the maximum level for a heterogeneous union of 27 (28) Member States. The mismatch between social justice in a nation-state context and social justice in a transnational quasi-statutory entity remained long unobserved.

---

[124] K. I. Schmidt, 'Henry Maine's "Modern Law": From Status to Contract and Back Again?' (2017) 65 *The American Journal of Comparative Law* 145-186.
[125] This is particularly true for the United Kingdom, where collective bargaining served as a substitute for statutory regulation; see Part I. 1.2.4.
[126] C. R. Sunstein and R. H. Thaler, 'Libertarian Paternalism Is Not an Oxymoron' (2003) 70 *The University of Chicago Law Review* 1159-1202.

The transfer of national patterns of justice to the EU blinded us (I include myself) to the potential differences between the Member State arena vis-à-vis the EU.[127] The European Union brings reality back in – the 'who pays' and the 'how to compete'. The EU highlights the complicated link between the rise of the welfare state and the rise of sovereign debt; it brings the difficulties to the fore under which national economies with high labour and social costs may survive in a more competitive global market. In light of these claims and expectations, the true reach of the European integration process can be properly assessed. The 'nation-state' is objectified through a quasi-statutory entity viz. the EU, which has a genuine 'legal (constitutional) order' and institutions that yield their own standard of justice. Therefore, the EU has to be measured against normative standards that comply with its constitutional and institutional status.[128]

Both the Member States and the EU use, more or less, the same tools for achieving justice through public regulation: first, materialisation of private law[129] through mandatory standards; second, by inserting general concepts on good faith, reasonableness and fairness;[130] and third, through constitutionalisation via fundamental and human rights. Whatever the technique is, legislatures, courts and agencies have to transform the new European social moral into normative standards. Law is instrumentalised for social purposes beyond formal rationality. Whether materialisation through private law is possible at all is subject to a fierce debate that started in the early 1980s, when it became clear that statutory interventions in the name of the Social yielded all sorts of failures. That is why the analysis of the politics of justice has to openly address regulatory failure, governmental failure and the failure of enforcement, all of which endanger the success of social regulation in the late twentieth century.[131] EU law inherited this legacy from the Member States. In transforming social labour law and social consumer law into the law of the labour and consumer market society, the EU

---

[127] R. Sefton-Green, 'Social Justice and European Identity in European Contract Law' (2006) 2 *European Review of Contract Law* 275–286.
[128] Kochenov, 'The Ought of Justice', p. 26.
[129] In the sense of M. Weber, *Wirtschaft und Gesellschaft*, 5th rev. reprint (Tübingen: J. C. B. Mohr Siebeck, 1972), p. 387, in particular p. 503; Assmann, Brüggemeier, Hart and Joerges, *Wirtschaftsrecht als Kritik des Privatrechts*.
[130] Lord Sweyn, 'The Role of Good Faith and Fair Dealing in Contract Law: A Hair-Shirt Philosophy?' (1991) 6 *The Denning Law Journal* 131–141.
[131] With regard to the three nation-states under scrutiny, see Part I. 2; with regard to the EU, see Part II. 3.

opened up a new perspective that favours a more holistic perspective on the interplay between formal and material rationality, bringing the market and the society closer to each other. *Cassis de Dijon* serves as the benchmark for the rationality test. Non-discrimination law – the 'Darling Dogma of Bourgeois Europeanists'[132] – has transformed the prohibition of gender discrimination into a general principle, thereby stretching law to its limits. The EU has managed to yield a new, overarching European social moral. This does not mean, however, that it is necessarily for the law to transpose this social moral into societal reality. The ever harder litigation over the reach of the non-discrimination principle provides ample evidence.[133] There is need for politics, although politics might not necessarily be the cure to the claimed justice deficit. Politics and economics must go together. Niklas Luhmann's story of the twelfth camel provocatively claims that fair distribution is a mere fiction.[134] The way out of the claimed failure of the materialisation of law is said to be proceduralisation.[135]

From the 1980s onward, proceduralisation gained ground in the EU, most visibly through the turn to governance.[136] The conclusion would be that the state, be it the Member State or the EU, should lay down procedures under which the material standards of justice are elaborated. These procedures let the parties back in and allow for relational transactions within an EU-set quasi-statutory frame or even without a frame that governs proceduralisation. It is here where administrative governance and contract governance meet. As the results of the process are not predefined, there is room for experimentalism by all who are given a role in the procedure. Through the use of standardisation in private law, the EU is at the forefront of the

---

[132] A. Somek, 'The Darling Dogma of Bourgeois Europeanists' (2014) 20 *European Law Journal* 688–712.

[133] R. Xenidis, 'Shaking the Normative Foundations of EU Equality Law: Evolution and Hierarchy between Market Integration and Human Rights Rationales' (2017) *EUI-ERC Working Papers* Nr. 4.

[134] N. Luhmann, 'Die Rückgabe des zwölften Kamels. Zum Sinn einer soziologischen Analyse des Rechts (1985)', in G. Teubner (ed.), *Die Rückgabe des zwölften Kamels. Niklas Luhmann in der Diskussion über Gerechtigkeit* (Stuttgart: Lucius & Lucius, 2000), pp. 3–60.

[135] J. Habermas, *Faktizität und Geltung* (Franfurt a.M.: Suhrkamp 1992), p. 516; outspoken with regard to private law, D. Hart, 'Substantive and Reflective Elements in Modern Contract Law', in T. Bourgoignie (ed.), *Unfair Terms in Consumer Contracts* (Louvain-la-Neuve; Brussels: Cabay; Brulant: 1983), pp. 3–32.

[136] For a deeper discussion of governance as proceduralisation, M. Dawson, *New Governance and the Transformation of European Law. Coordinating EU social law and policy* (Cambridge: Cambridge University Press, 2011), p. 103.

development to overcome 'ignorance of state officials' (Sabel and Zeitlin) involved in the law-making.[137] This move, which yielded critique from a constitutional perspective, did not raise much attention among private law scholars. The same is true with regard to new modes of private and administrative governance in the enforcement of private law.[138]

3.2 The Post-Classical Move

The emergence of the genuine European model of justice in private law is explained through the move from the *classical* to the *post-classical*, from the idea of law as a *system*[139] in the nation-state to law as an *order* (Culver, Giudice)[140] that lacks coherence[141] and takes a neoformalist post-classical outlook (D. Kennedy). Part III is dedicated to give shape to the post-classical private law order. Its characteristics form its tripartite structure, which ties substance and procedure to a particular legal status. Such a private law beyond the nation-state merges contract and regulation, substance and procedure, rule-making and rule enforcement. Notwithstanding the blending of boundaries that characterises the post-classical move, this private legal order encapsulates a distinct form of justice that complements national patterns of social justice.

Inspired by M. Reimann,[142] I understand the loose and open structure of the European legal order as a promising experiment that allows study of the outlook of the post-nation-state, the private law order and the

---

[137] C. F. Sabel and J. Zeitlin, 'Experimentalism in the EU: Common Ground and Persistent Differences' (2012) 6 *Regulation & Governance* 410–426, draw a distinction between ignorance and uncertainty; the former is characterised by the lack of knowledge of the state officials which is compensated by knowledgeable parties, whereas uncertainty is characterised through an overall lack of knowledge.

[138] A notable exception is H. Schepel, *The Constitution of Private Governance* (Oxford: Hart Publishing, 2005); more recently in particular with regard to private law, B. van Leeuwen, *European Standardisation of Services and its Impact on Private Law* (Oxford: Hart Publishing, 2017).

[139] J. Dickson, 'Towards a Theory of European Union Legal Systems', in J. Dickson and P. Eleftheriadis (eds.), *Philosophical Foundations of European Union Law* (Oxford: Oxford University Press, 2012), pp. 25–53.

[140] K. Culver and M. Giudice, 'Not a System but an Order: An Inter-Institutional View of European Union Law', in J. Dickson and P. Eleftheriadis (eds.), *Philosophical Foundations of European Union Law* (Oxford: Oxford University Press, 2012), pp. 54–76.

[141] T. Wilhelmsson, 'The Contract Law Acquis: Towards More Coherence through Generalisations?', in 4. *Europäischer Juristentag* (Wien: Manz, 2008), pp. 111–145.

[142] M. Reimann, 'The American Advantage in Global Lawyering' (2014) 78 *Rabels Zeitschrift für ausländisches und internationales Privatrecht* 1–36.

patterns of justice.[143] The European experiment links to theories on proceduralisation (Luhmann and Teubner),[144] on competition and practice as a discovery procedure (*Entdeckungsverfahren Wettbewerb und Praxis*) (Hayek and Joerges),[145] on democratic and administrative (Sabel and Zeitlin),[146] on judicial (Gerstenberg and Frerichs)[147] and societal experimentalism (Ladeur),[148] or on *my* understanding of the European project as a laboratory.[149]

Each of the theoretical strands has its particular impact on private law discourse beyond the nation-state. Proceduralisation is the intellectual construct that embraces the society and the economy.[150] In the EU context it is most obviously reflected in the constitutionalisation process of the European legal order, in the constitutionalisation of European private law through human and fundamental rights, and through the rise of procedural elements within the European concept of justice.[151] The transfer of Hayek's competition as a discovery procedure nourishes fears of EU neoliberalism early on. Joerges' twist of the discovery procedure towards practice embraces social and societal processes beyond the market and helps to explain the emerging European private law.

Governance, not least through its broad umbrella, allows us to bring different strands of discourses together. Much of the new governance literature is written in the context of administration and regulation.

---

[143] H.-W. Micklitz, 'A European Advantage in Legal Scholarship?', in R. van Gestel, H.-W. Micklitz and Ed. L. Rubin (eds.), *Rethinking Legal Scholarship. A Transatlantic Dialogue* (New York: Cambridge University Press, 2016), pp. 262–309.

[144] G. Teubner, *Recht als autopoetisches System* (Frankfurt a.M.: Suhrkamp, 1989) and C. Joerges and G. Teubner (eds.), *Rechtsverfassungsrecht – Recht-Fertigung zwischen Privatrechtsdogmatik und Gesellschaftstheorie* (Baden-Baden: Nomos, 2003).

[145] C. Joerges, *Verbraucherschutz als Rechtsproblem* (Heidelberg: Verlagsgesellschaft Recht und Wirtschaft, 1981), pp. 133–134.

[146] Sabel and Zeitlin, 'Learning from Difference'.

[147] S. Frerichs, *Judicial Governance in der Europäischen Rechtsgemeinschaft* (Baden-Baden: Nomos, 2008); O. Gerstenberg, 'The Question of Standards for the EU: From "Democratic Deficit" to "Justice Deficit?"', in D. Kochenov, G. de Búrca and A. Williams (eds.), *Europe's Justice Deficit?* (Oxford: Hart Publishing, 2015), pp. 67–78.

[148] K.-H. Ladeur, 'Globalization and Public Governance – a Contradiction?', in K.-H. Ladeur (ed.), *Public Governance in the Age of Globalization* (Aldershot: Ashgate, 2004), pp. 1–24.

[149] H.-W. Micklitz, 'Philosophical Foundations of European Union Law. By Julie Dickson and Pavlos Eleftheriadis (eds.)' (2013) (32) *Yearbook of European Law* 538–554.

[150] A. Somek, *Rechtstheorie zur Einführung* (Hamburg: Junius, 2017), p. 22, argues that system theory is the very response to the decline of legal positivism.

[151] H.-W. Micklitz, 'Principles of Social Justice in European Private Law' (1999) 19 *Yearbook of European Law* 167–204.

However, there is an emerging second strand within the private law discourse. Its multi-faceted character grants governance a prominent position in the post-classical private law. Multi-level governance refers to the distribution of competence between Member States and the EU, and to transparency, accountability and legitimacy. The new approach on technical standards, later transferred to the Banking Union, paved the way for new modes of law-making that crossed the boundaries of public and private law. The Open Method of Coordination institutionalised bargaining processes in industrial and societal relations outside and beyond the treaty. New modes of enforcement within private law respond to regulatory failure resulting from the over-complexity of a multi-level structure of the EU. Governance in the EU is characterised through experimentalism rooted in the ignorance of the public officials.[152] The EU is experimenting with new forms of law-making, as documented in the evolution from the new approach over the Lamfalussy procedure to better regulation or in law enforcement through recommendations, guidelines or more formalised commitment decisions. Gerstenberg identified experimentalism in the European judiciary on the control of standard terms. Ladeur added societal experimentalism, with private law as a building block allowing for *relational* transaction without state interference.

The depths and array of legal thought is 'intimidating' (M. Dawson). However, for the purposes of this book, it suffices to highlight that the different theoretical strands are united in the search for the design of the legal order in the post-nation-state era. They are referred to in the unfolding of the overall argument, however, without discussing their pros and cons and without explicitly taking sides. The categorisation of the European project as an 'experiment' is meant to demonstrate that the European Union breaks away from the economic and philosophical foundations of the Member States and yields its own narrative.[153] The particular experimental character of the EU is enshrined in the constant change of paradigms, from integration through law in the early days, through integration without law once the ideal of building a European state on the model of the nineteenth century nation-state crumbled, up to the current stage of integration beyond the state.

---

[152] On that distinction, see Sabel and Zeitlin, 'Experimentalism in the EU'.
[153] Even the so far most ambitious project in the search for the European narrative is largely missing the point in that the European particularities are established through the lenses of nation-statenation-state political and moral philosophy; see my book review article 'Philosophical Foundations of European Union Law'.

Europe is constantly in the making, each stage leaving a particular footprint on the design of European labour, non-discrimination and consumer law. Its process is programme, and the foundations behind the European Union cannot be found in nation-state bound political philosophy alone.[154]

3.3 Intellectual History and Legal Consciousness

The reconstruction of the evolutionary process of the nation-states that are transforming through the European integration process and yielding a new genuine pattern of justice requires a methodology that embraces legal culture, legal thought, and the economic, political and social foundations of both the Member States and the EU. *Legal consciousness*[155] is the mode of thinking that typifies the social psychology of a particular society and is predominantly shaped by the understandings of the societies' most influential philosophers. Legal consciousness is inherently linked to *intellectual history*, the historiography of ideas and thinkers. History, this is the understanding, cannot be considered without the knowledge of the humans who created, discussed and wrote about it.[156]

The focal point around which legal consciousness and intellectual history is built is Wieacker's common European legal culture, characterised by personalism, legalism and intellectualism.[157] It will have to be shown that all three can be found in British, French and German societies. However, each one of these three European legal consciousnesses has professed one aspect of the general legal consciousness to the

---

[154] K. Tuori, *European Constitutionalism* (Cambridge: Cambridge University Press, 2015).
[155] U. Raulff (ed.), *Mentalitäten-Geschichte. Zur Historischen Rekonstruktion geistiger Prozesse* (Berlin: Wagenbach 1987); H. Schulze, 'Mentalitätsgeschichte – Chancen und Grenzen eines Paradigmas der französischen Geschichtswissenschaft' (1985) 36 *Geschichte in Wissenschaft und Unterricht* 247–270; Kennedy, 'Three Globalizations of Law and Legal Thought' and 'The Rule of Law, Political Choices and Developing Common Sense', in D. M. Trubek and A. Santos (eds.), *The New Law and Economic Development. A Critical Appraisal* (Cambridge; New York: Cambridge University Press, 2006), pp. 95–173.
In a European historical perspective, S. Conrad and S. Randeria, 'Geteilte Geschichten: Europa in einer postkolonialen Welt', in S. Conrad and S. Randeria (eds.), *Jenseits des Eurozentrismus: Postkoloniale Perspektiven in den Geschichts- und Kulturwissenschaften* (Frankfurt a.M.: Campus Verlag), pp. 9–49.
[156] Only indirectly it touches upon 'legal evolution' which is a distinct feature in Deakin's and Wilkinson's analysis of the (English) law of the labour market; Deakin and Wilkinson, *The Law of the Labour Market*, pp. 26–36.
[157] F. Wieacker, 'Voraussetzungen europäischer Rechtskultur' (Verlag Göttinger Tageblatt, 1985), translated into English by E. Bodenheimer and published as 'Foundations of European Legal Culture' (1990) 38 *The American Journal of Comparative Law* 1–29.

detriment of the others. The ideal type (Max Weber) looks like this: The English emphasised personalism, the French intellectualism, and the Germans legalism. The respective legal consciousness and the patterns of justice turn out to be rather stable over time. It is therefore possible to identify and determine differences and national particularities. This is notable, as the three countries underwent the same grand economic, social and political transformations in the seventeenth, eighteenth and nineteenth centuries.[158] The strong and stable exchange between the grand philosophers of Europe did not suffice to break down the national particularities.[159] During these times the Netherlands served as a refuge for many important philosophers, a place where they could escape political pressure in their respective home countries and freely speculate on moral and political philosophy. Personalism, legalism, intellectualism are enshrined in the *ius commune*,[160] which embraces not only continental European but also common law countries.[161]

After World War II, Wieacker's common European legal culture became the backbone of the then-established European Economic Community. Looking back in order to build the future of Europe, this

---

[158] There is a plethora of literature on the socioeconomic history: K. W. Nörr, *Die Republik der Wirtschaft, Part I and II* (Tübingen: Mohr Siebeck, 1999 and 2007). For the history of the Federal Republic of Germany, see C. Torp, *Konsum und Politik in der Weimarer Republik* (Göttingen: Vandenhoeck & Ruprecht, 2011); and Haupt and Torp (eds.), *Die Konsumgesellschaft in Deutschland 1890–1990*. With regard to the Consumer Society for the UK, see J. Darwin, *The Empire Project. The Rise and Fall of the British World-System. 1830–1970* (Cambridge; New York: Cambridge University Press, 2009), P. Mathias and S. Polland (eds.), *The Cambridge Economic History of Europe*, Volume VIII (Cambridge: University Press, 1989), p. 103.

[159] Q. Skinner, 'Thomas Hobbes and His Disciples in France and England' (1966) 8 *Comparative Studies in Society and History* 153–167; U. Wesel, *Geschichte des Rechts – Von den Frühformen bis zur Gegenwart*, 2nd ed. (München: C. H. Beck, 2001), p. 409; B. Russell, *A History of Western Philosophy* (Sydney: Unwin Hyman Paperbacks, 1979), in German, *Philosophie des Abendlandes* (München: Piper, 2004).

[160] R. Zimmermann, 'Savigny's Legacy: Legal History, Comparative Law, and the Emergence of a European Science' (1996) 112 *Law Quarterly Review* 576–605. On the critique against the European private law codification project which is inspired by and based on the destruction of the common philosophical ground of private law in the civil and common law systems, see H. Eidenmüller, F. Faust, H. C. Grigoleit, N. Jansen, G. Wagner and R. Zimmermann, 'The Common Frame of Reference for European Private Law – Policy Choices and Codification Problems' (2008) 28 *Oxford Journal of Legal Studies* 659–708.

[161] With regard to the Roman law foundations of the common law, R. Zimmermann, '"Heard melodies are sweet, but those unheard are sweeter . . . ": Condicio tacita, implied condition und die Fortbildung des europäischen Vertragsrechts' (1993) 193 *Archiv für die civilistische Praxis* 121–173.

was the post-war agenda of so many great politicians and also philosophers and lawyers. This does not mean that *legal consciousness* is a static concept. It is subject to change, just as the socioeconomic environment and the great ideas that shape the philosophical discourse. At some point in time, in the mid-1970s, there is a breakthrough in the general European legal consciousness. Scientists put in question the idea that the world can be explained with immutable, objective laws. They first changed their approach to legal norms. They no longer expected them to be coherent. General awareness of the scientific revolution coincided with the onset of the loosening impetus of the national welfare state and the rise of 'the Social' in the EU. EU legal scholars no longer wanted to build the United States of Europe, and they began deconstructing their status-related law. The result is a genuine EU model of justice, a genuine European legal culture and a genuine post-national European consciousness. The Eurobarometer surveys shed light on European consciousness in all its shakiness and contradictions.[162] This does not mean that the common heritage of Europe or the particular national variations of the three legal consciousnesses have vanished or are about to vanish. The new consciousness, as will be demonstrated, exists side by side with 'old' consciousnesses.[163] This process is far from being soft and without conflict. The much-debated Economic Constitution of Europe and its German construction provides ample evidence of the painstaking path from a national to a European concept.[164]

---

[162] L. Diez-Sanchez, 'Justice Index' Eurobarometer and the Issue of Justice. 1990 – 2015', manuscript 2017, on file with the author.

[163] With regard to the divided legal culture, H.-W. Micklitz, 'The (Un)-Systematics of (Private) Law as an Element of European Culture', in G. Hellerringer and K. Purnhagen (eds.), *Towards a European Legal Culture* (München; Oxford; Baden-Baden: C. H. Beck; Hart Publishing; Nomos, 2014), pp. 81–115; review from H. Collins 2016 (12) *European Review of Contract Law* 72–76.

[164] On the origins of ordo-liberalism and its impact on Germans with respect to the European Economic Constitution, D. Gerber, 'Constitutionalizing the Economy: German Neo-Liberalism, Competition Law and the "New" Europe' (1994) 42 *American Journal of Comparative Law* 25–84; and in a historical perspective, M. Stolleis, 'Prologue: Reluctance to Glance in the Mirror: The Changing Face of German Jurisprudence after 1933 and post-1945' and J. H. H. Weiler, 'Epilogue', in C. Joerges and N. S. Ghaleigh, *Darker Legacies of Law in Europe. The Shadow of National Socialism and Fascism over Europe and Its Legal Traditions* (Oxford: Hart Publishing 2003), pp. 1–18 and pp. 389–402, respectively; follow up in the Special Issue: 'European Integration in the Shadow of The "Darker Legacies of Law in Europe" Europe's Darker Pasts Revisited' (2006) 7 *German Law Journal*, D. Augenstein (guest editor); U. Beck, *German Europe* (Cambridge: Polity Press, 2013).

However, in the move from the classical to the post-classical in the EU legal order, a new intellectual current is appearing, which is much younger and which leads back to the shattering of national science and (legal) philosophy in the early twentieth century. Einstein questioned Newton's world of a logical and coherent natural science, and Nietzsche questioned the philosophical justification of the (nation-) state and the understanding of law as a system.[165] One may wonder to what extent this submerged strand of *European* (not national) commonality can be used to explain the post-national European consciousness and deeper intellectual foundations of the post-nation-state and the post-nation-state private (legal) order. This somewhat neglected part of the intellectual history remained all too often in the background or even underground of the mainstream political and moral philosophy. It must be regarded as an integral part of the common European legal culture.

4 How to Read the Book

The first part: The twentieth century is marked by the rise of the Social in private law. First labour law, then consumer law and today non-discrimination law: all three fields have considerably affected the concept of private law. The nation-state, later the welfare state, is seen to be in charge of providing social justice through appropriate legislative means and through courts monitoring the correct application. The limits of what the welfare state can do via private law to guarantee social justice became ever clearer from the late 1970s on. The enormous expectations nourished through the social democratisation of politics cannot be or at least cannot be fully met. The challenges coming from within – from what is possible and manageable to achieve via law, from the doubtful redistributive effects (the poor pay for the better off) – and from without – from the pressure globalisation and economic efficiency put on welfare states. The nation-state/welfare state is changing, so too is social justice. The intellectual history and the changing legal consciousness of the rise and decline of the Social will be told via a careful reconstruction of the private law orders of Germany, France and the United Kingdom.

The second part: The declining impetus of the welfare state goes hand in hand with an accelerating European integration process, which

---

[165] With regard to the parallel between Newton and the model of good governance (state), Russell, *A History of Western Philosophy*, pp. 652–653.

reached the Social through the Single European Act in the 1980s, exactly when nation-states started to realise the limits of what can be redistributed to the weaker party via law. The EU took over the Social from the Member States, thereby transforming the social dimension in private law, from social private law to the law of the labour and consumer market society, from social justice to access justice. The emergent European model of justice is to be explained through the decline of the nation/state welfare state and the gradual transformation of the EU into a quasi-statutory body. It does not replace or substitute national patterns of justice; it adds a new transnational dimension. Access justice captures what is distinctive about the European experiment, the building of a legal order with a 'social outlook' beyond the state through a supranational treaty, through transnational agencies and through an activist transnational Court.

The third part: The politics of justice can be retraced in private law beyond the nation-state. The key to its understanding is the differentiation of private law into a tripartite legal order – *universal services, social market law* and *societal private law*. Owing to the impact of the European Union, national social labour law, national social consumer law and national non-discrimination law differentiate in two directions. The nucleus remains, although the EU is turning social labour and social consumer law into the law of the labour and consumer market society. This move triggered hard ideological battles on the decline of social justice and on abolishing the protection of the weaker party. It is largely a battlefield over whether the EU minimum standard for access justice can and should be topped by higher national standards of social justice. However, the EU introduced two new layers: universal services as the bottom line for the protection of the vulnerable and a new 'societal private law' that imposes responsibilities on the market citizen, on civil society organisations and companies in building a market and a society beyond the nation-state. Access justice dominates universal services, whilst the new societal private law broadens the perspective towards societal justice.

The conclusions are built around four themes. First, the grand narratives hark back to the path dependence of national legal consciousness, the development of European legal consciousness and, as a consequence, the hybridisation of consciousness. Second, access justice and societal justice are claimed as *the great EU achievements* together with the tripartite European private law order of the labour and consumer market society, and the shared responsibilities of the EU, the Member States and private parties. Third, the drivers behind the transformation of the state, of labour and consumer law and of justice are economic, social and political forces. They help to clarify the role of the EU as a catalyst and a driver, the function of the rationality test and the constitutive importance of the European laboratory. Fourth, I discuss the remaining imponderables: the impact of Brexit on European legal consciousness, the relationship between the tripartite European legal order and the national private law orders, and the impact of the move from the 'geometric (Newton and Hobbes)' to the 'relative state' (Einstein and modern-state theories).

Part I

The Awakening of the Social and Its Transformation in England, France and Germany

The different national conceptions of justice are deeply embedded in legal consciousness and legal culture. Tracing back the intellectual history behind the different conceptions reveals particular patterns of justice that remain amazingly stable over time. The dream of social engineering through law became problematic from the 1970s and early 1980s onwards, calling into question the whole twentieth-century approach, in whatever national hue, just as the Single Market project arose. The welfare state is, if not declining, under pressure and so are the rules that advance the Social. The reverberations and convulsions have shattered the intellectual foundations of English, French and German private law. They irritate the different national models of justice and create a space that allows the EU to step in and develop its own pattern of justice.

The argument will be unfolded in three steps. First and foremost, I will dive into the intellectual history of the three countries and try to show how and why the English model of social justice can be called liberal and pragmatic, the French intellectual and the German paternalistic-legalistic. It goes without saying that these are ideal types. However, these ideal types help to explain the deeper foundations in the legal consciousness that are reflected in the way in which the citizens perceive justice, the role of the state and their own responsibilities. Secondly, I face the daunting task of looking into the successes of realising social justice through law and into the difficulties that the three countries have encountered more or less at the same time. Looking back from today into the 1970s and 1980s enables the disclosure of conceptual and maybe even theoretical deficiencies in the use of law. In that sense the analysis should be understood as an ideological critique. At the same time, stock-taking helps identify the frame of mind in the three states, their societies and their legal systems before the European Union started to engage in the Social. Here are the early signs of what I call the 'post-classical move' and what constitutes the third narrative of Part I: the irritations of path dependency at the foundational level of justice and the surface level of the social private laws. Both the analysis of the successes and difficulties of realising social justice through law as well as the deeper challenges to the national models of justice prepare the ground for Part II and its analysis of justice beyond the state with the European experiment.

1 Socioeconomic and Political Background of Social Justice in France, Germany and England

Where should one start in the search for the transformation of state, private law and justice? Following H. J. Berman,[1] the starting point for identifying legal consciousness should be the eleventh and twelfth centuries, when the conflict between the Catholic Church (the spiritual power) and the emperor (the temporal power) culminated in the conflict between Pope Gregory VII and Emperor Henry IV over the Church's independence from temporal power. The separation of spiritual and temporal power not only initiated the early state-building of first the Church and then the emperor, but also of legal scholasticism.[2] The Crusades already requested by Gregory VII in the eleventh century and the later fall of Constantinople in 1453 led to a much stronger exchange of ideas between the West and the East, and paved the way for the reinvigoration of the West with Greek and Roman philosophy.[3]

The French Constitution, together with the Declaration of Human Rights in 1789 and the adoption of the Code Civil in 1805, marked the development of the national private legal orders, in continental Europe and in the common law countries.[4] The legal nationalism which emerged from the French Revolution, of course, does not fully explain the development of English common law. If any, a parallel may be drawn between the French Revolution of the late eighteenth century and German state-building of the nineteenth century on the one hand, with the Civil War and the conflict between the English Crown and Oliver Cromwell in the seventeenth century, on the other. The Social in

---

[1] Berman, *Recht und Revolution*, p. 144.
[2] Berman, *Recht und Revolution*, pp. 146, 215.
[3] R. W. Southern, *The Making of the Middle Ages* (New Haven: Yale University Press, 1953), pp. 163–208.
[4] Wieacker, *A History of Private Law*, p. 339.

the way it is used throughout the book is linked to the nineteenth century. While intellectual history requires us to look beyond the French Revolution to the emergence of the state with the Westphalian Peace in the seventeenth century, the emergence of private law in our understanding corresponds to changes emerging in the late eighteenth and early nineteenth centuries, whereas the Social is the child of the late nineteenth century.

1.1 A Chart towards Orientation[5]

The following table (Table 1) reflects the findings of the forthcoming analysis of the three different countries. The analysis is built around

Table 1

	France	United Kingdom	Germany
Constitution	1789–1791 Fifth Republic	Republican commonwealth Declaration of Bill of Rights 1689	1848 failed/ 1870 Second Empire/1918 Weimar/1949 Bonn/1990 unification
Codification of civil law	1804 Code Civil	Common law	1900 Bürgerliches Gesetzbuch
Economic determinants	Mercantilism	The English Trading State (Handelsstaat)	Deutscher Bund Norddeutsche Bund Handelsstaat
Political determinants	Central state Corporatistic	Central state Liberal	Federal state
Social determinants	Revolution 1789	Evolution	Industrial revolution

---

[5] What follows in 1.1.–1.4 is a completely revised and fully worked through version of three previous publications: the 'Introduction' to the edited book, H.-W. Micklitz, The Many Concepts of Social Justice in European Private Law, (Elgar 2011), 3–57; H.-W. Micklitz, 'The (Un)-Systematics of (Private) Law as an Element of European Legal Culture', in G. Helleringer and K. Purnhagen (eds.), Towards a European Legal Culture, (München; Oxford; Baden-Baden: Beck; Hart; Nomos, 2014), 81–115; and H.-W. Micklitz, 'On the Intellectual History of Freedom of Contract and Regulation', (2015) 4 Penn State Journal of Law & International Affairs, 1–32.

Table 1 (cont.)

	France	United Kingdom	Germany
Philosophical determinants	Das Wahre ist das Nützliche ('what is right is useful') French Rationalism	Das Nützliche ist das Wahre ('what is useful is right') Empiricism, Utilitarianism	German Idealism German Romanticism
Legal consciousness	Intellectualism	Personalism	Legalism
Key actors	Executive and judges to a growing degree	Judges and QCs	Academia and judges to a growing degree
Model of distributive justice	Political and Paternalistic	Liberal and pragmatic	Authoritarian and paternalistic-libertarian
Labour law	Unity of social and labour law Code de travail	Statutory minimum protection and collective laissez faire	Social security laws (Bismarck) Labour constitution
Consumer law	Price regulation Code de la consommation	Piecemeal legislation in reaction to problems	Programmatic concepts Theoretical battles
Image	The individualistic politicised citizen worker/consumer	The self-determined market-biased worker/consumer	The worker/consumer as object of statutory regulation

the transformation of the state (the constitution) and the rise and transformation of private law-making in light of economic, political, social and philosophical determinants. The categories are to be understood as ideal types. The approach allows us to distinguish different types of legal consciousness and different types of social justice, as well as to identify the key actors in the transformation of private law and justice. The development of first labour law and later consumer law takes different paths in these three countries and is mirrored in different consumer images. Squeezing longstanding and complex developments into neat boxes is a dangerous undertaking and open to criticism. However, Table 1 allows for orientation, for looking backwards and forwards through the history of intellectual thoughts and legal consciousness.

1.2 The English Model: A Liberal and Pragmatic Design Fit for Commercial Use

In English history, there is no comparable event to the adoption of the Code Civil in France or in Germany. The Civil War took place in the seventeenth century and led to major changes in society and in the parliamentarian system. But it neither yielded a constitution nor a coherent codified body of civil law, notwithstanding the Declaration of the Bill of Rights in 1689. Seen through the eyes of a common law lawyer, the French and the German legal systems, and this remains to be shown, share a relatively homogenous view on the role and function of social justice in society. They are united in the idea of universal values that are reflected in legal principles and concepts. This is exactly where common law lawyers run into difficulties.

Thus, the true difference between continental law and common law must be deeper, and the reasons must date further back than the French revolution. The breaking point at which continental law and common law system diverge has to be identified. The socioeconomic and cultural environment in which the later development of social justice in England is embedded cannot be understood without appreciating the clash between continental *scholasticism* and its growing critique through *nominalism* in England. This is exactly when the relative cultural unity of Europe breaks into pieces.[6] *Empiricism* is responsible for the deep differences between continental and common law systems. Empiricism paved the way for utilitarianism. This is key to understanding English reservations about the realisation of social justice as a universal principle through law.

1.2.1 English Pragmatism and English Personalism

My view on the English legal system is imprinted by empirical research undertaken on the management of emergency situations with regard to unsafe consumer goods.[7] In our study,

---

[6] Berman, *Recht und Revolution*, p. 265.
[7] H.-W. Micklitz, T. Roethe and S. Weatherill (eds.), *Federalism and Responsibility. A Study on Product Safety Law and Practice in the European Community* (London: Graham & Trotmann, 1994).

We had to compare the management of emergency type of accidents: exploding office chairs in public buildings due to breakage-prone gas cylinders and the so-called glycol wine in inter alia France, Germany, and the United Kingdom. We analyzed the law in the books and the law in the action. The finding can be summed up in the following way: The French engineers and lawyers in the country were asking themselves, what Paris is doing, the German administrators were seeking the appropriate rules, the English administrators asked where the problem is. As far as Germany is concerned, we found our findings confirmed in a recent empirical study on product safety management in the Baltic Economic Area.[8]

As a visiting professor at Somerville College, University of Oxford, I benefitted from the opportunity to interview judges, barristers, solicitors and non-governmental organisations in the reconstruction of preliminary references from UK courts to the ECJ on Sunday trading, equal treatment and unfair contract terms.[9] The study visit and the research allowed for a deep insight into the English judicial system and the lawyers surrounding it. It is English *pragmatism* and English *personalism* that is characteristic in the handling of legal disputes. Two issues arise whenever one attempts to define the differences between civil law and common law: first, the use of case law in preference to legal principles; and, second, the use of purposive interpretation. Civil law lawyers reason *downwards* from abstract principles embodied in a code, whereas common law lawyers reason *upwards* from the facts, moving gradually from case to case. Civil law lawyers are searching for the *Zweck im Recht*, the purpose and objective behind the legal ruling. This occurs if the wording of the rule to be applied, its position in the broader framework of the code in which the rule is embedded or the history of the rule do not provide guidance. Common law lawyers view purposive interpretation as an alien element.[10] Lord Goff sums up these differences as follows:[11]

Continental lawyers love to proclaim some great principle, and then knock it into shape afterwards. Instead, the boring English want to find out first whether

---

[8] H.-W. Micklitz and T. Roethe, *Produktsicherheit und Marktüberwachung im Ostseeraum: Rechtsrahmen und Vollzugspraxis* (Baden-Baden: Nomos, 2008).
[9] H.-W. Micklitz, *The Politics of Judicial Co-operation in the EU. Sunday Trading, Equal Treatment, and Good Faith* (Cambridge: Cambridge University Press, 2005).
[10] Inter alia, Judge Bingham in *Customs and Excise Commissioners v. ApS Samex* (1983) 1 All ER 1042, at 1056.
[11] Lord Goff, 'The Future of the Common Law' (1997) 46 *International and Comparative Law Quarterly* 745–761, at 753; also R. Goode, 'Insularity or Leadership? The Role of the United Kingdom in the Harmonisation of Commercial Law' (2001) 50 *International and Comparative Law Quarterly* 751–765, quoting Lord Wilberforce at p. 761.

and, if so, how these great ideas are going to work in practice. This is not at all popular with the propagators of the great ideas.

The careful reasoning of English judges is admirable, as is their focus on the wording of the rule in question, the elaboration of the meaning of the rule and their careful explanation of the application of the rule to the particular facts of the case.[12] It is this peculiarly English pragmatism in looking at where the problem lies and at how to find an answer in case law and/or in the rules that is so startling to a civil law lawyer who is fixated on rules. The quotation from Lord Goff may find its deeper origin in three strands: (1) common law was and is, first and foremost, commercial law,[13] as the English legal system was never easily accessible for the person in the streets[14] because the costs of going to court were simply too high; (2) the practising lawyers select the judges, so judges benefitted from a strong commercial legal background; and (3) judges play a much more dominant role in the common law system than in the civil law systems, institutionally and individually.[15] This attitude can be transferred to social justice. There is a deep reservation against the existence of universal principles which enter into the common (commercial) law system from the outside, from politics or deeper from particular sociophilosophical ideas. With regard to potential differences in Europe, pragmatism is a helpful tool to handle differences. Therefore, a particular English view would be to simply accept that there are different concepts in Europe.

The hypothesis is that only by understanding English pragmatism can one comprehend English reservations against achieving social justice through law. The intellectual father is John Locke (1632–1704). The differences between the continental legal system and the common law system can only be explained by the drifting apart of two major

---

[12] B. S. Markesinis, 'Learning from Europe and Learning in Europe', in B. S. Markesinis (ed.), *The Gradual Convergence. Foreign Ideas, Foreign Influences and English Law on the Eve of the Twenty-First Century* (Oxford: Clarendon Press, 1994), pp. 1–32.

[13] H. Collins, 'Lord Hoffmann and the Common Law of Contract' (2009) 5 *European Review of Contract Law* 474–484 demonstrates the influence of one single judge, Lord Hoffman, to defend the traditional concept of contract law in today's time.

[14] R. Zimmermann and A. MacPherson, 'The Clapham Omnibus – Revisited' (2015) 23 *Zeitschrift für Europäisches Privatrecht* 685–688.

[15] Weber, *Wirtschaft und Gesellschaft*, p. 511; Part I. 1.1.5.1 and 2, those who subscribe to Rafael La Porta, Florencio Lopez-de-Silanes, Andrei Shleifer and Robert W. Vishny (LLSV) and claim the superiority of the liberal market economy over the coordinated market economy underline the key role of common law judges (US and UK) to guarantee legal certainty.

philosophical currents which are rooted in the socioeconomic environment of their respective centuries. This will not be possible without necessary simplifications:

- First, we must consider the clash between *scholasticism* and *nominalism*. The Crusades linked the Western world to the Arab world, helping to establish Italian cities (Venice) as world trade centers, and brought forth Arab discourse on ancient Greek philosophers (Aristotle and Plato) to Europe. The fall of Constantinople enhanced the influence of the Greek language and Greek philosophers on the Western world. These ideas questioned not only mainstream scholastic thinking (Thomas Aquinas' concept of universalism), but also the priority of the spiritual over the secular world in which trade should play a limited role. The critique against scholasticism found its expression in the growing importance of nominalism in the fourteenth and fifteenth centuries, particularly in England. Nominalism laid the groundwork for English reservations against *grandes idées* and universal legal principles.
- Second, the rise of *empiricism* is inseparably linked to the birth of the English trading state (Handelsstaat in the late sixteenth and early seventeenth century).[16] In continental Europe, feudalistic society gradually changed into societies of cities and merchants. Trade (i.e. the economy) turned into a function and a task to be managed by the state, and the mercantile system arose. Under Elizabeth I (1558–1603), England succeeded in breaking its dependence on the Hanseatic League with the help of the Merchant Adventurers, who got royal support in establishing worldwide operating trade companies.[17] Commercial law was needed to manage English trade internationally. The philosophical counterpart to social and economic change may be seen in the development from nominalism (Ockham) to empiricism (Bacon, Hume) to utilitarianism (A. Smith, Bentham). This might help to explain the powerful English combination of pragmatism and personalism.

Both historical strands justify the assumption that the continental European understanding of social justice in the meaning of distributive justice does not really correspond to the growth of philosophical,

---

[16] E. Schulin, *Handelsstaat England. Das politische Interesse der Nation im Außenhandel vom 16. bis ins frühe 18. Jahrhundert* (Wiesbaden: F. Steiner, 1969).
[17] L. James, *The Rise and Fall of the British Empire* (London: Little Brown, 1994), pp. 122, 169.

historical, economic and legal structures in England, or – to put it the other way around – England has yielded a legal system which is deeply rooted in nominalistic and utilitarian thinking. In this sense the English way of looking at the role and function of law is much more economic than German Idealism (Kant, Fichte, Hegel, Schelling) or French Rationalism (Descartes, Pascal, Voltaire, Rousseau). It is a shorter way from utility to economic efficiency and economic effectiveness than from duty, understanding, will, reason and spirit (Pflicht, Vernunft, Wille, Verstand, Geist). Utilitarian thinking, which will be shown here, could be more easily adapted to European 'integration through law', where judges and the judicial system are entrusted with a major role.[18]

1.2.2 Origins of Utilitarian Thinking

English law (common law) is less embedded in Christian logic, and that it is not has older origins than the discussions over scholasticism. Its legitimacy was not based on God or the Bible, but on a mixture of Celtic, Saxon, Danish and Norman customs and habits. The law *does* exist. It has only to be found by the judge. Its origin shielded English law against scholastic thinking and canon law. Canon law infiltrated English law via equity and the lord chancellors who were clergymen. These links were cut off during the English Reformation under Henry VIII, the dissolution of the monasteries and the break with Rome. Thomas More became the first non-cleric lord chancellor who resided in his own Court of Chancery. Due to the limited impact of scholasticism, nominalism could unfold in England. This goes together with the changing needs of the economy. Nominalism fit better into the mainstream of social life and growing trade than rigid scholastic thinking.

In essence, the old conflict (already between Aristotle and Plato) between nominalism and scholastic (here universalism) turns on the question of whether only individual things are real, whereas universals exist only in the minds of man, or whether the universals (general concepts) constitute the proper existence (*das eigentliche Sein*) from which the individual things are then deduced. Nominalism might contribute to explain at least two particularities of the English legal system: the aversion to *human rights*[19] and to the *idea of universal justice*. A human

---

[18] Part II, 1.2–1.4.
[19] Lord Hoffmann, 'The Universality of Human Rights', Judicial Studies Board Annual Lecture, March 19, 2009, available at: www.judiciary.gov.uk/announcements/speech-by-lord-hoffmann-the-universality-of-human-rights/.

has two arms and two legs and a head, which allows him or her to see and seize everything. That is the reason why the *Naturrechtslehre* (Grotius)[20] and ideas of human rights could not find acceptance in English legal thought. The second aversion is directed against *legal principles*. Legal principles are not real. They exist only in the idealistic minds of continental European lawyers. Ockham's razor: 'It is vain to do with more what can be done with fewer. *Pluralitas non est ponendo sine necessitate.*' Why do you need principles if you have to smash them before you can solve the case at issue?

The interplay between philosophy and English law can be identified in the grounding of empiricism by Francis Bacon (1561–1626), which paved the way for the development of utilitarianism.[21] The purpose of science is – according to Francis Bacon – to dominate nature for the utility of society. In order to understand the nature of things, man must get rid of all prejudices which hinder objective knowledge (*Erkenntnis*). The only true method to achieve objective knowledge is induction.[22] Such a methodical-experimental approach starts from collecting and comparing observations, in order to understand step by step the general nature of things. This runs contrary to scholastic thinking and contrary to Montaigne and Descartes, who start from deductive reasoning. Bacon's philosophy heavily influenced natural science (Isaac Newton 1643–1727)[23] and legal thinkers. Empiricism rendered the integration of moral considerations into the English legal system possible. Under the old common law, the judge was seen as the moral instance. Nominalism, however, lacks a moral dimension. Empiricism could not really close that gap, as it was meant to observe and analyse what man could see and grasp. This does not allow for the deduction of normative implications from facts. Bacon argued that the observations of the real things do not allow conclusions with how the things should be.

Later philosophers, not least in tumult of the Civil War, used empiricism to study the individual. Joy, envy, harm and utility could

---

[20] On Grotius and natural law, B. Straumann, *Roman Law in the State of Nature. The Classical Foundations of Hugo Grotius' Natural Law* (Cambridge: Cambridge University Press, 2015), p. 24.
[21] Russell, *A History of Western Philosophy*, p. 618 understands Locke as the founder of empiricism.
[22] Russell, *A History of Western Philosophy*, p. 551.
[23] On the relationship between natural science and philosophy, see Russell, *A History of Western Philosophy*, p. 534; for those who believe in the magic of numbers: Michelangelo 1475–1564, Galilei 1564–1642, Newton 1643–1727.

be observed. Now it was possible to define normative assumptions. Thomas Hobbes (1588–1679) argued that self-preservation is the most fundamental value, as each organism intends to avoid death. The concept of *summum bonum*, which for the scholastic ranks as the highest moral objective of a community, is replaced by the human striving for security. In the distinction between 'will' and 'reason', Hobbes characterised 'reason' as an instrument with which it is possible to find the appropriate means for the achievement of those purposes which are defined by the 'will' – so-called *utility motives*. His writings have to be placed into historical context. Hobbes was obviously supporting the king against Cromwell. Therefore, his philosophy cannot be understood in isolation from political events.[24] However, Hobbes has to be read in connection with Locke. For Locke, reason consists of two parts: the investigation (empiricism) of what we can know with certainty and the investigation of rules that we are wise to respect in practice, although we lack certainty and must start from probability.[25] Therefore, while Locke shares with Hobbes the key role of utility, he recognises the need to respect the limits of utility, which should not result in pure selfishness. In this sense, Lockean pragmatism helps to set limits on unbridled utilitarianism.

Now the way was cleared for later philosophers to set up a particular way of thinking, namely utilitarianism, which is often equated with the English way of thinking. Starting with Bacon, an individualistic social and moral philosophy arose in England which challenged, with great success, the dominant universalistic philosophy of the continent. This philosophy combines utilitarianism with pragmatism and laid the groundwork for an understanding under which the individual is responsible for his or her wealth and that it is not the task of the state to cushion social grievance.[26] The link to the reservations against social justice as the responsibility of the protective welfare state is obvious, although pragmatic interventions here and there are fully in line with the intellectual grounding.

---

[24] Menéndez, 'Whose Justice? Which Europe?', pp. 142–143.
[25] Russell, *A History of Western Philosophy*, p. 587: 'According to Locke, reason consists of two parts: first, the study of what we can know with certainty, and second, the exploration of sentences that are prudent in practice, though only probability does not speak for them.'
[26] Or to provide relief for famine, like in Ireland. A. Sen, *Development as Freedom* (Oxford: Oxford University Press, 1999), p. 15.

1.2.3 Societal Continuity and Economic Success

The continuity of the individualistic social and moral philosophy over centuries – which was grounded in the sixteenth century, deepened and reinforced in following centuries, and confirmed by the Anglican church through its puritan faith, a faith which made its way into the minds of the people (as a common unified scheme of thinking) – could possibly be explained by the success of the English trading state (*Handelsstaat*). The capitalistic colonisation through private companies contributed to the wealth of merchants and the Crown (by way of taxes and tariffs). The Civil War destroyed feudalistic structures in England, roughly one century prior in continental Europe, however, not in Ireland and the Scottish Highlands until the 1870s to 1880s. In England, merchants, citizens and craftsmen benefitted from the new (economic) freedoms. They, together with the aristocrats, paved the way for an 'industrial *evolution*' (not revolution).[27] In contrast to France and Germany, the English social and economic transformation from a trading state (*Handelsstaat*) to an industrial state (*Industriestaat*) occurred without a great revolution. Farmers who were no longer needed in agricultural production were largely absorbed by the growing industrial centers. This might also explain the late development – compared to the advanced level of industrialisation – of a labour movement and the Labour Party in England.

Not even the convulsions resulting from the loss of the American colonies, the loss of the hegemonic power, and the upsurge of competitors (France and Germany) and its negative impact on employment and working conditions produced a deep change of the individualistic social and moral philosophy. The social, political and economic turmoil in the late eighteenth and early nineteenth centuries, later on called the Age of Reform, did not end up in a movement towards a social protective welfare state similar to the developments in France and Germany at the end of the nineteenth century. There was, however, a political debate over whether poverty should be seen as a personal or as social misfortune. The new ideology was reflected in the 1834 English Poor Law Amendment Act.[28] The aim was to strengthen the labour market by distinguishing the paupers from the poor.

---

[27] K. Polanyi insists on the revolutionary character in England; see *The Great Transformation*, The Political and Economic Origins of Our Time, Beacon Press, Boston, Massachusetts, Second Paper Edition 2001), p. 72.

[28] Hepple, 'Welfare Legislation and Wage-Labour', p. 122; on the deeper background Polanyi, *The Great Transformation*, chapter 7; Speenhamland 1795, pp. 81–90.

Bentham and others called for a radical reform of the legal system. They claimed that the common law, which Bentham called the Demon of Chicane, was outdated and functioned as a barrier for citizens seeking advice in the law. Without legal counsel it was impossible to know how the law answers a particular problem (and this has not really changed over time). Therefore, Bentham and others advocated codification, which failed. This does not mean that the political debate on codification did not produce a change in the legal system. The Judicature Acts 1873–75 united common law and equity, which had developed in different directions. The separated courts were merged into one new court. Judges had to apply the common law and equity as well. The unification of the two different land laws, under which ownership could differ according to common law or equity, followed in 1925. There might be an indirect link to the dominating role the Social played in the post-war period in France. These pieces of codification could be interpreted as a late success of Bentham's critique. Codification had entered the realms of the English law tradition. The 'law' could no longer be found in the old customs and habits alone; it also resided in statutory form.

1.2.4 Intrusion of Social Justice into Labour Law

There was no big bang in English society which led to the development of social justice motivated legal regimes. The transformation from a feudalistic and corporative society to an open democracy occurred step by step. The Civil War constituted certainly a break-even point, but the transformation process was very much guided by conflicts between the nobles on the one hand and the merchants, on the other, who wanted to have their say in the political arena. The rise of the labour movement, in the legal theoretical language of D. Kennedy[29] the rise of the Social in the United Kingdom, is bound to the transformation from a trading state into an industrial state at the beginning of the nineteenth century – a few decades earlier than in continental Europe. The decline of feudalistic structures and the rise of an individualistic social and moral philosophy provided the ground on which the labour movement could grow.

Thilo Ramm[30] distinguishes two principles as a parameter of comparison in the new ordering of labour law in the nineteenth and twentieth

---

[29] Kennedy, 'Three Globalizations of Law and Legal Thought'.
[30] Ramm, 'Epilogue'.

centuries across the then nine Member States of the EU: *self-help* and *state-help*. Self-help was the basis of trade unions and strikes. This was close to the dominating liberal understanding of the economy in England, emphasising the free play of market forces. The system of self-help replaced individual laissez faire with *collective* laissez faire. Self-help and collective laissez faire is a noble circumscription for a period of fight and conflict which led to compromises at both ends, between the trade unions and the trade associations, and between the different political forces in Parliament. If Parliament took action, it did so in response to concrete problems via isolated statutes and ad hoc political decisions. This is the particular English way of dealing with matters of justice. The political programme of the Liberal Party to levy taxes and redistribute them would have indeed been a kind of revolution, a break away from longstanding traditions. However, while the draft budget passed the House of Commons, it was blocked by the House of Lords in 1910.

In the collective laissez faire system, health and safety laws as well as the social security system set up a stable system that lasted until the 1960s. In 1953 Otto Kahn-Freund[31] coined the term of 'policy of abstention' as a British particularity, where labour law and industrial relations was mainly shaped through the common law. Regulatory intervention from the late nineteenth and early twentieth century was aimed at eliminating barriers that the common law would have imposed on collective autonomy. Paul Davies and Mark Freedland underline in their analysis of UK labour legislation that Kahn-Freund's classification might not be totally correct, as the state had introduced by statute a social security system and health and safety legislation.[32] Therefore, it seems more precise to stress the interaction between collective bargaining as the dominant form of contract regulation and mandatory social insurance mechanisms.

The short period under the (old) Labour government in the 1960s is the only time in which statutory policy was used to strengthen

---

[31] P. Davies and M. Freedland (eds.), *Kahn-Freund's Labour and the Law*, 3rd ed. (London: Stevens, 1983), p. 37; contributions of O. Kahn-Freund, 'Legal Framework' and J. D. M. Bell, 'Trade Unions', in A. Flanders and H. A. Clegg (eds.), *The System of Industrial Relations in Great Britain. Its History, Law and Institutions* (Oxford: Basil Blackwell, 1954), pp. 42–127 and pp. 128–196; later H. A. Clegg, *The System of Industrial Relations in Great Britain* (Oxford: Basil Blackwell, 1972) with a strong focus on industrial relations, on the collective dimension of labor law.
[32] P. Davies and M. Freedland, *Labour Legislation and Public Policy* (Oxford: Oxford University Press, 1993), in particular chapter 1, 'Collective Laissez-Faire', pp. 8–59, pp. 8 and 35.

social institutions and distributive justice in labour law. This corresponds with the rise of Keynesianism to manage, and to shape, the economy as well as the growing importance of social justice concerns in the aftermath of the French 1968 revolution, partly triggered by the rise of bureaucratic power in the hands of ever bigger companies.[33] Three statutes were adopted to strengthen the rights of the individual in employment relations: the Race Relations Act 1968, the Equal Pay Act 1970 and the Unfair Dismissal Act 1972. While the Labour government did not reinstate the full collective autonomy of trade unions, it initiated a shift towards the contractualisation of employment relations. For Deakin and Wilkinson[34] this was the result of a particular mid-twentieth-century political consensus to break down the master–servant relation via statutory intervention. The Unfair Dismissal Act 1972, then, compensates for the non-binding character of collective bargaining agreements under the common law.[35]

These later legislative measures were elaborated, not least under influence of the EU. Employment equality law has been among the most important elements in UK employment law since 1970 onwards, and it has been the subject of a constructive interaction between English domestic law and EU law. Employment equality law survived Thatcherism,[36] contrary to collective self-help. This does not mean that the United Kingdom under Thatcher was ready to accept the European social policy which, from the United Kingdom's perspective, was perceived as a continuation of the 1970s. Quite the contrary is true. The rift between the emerging European social policy and the United Kingdom's move towards deregulation and increased freedom for economic actors to promote international competitiveness of the national economy became ever deeper and resulted in legal conflicts between the UK resistance to implementing European secondary law properly and/or between UK courts and the European Court of Justice. Trade unions and the Equal Opportunities Commission instrumentalised the preliminary reference procedure to defend and or to improve quite successfully individual labour rights for men and women in employment

---

[33] H. Collins, 'Against Abstentionism in Labour Law', in J. Eekelaar and J. Bell (eds.), *Oxford Essays in Jurisprudence* (Oxford: Oxford University Press, 1987), pp. 79–101.
[34] Deakin and Wilkinson, *The Law of the Labour Market*, 'preface', p. vii, chapter 1, 'Labour Markets and Legal Evolution', p. 24.
[35] Hepple and Veneziani, 'Introduction,' p. 19.
[36] Davies and Freedland, *Labour Legislation and Public Policy*, p. 237.

contracts.[37] The United Kingdom anticipated and later promoted the shift from the protective design of European labour regulation to market regulation. There is a link between the UK move and the European move from protection to regulating competiveness.[38] Davies and Freedland reject any correlation between the EU and the United Kingdom. They claim organic path dependence to be at the roots of the UK move towards the holistic perspective on the law of the labour market.[39] Even if there is no correlation, the resemblance strengthens the argument of those who criticise English–European neoliberalism. At the surface level, this might be plausible. If one understands the UK labour law as a blueprint for the development in the EU – what Deakin and Wilkinson claim –[40] one has to take into account not only Thatcherism but in particular the development of the English labour law after Thatcher under New Labour.

Outside the boundaries of EU law, the Thatcher government deregulated the labour market by withdrawing or weakening rights granted through statute (e.g. unfair dismissal) and, most importantly, through its attempt to reduce the collective autonomy of trade unions. The means to achieve this was not so much legislative intervention[41] but instrumentalisation of the common law as a means to hold the trade unions liable and to interfere with the inner democratic structure of trade unions to drive a wedge between the trade union and its members.[42] The overall aim remained the same: weakening collective bargaining as the mode of contractual governance and replacing it through 'individual' bargaining between employer and employees. The hard way

---

[37] With regard to equal treatment, Micklitz, *The Politics of Judicial Co-operation in the EU*, chapter 3, p. 165; informative is Davies and Freedland, *Labour Legislation and Public Policy*, 10.4. *The Impact of Membership of the European Community*, pp. 576–599.

[38] H. Collins, 'Regulating the Employment Relation for Competitiveness' (2001) 30 *Industrial Law Journal* 17–48; P. Davies and M. Freedland, *Towards a Flexible Labour Market. Labour Legislation and Regulation since the 1990s* (Oxford: Oxford University Press, 2007).

[39] Davies and Freedland, *Labour Legislation and Public Policy*, p. 14 with reference to the two key EU documents of the time, European Commission, White Paper, 'Growth, Competitiveness, Employment', COM(93) 700, 5.12.1993; European Commission, White Paper, 'European Social Policy', COM(94) 333, 27.7.1994 both adopted under the Presidency of Jacques Delors.

[40] Deakin and Wilkinson, *The Law of the Labour Market*, p. 26.

[41] Although the Thatcher government repealed the promotion of collective bargaining and the statutuory recognition procedure. Davies and Freedland, *Labour Legislation and Public Policy*, p. 658.

[42] Davies and Freedland, *Labour Legislation and Public Policy*, p. 519.

would have been to amend the Industrial Relations Act of 1971. However, the Thatcher government was quite reluctant, perhaps due to foreseeable resistance any amendment to the 1971 Act would have caused. The Conservative government under Prime Minister Heath had even intended to advance the spread of collective bargaining through public policy. This was no longer the collective autonomy Kahn-Freund had in mind; this was 'framed' autonomy politicised to the benefits of a conservative government. Under Thatcher collective bargaining lost its central role in governing industrial relations.[43]

What were the long-term effects of Thatcherism? Has collective bargaining lost its place in the UK economy, society and in politics independent from the party which is in power? Has labour law definitely and more strongly shifted from collective to individual bargaining with the consequence that labour law is now mainly about the reach and scope of individual rights? P. Davies and M. Freedland discuss the potential impact in practice as early as 1993 with regard to three dimensions: the Hayekian ideological (Lord Wedderburn), the short-term practical considerations (Auerbach) and their own distinction between ideological measures (against closed shops) and opportunistic measures (aimed directly at trade unions).[44] In 2007, the same authors presented an analysis of New Labour's policy. They provided a detailed account of the long-term effects of both the Thatcher and Blair policies. The UK law of the labour market is characterised by key elements that made their way into European social policy and contributed to the shaping of access justice.[45] First and foremost, New Labour should rather be understood as a continuation of Thatcher than a rupture with her policy. New Labour did not turn the clock back to collective autonomy. Whereas Thatcher aimed at moderating collective bargaining power and strengthening the protection of the individual, New Labour (1997–2006) turned social policy into the pursuit of labour market regulation in the interest of a free and competitive market economy. The truly innovative element of New Labour is the 'Fairness at Work' doctrine, which combines 'fairness (justice)' with (economic) 'efficiency'. Labour market and labour law is to be broadened to include

---

[43] Davies and Freedland, *Labour Legislation and Public Policy*, p. 656.
[44] Davies and Freedland, *Labour Legislation and Public Policy*, p. 521.
[45] Davies and Freedland, *Labour Legislation and Public Policy*, introduction in combination with the overall conclusions, p. 640.

taxation, social security, worker representation (as a substitute for collective bargaining power)[46] and unemployment policy. Flexible labour market rules should facilitate access of the unemployed or of all those who have difficulties in finding their way into the labour market. Promoting work ties in with the then-dominating rhetoric of the OECD and the EU. The slogan of the Blair government was 'money for modernization (the third way)', modernisation being understood as making the EU workers and employers (the holistic perspective) fit for raising international competitiveness. Davies and Freedland come to the conclusion that New Labour used the space left by the Thatcher government to develop a labour market policy that is no longer oriented towards the abolition of social inequity but to secure market inclusion in an ever more competitive global environment.

Why – compared to France – was it relatively easy for a Conservative government to change the regulatory paradigm, away from collective autonomy towards individualisation and contractualisation of labour relations, away from social justice to access justice? The simple answer would be that the shift from a manufacturing industry to a services-based economy effectively undercut trade unionism, i.e. trade unions developed in the shipyards, the coalmine, and the smelter. The more complicated one relates to the overall organic evolution of UK labour law from the twentieth into the twenty-first century. Such an interpretation sets aside that the path for the paradigm shift was only cleared once the Thatcher government had broken the dominant model of collective bargaining and of self-help. The collective power of the trade unions was not re-established, contrary to France, Italy, Spain and Portugal. However, civil organisations, human rights groups and women's organisations helped to counterbalance the loss of power of the trade unions, at least if one follows the new understanding that labour law is no longer limited to tackling social inequality, but is extended to managing the law of the labour market as a whole.[47]

---

[46] Hepple and Veneziani, 'Introduction', p. 26; more fully developed by U. Mückenberger, 'Workers' Representation at the Plant and Enterprise Level', in B. Hepple and B. Veneziani (eds.), *The Transformation of Labour Law in Europe. A Comparative Study of 15 Countries* 1945–2004 (Oxford: Hart Publishing, 2009), pp. 233–262; Davies and Freedland, *Towards a Flexible Labour Market*, p. 130 mandatory consultation of employee representatives; Deakin and Wilkinson, *The Law of the Labour Market*, Chapter 4 'Collective Bargaining and Social Regulation', p. 200.

[47] Hepple and Veneziani, 'Introduction', p. 26.

1.2.5. Intrusion of Social Justice into Consumer Law

The story of consumer law is a relatively new one; it is a post-war story, linked to the rise of the consumer society in the 1950s.[48] The emergence of consumer law is not linked to the labour movement. Trade unions and self-help did not play a role in the rise of consumer law in the United Kingdom. Neither were trade unions involved in the development of a consumer policy, nor were there bottom-up self-organised consumer associations that became a counterweight to trade and industrial organisation. Which?, a consumer association established in 1957 under the auspices of the Labour party, is a member-based and member-financed consumer journal that sells results of product testing and consumer advice. It fits all too well into the particular English economic and social history that consumer protection in the United Kingdom grew through self-organisation in the form of a state independent business.[49] This is remarkable if one compares the history of the sister institutions in France (Que Choisir) and Germany (Stiftung Warentest) where state subsidies still support the financing of the testing institutions today.

The debate over consumer law started in 1960 with the *Molony Report*, commissioned by the Labour government. It identified numerous deficiencies and injustices affecting individuals. It took until 1973 for consumer policy to be widely accepted across the political spectrum.[50] The United Kingdom did not formulate a comprehensive consumer policy programme in pursuit to the famous 1962 Kennedy declaration, unlike France and Germany, but instead reacted in a pragmatic-problem-bound way. Three major reforms took place in about four years: the Amendment of the Supply of Goods Act 1973, the adoption of the Consumer Credit Act in 1974 and the Unfair Contract Terms Act in 1977. All interventions created mandatory contract law, which was fully in line with mainstream thinking of using consumer law as a regulatory tool to limit contractual freedom.

There is a difference between the continental approach on the one hand, and the English approach on the other. The Unfair Contract Terms Act did not submit standard terms between business and consumers to a general fairness test, just as Germany and, some years later,

---

[48] Trentmann, *Empire of Things*, p. 78 going back to the sixteenth century.
[49] E. Roberts, *Which? 25: Consumers Association, 1957–82* (London: Consumers Association, 1982).
[50] M. Whincup, *Consumer Legislation in the United Kingdom and the Republic of Ireland. A Study prepared for the EC Commission* (London: Van Nostrand Reinhold, 1980), p. 7.

France did. It was not until Directive 93/13/EEC on unfair terms[51] that a good faith test was introduced in consumer contracts. The idea of placing a general concept of fairness in the hands of judges led to irritations.[52] The UK approach to consumer credit is less determined by a protective outlook than by guaranteeing a workable and feasible capital market. It combines private law and public law means. In Germany, consumer credit is certainly one of the areas where it is the courts, rather than the legislator, which played a predominant role in the protection of the weaker party. In 1993, the German Constitutional Court declared collateral guarantees between a bank and a debtor's daughter unconstitutional.[53] There is no counterpart in the case law of the House of Lords (now the Supreme Court). Initially, the UK courts had used equity and the common law to integrate consumer elements into contract law. After the intervention of the UK legislator, courts have become less active and even reversed mid-twentieth-century positions.[54] The Supreme Court became involved into consumer credit via the Unfair Terms Directive. Here it upheld its position that there is no need and no justification under English law to introduce an element of social justice into consumer contracts.[55]

The decision of the UK Supreme Court has to be read and understood against the distinction between the common law on contracts and market regulation. The former is the domain of commerce and freedom of contract to be governed and monitored by the English judiciary. Regulation has to be enforced by regulatory agencies. In line with American thinking, the United Kingdom put the protection of consumers into the hands of a regulatory agency, the UK Office of Fair Trading (1973–2014), now the Competition and Markets Authority (CMA).

---

[51] Council Directive 93/13/EEC of 5 April 1993 on unfair terms in consumer contracts, OJ No. L 95, 21.4.1993, p. 29.

[52] Helpful is G. Teubner, 'Legal Irritants: Good Faith in British Law or How Unifying Law Ends up in New Divergences' (1998) 61 *Modern Law Review* 11–32.

[53] M. R. Marella, 'The Old and the New Limits to Freedom of Contract in Europe' (2006) 2 *European Review of Contract Law* 257–274 in particular under reference to G. Teubner, 'Ein Fall von struktureller Korruption? Die Familienbürgschaft in der Kollision unverträglicher Handlungslogiken' (2000) 83 *Kritische Vierteljahresschrift für Gesetzgebung und Rechtswissenschaft* 388–404.

[54] E.g. *Cavendish v. Makdessi; ParkingEye v. Beavis* [2015] UKSC 67, joined cases on penalty clauses. ParkingEye is b2c, even contrary to EU law on unfair terms, Lord Toulson dissenting, for further information UKSC blog: http://ukscblog.com/the-supreme-court-on-the-penalties-doctrine-recast-and-restricted-but-not-rejected-in-full/.

[55] *Office of Fair Trading v. Abbey National plc & Others* [2009] UKSC 6 on appeal from [2009] EWCA Civ 116.

Regulatory agencies like CMA or the Financial Services Authority (FSA) monitor self-regulation by industry and trade as well as individual and collective claims of consumers.[56] The common law system dominated by judges and the consumer law system dominated by public authorities are kept separate from each other. Public enforcement allows for cross-fertilisation between labour and consumer law. Where the judiciary, in particular the House of Lords, became involved in consumer law matters, in particular in contract law, it promotes the freedom of contract ideology on consumer litigation.[57]

The Thatcher government in the 1970s and 1980s, the new Labour government of Blair in the 1990s, and the successive governments all failed to bring about substantial changes in consumer law, perhaps with the exception of a UK variation of the US class action in 2014.[58] Following the United States, the United Kingdom liberalised and privatised former state incumbents in the field of telecommunication, energy and transport in the 1970s. After a short period of a protective statutory policy under the Labour government in the 1960s, the English consumer had to face a new challenge which affected daily life considerably. In the field of regulated markets, the former customer turned into a market citizen rather than a protected consumer. The return to the market, to self-help instead of statutory regulation, has a long-standing history in the United Kingdom. Liberalisation and privatisation of former state monopolies is connected to *utilitarian* thinking.[59] The United Kingdom preceded and influenced these developments in the EU.[60] Hand in hand with the European Commission, the United Kingdom became the driving forces behind liberalisation and privatisation.

---

[56] C. Hodges, *The Reform of Class and Representative Actions in European Legal Systems. A New Framework for Collective Redress in Europe* (Oxford: Hart Publishing, 2008), p. 216.

[57] Collins, 'Lord Hoffmann and the Common Law of Contract'.

[58] L. Craig, T. Bolster, G. Chhokar, 'Living up to Expectations? The Consumer Rights Act 2015, a Year on' (2017) 31 *Global Competition Litigation Review* 1–9.

[59] G. Howells and S. Weatherill, *Consumer Protection Law* (Aldershot: Ashgate, 2005), p. 78, underlines the influence of F. v. Hayek in the way in which England administered the privatisation process under the Thatcher regime.

[60] J. Keßler and H.-W. Micklitz, *Kundenschutz auf liberalisierten Märkten. Energie. Vergleich der Konzepte, Maßnahmen und Wirkungen in Europa* (Baden-Baden: Nomos, 2008), p. 313; same authors, *Kundenschutz auf liberalisierten Märkten. Personenverkehr/Eisenbahn. Vergleich der Konzepte, Maßnahmen und Wirkungen in Europa* (Baden-Baden: Nomos, 2008), p. 233; same authors, *Kundenschutz auf liberalisierten Märkten. Telekommunikation. Vergleich der Konzepte, Maßnahmen und Wirkungen in Europa* (Baden-Baden: Nomos, 2008), p. 335.

The impact of this particular collaboration reaches far beyond the field of public services. The UK policy to execute enforcement via regulatory agencies – which are competent for a particular sector such as energy, telecommunication, transport or for a particular market design, competition and unfair commercial services – served for the European Commission as a blueprint for promoting the establishment of agencies all over Europe, first in the respective liberalised sectors and then in consumer law as a horizontal domain.[61] Today, the catchword 'agentification'[62] does the rounds in Europe. Not least due to the common law legacy, consumer law enforcement is moving much closer to an administrative enforcement model, even in private law matters.

1.3 The French Model: An Intellectual Political Design of a (Just) Society

France has a particular standing in the legal and theoretical discourse on the interrelationship between constitution building, private legal order building and matters of justice. It results from the French Revolution in 1789, the achievements of which are still shaping our understanding of 'a' constitution and 'a' civil code. The key events took place within two decades, contrary to England, where no such clear-cut events – at least not with regard to constitution-building and private legal order-making – can be identified. At the surface level, the difference between the ancient regime and the republic is striking; at the deeper level, there might well be continuity.[63] The revolution breaks definitively with feudalistic structures and institutes a bourgeois society, where the political power is centralised, governed by individual freedom and equality of rights, which became manifest in the Code Civil and in the French Constitution.[64] It is the French Revolution that, even today, provides the source of inspiration that guides French society, the French economy and French politics.

---

[61] Regulation (EC) No 2006/2004 of the European Parliament and of the Council of 27 October 2004; on cooperation between national authorities responsible for the enforcement of consumer protection laws, OJ No. L 364, 9.12.2004, p. 1.
[62] M. Scholten and M. van Rijsbergen, 'The Limits of Agencification in the European Union' (2014) 15 *German Law Journal* 1223–1256.
[63] A. de Tocqueville, *The Old Regime and the French Revolution* (New York: Anchor Books, 1955).
[64] Wieacker, *A History of Private Law*, p. 271.

Taking again scholasticism as the break-even point, the question is how France dispensed with the tight grip of the Church over the economy and society. What kind of conditions, economic, social, political, and philosophical, were needed to yield the two achievements that colour our understanding of the role and function of the law in France, namely universalism and constitutionalism? The answer lay in the declaration of human rights in 1789 with its emphasis on universality; the French constitution, which was based on Montesquieu's works (1689–1755), from which Rousseau (1712–1789) borrowed the separation of powers[65]; and the French Code Civil as the incarnation of a statutory order meant to organise the civil and economic life of the people. The answer to the question of universalism and constitutionalism can be found in French rationalism. This leads to Montaigne (1533–1596) and Descartes (1596–1650). French rationalism, in its two dimensions *'raison'* (Descartes, Voltaire) and 'imagination' (Rousseau), is the source of French intellectualism that explains the particular French worldview of the society, of the economy, of the demand for universalism and, in a way, also of the superiority of the French ideal: 'The power of reason expressed through law'.[66] Notwithstanding the appeal of French rationalism to Descartes in French academia and Voltaire in French politics, French rationalism is a broad philosophical and political concept, which leaves ample room for legend building.

1.3.1 French Intellectualism

Why do the French claim to think in the name of the world? Why are French intellectuals so convinced that their way of addressing the state, morality and the law is of such a universal interest? Why are French philosophers intellectual 'heroes' and integral to the nation-state and civil society?

My view on French law was shaped through two formative years I spent in France: one year in Paris as part of my apprenticeship at a French law firm in 1974 (what the Germans call *Referendariat* and what is part of the so-called second state exam), and one year at the University of Montpellier in 1979, where I worked as an assistant to Professor Jean Calais-Auloy. Luckily, S. Hazareesingh, in 2015,

---

[65] Russell, *History of Western Philosophy*, pp. 670–671.
[66] Nineteenth-century philosopher C. Dupont-White, *L'individu et l'État* (Paris: Guillaumin, 1865), p. lxvii, quoted in S. Hazareesingh, *How the French Think: An Affectionate Portrait of an Intellectual People* (London: Allen Lane, Penguin Random House, 2015), p. 11.

published his inspiring book *How the French Think*.⁶⁷ The methodology he uses is perfectly in line with 'legal consciousness'.⁶⁸ He refers to a British army manual issued before the Normandy landing, where the British soldiers were prepared for the singularities of the natives: 'By and large, Frenchmen enjoy intellectual argument more than we do. You will often think two Frenchmen are having a violent quarrel when they are simply arguing about some abstract point'.⁶⁹ This hint reminded me of an early experience at the University of Montpellier where a 'leftist' critical private law theorist and a 'right-wing' family lawyer were arguing in unfriendly words and with linguistic violence. Later, the same two were having lunch together, now in a very well-tempered mood, talking friendly to each other and smiling.

It is characteristic of French intellectualism that dispute is most visible in the public. S. Hazareesingh⁷⁰ opens his book with a quote from a speech French Foreign Minister Dominique de Villepin delivered at the Security Council debate at the United Nations in 2003 on whether to sanction the use of force against Saddam Hussein's regime. He forcefully argued against military intervention and concluded his speech with the following words:

We are the guardians of an ideal, the guardians of a conscience. The heavy responsibility and the immense honour which is ours should lead us to give priority to peaceful disarmament.

These two sentences condense what has survived over more than 200 years and what can be understood even today as the major characteristic of French intellectualism: the belief in logic; French universalism, the values to be defended are universal values, not French values; and French humanism, the conviction that politics should and must prevail over force. Numerous examples could be added, most of which would have to be taken from the public environment. S. Hazareesingh's book is full of entertaining little stories from the last few centuries.⁷¹

---

⁶⁷ The subtitle is equally important: *An Affectionate Portrait of an Intellectual People*.
⁶⁸ Hazareesingh, *How the French Think*, p. 18, where he describes his method to find French intellectualism.
⁶⁹ Hazareesingh, *How the French Think*, p. 9.
⁷⁰ Hazareesingh, *How the French Think*, p. 5. At p. 302 he writes, 'This was, *en passant*, an expression of two classics of Gallic repertoire: that something really became significant only when it happened in France, and that whatever occurred in France had universal significance.' Hazareesingh concludes the book with a similar statement from A. Siegfried in the immediate aftermath of World War II, at p. 312.
⁷¹ Hazareesingh, *How the French Think*, 'The Great Divide' between the confident and the anxious France, at p. 322, referring to Finkielkraut, is said 'to illustrate how far the

The French philosopher Michel Lacroix goes as far as to speak of 'an ontological understanding of Frenchness' in 2011.[72]

But what about the French judicial environment? What do judges say in defence of the French civil law system, the French constitution or human rights? Since 1789, France has changed her constitution five times. If any, the written constitution is the continuity. It is not a pragmatic solution like the British 'unwritten' constitution. However, the born candidate for stable and lasting French intellectualism and for French rationalism is the Code Civil. In the Panthéon, Napoléon holds the code in his hands. Despite many legislative interventions, mainly in the field of family law, the code survived by and large untouched in its overall architecture, not necessarily in its values until the major reform in 2016.[73] French civil lawyers (and not only French ones) understand the French Code Civil as a masterpiece of humankind, the integrity of which is undermined by European private law-making. This critique can be observed in a book that professors at Paris I and Paris II produced in 2004 to honour the bicentennial of the French Code Civil, particularly in the violent intellectual attacks from French academics against the Draft Common Frame of Reference or the forceful rejection of the World Bank Report that claimed the supremacy of the common law system over the continental (French) civil code.[74]

However, it would be wrong and misleading to emphasise that Frenchness is represented by pure rationalism alone. To be sure, the claim of reason is the starting point of French philosophical thought, and the prominence of deductive thinking since Descartes downgrades empiricism. There is a French saying *tant pis pour les faits*, which nicely expresses that reason, intellect and idea come first and that French rationalism enshrines, despite all emphasis on *raison*, the

---

declinist obsession [promoted by French intellectuals at the end of the twentieth century] has pushed mainstream French thought away from the Rosseauist and republican heritage' p. 311.

[72] M. Lacroix, *Éloge du patriotisme. Petite philosophie du sentiment national* (Paris: Robert Laffont, 2011), at p. 11.

[73] Special Issue: The New French Code Civil – In a Broader Context, *European Review of Contract Law*, (2017) 13.

[74] B. Fauvarque-Cosson and A.-J. Kerhuel, 'Is Law an Economic Contest? French Reactions to the Doing Business World Bank Reports and Economic Analysis of the Law' (2009) 57 *American Journal of Comparative Law* 811–830; also Special Issue of the (2002) 14 *European Journal of Law and Economics*, with an editorial of J. G. Backhaus and F. H. Stephen, 'The Code Napoléon after 200 years', 191–192. The six papers are discussing the economic, social and political circumstances under which the Civil Code was adopted and shaped.

opportunity for speculation, for imagination and for utopia. The other side of French rationalism is enshrined in Rousseau and his visionary *contrat social*. Rousseau paved the way for exactly this kind of utopian thinking which is 'abstract in design, systematic in its form and radical in its goals'.[75] There is a fierce debate on 'bullshit and French philosophy', triggered by G. A. Cohen.[76] What matters is the tension between order and revolution, between the constant striving for central power, be it the absolute monarchy under Louis XIV or the republican monarch under the Fifth Constitution, between Descartes enthroning Louis IV and Rousseau laying the ground for 'democracy'[77]. French rationalism allows both: justifying central power, construing a civil code through reason (both were the product of the French Revolution)[78] and the resistance of the French citizens against central power and even against the Code Civil, which is regarded as safeguarding and maintaining the power of bourgeoisie over society.

Therefore, a deeper analysis has to start from two premises:

- First, the vision of the French revolution, which was proclaimed in the Declaration of Human Rights, elaborated in a Constitution and later codified in the Code Civil, has deeper social, cultural, economic and intellectual roots. Today's conception of social justice in France can best be understood as a forward-looking political concept. This goes back to French Rationalism and Descartes and Voltaire.

- Second, French society is characterised by the tension between intellectual projects guided by *grandes idées* ('what is right is useful') – the French Constitution and the French Code, which strengthen the power of the executive to the detriment of the power of the judiciary – and the highly politicised bottom-up resistance against a too far-reaching executive power (Rousseau). The fight over 'the Social', and the political resistance in the early twenty-first century of public officials,

---

[75] Quote from Hazareesingh, *How the French Think*, p. 106.
[76] Late professor at All Souls, Oxford. G. A. Cohen, 'Complete Bullshit', in G. A. Cohen, *Finding Oneself in the Other* (Princeton, New Jersey: Princeton University Press, 2012), Chapter 5, pp. 94–114, available at: www.ditext.com/cohen/Cohen.pdf.
[77] Though a very particular democracy, where citizens can vote directly and are not represented through parties or institutions. Hegel later on uses Rousseau to legitimise the Prussian aristocracy, Russell, *A History of Western Philosophy*, p. 671.
[78] H.-G. Haupt, *Sozialgeschichte Frankreichs seit* 1789 (Frankfurt a.M.: Suhrkamp, 1989), p. 104 refers to the centralisation of the administration and the taxation.

workers or farmers[79] against 'change' in light of the growing budget deficit under three presidents Mitterrand, Sarkozy, and Hollande (maybe under Macron too),[80] demonstrates that social justice is a highly politicised matter throughout society and is subject to conflict, support or rejection.

Placing the two strands together helps explain the potential tensions between the French political and intellectual concept of a just society, which is deeply grounded in French rationalism, and the English utilitarian pragmatism that questions not only the legitimacy but also the feasibility of state-engineered distributive justice. One may go one step further and argue that contrasting the two models, the French and the English, helps understand the different approaches to the role and function of markets, state and society. French intellectualism understands the market as a political project that can and has to be governed by politics, by the French state which enjoys a degree of recognition in French society that is hardly to be imagined in England or in Germany and, last but not least, by a legal order (the Code Civil) which is construed as a visionary intellectual system.

The two strands of Frenchness are enlightening for the constitutive role France played in the founding period of the European Union. At the EU's birth, French rationalism and imagination are 'united'. The European Economic Community is both a project of 'reason expressed through law' – the link towards German ordo-liberalism springs to mind – and of utopia and imagination, European 'messianism'.[81] French intellectualism must be at odds with a judge-made European constitution, one which is not the product of a political process. But French intellectualism can easily adapt to the Internal Market as a 'social' project, to the rise of the executive power through 'Integration through Governance', and even more so, to the (failed) idea

---

[79] Haupt, *Sozialgeschichte Frankreichs seit* 1789, p. 8 refers to the anti-capitalistic attitude of the farmers in the nineteenth century. In today's time, French farmers have blocked the streets in order to demonstrate against EU rules that are said to harm their interests. A conflict which even involved the ECJ and led to the remarkable judgment that free trade prevails over the right to strike (under certain conditions), Case C-265/95, *Commission v. France* [1997] I-6959.

[80] The socialist Mitterrand followed aggressively Keynesian policy, increasing public spending, whilst Thatcher did exactly the opposite in the United Kingdom: Hepple and Veneziani, 'Introduction', p. 24. Conservative Sarkozy did the same in 2012, although the public deficit had reached a more critical stage: Hazareesingh, *How the French Think*, p. 298.

[81] Replaced by inward-looking French nationalism and ethnicity. Hazareesingh, *How the French Think*, Chapter 10, 'The Closing of the French Mind', p. 287.

of a European Civil Code – as long as the European Civil Code remains intellectually grounded in the architecture of the Code Civil.[82]

1.3.2 Origins of the Intellectual and Political Conception

Just like in England, the intellectual turning point was the fading influence of scholastic thinking. It liberated the French spirit from methodological scholastic circularity and enabled a particular rational method in philosophy. The founding father was Montaigne (1533–1592), the French counterpart to Francis Bacon (1561–1626). His epistemology went along with the zeitgeist of the sixteenth century and its radical scepticism: 'What do I know?'. His major contributions lay in the final collapse of existing knowledge by substituting for it a fully fledged scepticism; B. Russell speaks of 'in thought it prefers a large and fruitful disorder'[83] which was necessary to free himself from scholastic constraints and the attempt to find a generally binding moral and social peace. Montaigne set long-lasting incentives for the critical reflection of all existing knowledge and values, what has been later named 'Enlightenment'.

The sixteenth century may be regarded as a transitional period in which the old scholastic forms of thought were overcome, but where a new method to investigate the 'truth' and the concept of the truth was not yet developed. This was left to the seventeenth century, in a strong move towards subjectivism. Modern philosophy is said to begin with Descartes' *Discours de la Méthode*. He claimed that a particular method to acquire the truth is needed, which then allows one to solve all philosophical questions. It is a method of doubt: *cogito ergo sum* ('I think therefore I am'). The strongest part of Descartes' philosophy is the power of pervasive doubt. The link between reason and existence – 'I think therefore I exist' – reappeared in French existentialism (Sartre, de Beauvoir, Camus).[84] The consequences that he himself draws are largely deterministic and often subject to criticism. For Descartes, 'what is true is useful' – and not 'what is useful is true' like in utilitarianism – should be understood as his overall paradigm of political philosophy. This

---

[82] It is not my intention to revitalise the explanation of the French society via the tension between modernity and traditionalism. See Stanley Hoffmann's stalemate society, famously developed in 'Paradoxes of the French Political Community', in S. Hoffmann, C. P. Kindleberger, L. W. Wylie, J. R. Pitts, J.-B. Duroselle and F. Goguel, *In Search of France* (Cambridge, MA: Harvard University Press, 1963), pp. 1–117.
[83] Russell, *A History of Western Philosophy*, p. 18.
[84] Hazareesingh, *How the French Think*, p. 43.

contrast is key if we are to understand the particular French intellectual and political conception of the state, society and the market. Cartesian philosophy claims priority for theory over practice, which is the basis of French intellectualism. Cartesianism heavily influenced politics and the role and concept of what is today called the 'state'. The radical subjectivism in Descartes' philosophy is said to be the source of political anarchy. Radical subjectivism inherently questions existing institutions, be they the Church[85] or be they the statutory institutions. There is no such thing as French Rationalism per se; it is rather a way of seeing the world. Descartes has been used by all on the political spectrum as a source of legitimation for political purposes: from De Gaulle's appeal to the conscience of French citizens during the resistance,[86] to the French Communist Party after World War II claiming that Stalin is Cartesian.[87]

How could it be that Descartes legitimises the absolute monarchy of Louis XIV? Descartes was not anti-clerical. He was a faithful member of the Catholic Church, although he accepted Galileo's discovery, and although his 'method' was widely understood (by others) as being anti-clerical. Understanding this tension in Cartesian philosophy seems crucial because of the enduring admiration among French intellectuals for providential leaders, from Louis XIV the Sun King, to Napoléon, to de Gaulle and Mitterrand, a parallel which has attracted the attention of French cartoonists. The explanation can be found in Descartes' conviction that ultimate mathematical truths are grounded in the eternity of God: 'God has established these laws (the mathematical truths), like a King states laws in his kingdom' (my translation).[88] Hobbes and

---

[85] This is most obvious in belief and religion. When the Catholic Church is no longer in a position to determine what the official 'belief' is that people have to obey, then there is room for each and every believer to claim his or her version of religion. There are early predecessors to radical subjectivism: G. Savonarola (1452-1498) and St. Francis of (1182-1226), P. Sloterdijk, *Die schrecklichen Kinder der Neuzeit* (Berlin: Suhrkamp Verlag, 2014) in particular Chapter 6 'Die große Freisetzung', p. 312.

[86] Hazareesingh, *How the French Think*, p. 42; also the French existentialist would have said, 'I revolte therefore I exist', p. 45.

[87] Hazareesingh, *How the French Think*, p. 49.

[88] 'Gott hat diese Gesetze (die mathematischen Wahrheiten) festgesetzt, wie ein König in seinem Reich Gesetze festsetzt', K. T. Buddeberg, 'Descartes und der politische Absolutismus' (1936/37) 30 *Archiv für Rechts- und Sozialphilosophie* 541-560, where he opens his analysis with the quote from Descartes in his letter to Mersenne. The analysis was written in 1937 and is already influenced or inspired by Carl Schmitt, *Politische Theologie* (München; Leipzig: Duncker & Humblot, 1922), at p. 60 where he points to the link between Descartes metaphysic and the political theories of absolutism.

Descartes share the same conclusion. Hobbes claimed that the king must have absolute power, though his reasoning derives from political philosophy. Indeed, no other British king had more powers than James I.[89]

The fall of absolute monarchy goes hand in hand with a rising criticism of Descartes' philosophy – through Voltaire and Rousseau. Voltaire was inspired by Locke, with whom he constantly corresponded. Locke brought an element of pragmatism into French rationalism. He shared with Voltaire the inclination to keep the monarchy in power, though in the form of the 'enlightened king', for which the Prussian Frederic II served as an example. Rousseau represents more than any other French thinker the power of the Cartesian method: speculating about the future, dreaming of a utopian world that is to be found not on a remote island or a fictitious order, but in Paris itself. Mercier's *L'an deux mille quatre cent quarante*, written in 1771, wonderfully describes the future Paris as the ideal world, where all citizens communicate in French, although the utopia is claimed to be universal. For Rousseau, private property is the source of civil society and social inequality. In this sense, he differs sharply from Locke. That is the reason why Rousseau in his plea for equality and for basic democracy could turn into one of the key figures of the French Revolution. Both share, however, the belief in the existence of natural rights. Locke is said to have influenced the American Constitution and the anchoring of unalienable rights therein. In France, natural rights were mainly directed against the absolute power of a divine monarchy.

The innovative and creative potential of the French philosophy in the seventeenth century set the scene in social and moral philosophy. It overcame Cartesian metaphysics – revelation of natural laws through God, responsibility before God and reception of the power of the sovereign from God. Moral standards should be defined by themselves, not through God. They culminated in the declaration of the rights of man (natural rights) and citizen (political rights) in 1789 (*declaration de droit de l'homme et du citoyen*). The two parts of the declaration, the natural and the political rights, reflect the two strands of rationalism – pure reason and imagination, head and heart, Descartes and Rousseau. The two strains are united in the attempt to found a moral vision decoupled from theological and metaphysical requirements. This is claimed to be the core of French secularism (*laïcité*). Although, one might very well argue that, notwithstanding secularisation, French rationalism keeps

[89] Russell, *A History of Western Philosophy*, p. 539.

the providential leader, the sun king and the republican king alive – until today.

1.3.3 Constitution and Code beyond National Boundaries

Constitution-building and code-making went hand in hand in France. Rousseau and Voltaire were both members of the constituent assembly. French philosophers transformed political philosophy into politics. This turned out to be a far-reaching and long-lasting realisation of the Cartesian political concept, which constitutes one of the key constitutive elements of French society and the French legal system. In France, philosophers are not simply academics who write books which gather dust; rather, provided they become famous, they are public figures. It is hard to imagine another country besides France where more than 50,000 citizens attend the funeral of a great philosopher (here J.-P. Sartre).[90]

The Declaration of Human Rights, the Constitution and the Code Civil are read as the result of a democratic process.[91] This is partly true, as the drafts of the codes were made public in order to allow the French people to comment on them, a strategy already applied earlier on in Prussia and in Austria.[92] The particular democratic roots of the French Code Civil are an integral part of its political success story, which reaches far beyond France. Whether the democratic roots are a reality or whether these roots were overturned by the dictatorial drafting of Napoléon himself, who chaired 57 out of the 102 constitutive sessions, might be left for historians.[93] A number of countries have taken over the French Code Civil *because* of its democratic tradition.[94] Some German *Länder* kept the French Code Civil even after the defeat of France in the

---

[90] Hazareesingh, *How the French Think*, p. 230, under the telling title of Chapter 8, 'Writing for Everybody', pointing to the French tradition to present philsophy in prose.
[91] In the same vein, C. Joerges, 'Der Europäisierungsprozess als Herausforderung des Privatrechts: Plädoyer für eine neue Rechtsdisziplin', in A. Furrer (ed.), *Europäisches Privatrecht im wissenschaftlichen Diskurs* (Bern: Stämpfli, 2006), pp. 133–188, at p. 142.
[92] Wieacker, *A History of Private Law*, p. 271.
[93] In that context, Chapter 9, 'The End of History' in Hazareesingh, *How the French Think*, p. 258 is illuminating, as it helps to understand how history has been used in the nineteenth century for pedagogical purposes, later for scientific purposes and nowadays for promoting an inward-looking approach that centres around France.
[94] E. Fehrenbach, 'Der Einfluß des Code Napoléon auf das Rechtsbewußtsein in den Ländern des rheinischen Rechts', in J. Jurt, G. Krumeich and T. Würtenberger (eds.), *Wandel von Recht und Rechtsbewußtsein in Frankreich und Deutschland* (Berlin: Berlin-Verlag Spitz, 1999), pp. 133–142; Wieacker, *A History of Private Law*, p. 274.

battlefield.[95] This might be partly due to the political debate which surrounded the introduction of the Code Civil in these Länder. This debate did not take place in law journals alone. The Code Civil became a subject of the *Rheinbundöffentlichkeit*.[96]

Public awareness could only be raised because the Code Civil stood – in the light of the new French Constitution – for a bourgeois legal revolution. The Code ended feudalism by abolishing legal privileges. It relied on a liberalised property concept and stood firm against inequality (e.g. in the law of succession and in labour law through the groundbreaking idea of contractualising the relationship between the worker and the employer, contrary to the United Kingdom not in terms of master and servant, but of two persons who are formally equal[97]). It confirmed laïcité, secularised civil life (e.g. family law[98]) and established one set of rules for the French metropole. More than 100 years later than the same development in England, France had established a legal order that provided space for the development of an economy in the hands of merchants. Unlike in England, however, the French merchant could not benefit from a relatively stable political and economic environment. H.-G. Haupt[99] distinguishes between two phases of development after the revolution: the period until 1880, which he terms 'Notablengesellschaft' (society of the nobles), and from 1880 on until 'today' (the book was written in 1989), which he terms *Klassengesellschaft* ('society of classes'). Until 1880, agriculture dominated the country.

---

[95] The argument has been challenged by R. Schulze, 'Französisches Recht und Europäische Rechtsgeschichte im 19. Jahrhundert', in R. Schulze (ed.), *Französisches Zivilrecht in Europa während des 19. Jahrhunderts* (Berlin: Duncker und Humblot, 1994), pp. 9–36, at p. 17, because the German Länder were said to defend at the same time older traditions. With Berman, *Recht und Revolution*, I cannot recognise a contradiction, as the old and the new ideas merge.

[96] G. Schuck, *Rheinbundpatriotismus und politische Öffentlichkeit zwischen Aufklärung und Frühliberalismus. Kontinuitätsdenken und Diskontinuitätserfahrung in den Staatsrechts- und Verfassungsdebatten der Rheinbundpublizistik* (Stuttgart: Steiner, 1994).

[97] B. Hepple, 'Introduction', in B. Hepple (ed.), *The Making of Labour Law in Europe. A Comparative Study of Nine Countries up to 1945* (London: Mansell Publishing, 1986), pp. 1–30, at p. 2; although the Civil Code left all the arms in the hands of the employers, G. Aubin and J. Bouveresse, *Introduction historique au droit du travail* (Paris: Presses Universitaires de France, 1995), p. 123.

[98] Although the original version of the Code Civil allowed for a divorce on the basis of mutual consent. These rules were abrogated in 1815 and not restored until 1975.

[99] Haupt, *Sozialgeschichte Frankreichs seit 1789*; Aubin and Bouveresse, *Introduction historique au droit du travail* are following a similar distinction in time, also with regard to the emerging worker class after 1880, but they do not use the distinction between *Notabeln* and *Klassengesellschaft*.

The industrialisation of production was yet to occur. Political power remained in the hands of the aristocracy and the rich bourgeoisie.[100] In the nineteenth century, French society was shaken by three great revolutions (1830, 1848 and the French Commune) and the Franco-Prussian War 1870/1871. Both affected the way in which the French economy and the French legal order developed. Contrary to still prevailing prejudices, the French industrial revolution should be understood much more as an evolution in the English way than the economic revolution that shattered Germany in the late nineteenth century.[101]

The introduction of the new Code Civil went hand in hand with the establishment of new institutions, which resulted from the separation of powers. The new code had to be awoken, and it had to be applied in business practice, by lawyers and by judges. The role and function of the French judiciary, however, cannot be compared to the one it played and plays in England and the United Kingdom. The moral decline of the French society in the seventeenth century had reached the judiciary, where the post of a judge became subject to political and financial dealings. The profession of a judge was discredited because of a mixture of corruption and partisanship with the monarchy. The claim that the judge should act as *la bouche de la loi* is the direct result of this grievance. In civil law it is documented in the way judgments are formulated. The judges do not appear as individuals; their function is to mechanically apply the abstract rules of the code to the concrete case in hand.

This does not mean that today's reality complies with the formal appearance. In fact it seems that there is 'a vibrant and contested institutional and discursivie sphere' between French academics and justicial magistrates.[102] The adaptation of the Code Civil to the changing economic and social environment over the last two centuries has facilitated such transformation of the role of judges.[103] Most of the amendments introduced in the two centuries concerned family law and succession law.[104] The formal structure of the Code Civil as it was

---

[100] There was even a definition of the *societé des nobles* in the lexicon of the Académie française 1762, the most important and the most respected of a city, Haupt, *Sozialgeschichte Frankreichs seit 1789*, p. 115.
[101] Haupt, *Sozialgeschichte Frankreichs seit 1789*, pp. 80, 81.
[102] M. de S.-O.-l'E. Lasser, Judical (Self-) Portraits: Judicial Discourse in the French Legal System, (1995) 104 *The Yale Law Journal*, pp. 1325–1410, p. 1402.
[103] Weber, *Wirtschaft und Gesellschaft*, p. 510; Wieacker, *A History of Private Law*, p. 271.
[104] Critical G. Ripert, *Le Régime démocratique et le droit civil moderne*, 2nd ed. (Paris: Librairie générale de droit et de jurisprudence, 1948), my introduction in 'Demokratie und

adopted in 1804 remained the same until the reform of the law of obligations in 2016. The reform strengthened the role of judges, in line with overall developments in the Member States and the EU. Labour law and consumer law are different. Here the executive played and plays a key role.[105] The strong position of the Executive in the French constitution facilitated close co-operation between the French administration and European bureaucracy.

1.3.4 The Rise of 'The Social' via Self- and State Help

How was it possible that France managed to keep the spirit of the Code Civil as a prospective modern civil law concept for nearly 200 years as a democratic development of new civil order, which is even claimed to have navigated the social turmoil of the nineteenth and twentieth century? The Code Civil did not undergo many amendments – if any, they took place in the field of land law and family law.[106] The 2016 reform was not primarily inspired by the wish to give the Social more weight, although the reform is said to strengthen the position of the weaker party.[107] The major political objective seemed to adapt the French Code Civil to the needs of international commerce and make it more attractive for potential users.[108] Sagnac demonstrated that the reorganisation of land law during the French revolution, as enshrined into the Code Civil, must be understood as the beginning of the 'histoire sociale' of France.[109] It triggered and enabled the rise of the French gross

---

Privatrecht', in S. Grundmann, H.-W. Micklitz and M. Renner (eds.), *Privatrechtstheorie*, Band 1 (Tübingen: Mohr Siebeck, 2015), Kapitel 9, p. 708.

[105] Hepple, 'Introduction', p. 21: 'the most effective French labour regulation derived not from politics at all but from the activities of the bureaucracy', under reference to D. Thomson, *Europe Since Napoléon*, rev. ed. (Harmondsworth: Penguin, 1966), p. 357 (first published 1957).

[106] Wieacker, *A History of Private Law*, p. 273.

[107] M. Fabre-Magnan, 'What Is a Modern Law of Contracts? Elements for a New Manifesto for Social Justice in European Contract Law', (2017), 15 *European Review of Contract Law*, pp. 376–388.

[108] 'Rapport au Président de la République relatif à l'ordonnance n° 2016-131 du 10 février 2016 portant réforme du droit des contrats, du régime général et de la preuve des obligations', JORF n°0035 du 11 février 2016, texte n° 25, NOR JUSC1522466P, available at: www.legifrance.gouv.fr/eli/rapport/2016/2/11/JUSC1522466P/jo/texte; more sophisticated F. Rouvière, 'Les valeurs économiques de la réforme du droit des contrats' (2016) *Revue des contrats* 600–607.

[109] P. Sagnac, *La législation civile de la révolution française* (1789–1804). *Essai d'histoire sociale* (Paris: Hachette, 1898), p. II. Much more reluctant, Wieacker, *A History of Private Law*, p. 273: 'the rejection of publicity of landholdings constitutes the Achilles heel of the Code in its original form.'

income prior to industrialisation. Land law, however, is not at the core of this analysis.

The focus lay on the *social* outlook of the Code Civil in the field of contract law, more particularly labour and consumer law. From the ideology behind the Code Civil, its high degree of abstraction and its application via judges who were originally – i.e. under the spirit of the French revolution – given no leeway in interpreting the law, it is hard to imagine how such an abstract order, which was designed as a model regulation for a bourgeois society, could match the needs of the labour and, later, the consumer movement. There are two ways how the Social may be integrated into the French civil order. Both cannot explain the 'myth' of the Code Civil as a body of law that matches the needs of a 'Social' contract law. The first possibility would be that the judiciary took over the task to adapt the 'old' law to the 'new' needs, despite the original verdict. Law has to serve a particular objective as enshrined in naturalism *Duguit* (administrative law),[110] *Saleilles* (tort),[111] and *Josserand* (tort).[112] For *Gény* (theory and methodology)[113] law has a social function to fulfil (function sociale), which could be managed through a particular interpretative methodology. The second possibility would be to locate social legislation outside the Code Civil and to ensure the necessary adaption process via particular legislative acts as a result of political and social compromises. It seems as if France preferred the second option to the first, although the picture looks less clear in a tort lawyer's perpective. The French Code du Travail was adopted in 1910, though in the form of a compilation.[114] As if history could reiterate itself, the same

---

[110] L. Duguit, *Les Transformations Générales du Droit Privé depuis le Code Napoléon* (Alcan: Paris, 1912; 2nd ed. 1920); on Duguit, O. Motte, 'Duguit, Léon', in M. Stolleis (ed.), *Juristen. Ein biographisches Lexikon. Von der Antike bis zum 20. Jahrhundert*, 2nd ed. (München: C. H. Beck, 2001), pp. 187–188. In the aftermath of the political turmoil between 1870 and 1880 Duguit is proclaiming the need for a dominant objective order to ensure peace. He goes as far as rejecting the individual rights so forcefully introduced in the French revolution; see Aubin and Bouveresse, *Introduction historique au droit du travail*, p. 181.

[111] R. Saleilles, *Les accidents de travail et la responsabilité civile. Essai d'une théorie objective de la responsabilité délictuelle* (Paris: A. Rousseau, 1897).

[112] L. Josserand, 'L'évolution de la responsabilité (conférence donnée aux Facultés de Droit de Lisbonne, de Coimbre, de Belgrade, de Bucarest, d'Orades, de Bruxells, à l'institut français de Madrid, aux centres juridiques de L'Institut des Hautes Études marocaines à Rabat et á Casablanca)', in L. Josserand, *Évolutions et Actualités. Conférences de Droit Civil* (Paris: Recueil Sirey, 1936), 29–5.

[113] F. Gény, *Méthode d'Interprétation et Sources en Droit Privé Positif*, 2nd ed. (Paris: Librairie générale de droit et de jurisprudence, 1919); the first edition was published in 1899.

[114] Hepple, 'Introduction', p. 9; Ramm, 'Epilogue', p. 279, which goes all the way back to Richelieu.

fate was destined for the Code de la Consommation in 1992. The outsourcing through administrative regulation, which is then tied together in a compilation, fits into the conception of the French society, where substantive decisions are taken within the administration, but where the political decisions, however, have to be approved by the legislature in a democratic forum. French society places confidence in the executive as a law-maker, and as a law enforcement institution, perhaps more than in the legislature and the judiciary.

Just like in England, the development of labour law is tied to the labour movement, the establishment of trade unions and the rise of the *protective* welfare state. This does not mean that self-help and state-help took similar forms. The trade unions in France are close to the different political parties. They did not turn into an independent political movement. Trade unions grew out of the political parties and not vice versa as in the United Kingdom.[115] This might explain the very different role of collective autonomy in these two countries. In the nineteenth and twentieth centuries, UK trade unions were the dominant social actors in the field of labour law. In France, just as in Germany, trade unions remained closely connected to two political parties, socialist and communist – and via these political parties to the state. One may assume that each of the two political parties may be associated with a particular trade union and vice versa and that it is for the state – the government in place – to strike a balance between the parties or trade unions. That is why in France, social conflicts between workers and employers bear a political dimension that cuts across different parties, on each side of the poles. There is no *Einheitsgewerkschaft* (unified trade union) like in Germany, which looks after the interests of the workers as a whole. For decades the Einheitsgewerkschaft guaranteed stability and a rather smooth social environment without too many strikes.[116]

Overall, French unions are divided, which limits their influence as a political power. The French state on the other hand is much more the

---

[115] Hepple, 'Introduction', p. 25, refers to Germany, Netherlands, Belgium and Italy. He does not mention France.
[116] However, the Einheitsgewerkschaft is gradually falling apart in the twenty-first century. So-called *Spartengewerkschaften* (trade unions representing a particular profession even within the same sector, e.g. trade unions for pilots, for stewards, for the ground staff) have considerably gained importance.

protective welfare state in the German sense. Already in the nineteenth century, the French state learnt that it had to take workers' interests systematically into account. Aubin and Bouveresse call it the 'Le pacte Industriel':[117] 'la classe ouvriére se rallie tacitement à la république ... elle réclame avec insistence la légitime contrepartie'. In 1884, the working class was granted the right to association. In 1892, the French legislator introduced a facultative mechanism to settle conflicts, albeit with limited success. The early statutory intervention led to highly politicised collective bargaining and the constant involvement of the state, contrary to the United Kingdom. The so-called Matignon Agreements (French: Accords de Matignon) of 1936, concluded between the CGPF employers trade union confederation (Confédération Générale de la Production Française), the CGT trade union (Confédération Générale du Travail) and the French state set the course for the years to come: arbitration became mandatory, and in exchange, the rights of the workers were considerably improved.[118] The French government introduced legislation on limiting working hours to 40 hours and on granting paid vacation. The 'Magna Carta of French Labour' marks a break-even point in the triangular relationship of all three parties concerned. Since then, collective agreements have been nationalised and recognised as a means to negotiate salaries by sector.

From a French perspective, the notion of labour law does not make much sense. It is more correct to speak of *droit social,* which enshrines labour law (*droit du travail*) and social security (*sécurité sociale*). Like in Germany, droit social developed outside the civil law system and roughly at the same time.[119] The governments of the 'belle époque' adopted three major laws: they granted insurance against accidents at work in 1898, banned Sunday trading in 1906 and established the social insurance system (pension and invalidity) in 1910. The French social laws and French lawyers contributed substantially to the rise of droit social in Europe and beyond, in particular after World War I. The intellectual spirit of the Social in the late nineteenth and early

---

[117] Aubin and Bouveresse, *Introduction historique au droit du travail*, Chapter 2, 'Le ralliement du monde ouvrier', pp. 199–210.
[118] Haupt, *Sozialgeschichte Frankreichs seit 1789*, p. 280; Hepple, 'Introduction', p. 26, in more detail A. Jacobs, 'Collective Self-regulation', in B. Hepple (ed.), *The Making of Labour Law in Europe. A comparative Study of nine countries up to 1945* (London: Mansell Publishing, 1986), pp. 193–240.
[119] H.-G. Haupt, 'Sozialpolitik und ihre gesellschaftlichen Grenzen in Frankreich vor 1914', in *Jahrbuch für Wirtschaftsgeschichte* (Berlin: Akademie Verlag, 1995), pp. 171–192.

twentieth centuries is grounded in the idea of saving liberalism from itself.[120]

The comparison with German social security legislation could provoke the misleading impression that French social policy has to be understood as insurance policy. Initially, French social policy was rather based on voluntariness than compulsion or constraint. Only gradually did the French legislator turn social insurance into mandatory law: accidents at work in 1930, health insurance in 1930 after a painful process which started in 1898 and unemployment insurance in 1957.[121] The superficial similarities between Germany and France in social insurance policy should not overshadow the major differences. In nineteenth-century France, the political emphasis of statutory action in the field of social policy focused on protection for safety at work (including protection against accidents at work) and maintenance of the poor rather than on the establishment of a fully fledged insurance system.[122] Josserand and Saleilles analysed the consequences of accidents at work for the liability of the workers, the former focusing on the Code Civil, and the latter on the regulation outside the Code Civil. The preparedness of legal scholars and later courts to install strict liability in industrial and, later, in consumer relations led back to the French Revolution. Safety at work and maintenance of the poor may be easily identified as a legacy of 1789, equality as solidarity. They imbued French 'labour law' with the concept of droit social in the twentieth century and beyond.

1.3.5 Politicising Private Law as Social Law

Consumer law is a product of the consumer society, i.e. of the *market society*. For quite a long time, it was a commonplace in historical-

---

[120] D. Kennedy, 'Two Globalizations of Law & Legal Thought: 1850–1968' (2003) 36 *Suffolk University Law Review* 631–679, at 649.

[121] Even after the insurance system became mandatory, many gaps allowed the workers to get out of the system. See Haupt, *Sozialgeschichte Frankreichs seit* 1789, p. 271, in which all the exemptions to the binding laws are explained. His analysis is entirely in line with Aubin and Bouveresse, *Introduction historique au droit du travail*, Deuxième Partie Le Pacte Social, Chapitre 3 Audaces et timidité du legislateur, p. 222.

[122] F. Ewald, *L'Etat providence* (Paris: Grasset, 1986), p. 225; Haupt, *Sozialgeschichte Frankreichs seit* 1789, p. 27; Haupt, 'Sozialpolitik und ihre gesellschaftlichen Grenzen in Frankreich vor 1914', p. 171 is even more outspoken: 'die sozialpolitischen Interventionen [galten] stärker dem Arbeitsschutz und der Armenversorgung als dem Aufbau eines Versicherungssystems. In dieser Schwerpunktsetzung ist eine deutliche Differenz zum deutschen Modell des Sozialstaates zu sehen' (the policial interventions aimed much more at health and safety at work and caring for the poor rather than the establishment of a social security system).

economic research that France was considered a laggard vis-à-vis its neighbours on a number of performance indicators, inter alia in becoming a market society. Dynamic developments were said to occur outside France, in the United Kingdom, the Scandinavian countries and even in post–World War II Germany. Over the last decades, however, historians in France as well as in the Anglo-Saxon world produced a stream of books proclaiming the need for a radical revision of French (economic) history. It is now emphatically proposed that France had been remarkably successful in carving out its own path to development in the late nineteenth and early twentieth century.[123] The rewriting of the early period of industrialisation might equally affect the two post-war periods. Thus, in a way, the idea that France struggled to transform its more rural society into a market society in the second half of the twentieth century will have to be reinvestigated. It could explain why French statutory social law preceded the respective laws in Germany.

Two particularities deserve to be mentioned. The first is the different character of consumer policy and the different role of consumer law in France. Just like in France, Germany consumer policy arose as a statutory policy, but in France, the politicisation of consumer law is closely intertwined with the role and function of trade unions and other societal players in the public domain. When consumer policy reached the political agenda, the different trade unions entered the field and integrated the voice of consumers into their overall policy, at least to some extent. The rather strong political dimension of consumer policy was partly overcome when the French trade unions decided to support the state-initiated foundation of nationwide operating consumer organisations in the 1950s and 1960s, UFC Que Choisir (l'Union Féderale de la Consommation in 1951 – the equivalent to the German Verbraucherzentrale Bundesverband) and the Institut National de la Consommation (INC the equivalent to the English Which? and the German Stiftung Warentest in 1967).[124] Today, the institutional difference between France, on the one hand, and England and Germany, on the other, has lost importance. Consumer policy is largely formulated at a governmental level or by quasi-public consumer organisations. In France, however, each and every issue of consumer policy and law

---

[123] C. Heywood, *The Development of the French Economy, 1750–1914* (Cambridge: Cambridge University Press, 1995).

[124] J. Calais-Auloy and H. Temple, *Droit de la Consommation*, 9th edn. (Paris: Dalloz, 2015), nos. (numbers) 31 and 35.

could all too easily turn into a battlefield between trade unions and consumer organisations.

There is a close link between labour and consumption, maybe closer than in Germany and the United Kingdom, a link which can only be explained via the particularities of French socioeconomic and political history, especially the gradual evolution of a blossoming rural society that integrated ever more elements of the industrial society. Self-help and state help are much more deeply intertwined than in Germany and the United Kingdom. The post-war French consumer movement required the strong support of the French trade unions via their institutional infrastructure. Since 1983, the relationship between consumer organisations, trade organisations (*associations des professionelles*), the public services and the competent ministries is institutionalised in the Conseil National de la Consommation (CNC).[125] Trade unions are excluded from the forum. This is a form of nationalisation of consumer policy, together with business and consumer associations. The common roots of both fields of law are even more obvious in the second element of labour law – the role and function of state help, namely regulatory intervention through the state on behalf of the consumers. The resemblance between the two, labour and consumer law, can be demonstrated via reference to two constitutive elements – price control and health and safety – which point back to the French Revolution. It seems that there existed, and still exist, deep differences between France, the United Kingdom and Germany on how to organise a market society.

The first constitutive element is enshrined into the system of statutory price control, which was given up in the late seventies of the twentieth century under pressure from the EU. The system of price control had created strong and stable ties between the public and the private sphere. The rise of the consumer society allowed the French administrative authorities to use the regular yearly ritual of price-fixing as an opportunity to promote consumer protection. French consumer policy originated from price-fixing policy.[126] This is particularly true

---

[125] For more information on the CNC, see www.economie.gouv.fr/cnc; the members are listed here: www.economie.gouv.fr/files/files/directions_services/cnc/leCNC/Composition_2015_college_prof.pdf.

[126] Insightful are F. Steinmetz, Chapter 3, 'Prices' and J. Calais-Auloy, Chapter 5, 'Consumer information', in J. Calais-Auloy, M.-T. Calais-Auloy, J. Maury, H. Bricks, H. Temple and F. Steinmetz, *Consumer legislation in France* (Wokingham, Berkshire: Van Nostrand Reinhold, 1981), pp. 40–58 and pp. 83–84 respectively, where the latter gives examples on how the price mechanism was used to introduce information

with regard to contract law. The price-fixing *décrèts* combined the agreed increase with the obligation imposed on the respective business sectors to provide the consumer with proper product information and even grant mandatory extended warranties. Via the décrèts, the competent ministries supplemented the rules in the Code Civil and introduced mandatory protection for all consumers. Price-fixing itself, the idea of state control over prices, was regarded as an efficient way to protect consumers, in particular poor consumers. There is a clear line to the heritage of the French Revolution, the substantive notion of equality. The last product subject to price control was bread (baguette)! Its abolishment met strong objection from trade unions.

The second constitutive element of French consumer policy is product safety. As early as 1983, France adopted legislation to protect consumers against unsafe products.[127] This goes along with the strong tradition in guaranteeing health and safety at work. The French model heavily influenced the regulatory approach of the European Commission in Directive 92/59/EEC (which later became Directive 2001/95/EC).[128] The particular 'Frenchness' is to be identified in the way the safety standard is defined, which has to be respected by the manufacturers (and the dealers). It is no longer for the manufacturer to define the standard of safety. He has to take its 'foreseeable use' into account. Under pressure from France, consumers may rely on their legitimate safety expectations. Contrary to Germany and the United Kingdom, the level of safety is not automatically presumed to be defined via technical standards, elaborated by national, European or international standard bodies.

Opening up the market for consumer products, i.e. allowing the market to fix the price, meant for France the task of establishing a consumer policy to accompany market liberalisation. Consumer policy in France has always been and still is highly politicised. It is exposed

---

requirements. As price-fixing has been abolished, the mechanism is no longer discussed in Calais-Auloy and Temple, *Droit de la Consommation*, no. (number) 302.

[127] C. Joerges, J. Falke, H.-W. Micklitz and G. Brüggemeier, *Die Sicherheit von Konsumgütern und die Entwicklung der Europäischen Gemeinschaft* (Baden-Baden: Nomos, 1988); for the English version, 'European Product Safety, Completion of the Internal Market and the New Approach to Technical Harmonisation and Standards' (2010) 6 *Hanse Law Review*, available at: http://hanselawreview.eu/wp-content/uploads/2016/08/HanseLRVol6No02.pdf, at p. 137.

[128] Council Directive 92/59/EEC of 29 June 1992 on general product safety, OJ No. L 228, 11.8.1992, p. 24; Directive 2001/95/EC of the European Parliament and of the Council of 3 December 2001 on general product safety, OJ No. L 11, 15.1.2002, p. 4.

to strong political variations according to the political party which holds power and is closely related to social trends, as promoted by trade unions. Against the background of price-fixing rules, institutional policy-making is obviously centrally and bureaucratically organised. The societal counterpart is a proliferation of trade unions and semi-public consumer organisations. Similar to UK consumer law, enforcement is put in the hands of public authorities and – beyond the United Kingdom – in the hands of quasi-public consumer bodies. The judiciary plays a limited role in consumer protection, although if it intervenes, it does so to the benefit of consumers, sometimes in an innovative and path-breaking way.[129]

In Europe, France took a leading role in the field of consumer information and consumer contract law. Already in 1972, France established rules on door-to-door selling.[130] In Germany, it took until 1985. The respective legislation passed Parliament only after a highly conflictual confrontation with the direct-selling business. How could it happen that France claimed and took a leading role in formulating consumer policy even though it was not the most advanced market economy at the time? The reason can be identified in the strong ideological, philosophical and political roots of French law, which provide continuity and consistency in French social law-making.

That the Minister of Economics undertook a major effort in the early 1980s to set a benchmark for the future of consumer law in Europe fits such a perspective. The Commission de la Refonte, established by the government and headed by Jean Calais-Auloy, intended to develop a coherent body of rules that should stand side by side with the Code Civil.[131] The ambitious project, which would have given France a leading role in consumer law, failed for various reasons, not least because of the growing importance of European consumer law. However, the project was originally designed as a forward-looking

---

[129] Cour de Cassation, 22 October 1996, *Bancherau v. Chronopost*, D. 1997, Jur., p. 121, granted courts the power to exercise control over standard contract terms under the general notion of good faith; for more details, see Calais-Auloy and Temple, *Droit de la Consommation*, no. (number) 182.

[130] On the sources of consumer law see J. Calais-Auloy, M.-T. Calais-Auloy, J. Maury, H. Bricks, H. Temple and F. Steinmetz, *Consumer legislation in France* (Wokingham, Berkshire: Van Nostrand Reinhold, 1981), p. 7.

[131] Commission de refonte du droit de la consommation, Proposition pour un nouveau droit de la consommation, rapport de la commission de la refonte du droit de la consommation au secrétaire d'État auprès du ministre de l'Économie, des Finances et du Budget chargé du Budget et de la Consommation, 1985.

project that reached beyond the elaboration of technical rules but that should convey a political message, namely, that of the role and function of consumers as citizens in a market society. The drafters even intended to make collectively negotiated standard terms binding.[132]

The overall concept behind the draft goes along with the deeply rooted thinking that ideas prevail over market realities:[133]

> L'existence du droit de la consommation se fonde sur la nécessité de rétablir un équilibre dans les relations entre professionnels et consommateurs ...
>
> Or, pour assurer cette protection, le droit commun issue des codes napoléoniens ne suffit pas. En vertu du principe de l'autonomie de la volonté, une personne est engagée dès lors qu'elle a accepté de conclure un contrat, qu'elle que soit la fragilité de son acceptation ...

The decline of French consumer law as a forward-looking design for the future is obvious. The (failed) EU project on a European Code on Civil Law endangered French law's unique role, the role the Code Civil enjoys in Roman law countries. This might explain the sometimes nationalistic reactions against the European project. The project 'Catala',[134] now turned into the 2016 reform, was meant to bring intellectual leadership back to France. Even the European Commission had to consider the 'particular' position of France and the French Code Civil in the European codification project. The 'terminology group', being part of the French Academic Group constituted by the Société de Législation Comparée and the Association Henri Capitant des Amis de La Culture Juridique Française,[135] had to outweigh the English-Scottish-German-Polish Study and Acquis Group.[136]

---

[132] J. Calais-Auloy, 'Collectively Negotiated Agreements: Proposed Reforms in France' (1984) 7 *Journal of Consumer Policy* 115-123.

[133] Commission de refonte du droit de la consommation, Proposition pour un nouveau droit de la consommation, pp. 11 and 12.

[134] J. Cartwright, S. Vogenauer, S. Whittaker (eds.), *Reforming the French Law of Obligations. Comparative Reflections on the Avant-projet de réforme du droit des obligations et de la prescription ('the Avant-projet Catala')* (Oxford: Hart Publishing, 2009).

[135] B. Fauvarque-Cosson and D. Mazeaud (eds.), *European contract law. Materials for a Common Frame of Reference: Terminology, Guiding Principles, Model Rules* (München: Sellier European Law Publishers, 2008).

[136] C. v. Bar, E. Clive, H. Schulte-Nölke, H. Beale, J. Herre, J. Huet, M. Storme, S. Swann, P. Varul, A. Veneziano and F. Zoll (eds.), *Principles, Definitions and Model Rules of European Private Law. Draft Common Frame of Reference (DCFR)*, prepared by the Study Group on a European Civil Code and the Research Group on EC Private Law (Acquis Group), based in part on a revised version of the Principles of European Contract Law (München: Sellier European Law Publishers, 2009); Research Group on EC Private Law (Acquis Group), *Principles of the Existing EC Contract Law (Acquis Principles). Contract*

1.4 The German Model: A Paternalistic Market Design

The German Civil Code entered into force on 1 January 1900. The German Civil Code is a hundred years younger than the French Code Civil. It was developed and adopted at the high point of the second industrial revolution, in the last 20 years of the nineteenth century. New technologies allowed for mass production and mass communication, and companies mushroomed around Europe. These companies needed capital that no single person was able to provide. New organisational forms for companies had to be found to collect the capital from investors. These companies needed masses of workers. They came from the countryside. Most of them lacked education and were trained on the job. Working days lasted 10 to 12 hours, and often there was no Sunday break. Children were regarded as an effective workforce. This was the time when the working class emerged and when the working class found their voice in labour parties and trade unions around Europe.[137]

Germany had its particular role to play at the end of the nineteenth century. In the aftermath of the Vienna Congress (1814–1815), the scattered German regions (kingdoms, counties (earldoms), regions) failed to unite into a German state, united by its own constitution and giving political voice to the bourgeoisie and the working class, let alone men and women. All that the kingdoms, counties, earldoms and regions managed to agree upon in the Vienna Congress was the German Confederation (Deutscher Bund). The consequences were far reaching for the other European states (Austria, France, Italy, England, Netherlands, Belgium). The biggest country in the middle of Europe had been deprived of its political power.[138] It compensated its lacking political importance through idealised (Schiller, Herder Deutschland eine Kulturnation – Germany a cultural nation) and later nationalistic claims (Hegel, Fichte).[139]

I. Precontractual Obligations, Conclusion of Contract, Unfair Terms (München: Sellier European Law Publishers, 2007); *Contract II. General Provisions, Delivery of Goods, Package Travel and Payment Services* (München: Sellier European Law Publishers, 2009).

[137] On the metamorphosis of the world (not of Europe alone, though Europe had its particular role to play), J. Osterhammel, *Die Verwandlung der Welt. Eine Geschichte des 19. Jahrhunderts* (München: C. H. Beck, 2009), (here quoted after the 2011 special edition); particularly relevant in the context are the chapters XII Energie und Industrie, XIII Arbeit and XIV Netze, pp. 909–1055.

[138] Russell, *A History of Western Philosophy*, pp. 691–692 provides in two pages a short summary of the particular situation of the un-united Germany surrounded by nation-states and empires, which is helpful for non-German readers.

[139] I. Berlin understands German idealism as a sort of resentment, a response to the French enlightenment: 'Herder and the Enlightenment' in H. Hardy (ed.) *Three Critics of*

The French Revolution of February 1848, which swept away the Orleans monarchy (in English referred to as the Bourbon Monarchy), established the Second Republic in France, but more importantly triggered turmoil in many European countries, in the Deutsche Bund, and more particularly in Southern Germany. With the help of the Prussian army, regional revolutions inspired by the French revolutionary spirit were suffocated.[140] The Deutsche Bund survived until 1866. This invasion was the entry card for Prussia to extend its influence as the only remaining powerful state of the mid-nineteenth century (within the Deutsche Bund). The Prussian King rejected the Frankfurt Constitution of 1848 that was supposed to establish a parliamentary democracy. He found philosophical backing in Hegel, who idealised the role and the function of the state[141] and strongly advocated against liberal conceptions of the state. Locke put the individual at the centre of his analysis and attributed to the state the task to serve the needs of the individuals. It took three wars with Denmark (1864), Austria (1866) and France (1870–1871) until the first German Reich under the regime of the Prussian emperor and his chancellor Bismarck was established. The 1871 constitution remained far behind the 1848 Frankfurt constitution. Germany remained a monarchy with limited parliamentary power under the tight authoritarian grip of Prussia. The codification of the German Bürgerliches Gesetzbuch (BGB) served to lay down a common legal order adapted to the needs of the blossoming economy for the now united Germany.

- The starting point for linking legal consciousness to the emerging German legal order and its social face differs considerably from England and France in all relevant dimensions: economic, social and political. In the second half of the nineteenth century, scholasticism was already overcome; Locke and Hobbes, Descartes, Voltaire and Rousseau had left their imprint on the British Empire and the first and second French constitutions, not least on the American Constitution. The deeper divide in Germany was the one between the protestant Prussian Kingdom as the only remaining political and military power and the scattered counties, earldoms and regions, which was also a divide between the

Enlightenment: Vico, Hamann & Herder (Princeton University Press: Princeton, 2013) pp. 208–300, p. 222.

[140] E. von Salomon, Der Tote Preusse. Roman einer Staatsidee (Frankfurt a.M.; Berlin: Ullstein, 1988).

[141] Russell, A History of Western Philosophy, pp. 708–710.

leading philosophers and the leading law professors located in Prussia (through targeted recruitment) and the sociologists, artists, musicians and poets located in the Western states.[142]
- Understanding the intellectual history behind the building of the German BGB, its strengths and its weaknesses, led to tensions between the remarkable rise of German industry and the democratic deficit that was only overcome after World War II. Much deeper is the intellectual, political and philosophical tension between Kant (1724–1804) and Savigny (1779–1861), who like Hegel (1770–1831) rejected codification. Thibaut (1772–1840) was in favour of codification. In the preparatory legislative work, the tensions between French rationalism (Descartes, Voltaire), English empiricism (Bacon, Locke, Hume) that had laid the ground for building the French and the English nations, and German idealism[143] and German romanticism[144] are illuminated. German legal naturalism, which the English would probably call legal functionalism (Jhering (1818–1892), Ehrlich (1862–1922), Weber (1864–1920), H. Kantorowicz (1877–1940)) served as a counterpart to formal rationality (Kant, Savigny) and brought the 'reality' of industrialisation back into politics and law. In the political and philosophical debates on the state, on society and on law, and *die soziale Frage* (the social question), the Social reached public attention, not least through the

---

[142] Russell, *A History of Western Philosophy*, pp. 692–693.
[143] R. Safranski, *Schiller oder die Erfindung des deutschen Idealismus* (München; Wien: Hanser, 2004) who uses Schiller, his life and his interaction with the eminent persons of his time (Goethe, Hölderlin, Schelling, Fichte, Hegel, Brentano) to explain what is to be understood by German idealism. In his prologue, Safranski provides a powerful definition of what idealism is (p. 11): '... wenn man mit der Kraft der Begeisterung länger lebt, als es der Körper erlaubt. Es der Triumpf eines erleuchteten, eines hellen Willens. Bei Schiller war der Wille das Organ der Freiheit' ('provided one lives longer through the power of enthusiasm than the body permits. It is the triumph of an illuminated, radiant will'). For an overview of German idealism in English, see P. Redding, 'German Idealism', in G. Klosko (eds.), *The Oxford Handbook of the History of Political Philosophy* (Oxford: Oxford University Press, 2011), pp. 348–368; not to forget the slightly scornful remarks on the German philosophers of J. Austin (1790–1859), *The Province of Jurisprudence Determined* (London: J. Murray, 1832), p. 370 as 'metaphysical speculators'.
[144] Russell, *A History of Western Philosophy*, p. 654; its origin might be in France, but the Romantic movement is German. Safranski argues that the best definition is still provided by Novalis, at p. 13: 'Indem ich dem Gemeinen einen hohen Sinn, dem Gewöhnlichen ein geheimnisvolles Ansehen, dem Bekannten die Würde des Unbekannten, dem Endlichen einen unendlichen Schein gebe, so romantisiere ich es' ('By giving the common a high meaning, the ordinary a mysterious esteem, the known the dignity of the unknown, the finite an infinite appearance, so I romanticise it').

publication of the Communist Manifesto in 1848 and the rising conflicts between the owners of the new companies and the working class.

1.4.1 The Axiomatic Role of Law

Why are the Germans so 'obsessed' with the role and the rule of law? There are endless examples for the very particular German approach to law, for the Deutschsein, for 'Germanness', and for the fixation on respect for law and order. In our abovementioned study on the emergency management of product and food safety,[145] I was for the first time confronted empirically with the phenomenon that German lawyers, when they have to face a deep and highly conflictual phenomenon, are intuitively first and foremost looking for rules, whether or not there is guidance enshrined in rules, legislation, regulations or even internal administrative non-binding recommendations that can overcome the uncertainty, fill a gap and legitimate a reasonable decision. The fierce debate triggered by German lawyers in the aftermath of Lehman Brothers and the Eurozone crisis that the EU is infringing the no-bailout obligation in Art. 125 TFEU or that the Outright Monetary Transaction (OMT) decision of the ECB[146] is not in line with its legal mandate looks like Don Quixote's fight against windmills. German lawyers face severe difficulties in making themselves understood, in explaining why they insist so much on the role and the rule of law, even more so in a situation where the limits of law are so abundantly clear. This is not to say that the German lawyers are right or wrong in their interpretation of Art. 125 TFEU or the OMT decision of the ECB. There is something deeper in the German intellect, something which is particularly German and which makes Germans distinct from the English or the French.

The so-often maligned and discredited German national anthem,[147] written in 1841 by Heinrich Hoffmann von Fallersleben, contains in its third verse the original political message which expresses the will of the people: 'Einigkeit und Recht und Freiheit' (unity, law (right) and

---

[145] Micklitz and Roethe, *Produktsicherheit und Marktüberwachung im Ostseeraum*.

[146] L. P. Feld, C. Fuest, J. Haucap, H. Schweitzer, V. Wieland, B. U. Wigger (Kronberger Kreis), 'Das entgrenzte Mandat der EZB. Das OMT-Urteil des EuGH und seine Folgen' (2016) 61 *Stiftung Marktwirtschaft*.

[147] Fallersleben did not evince imperial dreams. These emerged later together with the rise of nationalism in Europe ever stronger at the end of the nineteenth century, Osterhammel, *Die Verwandlung der Welt*, VIII Imperien und Nationalstaaten, p. 565.

freedom).[148] 'Unity' refers to the scattered picture of kingdoms, counties and regions, and 'freedom' to the anti-feudalistic message of the French revolution. But why 'Recht', why 'law' or 'right'? The explanation given by Friedrich Ebert, the first *Reichspräsident* (president of the Weimar Republic), when he declared the song as the official German national anthem in 1922 is still telling. At a crucial moment in German history, after the end of World War I, when Germany had abolished the monarchy and was about to build its own democracy, the first freely elected president of the republic found the following words:[149]

Wir wollen Recht. Die Verfassung hat uns nach schweren Kämpfen Recht gegeben. Wir wollen Frieden. Recht soll vor Gewalt gehen. Wir wollen Freiheit. Recht soll uns Freiheit bringen. Wir wollen Einigkeit. Recht soll uns einig zusammenhalten. So soll die Verfassung von uns Einigkeit, Recht und Freiheit gewährleisten.
We want law. The constitution has given after heavy fights law. We want freedom. Law shall precede power/violence. We want freedom. Law shall bring us freedom. We want unity. Law shall tie us in unity together. That is why the constitution shall guarantee us unity, law and freedom (translation H.-W. M.).

One may wonder whether the strong emphasis on 'Recht', 'Recht' which has to guarantee unity and 'Recht' which has to enable freedom, guided its creator Hoffmann von Fallersleben. It finds expression in the third strophe only, 'Einigkeit und Recht und Freiheit' (often translated into 'unity, justice and freedom'), the most benign of the three, the least nationalistic, and the only one that Germans may sing in public after World War II.[150] Justice, however, does not catch the meaning of 'Recht'; justice is *Gerechtigkeit* rather than Recht. 'Recht' alludes to the body of laws, to rules and law as a societal system of justice.

One might understand 'Einigkeit und Recht und Freiheit' as a continuum, which condenses the difficulty of Germany over the last two centuries to become a nation-state, to remain a nation-state as well as the role and function law played and still plays in tying Germany

---

[148] J. Jurt, 'Die Rolle der Nationalsymbole in Deutschland und Frankreich', in J. Jurt, G. Krumeich and Th. Würtenberger (eds.), *Wandel von Recht und Rechtsbewußtsein in Frankreich und Deutschland* (Berlin: Berlin-Verl. Spitz, 1999), pp. 67–90.
[149] Jurt, 'Die Rolle der Nationalsymbole in Deutschland und Frankreich', p. 85.
[150] 'Einigkeit und Recht und Freiheit für das deutsche Vaterland! Danach lasst uns alle streben, brüderlich mit Herz und Hand! Einigkeit und Recht und Freiheit sind des Glückes Unterpfand. Blüh im Glanze dieses Glückes, blühe deutsches Vaterland' ('Unity and justice and freedom for the German fatherland! Let us all strive for this purpose. Brotherly with heart and hand! Unity and justice and freedom are the pledge of happiness; Bloom in the glow of this happiness, Bloom, German fatherland!').

together. The Nazi regime put emphasis on the first strophe 'Deutschland Deutschland über alles, von der Maas bis an die Memel, von der Etsch bis an den Belt' ('Germany, Germany above everything, above everything in the world. From the Meuse [Alsace-France] to the Memel [Lithuania], from the Adige [South Tyrol] to the Belt [Denmark]', on the territorial extension of what should be understood as Germany). During the 12 years between 1933 and 1945, there was no room for 'law' and 'freedom'. Germany turned into an *Unrechtsstaat* ('lawless state'). This deep historical burden led the first president of the newly founded Federal German Republic, Theodor Heuss, to advocate for replacing the Deutschlandlied with a new anthem. Schillers 'Ode an die Freude' ('ode to joy') would have been such a candidate, a masterpiece of mankind embodying and condensing German idealism. Until 1968, the two Germanys were requested by the International Olympic Committee to form a *gesamtdeutsche Mannschaft* (a unified team of Germany).[151] The attempt to replace the German anthem in 1949 failed, and the third strophe remained in the minds of the German people.[152]

The next occasion came with German unification, more precisely with the choice between various ways of implementing it once it was politically decided. The political decision of the Kohl government executed the unification of Germany through an act of law – *einen Rechtsakt*. The alternative, strongly promoted by the Green Party and left-wing academics, was to hold a referendum of the two Germanys. This would then have allowed for the replacement of the German Grundgesetz (the Basic Law) through a constitution on which the citizens would have the chance to vote. The elaboration of the German Basic Law had been initiated by France, the United Kingdom and the United States, together with the presidents of the German Länder. No vote had ever been organised. However, Kohl did not learn from Bismarck[153] and did not grant the German people a voice. 'Recht' (law) replaced 'political voice'.

---

[151] The English translation can hardly catch the sensitivities behind the carefully chosen wording of 'gesamtdeutsch', which is not unified – that would have been 'vereint'.
[152] 'Ich weiß heute, dass ich mich täuschte. Ich habe den Traditionalismus und das Beharrungsbedürfnis unterschätzt', quoted by Jurt, 'Die Rolle der Nationalsymbole in Deutschland und Frankreich', p. 85.
[153] To paraphrase H. James, 'Monetary and Fiscal Unification in Nineteenth-Century Germany: What Can Kohl Learn from Bismarck?' (1997) *Princeton Essays in International Finance* 2–38. Just like Bismarck used the economic and political power of Prussia to unite Germany, Kohl perhaps somewhat more delicately but in the end relied on the economic and political power of West Germany in the managing of the unification process.

The so-called Beitritt of the German Democratic Republic to the Federal Republic of Germany documents the strong continuity of the three strings – Einigkeit und Recht und Freiheit – that are inherently intertwined. No unity without law and no freedom without law. The third strophe holds it all together. The citizens of the former GDR did not protest when the new anthem of the GDR so forcefully promoted by the German communist party was abolished.

And the judiciary? What has been their role in the shaping and the maintenance of legal consciousness, of anchoring the axiomatic role of law in the minds of the German people since 1870? Through the lenses of the overall search for the particular role of law in the German design of justice, three phases may be distinguished, and in each of them the German judiciary played a key role. Wieacker had demonstrated in his seminal book *A History of Private Law in Europe* (*Privatrechtsgeschichte der Neuzeit* 1957) how the German Reichsgericht managed to adapt the formal structure of the 1900s BGB to the growing needs of the Social. During the Nazi regime, the same court was ready to use the formal structure of the BGB to justify and to legitimate arbitrary discrimination against Jews, Sinti and Roma in private law relations, in labour law, in tenant law and in consumer law. After World War II, the German Constitutional Court quickly gained a prominent role. Via its case law, the GCC paved the way for what is today called the constitutionalisation of private law,[154] via the potential direct effect of constitutional (fundamental and human rights)[155] and via the universal application of the proportionality principle as an ever more important technique to balance conflicting rights even in private law relations.[156] Habermas (and others) coined the German word *Verfassungspatriotismus* (constitutional patriotism) as a particular republican form of statehood.[157] There is, however, an undercurrent which links the legal consciousness, the role

---

[154] A. C. Ciacchi, G. Brüggemeier, G. Comandé (eds.), *Fundamental Rights and Private Law in the European Union*, Vols. I and II (Cambridge: Cambridge University Press, 2010).

[155] The famous *Lüth* judgment (BVerfG, 15.01.1958 – 1 BvR 400/51), H. Rösler, 'Harmonizing the German Civil Code of the Nineteenth Century with a Modern Constitution. The Lüth Revolution 50 Years Ago in Comparative Perspective' (2008) 23 *Tulane European and Civil Law Forum* 1–36.

[156] D. Kennedy, 'A Transnational Genealogy of Proportionality in Private Law', and N. Reich, 'Balancing in Private Law and the Imperatives of the Public Interest: National Experiences and (Missed?) European Opportunities', both in R. Brownsword, H.-W. Micklitz, L. Niglia and S. Weatherill (eds.), *The Foundations of European Private Law* (Oxford: Hart Publishing, 2011), pp. 185–220 and pp. 221–248 respectively.

[157] J. Habermas, 'Staatsbürgerschaft und nationale Identität', in J. Habermas, *Faktizität und Geltung* (Frankfurt a.M.: Suhrkamp 1992), pp. 632–660.

of law and the German Constitutional Court (GCC) together. The (West) citizens were proud of their court that was regarded as a bastion of 'law' understood as 'justice' (*Gerechtigkeit*).[158] This was due to the constitutional complaint (*Verfassungsbeschwerde*) that allows German citizens to directly approach the German Constitutional Court provided the basic rights have been infringed. The GCC is claimed to have been able to integrate into its design of 'law' and 'justice' the concerns of the former GDR.[159]

What can be taken from the axiomatic role of law in the minds of the German people? It seems as if 'law' bears exactly the twofold sense that is enshrined in the German word 'Recht' and that is untranslatable: 'law = order/Ordnung' and 'law Gerechtigkeit = justice'. What are the deeper roots? What are the economic, social and political underpinnings that verify or falsify such an interpretation of the German legal consciousness? The argument is built around two major guiding assumptions which mirror the tension between the axiomatic role of law that encompasses the authoritarian element of 'order' and the resistance against the dominance of 'law', which is best understood in German idealism and which can be more easily connected to matters of 'justice':

- First, there is a direct line from Kant to Savigny to the formal rationality of the private law system (Weber) which serves the execution of capitalist society. The Kantian philosophy inspired Savigny's 'Historische Schule', which gained dominating influence in the nineteenth century and which is still influential today.[160] It has created a particular way of thinking which allows for combining the formal rationality of law with the political dominance of the state to organise the market order and that is so characteristic for twentieth-century Germany. In such thinking, all social policy issues remain alien to the 'pure' private law system of the BGB and are better placed outside in separate laws.
- Second, there is the link between Hegel, Thibaut, German idealism, and legal naturalism, as expressed in Jhering, Ehrlich, Weber

---

[158] M. Jestaedt, O. Lepsius, C. Möllers and C. Schönberger, *Das entgrenzte Gericht. Eine kritische Bilanz nach sechzig Jahren Bundesverfassungsgericht* (Berlin: Suhrkamp, 2011), in particular the contributions of Jestaedt, 'Phänomen Bundesverfassungsgericht. Was das Gericht zu dem macht, was es ist', pp. 77–158 and Lepsius, 'Die maßstabsetzende Gewalt', pp. 159–280.

[159] S. Jaggi, *The 1989 Revolution in East Germany and Its Impact on Unified Germany's Constitutional Law: The Forgotten Revolution?* (Baden-Baden: Nomos, 2016).

[160] N. Jansen, *The Making of Legal Authority: Non-Legislative Codifications in Historical and Comparative Perspective* (Oxford: Oxford University Press, 2010).

and Kantorowicz, where the national ideals were tied to social ideals of a society and a nation. Such a vision can hardly be connected to the authoritarian German empire of the late nineteenth century which accepts the responsibility for guaranteeing protection in exchange for political participation of the working class (with the exception of Hegel). A counter-concept (*Gegenkonzept*) that complements the formal rationality through an economic constitution is promoted by Hugo Sinzheimer. It ties employers and employees to a 'just' social rationality. The German version of legal naturalism favours an instrumental use of the legal system for matters of justice. The ideological basis was laid in the 1920s.

1.4.2 Paternalistic Market Pragmatism and Idealistic Societal Visions

The intellectual quarrel of two nineteenth-century German law professors, Thibaut and Savigny, over the value of a codified German Civil Code is still of utmost relevance for understanding the tensions between formal and social rationality, between economic parternalism and social idealism, and between paternalistic market pragmatism and dreams of a different society. Understanding the reasons behind the tension explains why Germany holds the ideological middle ground between the pragmatic English and the intellectual French.

Thibaut was fighting from Heidelberg enthusiastically – inspired by German Idealism and *les grandes idées* of the French revolution – for a genuine German code; Savigny was fighting brilliantly (but not enthusiastically – he was not a good speaker unlike Thibaut) for the maintenance of the old Roman law.[161] Savigny is the founding father of the German Historische Schule, which argues that law should not, and cannot, be derived from 'nature' or 'reason' of the human being (*Natur und Vernunft*). Quite contrary to French rationalism (Montaigne, Descartes, Voltaire) and English empiricism (Bacon, Hobbes, Locke), law should and must be understood as a historical product of the spirit of the people (*Volksgeist*). The task of the lawyer is *not* to constitute a meaningful legal order for the human beings, but to collect and systemise the legal material produced by the spirit of the people. That is why it is somewhat misleadingly called 'Historische Schule'. History appears as rather static. Law in this sense is Kantian formal (kantisch-

---

[161] A. F. J. Thibaut and F. C. von Savigny, *Ihre programmatischen Schriften. Mit einer Einführung von Hans Hattenhauer* (München: Franz Vahlen, 1973); the long introduction by H. Hattenhauer wonderfully explains the overall context in which the debate took place, pp. 9–52.

formal), not inspired by nature and reason as Hegel claimed. Savigny wanted to become the Kant of the legal system (*der Kant der Rechtswissenschaft*).[162] The ideals of Thibaut were reflected in Hegel's philosophy. Hegel paved the way for studying history, its development and, 'most importantly', the dynamics of the development.[163] The rising legal naturalism (Jhering) contributed to a better understanding of the historical and present reality of legal orders. Most of the legal auxiliary sciences (*rechtliche Hilfswissenschaften*) such as criminology, *Rechtstatsachenforschung* (research on legal facts) and legal sociology (*Rechtssoziologie*) (Eugen Ehrlich and Max Weber) have their origin in legal naturalism, as well as the *Freirechtsschule* ('free law school').[164] The dark side of legal naturalism results from the strong belief in deducing from historical and present reality repercussions for a perfect model of justice, which has to be achieved by a politically guided law that is meant to realise a particular social purpose. Again, this darker side is a lesson worth recalling when it comes to discussing the achievements of social justice-related legislation and case law.[165]

Law-making was understood in Germany as an *academic* exercise, quite contrary to the beginning *democratic* discussion that surrounded the adoption and distribution of the French Code Civil. The Thibaut/Savigny conflict, this conflict between two leading professors, led to the creation of two law commissions by the Prussian state. The two professorial commissions paved the way for the adoption of the German Civil Code. The leading role of academics in Germany is associated with the *political* – democratic – vacuum that resulted from the failed attempt in 1848 to establish a German nation-state. The German professorship-model (*Professoren-Modell*) strongly influenced law-making in the nineteenth century and law application far beyond the nineteenth century until today.[166] However, this is not true with regard to the integration of consumer law into the BGB. There was no professorial discussion, nor was there a constitutive commission that was invited to draft rules and

---

[162] J. Q. Whitman, *The Legacy of Roman Law in the German Romantic Era: Historical Vision and Legal Change* (Princeton: Princeton University Press, 2014), Chapter IV, 'Imperial Tradition and the New Professorate after 1814', pp. 92–150.
[163] H.-P. Schwintowski, *Recht und Gerechtigkeit. Eine Einführung in Grundfragen des Rechts* (Berlin et al.: Springer, 1996), p. 35.
[164] Wieacker, *A History of Private Law*, p. 450.
[165] Part II. 2.
[166] My understanding of R. Zimmermann, 'Consumer Contract Law and General Contract Law: The German Experience' (2005) 58 *Current Legal Problems* 415–489; R. M. Kiesow, 'Rechtswissenschaft – was ist das?' (2010) 65 *JuristenZeitung* 586–591.

to discuss how such an integration could be achieved. The whole exercise was dominated by the German Ministry of Justice, with short and intense consultancies, but always under administrative guidance that was happy to make ad hoc decisions without a clear, conceptual underpinning.

The grand codification of the German BGB in 1900 could have ended the dominance of the German academia. This is all the more true as German academia had fulfilled its administrative mandate with the drafting of the rules. Quite the contrary transpired. The uncertainties the German judges faced in the early period after the adoption of the German Civil Code favoured academic support for the judiciary searching for the correct interpretation of the law.[167] In the making of what has been termed the Draft Common Frame of Reference (DCFR), the supposed precursor to a European Civil Code, the German Professoren-Modell re-emerged.[168]

The German Civil Code reiterated, more or less, the ideological substance of the French Code Civil. However, a hundred years later, the three pillars of the German civil order, the *Rechtssubjekt* (legal subject), *Eigentumsordnung* (private property) and *Vertrag* (contract), no longer conveyed a revolutionary message. The two commissions and the legislator missed the chance to respond to the challenges of the late nineteenth century, namely the development of a labour law to meet the needs of the industrial age and an appropriate tenancy (land) law, which takes into account the needs of the millions of workers who needed housing in the big cities (e.g. Wiener Wohnhöfe (Austria), Kruppsiedlungen (Germany) and Guinness (Ireland)). This does not mean that German academics spoke with one voice. Gierke, in 1889, published *Die soziale Aufgabe des Privatrechts*, in which he forcefully criticised the lack of communitarian thinking characteristic of Germanic law in the BGB as well as its 'missing socialist drop of oil'.[169] A. Menger even went further in his much-debated *Das Bürgerliche Recht und die besitzlosen Klassen*, published in 1890, in which he attacked a private legal order built on private

---

[167] Wieacker, *A History of Private Law*, p. 409.
[168] H. Schepel, 'Professorenrecht? The Field of European Private Law', in H. Schepel and A. Jettinghoff (eds.), *Lawyers' Circles. Lawyers and European Legal Integration* (The Hague: Elsevier Reed, 2004), pp. 115–124.
[169] O. v. Gierke, *Die soziale Aufgabe des Privatrechts. Vortrag gehalten am 5. April* 1889 *in der juristischen Gesellschaft zu Wien* (Berlin: Springer, 1889), p. 10; the same, *The Social Role of Private Law*, translated, with an introduction, by Ewan McGaughey, *German Law Journal* Volume 19 2018, pp. 1018–1114.

property and freedom of contract, which excludes four-fifths of the society.[170] The drafters of the code were not open to such a critique and more or less set the social question aside. These issues were debated in a context of a very limited male franchise; women were entirely excluded from the right to vote. The open problems of the Second Reich left a deep imprint on how German civil law developed in the twentieth century.

1.4.3 From Authoritarian to (Ordo-)Liberalism

Social justice issues did not make their way into the German Civil Code. This does not mean that social policy did not gain importance in the late nineteenth and early twentieth century. However, self-help and state help took a peculiar form in Germany which was very distinct from England and France. Under the strong Prussian regime, the German Reichstag in 1878 adopted the so-called *Sozialistengesetz*, which prohibited political activities of socialists and social democrats. This was a harsh reaction to tame the growing voice of the working class. The explicit objective was to undermine the rise of the labour movement. It set the path of development for decades if not for the whole twentieth century. Until 1890, when the ban was lifted, there was no room to unfold political activities, and even after 1890 the left-wing political parties remained under strong surveillance. Law was just one way to make their life difficult. The working class was not able to develop its own societal forum. The only safe way for workers to organise themselves was to unite in educational circles, in the so-called *Arbeiterbildungsvereine* (worker's educational associations). They constituted the nucleus for the organisation of the labour force after the collapse of the second German empire with the end of World War I. A legacy of these times is the Büchergilde Gutenberg, established in 1924, which survived World War II and whose aim was, and is, to make high-brow literature (poetry mostly with a critical undertone towards the authoritarian German society or the capitalist economy) available to workers at low prices.[171]

The second limb, state help, set standards for social policy far beyond Germany and impacted the design of social policy in all industrialised

---

[170] A. Menger, *Das Bürgerliche Recht und die besitzlosen Volksklassen. Eine Kritik des Entwurfs eines Bürgerlichen Gesetzbuches für das Deutsche Reich* (Tübingen: Laupp, 1890).

[171] There is no English translation, but the German entry in Wikipedia provides a short summary of its history https://de.wikipedia.org/wiki/B%C3%BCchergilde_Gutenberg.

Western (democratic) economies.[172] In response to distortions of the industrial revolution, the expropriation of the labour force and its disastrous effects on health and safety, the German empire introduced a dense and mandatory social security system. Between 1881 and 1889 the German Reichstag adopted the law on health insurance (1881), accident insurance (1883), and old-age and disability insurance (1889). In 1891, the introduction of the pension funds was secured. These protective welfare activities were meant to compensate for the exclusion of the fourth class (the workers) from political power by the Sozialistengesetze (Anti-Socialist Laws). The state adopted a mandatory social security system, which by and large survived the twentieth century and is paradigmatic for the very German version of how to deal politically with the social question. Under the German model, it is not citizens who organise themselves and who fight for their rights with their employers. The state accepts responsibility and sets the framework under which the working class and employers have to organise themselves. Hepple reads the protective legislation of the Prussian state as rights and not gifts. However, before World War I, the social security systems looked like a payoff to keep socialists and communists at bay.[173]

The Weimar Republic brought a democratic constitution. A number of high-ranked academics were involved in the making of it.[174] The legal recognition of collective agreements in Art. 165 and many other social rights owed their inspiration to Hugo Sinzheimer (1875–1945) who had forcefully advocated for the introduction of legislative means to declare collectively negotiated tariffs generally applicable as early as 1915.[175] It is worth pausing and considering the genealogy of labour lawyers in Europe: Kahn-Freund was a desciple of Hugo Sinzheimer; Kahn-Freund had two disciples, Paul Davies and Mark Freedland, who had Hugh Collins as his disciple. Each of them has left deep imprints on the development of labour law. The formation of labour law as a separate legal discipline that cuts across the public/private divide goes back to

---

[172] Aubin and Bouveresse, *Introduction historique au droit du travail*, p. 183, underline the progress that Bismarck brought to social policy and that France took more than 30 years to catch up with the German social security standards; Hepple, 'Introduction', under 'The Modernisation of the State', pp. 15, 16.

[173] Hepple, 'Introduction', p. 21.

[174] A chronology, G. Jasper, 'Improvisierte Demokratie? Die Entstehung der Weimarer Verfassung', in T. Stammen (ed.), *Die Weimarer Republik. Band I – 1918–23. Das schwere Erbe* (München: Bayerische Landeszentrale für Politische Bildungsarbeit, 1992), pp. 117–146, available at www.blz.bayern.de/blz/web/100081/03.pdf.

[175] H. Sinzheimer, *Grundzüge des Arbeitsrechts* (Jena: G. Fischer, 1921).

Sinzheimer.[176] No less a figure than him coined the word *Wirtschaftsverfassung* (economic constitution). It is here that self-help and state speak to each other. The idea of an economic constitution made a prominent career under the influence of ordo-liberalism, first in post-war Germany and later in the European Economic Community (today the European Union).

The concrete legislative measures remained far behind the ambitious projects that the Weimar Constitution had set into motion. However limited, reassuring or disappointing it might have been, Germany set decisive incentives for a development that is constitutive for the twentieth century: the separation of economic policy from social policy, or in legal terms, of economic and private law from labour law.[177] The *Vereinigung für Sozialpolitik* (the *Kathedersozialisten* or the 'academic socialists' as they were somewhat pejoratively denominated) turned into the key conceptual player. The economic dependence of the worker had to be compensated for by statutory activities.[178] The 1922 Act on Work Councils (*Betriebsrätegesetz*) granted workers the right to participate in the decision-making of companies. Whilst this was certainly a major step in the development of labour law, workers did not reach parity with employers. The Weimar Republic provided a fertile ground for ideas and concepts to give the economy a more democratic outlook (*Naphtali*).[179] These ideas and concepts were only realised in the 1970s when the now Federal Republic of Germany elected the first government in which the Social Democrats obtained a majority in the elections and adopted, in 1976, the law on codetermination (*Mitbestimmungsgesetz*). The time frame is characteristic for the delayed transposition of intellectual concepts into legal means. In 1933, this is the rather disappointing conclusive summary: German labour law stood by and large where it was prior to World War I. The drive and inspiration of the Weimar Constitution had evaporated.[180] National Socialism deeply transformed industrial relations, destroyed trade unions and created a body of law that was deeply engrained in the Nazi ideology of the Volksgemeinschaft. Labour and employers were

---

[176] Hepple, 'Introduction', p. 8.
[177] Hepple, 'Introduction', p. 24.
[178] Hepple, 'Introduction', p. 7.
[179] On the long-lasting intellectual impact of Weimar, see U. Greenberg, *The Weimar Century. German Émigrés and the Ideological Foundations of the Cold War* (Princeton University Press, 2014); F. Naphtali, *Wirtschaftsdemokratie, ihr Wesen, Weg und Ziel* (Berlin: Verlagsgesellschaft des Allgemeinen Deutschen Gewerkschaftsbundes, 1928).
[180] Ramm, 'Epilogue', p. 288.

organised in forced communities. These laws were abolished after 1945.[181] The Nazi regime promised prosperity to consumers and realised it by providing a radio to everybody (*Volksempfänger*). 'Law' played a role in that prices were politically fixed.[182]

1.4.4 Turmoil and Continuity

The twentieth century with its two world wars seems to exclude the idea of continuity. However, the caretaking welfare state is deeply anchored in the minds of German citizens. There is a German saying: 'Der Rock des Staates ist warm, aber eng' ('the clothes of the state [a metaphor for public officials working for the German state] are warm but narrow'). It sums up correctly the spirit that governed the relationship between German citizens and *Vater Staat* (father state or fatherland) in the German anthem. *Der Fürsorgestaat, l'état providence* is not exactly identical with the welfare state; the Fürsorgestaat rather takes care of its citizens, of its weaknesses and its sorrows. There is an authoritarian element in *Fürsorge*, one that is deeply enshrined in Bismarckian social security and backed by catholic social theory.

In the German empire, taking care went hand in hand with deprivation of political participation. This does not mean that the mentality of German citizens did not change over the last hundred years, visibly via the different constitutions and laws that enhanced political participation and invisibly via the educational democratic training, from which the West German citizens benefitted after World War II.[183] The student revolt of 1968 and the move from the Christian Democrats to the Social Democrats, from Adenauer/Erhard to Brandt/Schmidt (*mehr Demokratie wagen*, literally 'dare more democracy'; let us try more and deeper democracy, directed against post-war Adenauer Germany),[184] initiated

---

[181] G. Brüggemeier, *Entwicklung des Rechts im organisierten Kapitalismus. Band 1. Von der Gründerzeit bis zur Weimarer Republik* (Frankfurt a.M.: Syndikat, 1977), pp. 239–290; *Band 2. Vom Faschismus bis zur Gegenwart* (Frankfurt a.M.: Syndikat, 1979), pp. 32–69, in particular 35–49.

[182] C. Torp, Wachstum, Sicherheit, Moral. Politische Legitimation des Konsums im 20. Jahrhundert (Göttingen: Wallstein-Verl., 2012), pp. 59–91.

[183] *Instructions for British Servicemen in Germany 1944*, prepared by the British Warfare Executive, first published by the Foreign Office in London, reprint in 2007 by the Bodleian Library.

[184] It is striking that the collection of articles edited by D. Simon (ed.), *Rechtswissenschaft in der Bonner Republik. Studien zur Wissenschaftsgeschichte der Jurisprudenz* (Frankfurt a.M.: Suhrkamp, 1994), although it aims at giving an account of what has been achieved in the Rechtswissenschaft between 1945–1991 (the unification of the two Germanies), does not contain a contribution on 'democracy' or on 'democratic theories'.

grassroots initiatives all over the country and enhanced democratisation from the bottom-up.[185] Yet, the idea that the state is caring for you (*der Staat sorgt für Dich*) and even stronger that the state is obliged to do so, is deep in the minds of German citizens. The expectations remained constant, but the legal subject behind it changed from gift-taker to rights-holder. Whilst this might not be in itself problematic, as the changing attitude mirrors the more general development in the EU Member States, the unification of the two German states in 1990 reinvigorated the expectations of a strong and authoritarian state.[186] Haselbach had already argued that there is a direct path from 'authoritarian liberalism' (an oxymoron) of the Second Empire (the Kaiserreich 1870–1918) to the *Soziale Marktwirtschaft* (social market economy) after 1949, which so successfully established the market economy in postwar Germany and integrated the trade unions into politics.[187]

Such an understanding of the coincidence of market economy and a strong statutory authoritarian outlook might explain the particular role German *courts* played in adapting the German BGB to the social needs of the twentieth century, which is so blatantly neglected in its original design. Already during the Weimar Republic, but even more so after World War II, German courts took a strong protective stand (*Fürsorge*) towards the weaker party in individual contractual relations.[188] The courts were much more reluctant when the problem to be decided bore a strong collective political dimension. Taking

---

[185] Governmental policy statement by Willy Brandt in 1969, available at: www.willy-brandt.de/fileadmin/brandt/Downloads/Regierungserklaerung_Willy_Brandt_1969.pdf.

[186] T. Roethe, *Arbeiten wie bei Honecker, leben wie bei Kohl. Ein Plädoyer für das Ende der Schonzeit* (Frankfurt a.M.: Eichborn, 1999).

[187] D. Haselbach, *Autoritärer Liberalismus und Soziale Marktwirtschaft. Gesellschaft und Politik im Ordoliberalismus* (Baden-Baden: Nomos, 1991); Hepple and Veneziani, 'Introduction', p. 6, argue that 'some countries had inherited a system of labour relations and labour law from the pre-war period or in the immediate aftermath of the war that could be relatively easily adapted to the needs of post-war reconstruction and growth and later to achieve the labour 'flexibilty' demanded by firms who relied on technological innovation in order to improve productivity in the face of increased global competition'.

[188] Wieacker, *A History of Private Law*, p. 410, provides a summary of the landmark decisions the Reichsgericht and later the Bundesgerichtshof have taken to integrate social elements in the German Civil Code. D. Hart, *Allgemeine Geschäftsbedingungen und Justizsystem* (Kronberg: Scriptor-Verlag, 1975), uses the role of courts in the control of unfair contract terms as a paradigmatic example for the authoritarian protective policy; see A. Somma, 'Social Justice and the Market in European Contract Law' (2006) 2 *European Review of Contract Law* 181–198, on the relationship between authoritarian liberalism and courts.

France as a reference point helps us understand the implications. In France, social policy issues enshrine a genuine political dimension that may end up in some form of social turmoil, whereas in Germany, social policy issues still have a technical-instrumental focus, which goes back to the Sozialistengesetze. Individualised social protection contributes to appease the workers and later consumers. The collective political dimension is downgraded if not excluded. In 1957, the German Supreme Court held the largest trade union (IG-Metall) liable for an 'illegal strike' that resulted in compensation of more than 38,476 million German marks.[189] The employers renounced their right to be compensated in exchange for a conciliation procedure that had to advance a 'legal strike'. There is a striking coincidence with the logic enshrined in the ECJ's *Viking* and *Laval* judgments that a strike is bound to particular thresholds that are to be derived from law.[190]

German consumer policy goes hand in hand with the rise of the social welfare state in the late sixties and the seventies of the twentieth century. The German consumer policy was shaped and elaborated under the first post-war Social Democrat government.[191] This was more by coincidence than subject to a strategic decision. The *Kennedy* declaration dates back to 1962, while consumer policy in the OECD – the catalyst for the transferral of US policy to Europe – started in 1972.[192] The first consumer policy report was adopted in 1971 under the then sociliberal German government headed by Willy Brandt.[193] The political debate focussed on two issues, on the so-called thalidomide catastrophe that affected 6,000 children in Germany alone and the heated discussion over the pros and cons of controlling standard contract terms. Ludwig Raiser accomplished his

---

[189] Bundesarbeitsgericht, Urteil vom 31.10.1958 – 1 AZR 632/57 – Friedenspflicht – Schlichtungsvereinbarung der IG Metall, BAGE 6, 321; AP Nr. 2 zu § 1 TVG Friedenspflicht; NJW 1959, 356, 908; BB 1958, 1132; Betrieb 1959, 143; T. Ramm, 'Pluralismus ohne Kodifikation. Die Arbeitsrechtswissenschaft nach 1945', in D. Simon (ed.), *Rechtswissenschaft in der Bonner Republik. Studien zur Wissenschaftsgeschichte der Jurisprudenz* (Frankfurt a.M.: Suhrkamp, 1994), pp. 449–528, at p. 468 and pp. 476–486.
[190] Case C-438/05, *The International Transport Workers' Federation und The Finnish Seamen's Union* [2007] ECR I-10779; Case C-341/05, *Laval un Partneri* [2007] ECR I-11767.
[191] In particular, N. Reich, K. Tonner, H. Wegener, *Verbraucher und Recht* (Göttingen: Schwartz, 1976).
[192] Reprinted in E. v. Hippel, *Verbraucherschutz*, 3rd ed. (Tübingen: Mohr, 1986), p. 414.
[193] Bundestag-Drucksache 4/2724, 18.10.1971.

habilitation on the control of standard terms at the very end of the Weimar Republic.[194]

The success of the German Civil Code neither results from its grand vision of a new (market) society, nor from its (missing) social outlook. It results from its usability and usefulness for effectively and efficiently organising the economy in the industrial age. Ensuring a smoothly functioning market includes the need to protect weaker parties in response to the changing ideological patterns of the twentieth century. The default rules enshrined in the code functioned as standards of justice, at least in contracts based on standard contract terms. This is not the drop of socialist oil O. v. Gierke or A. Menger had in mind. It is the oil which is needed to guarantee the proper working of the market economy. Social protection is the exception to the rule, and it is granted on an individual basis only. This strength (or weakness) characterises the German civil law system – until today. It is pragmatic in that it is bound to a market-oriented model, while it is authoritarian protective insofar as it ensures a ground level of protection for people in need.

1.4.5 The German Civil Code and Sonderprivatrecht

The rise of consumer law brought a discussion between two academics camps back to the fore (Professoren-Modell), a discussion which could only take place in Germany, as it is only in Germany that academics still hold a position which allows them to turn a political debate into a legal debate. The stakes are seemingly high: on the one hand there is the German Civil Code guided by the liberal regulatory philosophy that intends to provide guidance to the market participants via default rules; on the other hand there is the so-called *Sonderprivatrecht*, which ties protection to the consumer status through mandatory private law rules.

Gierke wrote clairvoyantly as early as 1889 on the relationship between the then envisaged codification of the civil law and the already existing laws and regulations that have been adopted in response to the changing economy (the industrial state):[195]

---

[194] H. Grossmann-Doerth, *Selbstgeschaffenes Recht der Wirtschaft und staatliches Recht* (Freiburg: Wagner'sche Univ. Buchh., 1933); L. Raiser's *Das Recht der Allgemeinen Geschäftsbedingungen* (Hamburg: Hanseat. Verl. AnS., 1935) is the book version of his 1933 habilitation. For a deeper analysis of the role and function of 'economic democracy' (*Wirtschaftsdemokratie*) in the period after World War II, Brüggemeier, *Entwicklung des Rechts im organisierten Kapitalismus. Band I*, p. 379.

[195] Gierke, *Die soziale Aufgabe des Privatrechts*, p. 13.

One receives two systems which are dominated by a totally different philosophy: a system of a common civil law, which enshrines the 'pure' private law, and a bulk of special rules, which is governed by a cloudy mixture of public and private law. Here a vivid, popular, socially coloured law full of inner dynamic – there an abstract model, romanistic, individualistic, ossified in dead legal doctrine (translation H.-W. M.).

The question behind the question was whether the regulatory spirit of the old German Civil Code should be amended so as to integrate the missing social(ist) oil into the German Civil Code – not labour law but consumer law, which had grown to a separate field of law outside the German Civil Code. There is one notable effort to be reported from German academia to develop a coherent intellectual concept for a socially integrated approach to the interpretation of the German Civil Law. The so-called *Alternativkommentar* (alternative commentary to the Civil Code), edited by former president of the Court of Appeal in Braunschweig R. Wassermann, united critical academics in order to realise via interpretation what has not been achieved via the legislature.[196] The project did not survive its first edition, although the contributions provide a different view of German contract, tort and property law, one which is inspired by legal naturalism in its various forms and one which fits nicely into attempts by Gény and others in the early twentieth century. Thirty years later the commentary is largely forgotten, although it is still a source of inspiration. The Alternativkommentar was discredited as a socialist project, shaking the foundations of the German private law system. Even this debate remained purely academic. It did not reach the public forum. That might help to understand why the German Parliament did not discuss the political implications of inserting consumer law into the Civil Code, at least not between the 1960s and the year 2000. The legal-political response to the consumer society which grew and grew in the aftermath of World War II remained timid and half-hearted. In an amazing historical continuity, consumer law developed outside the Civil Code in special laws and regulations (*Sonderregelungen* = Sonderprivatrecht), commented and documented by a critical

---

[196] R. Wassermann (ed.), *Kommentar zum BGB (Reihe Alternativkommentare)*, multiple volumes (Neuwied: Luchterhand, 1980–1990). It was a unique exercise by critical German scholars to use interpretation as a means to give the whole BGB a more social outlook. Of lasting intellectual value are the introductions to concepts the BGB is using. Even in Google, the commentary does not bring valuable results to light. Today's generation of undergraduates and young scholars do not know what it means.

academia. Kahn-Freund's five criteria that justified treating labour law as a separate field of law could, by and large, be transferred to consumer law.[197]

Contrary to England and France, the enforcement of consumer law was not put into the hands of public agencies, but was largely left in the hands of the judiciary. The simple explanation might be that it is much harder to centralise enforcement in a federal state like Germany than in France. Traditionally, enforcement lay with the German Länder. It is characteristic of the German legal system that the enforcement of special laws and regulations, the so-called *Wirtschaftsprivatrecht* (economic law), was delegated to private organisations. The break-even point was the adoption of the German Act on unfair advertising in 1896/1906, which turned business organisations into law enforcers. Consumer organisations were granted standing in 1965.[198] In 1976, private enforcement was extended to the control of unfair standard contract terms. Bakardjieva-Engelbrekt[199] explains the particularities of the German enforcement structure through the strong role of medium-sized business in the economy and – again a phenomenon which relates to the German history – the scattered picture of regions, counties, etc. in the first half of the nineteenth century.[200]

Germany did not make a single political effort to condense the consumer protection rules in a coherent legal body. In a certain way, such an exercise would have fit into the tradition of the Historische Schule, not so much in the sense that consumer law can be found in the existing

---

[197] Hepple, 'Introduction', under reference to Kahn-Freund, pp. 8–9: (1) the (social) importance of the subject matter – the heart of their social existence, (2) the special nature of the subject matter – the missing public/private divide, (3) the special treatment which labour law demands – advocacy of sociology and legal policy, (4) the necessity of auxiliary sciences – sociology, social policy and theory of business organisations (!!), (5) the unity of the goal – embodiment of the human personality, labour law based on the needs of employment relationship. The first four criteria could easily be applied to consumer law. Only the fifth might be somewhat problematic, as I hesitate to grant consumption the same social status as labour. However, consumption has turned into a stabilising factor of the economy. This has changed also the political legitimation of consumption; see C. Torp, *Wachstum, Sicherheit, Moral. Politische Legitimation des Konsums im 20. Jahrhundert*.

[198] For a summary of the historical development, C. Alexander, *Schadensersatz und Abschöpfung im Lauterkeits- und Kartellrecht* (Tübingen: Mohr Siebeck, 2010), p. 18.

[199] A. Bakardjieva Engelbrekt, *Fair Trading Law in Flux?: National Legacies and Institutional Choice and the Process of Europeanisation*, PhD thesis, Stockholm University (2003).

[200] Although there is a cautious move towards administrative enforcement, whether it will lead to legislative activities is open. But politics and academics are starting to discuss administrative enforcement of private law.

law already but in the strong reliance (of the majority of German academics until today) on the power of systems and coherence. However, those academics who defended the idea of a consumer law did not share the conceptual ideals of the Historische Schule. Consumer law in this part of the academia was seen as a political instrument of change for society. One may easily build a link backwards to Jhering, Weber, Sinzheimer and legal naturalism. In light of the social welfare state losing impetus in the late seventies of the twentieth century, Germany was politically all too ready to delegate consumer policy to the European Union. Since then, there is no longer such a thing as a forward-looking German consumer policy, at least not in the field of private law. A certain revival of the national consumer movement – a grand word for a small exercise – results from institutional change, through the establishment of consumer policy commissions in the German Länder (Bavaria in 2009, Baden-Württemberg in 2008 and Niedersachsen in 2014) and at the federal level through the Sachverständigenrat für Verbraucherfragen (2014; its predecessor was the Wissenschaftliche Beirat starting in 2002).[201]

As of 2002, consumer law provisions form part of the German Civil Code. This time,[202] there was no outcry in academia, although the integration of the consumer contract law rules challenged the system and the coherence of the German Civil Code.[203] The integration was prepared by the backdoor through the introduction of the concept of the consumer and the right to withdrawal into the German Civil Code in 2000, along the line of the implementation of the Distant Selling Directive 97/7/EC.[204] This major amendment is certainly due to the change in political power in 1998, which gave the red-green coalition

---

[201] For the working papers of the Sachverständigenrat für Verbraucherfragen, www.svr-verbraucherfragen.de/dokumente/.

[202] For an overall account of the development of consumer contract law in Germany and its integration into the BGB, see Zimmermann, 'Consumer Contract Law and General Contract Law'; critical with regard to the integration into the BGB is K. Adomeit, 'Die gestörte Vertragsparität – ein Trugbild' (1994) *Neue Juristische Wochenschrift* 2467; K. Adomeit, 'Herbert Marcuse, der Verbraucherschutz und das BGB' (2004) *Neue Juristische Wochenschrift* 579–582; W. Flume, 'Vom Beruf unserer Zeit für die Gesetzgebung' (2000) *Zeitschrift für Wirtschaftsrecht* 1427–1430.

[203] The attempt to initiate a political debate in the German community on the pros and cons of the integration of consumer law into the BGB via the 67. German Juristentag in 2012 failed completely; Micklitz, 'Do Consumers and Businesses need a New Architecture for Consumer Law?'.

[204] Directive 97/7/EC of the European Parliament and of the Council of 20 May 1997 on the protection of consumers in respect of distance contracts, OJ No. L 144, 4.6.1997, p. 19.

the opportunity to catch up with what was missed during the codification of the German Civil Code – the insertion of the famous 'drop of social(ist) oil'.[205] Two years later, in 2002, in the shadow of the long-debated project on modernisation of German contract law (Schuldrechts-Modernisierungsgesetz), the executive, i.e. the Ministry of Justice, smuggled the bulk of consumer contract law rules into the German Civil Code. It is telling that the academic attention of civil law professors and leading judges focused on the revision of prescription rules, on *Leistungsstörungsrecht* (interference with or impairment of the performance of an obligation) and on sales law. The proclaimed reform of the prescription rules was overwhelmingly discussed as a matter of coherence and consistency, not as a matter of justice.[206] The major shift – the integration of the Sonderprivatrecht into terra sancta of the BGB – raised less attention.

The more political dimension, the merging of technical, formalistic civil law (Savigny) and value-loaded consumer law (Gierke), attracted neither much public nor much academic awareness. The integration of consumer law into the German Civil Code was performed as a technical bureaucratic exercise. Even today, German academia tends to downplay the possible long-term effects of the materialisation of private law through mandatory contract law rules and its Europeanisation through the integration of harmonised consumer contract law rules on the traditional body of consumer law. The old fractions in civil law scholarship are still encamped, only the language used has been sanitised. The majority of academics reflect on how to integrate the new rules of the law on modernisation of the Civil Code into the existing dogmatic structure – just as it was in the early twentieth century. But the same is true for the other fraction. Consumer lawyers do not try to link the particular fields of consumer law to the general structure of the civil system.[207] Regulatory private law on services (telecom, postal services, energy, transport, financial services), in all its implications for contract law, remains outside the German Civil Code. Here Gierke's dictum still holds true. It seems as if institutional choice between integration of

---

[205] The wording goes back to Gierke, *Die soziale Aufgabe des Privatrechts*.
[206] As to the background in the German reform debate, see P. Bydlinski, 'Die geplante Modernisierung des Verjährungsrechts' und H. Eidenmüller, 'Ökonomik der Verjährungsregeln', in R. Schulze and H. Schulte-Nölke (eds.), *Die Schuldrechtsreform vor dem Hintergrund des Gemeinschaftsrechts* (Tübingen: Mohr Siebeck, 2001), pp. 381–404 and pp. 405–415 respectively.
[207] There are exceptions: K. Tonner, A. Willingmann, and M. Tamm, *Vertragsrecht. Kommentar* (Köln: Luchterhand Verlag, 2010).

consumer law into the Civil Code or outsourcing consumer law into a separate body of law does not matter. Consumer law remains alien to the Civil Code.

It remains for the courts to handle the difficulties, inconsistencies, overlaps and adaptations which result from the somewhat hastened integration of consumer law rules into the Civil Code, hastened because the German legislator did not find the time and did not have the willingness or the power (?) to adapt the new rules to the old system.[208] Although formally integrated into the BGB, consumer law remains distinct from traditional civil law rules, a bit like a foreign element. The extent to which there are similarities between the three countries in ad hoc legislative amendments, tensions running through the law, and the lack of a basic norm that orients the whole system will now be investigated.

1.5 Conceptions of Social Justice in Comparison

The chart towards orientation in Table 1 can be read vertically and horizontally. So far, emphasis has been placed on the vertical dimension and on the presentation and analysis of each of the three countries and their particular design, with horizontal sidesteps here and there. Now it is time to engage in a horizontal comparison of the different patterns of justice. This will be done by undertaking the onerous task of categorising the perceived patterns of justice, of the function of law in remedying deficits, and of categorising the interaction between the market order and society, as well as the mutual social expectations of states and their citizens. This is an exercise in overt simplification. The reference point is legal consciousness, which might be homogeneous neither among the citizens of the country nor over time. Overall, however, I argue that the particular patterns of justice remain remarkably stable over time, demonstrating the inertia of culture and tradition in a given society.

1.5.1 *Perceived Patterns of Justice*

The legal consciousness in the three countries could be caught in three parameters: the perception of the people of their countries, the degree

---

[208] M. Schirmbacher, *Verbrauchervertriebsrecht. Die Vereinheitlichung der Vorschriften über Haustürgeschäfte, Fernabsatzverträge und Verträge im elektronischen Geschäftsverkehr* (Baden-Baden: Nomos, 2005).

Table 2

	Perception	Scale	Key actors
England	Liberal utilitarian	Corrective	Self-help
France	Rational political	Societal/political	Executive
Germany	Idealistic authoritarian	Distributive	Judiciary

of justice they expect and the potential addressee of the perception and the expectation. The overview is largely self-explanatory: the English consciousness is rooted in liberal utilitarian thinking, expecting corrective justice, for which citizens have to fight for by themselves before the courts or Alternative Dispute Resolution (ADR) bodies; the French consciousness is rooted in rational political thinking, expecting distributive justice politically from the state, i.e. the executive; and the German consciousness is rooted in idealistic authoritarian thinking, expecting distributive justice not only from the state but also from private companies.

Such a reading finds support in the groundbreaking analysis by Rafael La Porta, Florencio Lopez-de-Silanes, Andrej Shleifer and Robert W. Vishny (LLSV) of financial markets using legal families as a starting point for comparison.[209] Their work can be assigned to the line of research called LOT – i.e. legal origin theory.[210] The authors' most important statement is that the historical origins of a legal system have an essential impact on the economic development and opportunities for future development. Their approach correlates with the idea of a common European legal culture. However, the crucial difference is that the *ius commune* highlights European commonalities, beyond the moats of continental European and common law, whereas LOT declares the differences between continental European and common law systems to be the central parameter of analysis.

The analysis of the variables is characterised by a clear preference for the common law system compared to the French Civil Law countries.

---

[209] R. La Porta, F. Lopez-de-Silanes, A. Shleifer and R. W. Vishny, 'Law and Finance' (1998) 106 *The Journal of Political Economy* 1113–1155; R. La Porta, F. Lopez-de-Silanes and A. Shleifer, 'The Economic Consequences of Legal Origins' (2008) 46 *Journal of Economic Literature* 285–332, at 288.

[210] The origins of LOT can be found in the economic analysis of law; A. T. F. Lang, 'The Legal Construction of Economic Rationalities?' (2013) 40 *Journal of Law and Society* 155–171. For an account of the different currents of LOT with reprint of original texts, S. Deakin and K. Pistor (eds.), *Legal Origin Theory* (Cheltenham: Edward Elgar, 2012).

Germany is not dealt with separately. LLSV has provided the impulse for a variety of research projects, which use the same method and go beyond business financing, the ownership structures of banks, rules about market access, labour market provisions, media ownership structures, formal requirements for judicial procedures, and the relative independence of courts. They are listed and explained in more detail by LLS (without Vishny) in the 2008 text. These examinations are meant to sharpen the original findings of 1998 and reinforce the superiority of common law:[211] 'In all these spheres, civil law is associated with a heavier hand of government ownership and regulation than common law. Many of these indicators of government ownership and regulation are associated with adverse impacts on markets, such as greater corruption, a larger unofficial economy, and higher unemployment', and further:[212] 'in strong form (later to be supplemented by a variety of caveats), we argue that common law stands for a strategy of social control that seeks to support private market outcomes, whereas civil law seeks to replace such outcomes with state-desired allocations'. In the words of M. Damaška, civil law is 'policy implementing', while common law is 'dispute resolving';[213] in those of K. Pistor, French civil law embraces 'socially-conditioned private contracting', in contrast to common law's support for 'unconstrained private contracting'.[214]

1.5.2 *Perceived Function of the Role of Law in Remedying Social Justice Deficits*

A more nuanced view, one more encompassing than the crude generalisations of LLSV, is possible. The English legal order is liberal and pragmatic; if statutory intervention is needed it occurs ad hoc. It is problem-orientated public regulation. Here we find the typical pragmatism so characteristic of the English liberals (Locke and Hume). It is neither ideology nor the purity of the idea that decides whether the

---

[211] La Porta, Lopez-de-Silanes and Shleifer, 'The Economic Consequences of Legal Origins', p. 286 left column.
[212] La Porta, Lopez-de-Silanes and Shleifer, 'The Economic Consequences of Legal Origins', p. 286 right column.
[213] M. Damaška, *The Faces of Justice and State Authority: A Comparative Approach to the Legal Process* (New Haven: Yale University Press, 1986), IV. Conflict-Solving Type of Proceeding, p. 97 and V. The Policy Implementing Type of Proceeding, p. 147.
[214] K. Pistor, 'Legal Ground Rules in Coordinated and Liberal Market Economies', in K. J. Hopt, E. Wymeersch, H. Kanada and H. Baum (eds.), *Corporate Governance in Context: Corporations, States, and Markets in Europe, Japan and the US* (Oxford: Oxford University Press, 2005), pp. 249–280, at pp. 255, 256.

envisaged use of the law contributes to problem-solving. This is not to say that different ideologies do not compete within the common law of contract; they most certainly do.[215] However, in the final analysis, the judge's resort is usually to dispute resolution as justice on the facts of the case, according to the standard of reasonableness and all things considered. This is in essence a pragmatic method. That helps us understand the clear distinction common lawyers tend to defend between contract as private ordering and regulation as public ordering.[216]

The French legal order is protective and paternalistic, ambitious in its form – the allusion to the Code Civil is obvious – but poor in substance, as both new codes that are meant to enshrine the Social, the Code de Travail and the Code de la Consommation, are no more than compilations of all sorts of rules, with little or no attempt to unite them into a 'system'. The French model should be distinguished from the German model, although both are more closely aligned in comparison to the English one. The French state has always had a strong protective and paternalistic hand in the economy. It is libertarian in the sense that French society devotes much attention to individualism and autonomy. It is 'grassroots libertarian paternalism', as it bears a highly political dimension which derives from bottom-up action.[217] Statutory paternalism is counterbalanced by the highly politicised conception of the law. There is always a citizen dimension in labour law and even in consumer law. This is the legacy of French rationalism.

The German legal order is protective but authoritarian. Legal solutions oscillate between problem-solving and 'grand' solutions; most of the time civil law thinking prevails over intervention via public regulation. This is a very particular form of protection which differs from the

---

[215] Adams and Brownsword, 'The Ideologies of Contract'.
[216] Adams and Brownsword, *Understanding Contract Law*, 5th ed. (London: Sweet & Maxwell, 2007): 'Sometimes judges' decisions are underwritten by considerations of commercial convenience, at others by considerations of fairness and reasonableness. One key to understanding contract law is to understand the complex interplay between these competing considerations or ideologies (...). Inevitably, these conflicting ideologies inject inconsistent doctrines into the contract rule-book. Attempting to reconcile conflicting precedents, it may be argued, is misguided rather than heroic ... In our view, it is a mistake to think of contract law as a train-load of doctrine chugging along in one direction. Rather, it is carried on several trains, some bound on collision courses with one another.'
[217] French grassroots libertarian paternalism should not be conflated with the libertarian paternalism that Sunstein and Thaler ('Libertarian Paternalism Is Not an Oxymoron') have in mind, when they discuss modes to 'nudge' consumers into the – politically and economically – correct direction.

Table 3

	Legal order	Form	Substance
England	Liberal and pragmatic	Ad hoc intervention	Contract regulation vs. common law
France	Protective and paternalistic or political	Code de Travail Code de la Consommation	Compilation
Germany	Protective and authoritarian	No ad hoc, no code	Civil law

French attitude. It could be called 'authoritarian' protection, as the citizen (still) is much more the object of statutory action than the addressee of political participation. German uncertainty on the choice of the appropriate form documents its mid-term position between England and France. With England, Germany shares a reluctance to intervene too deeply into the market – that is the liberal side; with France it shares the striving for unity – a codified legal system (code), though more in an idealistic than in a rationalistic mode. The difference between French grassroots paternalistic liberalism and German authoritarian liberalism explains why the German model is constantly oscillating back and forth between the French political and the English pragmatic models.

1.5.3 Interaction Between Market Order, Society and the Social

The English market is liberal and embedded in an evolving society that did not undergo disruptive revolutionary changes in the last three centuries; a society where the economic and social development remains strongly interconnected through the combination of self-help and state help, binding statutory distributive interventions to financial affordability. The biggest French–German similarities result from the divide between economic and social policy – the attempt to bifurcate matters of justice from affordability. In Germany, this is due to the strong impact of idealism; in France, it is the Rousseauean side of French rationalism.

The German market order, however, does not function and has not functioned historically in the same way as the French market order. The German state and the German market order contain an authoritarian element which survived two world wars and is still present today. The particularity of the German legal order lies in the (ordo-)libertarian momentum, which is less developed in the French market order, and which brings the German market order nearer to the English one. In France, the market ideology was strengthened considerably through the European Union in the form of post-war German ordo-liberalism.[218] The French-German differences in the conception and the perception of the market order correlate with their particular design of society. The French market order must be seen in the light of the long shadow of the French Revolution, which was a bottom-up political revolution. The French market order is first and foremost a political order. The German market order is the product of the industrial revolution, which was enabled via the Prussian state but which unfolds its own dynamic once established and which has blown away barriers to trade resulting from state legislation. H. James argues that the German identity is deeply connected to the economic power Germany derives from its market economy.[219]

The more pragmatic conception of the market order, the persistence of economic power and its deep anchoring in the German minds as an integral part of the German identity might help us to understand why Germany was able to reform the economy under the lead of Social-Democrat Chancellor Schröder's agenda 2010.[220] Whereas the German people voted chancellor Schröder out of office, they benefitted from the 'modernised' German social welfare state.[221] The bias between German idealism – the defence of the welfare state against Schröder – and the remaining portion of English pragmatism in implementing Agenda 2010 is striking. In France, resistance in the streets prevented and still prevents the government from engaging in deeper social reforms. One may speculate as to whether Macron will succeed this time. Until today, the political agenda, the utopia of a just society, not only dominates public discourse; it leaves its footprint on a French economy that is

---

[218] Gerber, 'Constitutionalizing the Economy'.
[219] H. James, *A German Identity 1770–1990* (New York: Routledge, 1989); *Deutsche Identität 1770–1990* (Frankfurt a.M.: Campus-Verlag, 1991), book review, H. Schulze, 'German Identity' (1989) 32 *The Historical Journal* 1005–1011.
[220] The link provides access not only to Schröder's speech in the German Bundestag, but also to the legislative measures taken and a resume ten years after: www.bundestag.de/dokumente/textarchiv/2013/43257637_kw11_kalenderblatt_agenda2010/211202.
[221] He delivered the data, but his intention is to demonstrate the decline of the German social welfare state; Scharpf, 'Monetary Union, Fiscal Crisis and the Pre-Emption of Democracy'.

Table 4

	Market	Society	The Social
England	Liberal	Evolutionary	Connected to the market
France	Liberal under EU influence	Politically disruptive	Disconnected from the market
Germany	Liberal via national intervention	Economically disruptive	Disconnected from and then reconnected to the market

struggling with the social costs of defending a just society in the face of global competition.

1.5.4 Social Expectations, Relationship between State and Individuals

It is in this category where the three states under review seem to differ most. The English society is historically built on self-help. English and UK citizens do not so much rely on the state to protect them against social grievance. They have learnt over centuries that they are first and foremost self-responsible – although today even the English/UK state provides a basic minimum protection. This is equally true for the English entrepreneur. The small state facilitates ethical business. The French expect the state not only to look after their social interests, but to solve the problems behind social grievance. At the most they require the state to create a different society, while at a more pragmatic level they expect the executive to solve their problems. These high expectations may easily end up in frustrations, which are then turned into political action against the very same government. Germans, in contrast, have over the last century delegated responsibility for social matters to the state, first to the judiciary and later to the executive. The judiciary managed to adapt the formal German BGB to the material needs of the underprivileged by imposing more and more responsibilities on entrepreneurs. Over time, the state, the legislature and the executive have taken a much more interventionist stand.

Despite the different addressees, France and Germany share political dreams of a state-made better society, the French pushing and the Germans expecting. Unlike the French, the Germans do not fight for their rights in the political arena. Recall the famous saying attributed to Lenin or Stalin: 'In Deutschland findet die Revolution nicht statt, weil das

Table 5

	Parameters	Objective	Addressee
England	Self-help and state help	Social grievance	Society and judiciary
France	State help and self-help	Political problems (a different society)	State/executive
Germany	State-help, third party help and self-help	Economic problems (a different market)	State/judiciary Entrepreneur

Betreten des Rasens verboten ist' ('In Germany the revolution does not take place, because entering the lawn is prohibited').[222] Germans do not revolt in the streets against the government like the French do. This was even true in the moment of economic crisis that triggered Agenda 2010. The student revolt of 1968 has not yielded a long-term impact on the German political system, at least not if one compares the constant grassroots resistance in France to Germany. The German unification process undermined societal resistance and reinvigorated authoritarian thinking.[223] This is not to deny the potential impact of unification on constitutional law. What is missing in such a perspective, however, is a democratic dimension. Therefore, focusing on constitutional law and even more so on 'law' in the making of a new constitution fits all too well in the role 'law' played throughout the twentieth century in the formation of a German state.[224] One might go as far as saying that the whole German unification process was much too legalistic and not democratic enough.

In sum: the higher the expectations in the respective countries are, the shakier the position of the respective government, if not the state. The lower the expectations, the easier is it for the respective government to handle social policy issues without undermining its own legitimacy.

---

[222] Who said it is not clear. G. Grass used it during the 1970s.
[223] For a critical view on the revolution that is claimed to have taken place in the GDR, Roethe, *Arbeiten wie bei Honecker, leben wie bei Kohl*; and R. Wieland, *Ich schlage vor, dass wir uns küssen* (München: Kunstmann, 2009).
[224] Relying on B. Ackermann's theory of intergenerational synthesis, Jaggi analyses the impact of the unified Germany on the German constitutional order – via the German Constitutional Court: Jaggi, *The 1989 Revolution in East Germany and Its Impact on Unified Germany's Constitutional Law*.

2 Success and Failure of Social Justice through Private Law

So far, I have analysed the rise of the Social in labour and in consumer law through the lenses of a national perspective. The focus has been laid on the nation-state, on national markets, national societies and national variations in the use of law to compensate for deficiencies in the labour and the consumer market. This was to test the overall hypothesis of national patterns of social justice that are deeply ingrained in national culture and national tradition and that are reflected in the way the law is used to raise (or not) social standards in the labour and the consumer market. Thinking about the success or even the failure of the different national patterns of justice through the lenses of the *law* serves a twofold purpose:[1] it is an ideological critique and it is a way to identify the state of mind in the three states, their societies and their legal systems when the European Union began to become gradually involved in developing a social Europe.

2.1 The 'Social' Effective, Desirable, Affordable and Efficient

Historically, the crisis of the social welfare state was triggered long before the fall of the Berlin Wall and the rise of the global economy. This becomes visible in the way social movements in the three countries stagnated in the 1970s already, when social democratic thinking started to lose ground as the dominating ideology and when the three states began to reconsider the design of their welfare system. The debate started rather softly, not about the yes or no of social policy, but about its *effectiveness*. Already in the 1970s, it became clear that the good

---

[1] Introduction 3.1.

political intention to transform the economy and society via law meets barriers. They were discussed in the language of 'failures'. 'Regulatory failure'[2] addressed the role of the state, more particularly the executive. This is not at all surprising, as the rise of the Social increased statutory powers to intervene in the market and the society via law. It turned out that neither ministries nor specialised agencies established to look after the collective interests of the workers and the consumers were able to fully implement the social objectives enshrined in the various laws. There was but a small step from regulatory failure to governmental failure[3] or regulatory capture,[4] arguing that the state and the executive engage in collusive relations with business. From the 1970s onwards, the academic and political debate has been dominated by proposals concerning new forms of more effective social regulation – responsive regulation, better regulation, smart regulation, and most recently, 'nudging'.[5] The deeper theoretical debate in private law and in legal theory questioned materialisation in the Weberian sense and promoted proceduralisation. The debate shifted from material justice to procedural justice, from Habermas' 'facts and norms' to Luhmann's 'system theory' and Teubner's 'autopoeitic' law.[6]

The broader political and economic environment had changed, too. The reform drive that spread over Europe after 1968 and pushed governments into action came gradually to a halt. Conservative thinking gained ground, and conservative parties came to power first in the United Kingdom, then in Germany and, in the end, in France. The political critique was directed against the impact of the social welfare ideology on society, the decline of individual self-responsibility, the over-reliance of citizens on the state and the nation-state's unfitness for a globalised world.[7] The political question

---

[2] R. Coase, 'Discussion' (1964) 54 *American Economic Review* 195–197. Discussion of three papers on 'Regulated Industries' published in 54 *American Economic Review*.

[3] N. Reich, 'The Regulatory Crisis: Does It Exist and Can It Be Solved? Some Comparative Remarks on the Situation of Social Regulation in the USA and the EEC' (1984) 2 *Environment and Planning C: Government and Policy* 177–197.

[4] J.-J. Laffont and J. Tirole, 'The Politics of Government Decision-Making. A Theory of Regulatory Capture' (1991) 106 *Quarterly Journal of Economics* 1089–1127.

[5] R. Baldwin and J. Black, 'Really Responsive Regulation' (2007) *LSE Law. Society and Economy Working Paper* No. 15, available at: www.lse.ac.uk/law/working-paper-series/2007–08/WPS15-2007BlackandBaldwin.pdf.

[6] G. Teubner, *Law as an Autopoietic System* (Oxford: Blackwell, 1993).

[7] F. Josef Strauss coined the word from the 'Soziale Hängematte' (the social hammock), www.utv.de/zitate-von-franz-josef-strausz.html.

became how much social policy and how much social welfare do we want? The debate shifted from *effectiveness* to *desirability* and *feasibility*.

The economic environment had changed, too. The oil price shock of 1973 had not only left deep traces in the minds of the people and the belief in the market economy, but it had also brought *Keynes* to the forefront of the political agenda and triggered public spending as a means to relaunch the economy. Keynesian economic policy had to be financed just as social policy did. Gradually, affordability became an issue due to the costs of social welfare state measures and the 'who pays'. In the long run Keynesianism paved the way for economic efficiency thinking into politics. However, Keynesianism was sidelined and the Chicago School came to dominance in promoting economic efficiency. Scarce resources had to be allocated whilst social policy had grown into the biggest post in national budgets. Gradually social policy became connected to *affordability* and to *economic efficiency*. The financial implications of a social policy had been somewhat downgraded in the heydays of the social welfare state in light of the then blossoming economy. People began to realise that the benefits of the social welfare state had to be financed; social policies started to compete with economic policies.

How did the move towards effectiveness, desirability, affordability and efficiency affect legal consciousness in the three states under scrutiny? The reactions to the new challenges of the welfare paradigm in the late 1970s differed widely in all three countries, but they reflect the deeper patterns identified in the reconstruction of legal consciousness throughout the centuries: the English tackled the new challenge via Thatcherism in solving the 'problem' through budget cuts and downgrading social policy and social law (from 1979 on). Gradually, labour law was turned into labour market law, and English society adapted to the new challenges. The French rejected the hard economic facts, maintaining the ideal of the welfare state (from 1981 Mitterrand). There is a long list of political attempts of the different French conservative and socialist governments after 1980 to transform the labour market in particular. All these efforts were rejected through political resistance in the streets. At the time of this writing, Macron has launched a new initiative. It remains to be seen whether he will succeed where so many French presidents have failed before him. Germans (from 1982 Kohl/Genscher on), whilst not relinquishing their idealism for the realisation of a more just society, were ready to engage in a serious reform of the labour market and the social security system under Schröder (Agenda 2010).[8] This does not mean that there were, and that there are, no conflicts and fights in these three societies. The historical reconstruction of the way in which the three states and their peoples came to grips with the transformation of the welfare state allows for labelling legal consciousness. The crucial point is certainly the economic dimension of the who pays. The English people are guided via pragmatism: we the taxpayers have to pay, and we are ready to accept our remaining self-responsibility, as well as less state and more individual self-help, contrary to the Danish society for instance.[9] The French know that the country is facing serious economic difficulties but refuse to give up their political rights. They view rights as political, and by giving up those political achievements, they lose out – at a deeper level it is a step backwards from Rousseau and the idea of progression towards an ideal that the Enlightenment promises. Germans are somewhere in between the two. It dawns on the Germans that they have to pay for the social welfare benefits in the end, but they believe and hope that the German economy is strong enough to cope with the additional burden. The deeply rooted striving for economic power as an integral part of the German identity explains that the Germans tend to set aside the detrimental effects the prerogative of financial stability in the EU produces for other Member States.

This flows through to the perception of the Social in each country, most certainly with regard to social security, health insurance, pensions and employment contracts. In the latter, the tensions between social policy and market economy culminate. It suffices to recall the struggle over unfair dismissals. There is no comparable phenomenon in consumer contract law, although the two fields of law were originally united under the label of social policy. The economic and political decline of the social policy in the 1970s/1980s started in labour law (labour policy, employment policy) and migrated from there into consumer law and policy. The inner link between the two fields loosened through the dislocation of the production of consumer goods outside Europe: 56 per cent of the gross income in Europe results from private

---

[8] C. Crouch, *Can Neoliberalism Be Saved from Itself?* (Social Europe Edition, 2017).
[9] S. Steinmo, *The Evolution of Modern States, Sweden, Japan and the United States.*

consumption;[10] 80 per cent of consumer goods are said to be imported into the EU.[11]

The historic crisis of the national welfare state coincides with the European Union entering the political arena with its 1985 White Paper on the Completion of the Internal Market[12] that combined market building with social protection. It will have to be demonstrated that the European Union did not have much 'time' to develop a genuine European social policy that could focus on the EU alone, along the line of what the Member States were able to do in the 1960s and 1970s, prior to the new globalisation wave after 1989.[13] This would have needed a much deeper debate of what a European social policy could and should look like and who – the Member States or the EU – should be responsible for what and how a European social policy should be financed. The collapse of Communism in 1989, the rise of the global economy and financialisation dramatically changed the economic, social and political environment in which the nation-states and the EU were operating. European social policy had to match the transnational dimension of a European social policy in an ever more competitive environment, just five years after its 'constitutionalisation' in the Single European Act.

The first and most powerful blow against the promises of social welfare states arose from external competitive pressure on the EU, evidenced by the rise of the efficiency doctrine that shattered the social welfare doctrine. Somewhat overstated, it is a shift from justice to efficiency, from politics to economics, from the national welfare state to the European market state. European social policy thinking is dominated by *effectiveness* and *efficiency* rather than *desirability*. The second, less visible but in the long run most powerful change occurred in society. Collective self-help as a form of political participation lost ground, for better or worse, to the individualisation of rights. The national welfare

---

[10] Consumption expenditure by households and non-profit institutions serving households contributed 56.0 per cent of the EU-28's GDP in 2016; Figure 9 on 'Expenditure components of GDP at current market prices, EU-28, 2016 (% share of GDP) on the website of Eurostat, available at: http://ec.europa.eu/eurostat/statistics-explained/index.php/National_accounts_and_GDP.

[11] Estimation by public officials, no concrete figures, http://ec.europa.eu/eurostat/statistics-explained/index.php/International_trade_in_goods and https://wits.worldbank.org/CountryProfile/en/Compare/Country/EUN/Indicator/MPRT-PRDCT-SHR/partner/WLD/product/UNCTAD-SoP3/region/EUN/show/line.

[12] COM (85) 310 final, 14.6.1985.

[13] Part II. 1.

state is a passive party in this change. Pushed into action via the labour movement, the nation-states supported and framed but also undermined the self-organisational power of workers and later of consumers through extensive welfare programs, in labour law more indirectly through the involvement of the state in the organisation of industrial relations, and in consumer law directly through the financing of state-established consumer institutions.[14] The development of labour law in the United Kingdom is paradigmatic for the rest of Europe. Both 'blows' have left deep traces in law and the legal system: the first is condensed in the efficiency-driven comparison of legal systems; the second in the move towards individual rights.

I will begin by asking whether the protective policies in labour and consumer law have achieved the objectives they intended to achieve. Emphasis is placed on the private law dimension, on employment contracts and on consumer contracts. This is not a full account of the national law of the labour market or the national law of the consumer market. It is therefore necessary to define the objective of the respective policies and develop a design against which the measures can be evaluated. This is, in essence, an empirical question that aims to test the effectiveness of social policy implemented through law. The analysis is broken down into the collective distributive effects, the individual social effects and the potential non-economic societal effects. The first two are dealing with effectiveness; the third contrasts effectiveness with efficiency.

2.2 Measuring the Distributive (Collective) Effectiveness of Private Law

None of the three Member States undertook a serious and comprehensive attempt to evaluate the respective national policies and to assess them against the political programmes of the respective governments. The well-known difficulty of defining a sound methodological design that allows for the verification or falsification of a legal measure could neither explain nor justify this absence.[15] In the 1980s, and even in the

---

[14] T. Becker, 'Finanzierungsmodelle für die Verbraucherarbeit in Deutschland', Gutachten im Auftrag des Bundesministeriums für Ernährung, Landwirtschaft und Verbraucherschutz, 2009, available at: https://service.ble.de/ptdb/index2.php?detail_id=11027&site_key=145&stichw=finanzierungsmodelle&zeilenzahl_zaehler=2#newContent, with data on the financing of the German consumer association.

[15] As to the difficulties, see C. Meller-Hannich and A. Höland, 'Evaluierung der Effektivität kollektiver Rechtsschutzinstrumente', Gutachten im Auftrag des Bundesministerium

1990s, in the euphoria of the collapse of communism, the kind of thinking in impact assessments,[16] in testing the economic (since 1992), social and environmental (since 2005) impact of a certain measure had not yet fully reached the minds of politicians, of legislatures and of executive bodies. This is particularly true for the US approach of putting consumer protection rules to the sword of an efficiency test, not by an articulated public policy but via academic research initiated by the Chicago School.[17] Getting into the facts would have made it indispensable to clarify not only what exactly the policy objective was, but also how social justice and the distributional effects should be understood, in economic terms, in legal terms and social terms. Even the policy changes of the late 1970s and the early 1990s were not based on hard facts. They were based on political decisions and political judgments (if not prejudices) about individual behaviour of the people. The idea of 'evidence-based policy' is a legacy of the impact of political science on the law and bears in itself new risks for politicians and democratic powers.[18]

2.2.1 A Blind Eye on Facts

Trying to assess the distributive effects of the materialisation of private law through mandatory rules on information disclosure, through state-set minimum rights and duties for consumers and employees and, last but not least, through the increased attention of access to justice through individual and collective redress has to be based on second-best information – namely on the few empirical studies that have been initiated via non-lawyers and anecdotal evidence from those academics who have been working in the field for years. Why have those who promoted the development of social policies in the 1970s stayed away from engaging in a serious empirical assessment of whatever kind? Simply because of an unwillingness of governments and parliaments to finance such research? Why have left-wing politicians and left-wing

---

für Ernährung, Landwirtschaft und Verbraucherschutz, Schriftenreihe Angewandte Wissenschaft, Heft 523, 2011, availabe at: http://download.ble.de/09HS011. Pdf., p. 5.

[16] C. Strünck, K. Hagen, H.-W. Micklitz, A. Oehler and L. A. Reisch, 'Was nützt die Verbraucherpolitik den Verbrauchern? Plädoyer für eine systematische Evidenzbasierung der Verbraucherpolitik', WISO direkt, Friedrich-Ebert-Stiftung, April 2013, available at: http://library.fes.de/pdf-files/wiso/09837.pdf.

[17] N. Olsen, 'From Choice To Welfare: The Concept of the Consumer in the Chicago School of Economics' (2017) 14 *Modern Intellectual History* 507–535.

[18] P. Cairney, *The Politics of Evidence-Based Policy Making* (Basingstoke: Palgrave MacMillan, 2017).

scholars kept such a low profile, even though it became ever clearer – through hindsight – that the ambitious policy objectives of making private law more just were much harder to achieve than expected? To be sure, the effects of intervention were difficult to assess in their breadth and depth; for example, whether employees and consumers really benefitted from all the new legislation and even more specifically 'who' benefitted. Social policy right from its beginning suffered from the prejudice that the 'haves' would be the major beneficiaries: the employed and not the unemployed, middle class consumers and not poorer consumers. Is the deeper reason that the left did not want to know the full facts out of fear of admitting the failure not of the state, of the government, not of the failure of 'others', but maybe the much deeper failure of the feasibility of shaping social policy through the means of private law? Or even more problematic, that they – the employed and the middle class consumers – turned out to be the primary beneficiaries of all the social measures that had been promoted in the name of the under-privileged, the unemployed or the discriminated and poor consumers? Yet, the opposite could be true. Left-wing politicians and left-wing scholars were by and large satisfied with the achieved policies, not so much looking into their practical effects but the ideology they defended and defend, or positively speaking with the more invisible achievements in the culture and in the minds of the people that they are living in a society which defends social values even if it is not entirely clear who benefits or if the 'right people' benefit. This is the legacy of French rationalism, which puts emphasis on the distributive effects of universal entitlements, notwithstanding possible adverse effects.

In his controversial book 'France in Crisis' from 2004 Timothy B. Smith[19] argues on the basis of comprehensive research underscored by a wealth of quantitative data with regard to the French – and to some extent – the German social security system:

Today solidarity usually means 'security'. Continued security that is for one quarter of the workforce (state employees), which has lifelong job security and 'special social' benefits, financed by the general regressive tax system ... French

---

[19] T. B. Smith, *France in Crisis. Welfare, Inequality, and Globalization since 1980* (Cambridge; New York: Cambridge University Press, 2004), p. 10, translated *La France injuste. 1975–2006. Pourquoi le modèle social français ne fonctionne plus* (Paris: Autrement, 2006); for a forceful critique, 'Sous-titre: Critique d'un livre injuste' on the Blog *Regain 2012*, 29.2.2012, available at www.regain2012.com/article-la-france-injuste-1-100442810.html.

'solidarity' is better understood as state-mandated job protection and insurance. This is an entirely different thing than the redistribution of wealth.

Much of the critique is directed against the politics behind the possible consequences, challenging the privileges of public servants. However, the critique does not engage with the facts that are the basis of T. B. Smith's assessment. The key message of the critique is that politics must prevail over economics. His argument, taken for granted, would mean that the concept of social justice had been corrupted – those who defend social justice defend, economically speaking, their status and, legally speaking, their status of possession. This begs the question of who is *in* and who is *out*? Those not belonging to the social security systems fall by the wayside. What is most striking is that the protests in the streets unite the privileged and young people who might hope for similar positions but are still on the outside. These facts underpin the genuine political character of social justice in France. Whilst this statement needs to be deepened and aligned with the different models of social justice in the various countries, it highlights the legal conceptual difficulties when it comes down to defining solidarity between the members of the social security systems and between those who are in, or solidarity with those who are excluded.[20]

Do we have the same or a similar phenomenon in consumer policy?[21] There is no research in the three countries, which has made the attempt to empirically evaluate the effects of consumer protection rules on a broader scale difficult. The drive comes from the United States and from the distributive effects of consumer law and consumer finance, which puts ever stronger pressure on the EU.[22] Research, but also politics and even the mass media, take consumer policy as sacrosanct. After the collapse of Lehman Brothers, the banks which had sold the securities came under fire. Why did they advise private investors to engage in such risky transactions? Overnight, the quality of advice in financial services became a public issue, which eventually led to the

---

[20] A. Wunder, *The Usage of Solidarity in the Jurisdiction of the ECJ: Symbolism or a European Legal Concept?*, LLM thesis, European University Institute (2008); D. Grimm, *Solidarität als Rechtsprinzip* (Frankfurt a.M.: Athenäum-Verlag, 1973); A. Sangiovanni 'Solidarity in the European Union. Problems and Prospects', in J. Dickson and P. Eleftheriadis (eds.), *Philosophical Foundations of European Union Law* (Oxford: Oxford University Press, 2012), pp. 384–411.

[21] For a critical account of distributive effects from the early days of consumer law, Whincup, *Consumer Legislation in the United Kingdom and the Republic of Ireland*, p. 4.

[22] H.-W. Micklitz, A.-L. Sibony and F. Esposito (eds.), *Research Methods in Law and in Consumer Research*, 2018 forthcoming.

adoption of a new law that obliges bankers to write a protocol on the interview.[23] Neither the banks nor the mass media opposed German consumer organisations, questioning the quality of their financial and legal advice, claiming co-responsibility or even initiating a little project – 'mystery shopping' in consumer organisations. The problem was known to insiders,[24] but the storm passed by and nothing happened.

If anything, consumer research addressed access to justice, the question whether consumers are in a position to defend their rights and whether the necessary institutions, courts and non-courts, are accessible to consumers.[25] That is why it is not possible to make empirically verifiable statements whether and to what extent the three models yield different distributive effects to the benefits of those in whose names these measures have been taken or whether despite all differences they are united in the failure of distributing welfare via consumer contract law.

2.2.2 Expert Statements

Two statements by members of the Social Justice Group, one from an Italian and the other from an English lawyer, which are both published in a separate issue of the *European Review of Contract Law*, serve as

---

[23] § 34 Abs. 2a WpHG Wertpapierhandelsgesetz obliges the banks to produce a protocol after each investment advisory service. Commission Regulation No 1287/2006 of 10 August 2006 implementing Directive 2004/39/EC of the European Parliament and of the Council as regards record-keeping obligations for investment firms, transaction reporting, market transparency, admission of financial instruments to trading, and defined terms for the purposes of that Directive, OJ No. L 241, 2.9.2006, p. 1 (Articles 7 and 8).

[24] There was even a meeting of the heads of the 16 German consumer advice centres where they discussed potential counter strategies. When the head of the Verbraucherzentrale Hamburg, one of the most active regional consumer organisations, retired, the echo in the media was unanimously positive: press release 'Stabwechsel bei der Verbraucherzentrale' of the Verbraucherzentrale Hamburg, 1.3.2016, at vzhh.de: www.vzhh.de/vzhh/444556/stabwechsel-bei-der-verbraucherzentrale.aspx?sid=eb9c509b-64f3-4dfd-8eae-8e09bfa1b16f; and the following newspaper articles: 'Die neun größten Betrugsfälle des Günter Hörmann', Die Welt, 26.2.2017: www.welt.de/regionales/hamburg/article152663825/Die-neun-groessten-Betrugsfaelle-des-Guenter-Hoermann.html, 'Günter Hörmann: Ein Leben für den Verbraucherschutz', Hamburger Abendblatt, 26.2.2016: www.abendblatt.de/hamburg/article207093733/Guenter-Hoermann-Ein-Leben-fuer-den-Verbraucherschutz.html, 'Schnaps-Schnitte und Co. Verbraucherschutz-Boss: Das waren meine krassesten Fälle', Mopo, 28.02.2016: www.mopo.de/hamburg/schnaps-schnitte-und-co-verbraucher schutz-boss-das-waren-meine-krassesten-faelle-23632172.

[25] Final report of a year-long project on new forms of individual and collective consumer advice, U. Reifner and M. Volkmer, *Neue Formen der der Verbraucherrechtsberatung* (Frankfurt a.M.: Campus Verlag, 1988).

a starting point. Both assessments are not based on facts and do not go deeper into distributive effects of private law, but they seem to suggest that there is/can be a link between the social regulation through private law and potential distributive effects.

Marisa Meli[26] argues that, in theory, contract law could have a redistributive effect, depending on the type of welfarism contract law is embedded in (Thomas Wilhelmsson). She does not engage with the varieties of capitalism and the distinction between liberal market economies and co-ordinated market economies. But referring to welfarism would imply that the continental legal systems, in particular in France, are more open to redistribution via contract law than the English legal system, which is associated with liberal market economy. She writes with a view to the outlook of the future of European contract law:

> In such a new context [control of standard contract terms under the assumption that the party is deemed to need protection insertion], the concept of social justice no longer has anything to do with social inequalities of contracting parties and with wealth redistribution goals. Contractual justice is today referred together with efficiency. Justice and efficiency become, indeed, the two parameters for assessing whether the market is functioning smoothly ...
>
> Such considerations bring us to a central point: which kind of welfarism are we searching for in European contract law? It is obvious enough that a central concern is devoted to consumer protection and to what has been correctly called market-rational welfare [Thomas Wilhelmsson].[27] The present *acquis*, by improving party autonomy and the function of the market itself (e.g. information rules), emphasises market-rational welfarism and shows a negative attitude towards attempts to achieve internally redistributive welfarism.

Hugh Collins[28] dwells on the difference between private law – common law, party autonomy, freedom of contract – and regulation – consumer contract law and employment contracts. He is cautious in his language but again he seems not to exclude potential redistributive effects:

---

[26] M. Meli, 'Social Justice, Constitutional Principles and Protection of the Weaker Party' (2006) 2 *European Review of Contract Law* 159–166, at 165, 166.

[27] T. Wilhelmsson, 'Varieties of Welfarism in European Contract Law' (2004) 10 *European Law Journal* 712–733; for an attempt to transfer the different forms of welfarism to the design of consumer law, Micklitz, 'Do Consumers and Business need a New Architecture for Consumer Law?'.

[28] H. Collins, 'The Alchemy of Deriving General Principles of Contract Law from European Legislation: In Search of the Philosopher's Stone' (2006) 2 *European Review of Contract Law* 213–226, at 219.

In relation to questions of fairness, we can detect many contrasts between private law and regulation. Private law examines the particular case, whereas regulation contemplates the distributive effects on groups in the market of a type of market transaction; private law is concerned with the outcome between individuals, regulation with consequences on the operation of the market and on economic groups. These contrasts in modes of governance indicate the nature of the difficulty in translating the concerns of one mode into the other.

Collins is focusing on the question of aims to be pursued by courts, and not so much on practical consequences. His interest is more what private law is for/about and whether it could be a means to achieve distributive justice. Both authors do not discuss different models of justice. Their statements seem nevertheless to address the distributive effects of private law, notwithstanding the respective national regulatory context. They are united in the idea that social justice bears a strong connotation of *collective* justice, which is granted to particular groups in society, in our case consumers or employees. This is achieved mostly by way of regulatory contract law in all Member States, i.e. through the means of setting binding standards. But nothing in the statements tells us whether the distributive effects have been *really* achieved or whether consumers and employees are *really* the beneficiaries to the detriment of the employers and the suppliers. This is not explicitly Collins' aim, contrary to Meli. She leaves open what she means by distribution or distributive effects.

2.2.3 Collective Control of Standard Contract Terms

From my own research over decades,[29] I would like to use the collective control of unfair contract terms as an example of potential distributive effects. This seems not only academically interesting, but also politically important. Here lies the biggest difference between US and EU consumer law. Germany has strongly influenced legislation on unfair terms. Directive 93/13/EEC is inspired by the German model. The directive established a union-wide mechanism for the collective control of standard terms. The German situation might be paradigmatic for the state of affairs in France and the United Kingdom despite the

---

[29] N. Reich and H.-W. Micklitz, *Consumer Legislation in the EC Countries. A Comparative Analysis* (New York: Van Nostrand Reinhold, 1980); H.-W. Micklitz and M. Radeideh, 'CLAB-Europe – The European Database on Unfair Terms in Consumer Contracts' (2005) 28 *Journal of Consumer Policy* 325–360; H.-W. Micklitz and N. Reich, 'The Court and Sleeping Beauty: The Revival of the Unfair Contract Terms Directive (UCTD)' (2014) 51 *Common Market Law Review* 771–808.

different enforcement structures, or if not paradigmatic, it might at least be indicative. The following quote is based on prior research, mainly in regard to the experience gained in the management of Clabus (1995–2003) – the European database, and the interaction with the partner institutions from all over Europe who were responsible for their countries.[30]

The German model suffers from the distinction between the control of unfair contract terms in individual and collective litigation. At a first glance, the balance sheet of the control of unfair contract terms in Germany is impressive. Since the adoption of the German Unfair Terms Act (AGBG) in 1976 an estimated figure of more than 10,000 judgments seem to provide evidence of how serious Germany is controlling standard contract terms, although the figure has to be set into correlation to the estimated more than 80,000 standard terms that exist.[31]

The true problem of the German control mechanism lies in what I would like to call a 'phantom control'. Individual litigation deals with facts and real problems. Collective litigation deals with contracts terms outside facts and reality. It suffices to compare two cases in similar or identical matters in order to understand that judicial control operates at two different levels if not in two different worlds. In collective litigation German courts have coined the term of 'kundenfeindlichste' Auslegung, i.e. the most unfavourable interpretation of standardised contract terms is taken as the starting point to assess its fairness. If such an interpretation rule (i.e. 'kundenfeindlichste Auslegung') is combined with the Leitbild of the legally ignorant consumer as a yardstick for comprehension, standardised terms can relatively easily be declared unfair. The result is ambiguous. The courts may take 'fictitious' modes of interpretation into consideration, in order to be able to argue that the clause in question is unfair. Under such circumstances a contract term might be declared unfair in a collective litigation although its factual (economic and legal) background has never come to the attendance of the court. One might argue that the elimination of each and every 'unfair' contract term is one step further into the reestablishment of party autonomy, whatever the argumentation might be and how far-fetched legal considerations appear.

However, at least two constellations are imaginable which demonstrate possible detrimental effects to the system of control of unfair terms. It might be that the courts eliminate contract terms which are of absolutely no importance in business practice. Clearing the market from this sort of terms does not affect the

---

[30] H.-W. Micklitz, 'Some Considerations on Cassis de Dijon and the Control of Unfair Contract Terms in Consumer Contracts', in K. Boele-Woelki and F. W. Grosheide (eds.), *The Future of European Contract Law* (The Hague: Kluwer Law International, 2007), pp. 387–410. reprinted in H. Collins (ed.), *Standard Contract Terms in Europe: A Basis for and a Challenge to European Contract law* (Alphen aan den Rijn: Kluwer Law International, 2008), pp. 19–42.
[31] In fact there are no hard data, only estimations.

usefulness of the legal mechanism. The making of standard terms, its use and its control by consumer organisations, lawyers and judges then is the ideal type of a self-referential system in the meaning of Teubner. Then terms are elaborated, introduced into business, attacked by consumer organisations and declared void by the courts. At least in the long run, the rationality of control is in jeopardy, at least once the 'phantom' character of the control has come clear. Or – and this is the second variant, the same or a similar term is brought to court in individual litigation, where the neglected economic and social background reappears. Then the second litigation has to compensate for possible deficiencies of the first. German courts are aware of the legitimacy gap and responded by way of applying the same standards of interpretation in individual and collective litigation.

Such a finding, if confirmed through sound empirical research, would be grist to the mill for all those who criticise the inefficiency of unfair terms control, or at least collective unfair terms control. It would mean that unfair terms control if applied in the way analysed is costly, inefficient and at times counterproductive. This comes very close to the arguments brought forward by law and economics against mandatory disclosure rules.[32] Neither Member States nor the European Commission have initiated research that looks deeper into the potential effects of the *collective* control mechanism. If research is undertaken at all, it remains conclusory, aiming at the justification of how 'good' and how 'useful' unfair terms control is for the consumers. In 2006, the German Ministry of Justice organised a workshop to celebrate 30 years of unfair terms control in Germany. The whole event served window-dressing purposes. Anecdotal evidence replaced hard facts, and the carefully chosen list of speakers avoided all sorts of potentially critical questions that would go down to the substantive design of the German solution. The empirical research, initiated three years later, focused on the 'effectiveness' of the unfair terms control, which is obviously equated with the intended social distributive effects.[33] Does it mean that politics is satisfied provided the intended policy goal – protection of the consumer against unfair terms – produces unspecifiable effects to the benefit of consumers and therefore remains symbolic?

There is a growing academic debate, which is inspired by two different sources, all aiming at increasing the effectiveness of unfair terms control. The first strain is embedded in the discussion on responsive

---

[32] O. Ben-Shahar, 'The Myth of the "Opportunity to Read" in Contract Law' (2009) 5 *European Review of Contract Law* 1-28.
[33] Meller-Hannich and Höland, 'Evaluierung der Effektivität kollektiver Rechtsschutzinstrumente'.

regulation, on whether and how public agencies could become involved in a more efficient settlement of conflicts that bear a collective dimension.[34] The other takes a fresh look at consumer and business organisations as well as chambers of commerce and their opportunities to become involved in collective bargaining and collective enforcement of consumer law more broadly beyond unfair terms. In this strain of discussion, collective compensation schemes play a crucial role, an instrument by and large underdeveloped in the Member States.[35]

Breaking down the debate on how to increase effectiveness, the three countries and the dominating pattern of justice, one may identify an element of continuity that goes back to culture and tradition. In the United Kingdom, the control is in the hands of an agency, first the Office of Fair Trading (OFT) and now the Competition and Markets Authority. Courts are not the main actors. The unfair terms regulation and the common law are largely kept apart. Therefore, it is not surprising that the United Kingdom is at the forefront of searching for new modes of enforcement outside and beyond command and control. A pragmatic solution is needed to the problem of unfair control of contract terms, not a legally perfect one. This is already visible in the way the Office of Fair Trading handled the new regulatory device of collective control. Not so much phantom control, but control linked to the concrete economic and legal circumstances dominates the control philosophy. The few occasions where the then Office of Fair Trading went to court, demonstrate the OFT's willingness to select high-profile cases and to seek solutions to the benefit of consumers even *ex post* after their apparent failure before the House of Lords.[36] In France, the enforcement responsibility is split between an administrative body, the Commission des Clauses Abusives[37] and consumer organisations which seek an injunction in court. Nevertheless, the dominant actor is the Commission des Clauses Abusives. It is a political actor, operating through 'opinions' and 'recommendations', composed of judges, academics and

---

[34] Hodges, *The Reform of Class and Representative Actions in European Legal Systems*, p. 223.
[35] F. Cafaggi and H.-W. Micklitz (eds.), *New Frontiers of Consumer Protection. The Interplay between Private and Public Enforcement* (Antwerp: Intersentia, 2009).
[36] The OFT lost before the House of Lords but then negotiated with the banking sector a reduction of the costs for running a bank account that are imposed on the consumers; H.-W. Micklitz, 'House of Lords – Fair Trading v National Bank' 2006 (2) *European Review of Contract Law* 471–480.
[37] For the website of the Commission des Clauses Abusives, www.clauses-abusives.fr/.

representatives of businesses and consumers.[38] The yardstick for control is much more a political one or a judicial one, although the French judiciary plays a more important role today than it played in the past. The composition of the Commission des Clauses Abusives reflects the deeper understanding of French politics by involving the stakeholders in the monitoring of the market and not leaving it to private parties and or the judiciary alone.[39] In Germany, consumer and trade organisations are the only institutions that enjoy legal standing. They need to involve courts in order to strike down unfair terms. The German government subsidises consumer organisations in exchange for what must be understood as a statutory task. From the outside, they look like hybrids, private bodies but fully funded by the state, a construction which yields tensions between the ministry in charge and the consumer organisations. The institutional reorganisation of the consumer organisations has led to a change in the control philosophy. Today, they search for key cases, for key problems only, where an injunction might help to solve a collective consumer problem. The 'phantom' control is certainly on the retreat, though not abolished. The last government triggered a debate whether Germany should establish a consumer agency with regulatory powers and with legal standing.[40]

2.3 Measuring the Social (Individual) Effectiveness in Private Law

The *individual* dimension concerns the question as to whether mandatory consumer protection rules designed to protect consumers reach

---

[38] Instituée par l'article L. 132-2 du code de la consommation, la Commission des clauses abusives est placée auprès du ministre chargé de la consommation. Elle est composée de magistrats, de personnalités qualifiées en droit ou technique des contrats, de représentants des consommateurs, de représentants des professionnels ('Established by Article L. 132-2 of the Consumer Code, the Unfair Contract Terms Commission is placed with the Minister of Consumer Affairs. It is composed of magistrats, persons qualified in law or technical contracts, representatives of consumers, representatives of professionals').

[39] A. Héritier, 'Market Integration and Social Cohesion: the Politics of Public Services in European Regulation' (2001) 8 *Journal of European Public Policy* 825–852, discusses public services, but her findings are equally relevant for the overall understanding to politicise the control of social policies.

[40] On the feasibility of public enforcement in consumer matters, H. Schulte-Nölke und Bundesministerium der Justiz und für Verbraucherschutz (eds.), *Neue Wege zur Durchsetzung des Verbraucherrechts* (Berlin: Springer, 2017).

the weaker party. This bring us back to the strong critique raised by T. B. Smith that social regulation serves mainly the 'haves' (*Habenden*), a finding which is not really surprising after Galanter had convincingly demonstrated that the 'haves come out ahead'.[41] It is one thing if mandatory rules do not yield or do yield only limited collective redistributive effects; however, it is politically, economically, socially and legally much more difficult if the individual weaker party does not benefit from social protection. Individual effectiveness invokes both dimensions of social justice – political social justice and economic distributive justice. In the following, three dimensions of measuring will be investigated: 1) the weaker party rhetoric and the imbalance of power, 2) the status of the weaker party in the contractual relation and 3) access to justice.

2.3.1 Imbalance of Power

The common denominator of labour and consumer law is that mandatory protection rules are said to protect the weaker party. This formula is so vague that it seems to fit into each of three patterns of social justice, independent of the country and independent of the addressee, legislature, executive and courts. Weakness suggests an imbalance of power between an employee and her employer, the consumer and her supplier. The fight of the labour movement for better protection through law was historically also a fight for the recognition of the structural difference between the two sides, of employers and employees. This is behind all the rhetoric on the economic constitution that started with Sinzheimer and went through the whole twentieth century. The separation of labour law from civil law and common law is the visible expression of the differences between normal citizens and labour relations. This might explain why the fight over dismissal rights always takes such a harsh form. Here the privileged status of the worker being recognised as the weaker party is most visible.

Consumer law took a different avenue. Maybe this is already enshrined in President Kennedy's starting formula 'consumers, by definition, include us all'. Until today, it is an open issue whether the imbalance of power is *structural* – meaning consumers are on a par with workers with regard to their particular weaker status – or whether the power is

---

[41] M. Galanter, 'Why the Haves Come out Ahead: Speculations on the Limits of Legal Change' (1974) 9 *Law and Society Review* 95–160, reprinted (with corrections) in R. Cotterrell (ed.), *Law and Society* (Aldershot: Dartmouth, 1994), pp. 165–230.

situational. If the latter is true, the recognition of the status of being a consumer tells only half the story. What is needed on top is evidence for the imbalance in the concrete *situational* circumstances of the case at issue. In a groundbreaking decision from 1994, the German Constitutional Court recognised[42] that the imbalance between the consumer debtor and the bank creditor is *structural* in nature, which implies that there is at least a presumption of weakness to the benefit of the consumer. Consumers are regarded as a collective entity that deserves protection essentially per se. This understanding is certainly not shared by the UK Supreme Court, which insisted on the predominance of freedom of contract and the self-responsibility of the consumer debtor, somewhat counterbalanced by rules on undue influence, duress and unconscionable bargain in equity. The conflict has reached the European Court of Justice. Evidence can be found for both positions, the more protective one of the German Constitutional Court (structural in Aziz)[43] and the stricter one of the UK Supreme Court (situational in Herron).[44]

The difference between structural and situational imbalance is crucial for the footprint the respective systems leave in the minds of the people. If I am regarded by the legal order as structurally weak, I will tend to regard myself as being 'weak'. If I can be the weaker party subject to the concrete circumstance, I will tend to regard myself as a 'could be' weaker party. It is striking to see how different the courts in the three countries under investigation deal with the 'power' argument. In Germany, it needed the interference of the Constitutional Court to remind the higher civil courts that there is an 'imbalance' (*Ungleichgewicht*) in lending contracts. The court does not speak of 'power' (*Macht*); it uses 'imbalance'. Language matters. In German civil law doctrine, much effort has been made to circumvent the power argument in the control of unfair standard terms.[45] English courts and the English legislature have no difficulty naming the phenomenon 'power', which does not mean that they are more inclined to protect

---

[42] BVerfGE 89, 214 – Bürgschaftsverträge (consumer guarantees).
[43] Case C-415/11, *Aziz* [2013] ECR I-000.
[44] Case C-426/11, *Alemo-Herron and Others* [2013] ECR I-000.
[45] There was a harsh conflict between two German academics on whether the word 'stellen' enshrines an element of power or not: N. Reich, 'Verbraucherpolitische Probleme bei der Anwendung des Gesetzes zur Regelung des Rechts der Allgemeinen Geschäftsbedingungen (AGBG)' (1978) 2 *Zeitschrift für Verbraucherpolitik* 236–248; and the response by P. Ulmer, 'Schutz vor unbilligen Allgemeinen Geschäftsbedingungen als Aufgabe eines speziellen Verbraucherrechts oder des allgemeinen Zivilrechts? Zu Reichs Beitrag'(1978) 2 *Zeitschrift für Verbraucherpolitik* 248–252.

the weaker party. Quite the contrary seems true. German courts are more protective, whilst they deliberately avoid the language of power, whereas English courts are less protective, although they do not shy away from using the power argument. It is again an instance of English pragmatism and German idealism. If D. Kennedy is correct, the power argument will lose when each and every person, in whatever capacity claims or can claim (and might be heard with the argument) to be weak.[46]

2.3.2 Status

Whether structural or situational, the legal recognition of status of the worker or the consumer constitutes the foundation on which the whole design of the contractual relation rests.

In labour law, the debate circled around the master–servant relationship, which implies an element of domination and which entitles the master to instruct the servant what to do. Despite the changes in language from master–servant to employer/employee, it is the particular kind of relationship that ties the two together, which legitimated the move from contract to status, from treating the employee as a 'normal' person under contract law to treating her as somebody with a special status. The separation of labour law from general private law goes back to that distinction. During the twentieth century, however, the status of the employee changed dramatically. The former life-long employment relationship lost ground, not least through the transformation of the industrial economy to the service and digital economy. Politics has promoted this development through changes in the employment contracts. Today, the employment relationship can take many forms, from the old-fashioned master–servant relationship to self-employment.[47] They all have in common that the former employee has to undertake more and more self-responsibility. The loosening ties to the entrepreneur are reflected in the much looser contractual shaping of rights and duties. Gradually, but steadily, the employee loses her particular status as a weaker party to the contract: from status (the guilds) to contract (the verdict of the equal parties in the industrial age) to status (with the rise of the Social) to contract (via the new forms of contractualisation in the working

---

[46] Kennedy, 'Three Globalizations of Law and Legal Thought', p. 65.
[47] To a hybrid or legal fiction; see High Court of Australia judgment *Hollis v. Vabu* [2001] HCA 44, for more information, see: www.unistudyguides.com/wiki/Hollis_v_Vabu.

relation).[48] These new forms have been given many names: flexicurity, precarious work – and they are subject to empirical research. The transformation is due to economic and political pressure on the labour movement, most prominently since the adoption of the Lisbon Agenda 2000.[49]

Consumer law took a different path. The consumer is not defined via the type of relationship she undertakes with the supplier. There is no structural personal dependence; in a competitive market, the supplier cannot tell the consumer what to buy. In theory, the consumer is free to choose the supplier from whom she wants to buy and the product she desires. In practice, marketing and sales promotion has turned into an ever more powerful machinery to exert indirect and invisible influence on the decision of the consumer. In the digital age this is achieved through consumer individualisation.[50] There is dependence, but the dependence is less visible, less tangible: it is an anonymous dependence reflected in the particular form of power that the market and the suppliers hold over the consumers. Thus, when it comes to the definition of the consumer, the dependence/power element is difficult to grasp. How, then, can one catch in legal terms this dependence or power?

The answer to the challenge was more or less the same in all countries that had launched a consumer policy in the 1960s or 1970s. The consumer was defined not via her personal relations like in labour law but via the relevant economic transaction. Even these economic transactions were more often than not defined negatively, typically via reference to the purpose of the transaction, which must be 'outside trade, business, craft or profession'.[51] Whilst the negative approach managed to lay down a kind of minimum standard all over Europe, there are still major differences, with regard to the correct classification of dual-use products, of non-profit organisations or of SMEs. Consumer law and policy is much younger than labour law and policy. Nevertheless, in consumer law the grand transformations of the post-

---

[48] Quite critical on the moves back and forth between status and contract: Schmidt, 'Henry Maine's "Modern Law": From Status to Contract and Back Again?', however, without discussing the particular transformations in European private law.
[49] In detail Part II. 1, with regard to flexicurity website of the Hans-Böckler Stiftung (foundation), available at: www.boeckler.de/themen_35424.htm.
[50] P. Rott, 'Der "Durchschnittsverbraucher" – ein Auslaufmodell angesichts personalisierten Marketings?' (2015) *Verbraucher und Recht* 163–167.
[51] Lately Art. 2 (1) Directive 2011/83 of the European Parliament and of the Council of 25 October 2011 on consumer rights, OJ No. L 304, 22.11.2011, p. 64.

war consumer society via servicification and digitalisation (shared economy) can be observed. The tendency is the same as in labour law. The consumer being regarded as the prototype of the weaker party – the judgment of the GCC is only 24 years old – is gradually turning into a societal figure (*Rechtsfigur*) that can take many forms, from the vulnerable consumer in need of protection to the consumer entrepreneur (prosumer) who transacts via the Internet. Contrary to labour law and labour policy, however, there is much less empirical research available on the degree of transformation in the consumer society or on the impact of the economy and society, let alone the potential legal consequences of the loss of the legal contours of the notion of the consumer.[52]

Status-related rights immediately produce a legal bias. Those who fall under the criteria benefit from special rights and special protection; those outside the scope of the definition fall by the wayside. This is the downside of status-related rights and the merit of generally applicable law. Seen through the lenses of the party who is seeking protection, there is a strong incentive to make all possible efforts to belong to the beneficiary group. This entails the tendency of broadening the notion of the worker/consumer. However, the broader the scope, the less precise the contours and the more the exception – the status-related protection – turns into a general rule. There is a line of critique which focuses on the question of whether the courts manage to fairly decide who is in need, who is weak or who is not weak. M. Marella raises two important questions in the context of her analysis on 'The Old and the New Limits to Freedom of Contract in Europe':[53]

> There are two classical arguments against the social model and rhetoric of weak parties. One is that new limits to freedom of contract for family guarantees ... for instance, generate the indirect effect of restricting access to credit ... at the expense of the beneficiaries of the protecting policy themselves. The second argument is that strong protection of weak parties generates a pattern of cross-subsidies at the expense of the weakest social groups. The protection of weak parties turns to exclude people at the bottom of the social pyramid: there will

---

[52] For a first though not representative overview, K. Purnhagen and S. Wahlen, 'Der Verbraucherbegriff, § 13 BGB und die Sharing Economy', in H.-W. Micklitz, L. Reisch, G. Joost, H. Zander-Hayat (eds.), *Verbraucherrecht 2.0 – Verbraucher in der digitalen Welt* (Baden-Baden: Nomos, 2017), pp. 185–220.

[53] Marella, 'The Old and the New Limits to Freedom of Contract in Europe', 266, 268, under reference to D. Kennedy, 'Thoughts on Coherence, Social Values and National Traditions in Private Law', in M. W. Hesselink (ed.), *The Politics of a European Civil Code* (The Hague: Kluwer, 2006), pp. 9–31.

always be weak parties that are weaker than the weak parties protected by protecting policy. Or there are always weak parties that are not acknowledged as such. How about mistresses or best friends, as in the case of family guarantees? ... And what about domestic contracts concluded by unmarried partners?

The awareness on the countereffects of the status-related laws is growing. Status implies both inclusion and exclusion. It has become clear in the European codification projects through the difficulty to define a consumer, not only in the narrow boundaries of European law, but for all Member States.[54] Status-related positions may become static, and, if the standard of protection is lowered due to the unclear reach of the personal scope, might even deprive the individual of protection. In the long run, those in need of protection – be they vulnerable consumers or workers in precarious relationships – might be better off if they argue that they do not belong to the status group, in order to gain protection under the general contract law system, within the particular factual circumstances. F. Zoll coined the wonderful saying: 'I am NOT a consumer, I need protection'.[55]

2.3.3 Access to Justice

The three countries differ considerably in the degree to which they grant access to justice.[56] Already the question might sound strange at least if access to justice is put on an equal footing with access to courts. Access to court implies that there are individual enforceable rights that can be defended in courts. The individualisation of rights, however, is a rather recent development, which leads to a certain approximation of the different legal systems – at least in light of the direction EU law has taken. Let us recall the three different approaches in light of the historical reconstruction of the rise of labour law and consumer law in the three countries. This might explain why, even if there were data for each country, it is extremely hard to engage in a comparative assessment, claiming that judicial enforcement prevails over out-of-court

---

[54] This is exactly the concept of the European Principles of Contract Law, H.-W. Micklitz, 'The Principles of European Contract Law and the Protection of the Weaker Party' (2004) 27 *Journal of Consumer Policy* 339–356.
[55] At a conference that has taken place in Manchester on targeted consumer protection, G. Howells and R. Schulze (eds.), *Modernising and Harmonising Consumer Contract Law* (München: Sellier European Law Publishers, 2009).
[56] E. Kocher, *Funktionen der Rechtsprechung. Konfliktlösung im deutschen und englischen Verbraucherprozessrecht* (Tübingen: Mohr Siebeck, 2007).

settlement or over self-help and political solutions fought out in the streets.

The UK relies on a self-help conception of enforcement. Litigation is the exception to the rule. If it takes place, the litigant is not a private party, or if the litigant is a private party, the litigation is promoted and paid for by non-governmental organisations. This is most obvious in UK labour law. As long as the self-help paradigm dominated, solutions to conflicts affecting employment relations were left to the trade unions and the trade associations. They had to find a mutually satisfactory way out. Under the common law, collective agreements could not even be enforced before the courts.[57] Since 1964, workers can launch a complaint before the employment tribunals. In the field of labour law, courts started to play a major role after Thatcher began to transform labour law. Trade unions and women's organisations discovered the potential of EU law to be mobilised against national restrictions, which were in conflict with EU non-discrimination law. The Equal Opportunities Commission turned into a key player before the employment tribunals. The exaggerated expectations of public interest groups yielded disappointment and a certain withdrawal from the Luxembourg Court as the forum where national UK labour rights could be promoted.[58] The 2013 reform introduced large costs for claims before the employment tribunals, thereby greatly reducing the volume of claims.[59]

The picture looks totally different in consumer law. UK consumers would not seriously consider bringing a standard consumer case to the general court. However, consumers may – as everybody else – bring a claim to small claims court. They were initiated by the Consumer Council and meant to offer easy access to a rather informal procedure, which is very much managed by the judge. Baldwin investigated small claims court via interviews with judges and the parties. He identified a high degree of satisfaction so long as lawyers were not involved in the procedure.[60] ADR mechanisms monitored and surveyed by national

---

[57] Ford v A.U.E.W. [1969] 2 QB 303. Changed by the Industrial Relations Act 1971.
[58] On the litigation in equal treatment: Micklitz, *The Politics of Judicial Co-operation in the EU*, Chapter 3, p. 165, where the interplay between UK courts and the ECJ, as well as the role of the trade unions and the Equal Opportunities Commission is analysed in detail.
[59] www.citizensadvice.org.uk/work/problems-at-work/employment-tribunals-from-29-july-2013/what-will-it-cost-to-make-a-claim-to-an-employment-tribunal/employment-tribunals-how-much-will-it-cost-to-make-a-claim/.
[60] J. Baldwin, *Small Claims in the County Courts in England and Wales: The Bargain Basement of Civil Justice* (Oxford: Oxford University Press, 1997); also Kocher, *Funktionen der Rechtsprechung*, pp. 234–244.

agencies are largely replacing general courts and also the county courts which are responsible for the small claims.[61] ADR does not end up in a legal decision, which is made public and where the search for a legal solution dominates. The dominating philosophy in ADR is to look for a quick and reasonable solution, which in practice might often be a compromise. The immediate prejudice is that consumers do not get what they are entitled to. However, the different accessibility has to be taken into account. Sound empirical research in the 1960s has revealed that the different access barriers work as a filter.[62] Launching a complaint against the supplier is quite often a hard barrier; approaching ADR mechanism means that consumers must mobilise extra energies, and going to court is often unreachable, not only because of the costs, but also because of the deeper psychological barriers. In short, easy access to ADR might well compensate for expensive and difficult access to court. Similar to labour law and also in consumer law agencies, the former OFT could go to court in hard cases. However, the OFT was less successful than the Equal Opportunities Commission and did not even manage to convince the competent English court to refer a key case to Luxembourg.[63] There is only one clear example, which runs in the other direction. *Which?*, the UK consumer organisation, succeeded in getting a complaint that consumer organisations must be granted standing under the Directive 93/13/EEC on unfair terms referred to Luxembourg. The conflict was settled politically, as the incoming new Labour government changed the law to the benefit of consumer organisations.[64] The granting of powers remained symbolic but might have pushed OFT into action.

In the French legal system, a certain ambivalence towards courts can be observed. This might go back to the pre-revolutionary times and the distrust against a corrupt judiciary, deeply anchored in the minds of the people. Even today, French courts play a limited, though increasing, role in the handling of labour and consumer conflicts. In employment relations, just as in the United Kingdom, there is a special jurisdiction. The Conseil de Prud'hommes was established in 1806. The French legal

---

[61] The particular philosophy behind ADR is explained by Kocher, *Funktionen der Rechtsprechung*, pp. 247–274.
[62] E. Blankenburg und U. Reifner, *Rechtsberatung. Soziale Definition von Rechtsproblemen durch Rechtsberatungsangebote* (Neuwied; Darmstadt: Luchterhand, 1982).
[63] Micklitz, 'House of Lords – Fair Trading v National Bank', 471
[64] J. Dickie, 'Article 7 of the Unfair Terms in Consumer Contracts Directive' (1996) 4 *Consumer Law Journal* 112–117.

system leaves much space for political solutions outside of court through the involvement of ministries, semi-public commissions or even the government. Whilst political solutions exist in all countries, in France the political resistance in the street has often managed to tilt the balance. There is a difference between the role of the executive in France and in the United Kingdom. Contrary to the United Kingdom, France never established a public agency in charge of the enforcement of consumer law. The *Direction génerale de la concurrence, de la consommation et de la répression des fraudes* (DGCCRF) looks somewhat similar, but in fact the DGCCRF differs considerably from the Office of Fair Trading/the Competition and Market Authority.[65] The history of the DGCCRF is linked to its investigative powers in the fight against fraud. Over time, the very same body integrated consumer protection first and competition policy later. The DGCCRF remains first and foremost a public authority with investigative powers. It has no regulatory powers and no legal standing. Therefore, it resembles more a political institution than a regulatory agency in the US-UK mould. The different French and UK models of enforcement clashed when the European Commission started liberalising public services and required Member States to set up regulatory bodies. France fought hard politically and judicially to leave space for the involvement of stakeholders, a move away from technocracy to politicisation. The existence of a tripartite system is a common characteristic of the French legal system. It brings together the state, business and consumers. The French term for this particular form of co-operation is 'organes de concertation'.

The same ideology dominates the enforcement of consumer law. The Commission des Clauses Abusives deserves mention. Just as in Germany, France did not follow the United Kingdom in setting up specialised courts for consumer affairs. Instead the French legislature started experimenting with new forms of ADR. The Boîte Postal 5000 was established in 1977, as a French variant of an ADR mechanism.[66] Again, there is a difference between the United Kingdom and France. In the United Kingdom, there is much room for publically supervised self-regulation and self-established dispute settlement procedures. However, in France, the public authorities directly run the ADR system, very much in line with the tripartite thinking.

---

[65] Calais-Auloy and Temple, *Droit de la Consommation*, nos. (numbers) 33, 361.
[66] Calais-Auloy and Temple, *Droit de la Consommation*, no. (number) 596; with regard to Boîte Postal 5000, http://terroirs.denfrance.free.fr/p/defense_consommateur/boite_postale_5000.html.

Contrary to the United Kingdom, the German legal system is strongly court-centered. Neither administrative enforcement nor ADR mechanisms play a major role. This overall finding is true for both labour law and consumer law. An easy explanation is that in comparison at least to the United Kingdom, access to courts is cheap, and a developed legal aid mechanism renders the financial risks for litigants calculable. The deeper reason has to be found in the particular role the German courts played in adapting the BGB to the challenge of the Social, the legitimation for judicial interference provided by the Weimar Constitution in labour law, and by the Basic Law (Grundgesetz) in consumer law. Despite two world wars and despite the disastrous role of the judiciary during the Nazi regime (1933–1945),[67] the judiciary appears as a constant in the German political system. This does not mean that there was no resistance from the labour movement against the Bismarckian authoritarian courts. Before and after World War I, courts and judges were blamed for exercising *Klassenjustiz*: the bourgeois class provided the judges, who tended to decide against the working class.[68] There was socioempirical research undertaken that provides evidence of justice as a two-class system. After World War II, this kind of argument enjoyed a revival. It is certainly one of the major achievements of the German Constitutional Court[69] to have brought this critique to a halt, not least due to a much more balanced approach with regard to the deep social conflicts between employers and employees (the judgment on co-determination in 1979) and later suppliers and consumers (the judgment on consumer loans in 1994). In labour law, the new Federal Republic of Germany established a particular jurisdiction, which is institutionally separated from the civil courts. No such equivalent exists with regard to consumer litigation. The German legislature never seriously considered introducing a separate consumer court like in the United Kingdom.

German consumers ever since have understood access to court as a right entitling them to cheap access and fast decision-making. Expectations are high of being granted 'justice' in the courtroom.

---

[67] Seminal, B. Rüthers, *Die unbegrenzte Auslegung. Zum Wandel der Privatrechtsordnung im Nationalsozialismus*, 8th ed. (Tübingen: Mohr Siebeck, 2017).

[68] E. Fraenkel, *Zur Soziologie der Klassenjustiz* (Berlin: E. Laub, 1927); Th. Rasehorn, *Recht und Klassen. Zur Klassenjustiz in der Bundesrepublik* (Darmstadt; Neuwied: Luchterhand, 1974).

[69] For a sophisticated analysis of the role and function of the German Constitutional Court in the formative stage of the Federal Republic of Germany, Jestaedt, Lepsius, Möllers and Schönberger, *Das entgrenzte Gericht*.

Despite a forty-year debate, Germany did not manage to set up a regulatory agency whether self-standing or linked to other agencies like the cartel office.[70] Not even ADR has gained ground. ADR is viewed as substandard to litigation in court. This does not mean that there are no ADR bodies.[71] Quite the contrary is true: there are many, maybe too many, and they do not follow a common design. Their role and practical importance is very much subject related. The German Automobile Club (ADAC) funds a particular conciliation procedure for car repairs, which operates successfully. Another example is the ADR bodies dealing with medical malpractice, which is based on a conciliation model. Attempts by the incumbent social-liberal government to set up a conciliation body in the construction business largely failed.[72] Characteristic for the German understanding of ADR bodies is the overall attempt to design them as quasi-courts that make non-binding decisions, despite well-established research that more formalised structures render dispute resolution in ADR bodies more difficult.[73] The German inclination for a decision based on 'law' (*Recht und Gesetz*) prevails over common sense or mutual compromise.

2.4 Social Effectiveness vs. Economic Efficiency

Politicians, labour and consumer activists, most labour and consumer lawyers apart, perhaps, from doctrinal purists show little concern for these developments, which seems to suggest that most of them are happy or can live with the degree of effectiveness that had been achieved through social regulation. In the final analysis, this could mean that there is a common denominator of social effectiveness that cuts across the three Member States and that might manifest a kind of minimum denominator for European legal consciousness.[74] This harmonious perspective comes under pressure from across the Atlantic. In the United States, law and economics and behaviour economics is submitting consumer laws to an efficiency test. This is a much

---

[70] Reich, Tonner, Wegener, *Verbraucher und Recht*; now Schulte-Nölke and Bundesministerium der Justiz und für Verbraucherschutz (eds.), *Neue Wege zur Durchsetzung des Verbraucherrechts*.
[71] T. Brönneke, P. Rott, M. Tamm and K. Tonner (eds.), Verbraucher und Recht (VuR) – Sonderheft zur Einführung des VSBG (2016), pp. 1–59.
[72] U. Boysen and K. Plett, *Bauschlichtung in der Praxis* (Düsseldorf: Werner, 2000).
[73] D. Eidmann, *Schlichtung. Zur Logik außergerichtlicher Konfliktregelung* (Baden-Baden: Nomos, 1994).
[74] Collins, 'Book Review', 76.

harsher and maybe a more measurable yardstick that could affect the social substance enshrined in consumer and labour law and lay bare the differences between the legal consciousnesses of the different countries.

2.4.1 Relaxed Attention: Socially Achieved?

In her book on European private law, Bettina Heiderhoff identifies a European version of the consumer against which effectiveness could be measured. It is suggested that her model is equally and more generally relevant to the citizen-worker and the citizen consumer. This is what Heiderhoff writes as a summary of EU consumer law:[75]

> Der Verbraucher ist wie ein Fußgänger eben schutzbedürftiger und ihm können weniger Pflichten aufgehalst werden als dem gleichen Menschen wenn er im Auto sitzt. In diesem Bild geht es nicht um den Ausgleich von Imparität, sondern es wird auch dem Fußgänger, der ein perfekter Autofahrer ist, zugestanden, sich als Fußgänger entspannt und vergleichsweise unvorsichtig zu verhalten. ...
>
> Klar tritt am Bild des "Spaziergängers" hervor, dass ein Wohlfahrtsideal des angenehmen und ungefährlichen Marktes geschaffen werden soll, von dem natürlich zugleich vermutet wird, dass er am meisten genutzt wird und damit auch wirtschaftlich am besten funktioniert ... Das Leitbild ist der vernünftige Bürger in entspannter Aufmerksamkeit.
>
> [The consumer is like a pedestrian in need of more protection. On him less duties can be put than on the same person sitting in a car. In this picture the point is not the balance of imparity, also the pedestrian who is a perfect driver is conceded to behave as a pedestrian in a relaxed way and comparatively inattentive ...
>
> The image of the stroller illustrates that an ideal of the welfare state is created, one of a comfortable and harmless market, an ideal from it is equally presumed that it is used the most and functions economically in the best way. ... The overall image is the reasonable citizen in a spirit of relaxed attention.]

A legal system which is based on a spirit of relaxed attention aims at creating a 'carefree, light-hearted and credulous' society in which the different activities of the people are embedded. Is this the model that has reached at least a certain degree of effectiveness in all three countries under scrutiny or is this only a normative image which exists in the minds of law- and policy-makers? Is national consciousness converging through social regulation, to paraphrase Legrand?[76] If yes, how could

---

[75] Quoted after B. Heiderhoff, *Europäisches Privatrecht* (Heidelberg: C. F. Müller, 2004), p. 288 (in the meantime 4th ed. 2016 has been published).

[76] To use P. Legrand's formula, 'European Legal Systems Are Not Converging' (1996) 45 *International and Comparative Law Quarterly* 52–81.

that be verified? If the image of relaxed attention captures reality or, at least parts of it, then what remains for the differing perceptions of English, French and German consumer-worker-citizens so carefully analysed in the Member States? Have they become obsolete? Or is it (still) a normative model, the advocacy of the new carefree, light-hearted and credulous citizen, the dream of a social model that burst all limits, even those between cultures and traditions, a modern version of the communist dream of 'workers of all the world, unite'? If the image remains a normative fiction, there is ample space for national consciousness. The reasonable citizen in a spirit of relaxed attention would clash with the different mindsets of the English, the French and the Germans. The common benchmark helps at least to clarify the type of questions which have to be raised in the three countries to shed light on the possible mismatch between the politically intended common denominator (however diffuse it might be) and national legal consciousness.

Then there are questions above questions. Are the English happy to have the reputation that they are tougher than their continental counterparts – a prejudice/truth (?) that has made its way into Belgian courts in *Duchesne*, a conflict between a Belgian advertising company which addresses UK consumers?[77] Is this a normative statement of what a Belgian court believes the English to be or does it capture English reality? If it captures reality, the English might feel overprotected and patronised by social regulation that takes too much of their responsibility away. Do German and French consumer-worker-citizens feel comfortable with the image of the reasonable citizen in a spirit of relaxed attention, or is the benchmark too low? Germans might tend to agree, as it seems to comply with the high expectations they set for the welfare state. Overall, the French might share German perceptions, but they might feel patronised by the image for a different reason than the English do. The image of relaxed attention takes away the political dimension of social regulation and might therefore diminish the possibility of resistance.

So far nobody, neither in the EU nor in the Member States, is in a position to provide an answer on where the English, the French and the Germans stand. There are no facts that provide evidence on effectiveness, neither with regard to the reasonable citizen in a spirit of relaxed attention as a common denominator that unites the people

---

[77] Appeal Court of Brussels, 8.12.2005, *D. Duchesne v. Office of Fair Trading*.

across the border nor with regard to the different mindsets of the English, the French and the Germans that survive any attempts of convergence through social regulation.

2.4.2 *Efficiency and Society*

A much more powerful challenge to the Social and social regulation in all its national variations results from the *efficiency* paradigm so amply promoted by the law and economics movement. The deeper link between law and economics is old; in Germany, economics and law (together with political science, sociology and history) were long united in one and the same faculty – Staatswissenschaften.[78] Here, however, a different strand of debate has to be highlighted, one that started with Coase in the 1930 and that led to what became known worldwide in the 1970s and 1980s as 'the Chicago School of Economics'.[79] Law and economics is understood as a political project designed and promoted to academically and scientifically question the impact of the New Deal on American society and economy, and to legitimate deregulation and promote competition.[80] Therefore, competition law and the degree to which the Federal Trade Commission should regulate market power became the major target. Law and economics advocate economic efficiency, which is claimed to be a neutral and objective yardstick against which statutory regulation should be measured. Contrary to the New Deal, markets and democracy were separated from each other. The New Deal *citizen consumer* is supposed to make 'democratic' decisions[81] The Chicago School advocated the consumer purchaser, the efficient

---

[78] W. Drechsler, 'On the Viability of the Concept of Staatswissenschaften' (2011) 12 *European Journal of Law and Economics* 105–111.

[79] For a careful and sophisticated reconstruction of the law and economics movement (which shows many nuances that reach far beyond popular attributions of neoliberalism), in particular with regard to the shift from the consumer citizen to the consumer purchaser, and from rational choice to consumer welfare and its implications on American politics and economics, see Olsen, 'From Choice To Welfare'.

[80] On the politics of the Olin Foundation in conquering intellectuals via sponsoring academic research in the US Ivy League so as to influence politics, J. Mayer, *Dark Money. The Hidden History of the Billionaires Behind the Rises of the Radical Right* (New York et al.: Doubleday, 2016), p. 100 (pointing to how Hayek's essay 'The Intellectuals and Socialism' serve as a source of inspiration for foundations), pp. 107–119 on how the Olin Foundation managed to establish what they called beachheads in American law schools to promote law and economics against the then dominating leftist thinking in the US top law schools.

[81] L. Cohen, *A Consumers' Republic: The Politics of Mass Consumption in Postwar America* (New York: Knopf, 2003), pp. 17–61; S. Schwarzkopf, 'The Consumer as "Voter", "Judge" and "Jury": Historical Origins and Political Consequences of a Marketing Myth' (2011)

consumer and the rational consumer as the new Leitbild of the economy. Distributional (justice) concerns were placed outside the realms of economics into tax law.[82] The intellectual ground was prepared over decades, from the 1930s on. Politically it needed the move from Carter to Reagan, from the American welfare regulation in the 1960s and 1970s[83] to questioning these very achievements, not least due to its impact on the American economy. The Republicans put economic efficiency at the forefront of politics, in line with the Chicago School.

The first field here of interest where the European and the American understanding on social regulation clashed was the attack mounted by law and economics against strict product liability. The 3rd restatement coincided with the adoption of the product liability directive in 1985.[84] It led to the reintroduction of negligence in product liability law. Gradually law and economics entered ever-new areas. The methodology used was, strictly speaking, not empirical; it was numerical and mathematical. With regard to consumer law, the rise of behavioural sciences (BS) and more particularly behavioural law and economics (BLE) became much more important. BLE brought reality (empirics) back in to economics, mainly through cognitive psychology.[85] With rigour and enthusiasm, American scholars started dense and deep empirical research on the economic effects of social regulation, first on mandatory information disclosure rules. The findings brought uncomfortable results to all those advocating social policy via law. There are variations in argument but, in

---

31 *Journal of Macromarketing* 8-18. It has to be underlined that the notion of the citizen-consumer has not been invented by the EU; it is much older and dates back to the 1930s.

[82] G. Stigler, *The Theory of Competitive Price* (New York: Macmillan, 1942).

[83] V. Packard, *The Hidden Persuaders* (Harmondsworth: Penguin, 1957) and J. K. Galbraith, *The Affluent Society* (London: Hamish Hamilton, 1958) were both concerned with how the desires and needs of consumers were manipulated.

[84] Council Directive 85/374/EEC of 25 July 1985 on the approximation of the laws, regulations and administrative provisions of the Member States concerning liability for defective products, OJ No. L 210, 7.8.1985, p. 29; H.-W. Mickitz, ' ... und die USA?', Kolloquium zur Zukunft der Produkthaftung aus Anlaß des 70. Geburtstages von Prof. Dr. Hans-Claudius Taschner, (2002) *Zeitschrift für europarechtliche Studien* 75–102.

[85] It is a particular kind of empirical research mostly aimed at shattering the leading philosophy in law and economics that consumers are making rational choices and rational decisions. This bias might explain why psychology is playing such a dominant role in the type of research undertaken. It is only more recently that the societal dimension of 'rational choice' research is gaining importance in empirical research, P. Mascini, *Law and Behavioral Sciences. Why We Need Less Purity Rather than More*, Erasmus Law Lectures 41 (The Hague: Eleven International Publishing, 2016), demonstrates that sociology is needed to fully embrace the social environment in which consumers are taking decisions.

essence, the critique is directed against the problematic *distributive* results of mandatory contract law, which not only works to the benefit of the more privileged parts of society, but which is paid for by the less privileged (this means those in whose names all the regulatory measures have been introduced).[86] The sole means to remedy the uncomfortable results, provided they find confirmation in European research, is said protection through a collective remedy such as the US class action.[87] However, to be abundantly clear: the argument is that social regulation fails because the 'wrong' people benefit and the 'wrong' people pay for the benefits. The whole ideology of a more just, better society in which wealth is distributed more equally between rich and poor, vanishes in the haze. However, easy access to the credit market is equally no substitute for statutory social regulation.[88] The only field where US research is less developed is in the area of how best to control standard terms. However, there seems to be a growing interest, not least through the involvement of the American Law Institute.[89]

The limited empirical research performed in France, Germany and the United Kingdom[90] under the new label of behavioural law and economics or behavioural science tends to focus on the behaviour of consumers and not so much on potential distributive effects. This type of research goes along with the search for more effective rules. BLE might then even justify stronger statutory intervention to protect the consumer.[91] This research misses the key question that the law and economics movement has raised: is social regulation the wrong means

---

[86] Ben-Shahar, 'The Myth of the "Opportunity to Read" in Contract Law'.
[87] O. Ben-Shahar, 'The Paradox of Access Justice, and Its Application to Mandatory Arbitration' (2016) 83 *The University of Chicago Law Review* 1755–1817; H. Luth, *Behavioural Economics in Consumer Policy. The Economic Analysis of Standard Terms in Consumer Contracts Revisited* (Antwerp: Intersentia, 2010); N. Jansen, 'Klauselkontrolle im Europäischen Privatrecht' (2010) *Zeitschrift für europäisches Privatrecht* 69–106; G. Wagner, 'Zwingendes Privatrecht – Eine Analyse anhand des Vorschlags einer Richtlinie über Rechte der Verbraucher' (2010) *Zeitschrift für europäisches Privatrecht* 243–278.
[88] G. Trumbull, *Consumer Lending in France and America: Credit and Welfare* (Cambridge: Cambridge University Press, 2014).
[89] However, the American Law Institute is working on a restatement to consumer contract law, which deals with the application of the unconscionability doctrine; I. Ayres and A. Schwartz, 'The No-Reading Problem in Consumer Contract Law' (2014) 66 *Stanford Law Review* 545–610; Y. Bakos, F. Marotta-Wurgler and D. R. Trossen, 'Does Anyone Read the Fine Print? Consumer Attention to Standard Form Contracts' (2014) *New York University Law and Economics Research Paper* No. 195.
[90] With regard to Europe, A. Alemanno and A.-L. Sibony (eds.), *Nudge and the Law* (Oxford: Hart Publishing, 2015).
[91] Luth, *Behavioural Economics in Consumer Policy*.

by which to promote social distributive justice? Is tax law the better and preferable tool for regulating the consumer market? Before European states throw out the baby with the bathwater, they have to find out whether economic efficiency could be legitimately accepted as being the key parameter to test patterns of social justice through law or whether the societal dimension of social justice needs to be more actively promoted. The exchange of letters between Rawls and van Parijs from 2003 has not lost its significance:[92]

> One question the Europeans should ask themselves ... is how far reaching they want their union to be ... The long term result of this [the US federal union driven by market efficiency] ... is a civil society awash in a meaningless consumerism of some kind. I can't believe that that is what you want.

The good old times are over. The welfare state is, if not declining, under pressure and so are the rules that advance the Social.

---

[92] J. Rawls and P. Van Parijs, 'Three Letters on the Law of Peoples and the European Union' (2003) 4 *Revue de philosophie économique* 7-20, available at: www.uclouvain.be/cps/ucl/doc/etes/documents/RawlsVanParijs1.Rev.phil.Econ.pdf.

3 Path Dependency, Irritations: The Post-Classical Move?

The reverberations and convulsions shatter the intellectual foundations of English liberal pragmatism, French intellectualism and German idealism, and that affects labour law and consumer law. It is exactly here where the move from the classical legal order to the post-classical legal order can be observed – the gradual falling apart of law as a system and the move towards neoformalism. The idea is to clarify how and where the move from the classical to the post-classical can be traced, using the distinction between foundational (intellectual history and legal consciousness) and surface level (the transformation of labour and consumer law).[1]

The political economy of the overall transformations is to be found in globalisation. The challenge for the post-nation-state is how to respond to reverberations and convulsions. Currently two strands in the academic and the political debate can be observed: those who want to turn the clock back to the glorified wonderland of the 1970s, the heyday of the welfare state, the heyday of social regulation and the heyday of the expectations set into law as a transformative power for a better more just society; and the other strand of those who try to understand the transformations of the state and the Social and are faced with the critique to support neoliberalism, the downturn of the Social and the deconstruction of national democracies. The more problematic one, however, is intellectually the more interesting and the more promising. It offers opportunities to better understand how the transformations in the three states and the changing paradigms of European integration are interconnected.

---

[1] H.-W. Micklitz, 'The Constitutional Transformation of Private Law Pillars through the CJEU', in H. Collins (ed.), *European Contract Law and the EU Charter of Fundamental Rights* (Cambridge; Antwerp; Portland: Intersentia, 2017), pp. 49–91.

3.1 Irritations at the Foundational Level of the Three Models

The claim is ambitious. It requires evidence that the intellectual history and legal consciousness have undergone substantive changes in the last couple of decades that become ever more visible. A disclaimer is needed. It is plain that trying to understand and to explain the present is much more difficult than analyzing the past. The necessary distance in time is missing. As Hegel puts it, the owl cannot fly high enough to fully recognise ongoing processes. This is slippery ground. Therefore, I will be short and apodictic in statements and questions.

Is English pragmatism and utilitarianism vanishing? Research on the intellectual history of the common law in England since the seventeenth century could have led to the conviction that the United Kingdom would not leave the EU. This implies the seemingly wrong assumption that the majority of the voters would make a pragmatic choice and decide in favour of the economic advantages resulting from having access to the internal market. In such a long perspective, the UK citizens, maybe not with their hearts but with their minds, were assumed to share the overall goal of European integration, which remains first and foremost an Internal Market now supplemented with the Banking Union. From such a perspective Brexit is amazing.[2]

HAMLET	Ay, marry, why was he sent into England?
FIRST CLOWN	Why, because he was mad: he shall recover his wits there; or, if he do not, it's no great matter there.
HAMLET	Why?
FIRST CLOWN	'Twill not be seen in him there; there the men are as mad as he.

Fear and insecurity prevailed over pragmatism and this even in the northeast of England, where people are most dependent from subsidies through the various EU funds. How could that happen and will it affect the legal system? Put this way, Brexit might affect legal pragmatism and shatter utilitarian thinking. But it could also be the other way round. Brexit could be understood as a pragmatic decision at times when the EU is sinking. The British are not wedded to the European project, to French rationalism (an ever closer union) and German idealism (a united Europe in peace and prosperity). Brexit would then be a bit of British *sang froid*, the return of Britain to its roots – the pragmatic liberal Handelsstaat. The Brexiteers mobilised emotions and made false

---

[2] I am grateful to Mark Freedland.

promises on the costs of the EU for the British people, on the potential savings, and even more fundamentally they were able to play upon a certain kind of resentful individualism and upon a spirit of deregulation which has been the legacy of Thatcherism. But this is only one side of the coin. The elite classes might be more interested in the Handelsstaat that reaches even further than Thatcherism.

What about French intellectualism and French rationalism? Hazareesingh entitled the last chapter of his book 'The Closing of the French Mind' and the Conclusions 'Anxiety and Optimism'.[3] This is exactly what can be found in the writings of those who engage with the French mindset after the millennium. Right at the beginning he refers to Largeaud *La Defaite Glorieuse*[4] in order to underpin what he calls the French love of paradox:

> Thanks to this trait, France has given us passionate rationalists, conservative revolutionaries (and revolutionary traditions), violent moderates, secular missionaries, spiritual materialists, *spectateurs engages,* patriotic internationalists, conflictual allies and collective-minded individualists – and, by virtue of the sometimes unfortunate fate of French armies on the battlefield, from Vercingetorix to the Battle of Waterloo, perhaps the most exquisite of them all: the glorious defeat.

It is easy to link the great French thinkers to the different categories evoked. The more positive reading, however, contrasts with the reference to R. Frank's *La Hantise du Déclin*[5] at the very end of the book, where he writes under the heading of 'The Weight of the Past';[6]

---

[3] Hazareesingh, *How the French Think*, p. 287 and p. 312.
[4] P. 16 under reference to J.-M. Largeaud, *Napoléon et Waterloo: la défaite glorieuses de 1815 à nos jours* (Paris: Boutique De L'histoire, 2006) advertised as 'cette remarquable étude nous offre un panorama complet des conséquences et du souvenir de cette bataille dans l'imaginaire collectif. L'auteur y démontre comment une défaite peut être 'glorieuse et insérée positivement dans la mémoire nationale' ('this remarkable study offers us a complete overview of the consequences and of the memory of this battle in the collective imagination. The author shows how a defeat can be 'glorious and positively inserted into the national memory' – translation HWM).
[5] R. Frank, *La hantise du déclin. La France de 1914 à 2014* (Paris: Belin, 2014), advertised as 'l'auteur ne cherche pas à apporter de l'eau au moulin des déclinologues. Son propos se veut même optimiste. Il montre comment cette hantise peut prévenir le risque de dégradation effective, voire comment elle gagnerait à devenir européenne, incitant le Vieux Continent à sortir de son statut de nain politique face aux émergents' ('the author does not seek to add weight to the arguments of those who believe in the decline. His words are even optimistic. It shows how this obsessive fear can prevent the risk of effective degradation, how it could become European, encouraging the Old Continent to get out of its status as a political dwarf facing emerging countries' – translation HWM).
[6] Hazareesingh, *How the French Think*, pp. 319–320.

... the French have been 'haunted by decline' not only because of their defeat in 1940 but because of this calamity was followed by two further catastrophes which were not fully internalized: the loss of Indochina and the withdrawal from Algeria ... The other much-noted change to the French collective outlook is the disintegration of the progressive eschatology (a mixture of Cartesian rationalism, republicanism and Marxism) that dominated the mindset of the nation's elites for much of the modern era ... Not coincidently the French penchant for utopianism came to an end in the late twentieth century, at least for the time being, as communism imploded and Parisian thinkers turned away from the kind of sweeping visions which has so long typified the constructs of the Left Bank.

Hazareesingh leaves us with an ambiguous conclusion: A proclaimed tension between anxiety and intellectual optimism which reflects the spirit of Frank's *Hantise du Déclin*. His book ends with a rather positive and forward-looking perspective, one which builds on French rationalism and which might gain ground under the Macron government. The link to the legal system is more obvious and easier to grasp than in the United Kingdom. Is the DCFR 'the glorious defeat' of the French Code Civil? French lawyers were in favour of a European Civil Code provided it would copy/paste the French Code Civil. French lawyers might understand the failure of the European project as a glorious success. In this sense, the metaphor might be wrong. But is this really so? The attraction of the past glory – the French Code Civil – is just another variation of the long-standing and widely spread attempt to question the economic, social and political reality in France and in Europe. This holds true even after the 2016 reform, which is strongly inspired by international competitiveness.

What about German idealism and the German belief in the 'law' as a means to unite the country and to transform the society? Where is the authority of the law going in times when leading companies and leading politicians openly infringe the law for 'higher' economic or political values? It suffices to recall the involvement of Deutsche Bank in the Libor scandal[7] or Dieselgate, where Volkswagen has been manipulating the emission tests in order to promote its green car campaign.[8] Not to forget Angela Merkel's statement 'wir schaffen das', which was based on a doubtful interpretation of the EU rules

---

[7] M. Foster, 'Deutsche Bank Fined for LIBOR Fraud' available on Investopedia, 29.3.2017, available at: www.investopedia.com/news/deutsche-bank-fined-libor-fraud-db/.
[8] P. Kolba, *David gegen Goliath. Der VW Skandal und die Möglichkeit von Sammelklagen* (Wien; Berlin: Mandelbaum, 2017).

and the German Basic Law.[9] The 'wir schaffen das' ('we will make it') fits all too well into German idealism that turns into German Ideology, the way Marx had criticised it.[10] There seems to be a disquieting continuity including the rather authoritarian decision the German chancellor took without consulting the German Parliament.[11] The post-classical irritations are to be found elsewhere, although there is a connection. Academics, but not only academics, around Europe are raising in variations the same question: The Germans are thought to abide by the law. This is the legacy of Lutheranism in its literal approach to morals and ethics. However, German politicians and German companies behave exactly the way southern Catholic European Member States and southern European companies do in their more flexible attitude to rules. The Germans love to criticise such a behaviour ever since and even stronger after the economic and the Eurozone crisis.

What does it mean for Germany and for the German legal consciousness if the 'law' in the German anthem, in 'Einigkeit und Recht und Freiheit' is fading? German politicians constantly remind other Member States of the EU, in particular those from southern Europe to respect the 3 per cent threshold for public debts – although it was Germany and its finance minister who mobilised the ECJ in Luxembourg to challenge the binding character of the 3 per cent rule in the treaty.[12] The only remaining constant seems to be 'economic power' as part of the German identity.

3.2 Irritations at the Surface Level of Labour and Consumer Law

During the heyday of labour and consumer law, many supporters of social regulation dreamed of or advocated for the separation of labour/

---

[9] https://jaegercvm2.wordpress.com/2015/09/24/merkels-einwanderungspolitik-ist-verfassungswidrig-prof-schachtschneider/ for a more reluctant assessment C. Langenfeld, 'Merkels Politik ist kein Rechtsbruch', published on ZeitOnline, 2.2.2016, available at: www.zeit.de/politik/deutschland/2016-01/angela-merkel-fluechtlingspolitik-verfassung.

[10] Directed against the young Hegelians and German socialists, K. Marx, *Die deutsche Ideologie*, Band I. Kapitel I. Feuerbach. Gegensatz von materialistischer und idealistischer Anschauung (Dietz Verlag: Berlin, 1972), pp. 31–119 and pp. 399–507.

[11] W. Streeck, 'Scenario for a Wonderful Tomorrow', Book review of Europe's Orphan: The Future of the Euro and the Politics of Debt by Martin Sandbu (Princeton: Princeton University Press 2015), (2016) 38 *London Review of Books* 7–10, available at: www.lrb.co.uk/v38/n07/wolfgang-streeck/scenario-for-a-wonderful-tomorrow.

[12] Case C-27/04, *Commission v. Council* [2004] I-6649.

consumer law from traditional civil/common law. From a continental perspective, it is the dream of a Code de Travail and a Code de la Consommation as counterpart and supplement to the Code Civil or the German Bürgerliches Gesetzbuch – to unite the rights of the weaker parties, the workers and the consumers in a *coherent and systematic legal construct*. No such dreams were dreamt in the United Kingdom, with the exception of Brian Bercusson, who established European – not UK – labour law as a discipline.[13] In the three old Member States, the Social came unstuck; first, in the United Kingdom which turned into a forerunner in understanding labour law as the law of the labour market; then, in Germany, which delegated the Social readily to the EU level and allowed its transformation and adaptations to globalisation, not least through the decline of codetermination, a building block of German social policy since Sinzheimer; then, in France, which pushed for a European Social Model in line with the social welfare state and is now trapped politically in the tension between economic affordability and less and the universality of social rights.

S. Deakin and F. Wilkinson provide the following realistic account:[14]

The employment model took shape against the background of the vertical integration of the enterprise and the traditional division of labour within the nuclear family. The power of the nation-state to regulate social and economic relations through legislation was more or less taken for granted. In all these respects the contract of employment was a product of midtwentieth century consensus which is not being called into question. The disintegration of the enterprise, changing family structures, and the realisation of the limits to the effectiveness of social regulation together mean that the employment model is increasingly unable to fulfil its essential role of ensuring social protection and cohesion while also providing for the governance of work relations.

They demonstrate how deep the irritations go. The overall picture looks even more dramatic if one takes the impact of the service society and the information society into account. The employment contract relates to industrialisation and to mass production in firmly established companies. The move from the production of goods to providing services is one of the reasons behind the change of the 'model worker' and the rise

---

[13] B. Bercusson, *European Labour Law*, 2nd ed. (Cambridge: Cambridge University Press, 2009), read the obituary in the Guardian, available at: www.theguardian.com/uk/2008/sep/26/law.

[14] Deakin and Wilkinson, *The Law of the Labour Market*, p. vii.

of precarious employment relationships.[15] The dramatic consequences of the digitisation of the economy on employment and employment contracts have not yet reached the limelight of academic scrutiny. The predictions vary but it is plain that the digitisation will substitute and transform the labour force to a large extent.

As a discipline, consumer law is 50 years younger than labour law, but it shows the same transformations.[16] Consumers are confronted with the disintegration of the enterprise through the unclear responsibilities in supply chains, which have replaced or are about to replace corporations as the main unit of legal analysis. They do not know whom to sue. The remedies are grouped around the last contracting partner, the retailer, which is more often than not the weakest link in the chain. The breadwinner model, the male employee, the woman looking after the children, might still exist, but it is complemented via a broad variation of family structures, heterosexual, homosexual and transsexual, a patch work of 'blended' families with or without children. Many different members of a family with different responsibilities are now involved in the consumption process. Twentieth-century consumer law was at least implicitly connected to the old-fashioned division of tasks between the breadwinner and his wife; its dissolution creates all sorts of tensions, e.g. in sustainable consumption when cooking time has to be weighed against working time. The limits to the effectiveness of social welfare consumer law have been amply demonstrated.

The service society and the information society undermine the twentieth century consumer model, whose flagship is the consumer sales contract, the contract between the consumer and a local retailer on the exchange of money against the acquisition of a product. The move to the service society seems more dramatic than the effects of the disintegration of the enterprises and its substitutes, the supply chains. Contrary to the sales contract, there is no clear model of a consumer services contract. There are many service contracts depending on the structure of the regulated market. More importantly service contracts are long-term contracts, which tie the consumer to the customer for years if not decades. A mirror-inverted development can be observed between employment contracts and consumer service contracts.

---

[15] A. Adams, M. Freedland and J. Prassl, 'The "Zero-Hours Contract": Regulating casual work, or legitimating precarity?' (2015) *European Labour Law Network Working Paper* No. 5, *Oxford Legal Studies Research Paper* No. 11.

[16] Not to be equated with the development of consumer policy, Trentmann, *Empire of Things* and Torp, *Wachstum, Sicherheit, Moral*.

The former turn into ever more unstable relations and the latter move towards relational contracts with all its consequences for the limits of the law to solve conflicts during the duration of the contract. The Internet of Things promotes the servicification of goods and blurs the boundaries between the constitutive distinction of a consumer and a supplier.

Both labour law and consumer law are status related. The entrance door to benefit from social protection is the concept of the worker and the consumer. When the status loses its contours, the concept of labour law and consumer law as separate and self-standing disciplines becomes shaky. Social regulation in the form of labour and consumer law gets ever more liquid and slips through the fingers of all those who would like to give it a solid graspable form.

Part II

Justice beyond the Nation-State: The European Experiment

Thus far, the focus has been placed on three leading nation-states. I observed how the Social rose, lost impetus and even declined together with the transformation of the state, and, secondly, how this trajectory is reflected in the private legal order and in the different patterns of justice. In this part of my analysis, the perspective shifts from the national to the European level. The EU emerges as an actor and gradually becomes involved in the domain of the Social exactly at a moment when the Social is in the throes of difficulties. The two narratives, the national and the European, overlap. I argue that they become entangled and, in the final analysis, they generate access justice as the genuine European pattern of justice and, *in nuce*, societal justice.

The argument will be developed in four steps. First, I will reconstruct 60 years of European integration in three steps: the founding years, the heyday of the European Social and what I call the post-classical move. Wieacker's European common heritage thesis propelled the integration process for 40 years, guiding it through the founding years and the beginning of the European Social. However, the common heritage does not suffice to build a European constitution and a European civil code, let alone to manage the current crisis. The intellectual history and legal consciousness of Member States has reached a turning point. Against this bigger frame of Europe building, the development of European private law is unpacked. This is the task of the second step. I use the same three-step structure to present an account of social regulation, to demonstrate how the EU first tried to mimic national patterns of social justice and, then, transformed labour protection and consumer protection law into the law of the labour and consumer market society. This is the break-even point for the development of European access justice and European societal justice, namely, not only to open up markets on fair conditions but to guarantee European citizens the opportunity to participate in European society building beyond the market. The result of this transformation is post-classical labour, non-discrimination and consumer law.

The third step is descriptive and should be understood as a kind of stocktaking, in parallel to the analysis of the success and failures of national social welfare regulation. The purpose is to lay down the general features of the post-classical private law of labour, non-discrimination and consumer law in a cross-cutting perspective. I thereby distinguish between its substantive and procedural features. The substance of post-classical private law may be characterised in terms of quantity, rationalities, regulatory cascades and their legal nature. The procedural features of the post-classical private law are shaped through its laboratorian character, enshrined in its shaky infrastructure and by experimentalism in lawmaking and enforcement. The fourth step points to the prescriptive potential of the post-classical European private law by combining access justice and societal justice. The key features around which the European private law shall be built are the rationality test rooted in *Cassis de Dijon*; shared public-private competences and responsibilities between the EU, the Member States and private business; and, last but not least, the fragmentation of the legal status of the person with implications for justice and legal consciousness. The fourth step prepares the ground for the last part of the book, the implementation of the theoretical findings into the tentative concept of a tripartite European private law order. Part II concludes with a short summary of the overall impact on the EU patterns of justice.

1 Socioeconomic and Political Background of Social Justice in the EU

When it comes to the intellectual and philosophical foundations of the EU, three different narratives compete with each other, but read together they explain and structure the emergence of the European pattern of justice engrained in European private law: the first is the common European intellectual and philosophical heritage, the second is the integration through law paradigm, and the third is the post-classical move in the European integration

A protagonist for the common heritage in private law is Wieacker[1] who highlights three constants of European legal culture: personalism, intellectualism and legalism. The three constants reflect the common denominator of English utilitarianism-individualism, French intellectualism and German legalism. They lie behind the overall rhetoric of 'united in diversity'. They explain the commonality of the different patterns of social justice and, more importantly, they serve as the deeper spiritual platform of the post-war initiative to build a 'united Europe' based on nation-states and national legal orders, not despite but because of their differences.

The genealogy of the EU reconstructed around the interplay of 'integration', 'law' and 'goverance' constitutes the second narrative. Walter Hallstein famously and influentially stated in 1969: 'The European Community is a remarkable legal phenomenon. It is a creation of law; it is a source of law; and it is a legal system'.[2] There is a direct line from Hallstein to the formula Mauro Cappelletti, Monica Seccombe and Joseph H. H. Weiler so powerfully coined in their vast project

---

[1] Wieacker, 'Foundations of European Legal Culture', 20.
[2] W. Hallstein, *Europe in the Making* (translated from German by C. Roetter; originally published under the title *Der unvollendete Bundesstaat* (Düsseldorf; Wien: ECON, 1969) (London: George Allen & Unwin Ltd, 1972), p. 30.

'Integration Through Law: Europe and the American Federal Experience'.[3] Private law remains at the border of the integration through law paradigm, although private law strongly interacts with what could be called the EU state-building process.

The third narrative identifies the break-even point in the post-classical move as being enshrined in the Lisbon Agenda, the Charter on Fundamental Rights and the White Paper on Governance. The three read together insinuate a paradigm shift, away from European state-building through ever closer integration towards a trans- or post-nation-state laboratory. Broken down to private law, it is the change from law as a *system* to a post-classical understanding of a private legal order, from a nineteenth-century understanding of law in line with Newton's *lex geometrica* towards a twenty-first-century understanding of law as a neoformal, incoherent and unsystematic European legal *order* in the meaning of D. Kennedy,[4] which comes closer to revolution in twentieth-century physics.

1.1 A Chart towards Orientation

On the basis of the three narratives, the evolution of the European legal order can be broken down into the founding phase, the heyday of the legal order, and the post-classical move. The founding phase is determined by a clear separation of the European common market from the Member States' social competences. There was no need for a Europeanised private law. The second phase is determined by the Internal Market programme, by the rise of the Social in the EU, and by the growing intrusion of EU law in all policy fields, manifest in the short dream of a European Social Model. It culminates in the failed attempt to transform the European Union into a constitution and to give its own European civil code. The third phase starts with the Lisbon agenda and ends in the current economic, social and political crisis of the EU. In all its insufficiencies one might glimpse the dawn of a post-classical legal order that underpins the laboratorian character of the EU, and explains the emergence of the EU market state and the European model of access justice.

---

[3] M. Cappelletti, M. Seccombe and J. H. H. Weiler, 'Integration Through Law: Europe and the American Federal Experience', in M. Cappelletti, M. Seccombe and J. H. H. Weiler (eds.), *Integration Through Law* Vol. 1, Book 1 (Berlin: de Gruyter, 1986), pp. 4–68.

[4] Kennedy, 'Three Globalizations of Law and Legal Thought'.

Table 6

	Origins 1957–1986	In transition 1986–2000	Towards a post-classical legal order
Constitution	Economic constitution (1957)	Political constitution (2005)	Many constitutions
Codification of civil law	National level	DCFR, CFR, CESL Regulatory private law	Constitutionalisation of private law
Economic determinants	Four market freedoms and competition law	Social market economy	Globalisation, financialisation, efficiency
Political determinants	Separation of powers between MS and the EU	EU federal state	Multi-level governance Technocracy and juristocracy
Social determinants	In the hands of the Member States	European Social Model	Social inclusion Non-discrimination
Philosophical determinants	Personalism, intellectualism, legalism	The twilight in the common heritage	Post-classical philosophy
Legal consciousness	National	National European	National European divided
Key Actors	ECJ Judges European elite	European Commission + Member States	European agencies National/European courts, private actors
Model of justice	National models of justice	Transnational welfare justice	Access justice
Labour/consumer law	National models	Social private law	Law on the labour/consumer market
Worker/consumer image	National models	Rational worker + consumer	Citizen-worker-citizen-consumer
Producer/supplier image	National models	Market bound producer supplier	The citizen-producer + citizen-supplier

The above table (Table 6) has to be read in conjunction with the table on the intellectual history of the three states (Table 1).[5] The vertical column mirrors the criteria chosen to analyse the three countries. The horizontal one documents the historical development of the EU broken down into three steps. Again the analysis is not exhaustive; rather, the table is meant to serve as guidance and orientation.

---

[5] Part I. 1.1.

1.2 The First Thirty Years Built on the Common Intellectual History

When it comes to assess the first thirty years, the post-war conditions have to be recalled. The nation-states were gradually recovering from the economic, political, social and, not least, psychological consequences of war. The Franco-Italian initiative of leading politicians to remedy the wounds of the peoples and their citizens through the building of the steel and coal union in 1950 and the European Economic Community in 1957 still deserves the highest respect and recognition. The recovery of the states, the economies and the peoples went hand in hand with 'European integration', a combination of words that was meant to send a message to the peoples of Europe: peace and prosperity would come through trade under a common institutional umbrella that domesticises the destructive power of the war industries on both sides of the Rhine. The idea of European integration rested on two sound pillars: the market for the EU and the Social for the Member States.[6] The EU was built on nation-states that autonomously decided to engage in the joint project of European integration and that guaranteed smooth cross-border trade through the interaction between their national legal orders. The common heritage, the post-Westphalian state nation, which turned into the nineteenth-century nation-state and the respective national private law orders underpinned the distinction and stabilised the EU. Legal integration through the market was counterbalanced through political integration in intergovernmental fora.[7]

1.2.1 The First Thirty Years, 1957–1986

The European Union was set up in 1957. It laid down the structure of what has been termed, particularly by German lawyers, the European Economic Constitution.[8] The latter rests on two pillars: the four market freedoms and competition law. It remained for the

---

[6] Spaak Report.
[7] J. H. H. Weiler, *Supranational law and the supranational system. Legal Structure and Political Process in the European Community*, unpublished PhD thesis, European University Institute (1982).
[8] E.-J. Mestmäcker, 'Auf dem Wege zu einer Ordnungspolitik für Europa', in E.-J. Mestmäcker, H. Möller, H. P. Schwartz (eds.), *Eine Ordnungspolitik für Europa: Festschrift für Hans von der Groeben* (Baden-Baden: Nomos, 1987), pp. 9–49.

ECJ[9] to turn an international treaty into 'a genuine legal order', which is characterised by supremacy of EU law over national law and by the direct effect of EU law to the benefit of individual parties. Private parties, the holders of the rights and their recipients, are legally entitled to strike down national laws and regulations which hinder the four freedoms. It seems as if the idea of a genuine European legal order is, in fact, a product of French intellectualism represented in R. Lecourt.[10]

In the founding years, the ECJ became the key player and the forceful driver of European integration. An endless chain of references to the ECJ allowed the Court to build and shape a common market without quantitative restrictions and without barriers to trade. The Social did not really play a role at that stage, at least not at the EU level. The European Economic Community has been established on the basis of a *functional separation of powers* between the EEC and the Member States. The EEC was granted enumerated powers only as far as they were needed to establish the Common Market to overcome economic nationalism. The establishment and the development of social welfare systems and of social justice was left to the Member States.[11] Redistributive policies were to remain subject to national politics, with the exception of the Common Agricultural Policy (CAP).[12]

This does not mean that the European Union did not attempt to get involved into social matters. However, it did so, and had to do so, exactly within the boundaries of the economic constitution and the distribution of powers. Legislative measures initiated by the European Commission could only pass with the unanimous agreement of the Member States in the Council, Art. 100 EC (now Art. 115 TFEU). The European Parliament had no decision-making power until 1986. Despite these tight restrictions, the European Regional Development Fund was set up in 1973 and started operating in 1975. In 1974, the European Commission developed a social policy programme[13] and, in

---

[9] E. Stein, 'Lawyers, Judges and the Making of a Transnational Constitution' (1981) 75 *American Journal of International Law* 1–27.
[10] W. Phelan, 'The Revolutionary Doctrines of European Law and the Legal Philosophy of Robert Lecourt' (2016) *EUI Working Paper Law* No. 18.
[11] Dawson, *New Governance and the Transformation of European Law*, p. 34.
[12] The CAP and structural funds were (are) proper redistributive policies with tangible economic impact – just not very socially salient. They were financed out of the EU budget and decided by majority voting. The subjects of these policies are not akin to classic welfare state schemes.
[13] OJ No. C 13, 12.2.1974, pp. 1.

1975, a consumer policy programme.[14] Both were unanimously approved by the Council of Ministers and published in the EC Official Journal. The Council of Ministers' approval provided legitimacy to the European Commission to elaborate legislative means. Whether it was the lack of an appropriate legal basis or whether the Member States deliberately decided to link market building to social policies, this has been subject to endless debates. However, the choice of competence had long-lasting effects on how social policies could be realised and how they were perceived. It is here that we find the roots for the success and the critique of the pick-a-pack procedure, where social policies became dependent on a market-building competence, linking economic and social policy. Others would argue that this approach submits social policy to the market logic.

Quite a number of remarkable directives were adopted in both fields: in labour and non-discrimination law, Directive 75/117 on equal pay[15] and Directive 76/207 on equal access to employment;[16] in consumer law Directive 85/374 on product liability, Directive 85/577 on doorstep selling[17] and Directive 87/102 on consumer credit.[18]

1.2.2 The Common Heritage

The building of the EU rests on two pillars. The first is the political will of the six founding members and their decision to build a peaceful Europe through trade. The second is the deeper common intellectual history and legal consciousness that provided the foundations on which political action could be taken.

The political foundation of the Treaty of Rome is to be found in the Schuman Declaration of May 1950. It is only 132 lines long (extract).[19]

---

[14] OJ No. C 92, 24.4.1975, p. 2.

[15] Council Directive 75/117/EEC of 10 February 1975 on the approximation of the laws of the Member States relating to the application of the principle of equal pay for men and women, OJ No. L 45, 19.2.1975, p. 19.

[16] Council Directive 76/207/EEC of 9 February 1976 on the implementation of the principle of equal treatment for men and women as regards access to employment, vocational training and promotion, and working conditions, OJ No. L 39, 14.2.1976, p. 40.

[17] Council Directive 85/577/EEC of 20 December 1985 to protect the consumer in respect of contracts negotiated away from business premises, OJ No. L 372, 31.12.1985, p. 31.

[18] Council Directive 87/102/EEC of 22 December 1986 for the approximation of the laws, regulations and administrative provisions of the Member States concerning consumer credit, OJ No. L 42, 12.02.1987, p. 48.

[19] The Schuman Declaration is available on the website of the Robert Schuman Foundation at: www.robert-schuman.eu/en/declaration-of-9-may-1950.

Schuman refers to civilisation but not to democracy.[20] The 'peace through trade' formula embraces a common European history, sparked by centuries' long interconnectivity of states and commerce. Schuman implicitly presupposes the existence of a national private law, which is organising trade. P. Pescatore[21] has analysed, with masterly precision, the differences between international law and the European law of integration. Without the existence and without deep reliance on the viability of nation-states, their constitutions and the private law order, trade cannot be organised. Schuman, and indeed the Treaty of Rome, presuppose the functionality of nation-states, of their democratic constitutional legal order and of their private law orders.

The deeper philosophical foundations, the common heritage of Europe, rendered the Schuman plan politically feasible. There is the nation-state, a heritage of the Westphalian peace, which developed over the centuries. The early Westphalian state transformed into a nation-state, and later a democratic state.[22] The key role of the state in inserting the Social into the private law systems is shown in Part II of this book. Wieacker and Paolo Grossi have analysed and written at length on the modern history of private law. Wieacker highlights the invariables of the historical development that are enshrined in the European legal culture: personalism, legalism and intellectualism.[23] Justice should be understood as an integral part of the legal culture.[24] Based on our analysis, it is legitimate to use Wieacker's trinity to understand the place of Europe's common heritage in shaping legal developments. To be clear, personalism connects to the English intellectual history, legalism to the German and intellectualism to the French.

Personalism describes the separation of subject and object, the theoretical conception of human relations in 'opposition' and not in the 'we' sense, which Wieacker traces back to Judaism and Christianity. In the Judeo-Christian tradition, man knows only one God and considers himself as 'I' towards the demanding and granting 'you'. The religious experience is the birthplace of the ultimate liberty of the decision of

---

[20] J. H. H. Weiler, 'Deciphering the Political and Legal DNA of European Integration: An Exploratory Essay', in J. Dickson and P. Eleftheriadis (eds.), *Philosophical Foundations of European Union Law* (Oxford: Oxford University Press, 2012), pp. 137–158, at p. 139.
[21] P. Pescatore, *The Law of Integration: Emergence of New Phenomenon in International Relations, Based on Experience of the European Communities* (Leiden: Sijthoff, 1974), originally published in French 1972.
[22] Micklitz and Patterson, 'From the Nation-State to the Market'.
[23] Wieacker, 'Foundations of European Legal Culture', 20.
[24] Micklitz, 'The (Un)-Systematics of (Private) Law as an Element of European Culture'.

the 'I', which correlates with personal responsibility as an answer to the demanding and granting 'you'.[25] Personalism manifests itself in the conception of law, particularly in private law, in the idea of liberty and self-determination instead of magic or collective compulsion. It is here one finds the common origins for the reason-based freedom of will, the autonomy of decision, and private autonomy, notwithstanding its different national guises.[26] In the 'I versus You', in 'Rights versus Duties', and in 'Autonomy versus Responsibility', there is a tension which kept the European legal and political philosophy in suspense ever since. E. Bodenheimer's comment on the relationship between republicanism and liberalism, between 'individual rights theory' and 'public interest thinking',[27] is instructive and illuminating. The increasingly strong orientation to individual rights in Europe's quasi-statutory construction provokes counterreactions that proclaim the priority of the public interest (public goods) over individual rights.[28]

The second invariable of European legal culture is legalism. Decisions about social relations and conflicts have to be submitted to rules of law, the validity and acceptance of which does not depend on external moral, social and political values or purposes. Law and legal rules are separated from other social rules and values, among which include religious convictions, moral imperatives, habits and customs. Wieacker traces the separation of law and morals back to the development of a specific professional administration in Ancient Rome. Thomasius and Kant have reshaped this tradition for the Modern Age. Legalism considers social obligations, rights and privileges as non-arbitrary objectified legal rules. Legalism in private law manifests itself in the transition from 'status to contract'.[29] Wieacker recognises and broaches the issue to the downside of legalism, which sacrifices material moral concepts, social rights and, last but not least, justice for the sake of the formal rationality of law. He deals thoroughly with

---

[25] Wieacker, 'Foundations of European Legal Culture', 20-21. The far-reaching implications of the distinction between 'I' and 'You' as a legacy of Christianism are analysed by P. Sloterdijk, *Die schrecklichen Kinder der Neuzeit*, p. 278.

[26] Micklitz, 'On the Intellectual History of Freedom of Contract and Regulation'.

[27] Wieacker, 'Foundations of European Legal Culture', 22; M. J. Horwitz, 'Republicanism and Liberalism in American Constitutional Thought' (1987) 29 *William & Mary Law Review* 57-74; 'Symposium on Republicanism', (1988) 97 *Yale Law Journal* 1493.

[28] For an analysis of European public interest litigation, D. Kelemen, *Eurolegalism. The Transformation of Law and Regulation in the European Union* (Cambridge, MA: Harvard University Press, 2011).

[29] H. Maine, *Ancient Law: Its Connection with the Early History of Society, and Its Relation to Modern Ideas* (J. H. Morgan ed., London: J. M. Dent & Sons Ltd., 1917) (1861), p. 101.

antinomies and justifies the necessity of the correction of formal law through interpretation by judges and legislative corrections.[30] Whether and to what extent cutting the boundaries between law and morals, in particular through the non-discrimination paradigm, endangers the 'integrity of the law', is the subject of ideological critique.[31]

The third invariable of European legal culture is intellectualism, which refers to the particular way in which the phenomenon of law is understood and interpreted: as epistemological idealism, as European cognitive thinking aiming at conceptualisation, or as unambiguous consistency of the empirical legal material.[32] According to this line of thinking, the codification of private law appears to be the crowning glory of European intellectualism.[33] A common law system will face difficulties against such an understanding of European intellectualism. It seems more appropriate to stress the commonality between the continental codifications and the common law in their joint search for inner consistency and systematic structures.[34] The formal side of European intellectualism is balanced by the idea of justice. Wieacker considers the distinction between corrective and distributive justice to be the cornerstone of European intellectualism. The intellectual history of the three variations of social justice in English, French and German private law underpins such an understanding.

J. H. H. Weiler[35] has explained the success of the first 30 years through the balance between forceful integration through law and supranational intergovernamentalism. The driver of integration through law

---

[30] Wieacker, *The History of Private Law*, more particularly § 30 Search for Justice, p. 586; respectively F. Wieacker, *Das Sozialmodell der klassischen Privatrechtsgesetzbücher und die Entwicklung der modernen Gesellschaft* (Karlsruhe: C. F. Müller, 1953), thereto M. Renner, 'Formalisierung, Materialisierung, Prozeduralisierung', in S. Grundmann, H.-W. Micklitz and M. Renner (eds.), *Privatrechtstheorie*, Band 1 (Tübingen: Mohr Siebeck, 2015), Kapitel 10, pp. 821–873.

[31] Introduction 3.1. R. Dworkin, 'Integrity in Law', in *Law's Empire* (Cambridge, MA: Harvard University Press, 1986), also on the 'Theory of Jurisprudence' blog: http://the oryofjurisprudence.blogspot.it/2007/12/ronald-dworkin-law-as-integrity.html;
L. Fuller's eight desiderata in the *Morality of the Law* (New Haven: Yale University Press, 1964); A. Somek, *Engineering Equality. An Essay on European Non-discrimination Law* (Oxford: Oxford University Press 2011), p. 83.

[32] Wieacker, 'Foundations of European Legal Culture', 25.

[33] Wieacker, 'Foundations of European Legal Culture', 26 'ultimate triumph'.

[34] T. Tridimas, 'Precedent and the Court of Justice: A Jurisprudence of Doubt?', in J. Dickson and P. Eleftheriadis (eds.), *Philosophical Foundations of European Union Law* (Oxford: Oxford University Press, 2012), pp. 307–330.

[35] J. H. H. Weiler, 'The Transformation of Europe' (1991) 100 *The Yale Law Journal* 2403–2483.

was the ECJ, European politics were enshrined and guaranteed through the unanimity principle. Personalism, intellectualism and legalism could unfold an integrative power beyond national particularities – *because* the national private law orders remained largely untouched and because the Member States could maintain their particular model of the Social.

1.3 The Heyday of the Social, 1986 until 2000 and Beyond

The post-war period until the oil crisis of 1974 brought with it prosperity and social and political stability. The Common Market worked to the benefit of the Member States and the European peoples. Increased choice was equated with a better life and capabilities, which were viewed as the valid currency of justice in the EU.[36] The Social in the Member States reached a new peak, first by stabilising labour relations, later in the consumer society that emerged from the 1960s on and reached ever broader parts of the society. Politically, it was a time where the Member States and the EU were promoting a more homogeneous society where the opportunities of the European market were, in principle, open to everybody. These hopes gradually evaporated in the second half of the 1970s, exactly at the time when the ECJ via *Dassonville* and *Cassis de Dijon* set a new round of integration into motion.[37] The idea of a better life through increased choice is subject to fierce criticism today, theoretically and empirically.[38] However, the second stage of European integration was still one of hope that provided political leeway for stronger social integration.

The philosophy and the hope was to build a Europe with a social outlook, a formation of nation-states that enshrines a social dimension, both in labour law and consumer law. There were strong expectations for a social Europe that could compensate for the decline at a national level. Initially, the competence transfer from the Member States to the EU nourished these hopes and expectations not least through a whole wave of secondary legislation adopted in the aftermath of the Single

---

[36] F. de Witte, *Justice in the EU*, pp. 61, 200.
[37] Case 8/74, *Dassonville* [1974] ECR 837; Case 120/78, *Rewe-Zentral AG v Bundesmonopolverwaltung für Branntwein*.
[38] G. Davies, 'Social Legitimacy and Purposive Power: The End, the Means and the Consent of the People', in D. Kochenov, G. de Búrca and A. Williams (eds.), *Europe's Justice Deficit?* (Oxford: Hart Publishing, 2015), pp. 259–276; empirically via the findings of the Eurobarometer, Diez-Sanchez, 'Justice Index' Eurobarometer and the Issue of Justice', conclusions.

European Act (SEA). Over time, it became clear that the European social could not be equated to its national predecessor. For one thing, the EU grew politically lopsided. The fragile balance between forceful integration through law and strong political inter-governmentalism faded away.[39] Majority voting facilitated secondary law-making but worked as a destabilising factor. The new division of competences and responsibilities between the EU market and the 'national Social' rendered integration increasingly complicated. Eventually, the over-promotion and over-instrumentalisation of law as a means of political integration brought politics back in, through governance. Out of this ever more complex legal and political environment, a new concept of justice emerged that altered redistributive schemes by emphasising equal access. This new concept is not entrenched in a particular redistributive ethos; however, this does not exclude redistributive implications.[40]

The Single European Act, indeed, marks the birth of access justice. The emergence of access justice, however, is overshadowed by a grander and all the more pompous project. In the aftermath of the fall of the Berlin Wall and the collapse of Communism, the post-war idea of a United States of Europe was revitalised through the attempt to build a European Constitution and a European Civil Code. To achieve this grand vision, the common heritage of Europe was mobilised to shape a European Union on the model of the nineteenth-century nation-state, through a constitution and a civil code. Yet, the common heritage alone does not suffice to realise such a leap. Building a European Constitution and a European Civil Code requires different foundations. The failure of the two grand projects demonstrates the limits of the common heritage. The past cannot build the future. The messy upshot of the second stage of the European integration process is 'integration through governance'. The far-reaching implications and consequences with regard to the design of the European Social are only gradually emerging from the mist of the many rules so complacently termed multi-level governance.

1.3.1 *The Second Phase*

The second phase is characterised by the growing importance of the Social in the constitutionalisation process of the EU. The famous White Paper on the Completion of the Internal Market developed under the

---

[39] Weiler, 'The Transformation of Europe', 2403; Mestmäcker, 'Auf dem Wege zu einer Ordnungspolitik für Europa', p. 20 Der Binnenmarkt.
[40] As documented in the tripartite legal order; Part III.

presidency of Jacques Delors provided the ground for the adoption of the Single European Act. It is a wonderful combination of French intellectualism and British pragmatism. The overall message addressed to the Member States was that the realisation of the Internal Market could not be achieved without the establishment of minimum standards to protect workers and consumers. One may wonder how it was possible that Member States agreed to such a far-reaching paradigm change, which reshuffled the distribution of economic and social competences between the EU and Member States, and which had been so firmly established in 1957. It should be recalled, however, that by the late 1970s, the European Union lacked any clear vision on its future. The Internal Market Programme broke the impasse. The integration of the social dimension is not least due to the functional logic of the market integration process where the distinction between the economic and the Social became more and more difficult to sustain. The European integration process seemed to provide evidence for Polanyi's theory of the social embeddedness of the capitalist market.[41] The ECJ played a crucial role in paving the way for a reorientation of the EU policy in the mid 1990s through its understanding of the treaty not only as an autonomous legal order, but as a constitutional charter that enshrines and encompasses fundamental and human rights as the common constitutional heritage.[42] The most obvious changes in the Single European Act were enlarged competences and the introduction of majority voting. Art. 100(a) Single European Act (Art. 114 TFEU) turned into the key instrument that legitimated and justified European secondary legislative measures in both labour and consumer law. Indeed, majority voting helped to unblock long-standing legislative projects that could not find unanimous agreement. The social forces in the Member States placed much hope on Art. 118 a) (Art. 153 TFEU) and, in particular, on Art. 118(b) (Art. 152 TFEU), which was meant to promote dialogue between social partners.

The agreement on the European Monetary Union in Maastricht 1991 triggered a debate over the need to compensate the Member States for the loss of their autonomy, to use monetary policy for devaluation of their currencies by the introduction of a Social Policy Agreement. The project failed in 1991 due to the resistance of the United Kingdom and

---

[41] For critical account on the achievements, see M. Höpner and A. Schäfer, 'Embeddedness and Regional Integration: Waiting for Polanyi in a Hayekian Setting' (2012) 66 *International Organization* 429–455.

[42] Pescatore, *The Law of Integration*, p. 78.

was adopted only as a Protocol on Social Policy by the remaining 11 Member States.[43] However, it led to the establishment of the Cohesion Fund in 1994. The 1999 Amsterdam Treaty not only integrates the Social Policy Agreement as Art. 137 (Art. 153 TFEU) into the treaty, but also extended the legislative powers of the EU in the field of equal treatment, Art. 13 ET (Art. 19 TFEU) and Art. 141 (3) (Art. 157 TFEU). Consumer policy too was upgraded and received a separate chapter in Maastricht, Art. 129 (a) ET[44] as amended and slightly adjusted by Art. 153 ET in Amsterdam (today Art. 169 TFEU). In consumer law, the newly introduced competences were of limited practical significance, but they were highly symbolic, as Art. 95 ET (Art. 104 TFEU) remained the key competence rule. Art. 13 (Art. 19 TFEU) and Art. 141 (3) (Art. 157 TFEU) triggered the adoption of three directives in the field of equal treatment, namely Directives 2000/43 on race equality,[45] 2000/78 on equal treatment[46] and 2004/113 on gender equality in the provision of goods and services.[47]

The social drive in the constitutionalisation process reached its high point with the introduction of the Social Charter in 1989 and, in 2000, through the EU Charter on Fundamental Rights,[48] which integrated consumer policy, though to a lesser extent than social rights. By the end of the millennium, the Social had gained standing in the EU constitution. However, a closer look shows that competence rules are either bound to the completion of the Internal Market or are wholly lacking. They did not provide enough substance for realising the dream of a European Social Model or to use the words of Tuori[49] of a 'social constitution'. Rödl[50] concludes with regard to labour law and policy, the

---

[43] F. Rödl, 'Labour Constitution', p. 640.
[44] H.-W. Micklitz and N. Reich, 'Verbraucherschutz im Vertrag über die Europäische Union. Perspektiven für 1993' (1992) Europäische Zeitschrift für Wirtschaftsrecht 593–598.
[45] Council Directive 2000/43/EC of 29 June 2000 implementing the principle of equal treatment between persons irrespective of racial or ethnic origin, OJ No. L 180, 19.07.2000, p. 22.
[46] Council Directive 2000/78/EC of 27 November 2000 establishing a general framework for equal treatment in employment and occupation, OJ No. L 303, 02.12.2000, p. 16.
[47] Council Directive 2004/113/EC of 13 December 2004 implementing the principle of equal treatment between men and women in the access to and supply of goods and services, OJ No. L 373, 21.12.2004, p. 37
[48] OJ No. C 364, 18.12.2000, p. 1.
[49] On the struggle of the EU, K. Tuori, 'European Social Constitution: Between Solidarity and Access Justice,' in K. Purnhagen/P. Rott (eds.), Varieties of European Economic Law and Regulation. Liber Amicorum for Hans Micklitz, pp. 371–400.
[50] Rödl, 'Labour Constitution', p. 638.

higher the social relevance, the lesser-developed are the EU competences. Even during the heyday of the Social, the EU did not succeed in conquering the mainland of labour law. The law on employment contracts and collective labour law remained, by and large, in the hands of the Member States. The picture looks different with regard to consumer law. The competence rules largely sufficed to 'rescue' consumer law, which has lost ground together with the decline of the welfare state. The price paid was the shift from consumer protection law to consumer law without protection, or to use Deakin and Wilkinson's terminology – the shift towards the law of the consumer market.[51] Most remarkable is the success story of the EU's non-discrimination policy. In non-discrimination law, the EU set a new agenda that went far beyond what Member States had achieved, and that applies to both labour law and consumer law.

1.3.2 The Limits of the Common Heritage

Since the late 1990s, two legal-political issues have dominated European legal discourse,[52] namely the development of a European Constitution and the making of a European Civil Code. If both the Constitution and the Civil Code had been realised, they would have brought the European Union much nearer to the concept of a nation-state as developed in the seventeenth century. The fall of the wall and the breakdown of the Soviet Union had liberated Middle and Eastern European countries. In their striving for sovereignty, these countries adopted national constitutions and national civil codes. Looking back, the 2002 White Paper on Governance appears like a swan song to the political project of a United Europe long before the new Member States officially joined the EU. At a surface level, constitution building and private law building can be associated with the common heritage of the Westphalian peace and of what Wieacker called the 'ultimate triumph'[53] – a codified private law order.

At a first, but superficial, glance, the historical similarities between state-building and code-making in France at the end of the eighteenth to

---

[51] Micklitz, 'The Expulsion of the Concept of Protection from the Consumer Law and the Return of Social Elements in the Civil Law'; Deakin and Wilkinson, *The Law of the Labour Market*.

[52] For an account of the theoretical strains in the debate, N. Walker, 'Legal Theory and the European Union: A 25th Anniversary Essay' (2005) 25 *Oxford Journal of Legal Studies* 581–601.

[53] Wieacker, 'Foundations of European Legal Culture', 26.

the beginning of the nineteenth century and the current debate on Europe's future are striking. These similarities have not been openly addressed, neither politically nor theoretically. In fact, both grand projects are strongly interconnected via questions of their feasibility at the end of the twentieth century, of the degree to which they take into account the Social, of their shaky legitimacy, of unclear mandates/ competencies given to the drafters, and of the ambitious though somewhat misleading use of the words 'constitution' and 'civil code'. In sum, they were driven by ideological preconceptions.[54] In particular, the European Parliament, which was the main driver behind the constitution/private law building as the last step for the European integration project, seemed to be guided by rather simplistic ideologies.

In the meantime, both the grand constitutional project and the grand civil law project 'failed'. The common heritage and the deeper foundations could not carry such a fundamental change. Personalism, intellectualism and legalism might have sufficed to build a national constitution and a national private legal order. It might even have sufficed to adopt the Treaty of Rome with its clear division between the market and the Social. However, it would have needed a political decision to go beyond the common heritage and to open up a new page in the intellectual history of Europe, a discussion in the respective democratic fora on justice, on the kind of justice to be achieved at what level and by whom.[55] Both grand projects were guided by a similar philosophy, one where European integration is regarded very much like a technical process in which it comes down to develop the correct rules that fit into the furtherance of market integration, rather than a controversy over social political aims and perspectives and their feasibility in a supranational environment.[56] This does not mean that the grand

---

[54] H.-W. Micklitz, 'Failures or Ideological Preconceptions? Thoughts on Two Grand Projects: The European Constitution and the European Civil Code', in K. Tuori and S. Sankari (eds.), *The Many Constitutions of Europe* (Farnham: Ashgate, 2010), pp. 109–142.

[55] M. A. Wilkinson, 'Politicising Europe's Justice Deficit: Some Preliminaries', in D. Kochenov, G. de Búrca and A. Williams (eds.), *Europe's Justice Deficit?* (Oxford: Hart Publishing, 2015), pp. 111–136.

[56] For an early critique of the technical apolitical character of the codification project. See The Manifesto of the Study Group on Social Justice in European Private Law, 'Social Justice in European Contract Law: A Manifesto' (2004) 10 *European Law Journal* 653–674; and on the outcome of the project, M. W. Hesselink, *CFR & Social Justice. A short study for the European Parliament on the values underlying the draft Common Frame of Reference for European private law: what roles for fairness and social justice?* (München: Sellier, 2008), who gives a relatively positive account of the degree to which social justice has been taken into account.

projects did not deal with 'justice' or did not enshrine a particular model of justice, but such thinking remains hidden behind either technicalities or 'grand words' without any specification.[57]

The European Constitution was rejected in the Dutch and French referenda. Notwithstanding the question as to whether the project deserved to be called a constitution, the peoples of these two Member States were not willing to give way to a further step in the development of the United States of Europe. Without much deeper political discussion on the reasons behind the rejection, the Member States and their governments 'saved' the core of the constitutional project in the Lisbon Treaty. By contrast, the European Civil Code project led to intensive academic debates and the production of the Acquis Principles[58] and the Draft Common Frame of Reference.[59] The latter comes near to a fully fledged European Civil Code disguised as an 'academic exercise'. With the help and support of legal experts, the European Commission transformed the DCFR into a draft regulation on a Common European Sales Law (CESL). The collaboration between the European Commission and European Academia resembles, in an ominous way, the German Professorenmodell where academia cooperated with an authoritarian executive, overstepping a weak parliament.[60] However, the European Parliament did not complain about or criticise this undemocratic lawmaking behind closed doors. Resistance came from six governments that forced the European Commission to officially withdraw its proposal.[61] The third attempt of the European Commission to save the overall project is to be found in the still-pending proposal on transborder sales.[62] Both failures tell one single story: the common heritage has reached its limits. Constitution and private law building stretches the boundaries too far.

---

[57] Art. 2 of the Lisbon Treaty, where 'justice' as one of the EU values is listed up.
[58] Research Group on EC Private Law, *Principles of the Existing EC Contract Law (Acquis Principles). Contract I.; Contract II.*
[59] v. Bar, Clive, Schulte-Nölke, Beale, Herre, Huet, Storme, Swann, Varul, Veneziano and Zoll (eds.), *Principles, Definitions and Model Rules of European Private Law. (DCFR).*
[60] H. Schepel, 'The European Brotherhood of Lawyers: The Reinvention of Legal Science in the Making of European Private Law Law' (2007) 32 *Law & Social Inquiry* 183–199, U. Mattei and F. Nicola, 'A 'Social Dimension' in European Private Law? The Call for Setting a Progressive Agenda', (2006) 41 *New England Law Review*, pp. 1–65, p. 3, calling 'for self-critique of the role of legal academia in the process of Europeanisation of private law'.
[61] E. Clive, 'Proposal for a Common European Sales Law withdrawn', European Private Law News blog, available at: www.epln.law.ed.ac.uk/2015/01/07/proposal-for-a-common-european-sales-law-withdrawn/.
[62] COM (2015) 634 final, 9.12.15; COM (2015) 635 final, 9.12.2015.

European public opinion – if we can speak of a public opinion with regard to the discussion of the two projects – was divided over the idea of whether constitution building and civil code building at the European level is needed, feasible and useful. There are questions that deserve to be further explored with regard to the role and function of legal consciousness in the failure of the two projects. It seems as if the common heritage that unites the Member States and that allowed for building the EU sets barriers to political attempts to promote further integration against the wishes of the European peoples. The civil law codification project has yielded strong reactions among European private lawyers due to its anti-social and anti-democratic character.[63] Most of the resistance, however, came from national academia defending the national civil code as an integral part of their national identity[64] and from national governments. The debate over the DCFR and CESL never reached the broader public, at least if we equate the broader public with citizens. The Eurobarometer data shows that Europeans were always supportive of harmonisation of consumer legislation at the EU level. Resistance resulted more particularly from political elites rather than the public at large.[65] The 'zeitgeist' (Hegel and Constant) opts for social justice as enshrined to a varying degree in the Member States'

---

[63] M. W. Hesselink, 'The Politics of a European Civil Code' (2004) 10 *European Law Journal* 675-697; C. Joerges, 'Der Europäisierungsprozess als Herausforderung des Privatrechts: Plädoyer für eine neue Rechtsdisziplin', in A. Furrer (ed.), *Europäisches Privatrecht im wissenschaftlichen Diskurs* (Bern: Stämpfli, 2006), pp. 133–188, at p. 142; contributions of A. Somma, G. Vettori, St. Grundmann, N. Reich, J. Smits, F. Gomez, N. Jansen, F. Möslein, H. Muir Watt/R. Sefton-Green in H.-W. Micklitz and F. Cafaggi (eds.), *European Private Law after the Common Frame of References* (Cheltenham; Northampton, MA: Edward Elgar, 2010); Study Group on Social Justice in European Private Law, 'Social Justice in European Contract Law', 653.

[64] H. Honsell, 'Die Erosion des Privatrechts durch das Europarecht' (2008) *Zeitschrift für Wirtschaftsrecht (ZIP)* 621-630 and maybe even more forcefully in France, Y. Lequette, 'Quelques remarques à propos du projet de code civil européen de Monsieur von Bar' (2002) *Recueil Le Dalloz* 2202-2214; B. Fauvarque-Cosson, 'Faut-il un code civil européen?' (2002) *Revue Trimestrielle De Droit Civil* 463; B. Fauvarque-Cosson, 'Droit européen des contrats: première réaction au plan d'action de la Commission' (2003) *Recueil Le Dalloz* 1171-1173; Ph. Malinvaud, 'Réponse - hors délai - à la Commission européenne: à propos d'un code européen des contracts' (2002) *Recueil Le Dalloz* 2542-2551; J. Heut, 'Nous faut-il un 'euro' droit civil?' (2002) *Receuil Le Dalloz* 2611-2614 thereto also W. Wurmnest, 'Common Core, Grundregeln, Kodifikationsentwürfe, Acquis-Grundsätze – Ansätze internationaler Wissenschaftlergruppen zur Privatrechtsvereinheitlichung in Europa' (2003) *Zeitschrift für Europäisches Privatrecht* 714-744.

[65] Diez-Sanchez, 'Justice Index' Eurobarometer and the Issue of Justice'.

legal order.⁶⁶ The emergence of the European pattern of social justice is obviously not the joint product of European Constitution and European Code building, but the result of an incremental process.

1.4 The Post-Classical Move in the European Integration

It is paradigmatic for the current state of affairs that the third stage of European integration cannot be associated with a big bang, contrary to the Treaty of Rome that shaped the first stage and the Single Europe Act that set the Social into motion. Three major documents are constitutive for what is termed the post-classical move and what might be associated to the transformation of the European legal order into a neoformalistic order: the Lisbon Council 2000, the Constitutional Charter 2000 and European Governance 2002. The Lisbon Treaty from 2007 has not initiated a new social discourse, perhaps with the exception of the formal integration of the Charter of Fundamental Rights into the EU legal order. The economic and the Eurozone crisis, however, have set their own agenda. In the establishment of the Banking Union, the contours of a new economic constitution emerges, which upgrades finance and downgrades the Social.

All three documents, strictly speaking, are not legally binding. Legalism is set aside in favour of politics. Their impact, however, is even more palpable than many articles that made their way into the treaties, such as the competence rules on social dialogue or on consumer policy. The first document is the 'The Presidential Conclusions' of the European Council in Lisbon in March 2000, where the heads of the then 17 Member States (without the 10 new member states and without Croatia) were responding to 'a quantum shift resulting from globalisation and the challenges of a new knowledge-driven economy'.⁶⁷ The Lisbon Council indicates the move towards economic efficiency *and* social inclusion as key paradigms for the new millennium. One might wonder as to the extent to which it is linked to the accession of the new Member States, namely the potential impact on the labour force and on the EU budget, if a proper redistributive approach were taken. The Lisbon Council promotes economics and social inclusion. The second document, formally unrelated, but politically strongly interrelated with the Lisbon

---

⁶⁶ B. Constant, 'De la Liberté des brochures, des pamphlets et des journaux', in Alfred Roulin (ed.), *Œuvres* (Paris: Gallimard, 1957), pp. 1219–1243.
⁶⁷ The Lisbon Strategy of 2000, para. 1.

Council, is the adoption of the Charter of Fundamental Rights in December 2000 by the European Parliament, the Council and the Commission. This is the prolongation of the integration through law saga, now via constitutionalisation through rights. Economic efficiency is to be counterbalanced through fundamental and human rights. However, the rights holder is not the individual of the nineteenth or twentieth century. The individual is a placeholder, not an end in itself. She is characterised by her representativeness.[68] The third document is the 2002 White Paper of the European Commission on 'European Governance', meant to 'fac[e] a real paradox. On the one hand, Europeans want them to find solutions to the major problems confronting our societies. On the other hand, people increasingly distrust institutions and politics or are simply not interested in them' (preamble). This is a thin version of French intellectualism.[69] Governance brings politics into the management of the European integration process. The three documents together unite economics (Lisbon Summit), law (Charter of Fundamental Rights) and politics (Governance). The new institutional and 'constitutional' structure is currently challenged by the measures taken through the EU, Member States and the Troika, to manage the repercussions on the economic and social crisis.

1.4.1 *The Lisbon Council, Economic Efficiency and Social Inclusion*

The Lisbon Council 2000 marked the break-even point in the further development of the European legal order in general, and the Social in particular. It is here that the EU developed its rhetoric on the EU becoming 'the most competitive and most dynamic knowledge-based economy'. The Lisbon Council 2000 must be regarded as the contemporary backbone of EU policy, at least the one which is favoured and advocated for by the European Commission. It has found its way into the reasoning of the ECJ.[70] The 'new economic approach' is deeply anchored in the Lisbon Agenda. Not only does it put competition law under pressure, but the new economic approach affects all policy fields, including social policy and consumer policy. Its political importance

---

[68] Part II. 3.1 below.
[69] K. A. Armstrong, 'Civil Society and the White Paper – Bridging or Jumping the Gaps?', in C. Joerges, Y. Mény and J. H. H. Weiler (eds.), 'Mountain or Molehill? A Critical Appraisal of the Commission White Paper on Governance' (2001) *Jean Monnet Working Paper* No. 6, 119.
[70] S. Smismans, 'From Harmonization to Co-ordination? EU law in the Lisbon Governance Architecture' (2011) 18 *Journal of European Public Policy* 504–524.

comes close to the Schuman declaration. In the presidential conclusion of the Lisbon Council decision we find the following statement:

> An effective framework for ongoing review and improvement, based on the Internal Market Strategy endorsed by the Helsinki Council, *is also essential if the full benefits of market liberalization are to be reaped* [emphasis added]. Moreover, fair and uniformly applied competition and state aid rules are essential for ensuring that businesses can thrive and operative effectively on a level playing field in the internal market.[71]

The renewed paradigm shift, from the Internal Market to globalisation, yielded the need to respond to social concerns. The new formula found is *social inclusion*:

> The European social model, with its developed systems of social protection, must underpin the transformation to the knowledge economy. However, these systems *need to be adapted as part of an active welfare state* to ensure that work pays, to secure their long-term sustainability in the face of an ageing population, *to promote social inclusion and gender equality*, and to provide quality health services [emphasis added].[72]

The promotion of *social inclusion* responds to *social exclusion*. Those citizens, workers, consumers who are not able to meet the challenges resulting from the increased competitive pressure in the labour and the consumer market run the risk of being cut off from the labour market and the consumer market. Since 2000, the European Union has developed and adopted a huge amount of policy documents that are meant to fight social exclusion. Without explicitly saying so, the agenda recognises the failure of 'a better life through increased choice'. It calls for active political involvement in looking after those who have fallen behind and who have not acquired the necessary capabilities. The paradigm shift in consumer policy is relevant far beyond consumer policy. It explains the spirit behind *Viking, Laval* and now *Aget Iraklis*.[73] The Communication from the Commission to the European Parliament, the Council, the Economic and Social Committee and the Committee of the Regions on a consumer policy strategy 2002–2006 transformed the Lisbon mandate into a concrete objective.[74] Social exclusion shall be overcome through 'access', 'knowledge' and 'investment in people':

---

[71] The Lisbon Strategy of 2000, para. 16.
[72] The Lisbon Strategy of 2000, para. 31.
[73] Part II. 2.2.
[74] OJ No. C 137, 8.6.2002, pp. 2, for a full comparison between the language of the Lisbon Agenda and the Consumer Policy 2002–2006, H.-W. Micklitz, 'The Targeted Full

Different means of *access* must prevent from info-exclusion. The combat against illiteracy must be reinforced. Special attention must be given to disabled people ... The new *knowledge* based society offers tremendous potential for reducing social exclusions ... At the same time, it brings a risk of an ever widening-gap between those who have access to the new knowledge, and those who are excluded ... *Investing in people* and developing an active and dynamic welfare state will be crucial both to Europe's place in the knowledge economy and for ensuring that the emergence of this new economy does not compound the existing problems of unemployment, social exclusion and poverty [emphasis added].[75]

Condensed in a nutshell, the major paradigm shift results from the welfare state to the market state, from social redistribution to social inclusion, from social justice to access justice. It has to be recalled that proclaiming the need for adapting the welfare state to the increased international competitiveness results from a unanimous policy declaration by the heads of the states. This is not just a Commission policy instrument. The Lisbon Agenda has been agreed upon at the highest political level in consultation with the president of the European Parliament. For our purposes, the question is not whether the Lisbon Agenda was successful or not;[76] the focus is rather put on the long-term paradigm shift of key parameters of the European legal order. The Lisbon Agenda requests a transformation of the welfare state, an adjustment of welfare measures to meet the challenges of increased international competition. Even Agriculture and Structural Funds must provide a fair return principle.[77] This exactly is what is behind the formula of the 'market state'. Under such a perspective, it needs only to go one step further to promote social inclusion instead of social distribution. International competition puts pressure on the labour market, and

---

Harmonisation Approach: Looking behind The Curtain', in G. Howells and R. Schulze (eds.), *Modernising and Harmonising Consumer Contract Law* (München: Sellier European Law Publishers, 2009), pp. 47–86, in particular the table at p. 80.

[75] The Lisbon Strategy of 2000, paras. 9 (access), 32 (knowledge), 24 (investment).

[76] In terms of promoting growth and increasing employment it was not a success, Commission Staff Working Document, Lisbon Strategy evaluation document, SEC(2010) 114 final, 2.2.2010.

[77] Agricultural assistance to new Member States was much curtailed, and efforts to modernise the CAP got momentum. Structural funds evolved towards a logic of 'everybody gets something,' which comes close to the fair return principle. The new policy departed from former emphasis on developing regions. They became another instrument of efficiency, which culminated with the introduction of macroeconomic conditionality in the aftermath of the Eurozone crisis. If a Member State breaches the Six Pack and the instructions given in the European semester, they might lose their access to structural funds.

investment is needed to keep or include people in the labour market with such a policy turning against redistributing capital among the employed. The political objective is no longer social distributive justice but access justice. How the paradigm shift affects the substance of labour law, non-discrimination law and consumer law will have to be demonstrated later on.

The shift in social policy required new means for its implementation. The Lisbon Council relied heavily on the Open Method for Co-Ordination (OMC),[78] which was already introduced in the Treaty of Amsterdam 1999, but which needed to be developed. The Head of the States recognised OMC as the major tool to achieve 'social inclusion'. The OMC operates in those areas of the social policy where the European Union has no competences – for example, in the mainland of Labour Law. National governments remain the key actors, able to control the process. The OMC does not produce binding results. Indeed, the exclusion of the ECJ was vital for the establishment of the OMC. OMC is far removed from legalism. The European Commission manages a comprehensive website on ongoing activities under the OMC. The evaluation of the Lisbon Strategy in 2010 provides for a detailed account of what has been achieved through the OMC and where the OMC has failed. On top of this, there is a rich academic debate on the success or failure of the OMC; on its practical effects; on the role and function of Member States, the European Commission and NGO's; and on the impact of the OMC on European integration 'without law'.[79]

Through the 2002 White Paper on European Governance, the European Commission generalised the overall idea behind the OMC to use political cooperation outside treaty competences. The debate reached the European Civil Code project in that leading academics were

---

[78] Information on the OMC and its cycles is available at: http://ec.europa.eu/invest-in-research/coordination/coordination01_en.htm#1.

[79] Substantiated analysis of the OMC and its potential for the EU (contract law), D. M. Trubek and L. G. Trubek, 'Hard and Soft Law in the Construction of Social Europe: the Role of the Open Method of Co-ordination' (2005) *European Law Journal* 343–364; and engagement of N. Reich with their arguments, '"Reflexive Contract Governance in the EU'- David Trubek's Contribution to a More Focused Approach to EU Contract Legislation', in G. de Búrca, C. Kilpatrick and J. Scott (eds.), *Critical Legal Perspectives on Global Governance; Liber amicorum David M. Trubek* (Oxford: Hart Publishing, 2014), pp. 273–294. Höpner and Schäfer, 'Embeddedness and Regional Integration', 439, concede early successes; in the same vein under consideration of the situation before and after the crisis, J. Zeitlin and B. Venhercke, *Socialising the European Semester? Economic Governance and Social Policy Considerations in Europe 2020*, Swedish Institute for European Policy Studies 2014:7.

promoting OMC as a possible alternative to the European Civil Code project. One of the key figures was the late advocate general Walter van Gerven, who initiated the Ius Commune project. Contrary to the prevailing opinion that favoured top-down regulation via the adoption of a European Civil Code or something similar, the Ius Commune project advocated a bottom-up approach, through convergence via denser cooperation and exchange between courts beyond national borders.[80] This comes close to pragmatism. The European Commission never provided support for van Gerven's initiative. This is all the more astonishing, as the European Commission only half-heartedly supported the European Civil Code project. In the meanwhile, a whole series of textbooks have been published, none of which received any funding from the European Commission.[81] More implicitly than explicitly, 'governance' has made its way into European private law.[82] This is documented in consumer law and non-discrimination law, where the potential of European governance remains under-explored.[83]

The last document that underpins the post-classical move is the Charter on Fundamental Rights. Adopted nine months after the Lisbon Agenda in a solemn declaration at the end of 2000, it has no direct link to the agenda. Indeed, the text does not refer to human rights or fundamental rights. The charter counterbalances the efficiency paradigm through the values enshrined in fundamental and human rights. The integration of the charter into the Treaty of Lisbon was required to boost the preparedness of the ECJ to give whatever conflict came before it a human rights and fundamental rights outlook. Today, more than 50 per cent of all ECJ cases are said to contain a reference to the Charter.[84]

---

[80] W. v. Gerven, 'Needed: A Method of Convergence for Private Law', in Furrer (ed.), *Europäisches Privatrecht im wissenschaftlichen Diskurs*, pp. 437–460 and F. Cafaggi, 'Rethinking Private Regulation in the European Regulatory Space', in F. Cafaggi (ed.), *Reframing Self-Regulation in European Private Law* (Alphen aan den Rijn: Kluwer Law International, 2006), pp. 3–75.

[81] For an overview of the Ius Commune Casebooks for the Common Law of Europe (D. Droshout ed.), see www.bloomsburyprofessional.com/uk/series/ius-commune-case books-for-the-common-law-of-europe/?SeriesName=Ius+Commune+Casebooks+for+th e+Common+Law+of+Europe&SeriesFullTitle=Ius+Commune+Casebooks+for+the+Co mmon+Law+of+Europe/.

[82] Cafaggi and Muir-Watt (eds.), *Making European Private Law*; F. Cafaggi and H. Muir-Watt (eds.), *The Regulatory Function of European Private Law* (Cheltenham: Edward Elgar, 2009).

[83] H. Collins, 'Discrimination, Equality and Social Inclusion' (2003) 66 *The Modern Law Review* 16–43. See also Part III. 2.5, 3.5, 4.5.

[84] M. Safjan and D. Düsterhaus, 'A Union of Effective Judicial Protection: Addressing a Multi-level Challenge through the Lens of Art 47 CFREU' (2014) 33 *Yearbook of European Law* 3–40.

The ongoing 'contitutionalisation' of labour law, non-discrimination law and consumer law[85] through fundamental and human rights before national and European courts has led to a fierce academic debate. The 'believers' understand fundamental rights and human rights as a means to counterbalance the global power of economic efficiency in the post-nation-state area, to lay down the foundations of a global constitution and to guarantee justice through fundamental rights.[86] Academic critiques, in contrast, question the use and usefulness of human rights and fundamental rights to remedy the vanishing social values of the European legal order, and underpin the need to separate the constitutional order from the private law order as two semi-detached houses – or even more fundamentally claim that fundamental/human rights and justice are different and have to be kept distinct.[87] In Part III it will have to be shown that European access justice is much more than constitutionlisation of private law through human and fundamental rights.

1.4.2 Constitutional Standstill and Political Move to Financial Inclusion

The current situation appears to be a standstill, at least if one uses the development of EU integration via extending the powers of the EU in social matters as the decisive yardstick.[88] The Treaty of Nice, which was meant to give the enlarged EU a new institutional structure, turned out to be a complete failure. Minor amendments were introduced in the

---

[85] O. O. Cherednychenko, *Fundamental Rights, Contract Law and the Protection of the Weaker Party: A Comparative Analysis of the Constitutionalisation of the Contract Law, with Emphasis on Risky Financial Transactions* (München: Sellier. European Law Publishers, 2007); C. Mak, *Fundamental Rights in European Contract Law. A Comparison of the Impact of Fundamental Rights on Contractual Relationships in Germany, the Netherlands, Italy and England* (Alphen aan den Rijn: Kluwer Law International, 2008); Ciacchi, Brüggemeier and Comandé (eds.), *Fundamental Rights and Private Law in the European Union*.

[86] M. Kumm, 'The Moral Point of Constitutional Pluralism: Defining the Domain of Legitimate Institutional Civil Disobedience and Conscientious Objection', in J. Dickson and P. Eleftheriadis (eds.), *Philosophical Foundations of European Union Law* (Oxford: Oxford University Press, 2012), pp. 216–246; A. Somek, 'The Preoccupation with Rights and the Embrace of Inclusion: A Critique', in D. Kochenov, G. de Búrca and A. Williams (eds.), *Europe's Justice Deficit?* (Oxford: Hart Publishing, 2015), pp. 295–310 with a reply from A. Williams, 'A reply to Somek', in Kochenov, de Búrca and Williams (eds.), *Europe's Justice Deficit?*, pp. 311–318.

[87] Critical with regard to the constitutionalisation of private law; Collins, 'The Constitutionalization of European Private Law as a Path to Social Justice'.

[88] I do not deal with the institutional amendments; see I. Pernice and S. Hindelang, 'Potenziale europäischer Politik nach Lissabon – Europapolitische Perspektiven für Deutschland, seine Institutionen, seine Wirtschaft und seine Bürger nach dem Inkrafttreten des Vertrags von Lissabon' (2010) 21 *Europäische Zeitschrift für Wirtschaftsrecht* 407–413.

field of social policy. Art. 13 (2) (Art. 19 TFEU) grants the European Union a stronger role in the field of equal treatment, and Art. 137 (2). Art. 153 TFEU allows the Council to unanimously decide on the extension of the cooperation procedure (Art. 251/ 294 TFEU) to the protection against termination, as well as to rules on the representation and collective defence of the interests of workers and employers. The integration of the OMC was envisaged under Art. I-14 (4) of the European Constitution, but did not receive the support of the Member States. The Lisbon Treaty does not bring about much change in labour and consumer law.[89] Changes did not result from a different set of 'Leitlinien' in Art. 2 TFEU (new) and Art. 3 (3) TFEU, or from the extension of standing against directly effective legal acts, Art. 263 (4) TFEU, but from the formal integration of the EU Charter of Fundamental Rights. Art. 3 (3) TFEU introduced the concept of a 'highly competitive social market economy'. Whether or not this reference is apt to support the development of a genuine European Social Model, without any further shift of competences from the Member States to the European Union, is subject to controversy.[90]

Underneath constitution building, the established mechanisms of law-making and rule protection remained by and large unaffected. The European Commission, the Council, and the European Parliament continued to adopt secondary community law. The ECJ produced ever more judgments. The European Commission discovered OMC as a new form of competence creep, and business benefitted from the modes of new governance in labour, non-discrimination and consumer law. The consequences are far-reaching. As a clear institutional and constitutional framework is missing, social conflicts migrate to the European Court. There is a dramatic increase of preliminary references in non-discrimination and consumer law, albeit fewer in labour law. Knowledge of most of these developments remain within the inner circle of European and national lawyers. From time to time, however,

---

[89] But not in consumer law; H.-W. Micklitz, N. Reich, St. Weatherill, 'EU Treaty Revision and Consumer Protection' (2004) 27 *Journal of Consumer Policy* 367-399.

[90] For a rather pessimistic perspective, Joerges, 'A Renaissance of the European Economic Constitution'; for an attempt that the introduced changes do not undermine the ordo-liberal European Economic Constitution, J. Drexl, 'Wettbewerbsverfassung', in A. v. Bogdandy and J. Bast (eds.), *Europäisches Verfassungsrecht*, 2nd ed. (Berlin: Springer, 2009), pp. 905-960; for a more optimistic view, D. Damjanovic and B. de Witte, 'Welfare Integration through EU Law: The Overall Picture in the Light of the Lisbon Treaty', in U. Neergaard, R. Nielsen, L. M. Roseberry (eds.), *Integrating Welfare Functions into EU Law. From Rome to Lisbon* (Copenhagen: Djøf Publishing, 2009), pp. 53-96.

the ECJ comes to public attention,[91] mainly when its judgments are accused of having been decided ultra vires, or have neglected the social dimension in the interpretation of Community law.[92] There are few judgments of the ECJ taken in the social domain that have raised as much concern as *Viking*,[93] *Laval*[94] and *Aget Iraklis*[95] in employment law, or *Mangold*[96], *Kücükdevici*[97] and *Test Achats*[98] in non-discrimination law. They are criticised because the ECJ is said to undermine national autonomy in setting social standards and, even more so, in deconstructing the achievements of labour movements. There is no judgment of the ECJ in the field of consumer law that has ever raised a similar concern, perhaps with the exception of *Sanchez*[99] and *Mohamed Aziz*.[100] In *Sanchez* the ECJ held that the Directive 85/374 on product liability provides for full harmonisation, what was fiercely rejected by the Member States. In *Mohamed Aziz*, the ECJ plays a different and more promising role, at least seen through the eyes of the social justice advocates. Overall there is no clear line in the case law of the ECJ, whose judgments are sometimes for the better (more social) and sometimes for the worse (more market liberal).[101]

The economic crisis and the Eurozone crisis has led to distortions and disruptions in the EU, in particular between the northern and the southern member states, which have their own understanding of social justice, of labour, non-discrimination and consumer law.[102] The measures taken by the Troika, Member States and the EU to remedy the negative impact of the crisis on over-indebted Member States are

---

[91] Most prominently the public attack by the former president of the Federal Republic of Germany and former president of the German Constitutional Court; Roman Herzog, 'Stoppt den Europäischen Gerichtshof' in *Frankfurter Allgemeine Zeitung*, 8.9.2008, pp. 8. 'Stop the European Court of Justice'.

[92] Contributions in H.-W. Micklitz and B. de Witte (eds.), *The European Court of Justice and the autonomy of the Member States* (Cambridge; Antwerp: Intersentia, 2012).

[93] Case C-438/05, *The International Transport Workers' Federation und The Finnish Seamen's Union*.

[94] Case C-341/05, *Laval un Partneri*.

[95] Case C-201/15, *AGET Iraklis* [2016] ECR I-000.

[96] Case C-144/04, *Mangold* [2005] ECR I-9981; Case C-411/05, *Palacios de la Villa* [2007] I-8531.

[97] Case C-555/07, *Kücükdeveci* [2010] ECR I-00365.

[98] Opinion of Advocate General Kokott – Case C-236/09, *Association Belge des Consommateurs Test-Achats and Others* [2011] ECR I-773.

[99] Case C-183/00, *González Sánchez*.

[100] Case C-415/11, *Aziz*.

[101] For a nuanced account S. Weatherill, *Contract Law of the Internal Market* (Cambridge: Intersentia, 2016), Chapter 4, pp. 95.

[102] Documented in Diez-Sanchez, 'Justice Index' Eurobarometer and the Issue of Justice'.

putting pressure on social distributive justice. The establishment of the Banking Union – if not triggered then legitimised[103] when ECB President Draghi in July 2012 said, 'Within our mandate, the ECB is ready to do whatever it takes to preserve the euro'[104] – stands out as a symbol that shifts the focus from competition as the leading paradigm of the EU constitution to financial stability.[105] Much of the fierce critique raised against the Troika is directed towards the macro economic effects of the austerity policy that hits the South ('the poor') and privileges the North ('the rich'). At the micro level, the conflict culminates in the mobilisation of property rights in private law relations for the sake of justice. In a whole series of references, in particular from Spain, the ECJ granted the right to housing constitutional standing that corrects the detrimental effects of contractually founded foreclosure.[106] Those who can no longer pay their mortgages because they lost their jobs in the aftermath of the crises cannot be evicted from their homes. However sympathetic that might be and how it may even help the ECJ to increase its image around Europe as a court of last resort that protects social rights, the maintenance of private law relations might be disruptive and counterproductive from a macro economic perspective.[107] The latter argument was put forward by the Spanish Tribunal Supremo, but clearly rejected by the ECJ in the follow-on judgment *Gutiérrez Naranjo*.[108] To put it in blunt language: the overall objective of financial stability might require measures to the detriment of both the creditors and the debtors that are not in line with private law doctrine. The

---

[103] H.-W. Micklitz, 'The Internal Market and the Banking Union', in S. Grundmann and H.-W. Micklitz (eds.) *The European Banking Union Beacon for Advanced Integration or Death-Knell for Democracy* (Oxford: Hart Publishing, 2018 forthcoming).

[104] President M. Draghi's speech is available at: www.ecb.europa.eu/press/key/date/2012/html/sp120726.en.html.

[105] S. Grundmann, 'Europäisches Wirtschaftsrecht im Wandel – von der Wettbewerbsunion zur Finanzunion', in B. Limperg, J. Bormann, A. C. Filges, M. L. Graf-Schlicker and H. Prütting (eds.), *Recht im Wandel deutscher und europäischer Rechtspolitik. Festschrift 200 Jahre Carl Heymanns Verlag* (Köln: Carl Heymanns Verlag, 2015), pp. 193–209.

[106] F. Della Negra, 'The Uncertain Development of the Case Law on Consumer Protection in Mortgage Enforcement Proceedings: Sánchez Morcillo and Kušionová' (2015) 52 *Common Market Law Review* 1009–1032.

[107] With regard to the impact of the economic and the Euro-crisis on consumers, Micklitz and Domurath (eds.), *Consumer Debt and Social Exclusion in Europe*; also e.g. Bank of America's shareholders' suit for having taken over Merrill Lynch at the height of the crisis here: http://dealbook.nytimes.com/2012/09/28/bank-of-america-to-pay-2-43-billion-to-settle-class-action-over-merrill-deal/?_r=0

[108] Joined Cases C-154/15, C-307/15 and C-308/15, *Gutiérrez Naranjo* [2013] ECR I-000.

protection of constitutionalised property rights might endanger financial stability. This is what the ECJ decided in compensation claims of private bondholders against the European Commission.[109] In the *Mohamed Aziz* saga, the creditor is in most cases the Caixa Bank, which has been bailed out by the Spanish government. The Spanish government, the Spanish state and the Spanish taxpayer, then, has to raise the money not only to save the banks but to finance the right to housing. One might wonder whether this is the fairest solution, as taxes are paid according to income levels. *De Schutter* and *Salomon* have proposed to tie macro and micro together with a procedure that respects social human rights.[110]

The political answer of the EU to the growing risk of consumer overindebtedness or even consumer insolvency is an ever stronger pursuit of financial inclusion. It took a while before the catchword reached the political fora. At the time of the Lisbon Council in 2000, the economic environment looked much more stable than today.[111] Already, the first directives on consumer credit were an instrument to promote financial inclusion, although the term was not used. The 1999 Commission's Financial Services Action Plan mentioned the importance for consumers to obtain safe and transparent basic financial products in an integrated financial market.[112] The first EU document recognising the overall political and economic advantages of including the citizens in the financial market more explicitly, was the 2005 Commission's White Paper on Financial Services Policy 2005–2010.[113] Starting only in 2007/2008 was the term 'financial inclusion' employed in various documents, like the FIN-USE annual report 2007/

---

[109] Case C-105/15 P, *Mallis and Malli v. Commission and the ECB* [2016] ECR I-000; similar ECHR, *Grainger v. the UK*, application no. 34940/10, for a comment M. Waibel, 'ECHR leaves Northern Rock shareholders out in the cold', available at: www.ejiltalk.org/ec hr-leaves-northern-rock-shareholders-out-in-the-cold/, for a deeper analysis K. Pistor, 'Contesting Property Rights: Towards an Integrated Theory of Institutional and System Change' (2011) 11 *Global Jurist (Frontiers)*, Article 6, 1–26; A. Mian and A. Sufi, *House of Debt* (Chicago: The University of Chicago Press, 2014) argue that a better allocation of risk between creditor and debtor would have avoided the economic crisis like the one we have experienced.

[110] O. De Schutter and M. E. Salomon, 'Economic Policy Conditionality, Socio-Economic Rights and International Legal Responsibility: The Case of Greece 2010–2015', Legal Brief prepared for the Special Committee of the Hellenic Parliament on the Audit of the Greek Debt (Debt Truth Committee), 15 June 2015, available at: http://cadtm.org/Legal-Brief-Prepared-for-the.

[111] Comparato, *The Financialisation of the Citizen*.

[112] COM(1999) 232 final, 11.05.1999, p. 8.

[113] COM(2005) 629 final, 1.12.2005.

2008.[114] The turn towards financial inclusion is reflected in the European Barometer. In 2009, the Special Eurobarometer 321 on Poverty and Social Inclusion had, for the first time, sections devoted to financial aspects.[115]

Financial inclusion might not help manage post-crisis effects, as this would require a more proactive policy with regard to consumer insolvency. However, the promotion of financial inclusion is no coincidence. Social inclusion is the answer to social discrimination through gender, race, disability, age, religion and so on. The Lisbon Agenda makes the deeper links abundantly clear. Financial inclusion is the political reaction to financial economic discrimination. This is what the crisis adds to the post-classical legal system. From now on, matters of justice have to deal with social inclusion or social discrimination and financial inclusion or economic discrimination. These measures are hard to reconcile with a legal order based on competition and private autonomy.

1.4.3 *The Post-Classical Foundations*

D. Kennedy[116] characterises the current state of private legal thought (the third globalisation) as 'neoformalism'. As he explicitly refers to legal consciousness, his findings and his analysis provide for a fruitful basis on which to develop a first understanding of what could be understood by 'post-classical'. Neoformalism is 'neo' because it transfers private law thinking to the public sector, to policies and institutions,

---

[114] Forum of User Experts in the Area of Financial Services (FIN-USE), annual reports are available at: http://ec.europa.eu/internal_market/fin-use_forum/reports/index_en.htm.

[115] Diez-Sanchez, 'Justice Index Eurobarometer and the Issue of Justice', Special EB 321 on Poverty and Social Inclusion. One of these sections, 'Financial Exclusion', concluded that of 'Europeans with difficulties paying bills on time: close to three quarters of these citizens (72 per cent) find it difficult to get a mortgage, 64 per cent find it difficult to get a loan, and 55 per cent have difficulties getting a credit card. The unemployed: seven out of ten unemployed Europeans (70 per cent) have difficulties getting a mortgage; a further 58 per cent have problems getting a loan and 47 per cent find it difficult to get a credit card.' The section 'Access to financial services' concluded that 'Europeans believe in fair but strictly regulated access to financial services for poor people. According to 88 per cent poor people should have free personalised financial advice, given by an official source. Furthermore, eight in ten feel that every financial institution should allow anyone to open a basic bank account and 76 per cent are of the view that unemployed people who want to start up a business activity should have easier access to loans. At the same time, 86 per cent are of the view that credit institutions should check the financial capacity of potential borrowers much more carefully and there is slightly less support for giving poor people access to interest free loans (56 per cent 'agree' versus 38 per cent 'disagree').

[116] Kennedy, 'Three Globalizations of Law and Legal Thought'.

without taking into account that 'policy analysis' is structurally bound to a particular policy subject and/or to a particular object (e.g. a sector of the economy), and that coherence or something similar can be achieved, if at all, only in narrow policy fields that are kept distinct from overarching influences from other policy fields. This fits nicely with Luhmann and Teubner,[117] who stress the irreversibility of the differentiation and fragmentation of society or with K. Tuori[118] who uses the metaphor of the 'many constitutions of the European Union' or L. Niglia[119] who stresses 'pluralism and European private law'.

The three non-binding documents (the Lisbon Agenda, the Charter 2000 (now integrated into the treaty) and the 2002 White Paper on Governance) read together exemplify a major change in the European integration process, not only at the surface level but also at the foundational level. Neoformalist European private law does not resemble a legal *system* anymore. It should be understood as a legal *order*.[120] There is no, or very limited coherence, not even in between the various policy-driven fields of European private law. Non-discrimination law and consumer law are often conceived of as a new domains of law that can and should be governed by a particular rationale. However, a more detailed analysis of secondary EU law will reveal that it might be even misleading to understand non-discrimination law or consumer law as a coherent legal order. There is no coherence given the forms of discrimination and the identities to be protected.[121] In private law beyond the nation-state, there are 'many private legal orders' – to paraphrase Tuori – that are only loosely knit together via access justice. The relationship between access justice and the pluralilty of legal orders will have to be investigated. The key question is whether access justice can serve as the bracket that cuts accrross the functionally differentiated areas of European private law. This, however, remains for Part III of the book.

---

[117] T. Prien, 'Under the Spell of Society. System Theoretical Perspective of Justice', in W. Matiaske, S. Costa and H. Brunkhorst (eds.), *Contemporary Perspectives on Justice* (München: Rainer Hampp Verlag, 2010), pp. 41–68, at p. 47.

[118] Tuori, *European Constitutionalism*, p. 10; Tuori, 'European Social Constitution: Between Solidarity and Access Justice', pp. 371–400.

[119] L. Niglia (ed.), *Pluralism and European Private Law* (Oxford: Hart Publishing, 2013), in particular his contribution 'The Double Life of Pluralism in Europe', pp. 13–28, as well as M. W. Hesselink 'Pluralism in a New Key – Between Plurality and Normativity', pp. 249–260.

[120] Dickson, 'Towards a Theory of European Union Legal Systems' against Culver and Giudice, 'Not a System but an Order'.

[121] Xenidis, 'Shaking the Normative Foundations of EU Equality Law'.

What is missing, however, is an explanation of the post-classical move, a deeper philosophical foundation similar to the ones used for making the intellectual history of social justice accessible in the three Member States. The philosophical foundations of EU cannot be found in J. Dickson and P. Eleftheriadis, contrary to the ambitious title of the book.[122] Looking into transformations of the economy, technology and society helps to explain what is going on in the nation-states and the EU, but does not really bring clarity on the deeper foundations of the now Europeanised intellectual history.[123] M. Reimann provides two reasons as to why American law is ahead of the EU:[124] (1) 'dumb luck', the advantage of global lawyering fell into the American lap'; and (2) much deeper and much more sophisticated, the move from classical to post-classical law, which is claimed to be in harmony with broader intellectual trends. The continental European tradition is still deeply rooted in universalism and rationalism which stands behind the classical concept of law and which goes back to scientific and philosophical developments from the seventeenth century onwards.[125] In this intellectual climate, knowledge is objective, absolute, universal and consistent. Over the twentieth century this conception of knowledge was overtaken in natural science through Einstein and Heisenberg,[126] and in philosophy through Nietzsche and Heidegger. Knowledge is not hierarchical, but the result of flat networks. In law, Sousa Santos[127] denies the existence of one objective truth (or law) and advocates pluralism of competing orders and values.

The cracks in the classical continental systems were visible and voiced before World War I and even more forcefully in the 20 years between the two world wars. Raymond Aron, the French sociologist and Fritz Stern, the legal historian agreed in a public debate held in 1979

[122] Micklitz, 'Philosophical Foundations of European Union Law'.
[123] H.-W. Micklitz and Y. Svetiev, 'The Transformation(s) of Private Law', in H.-W. Micklitz, Y. Svetiev and G. Comparato (eds.), 'European Regulatory Private Law – The Paradigm Tested' (2014) EUI-ERC Working Paper No. 4, 69–97.
[124] Reimann, 'The American Advantage in Global Lawyering', 32–33.
[125] A. Somek, 'Zwei Welten der Rechtslehre und der Philosophie des Rechts' (2016) 71 Juristen Zeitung 481–486.
[126] H.-P. Dürr (ed.), Physik und Transzendenz. Die Großen Physiker unserer Zeit über ihre Begegnung mit dem Wunderbaren (Bern et al.: Scherz, 1986), cited according to the renewed edition (Bad Essen: Driediger, 2010), with contributions of D. Bohm, N. Bohr, M. Born, A. Einstein, W. Heisenberg, P. Jordan, W. Pauli, M. Planck, E. Schrödinger, C. F. v. Weizsäcker.
[127] B. de Sousa Santos, 'Law: A Map of Misreading: Toward a Postmodern Conception of Law' (1987) 14 Journal of Law and Society 279–302, at 282.

that at the turn of the twentieth century one could have expected that Germany would leave its footprint on the twentieth century, though not through two world wars.[128] This would have implied that Germany might and could have been at the forefront of the move from the classical to the post-classical law.[129] Indeed, Reimann's references to key figures in natural sciences and philosophy seem to be in line with the statement. Taking France and Germany as paradigmatic for the development in other continental European legal systems, it seems safe to argue that the subterranean and surface cracks in the classical tradition, exploded by 1968, shattered the classical continental legal tradition, but did not lead to a turnaround. The move from the classical to the post-classical occurred silently and less dramatically via and through the building of Europe – through law, through governance (without law) and beyond law.

Europe and European legal scholarship did not reconnect to the early beginnings of the post-classical move after World War II. In the search for a European future, Europe looked into its past, into the deeper cultural foundations that united the legal systems not only of the continent but also of the common law. One might term this a form of revitalisation of the classical understanding. Wieacker's work 'Voraussetzungen europäischer Rechtskultur' ('Foundations of European Legal Culture')[130] focuses on the common European legal culture. The title implies a community of Europe, with roots in history and in law. Thus, Wieacker adheres to the tradition of *ius commune*, to a concept of law uniting legal history and comparative law – in the European legal culture. R. Zimmermann made a powerful plea for the importance of the *ius commune* as a basis and source of knowledge of European private law, codified continental law *and* common law:[131]

In defiance of all differences of modern legal dogmatics, European contract law is at the end of the day from the same mould. Over centuries lawyers have worked/operated on the basis of the same rules, institutions and ways of thinking, and everywhere the profession has been shaped by the same values and philosophical currents.... England has to be considered as a part of Europe as well.

---

[128] E. Jäckel, *Das deutsche Jahrhundert: Eine historische Bilanz* (Stuttgart: Deutsche Verlags-Anstalt, 1996), review by A. Baring, 'Wem gehört das Jahrhundert?', Frankfurter Allgemeine Zeitung, 29.01.1997, No. 24, pp. 12, available at: www.faz.net/aktuell/feuilleton/politik/rezension-sachbuch-wem-gehoert-das-jahrhundert-11304465.html

[129] Kantorowicz' doctrine of free law (Freirechtsschule) instead of Savigny's Historical School.

[130] Wieacker, 'Foundations of European Legal Culture'.

[131] Zimmermann, 'Heard melodies are sweet, but those unheard are sweeter ... ', 173.

If we have entered a new world, one where the *lex geometrica* sustains but not as the sole parameter, instead supplemented by the *lex 'relativa'*, then we need to develop a different understanding of why Europe serves as a laboratory for the post-nation-state and for the post-nation-state legal order. Isaac Newton was not only the builder of the new world of physics, he was also an alchemist.[132] At the end of Part II, I will elaborate the potential that the EU offers through the rationality test and the concept of shared responsibilities. The risks are enshrined in the fragmented status-related justice and the divide between European and national consciousnesses.[133]

---

[132] 'Isaac Newton's occult studies', available at: https://en.wikipedia.org/wiki/Isaac_Newton%27s_occult_studies.
[133] Conclusions under Part II. 3.

2 The Impact of EU Law on Employment, Non-Discrimination and Consumer Law

Whilst the reconstruction of the three stages of integration helps us to understand the bigger picture, namely what is behind the different moves and perhaps a tentative explanation of the deeper foundations, it now comes time to analyse the concrete impact of the EU law on the three major fields of analysis where the new justice paradigm is located in the European private law. The three stages of European integration are translated into the evolution of labour, non-discrimination and consumer law from 1957 until today. The first 30 years into 'the building process governed by primary EU law, the heydays of the Social into labour, non-discrimination and consumer law and the post-classical move in European integration after 2000 into the shift from social protection to the law of the labour and consumer market. The analysis distinguishes between labour and non discrimination law on the hand, and consumer law on the other. Each of the two separate subsections concludes with a summary of the post-classical labour, non-discrimination and consumer law. This burdensome analysis is crucial in understanding the transformation from protective social regulation to regulation that aims at the extablishment of a European law of the labour and consumer market *society*. It is this double move towards the market and the society beyond the market that explains the emergence of access justice and – in its most promising outlook – societal justice.

2.1 A Chart for an Overview of Primary and Secondary EU Law

Table 7 is based on the three major steps of the socio-economic and political background of social justice in the EU: the formative years of the EU, where the Social did not play a prominent role and where

Table 7

	Labour PEUL	Labour SEUL	Non-Discrim PEUL	Non-Discrim SEUL	Consumer PEUL	Consumer SEUL
1957 Rome (57) Economic constitution	Art. 100 (Art. 113 TFEU) Art. 119 (Art. 141 TCE, 157 TFEU) Art. 235 (Art. 352 TFEU)	Dir. 75/129 (92/50 + 98/59) collective redundancies Dir. 77/187 (98/50 + 01/23) transfer of undertakings Dir. 80/987 (08/94 Insolvency protection)		Directive 75/117 EEC (equal pay for men and women) Dir. 76/207 ECC, 2002/73 (equal access to employment) Directive 79/7/EEC (ET social security) Directive 86/378/ EEC (ET social security) Directive 86/613 EEC (ET self-employed)	Art. 100 (Art. 94)	Dir 84/450 (misleading advertising) Dir. 85/577 (door step) Dir. 85/374 (product liability) Dir. 87/107 (consumer credit)
1986–1999 SEA (86) Maastricht (91) Amsterdam (99) Emergence of the Social	Art. 95 (SEA) Art. 118 a) SEA (86) Social Charter (89) Protocol on Social Policy Maastricht (91) EU Charter (2000)	Dir. 89/301 (health and safety at work) Dir. 91/533 (information on rights) Dir. 93/104 (03/88) working time	New paragraphs 3 and 4 Art 141 + Art 13 TEC (Amsterdam 99) competence to combat discrimination beyond	Directive 92/85/EEC (pregnant workers protection) Directive 96/34/EC (97/75) (parental leave) Directive 97/81/EC	Art. 95 (SEA) Art. 129 a, Art. 153, Art. 169 TFEU Art. 36 EU Charter (2000)	Dir. 90/314 (package tours) Dir. 92/59 consumer safety) Dir. 93/13 (unfair terms) Dir. 94/47 (time share)

Table 7 (cont.)

Labour PEUL	Labour SEUL	Non-Discrim PEUL	Non-Discrim SEUL	Consumer PEUL	Consumer SEUL
	Dir. 94/33 (young people) Dir. 94/45 (97/74) working council Dir. 96/71 (posting of workers)	employment (= now Art 19 TFEU) + new Title XI TEC integrating the Social Protocol Art 3(3) TEU (ex-Article 2 TEU, Amsterdam Treaty): promote equality Art 3(2) gender mainstreaming as horizontal objective Article 2 TEU: non-discrimination Articles 12 and 18 (1) TEC (now Articles 18 and 21 TFEU) Art 8 TFEU (ex Art 3 (2) TEC): equality between men and women	(98/23) (part time work) Directive 97/80/EC (on the burden of proof in cases of discrimination based on sex) Directive 2000/43 on racial equality Framework Directive 2000/78/EC (ET in employment and occupation)		Dir. 97/7 (distant sales) Dir. 98/27 (action of injunction) Dir. 99/44 (consumer sales)

2000 Lisbon Council Globalisation – 'the most competitive and dynamic knowledge-based economy'	Social Inclusion Enhancing OMC	Soft means minimum harmonisation		Promote gender equality and provide quality health services		Shift from minimum to full harmonisation Together with Consumer Strategy 2002–2006
Treaty of Nice (04) Lisbon Treaty (09) 'Social Economic Constitution' + 'EU Charter'	Art. 13 (2) (Art. 19 TFEU), Art. 137 (2) (Art. 153 TFEU) Nice (04), Lisbon (09) Leitnormen Art. 3 (3) 'social economic constitution' Art. 2 'solidarity' Art. I – 14 (4) OMC repealed	Dir. 2001/23 (rights in transfers) Dir. 2003/88 (working time) Dir. 2008/94 (insolvency of employer) Dir. 2009/38 (working council) Directive 2010/18 repealing Directive of 3 June 1996 (parental leave)	EU Charter of fundamental rights (2000) → binding since Lisbon Treaty Art 6 + Art 6 'EU shall accede ECHR' (put into question by ECJ Opinion 2/13) Art. 20 = general equality principle Art. 21: non-exhaustive list of explicit prohibitions of discrimination Art 23	Dir. 2002/73 EC amending previous Dir. 76/207 on equal treatment (def. direct/indirect discrimination) Directive 2004/113 EC on gender equality in provision of goods and services (Directive 2004/38/EC citizens and family members to move and reside freely) Dir. 2006/54 EC repealing Dir. 2002/73 on equal opportunities	Leitnormen Art. 3 (3) 'social economic constitution' Art. 2 'justice'	Dir. 2001/95 consumer safety Dir. 2002/65 (distant selling financial products) Dir. 2002/22 and 2009/136 (telecom) Dir. 2003 54 + 55, 2007/92 + 93 (energy) Dir. 2005/29 (unfair commercial practices) Dir. 2008/48 (consumer credit) Dir. 2008/122 (time share) Dir. 2009/22 (action of injunction recast)

Table 7 (cont.)

Labour PEUL	Labour SEUL	Non-Discrim PEUL	Non-Discrim SEUL	Consumer PEUL	Consumer SEUL
			Proposal 2008 against discrimination beyond the workplace (**rejected**) Directive 2010/41 ET self-employed repealing Directive 1986 Accession UN Convention on Disabilities (2010)		Dir 2011/83 (consumer rights) Dir. 2014/17 (mortgage credit) Dir 2014/92 (payment account) Dir 2015/2302 (package travel)

legislative measures required unanimity. The rise of the Social foreshadowing the Single European Act in the 1986s and 1990s demonstrates how the EU based on the scarce amendments in the treaties started mimicking the social welfare policy of the Member States. The Lisbon Agenda gave the Social a new direction and made the distinction between the welfare state regulation and the regulation of the labour and consumer market ever clearer.

The table translates the major constitutional developments (PEUL – Primary EU Law) and the specific measures taken by the EU (SEUL – Secondary EU Law) into an overview. It is meant to help the reader to locate the point at which specific measures were taken and why they are associated with a particular step in the integration process. The sheer quantity of all these treaty amendments and the legislative measures adopted is apparent.

2.2 The Impact of the Determinants on Labour and Non-Discrimination Law

The development of the substantive EU labour and non-discrimination law starts with the free movement of workers, which is one of the major achievements of the European legal order. It is only against the background of the groundbreaking case law of the ECJ that the development of labour and non-discrimination law can be understood. More narrowly the development in labour and non-discrimination law may be broken down into three major trends.

The Rome Treaty was introduced under pressure from France (Art. 119 (Art. 141, Art. 157 TFEU) on equal payment of men and women). During the negotiations of the Rome Treaty, France argued that a principle of equal pay for women and men was necessary to avoid market and competition distortions among Member States. Thus, the Rome Treaty legitimated the European Commission and the ECJ to actively promoting gender equality. A most active court and a responsive EU legislator backed by a number of treaty amendments, in particular via the Treaty of Amsterdam, took an active stand. Art. 13 (Art. 19 TFEU) and Art. 141 (3) (Art. 157 TFEU) transformed the rules on equal payment into a principle of non-discrimination which reached far beyond discrimination in labour relations, by treaty amendments and secondary community law. The role, function and reach of the non-discrimination principle in private law is subject to a controversial debate.¹ The DCFR proposed to introduce the non-discrimination principle. What could have become one of the major achievements in European private law was demoted in the political agenda, when the DCFR was transformed into the draft proposal of a Common European Sales Law. After the failure of the 2008 proposal to extend the non-discrimination principle beyond the workplace, any generalisation of the non-discrimination principle through explicit legislative action is out of reach for the time being. Despite the imperfections and inconsistencies, the gradual extension of the non-discrimination principle in ever more areas constitutes a building block in the concept of access justice (Zugangsgerechtigkeit).

The second area, the OMC, is rather broad and covers a whole range of legal issues, which demonstrate that despite all the impressive activities of the EU since the mid 1980s in the mainland of labour law, in employment law and industrial relations, intervention remains rather pointillistic. The OMC, meant to fill the competence gap, can certainly not serve as a major tool to build a social Europe. The widely felt failure to construe a European version of the social welfare state, however, is deeper. It suffices to look into the EU's legislative activities to recognise that the European drive has lost considerable impetus. If anything, it remains for the ECJ then to set a reform development in motion. The EU opens up markets for workers and fights against discrimination in access requirements, but the Member States remain responsible for the social welfare 'aftercare', for post-market distribution.²

The third relatively stable and coherent field where the EU holds competence, since the introduction of Art. 118 (a) (Art. 137, Art. 153 TFEU) into the Single European Act, is health and safety at work. The EU has engaged in considerable law-making activities that have bypassed public attention. The overall picture, however, looks rather mixed, despite explicit competence in the field. From a private law perspective, health and safety at work issues come to the fore in the case of accidents. Indeed, here, the European Commission failed to read a mandatory obligation of the employer to insure employees into

---

[1] Critical is F. J. Säcker, 'Vertragsfreiheit und Schutz vor Diskriminierung' (2006) *Zeitschrift für Europäisches Privatrecht* 1-6 and J. Basedow, 'Grundsatz der Nichtdiskriminierung im europäischen Privatrecht' (2008) *Zeitschrift für Europäisches Privatrecht* 230-251; supportive, A. S. Vandenberghe, 'The Economics of the Non-Discrimination Principle in General Contract Law' (2007) 3 *European Review of Contract Law* 410-431.

[2] R. Münch, *Die Konstruktion der Europäischen Gesellschaft. Zur Dialektik von transnationaler Integration und nationaler Desintegration* (Frankfurt a.M.: Campus Verlag, 2008), pp. 368-370.

Directive 89/381.³ In contrast to Consumer Law, the question as to who pays for accidents at work did not reach the EU level.

Three phases can be identified: coordination of national laws and policies in the shadow of the equal pay approach, European legislative activism in the aftermath of the Single European Act to build a social model and, last but not least, the decline of the European Social Model and the rise of the non-discrimination principle beyond the labour market. Coordination and legislative activism are still related to the 'classical' law, although legislative activism already embraces the post-classical in its inherent failures, which then takes shape in the EU's non-discrimination policy to demarcate between the EU and the Member States.

2.2.1 Establishing the Free Movement of Workers

The treaties of Rome introduced the free movement of workers through Art. 49 (now Art. 45 TFEU).⁴ Recital 3 of Regulation 1612/68 underlines its crucial importance:⁵

> Whereas freedom of movement constitutes a fundamental right of workers and their families; whereas mobility of labour within the Community must be one of the means by which the worker is guaranteed the possibility of improving his living and working conditions and promoting his social advancement, while helping to satisfy the requirements of the economies of the Member States; whereas the right of all workers in the Member States to pursue the activity of their choice within the Community should be affirmed.

The free movement of workers is meant to guarantee the freedom of employees, meaning persons in dependent employment. It turned into a building block of 'a better life' in Europe.⁶ The free movement of establishment in Art. 52 Treaty of Rome (Art. 49 TFEU) is aimed at self-employed persons. The freedom to provide services Art. 59 (Art. 56 TFEU) supplements the other two freedoms. All three freedoms read together have market citizens in mind, namely those who earn their living through their labour, professional qualifications or any other

---

[3] Case C-127/05, *Commission v. United Kingdom* [2007] ECR I-4619.
[4] Relationship between the free movement of workers and private law, N. Reich, *Bürgerrechte in der Europäischen Union* (Baden-Baden: Nomos, 1999), § 11, pp. 158 and the same, 'The public/private divide in European law', in H.-W. Micklitz and F. Cafaggi (eds.), *European Private Law after the Common Frame of Reference* (Cheltenham: Elgar, 2010), pp. 56–89.
[5] Regulation (EEC) No 1612/68 of the Council of 15 October 1968 on freedom of movement for workers within the Community, OJ No. L 257, 19.10.1968, p. 2.
[6] F. de Witte, *Justice in the EU*, pp. 171–173.

services to be performed in exchange for payment. The freedom of movement entails the abolition of *any discrimination based on nationality* between workers of the Member States with regard to employment, remuneration and other conditions of work and employment, subject to legitimate restrictions. 'The key to defining an autonomous role for private law within the European legal order is the theory of direct effect.'[7] The saga started with the case law on the vertical direct effect that allowed private parties to set aside restrictions based on nationality. The move towards horizontal direct effect began with *Walrave* in 1974.[8] In *Bosman*,[9] *Angonese*,[10] *Viking, Laval,* and *Olympique Lyonnais*,[11] the ECJ recognised the directly applicability of Art. 39 (Art. 45 TFEU), the freedom of movement for workers, respectively freedom of establishment in *Viking* Art. 43 (Art. 49 TFEU) and freedom of services in *Laval,* Art. 49 (Art. 56 TFEU). There is a direct line from *Walrave* to *Bosman, Agnonese,* even *Viking* and *Laval*, and finally *Olympique Lyonnais* in that the ECJ eliminated discriminatory collective agreements with the help of Articles 39, 49, 56 TFEU, against the fierce resistance of private associations and Member States. The key argument in *Wouters* deserves to be recalled:[12]

> It should be observed at the outset that compliance with Articles 52 and 59 of the Treaty is also required in the case of rules which are not public in nature but which are designed to regulate, collectively, self-employment and the provision of services. The abolition, as between Member States, of obstacles to freedom of movement for persons would be compromised if the abolition of State barriers could be neutralised by obstacles resulting from the exercise of their legal autonomy by associations or organisations not governed by public law (Case 36/74 Walrave and Koch [1974] ECR 1405, paragraphs 17, 23 and 24; Case 13/76 Dona [1976] ECR 1333, paragraphs 17 and 18; Case C-415/93 Bosman [1995] ECR I-4921, paragraphs 83 and 84, and Case C-281/98 Angonese [2000] ECR I-4139, paragraph 32).

Against the background of the gradual move towards horizontal direct effect of the free movement of workers, the right to establishment and

---

[7] Reich, 'The Public/Private Divide In European Law', p. 61.
[8] Case 36/74, *Walrave and Koch v. Association Union Cycliste Internationale and Others* [1974] ECR 1405.
[9] Case C-415/93, *Union royale belge des sociétés de football association and Others v Bosman and Others* [1995] ECR I-4921.
[10] Case C-281/98, *Angonese* [2000] ECR I-4139.
[11] Case C-438/05, *The International Transport Workers' Federation and The Finnish Seamen's Union*; Case C-341/05, *Laval un Partneri*; Case C-325/08 *Olympique Lyonnais* [2010] ECR I-02177
[12] Case C-309/99, *Wouters and Others* [2000] ECR I-1577, at para. 120.

the right to provide services, the equal pay doctrine enshrined in Art. 119/Art. 141 (Art. 157 TFEU) appears in a different light. Provided Art. 119 has horizontal direct effect, it would lay down a common standard for equal pay to men and women in employment contracts whether the employer is public or private. The ECJ took this decisive step only one year after *Walrave* in *Defrenne II*.[13] The parallel move indicates that the ECJ deliberately connected the horizontal direct effect of mobility of workers to equal payment of men and women. Discrimination by nationality and discrimination by gender are put on an equal footing. The message is crystal-clear. Wherever workers move within the territory of the EU, they can start from the premise that men and women are paid the same salary. Non-discrimination law and the case law is not grounded in the protection of fundamental or human rights.

Art. 119 did not (yet) provide for legislative competences in the version it was given under the Rome Treaty. This had to wait until the Treaty of Amsterdam in 1999. Another competence rule was needed. On the basis of Art. 100 EC (Art. 94, today Art. 113 TFEU), the EEC, as it then was, *unanimously* adopted six directives which can be grouped around three topics: (1) Directive 75/117 on equal pay and Directive 76/207 (today Directive 2002/73) on access to employment, which are strongly connected to the principle of equal pay per Art. 119; (2) Directive 75/129 on collective redundancies (amended via Directives 92/56 and 98/59),[14] Directive 80/987 on insolvency protection (amended by Directive 2008/94)[15] and Directive 77/187 on transfer of rights;[16] (3) Directive 91/533 on

---

[13] Case 43/75, *Defrenne v. Sabena* [1976] ECR 455.
[14] Council Directive 75/129/EEC of 17 February 1975 on the approximation of the laws of the Member States relating to collective redundancies, OJ No. L 48, 22.2.1975, p. 29; Council Directive 92/56/EEC of 24 June 1992 amending Directive 75/129/EEC on the approximation of the laws of the Member States relating to collective redundancies, OJ No. L 245, 26.8.1992, p. 3; Council Directive 98/59/EC of 20 July 1998 on the approximation of the laws of the Member States relating to collective redundancies, OJ L 225, 12.8.1998, p. 16.
[15] Council Directive 80/987/EEC of 20 October 1980 on the approximation of the laws of the Member States relating to the protection of employees in the event of the insolvency of their employer, OJ No. L 283, 28.10.1980, p. 23; Directive 2008/94/EC of the European Parliament and of the Council of 22 October 2008 on the protection of employees in the event of the insolvency of their employer, OJ No. L 283, 28.10.2008, p. 36.
[16] Council Directive 77/187/EEC of 14 February 1977 on the approximation of the laws of the Member States relating to the safeguarding of employees' rights in the event of transfers of undertakings, businesses or parts of businesses, OJ No. L 61, 5.3.1977, p. 26.

information of worker rights.[17] The last three directives establish a kind of safety net for workers, which complement the equal pay policy enshrined in Art. 141, today Art. 157 TFEU, and Directives 75/117 as well as 76/207 (today Directive 2002/73).[18]

The six directives triggered an endless chain of references to the ECJ. The first two directives encouraged, in particular, trade unions and the Equal Opportunities Commission in the United Kingdom to mobilise EU law against the austerity policy of the Thatcher government. Within the framework of the two directives, the ECJ developed ground rules for the judicial protection of individually enforceable rights,[19] ground rules which the ECJ transferred from the field of equal pay and access to employment into all other fields of European law where the enforceability of subjective rights was at stake.[20] The directives and the conflicts that lay behind them triggered an increasing emphasis on gender equality, reflected at the institutional level with the creation of several bodies: the Equal Opportunities Unit (1981) at the Commission and a Committee on Women's Rights and Equal Opportunities at the Parliament (1984), and an Equal Opportunities Action Programme from 1982–1985. Prior to the adoption of the Single European Act, and based on Art. 100 and Art. 235 (Treaty of Rome), the EU adopted Directive 86/378 on equal treatment in occupational social security schemes[21] in direct response to the ongoing battle on the reach of Art. 119/141 (Art. 157 TFEU). Quite a number of preliminary references clarified whether social security schemes are to be qualified as equal pay. In *Barber*,[22] the ECJ answered the preliminary question in the affirmative. In the same year, Directive 86/613 on equal treatment for self-employed

---

[17] Council Directive 91/533/EEC of 14 October 1991 on an employer's obligation to inform employees of the conditions applicable to the contract or employment relationship, OJ No. L 288, 18.10.1991, p. 32.

[18] Directive 2002/73/EC of the European Parliament and of the Council of 23 September 2002 amending Council Directive 76/207/EEC on the implementation of the principle of equal treatment for men and women as regards access to employment, vocational training and promotion, and working conditions, OJ No. L 269, 5.10.2002, p. 15; F. de Witte distinguishes between three waves of regulation. He would associate the six Directives to what he calls the 'floor of rights', F. de Witte, *Justice in the EU*, p. 102.

[19] Micklitz, *The Politics of Judicial Co-operation in the EU*, p. 202.

[20] Reich, *Bürgerrechte*, §§ 8, 9, 14, p. 228.

[21] Council Directive 86/378/EEC of 24 July 1986 on the implementation of the principle of equal treatment for men and women in occupational social security schemes, OJ No. L 225, 12.08.1986, p. 40.

[22] Case C-262/88, *Barber v Guardian Royal Exchange Assurance Group* [1990] ECR I-1889.

people was enacted.[23] The EU thereby reacted to the growing trend in the Member States to transform long-term stable employment relations into precarious ones.

The second set of directives granted *minimum protection* to workers in the EU where they run the risk of losing their job due to employers getting into economic difficulties, be it an imminent inability to pay or be it in the event of the transfer of the undertaking or parts of it. It suffices to recall *Schmidt*[24] to highlight the explosive potential that lies in the directive on the transfer of rights. Directive 91/533 on the information of worker rights, though adopted many years after Directive 80/987, is still based on Art. 100 (now Art. 113 TFEU). It is guided by the same spirit as the previous five adopted between 1975 and 1980. The idea of relying on individual information instead of collective protection is very much in line with the transformation of labour law to the law of the labour market society. The worker is to be informed about his or her rights. This is not protection via collective action, but rather individualisation through the granting of rights that have to be enforced. Yet, one should be cautious. Individuation is not the pivot of post-classical EU law. Whilst stressing the individual, post-classical EU law is based on identity rights, as will have to be shown.[25]

2.2.2 Building Social Europe after 1986

The second phase – termed in the background analysis 'the emergence of the Social' – covers a whole series of activities, which can be broken down into three fields: the establishment of health and safety at work as a European policy and, most of all, the half-hearted attempt to elaborate on a European labour law.

The Single European Act introduced competences for the EU in the regulation of health and safety at work. The European Commission rushed to get a series of directives adopted under the newly introduced Art. 118 (a) (Art. Art. 153 TFEU), thereby taking possession of at least one of the central issues of labour policy via minimum standards:

---

[23] Directive 2010/41/EU of the European Parliament and of the Council of 7 July 2010 on the application of the principle of equal treatment between men and women engaged in an activity in a self-employed capacity and repealing Council Directive 86/613/EEC, OJ No. L 180, 15.7.2010, pp. 1.
[24] Case C-392/92, *Schmidt v. Spar- und Leihkasse der früheren Ämter Bordesholm, Kiel und Cronshagen* [1994] ECR I-1311.
[25] Part III. 2.1, 3.1, 4.1.

framework Directive 89/391 health and safety of workers,[26] Directive 92/85 on the protection of pregnant women at work,[27] Directive 93/104 on working time (amended by Directive 2003/88)[28] and Directive 94/33 on the protection of young people at work.[29] These directives are protective in nature. They fit into, and they complement, the overall policy developed in the first stage of the EU between 1975 and 1989. The particularly vulnerable worker, the ones exposed to dangerous work facilities, or pregnant women or young people are the addressees of EU legislation. EU directives enacted to improve health and safety at work coincided with the adoption of the Directive 92/59 on general product safety. Again, numerous ECJ judgments could be recalled where the court, in an activist mood, stretched the boundaries of the scope of application of harmonised EU rules.[30]

The 1991 Maastricht Treaty brought with it the EMU, but also Union citizenship and new competences in the field of social policy. Union citizenship bestowed a new dimension on freedom of workers. The worker as a pure market citizen turned into a citizen of the Union to whom a whole series of rights are granted.[31] There are two ways to look at the development in the 1990s, which was again actively promoted by the ECJ. One way is to insist on the particularities of the status of the worker. This focuses on whether the claimant is a worker, self-employed, a student, an apprentice, a trainee, and aims to concretise his or her legal position under primary and secondary EU law, particularly through the case law of the ECJ. The other perspective is to stress the common element in the extension of the freedom of workers despite all the sector-specific differences. In this vein, EU citizenship serves as an umbrella under which all these status-related positions

---

[26] Council Directive 89/391/EEC of 12 June 1989 on the introduction of measures to encourage improvements in the safety and health of workers at work, OJ No. L 183, 29.6.1989, pp. 1.

[27] Council Directive 92/85/EEC of 19 October 1992 on the introduction of measures to encourage improvements in the safety and health at work of pregnant workers and workers who have recently given birth or are breastfeeding, OJ No. L 348, 28.11.1992, pp. 1.

[28] Council Directive 93/104/EC of 23 November 1993 concerning certain aspects of the organization of working time, OJ No. L 307, 13.12.1993, p. 18; Directive 2003/88/EC of the European Parliament and of the Council of 4 November 2003 concerning certain aspects of the organisation of working time, OJ No. L 299, 18.11.2003, p. 9.

[29] Council Directive 94/33/EC of 22 June 1994 on the protection of young people at work, OJ No. L 216, 20.8.1994, p. 12.

[30] Case C-183/00, *González Sánchez* with regard to the product liability directive.

[31] Case C-85/96, *Martínez Sala v. Freistaat Bayern* [1998] ECR I-2691.

could be united, though still differing in reach.³² Both readings agree that the key role of union citizenship is to upgrade and to extend the freedom of workers in the EU. This is needed if the concept of union citizen is not to remain an empty shell.

The new competences introduced through the social protocol originally affected only 11 Member States. This constitutional deficit was remedied in the Treaty of Amsterdam and paved the way for the United Kingdom, transposing the four relevant directives between 1994 and 1997. Art. 2 (2) of the protocol led to the adoption of Directive 94/45 on the working council (as amended by Directive 2009/38)³³ and Directive 97/80 on the burden of proof (the latter was repealed by Directive 2006/54).³⁴ Whilst Directive 97/80 largely codified the ECJ case law,³⁵ the former set a provisional end to a decade-long debate on the appropriate form of co-determination in the EU.³⁶ The debate reemerged in the context of the Societas Europaea³⁷ and has gained pace after the ECJ's judgment in *Viking* and *Laval*. Art. 4 (2) of the protocol allowed for the introduction of Directive 96/34 on parental leave and 97/81 on part-time workers. Both directives are meant to strike down particular modes of discrimination. The last major Directive, Directive 96/71 on the posting of

---

[32] Reich, *Bürgerrechte* stands for the later perspective, §§ 11–16, p. 159 'ungeachtet des immer noch sektorenspezifischen Vorgehens des EG-Rechts gehen wir von einem einheitlichen Bürgerrecht auf Freizügigkeit aus' ('Notwithstanding the still sector specific approach of EC law, we start from the existence of a coherent union right to freedom of movement').

[33] Council Directive 94/45/EC of 22 September 1994 on the establishment of a European Works Council or a procedure in Community-scale undertakings and Community-scale groups of undertakings for the purposes of informing and consulting employees, OJ No. L 254, 30.09.1994, p. 64; Directive 2009/38/EC of the European Parliament and of the Council of 6 May 2009 on the establishment of a European Works Council or a procedure in Community-scale undertakings and Community-scale groups of undertakings for the purposes of informing and consulting employees, OJ No. L 122, 16.5.2009, p. 28.

[34] Council Directive 97/80/EC of 15 December 1997 on the burden of proof in cases of discrimination based on sex, OJ No. L 14, 20.1.1998, p. 6; Directive 2006/54/EC of the European Parliament and of the Council of 5 July 2006 on the implementation of the principle of equal opportunities and equal treatment of men and women in matters of employment and occupation, OJ No. L 204, 26.7.2006, p. 23.

[35] Opinion of Advocate General Lenz delivered on 14 July 1993 – Case C-127/92, *Enderby v. Frenchay Health Authority and Secretary of State for Health* [1993] ECR I-5535, at 5556, Micklitz, *The Politics of Judicial Co-operation in the EU*, p. 251.

[36] Reich, *Bürgerrechte*, § 21, p. 253 proposal of the *Vredeling* Directive.

[37] Regulation (EC) No 2157/2001 of 8 October 2001 on the Statute for a European company (SE), OJ No. L 294, 10.11.2001, p. 1.

workers,[38] was even more controversial than the others, and was based on Articles 57 (2) and 66 ET. In *Laval*, the ECJ interpreted the posting workers directive *de facto* and *de jure* as laying down fully harmonised standards, although the directive was meant to formulate minimum standards only.[39] *Viking* and *Laval*, both decided in 2007, are regarded by labour lawyers and social activists as the death knell of social labour law and of social justice, if not of the democratic sovereignty of the nation-states to design their social policies. According to these judgments, the fundamental freedoms apply horizontally 'to rules of any other nature aimed at regulation in a collective manner gainful employment, self-employment and the provision of services'.[40] Collective private regulation is to be assessed via the directly applicable freedom of workers, the freedom of establishment and the freedom to provide services. They confer rights on individuals whose freedoms are violated by collective action. This is the market-liberating side. However, the argument can be turned upside down. By the same logic, individuals become addressees of social rights. L. Azoulai stressed the potential of the case law for promoting social rights. I will come back to such an understanding of the controversial case law of the ECJ.[41]

The community of labour lawyers placed much hope on 'Social Dialogue' Art 118 b) (now Art. 152 TFEU), which was meant to compensate for the failure of the *Vredeling* Directive and rather modest co determination rights granted under the working council Directive 94/45. However, only a very few initiatives have been taken, and those which have been taken did not lead to encouraging results.[42] The new set of directives enshrined a new spirit in EU labour law-making right

---

[38] Directive 96/71/EC of the European Parliament and of the Council of 16 December 1996 concerning the posting of workers in the framework of the provision of services, OJ No. L 18, 21.1.1997, pp. 1.

[39] Case C-341/05, *Laval un Partneri*, paras. 51–111; there is an interesting and controversial debate on how to read the Directive 96/71 of the European Parliament and of the Council of 16 December 1996 concerning the posting of workers in the framework of the provision of services (OJ No. L 18, 21.1.1997, p. 1), in particular on whether the minimax debate fits to the directive at all (2008) 10 *Cambridge Yearbook of European Legal Studies*, pp. 463–609.

[40] Case C-438/05, *The International Transport Workers' Federation and The Finnish Seamen's Union*, para. 33; Case C-341/05, *Laval un Partneri*, para. 96; Reich, 'The public/private divide in European law', p. 61.

[41] Part III. 4.5.

[42] A. Bogg, C. Costello, A. C. L. Davies, *Research Handbook on EU Labour Law* (Cheltenham: Edward Elgar, 2016), p. 97.

from the beginning. This new spirit is already evident in Directive 91/533 information on rights and, later, in Directive 94/45 on working council and Directive 96/17 on the posting of workers adopted under the Social Protocol. They contain a strong cross-border element, and they rely on the 'leitbild' of a worker who resembles the circumspect and responsible consumer. One might even build a link to the Social Charter. The new ideal of the European worker demands a person who enforces her rights herself, which is perhaps most prominently displayed in *Bosman*.[43] The shift in focus sheds new light on the more 'protective' outlook of the former set of EU directives. Protecting pregnant women, securing the rights of the youth and granting parental leave, all bear a strong economic element insofar as the EU's law of the labour market is meant to keep access open to everybody, not only for the male full-time worker. There is definitely an element of protection present.[44] However, the protective regulation serves the purpose of market integration. Whatever measure the EU adopted in the aftermath of the SEA, it provoked a considerable volume of litigation, in particular on the scope ratio personae and ratio materiae of EU law, as well as on the minimum mandatory level of protection to be granted. An endless chain of ECJ judgments shaped the European labour law acquis and contributed to the development of a new leitbild of the worker that oscillates between the Bosman-type worker and the worker who needs help and support in getting access to the market.

2.2.3 *From Labour to Non-Discrimination Law after Lisbon 2000*

The third phase can be characterised by three modes of regulation, a hidden mode, a new mode, and an old mode in a new disguise. The contours of the Social are becoming clearer now. The stronger the EU intervenes in the social domain, the more it becomes obvious that the EU can set only a frame, which must be filled in – and paid for – by the Member States. The frame follows the well-established distinction between pre- and post-market control in product regulation. The EU is meant to establish access and accessibility to the labour market. This comes close to pre-market control. It then remains for the Member States to decide whether to take or not take social redistributive measures ex post. R. Münch describes this as 'premarket activation' of each

---

[43] Case C-415/93, *Union royale belge des sociétés de football association and Others v Bosman and Others.*
[44] Reich, *General Principles of EU Civil Law*, p. 41.

individual and 'the guarantee of equal opportunity' instead of 'post-market redistribution with the aim of approaching an equality of results'.[45] *Viking* and *Laval* are more than ten years old. The impact of the two decisions in the Member States varies considerably and so too do the compensatory redistributive measures taken by Member States.[46] The ECJ had neither developed nor retrieved its line of argument, with one exception – *Aget Iraklis*, decided in 2015. A European social policy that enshrines post-market redistribution is hard to imagine. A major amendment of the treaty would be needed to unblock the deadlock in European social policy.

The *hidden* mode refers to cold harmonisation that results from the introduction of a single currency. Whilst the EU has limited power to adopt minimum standards in the fields of labour law and policy, the practical effects of the EMU became clear after the economic and social crisis in 2008. Member States are deprived of a particular remedy which belonged to the national regulatory armoury in fighting social imbalances, namely the devaluation of the national currency. The national welfare state is 'transformed' by the back door and through the EU. The Member States have to obey the rules of the EMU, vigorously enforced through the Troika. The conflict between measures to secure financial stability and measures to preserve social distributive justices comes into stark relief. Those who are affected via the austerity policy of the Troika mobilise social property rights in order to defend the status quo against policy-driven haircuts of their salaries or their pension rights. The ECJ has been approached in *Pringle*, *Mallis* and *Mohamed Aziz*.[47] The prime addressees of such social rights claims are nevertheless national constitutional courts. In line with institutional choice theory, claimants approached the European Court of Human Rights from which they expected 'better' protection of their property rights. This major carrier of hope, however, did not meet the far-reaching expectations.[48]

---

[45] R. Münch, *European Governmentality. The liberal drift of multilevel governance* (London, New York: Routledge, 2010), p. 151.

[46] M. Freedland and J. Prassl (eds.), *Viking, Laval and Beyond* (Oxford: Hart Publishing, 2014) in which the impact of the two decisions on ten national legal orders is analysed, with varying results.

[47] Case C-370/12, *Pringle* [2012] I-000; Case C-105/15 P, *Mallis and Malli v. Commission and the ECB*; Case C-415/11, *Aziz*; regarding consumer protection after *Aziz*, Joined Cases C-154/15, C-307/15 and C-308/15, *Gutiérrez Naranjo*.

[48] A. Nannery, *The 'conscience of Europe' in the European sovereign debt crisis: an analysis of the judgments of the European Court of Human Rights and the European Committee of Social Rights on austerity measures*, LLM thesis, European University Institute (2015).

The *new* mode results from the introduction of the OMC in 2000 and its growing importance even outside core fields of labour policy such as social inclusion (OMC SPIC) and the European Employment Strategy (EES).[49] The new mode might lead to less litigation before the ECJ and more enforcement through the newly established administrative agencies that have to fight against discrimination. In light of the potential effects of the EMU on national social policies, one might read the OMC as an attempt, in particular by the European Commission, to develop a social policy outside the formal structure of the EU treaties in order to give shape to the mandate of the Lisbon Council – i.e. the fight against social exclusion. The OMC proceduralises social policy-making and social policy enforcement by new modes of governance. The European Commission is not the primary actor, unlike areas where it has the discretion and the monopoly to introduce legislative action. OMC activities are contingent upon the preparedness of national governments to cooperate, and of NGO's to participate in the undertaking. Proceduralisation within new governance does not allow for setting clear-cut standards on social justice. The OMC is much nearer to the model of 'access justice'. Since the integration of the OMC in the Lisbon Treaty failed, its (legal) future has become uncertain. Various proposals are under way to increase its transparency, to enhance accessibility in particular for NGOs, to entrust the European Parliament with a voice, and to use the European Ombudsman as a redress scheme.[50] Legally speaking, these proposals aim at constitutionalising the procedural element in the OMC.

There is one area of labour law and policy, however, in which the European Union has been able to set the tone since the insertion of Art. 119 Treaty of Rome. Largely independent from the ups and downs of social politics, the EU extended its regulatory powers through treaty amendments on non-discrimination. A proactive ECJ, in strong interaction with the EU legislator, struck down old and new forms of discrimination. This process has slowed down and seems to have come to rest. Yet, despite the current deadlock, non-discrimination rules form the third and most prominent mode of European social regulation. The Treaty of Amsterdam extended community powers in Art. 141 (3) (now Art. 157 TFEU) and introduced Art. 13 (now Art. 19 TFEU). Both new competences strengthened the role of the EU and led to a series of

---

[49] http://ec.europa.eu/employment_social/spsi/joint_reports_en.htm.
[50] Dawson, *New Governance and the Transformation of European Law*, Epilogue, p. 311.

directives which formulate a dense network of EU rules, overreaching the boundaries of EU labour law and policy by establishing minimum standards in the fight against discrimination. Art. 141 (3) (Art. 157 TFEU) was used by the EU to amend Directive 76/207 by Directive 2002/73 and to recast Directive 76/207 via Directive 2006/54. The EU competence changed from Art. 100 (Art. 94) to the more specific rule in Art. 141 (3) (Art. 157 TFEU). Art. 13 (now Art. 19 TFEU) initiated three directives, 2002/43 on equal treatment between persons irrespective of race and ethnic origin, 2000/78, establishing a general framework for equal treatment in employment and occupation, and, last but not least, Directive 2004/113 on equal treatment between men and women in the access to the supply of goods and services.[51] All directives required *unanimity* in the Council, which was easily obtained with regard to directives 2000/43 and 2000/78, whereas Directive 2004/113 received the necessary support only once certain areas such as the media were exempted from its scope of application. Bringing this series of directives through the political procedure results from a unique combination of forces, the so-called velvet triangle of EU institutions, Commission and Parliament, civil society and academia.[52] The 2008 proposal meant to extend the non-discrimination principle beyond the labour market failed due to the fierce resistance of Germany.[53] The velvet triangle had collapsed. That is why, with the exception of Directive 2004/113, the EU legislator has focused, until now, on the elimination of discrimination in the labour market. There is quite a gap between the pompous political rhetoric on the reach of the non-discrimination law and its rather limited extension into civil society.[54]

---

[51] Summary of the EC law on non-discrimination, U. Rust and J. Falke (eds.), *AGG. Allgemeines Gleichbehandlungsgesetz mit weiterführenden Vorschriften. Kommentar* (Berlin: Erich Schmidt Verlag, 2007), p. 198.

[52] E. M. Hinterhuber and V. Vasterling, 'Gender and Diversity Studies in European Perspectives: International conference, 8-10 January 2015, Rhine-Waal University of Applied Sciences, Kleve' (2015) 7 *Gender: Zeitschrift für Geschlecht, Kultur und Gesellschaft* 136-142.

[53] Proposal for a Council Directive on implementing the principle of equal treatment between persons irrespective of religion or belief, disability, age or sexual orientation, COM(2008) 426 final, 2.7.2008.

[54] Commission Staff Working Document accompanying the Proposal for a council directive on implementing the principle of equal treatment between persons irrespective of religion or belief, disability, age or sexual orientation, Impact Assessment, SEC(2008) 2180. Even if the rhetoric is about a general principle of non-discrimination and 'all areas of life', the EU has a limited scope of competence (i.e. labour and consumer law).

The limited scope of EU non-discrimination law was extended via the Charter on Fundamental Rights in 2000/2009.[55] Provided the principle of equality operates in conjunction with the Charter of Fundamental Rights as self-standing legal sources, the ECJ bears the responsibility to decide whether non-discrimination lies in its competences or not. The ECJ uses the Charter as a Bill of Rights.[56] The court has done so only pointillistically, as will have to be demonstrated. For the Court, there is a high risk of political overexposure and loss of legitimacy.[57] The Charter of Fundamental Rights cannot compensate for the lack of the Social in primary and secondary EU law. The limits of constitutionalising anti-discrimination law are evident.

2.2.4 The Post-Classical EU Labour and Non-Discrimination Law

The non-discrimination principle has become a core social moral that ties the European Union together. It has found its way into the draft of the European Constitution; it is anchored in Art. 2 of the Union Treaty and Art. 21 of Charter of Fundamental Rights;[58] it played a prominent, though highly contested role,[59] in the Acquis Principles (ACQP) and the DCFR.[60]

The post-classical move can be crystallised into four dimensions: first, the rise of non-discrimination as a *legal principle* hand in hand with the decline of classical social policy that cuts across the boundaries of vertical and horizontal direct effect of EU law and that links the EU non-discrimination policy to international standards on human rights; second, the focus of ECJ case law on non-discrimination and labour law on granting *access* to the EU market and transnational society that leaves the Member States with the responsibility for possible ex post redistributive measures; third, the extension of non-discrimination beyond nationality and gender, which not only leads to *hierarchies* and intersectionality in EU non-discrimination law but also to *group-based identities*

---

[55] Bell, 'The Principle of Equal Treatment: Widening and Deepening', p. 629.
[56] On the origins of the lack of the democratic element and how the ECJ is trying to build a legal order nevertheless, Weiler, 'Deciphering the Political and Legal DNA of European Integration'.
[57] Xenidis, 'Shaking the normative foundations of EU equality law'.
[58] For a deeper analysis, J. Falke, 'AGG Einleitung', in Rust and Falke (eds.), *AGG*, paras. 291 and Basedow, 'Grundsatz der Nichtdiskriminierung im europäischen Privatrecht', 248.
[59] Säcker, 'Vertragsfreiheit und Schutz vor Diskriminierung' and Basedow, 'Grundsatz der Nichtdiskriminierung im europäischen Privatrecht'.
[60] Art. 3:101 till 3:103 ACQP; II.-2:101 DCFR.

that compete with each other for priority;[61] and fourth, the move away from court-based litigation over the scope and reach to the non-discrimination through 'acquisitive individualism'[62] to the administrative management of collectively shared identities for the purpose of social inclusion. The four read together indicate the fading importance of status-based law, deep-going fragmentation, a lack of coherence, and a move away from courts to new forms of conflict resolution.

First, the *Mangold* judgment[63] has raised a highly controversial debate on whether EU law knows a *self-standing binding general principle of non-discrimination,* and whether such a principle is not only applicable vertically in citizen-state relations but also horizontally in citizen-to-citizen relationship. The pillars would be 'self-standing' and 'general'; 'self-standing' means independent or at least embracing primary and secondary EU law, and 'general' reaches beyond particular forms of discrimination and covers each and every form of discrimination. The breathtaking perspective would need additional input, and it is obviously derived from the rise of the human rights movement internationally and, in Europe, through the Charter of Fundamental Rights and the failed attempt to link the European Convention of Human Rights and the Treaty of Lisbon together. However, this is exactly what the ECJ did in a number of judgments, starting with *Mangold*. In its broadest reading, *Mangold* could be at the heart of European *access justice*. It would guarantee access of EU workers to the labour market, access of EU consumers to the consumer market and access of EU citizens to all sorts of services, insofar as they come under the scope of EU law. Even further, it would reach beyond the market-bound logic of the EU and could and would deliver access to European society. N. Reich understands non-discrimination as one of seven general principles of EU civil law.[64] Such a principle would still be market bound. Reich does not discuss family law, which could be regarded as being part of private law.

---

[61] A.-M. Hancock, *Intersectionality. An intellectual history* (New York: Oxford University Press, 2016).
[62] Münch, *European Governmentality*, pp. 142–143.
[63] Case C-144/04, *Mangold*; Case C-411/05, *Palacios de la Villa*.
[64] Reich, *General Principles of EU Civil Law*, p. 62, explicitly rejects Basedow, 'Grundsatz der Nichtdiskriminierung im europäischen Privatrecht', in particular that 'the principles of equality or the prohibition of discrimination are not part of the traditional principles of civil law' and later with regard to EU law that 'there are only limited and selective prohibitions of discrimination, usually aimed at creating balance in situation of power, and not a general prohibition of discrimination in the conclusion of contracts' (translation of Basedow by Reich).

In a modest version, non-discrimination would be a general principle limited to particular forms of nationality or market discrimination. Yet, certain scholars reject the idea of a general principle at all. The ECJ provides arguments for all sorts of different positions.[65]

Mangold produced strong reactions. German lawyers, including the former president of the German Constitutional Court, publicly appealed to 'Stop the ECJ!', claiming that the decision was 'only one of many judgments significantly interfering with competences of the member states'.[66] In *Kücükdevici*, the ECJ reacted to the critique in anchoring horizontal direct effect in the Charter of Fundamental Rights. By referring to the charter, the ECJ elegantly set aside the criticism that *Mangold* has been decided *ultra vires* and opened a debate on the reach of the interaction between 'a general principle' and role and function of the charter.[67] A related battlefield has come up in *Test Achats*,[68] where the ECJ submitted secondary EU law to a compliance test with Art. 21 and 23 of the Charter of Fundamental Rights. Here the ECJ seeks to tie the general principle to the charter. However, there is also counterevidence, more implicit in cases where there is no reference although the link would be obvious and in a way evident (*Römer, Rosenbladt, Georgiev*)[69] or where the court explicitly rejects the existence like in *Navas*.[70] Let us assume that there is such a principle and test its implications.

Mangold, Kücükdevici, Test Achats could serve as a tool to overrule the reservations of the United Kingdom (after Brexit, no longer relevant), Poland and the Czech Republic against the integration of the Charter of Fundamental Rights into Union law. This is the the ECJ's approach in

---

[65] Building on Xenidis, 'Shaking the Normative Foundations of EU Equality Law'.
[66] R. Herzog and L. Gerken, 'Stop the European Court of Justice', *euobserver*, 10 September 2008, available at: https://euobserver.com/opinion/26714.
[67] Case C-555/07, *Kücükdeveci*, at paras. 21–22: '(21) In that context, the Court has acknowledged the existence of a principle of non-discrimination on grounds of age which must be regarded as a general principle of European Union law (see, to that effect, *Mangold*, paragraph 75). Directive 2000/78 gives specific expression to that principle (see, by analogy, Case 43/75, *Defrenne* [1976] ECR 455, paragraph 54). (22) It should *also* (emphasis added H.-W. Micklitz) be noted that Article 6(1) TEU provides that the Charter of Fundamental Rights of the European Union is to have the same legal value as the Treaties. Under Article 21(1) of the charter, '[a]ny discrimination based on ... age ... shall be prohibited.'
[68] ECJ Case C-236/09, *Association Belge des Consommateurs Test-Achats and Other*.
[69] Case C-147/08, *Römer* [2011] ECR I-3591; Case C-45/09, *Rosenbladt* [2010] ECR I-9391; Case C-250/09, *Georgiev* [2010] ECR I-11869.
[70] Case C-13/05, *Chacón Navas* [2006] ECR I-6467.

Viking, where it deduced the right to strike out of the constitutional traditions of the Member States and international agreements, thereby ignoring reservations in the United Kingdom where no such right to strike exists. *Kücükdevici* is far from clear. It seems as if the ECJ uses the charter as a supportive argument (*'also'*)[71] to back the position developed in *Mangold*. If the treaty enshrines a general principle, then, the rather inconsistent scope of the various non-discrimination rules does not matter anymore. The non-discrimination principle is generally applicable, also in private law relations. The different reach of these judgments, and the degree to which EU law allows for legitimate restrictions, would not endanger the existence of the general principle per se. One way to overcome the deeper conceptual differences is to understand the ECJ case law as a form of judicial experimentalism, a phenomenon that can also be found in consumer law.[72]

Second, when it comes to access to the labour market, EU labour law and EU anti-discrimination law are uniting. The ex-ante conditionality of the European Social Fund supports such an understanding.[73] The market-opening perspective dominates EU law. All those who are excluded from the labour market or face difficulties in getting access to the labour market have successfully relied in the past decades on EU law and the ECJ to strike down national legal barriers in private or public employment contracts. More often than not, litigating parties are tied together via contract. Based on the existing case law of the ECJ, two types of barriers may be distinguished: those which result from gender, transgender, nationality, race, age, disability or religious discrimination; and those which result from collective private regulation. In most of the cases, barriers result from national legislation that leaves the 'weaker party' in a less favourable position. This legislation finds its way directly into the employment contract or frames the social and economic environment in which the contract is embedded. It is here

---

[71] Case C-144/04, *Mangold*, para. 22.
[72] Introduction 3.1.
[73] A main aim of the ESF concerns advancing the European Employment Strategy (EES). To this end, Article 2 of the ESF Regulation No. 1262/1999 (OJ No. L 161, 26.6.1999, p. 48) outlines five key policy areas. The Eurofund website states: 'This new legal base allows the Commission to use the ESF to be more active in the area of gender mainstreaming. Discrimination represents a major concern of the ESF. Since 2001, the ESF has financed the EQUAL programme, an initiative designed to fight employment exclusion due to discrimination based on sex, race, ethnic origin, religion, disability, age or sexual orientation', available at: www.eurofound.europa.eu/observatories/eurwork/industrial-relations-dictionary/european-social-fund. In the meanwhile Regulation 1262/1999 has been replaced by Regulation 1304/2013 (OJ L 347, 20.12.2013, pp. 470).

one finds the deeper link between the freedom of workers, anti-discrimination law and private law. The active movers (the Bosmans of this world, so to speak) or the social activists (the women and later the human rights organisations) seek 'access' for themselves or for the minorities they intend to protect, quite often through test cases where the individual claimant represents a minority. They instrumentalise the free movement of workers and the non-discrimination rules to remove the national barriers that deprive the weaker parties of the opportunity of earning a living in 'barrier-free' conditions. What is true for goods and services is also true for the free movement of persons.[74] Contract law provides for the backstage of the conflicts.

Access barriers to the labour market are usually associated with a particular form of discrimination, historically nationality and gender, and then later on via other forms of discrimination on the basis of gender identity, race, age, disability and religion. The more EU law broadened the forms of discrimination, the more obvious the societal dimension, which reaches beyond access to the labour market, appeared. *Bosman, Angonese*,[75] *Viking, Laval* and *Olympique Lyonnais*[76] concern a different form of barrier. The facts of the cases have one element in common, namely that the workers mobilise the free movement rights in order to strike down *collective private agreements,* which are either established by private organisations that bear a quasi-statutory character (*Bosman, Olympique Lyonnais*) or by the states themselves (*Angonese*). *Viking* and *Laval* fit into that picture, although the perspective is different. Critics stress that the freedom of establishment is invoked by companies to challenge collective agreements or collective activities such as a strike.[77] Trade unions are treated in law like public actors. Such an analysis falls short of covering conflicts between workers – the ones defending their social status in the old Member States and the ones seeking access who typically reside in the new Member States – whose

---

[74] G. Davies, 'Freedom of Contract and the Horizontal Effect of Free Movement Law', in D. Leczykiewicz and S. Weatherill (eds.), *The Involvement of EU Law in Private Law Relationships* (Oxford: Hart Publishing, 2013), pp. 53–70; from a more doctrinal perspective St. Weatherill, 'Why There Is No 'Principle of Mutual Recognition in EU Law (and Why that Matters to Consumer Lawyers), in K. Purnhagen/P. Rott (eds.), *Varieties of European Economic Law and Regulation. Liber Amicorum for Hans Micklitz*, pp. 401–418.

[75] Case C-415/93, *Union royale belge des sociétés de football association and Others v. Bosman and Others*; Case C-281/98, *Angonese*.

[76] Case C-438/05, *The International Transport Workers' Federation and The Finnish Seamen's Union*; Case C-341/05, *Laval un Partneri*; Case C-325/08 *Olympique Lyonnais*.

[77] On this difference, see Azoulai, 'The Court of Justice and the Social Market Economy', p.1350.

interests are said to be (mis)-used to the benefit of the companies. The parties fight for access against 'abusive' collective private agreements, and the ECJ is granting access against the fierce opposition of trade associations and trade unions.[78] This recurring theme has a strong impact on consumer law.

The 'access' rhetoric of EU law is heavily criticised. Opening the labour market without setting EU-wide substantive standards of justice allows for downward competition between the different Member States' social policies to the detriment of workers.[79] Already in *Smith v. Advel*,[80] in 1994, the ECJ rejected the attempt of women and human rights organisations to fix the equality standard in gender conflicts at the most favourable level. Legal success before the ECJ on equal treatment or insurance premiums might be, in the end, a pyrrhic victory. Equal treatment might in practice mean equal treatment at a base level to the detriment of those who fought for their rights. The major argument that the ECJ provided ever since is that it remains for the Member States to define the level of protection. In Part III, I will go deeper into the argument and test its validity.

Third, the uneven level of protection against the different forms of discrimination and the different private collective regulation barriers yields two sorts of effects. On the surface level, there is a hierarchy in that certain forms of discrimination or certain barriers are prohibited per se, whereas others are subject to various restrictions. EU law stands firm when it comes to equal treatment between men and women, or nationality or race discrimination. Gender identity, age, disability and religion are subject to a complicated weighing procedure without a clear guidance from the ECJ. The form of discrimination reaching the ECJ for dispute depends on the national background of the conflict – age discrimination is an issue in Germany and in Denmark. Race and religion is not yet really a subject of concern for the ECJ, although the number of references is rising.[81] The same can be said with regard to the assessment of collective private regulation in light of the four freedoms.

---

[78] A. Saydé, 'Defining the Concept of Abuse of Union Law' (2014) 33 *Yearbook of European Law* 138–162.

[79] M. Bartl, 'Internal Market Rationality, Private Law and the Direction of the Union: Resuscitating the Market as the Object of the Political' (2015) 21 *European Law Journal* 572–598; Davies, 'Social Legitimacy and Purposive Power'; Kochenov, 'The Ought of Justice'; Rödl, 'Labour Constitution', just to name a few.

[80] Case C-408/92, *Smith and Others v Avdel Systems* [1994] ECR I-4435.

[81] The ECJ rendered until now only a few judgments in the area of racial and religious discrimination, Xenidis, 'Shaking the Normative Foundations of EU Equality Law'.

The differentiation and fragmentation, however, has a much deeper and a much more complicated dimension. The EU legal system unites social groups under particular legal categories and labels them as particularly vulnerable. This is most obvious in the field of non-discrimination; far beyond women and men, it includes sexual orientation and gender identity, age and youth, race, disability, and religion. As these groups do not enjoy the same legal treatment, they have to be defined one by one and have to be kept separated from each other. This finding goes along with identity-based rights in the meaning of D. Kennedy.[82]

Fourth, not only in labour law via the OMC but also in non-discrimination law there is an obvious move away from court litigation to administrative enforcement.[83] The development goes together with the rise of the anti-discrimination policy in the EU, Directives 2000/43 (race) and 2002/73 (equal treatment). Subsequently, equality bodies became a fixed ingredient of the EU non-discrimination policy that no longer relied on courts alone and pushed Member States to establish administrative bodies. They were integrated in Directives 2006/54 (repealing 2002/73) and 2004/113 (goods and services), and they were foreseen in the failed 2008 proposal meant to extend discrimination protections beyond employment. However, the Race Equality Directive does not refer to equality bodies. In 2007, the Fundamental Rights Agency was established at the EU level.[84] There is no equivalent body dealing with discrimination. Not surprisingly, human rights issues and anti-discrimination are amalgamated, outside formal competences. The competence creep is a double one. At a substantive level, the Fundamental Rights Agency might be tempted to use the Charter as the encompassing legal basis that integrates non-discrimination as a general principle, while at the enforcement level, the Fundamental Rights Agency might use a potential infringement of the Charter as a tool to use its competences for an assessment of practices outside the formal scope of non-discrimination law. Although the Fundamental Rights Agency has no regulatory powers to take action against individual wrongdoers, its assessments should not be underestimated in its impact on concrete practices.

---

[82] Kennedy, 'Three Globalizations of Law and Legal Thought', p. 65.
[83] B. de Witte, 'New Institutions for Promoting Equality in Europe: Legal Transfers, National Bricolage and European Governance' (2012) 60 *American Journal of Comparative Law* 49–74.
[84] Regulation (EC) No. 168/2007 of 15 February 2007 establishing a European Union Agency for Fundamental Rights, OJ No. L 53, 22.2.2007, p. 1.

What then are the reasons for the shift from litigation to management if it is not competence creep alone? G. de Búrca[85] has drawn a parallel to the United States. The decrease of the welfare state in the United States is said not only to have caused social rights to be enforced negatively through non-discrimination law on an individual basis but also to have provoked new forms of resistance. Novel, often non-court-centred, administrative and managerial means emerged that allow for going beyond acquisitive individualism to reach collective if not redistributive results. This is a quite ambitious claim at least in its descriptive dimension.

2.3 The Impact of the Determinants on Consumer Law

The consumer as a legal and social figure (*Rechtsfigur*) entered the European integration process through the deferrals in the production and consumption sphere. From the post-war period on, the share of the productive sector in the gross European product is declining, and the share of the consumptive sector is increasing. Today it is around 56 per cent of the overall gross income.[86] The shift is mirrored in the rise of the consumption society, a steadily increasing choice orientation, and – with the European integration process – the free choice between national products and those imported from EU member states and beyond. The freedom of goods and services is not at the heart of the analysis. However, the emergence, function and importance of consumer policy and consumer law in the EU is impossible to understand and to explain without the key role of the four freedoms. Again, it seems possible to identify three major trends that determine the development and the shaping of European consumer law.

The Treaty of Rome contains rules on production, trade and distribution, but not on consumption. The consumer appeared four times in the treaty, but the most important reference is to be found in ex-Art. 85 (3), today Art. 101 TFEU, which allows exemptions regarding the prohibition of cartels, provided an equitable share in the profit is reserved for

---

[85] G. de Búrca, 'The Trajectories of European and American Antidiscrimination Law' (2012) 60 *American Journal of Comparative Law* 1–22.
[86] In current price terms, consumption expenditure by households and non-profit institutions serving households contributed 56.0 per cent of the EU-28's GDP in 2016, Figure 9 on 'Expenditure Components of GDP at Current Market Prices, EU-28, 2016 (% share of GDP) on the website of Eurostat, available at: http://ec.europa.eu/eurostat/statistics-explained/index.php/National_accounts_and_GDP.

users (in the German version 'Verbraucher', the French 'consommateur'). Much effort has been put into the interpretation of Art. 2 of the Treaty of Rome as a basis for the development of a European Consumer Policy: 'It shall be the aim of the Community, by establishing a Common Market and progressively approximating the economic policies of Member States, to promote throughout the Community a harmonious development of economic activities, a continuous and balanced expansion, an increased stability, an accelerated raising of the standard of living and closer relations between its Member States.'[87] The rather vague language, however, sufficed to legitimate the adoption of the first and second consumer programmes in 1975 and 1981. Between the two programmes, in its famous *Cassis de Dijon* judgment in 1979, the ECJ recognised consumer protection as a legitimate reason to restrict the freedom of trade of goods under Art. 36 EEC (today Art. 36 TFEU).[88] However, the ECJ linked its affirmative action to strong requirements. Proper consumer information should replace sales prohibitions in the protection of the economic interests of consumers, but also in principle in the protection of health and safety. Increased consumer choice is contingent on the availability of proper information. Access to the market is bound to knowledge. The information paradigm survived all the ups and downs of the EU consumer policy. Pressure, if any, comes from behavioral economics and behavioral science that challenges the use and usefulness of information as a proper tool to empower consumers.[89]

The second stable element of European consumer law and policy is its comprehensiveness. It seems as if the EU succeeded in developing a genuine model for the protection of the consumers. Contrary to labour and non-discrimination law, Member States were willing to leave the field of consumer policy and law to the European Union once their national welfare policies ran into difficulties. The introduction of Art. 100 (a) Single European Act (now Art. 114 TFEU) triggered a whole wave of European legislative measures meant to protect the economic interests of consumers in the now Internal Market and to shield consumers against potential risks to their health and safety. The competence shift allowed the European Commission to take the driver's seat and to

---

[87] T. Bourgoignie, *Eléments pour une théorie du droit de la consommation* (Bruxelles: E. Story-Scientia, 1988), p. 215; L. Krämer, *EWG-Verbraucherrecht* (Baden-Baden: Nomos, 1985), pp. 17–18.
[88] Case 120/78, *Rewe-Zentral AG v Bundesmonopolverwaltung für Branntwein*, paras. 8 and 14.
[89] Part I. 2.2–2.4.

establish, over the last three decades, a consistent body of consumer law, originally for the sale of consumer goods but in the last 10 years increasingly with regard to the sale of services. Shortly after the new millennium, the EU took on digitisation and set the tone for the future development of consumer protection rules.[90] The move from minimum to maximum harmonisation in the Lisbon Agenda increased the powers of the EU. Where full harmonisation exists, Member States are deprived of their sovereignty. European consumer law and policy has not much to do with social-driven policy objectives, which Member States originally had in mind. Consumer protection law turned into consumer law, putting an emphasis on securing access to products and services.

The third relatively stable field of consumer policy where the EU sets the tone is the protection of health and safety against risks from unsafe products and unsafe services that are marketed throughout the EU.[91] The break-even point was the adoption of the new approach on technical standards in 1985.[92] After tariffs had been successfully abolished in the 1970s, the European Commission focused its attention on abolishing non-tariff barriers to trade. The new approach set out a regulatory framework. The EU adopted a number of directives laying down mandatory requirements which were then specified through technical standards elaborated under the Memorandum of Agreement concluded with the EU; it was, then, for the Comité Européen de Normalisation (CEN) and the Comité Européen de Normalisation Electronique (CENELEC) to organise the standardisation process. Originally the European Commission thought it had covered potential risks to consumers through the abolition of technical barriers to trade with the adoption of the Product Liability Directive 85/374 in 1985. However, it turned out that more was needed to meet the health and safety interests of consumers. Directive 92/59 (amended through Directive 2001/95) imposes on manufacturers and dealers, within limits, the obligation to market safe products only. Member States are equally obliged to entrust national regulatory agencies with post-market surveillance of

---

[90] COM (2015) 634 final and 635 final, 9.12.2015.
[91] Joerges, Falke, Micklitz and Brüggemeier, *Die Sicherheit von Konsumgütern und die Entwicklung der Europäischen Gemeinschaft*; for the shortened and updated English version: 'European Product Safety, Internal Market Policy and the New Approach to Technical Harmonisation and Standards'; H.-W. Micklitz (ed.), *Post Market Control of Consumer Goods* (Baden-Baden: Nomos, 1990); Micklitz, Roethe and Weatherill (eds.), *Federalism and Responsibility*.
[92] Council Resolution of 7 May 1985 on a new approach to technical harmonization and standards, OJ No. C 136, 4.6.1985, p. 1.

products. The regulatory design developed in product safety regulation set standards for other types of products, such as chemicals, pesticides and, today, 'toxic' financial products.

With hindsight, Europeanisation of consumer legal policy occurred in *three* phases just as European labour and non-discrimination law. Each phase can be linked to a particular model of justice and a particular consumer leitbild. The first phase is still dominated by the varying patterns of national social justice; the second already points to the development of an emergent European model of justice, which is subject to further specification and change in the third phase.

2.3.1 Establishing the Consumer Protection Paradigm

The *Cassis de Dijon* doctrine triggered an endless chain of follow-on cases where companies, for the most part, used the EU defence to strike down national legislation as a potential barrier to trade in the name of consumer protection. In *Cassis de Dijon*, the German government defended import restrictions with inexplicable arguments on the need to protect the health and safety of consumers against the consumption of the French liquor that did not comply with the German tax laws requiring a higher degree of alcohol for liquors (32 per cent instead of 15–20 in *Cassis*). Each Member State had its own *Cassis de Dijon* experience, each linked to particularly sensitive foodstuff: in France cheese, in Germany beer, in Italy noodles, in the UK milk. The most comprehensive analysis of the ECJ case law on the relationship between the freedom of goods/services and consumer protection is to be found in Johnston and Unberath.[93]

The case law of the ECJ showed a far-reaching understanding of consumer protection and of the consumer. The economic interests of the consumer are to be protected through information. Information and labelling is said to be an appropriate substitute for Member States' sales prohibitions. The former Common Market was opened for ever more products from the Member States. Through appropriate information, the consumer is in the position to make a rational choice between the increasing number of products. Sales restrictions can only be maintained in hard cases, mainly when health and safety serves as a legitimate reason. Barriers to trade resulting from differences in health and

---

[93] H. Unberath and A. Johnston, 'The Double-Headed Approach of the ECJ Concerning Consumer Protection' (2007) 44 *Common Market Law Review* 1237–1284, now Weatherill, *Contract Law of the Internal Market*, Chapter 2, p. 11.

safety standards can only be abolished through additional legislative measures, *in concreto* through the two directives on general product safety, but only after the adoption of the Single European Act. Gradually, the ECJ developed the notion of the average consumer as the leading normative figure against whom national laws that were claimed to set barriers to trade could and should be measured. The logic of the *Cassis de Dijon* doctrine is simple: The more demanding the normative standard of the average consumer, the higher the number of products that can circulate freely. Most of the leading cases that reached the ECJ via the preliminary reference procedure were decided in the 1980s. At that time, greater freedom and improved choice were regarded as an advantage to the cosmopolitan consumer who could select between an ever-greater assortment of products – of foodstuff, alcohol, cosmetics and spare parts.[94] It took nearly three decades before the critique on the role of the ECJ in establishing the Common Market for consumers gained ground. The blind thrust in opening markets to enable growth is now contrasted with its downside: the development of a uniform consumption culture and the loss of local habits, of local production and of local employment, all this to the advantage of fewer and fewer companies that reap the benefits of the market. The advocacy of a 'good life' through more choice is questioned.[95]

Whilst the market rhetoric seems to promote justice through access and to confirm all those who denounce access justice as substandard in relation to social justice, it should not be overlooked that the 1970s are characterised by a strong 'protection' bias. This becomes particularly clear in the first two consumer protection programmes in 1975 and 1981. The document does not mention the consumer as the weaker party, though. It refers to 'imbalance':[96]

N. 2. The wide range of experience in the countries of the enlarged Community favours the development of new ideas in the consumer field which, together with the many developments which have taken place in all Member States, point the way to a new deal for the consumer and *ways to find a better balance in the protection of his interests* [emphasis added].

---

[94] This is the undercurrent in all publications of European consumer law from the 1980s and 1990s.
[95] Bartl, 'Internal Market Rationality, Private Law and the Direction of the Union'; Davies, 'Social Legitimacy and Purposive Power'; Rödl, 'Labour Constitution'.
[96] Council Resolution of 14 April 1975 on a preliminary programme of the European Economic Community for a consumer protection and information policy, OJ No. C 92, 25.4.1975, pp. 1, under 2.

Balance refers to the imbalance of power which requires legislative intervention. Consequently, power is an issue. It is mentioned a couple of times, always in connection with contractual relations. This is exactly the social welfare rhetoric that stands behind the consumer protection programmes of the different Member States. The European Commission is zealous to please the Member States. EU consumer policy is embedded in national legal policies through coordination.[97] The 1981 programme strikes a different tone. The language no longer focuses on imbalance of power but on dialogue between consumers and business:[98]

> 4. Moreover, without in any way ceasing to ensure that the rights listed above are complied with, the consumer policy, which has hitherto been mainly defensive, should become more positive and more open to a dialogue in order to establish the conditions in which the consumer can become a participant in the preparation and implementation of important economic decisions which concern him first and foremost as a buyer or a user, and which very largely determine his individual or collective living conditions.

Whilst the change between the first and second programmes attracted attention in the relevante circles, it took a decade before the timid shift unfolded its consequences.

The imbalance of power rhetoric remained characteristic for the initiatives taken between 1975 and 1985, e.g. before the rise of the Internal Market. From the three directives adopted in this time span, two, Directive 85/577/EEC on contracts concluded away from business premises and Directive 87/102/EEC, bore a strong national protective bias. It is the weak consumer to whom regulatory action is addressed. Doorstep selling and claimed malpractices ranked high on the political agenda of the Member States. Consumer credit regulation, whilst certainly an issue around Europe, bore a different undertone. Contrary to the United States and the United Kingdom, consumer credit had not yet reached the continent as a means to use future income for the realisation of current purchase decisions. The directive intended to do both, encouraging consumers to make use of the credit business and also providing a safer legal environment. The initial legislation is more linked to considerations of social justice than to access justice. This is

---

[97] Critical as regards the objectives of consumer law, G.-P. Calliess, 'Nach der Schuldrechtsreform: Perspektiven des deutschen, europäischen und internationalen Verbrauchervertragsrechts', (2003) 203 *Archiv für die civilistische Praxis* 575–602.

[98] Council Resolution of 19 May 1981 on a second programme of the European Economic Community for a consumer protection and information policy, OJ No. C 133, 3.6.1981, p. 1.

in line with Unberath and Johnston, who stress the differences between the ECJ case law in primary and secondary EU law. Whilst the former promotes the average consumer, the second bears a protective undertone. The third directive on product liability has a very particular story. It relates to the US debate on strict liability and to the Convention of the Council of Europe. Originally, the European Commission intended to introduce a strict liability scheme that would have even included development risks. The compromise maintained the strict liability paradigm, though liability for development risks remained optional.

In the early years, there was little to no case law with regard to these three directives. There is a saying in European law circles that it takes ten years before the first cases reach the European Court of Justice. This holds true with regard to the doorstep selling and the product liability directives. Litigation, in both respects, arose in a context that nobody could imagine at the time of the adoption of the directives. The doorstep selling directive became famous in the aftermath of credit contracts concluded at the doorsteps to finance investments in the new Member States.[99] The product liability directive reached the level of public attention when the ECJ struck down more far-reaching national laws on the liability of dealers with the argument that the directive provided for full harmonisation.[100] In this period, the consumer credit directive did not reach beyond a mere shadow existence.

2.3.2 Building European Consumer Law after 1986

In implementing the two consumer programmes, the European Commission presented proposals and pushed hard to get them through the Council, as unanimity was still needed. However, many projects were stuck because consensus could not be reached. The history of the unfair terms directive is telling.[101] The United Kingdom on one side and France-Germany on the other side could not agree whether or not to include good faith into the fairness test. After the Single European Act, the European Commission needed 'only' the support of the majority of the Member States. Moreover, the European Commission benefited

---

[99] H.-W. Micklitz, 'The Relationship between National and European Consumer Policy – Challenges and Perspectives' in C. Twigg-Flesner, D. Parry, G. Howells and A. Nordhausen (eds.), *The Yearbook of Consumer Law 2008* (Aldershot: Ashgate, 2007), pp. 35–66.

[100] Case C-183/00 *González Sánchez*.

[101] H.-W. Micklitz, 'Unfair Terms in Consumer Contracts', in N. Reich, H.-W. Micklitz, P. Rott and K. Tonner (eds.), *European Consumer Law*, 2nd ed. (Antwerp: Intersentia, 2014), Chapter 3, pp. 125–164.

from the new competence rule, Article 100 (a) (3) (today Art. 104 TFEU) that referred to consumer protection.[102] To understand the link between the White Paper on the Completion of the Internal Market, the Single European Act, and the role and function consumer law in the building of the Internal Market, it is still worth reading the influential Sutherland report.[103] That is where the well-known rhetoric of 'an integrated market needs confident consumers' derives from.[104] The new competence rule and majority voting allowed the European Union to gradually take over the regulation of consumer law.[105]

Within a couple of years, the EU managed to get quite a number of directives though the legislative machinery, some of which were pending for years: Directive 90/314/EEC on package tours,[106] Directive 93/13 on unfair terms in consumer contracts, Directive 94/47/EC on time sharing,[107] 97/7/EC on distant selling, Directive 98/27 on injunctions[108] and Directive 99/44/EC on the sale of consumer goods.[109] Together with the four directives adopted under the old unanimity requirement (Directive 84/450 on misleading advertising,[110] 85/374 on product liability, 85/577 on doorstep selling and 87/102 on consumer credit), a kind of European legal order is emerging, composed of a general part and a

---

[102] H.-W. Micklitz and S. Weatherill, 'Consumer Policy in the European Community: Before and after Maastricht' (1993) 16 *Journal of Consumer Policy* 28–321.

[103] P. Sutherland, 'The Internal Market after 1992: Meeting the Challenge. Report Presented to the Commission by the High Level Group on the Functioning of the Internal Market', European Parliament Doc (SEC 92-final) 2277 (1992).

[104] S. Weatherill, 'The Evolution of European Consumer Law and Policy: From Well Informed Consumer to Confident Consumer', in H.-W. Micklitz (eds.), *Rechtseinheit oder Rechtsvielfalt in Europa? Rolle und Funktion des Verbraucherrechts in der EG und MOE-Staaten* (Baden-Baden, Nomos, 1996), pp. 423–468.

[105] S. Weatherill, *EU Consumer Law and Policy*, 2nd ed. (Cheltenham: Edward Elgar, 2005), p. 8; N. Reich, H.-W. Micklitz, P. Rott and K. Tonner (eds.), *European Consumer Law*, 2nd ed. (Antwerp: Intersentia, 2014), p. 11.

[106] Council Directive 90/314/EEC of 13 June 1990 on package travel, package holidays and package tours, OJ No. L 158, 23.6.1990, p. 59.

[107] Directive 94/47/EC of the European Parliament and the Council of 26 October 1994 on the protection of purchasers in respect of certain aspects of contracts relating to the purchase of the right to use immovable properties on a timeshare basis, OJ No. L 280, 29.10.1994, p. 83.

[108] Directive 98/27/EC of the European Parliament and of the Council of 19 May 1998 on injunctions for the protection of consumers' interests, OJ No. L 166, 11.6.1998, p. 51.

[109] Directive 1999/44/EC of the European Parliament and of the Council of 25 May 1999 on certain aspects of the sale of consumer goods and associated guarantees, OJ No. L 171, 07.07.1999, p. 12.

[110] Council Directive 84/450/EEC of 10 September 1984 relating to the approximation of the laws, regulations and administrative provisions of the Member States concerning misleading advertising, OJ No. L 250, 19.09.1984, p. 17.

specific part. The general part covers the directives on advertising, on standard terms control and on the regulation of the modalities of contract conclusion – doorstep and distant selling. The specific part unites the directives on particular types of contracts – credit, package tours, time sharing, consumer sales and liability and the directive on product liability. The Injunction Directive holds the specific part and the general part together through its annex. The introduction of Art. 129a into the Maastricht Treaty, together with the amendments in the Amsterdam Treaty, nourished hopes in academic circles of uniting and replacing the consumer law directives through a directly binding regulation based on the new competence provided for through Art. 153 Treaty of Amsterdam (Art. 169 TFEU).[111] However, this project never came near political concretisation. So far, only Directive 98/6 on price indications[112] has been based on ex-Art. 129 a). The new competence rule mainly served legitimatory purposes. The distinction between market-bound consumer law and consumer law that reaches beyond the market never gained political ground.

Despite these broken dreams, the 1990s were the heyday of European Consumer Policy. With enthusiasm and commitment, the European Commission gradually took over a leading role in the formulation of consumer policy. The Member States were not unhappy, as consumer policy had lost impetus in their home countries. This loss of support at the national level was compensated through legislative activism at an EU level. The political decision in the Paris Summit 1990 to open up the EU for the new Member States boosted the export of EU consumer law acquis into the then candidate states.[113] The European Commission took over the role and function the OECD had played in the 1960s and 1970s. The European Commission pushed the candidate states hard to integrate consumer law directives into their legal systems.[114]

---

[111] Reich, 'A European Contract Law, or an EU Contract Regulation for Consumers?'.
[112] Directive 98/6/EC of the European Parliament and of the Council of 16 February 1998 on consumer protection in the indication of the prices of products offered to consumers, OJ No. L 80, 18.3.1998, p. 27.
[113] Charter of Paris for a New Europe, Paris 1990, available at: www.oscepa.org/documents/all-documents/documents-1/historical-documents-1/673-1990-charter-of-paris-for-a-new-europe/file.
[114] H.-W. Micklitz, 'Divergente Ausgangsbedingungen des Verbraucherrechts in Ost und West', in H.-W. Micklitz (eds.), *Rechtseinheit oder Rechtsvielfalt in Europa? Rolle und Funktion des Verbraucherrechts in der EG und MOE-Staaten* (Baden-Baden, Nomos, 1996), pp. 3–22; M. Karanikic, H.-W. Micklitz, and N. Reich, (eds.), *Modernising Consumer Law: The Experience of the Western Balkan* (Baden-Baden: Nomos, 2012).

In the 1990s, the overall policy of the European Commission was to lay down minimum standards. The European Commission intended mainly to coordinate national consumer policies. Member States were to enjoy leeway to develop and maintain their own consumer policy and their own standards that could reach beyond the minimum. Minimum standards were to establish a common European platform, which each and every consumer could rely on to develop and build confidence in the Internal Market. 'Confidence' became the new buzzword and the confident consumer the new paradigm, promoted to maintain a minimum level of protection or criticised as abuse of consumer protection for market building purposes.[115] Politically, the minimum harmonisation approach helped to appease Member States in not shifting too much competence in social policy (!) to the EU. Some sort of 'minimum justice' for all European Citizens[116] – as they were called from the Treaty of Maastricht onwards – and an additional level of justice that reaches beyond the minimum, the reach and design of which was left to the Member States.

The link between the completion of the Internal Market and consumer protection, at first invisible, then increasingly obvious, changed the outlook of consumer law, its contents, its direction and its concept. The protective element of consumer policy lost priority to its benefit or detriment – depending on one's viewpoint. It now fell to the responsible consumer to play a central role within the European integration process.[117] Consumer protection and the consumer as an ideal type of a market citizen is submitted to the Internal Market philosophy. The weaker party, the consumer who needs to be protected, is not the ideal type who is able to make use of his or her rights and to contribute to the completion of the Internal Market.[118] This is where the genuine model

---

[115] Weatherill, 'The Evolution of European Consumer Law and Policy: From Well Informed Consumer to Confident Consumer'; Th. Wilhelmsson, 'The Abuse of the "Confident Consumer" as a Justification for EC Consumer Law' (2004) 27 *Journal of Consumer Policy* 317–337.

[116] J. Stuyck, 'Patterns of Justice in the European Constitutional Charter: Minimum Harmonisation in the Field of Consumer Law', in L. Krämer, H.-W. Micklitz and K. Tonner (eds.), *Law and Diffuse Interests in the European Legal Order / Recht und diffuse Interessen in der Europäischen Rechtsordnung: Liber amicorum Norbert Reich* (Baden-Baden: Nomos, 1997), pp. 279–289.

[117] Critical as regards the alleged change of the paradigm, H. Rösler, *Europäisches Konsumentenvertragsrecht. Grundkonzeption, Prinzipien und Fortentwicklung* (München: C. H. Beck, 2004), p. 76.

[118] Wilhelmsson, 'The Abuse of the "Confident Consumer" as a Justification for EC Consumer Law', 317.

of justice in EU has its roots. EU consumer law is *market behaviour law* – it is the law of the consumer market.[119] EU minimum justice is access justice.

Minimum harmonisation could hide the potential conflict between consumer protection law and the law of the consumer market for a long time. In practice, the demarcation line between EU minimum standards on market behaviour and national standards reaching beyond these minimum standards, which strengthen the protective outlook of consumer law, is less clear. First, there are Member States, such as the United Kingdom, which are nearer to the strong market bias of European policy. These countries, more often than not, simply made the EU minimum standards the national maximum standards, a tendency that gained momentum in the new Member States during the adaption process. EU directives were, more or less, literally copied into national law without paying too much attention as to whether or not the new EU rules comply with the existing body of consumer law.[120] At the other end, we find Member States who place more emphasis on the protective objective of consumer law and who used the leeway to upgrade the national standards of protection beyond the EU minimum level. Secondly, by the turn of the millennium, the ECJ oscillated back and forth between more market and more protection orientated interpretations of EU contract law directives. There are ECJ judgments which can be read as going beyond the image of the responsible consumer, approaching the image of the weaker, less knowledgeable consumer.[121] The distinction often drawn between the average consumer as the leitbild of primary EU law and the weak consumer as the leitbild of secondary EU consumer law somewhat overstates and simplifies the ECJ's case law.

Rather, national consumer law and policy and EU consumer law and policy start from different premises. Looking back, the rise of consumer law in the old Member States is inherently interwoven with the social welfare state paradigm. In the EU, consumer law bears the imprint of market building. The social dimension – the social outlook, the

---

[119] N. Reich, 'Protection of Consumers' Economic Interests by EC Contract Law – Some Follow-up Remarks', (2006) 28 *Sydney Law Review* 37–62; Wilhelmsson, 'The Contract Law Acquis', is quite critical about such attempts.

[120] The socialist countries had adopted consumer laws already before 1989, T. Roethe, 'Zum Konsumentenschutz in den MOE-Staaten – Transition und Rechtsvielfalt', in H.-W. Micklitz (eds.), *Rechtseinheit oder Rechtsvielfalt in Europa? Rolle und Funktion des Verbraucherrechts in der EG und MOE-Staaten*, pp. 205–240.

[121] Case C-240/98, *Océano Grupo Editorial and Salvat Editores* [2000] ECR I-4941, para. 25; Case C-96/00, *Gabriel* [2002] ECR I-6367, para. 58.

European Social Model – was tied up in market-building; it has never escaped the market logic. The EU 'rescued' consumer law as a policy paradigm, but there was a price to pay. The economic dimension of consumer law gained ground in the move from consumer protection law to the law of the consumer market society.

2.3.3 From Consumer Protection Law to Consumer Law and Back

The European ideal is the European consumer who shops across borders in a mood of relaxed, though attentive and self-responsible attention.[122] Yet, the hypothesis is that the current consumer law has lost a clear direction. Different trends can be distinguished. Indeed, at least in part, they even compete with each other. First, there is the move to full harmonisation promoted under the Lisbon Agenda. Second, there is the rise of the second generation of consumer law, i.e. the regulation of consumer services in regulated markets and the servicification of consumer goods through the digitalisation. Finally, the ECJ sometimes acts as a social engineer to manage the repercussions of the 2008 economic and Eurozone crisis on consumers.

The shift from consumer protection law to consumer law was initiated by the Lisbon Council and was fastened down in the 2002 consumer strategy. Since then, maximum harmonisation ranks high on the European Commission's political agenda. Directive 2002/65/EC on distant selling of financial services constituted the break-through in the realisation of the new paradigm. In a methodly interesting approach that transplants elements of Directive 2001/95/EC on general product safety, Directive 2005/29/EC on unfair commercial practices purports to harmonise unfair commercial practices with respect of B2C relationships.[123] The adoption of Directive 2008/48/EC on consumer credit followed suit[124] after a hard and long-lasting fight,

---

[122] B. Heiderhoff, *Grundstrukturen des nationalen und europäischen Verbrauchervertragsrechts: insbesondere zur Reichweite europäischer Auslegung* (München: Sellier European Law Publishers, 2004), pp. 289, 423 (new edition under preparation).

[123] Directive 2005/29/EC of the European Parliament and of the Council of 11 May 2005 concerning unfair business-to-consumer commercial practices in the internal market and amending Council Directive 84/450/EEC, Directives 97/7/EC, 98/27/EC and 2002/65/EC of the European Parliament and of the Council and Regulation (EC) No 2006/2004 of the European Parliament and of the Council, OJ No. L 149, 11.6.2005, p. 22; G. Howells, H.-W. Micklitz and T. Wilhelmsson, *European Fair Trading Law. The Unfair Commercial Practices Directive* (Aldershot: Ashgate, 2006), p. 83.

[124] Directive 2008/48/EC of the European Parliament and of the Council of 23 April 2008 on credit agreements for consumers and repealing Council Directive 87/102/EEC, OJ No. L 133, 22.5.2008, p. 66.

particularly as to whether a full harmonisation approach should be followed.[125] Directive 2008/122/EC[126] replaced Directive 94/47/EC on timesharing by an even more detailed set of fully harmonised rules. The European Commission presented a similar approach in its 2008 proposal on a directive on consumer rights, meant to substitute Directives 85/577/EEC on doorstep selling, 97/7/EC on distant selling, 93/13/EEC on unfair terms and 99/44/EC on consumer sales.[127] Not least due to forceful resistance from consumer advocates, the European Commission gave up the idea of fully harmonising unfair terms and consumer sales. Directive 2011/83, misleadingly called the Directive on Consumer Rights, however, fully harmonises direct selling and distant selling. The 2015 proposals of the European Commission on digital content[128] and on distance sales of consumer goods[129] both aim at full harmonisation. Directive 2014/17 on mortgage credit aims at maximum harmonisations.[130] Directive 2014/92 on payment accounts[131] and Directive 2015/2302 on package tours,[132] however, lay down minimum standards only.

In *Gysbrechts*, the ECJ argued for the first time ever in consumer contract law that particular national rules going beyond the EU minimum are not necessary to achieve an adequate level of protection and,

---

[125] H.-W. Micklitz, P. Rott and L. Tichy, *Impact Assessment of the Revised Proposal on Consumer Credit on the Member States Legislation in Czech Republic, Germany and the United Kingdom* (MS January, 2007) unpublished on file with the author.

[126] Directive 2008/122/EC of the European Parliament and of the Council of 14 January 2009 on the protection of consumers in respect of certain aspects of timeshare, long-term holiday product, resale and exchange contracts, OJ No. L 33, 3.2.2009, p. 10.

[127] COM (2008) 614 final, 8.10.2008; H.-W. Micklitz and N. Reich, 'Crónica de una muerte anunciada: The Commission Proposal for a "Directive on Consumer Rights"' (2009) 46 *Common Market Law Review* 471–519.

[128] COM (2015) 634 final, 9.12.2015.

[129] COM (2015) 635 final, 9.12.2015; C. Wendehorst and B. Zöchling-Jud (eds.), *Ein Neues Vertragsrecht für den digitalen Binnenmarkt?* (Wien: Manz, 2016).

[130] Directive 2014/17/EU of the European Parliament and of the Council of 4 February 2014 on credit agreements for consumers relating to residential immovable property and amending Directives 2008/48/EC and 2013/36/EU and Regulation (EU) No 1093/2010, OJ No. L 60, 28.2.2014, p. 34.

[131] Directive 2014/92/EU of the European Parliament and of the Council of 23 July 2014 on the comparability of fees related to payment accounts, payment account switching and access to payment accounts with basic features Text with EEA relevance, OJ L 257, 28.8.2014, p. 214.

[132] Directive (EU) 2015/2302 of the European Parliament and of the Council of 25 November 2015 on package travel and linked travel arrangements, amending Regulation (EC) No 2006/2004 and Directive 2011/83/EU of the European Parliament and of the Council and repealing Council Directive 90/314/EEC, OJ No. L 326, 11.12.2015, p. 1.

therefore, constitute disproportionate barriers to trade.[133] A second attempt initiated by business to strike down Spanish rules that allow for submitting price terms to judicial control, beyond the minimum standard in Directive 93/13, failed.[134] Today, it is unclear the extent to which the ECJ will apply the proportionality principle as a means to control national standards which reach beyond minimum EU protection or whether it is constitutionally permissible to do so. What does full harmonisation imply with regard to the separation of powers between the Member States and the EU in consumer law?[135] Full harmonisation takes away powers from the Member States. The hidden consensus between the European Commission and the Member States which boosted the adoption of minimum protection standards in the aftermath of the Internal Market programme collapsed, not silently, but publicly and widely. The new consumer leitbild is the economically efficient consumer which has to operate no longer merely in a European environment, but in an international one. Such an understanding becomes particularly clear in the two 2015 proposals on digital content and distance sales of consumer goods.[136]

The majority of the directives adopted and revised after 2000 still adhere in design to the first and second consumer programmes. The regulatory model they have in mind is the sales contract. However, the unfair terms directive applies to services as well, and the European banking sector is currently undergoing the painful experience of the control of its standard terms. At the time the directive was enacted, nobody thought about its potential impact on services. The idea behind the directive was to lay down general standards for all types of contracts. Gradually, however, service contracts sneaked into the scope of the directives on modalities of contract conclusion – direct and distant sales. There is no equivalent to the Consumer Sales Directive 99/44 and

[133] Case C-205/07, *Gysbrechts and Santurel Inter*; N. Reich and H.-W. Micklitz, 'Vollharmonisierung durch die Hintertür? – Zur Kritik der Schlussanträge der Generalanwältin Trstenjak in der Rs. Gysbrechts, C-205/07, v. 17.7.2008' (2008) 23 *Verbraucher und Recht* 349–351.
[134] Regarding Art. 4 (2) Directive 93/13/EC, Case C-484/08, *Caja de Ahorros y Monte de Piedad de Madrid* [2010] ECR I-4785.
[135] S. Weatherill, 'Minimum Harmonisation as Oxymoron? The Case of Consumer Law' and T. Wilhelmsson, 'European Consumer Law: Theses on the Task of the Member States', both in H.-W. Micklitz (ed.), *Verbraucherrecht in Deutschland – Stand und Perspektiven* (Baden-Baden: Nomos, 2005), pp. 15–36 and pp. 37–63, respectively.
[136] H.-W. Micklitz, 'Jack Is Out of the Box: The Efficient Consumer-Shopper' (2009) *Tidskrift Utgiven av Juridiska Föreningen i Finland* 417–436.

none to the Product Liability Directive 85/374. The ambitious project of a directive for the liability of services failed, and the Commission withdrew its proposal.[137]

The process of liberalisation and privatisation of former state monopolies in sectors such as telecommunication, energy and transport has significantly raised the importance of contract law, despite the fact that the bulk of the literature dealing with network services law predominantly focuses on its public law dimension. In fact, contract law is turned into a device to serve the overall purpose of liberalisation and privatisation of former public services, while the concept of universal services implants new principles into private law relations which may serve as nucleus for a genuine social European private law. The different directives and regulations shape network markets and network law: telecommunication (Directives 2009/22/EC, 2009/136/EC),[138] energy (2009/72/EC and 2007/93/EC)[139] and transport (passenger rights Reg. 261/2004 air,[140] Reg. 1371/2007 rail,[141] Reg. 1177/2010 ship,[142] Reg.

---

[137] U. Magnus and H.-W. Micklitz, *Liability for the Safety for Services* (Baden-Baden: Nomos, 2006) provide for an account of the state of affairs in a selected number of Member States and present at the end a proposal for an EU regulation dealing with the liability of services.

[138] Directive 2002/22/EC of the European Parliament and of the Council of 7 March 2002 on universal service and users' rights relating to electronic communications networks and services (Universal Service Directive), OJ No. L 108, 24.4.2002, p. 51; Directive 2009/136/EC of the European Parliament and of the Council of 25 November 2009 amending Directive 2002/22/EC on universal service and users' rights relating to electronic communications networks and services, Directive 2002/58/EC concerning the processing of personal data and the protection of privacy in the electronic communications sector and Regulation (EC) No 2006/2004 on cooperation between national authorities responsible for the enforcement of consumer protection laws, OJ No. L 337, 18.12.2009, p. 11.

[139] Directive 2009/72/EC of the European Parliament and of the Council of 13 July 2009 concerning common rules for the internal market in electricity and repealing Directive 2003/54/EC, OJ No. L 211, 14.8.2009, p. 55; Directive 2009/73/EC of the European Parliament and of the Council of 13 July 2009 concerning common rules for the internal market in natural gas and repealing Directive 2003/55/EC, OJ No. L 211, 14.8.2009, p. 94.

[140] Regulation (EC) No 261/2004 of the European Parliament and of the Council of 11 February 2004 establishing common rules on compensation and assistance to passengers in the event of denied boarding and of cancellation or long delay of flights, and repealing Regulation (EEC) No 295/91, OJ No. L 46, 17.2.2004, p. 1.

[141] Regulation (EC) No 1371/2007 of the European Parliament and of the Council of 23 October 2007 on rail passengers' rights and obligations, OJ No. L 315, 3.12.2007, p. 14.

[142] Regulation (EU) No 1177/2010 of the European Parliament and of the Council of 24 November 2010 concerning the rights of passengers when travelling by sea and inland waterway and amending Regulation (EC) No 2006/2004, OJ L 334, 17.12.2010, p. 1.

181/2011 bus[143]). The overwhelming bulk of the literature dealing with network law ignores this contractual dimension – whether it is B2B or B2C. This may be explained by the fact that the different sets of EC/EU directives deal only to a very limited extent with private law relations. The concept of universal services implants new principles and new legal concepts into private law relations, which may serve as nucleus for a genuine social European private law, reaching beyond access justice (Part III).

Insurance law (which is usually regarded as a subject of its own) and capital market law (investor protection law) resemble the approach chosen in the field of telecommunications, energy and transport. EC Directive 2004/39/EC on Markets in Financial Instruments[144] – the so-called MiFID Directive – lays down a broad framework, which aims to establish a coherent European capital market within level one of the Lamfalussy approach. After the financial crisis, MiFID II (Directive 2014/65/EU),[145] which repeals the MiFID I, and the MiFIR (Regulation (EU) 600/2014)[146] were enacted to make financial markets more efficient, resilient and transparent. Moreover, the MiFIR entrusts European and National Supervisory Authorities with the power to temporarily prohibit or restrict certain financial instrument activities when there is a significant investor protection concern or a threat to the orderly functioning of financial markets or the stability of the financial system in the Union. This amendment has led to litigation before the ECJ.[147] In line with the Lamfalussy procedure, two levels of law have been adopted: Directive 2006/73/EC on organisational requirements and operating conditions for investment firms,[148] and the implementing

---

[143] Regulation (EU) No 181/2011 of the European Parliament and of the Council of 16 February 2011 concerning the rights of passengers in bus and coach transport and amending Regulation (EC) No 2006/2004, OJ L 55, 28.2.2011, p. 1.

[144] Directive 2004/39/EC of the European Parliament and of the Council of 21 April 2004 on markets in financial instruments amending Council Directives 85/611/EEC and 93/6/EEC and Directive 2000/12/EC of the European Parliament and of the Council and repealing Council Directive 93/22/EEC, OJ L 145, 30.4.2004, p. 1.

[145] Directive 2014/65/EU of the European Parliament and of the Council of 15 May 2014 on markets in financial instruments and amending Directive 2002/92/EC and Directive 2011/61/EU Text with EEA relevance, OJ L 173, 12.6.2014, p. 349.

[146] Regulation (EU) No 600/2014 of the European Parliament and of the Council of 15 May 2014 on markets in financial instruments and amending Regulation (EU) No 648/2012, OJ No. L 173, 12.6.2014, p. 84.

[147] Case C-270/12, *United Kingdom v Parliament and Council* [2014] ECR I-000 on short selling.

[148] Commission Directive 2006/73/EC of 10 August 2006 implementing Directive 2004/39/EC of the European Parliament and of the Council as regards organisational

Regulation 2006/1287/EC. These combined measures already establish a dense network of rules, which contain strong links to contractual relations, where a professional or a private investor engages with his or her investment firm. The third level rules to be developed by national regulatory agencies are of primary concern for a deeper understanding of the transformation of private law rules. Again, the emphasis is placed on access rather than substance. Private law access rules are instrumentalised to establish a genuine European financial market.

The last characteristic is a kind of a double bifurcation. On the one hand, there is the EU consumer law on the sale of goods, and on the other, consumer rules on services contracts, broken down along the line of the different regulated markets. Whilst the first sector lies in the hand of the Directorate General, which is responsible for inter alia consumer policy, and despite the constant changing denomination (once DG Sanco (Santé Consommation) currently DG Just (Justice and Consumers)), the new field of services lies in the hands of the respective directorates. However, there does not seem to be much communication between DG Justice and the directorates responsible for the respective sectorial markets. The miscommunication, which mirrors the situation in the Member States, yields contract-related rules that follow the rationale of the respective sector, with no or little connection to the consumer law on sales or, more deeply, to traditional contract law. This is the first bifurcation. The second relates to the role of the ECJ in the two different fields. The ECJ has little or no role in the rules concerning regulated markets. The few judgments that exist provide little guidance on private law issues, whether B2b or B2c.[149] This is very different with regard to the established field of the first generation of consumer law. The effects of the economic and the Eurozone crisis have boosted the number of references to the ECJ via national courts, which often seek support for a more consumer-friendly interpretation of the respective national laws. The scope, reach and interpretation of the unfair terms directive lay at the heart of the litigation.

---

requirements and operating conditions for investment firms and defined terms for the purposes of that Directive, OJ No. L 241, 2.9.2006, p. 26.

[149] M. Cantero Gamito, *The Private Law Dimension of the EU Regulatory Framework for Electronic Communications: Evidence of the Self-Sufficiency of European Regulatory Private Law*, PhD thesis, European University Institute (2015); L. de Almeida, *Integration through Self-Standing European Private Law: Insights from the Internal Point of View to Harmonization in Energy Market*, PhD thesis, European University Institute (2017); Della Negra, *Private Law and Private Enforcement in the Post-Crisis EU Retail Financial Regulation*.

2.3.4 The Post-Classical Consumer Law

The analysis of the post-classical move in consumer law follows the same four parameters used in labour and anti-discrimination law: first, the rise of the consumer protection principle and the decline of its protective outlook that does *not* cut across vertical and horizontal direct effect of EU law; second, the focus of EU consumer law on granting access to the market for goods, services and to the transnational consumer society, whilst the leeway for the Member States to establish ex post redistributive measures is narrowed; third, the fragmentation of addressees of consumer protection, the move from consumer to customer and the differentiation between different groups of vulnerabilities; and fourth, the blurring line between court-based litigation and the increasing enforcement of private law through administrative agencies.

First, consumer protection has made its way into the Treaty of the Union. In the rhetoric of the ECJ, consumer protection is given constitutional standing. Until today, the implications of levelling up consumer protection to the constitutional level are still rather vague. Reich and I have tried to concretise the parameters of consumer protection in four directions:[150]

(1) Guarantees of the consumers' freedom of choice and decision, in particular by preventing fraudulent misrepresentation and by providing material information about products, services and markets;

(2) Protection of legitimate expectations against suppliers of products and services;

(3) Protection of special legal interests such as health and safety of products and services;

(4) Judicial protection and access to justice including collective legal protection and alternative dispute resolution mechanisms.

Art. 114 (3) TFEU shapes the Commission's attempts to complete the Internal Market (but not the Parliament or the Council) by specifying that EU law must reach '*a high level of protection* taking into account in particular of any new development based on scientific facts'. Art. 169 (1) TFEU is more outspoken: 'In order to promote the interests of consumers and to ensure a *high level of consumer protection*, the Community shall contribute to protecting the health, safety and economic interests of

---

[150] N. Reich and H.-W. Micklitz, 'Economic Law, Consumer Interests and EU Integration', in H.-W. Micklitz, N. Reich, P. Rott and K. Tonner (eds.), *European Consumer Law*, 2nd ed. (Antwerp; Cambridge; Portland: Intersentia, 2014), Chapter 1, pp. 6–65.

consumers as well as to promoting their right to information, education and to organise themselves in order to safeguard their interests'. Art. 38 of the Charter contains the principle of consumer protection whereby 'Union policies shall ensure a *high level of consumer protection*' without elevating it into the status of a subjective right in the sense of Art 52 (2) of the charter.

The four parameters focus on content. After the introduction of Art. 129(a) EC in the Treaty of Maastricht (now Art. 169 TFEU), the debate concentrated on the eventual self-standing character of consumer protection, independent from Art. 114 TFEU. In this view, the Social should gain a prominent constitutional standing, independent of Internal Market building. In *Corte Inglés*, the ECJ had to decide whether Art. 129(a) supports and legitimises the horizontal direct effect of Directive 87/102 on consumer credit. The Sixth Chamber denied any effect beyond regulating competences.[151] More important, seems to be the Court's '*obiter dicta*' in a decision on the validity of Directive 94/19/EC of 30 May 1994 on deposit-guarantee schemes.[152] The ECJ defined the relevance of consumer policy and the level of protection in the following words:

> In that regard it suffices to point out that, although consumer protection is one of the objectives of the Community, it is clearly not the sole objective ... Admittedly, there must be a high level of consumer protection concomitantly with those freedoms; however, no provision of the Treaty obliges the Community legislature to adopt the highest level of protection which can be found in a particular Member State ...

Therefore, the principle of consumer protection is not self-standing; it is connected to the Internal Market and needs to be concretised via secondary EU law. Consumer advocates reject the deep link between the market and consumer protection, insisting on the Social that has to prevail over the market logic. However, the uncoupling of the Social from social protection at EU level results from the transformation of the nation-state to the market state. The decreasing power of the nation-state creates leeway for civil society and for societal actors. Consumer

---

[151] Case C-192/94, *El Corte Inglés v. Blázquez Rivero* [1996] ECR I-1281, paras. 18–21, M. Jagielska and M. Jagielski, 'Are Consumer Rights Human Rights?', in J. Devenney and M. Kenny (eds.), *European Consumer Protection. Theory and Practice* (Cambridge: Cambridge University Press, 2012), pp. 336–353, at p. 349.

[152] Directive 94/19/EC of the European Parliament and of the Council of 30 May 1994 on deposit-guarantee schemes, OJ No. L 135, 31.5.1994, p. 5; Case C-233/94, *Germany v. Parliament and Council* [1997] ECR I-2405, para 48.

law oversteps the boundaries of the market towards post-nation-state citizenship, as will be explained in Part III.[153]

However, the ECJ refused to rule on social rights of weaker parties in national private laws. In *Alsthom Atlantique* and *CMC Motorradcenter*,[154] the ECJ exempted national private law from the scope of application of Art. 30 TFEU. If the ECJ would have answered the two preliminary references in the affirmative, binding national laws could have come under the compatibility test of Art. 30 TFEU. This would have been the most radical solution to remove national laws with a protective outlook. It would have provided the EU with the legitimacy to elaborate a 'European Civil Code'. At all events, the shift from consumer protection law to the law of the consumer market occurred less visibly. The guiding philosophy of EU consumer (and commercial) law is to increase competition through enhanced choice. Therefore, European consumer law is to be understood as competitive contract law.[155] Within the last 12 years, the European Commission has strengthened the competitive outlook of consumer contract law, not least through the shift from minimum to full harmonisation.

Second, the endless chain of the ECJ case law under Art. 30 TFEU is dominated by one single and outspoken objective: to strike down national laws that hinder the consumer to buy products goods and services from other countries. It is based on the premise that consumers are keen to buy foreign products and they have the resources to do so. The liberalisation of services follows the same line of argument, albeit with one important caveat. As far as former public services such as telecommunication, postal services, energy and transport are concerned, customers are dependent on access to these services for the organisation of their daily lives. Access depends, last but not least, on the price of these services. If the customer cannot afford to pay the market price, liberalisation and privatisation may turn into economic discrimination and financial exclusion. It will have to be shown in Part III that granting access

---

[153] Part III. 4.; more generally J. Davies, 'Consumer Protection in a Normative Context: The Building Blocks of a Consumer Citizenship Practice', in J. Devenney and M. Kenny (eds.), *European Consumer Protection. Theory and Practice* (Cambridge: Cambridge University Press, 2012), pp. 354–377; J. Davies, *The European Consumer Citizen in Law and Policy* (Houndmills; New York: Palgrave Macmillan, 2011).

[154] Case C-339/89, *Alsthom Atlantique* [1991] ECR I-107; Case C-93/92, *CMC Motorradcenter v. Baskiciogullari* [1993] ECR I-5009.

[155] H.-W. Micklitz, 'Concept of competitive contract law' (2005) 23 *Penn State International Law Review* 549–585.

requires more than choice and availability, that substantive minimum requirements have to be met.

There is potential in the ECJ case law to remove access barriers resulting from collective private regulation that limit the consumer's autonomy. This is the bright side of the *Cassis de Dijon* doctrine which put restrictions on the market under legitimacy pressure.[156] In *Frabo*, the ECJ had to deal with technical standards as possible barriers to the freedom of goods.[157] The regulatory focus within consumer law is on the regulation of the quality of goods and the rights and remedies consumers might and should have. Technical standards are a particular form of collective private regulation, which enjoys a privileged status under EU law. In the case at issue, they prevented an Italian company from getting access to the German market. The Court, contrary to the advocate general's opinion, denied horizontal direct effect. Could the developing doctrine be used to challenge the compatibility of standard contract terms with Art. 30 TFEU, in particular after *Elliot*?[158] What degree of collectivity is needed? When is the barrier to be determined as 'abusive'? *Bosman, Frabo,* and *Courage* provide an indication of the threshold of abusiveness each using a context-related understanding of abuse that requires clarification.[159]

Minimum harmonisation enabled the Member States to maintain ex post redistributive policies in form of higher standards to protect the particularly weak consumers who might not benefit from ever broader access to the market. With the move towards full harmonisation, EU consumer law undermines this opportunity, like in product liability after *Sanchez*. This does not matter so long as the EU provides for a 'high level of consumer protection' and a full-fledged set of EU remedies that allow the consumer to defend her rights. The different travel regulations stand on the other side of the spectrum. Whenever EU law fully harmonises whatever strand of EU law, the question arises as to who should then deal with the protection of the weaker party. The Member States are barred from taking action in fully harmonised fields of EU private law. In a legalistic perspective, they are free to take action only in areas that are not fully harmonised. Full harmonisation shifts to battlefield to enforcement. Member States and their courts might

---

[156] H.-W. Micklitz, 'Some Considerations on Cassis de Dijon and the Control of Unfair Contract Terms in Consumer Contracts'.
[157] Case C-171/11, *Fra.bo* [2012] ECR I-000.
[158] Case C-613/14, *James Elliott Construction* [2016] ECR I-000.
[159] For details Part III. 3.2.

simply resist and find ways to interpret EU law in a way that accommodates the interests of the weaker party. However, full harmonisation changes their responsibilities.[160] Within the fully harmonised area, the EU has not only absorbed competences from the Member States, but the EU has likewise accepted responsibility for looking after those who cannot meet the market standards. The EU regulation on universal services might serve as a blueprint for action. Here, EU law lays down basic standards to secure the supply of services to everyone, independent of the legal status and their degree of vulnerability, whereas Member States have to take measures to concretise concepts like 'affordability'. Via secondary EU law, the EU legislator achieves what the ECJ refused to grant in *Smith v. Advel* – a definition of the tolerable level of protection. This is a particular form of shared responsibility – the EU sets social standards via legislation (with the majority in the Council) that the Member States have to finance.[161]

Third, the differentiation between consumer and customer and between different groups of consumers, responsible, confident, vulnerable, leads to hierarchies in the level of protection – and along the lines of D. Kennedy to group-based identities. Customers have to be distinguished from consumers and vulnerable from responsible consumers. To accommodate the different groups of consumers, a flexible legal design of consumer law is needed so it can be adjusted to the needs of the different groups.[162] Provided collective regulation comes under the scope of Art. 30 TFEU, an additional complication arises. How should one define and delineate collective identities? Collective private regulations cover a broad range of activities, in particular when linked to governance. It resembles much more an umbrella term than a legal category, despite efforts such as those by F. Cafaggi,[163] to categorise the various phenomena. There is no case law yet, at least not at the EU level, although the ECJ is getting more and more involved in the assessment of 'private standards'. Both non-discrimination and consumer law deal with group or collective identities.[164] They engage in a competition over the best level

---

[160] Micklitz, Roethe and Weatherill (eds.), *Federalism and Responsibility*.
[161] Here is the difference between problematic case law of the ECJ on granting students the right to move freely in the EU and study medicine in Austria, Case C-147/03, *Commission v Austria* [2005] ECR I-5969.
[162] With regard to Germany, Micklitz, 'Do Consumers and Businesses need a New Architecture of Consumer Law?'.
[163] Cafaggi, 'Rethinking Private Regulation in the European Regulatory Space'.
[164] Schepel, *The Constitution of Private Governance*, where he discusses 'The Law on Standards', p. 403; H. Collins, The Revolutionary Trajectory of EU Contract Law towards Post-

of protection. Each group will claim that they need the highest protection available and will challenge any form of unequal treatment. Is it justifiable to distinguish between private regulation of trade unions, standard bodies, chambers of commerce, business, trade associations, consumer organisations, and civil society associations? The conflict lines are becoming even more complicated in intersectional discrimination or multi-reason collective private regulation barriers.[165]

Fourth, there is an obvious divide in the type and style of enforcement. In traditional consumer law, court-based litigation is stronger than ever. In the second generation of consumer law, the law on services and regulated markets, administrative enforcement gains ground even in private law. The liberalisation and privatisation of former public sectors went hand in hand with the establishment of regulatory agencies, first at the national level and today at the EU level through the establishment of sector-related agencies. Agentification is about to become a 'swearword' that enshrines in a nutshell the critique raised against the EU administrative state and EU technocracy.[166] There is evidence that the EU, via the European agencies, is trying to manage the enforcement policy of the respective national agencies. Independent from a degree of European influence, administrative authorities are interfering via soft or hard administrative action into existing contractual relations. They are shaping contractual relations in more than just B2C relations.[167] Most of these 'regulatory actions' have no formal legal status. They can only be reconstructed through careful empirical research, both in the vertical direction – the relationship between the agency and the addressee – and in the horizontal direction – the relationship between the parties to a contract or even third parties that are affected by the regulatory action.[168]

---

national law', in S. Worthington, A. Robertson and G. Virgo (eds.), *Revolution and Evolution in Private Law* (Oxford: Hart Publishing 2017), pp. 315–336, p. 321.

[165] Hancock, *Intersectionality*.
[166] Scholten and van Rijsbergen, 'The Limits of Agencification in the European Union'.
[167] ERC project on European Regulatory Private law, in particular the editorial of H.-W. Micklitz, 'The Public and the Private – European Regulatory Private Law and Financial Services' (2014) 10 *European Review of Contract Law* 473–475; the Special Issue contains contributions from O. O. Cherednychenko, Y. Svetiev and A. Ottow, H. Marjosola and F. della Negra; and Della Negra, *Private Law and Private Enforcement in the Post-Crisis EU Retail Financial Regulation*.
[168] Cantero Gamito, *The Private Law Dimension of the EU Regulatory Framework for Electronic Communications: Evidence of the Self-Sufficiency of European Regulatory Private Law*; De Almeida, *Integration through Self-Standing European Private Law: Insights from the Internal Point of View to Harmonization in Energy Market*; Della Negra, *Private Law and Private Enforcement in the Post-Crisis EU Retail Financial Regulation*.

Similar tendencies towards administrative enforcement can be reported outside regulated markets in fields where the European Commission has no enforcement competences at all: in consumer sales law, unfair commercial practices regulation or internet law. The European Commission has started to monitor compliance with the relevant EU rules via non-legal means of enforcement. Member States are free to decide whether they want to join the respective EU initiatives. Enforcement through administrative management seems to follow the distinction established in competition and environmental law. The European Commission focuses its attention on 'manifest infringements', to deliberately use the language of EU state liability or liability for anti-trust injuries. The Member States remain responsible for minor infringements of the EU law, which cannot be eliminated via the soft EU methods.[169] Contrary to labour and non-discrimination law, there is no preparedness to institutionalise consumer law enforcement at the EU level, with the exception of the cooperation in transborder conflicts under Regulation 2006/2004. The first draft proposal had proposed to considerably enlarge regulatory powers of the national competent authorities and even to grant the European Commission decision-making power.[170] The now-adopted revised regulation is much less ambitious, but it still strengthens the administrative enforcement of consumer law.[171]

---

[169] H.-W. Micklitz, 'Collective Private Enforcement in Antitrust Law – What Is Going Wrong in the Debate?', in J. Basedow, J. P. Terhechte, L. Tichý (eds.), *Private Enforcement of Competition law* (Baden-Baden, Nomos, 2011), pp. 101–119.

[170] Proposal for a Regulation of the European Parliament and of the Council on cooperation between national authorities responsible for the enforcement of consumer protection laws, COM(2016) 283 final, 25.5.2016.

[171] The final version is supposed to be published at the end of 2017, www.europarl.europa.eu/news/en/press-room/20171110IPR87814/buying-online-parliament-beefs-up-protection-against-fraudsters

3 Post-Classical European Private Law in Outline

The intermediate account is descriptive. It brings together the general features of labour, non-discrimination and consumer law under the same intellectual umbrella. The cross-subject perspective is broken down into its substantive and procedural dimensions. The substantive features of the post-classical private law deduced from the foregoing analysis are the following: quantity of regulatory law, the rationality and rationalities of sectorial regulation, the regulatory cascade from the legislature to 'technical standards', the legal nature of the rules and the revolutionary design of a rights-based approach. The procedural features are shaped through the laboratorian character of the European private law order, enshrined in its unstable constitutional infrastructure and through experimentalism in law-making and enforcement. This account reveals a rather messy field, replete with incoherence and uncertainties. In Part III, I will give shape to the post-classical private law that arises under these conditions.

3.1 General Features of Post-Classical Private Law

Quantity

The sheer quantity of rules that has to be mastered is stunning. In non-discrimination law, we have to deal with four directives, which have been amended over time. Then there is the first generation of consumer law and the growing number of ECJ judgments. Both fields of law, non-discrimination and first-generation consumer law, have been subjected to doctrinal treatment by academics in the last decades and have been put into a kind of 'order' to make it accessible.[1] The consumer law of the second generation adds a new layer to the debate. Angus Johnston framed it as follows:[2]

> One of the great difficulties presented by the combination of these two broad areas of EU law [the general EU law and EU energy law] is the array of terminology used by courts, legislators and commentators, often in a mutually inconsistent and overlapping fashion. A myriad of Venn diagrams[3] might be required to illustrate how these various terms [Johnston is concerned with the terminology of the consumer, customer and the like], might fit together and sit alongside each other ...

What is true for energy law is true for the other sectors too, telecommunication, postal services, transport, and financial services. It is not only secondary EU law, but also technical standards, guidelines and recommendations, which need to be checked with regard to their private law impact. In order to establish the Banking Union, the EU has produced more than 1,000 pages of EU law in less than three years.[4]

Rationality

Each sector is governed by its own rationality. Lawyers have to specialise in order to be able to participate in the sectorial communication between companies and regulatory agencies. The result of the specialisation is a further deepening of the ongoing fragmentation of law. Energy lawyers do not communicate with telecom lawyers, and banking

---

[1] C. Barnard, *EU Employment Law*, 4th ed. (Oxford; New York: Oxford University Press, 2012); Bercusson, *European Labour Law*; Bell, *Anti-Discrimination Law and the European Union*; Schiek, Waddington and Bell (eds.), *Cases, Materials and Text on National, Supranational and International Non-Discrimination Law*; H.-W. Micklitz, J. Stuyck and E. Terryn (eds.), *Cases, Materials and Text on Consumer Law* (Oxford: Hart Publishing, 2010); Reich, Micklitz, Rott and Tonner (eds.), *European Consumer Law*; G. Howells, C. Twigg-Flesner and T. Wilhelmsson, *Rethinking European Consumer Law* (Abingdon: Routledge, 2017).
[2] Johnston, 'Seeking the EU 'Consumer' in Services of General Economic Interest', p. 94.
[3] According to Wikipedia, a 'Venn diagram (also called a set diagram or logic diagram) is a diagram that shows all possible logical relations between a finite collection of different sets. Typically overlapping shapes, usually circles, are used, and an area-proportional or scaled Venn diagram is one in which the area of the shape is proportional to the number of elements it contains. These diagrams represent elements as points in the plane, and sets as regions inside curves. An element is in a set S just in case the corresponding point is in the region for S. They are thus a special case of Euler diagrams, which do not necessarily show all relations. Venn diagrams were conceived around 1880 by John Venn. They are used to teach elementary set theory, as well as illustrate simple set relationships in probability, logic, statistics, linguistics and computer science'; available at: https://en.wikipedia.org/wiki/Venn_diagram.
[4] Micklitz, 'The Internal Market and the Banking Union'.

lawyers do not communicate with transport lawyers. Whether a common denominator in private law relations can be distilled out of the European rules remains an open question. The tremendous monetary resources (nobody has ever made an effort to calculate the millions) and manpower (200 people were involved in its heyday from a limited number of Member States) poured into the elaboration of the European Civil Code through the Study Group and the Acquis Group is staggering. Yet, this academic exercise did not even touch the law of the regulated markets.

Non-discrimination law still looks like a field of law that is accessible and manageable. Such an assessment holds true at least with regard to social discrimination based on nationality, gender, race, age, disability, and religion. When it comes to economic discrimination, competition, energy, telecom, transport and financial lawyers enter the field.[5] Competition lawyers study the interplay between the EU ex post competition law and the ex ante EU law of the regulated market. Despite fascinating overlaps, social discrimination and economic discrimination are not studied together. Specialisation and fragmentation renders communication between lawyers difficult, if not impossible. One may wonder whether Dworkin's Hercules, immensely wise and with full knowledge of legal sources is not needed everywhere to drive a cut through the thicket of the legal undergrowth that has emerged in the last decades. EU law-making resembles Grimm's fairy tale of the sweet porridge. Nobody knows the secret words that stop the law cooking, though.[6]

---

[5] For a comprehensive overview: E. Deutscher, The Principle of Non-Discrimination in EU Economic Law, on file with author.

[6] English version of the fairy tale on the sweet porridge, available at www.grimmstories.com/language.php?grimm=103&l=de&r=en; 'There was a poor but good little girl who lived alone with her mother, and they no longer had anything to eat. So the child went into the forest, and there an aged woman met her who was aware of her sorrow, and presented her with a little pot, which when she said, "Cook, little pot, cook," would cook good, sweet porridge, and when she said, "Stop, little pot," it ceased to cook. The girl took the pot home to her mother, and now they were freed from their poverty and hunger, and ate sweet porridge as often as they chose. Once on a time when the girl had gone out, her mother said, "Cook, little pot, cook." And it did cook and she ate till she was satisfied, and then she wanted the pot to stop cooking, but did not know the word. So it went on cooking and the porridge rose over the edge, and still it cooked on until the kitchen and whole house were full, and then the next house, and then the whole street, just as if it wanted to satisfy the hunger of the whole world, and there was the greatest distress, but no one knew how to stop it. At last when only one single house remained, the child came home and just said, "Stop, little pot," and it stopped and gave up cooking, and whosoever wished to return to the town had to eat his way back.'

The existent European private law is no longer the law made by judges (in the common law), or by a highly selected group of specialised academics that develop an abstract system of law (France, Germany or the Draft Common Frame of Reference (DCFR)). The European private law looks more like a cascade that grows in terms of quantity and specification from each level to the next. There is not one cascade; there are many cascades, bigger and smaller ones, and they do not even unite in the same strong and wide river. The many law-making cascades produce legitimacy deficits due to the involvement of private parties and a lack of coordination and coherence. The cause behind the growth is the delegation mechanism, from parliaments to the executive and from there to experts in the respective fields. European integration and multi-level governance has made delegation even more complex. Many attempts have been undertaken at the nation-state level and the EU to reinstall parliamentary control. They have all largely failed. The increasing delegation documents the change of the nineteenth century society of individuals to the twenty-first century society of networks.[7] The extension of judicial review is supposed to compensate for legitimacy deficits. It is here that Dworkin's Herculean judge comes in.

Nature of the Law

The law-making machinery seems unstoppable. The delegation from Parliament to the executive and to economic and scientific experts seems irreversible. The question remains whether all these secondary EU rules that govern regulatory private law are still to be regarded as 'law'. ECJ case law provides ample evidence of the attempts of the advocate generals and judges to find 'law' in the sometimes self-contradictory directives and regulations. Yet, there are too many rules and not enough 'law'. Public officials in regulatory agencies, who are in charge of monitoring and supervising the regulated markets, face similar difficulties. How can a public official in a financial agency know 1,000 pages of 'law'? Administrative activities do not necessarily end up in formal regulatory actions that can be submitted to judicial review. This is what administrative authorities have in common with ADR bodies. Both are required to apply the law. European courts have to examine their arguments and submit them to justification. Even 'technical standards' are

---

[7] K.-H. Ladeur, 'The Evolution of General Administrative Law and the Emergence of Postmodern Administrative Law' (2011) *Comparative Research in Law & Political Economy*. Research Paper No. 16.

coming under judicial scrutiny. Ten years ago, H. Schepel had already identified an emerging 'law on standards' that requests courts to submit the governance structure of technical standard bodies to judicial review.[8] Habermas' critique is more far-reaching.[9] He calls EU law 'technolaw', as it is made by Eurocrats and lacks democratic legitimacy. Building on Habermas, Collins[10] distinguishes three features of technolaw: 'its high degree of instrumentalism, its applicable scope defined in terms of functional entities instead of persons and its incompleteness'.[11] European labour, non-discrimination and consumer law seem to be aligned with such an understanding of EU technolaw. European private law puts the person on the frontstage, though in the form of 'representatives'. Collins claims that there is a 'revolution' under way in European private law, a threefold change in the rule of recognition (Hart): technolaw, rights-based approach and a kind of transnational law. European private law is said to be distinct from Max Weber's materialisation. The balancing purpose does not serve the individuals but the Internal Market. Fundamental and human rights are instrumentalised for the market-building purposes in both directions – to the benefit of the employer, supplier or the benefit of the consumer, worker. The result is materialisation, thin social justice, viz. *access justice*.

However, the rights-based approach cannot replace the lack of values in EU private law. These have to be taken from European access and national social justice.[12] Constitutionalisation might allow for overcoming the fragmented EU law. Constitutionalisation serves as a tool in the search of where the law is in all these rules, how these rules are tied together and whether there is a common constitutional bottom line. The result might be a set of rules on 'constitutionalised' private law. These are not 'hierarchical' constitutional rules, in the public law Kumm-total constitutional sense, but more like Teubnerian-

---

[8] Schepel, *The Constitution of Private Governance*, p. 403.
[9] J. Habermas, *The Lure of Technocracy* (Cambridge: Polity Press, 2015).
[10] H. Collins, 'The Revolutionary Trajectory of EU Contract Law towards Post-national law', p. 318.
[11] R. Metz, 'Credit Scoring: Will Our Digital Identity Replace the Real Person?', in K. Purnhagen and P. Rott (eds.), *Varieties of European Economic Law and Regulation. Liber Amicorum for Hans Micklitz*, pp. 635–650; H.-W. Micklitz, 'The Legal Subject, Social Class and Identity Based Rights', in L. Azoulai, S. Barbou des Places and E. Pataut (eds.), *Constructing the Person in EU Law: Rights, Roles, Identities* (Oxford: Hart Publishing, 2016), pp. 285–310; same author, 'The Constitutional Transformation of Private Law Pillars through the CJEU'.
[12] Similar, R. Condon, *Tort Law beyond the Reasonable Man: Re-Thinking Tort Law beyond the State*, PhD thesis, European University Institute (2017).

Gerstenbergian side constraints on economisation, as will be developed in Part III.[13] The 'constitutionalised' private law should and must be taken into consideration, not only by courts but also by administrative bodies and out-of court settlement bodies. In this sense, there is indeed a revolution under way.

3.2 General Features of the Private Law Laboratory

The metaphor of a laboratory implies that there is a well-shielded closed device, scientists agreeing on a test procedure and substances used to get the test procedure going. Stepping back, one might add that there must be somebody in the background who has set up the laboratory and who is paying for it. Since its beginning, the EU has been in the 'making'. Its legal order and its constitution have been endlessly described as a 'process'. Whilst the Internal Market is and remained the focus, there was and there is always the hope or fear that the EU should or could go beyond the market, and should or could build a European Social Model, a European society or a European identity. The unstable structure of the EU and the inconsistency of the political element allow for and promote experimentalism: experimentalism in the law-making, experimentalism in the law-making, experimentalism in the judiciary and in the role of the executive. Experimentalism is inbuilt into a laboratory. Each new experiment should, in theory, help to improve the substance and procedure of European private law. The rationality logic that stands behind EU law enables the EU to raise important and timely questions, but not necessarily to find the correct answers. In this way, the EU suffers from a legitimacy deficit. Impact assessments are a tool to manage the uncertainty enshrined in experimentalism.

Institutional (Constitutional) Experimentalism

The EU has grown from 6 to 28 Member States, and is now shrinking to 27 or less. It is composed of what is called 'Europe', with all the difficulties of defining what Europe means and who belongs to Europe. There is (was), however, the deeper conviction that the old Member States and the new Member States share a common foundation, namely the common European legal culture. It turned out that the common foundation has

---

[13] M. Bell, 'Constitutionalization and EU Employment Law', in H.-W. Micklitz (ed.), *Constitutionalization of European Private Law* (Oxford: Oxford University Press, 2014), pp. 137–169, at p. 167.

become shaky and so has the whole European experiment. If it collapses, the remainders will be indispensable bricks for building the post-nation-state and the post-nation-state legal order. The United Kingdom will serve for the years to come as a blueprint for studying whether and to what extent a former empire that remains one of the five big economies of the world manages the adaptation process. In other words, how much will remain of EU law in the UK legal order after Brexit? With regard to first-generation consumer law, the predications are pretty clear. The current government does not intend to withdraw all the EU legislation.[14] It is equally hard to imagine that the United Kingdom will eliminate consumer protection out of the rules on the regulated markets. Since the late 1980s, the United Kingdom had strongly influenced the EU rules on liberalising and privatising the former public sector, on financial services and initially also on the anti-discrimination directives. But what will happen in the future, after Brexit? EU anti-discrimination law has come to a halt, but the acquis is not (yet) in jeopardy.

Law-making and Law Interpreting Experimentalism

The Single European Act had set the law-making machinery into motion that continues to shape the rules of the procedure. The new approach to technical standards and regulation, adopted in 1985, left a deep imprint on the drafting process of the DCFR and provided the backstage for European regulation of out-of-court dispute settlement.[15] The technical regulatory means of experimentalism started here. It is here where the script was written for the roles and responsibilities of the different actors in law-making: the division between law to be adopted via the normal EU legislative procedure and the technolaw that involved the European Commission as the spider in the web, the national administrations that gained power outside national constitutional procedures of accountability, the technical bodies providing the expertise for the

---

[14] G. Howells is currently undertaking research on exactly this question; see his lecture entitled 'Consumer Law in the UK after Brexit' at the European University Institute, 16 November 2017.

[15] H.-W. Micklitz, 'Review of Academic Approaches to the European Contract Law Codification Project', in M. Andenas, S. Diaz Alabart, Sir B. Markesinis, H.-W. Micklitz and N. Pasquino, *Liber Amicorum Guido Alpa: Private Law Beyond the National Systems* (London: British Institute of International and Comparative Law, 2007), pp. 699–728; with regard to ADR, H.-W. Micklitz, 'Privatisation of Access to Justice and Soft Law – Lessons from the European Community?', in T. Wilhelmsson and S. Hurri (eds.), *From Dissonance to Sense. Welfare State Expectations, Privatisation, and Private Law* (Aldershot: Ashgate, 1998), pp. 505–548.

development of the technical standards and the involvement of civil society associations that should legitimate technolaw.[16] Today technolaw, and the role of the Eurocrats, is at the heart of all the arguments of those who criticise the democratic, the political and the justice deficit of the EU.[17] In that sense, the European laboratory is said to produce untenable, unacceptable and illegitimate results to the detriment of the people, to the detriment of democracy and more important even to the detriment of the 'political'.[18] What is the alternative to technolaw? Is there an alternative at all? One might understand that technolaw is an experimental form of law-making/rule-making.

Embedding private law relations into the broader economic context allows for contextualising contractual relationships. Is this the true advantage of European laboratarian law-making? The pre- and the post-contractual phases are subject to all sorts of regulations that deal with the conditions under which a person has access and the conditions under which a contract is executed. Experimentalism does not stop at law-making/rule-making à la the New Approach. The European judiciary forms an integral part of the experiment. Judicial experimentalism can be found in consumer law[19] and in non-discrimination law.[20] Directive 2004/113, which extends in Art. 3 (1) beyond employment relations, might serve as a showcase:[21]

1. Within the limits of the powers conferred upon the Community, this Directive shall apply to all persons who provide goods and services, which are available to the public irrespective of the person concerned as regards both the public and private sectors, including public bodies, and which are offered outside the area of private and family life and the transactions carried out,

2. This Directive does not prejudice the individual's freedom to choose a contractual partner as long as an individual's choice of contractual partner is not based on that person's sex.

---

[16] H.-W. Micklitz, 'Produktsicherheit und technische Normung in der Europäischen Gemeinschaft – Zu den Leistungsmöglichkeiten und -grenzen des Selbstregulierungsmodells als Mittel des Verbraucherschutzes', in H. Paetow and K. Tonner (eds.), *Staatliche Wirtschaftsregulierung in der Krise* (Opladen: Westdeutscher Verlag, 1986), pp. 109–126; Micklitz, 'Services Standards: Defining the Core Consumer Elements and Their Minimum Requirements', study commissioned by ANEC (Brussels, 2007), available at: www.anec.eu/attachments/ANEC-R&T-2006-SERV-004final.pdf.
[17] Chalmers, Jachtenfuchs, Joerges (eds.), *The End of the Eurocrats' Dream*.
[18] S. Bartolini, *The Political*, forthcoming 2018.
[19] Gerstenberg, 'The Question of Standards for the EU', p. 73.
[20] As documented by Xenidis, 'Shaking the normative foundations of EU equality law'.
[21] OJ No. L 373, 21.12.2004, p. 40.

The directive embarks on new territory without having sounded out the implications and consequences – despite all the impact assessment rhetoric. With the unanimous support of all Member States, the EU combines non-discrimination and private law.[22] *Test-Achats* came as a bombshell. The judgment was a wake-up call for the Member States and the insurance business. However, the reach of the new rule is unclear. What the coming together of contract law and non-discrimination law will look like needs to be refined in many more test cases. The all-embracing perspective opens up new perspective and thereby necessarily yields experimentalism.

Is the incoherence of EU law a weakness or a strength? The German Ministry of Justice (at least parts of it) celebrates each parliamentary session where the BGB has *not* been amended as a success. Why? Because of the old fear that democratic intervention leads to a politicisation of the private law systems. It introduces foreign elements and destroys the inner logic.[23] The EU has no private law system to 'defend'. The EU can experiment at the borderlines of private law, at the periphery so to speak, where the economic character of private law is most obvious. The Internal Market project invites the European Commission to experiment on how to achieve that objective. The first and second generation of European consumer law, the move from sales law to the law of services, from traditional contract law rules to sectorial regulation, can and should be understood as a form of experimentalism. The EU reacts to a fast-moving economy and society together, and at least politically in agreement with the Member States, which have left the driver's seat to the European Commission.

Enforcement Experimentalism

The multi-level structure of the EU has turned enforcement into one of the largest laboratory.[24] The treaty does not provide the European

---

[22] D. Schiek, *Differenzierte Gerechtigkeit. Diskriminierungsschutz und Vertragsrecht* (Baden-Baden: Nomos, 2000).

[23] On democracy and private law comparing and analysing texts from Ripert, Kübler and Wilhelmsson, in Micklitz, 'Demokratie und Privatrecht'; also C. Joerges and T. Ralli (eds.), *European Constitutionalism without Private Law – Private Law without Democracy*, (2011) RECON Report No, 14, ARENA Report 3/11, available at: www.reconproject.eu/project web/portalproject/Report14_ConstitutionalismPrivateLawDemocracy.html.

[24] C. Hodges' empirical research on regulatory agencies, on ADR and on collective redress, C. Hodges, I. Benöhr, N. Creutzfeldt, *Consumer ADR in Europe* (Oxford: Hart Publishing, 2012) and C. Hodges, *The Reform of Class and Representative Actions in European Legal Systems*.

Commission with enforcement powers outside competition and agriculture. One way to look at the different efforts of the European Commission to get into enforcement through the infringement procedure in environmental protection or through new modes of public/private governance in consumer law is to categorise the phenomenon as competence creep. Is it the leviathan who awoke and who is grasping power, or is the EU at the forefront of the challenge all states are facing today, namely how to enforce the law beyond the nation-state?[25] The EU has very limited competences and that is why it has to be imaginative in developing enforcement policies, such as the distinction between minor and major infringements of the (EU) law. The regulatory private law is a wonderful field of study. Non-discrimination remains in the hands of the Member States. The Fundamental Rights Agency can only indirectly deal with discrimination issues. In the law on regulated markets, there are agencies, even at the EU level, but they have no regulatory power to take action – outside short selling.[26] That is why the European Commission uses guidelines and even less formal ways to coordinate enforcement all over Europe. Should there be coordinated enforcement, at least for major infringements of EU law, like in Dieselgate?[27] Is it not that, in particular in the United Kingdom, new modes of enforcement in regulated markets are tested, which affect private law and that could be called 'administrative enforcement of private law'?[28]

The EU is challenging legal orders like the German or the French one, where rights of workers, of consumers, of the discriminated against have to be enforced via the private law system. Administrative enforcement seems better suited to coordinate enforcement across borders than collective private enforcement. The shift towards administrative enforcement implies an open political discussion on how to best enforce non-discrimination and consumer law.[29]

---

[25] Contributions in H.-W. Micklitz and A. Wechsler (eds.), *The Transformation of Enforcement. European Economic Law in a Global Perspective* (Oxford: Hart Publishing, 2016).

[26] Case C-270/12, *United Kingdom v. Parliament and Council*.

[27] A. Beckers, 'The Regulation of Market Communication and Market Behaviour: Corporate Social Responsibility and the Directives on Unfair Commercial Practices and Unfair Contract Terms' (2017) 54 *Common Market Law Review* 475–515.

[28] H.-W. Micklitz, 'Administrative Enforcement of European Private Law', in R. Brownsword, H.-W. Micklitz, L. Niglia and S. Weatherill (eds.), *The Foundations of European Private Law* (Oxford: Hart Publishing, 2011), pp. 563–592.

[29] Schulte-Nölke and Bundesministerium der Justiz und für Verbraucherschutz (eds.), *Neue Wege zur Durchsetzung des Verbraucherrechts*.

Member States defend their sovereignty, but what happens if they are not even providing for the necessary infrastructure to organise enforcement effectively? Is the German system that relies on private law remedies and national courts really best suited to enforce the collective interests of consumers?

4 The Way Ahead: Rationality Test, Shared Responsibilities, Fragmented Status

It is clear from the foregoing that the EU should not be compared to a nation-state and, in particular, not to a nation-state which has undergone hundred(s) (of) years of development. Nor should EU private law be compared to the national private law order. Research that takes 'the' or 'an' idealised variation of the national welfare state or an idealised version of a social private law as an implicit or explicit yardstick has no difficulties identifying a social justice deficit. The normative potential of the European experiment can only unfold if there is leeway for experimentalism, if the EU does not turn into a fully fledged market or administrative state that centralises power, and if full harmonisation does not become the leading paradigm. Full harmonisation is not in line with the European competence order and, worse yet, full harmonisation prevents or controls efforts of redistribution through private law at a national level.[1] By enshrining all power in the hands of the EU, full harmonisation freezes the status quo and structurally limits the possibility of innovation aimed at improving the path already taken.[2]

The normative potential is broken down into three issues, namely the power and reach of the rationality test, the concept of shared responsibilities between the Member States, the EU and private parties, and the consequences that result from the fragmented status-related justice. The dialectics of *Cassis de Dijon* require that existing national rules on the Social need to be justified against the predominance of the economic freedoms before the European Commission and the ECJ. In secondary EU law, the rationality test requires potential addressees, not only Member States, but also the EU and private parties, to rationalise

---

[1] Introduction. 2.3.
[2] C. Twigg-Flesner, 'From REFIT to a Rethink: Time for Fundamental EU Consumer Law Reform?' (2017) 6 *Journal of European Consumer and Market Law* 185–189.

restrictions to individual freedoms. All three are involved in rule-making. All three share not only competences, but also responsibilities. Both the rationality test and the concept of shared responsibilities document this potential. The fragmented status relates to the overall tendency of EU law to break up the notion of the worker and the consumer and to differentiate between degrees of weaknesses that are reflected in the requirements of justice. The way ahead is an option – it is not (yet?) established EU law. The aim is to indicate the direction of European experimentalism.

4.1 The Power and Reach of the Rationality Test

The rationality test which follows from *Cassis de Dijon*[3] could be summed up as follows: if Member States decide to lawfully restrict the basic freedoms under the European legal order (European Constitution), they have to show that these restrictions are 'reasonable'.[4] Rationality refers to Max Weber's concept and understanding of the role and function of law.[5] The rationality of modern formal law is said to indicate its functionality for capitalist economies and the bureaucratic-legal system of government. By reference to Weber, Christian Joerges speaks 'of a law-making policy that is instrumentally and purposively rational'. The concept of rationality is said to replace practical and value-rational elements of law by methodically controlled argumentatively and systematically structured doctrines. Whilst this formula may serve as a starting point, it does not address the complexity of primary and secondary EU law, let alone the potential addressees of the modern formal rationality. The rationality test enshrined in *Cassis de Dijon*, this is my argument, cuts across primary and secondary EU law horizontally, and EU law and national laws vertically. The rationality test allows for placing each kind of restriction to the market and to personal autonomy, whether statutorily or privately induced, under scrutiny. This is the power behind the rationality test. It is the stronger the more harmonised the EU law is. It enables the court to ask uncomfortable questions, which does not mean that the rationality

---

[3] Case 120/78, *Rewe-Zentral AG v Bundesmonopolverwaltung für Branntwein*. K. Purnhagen discusses the many implications of the judgment but not the rationality doctrine, 'The Virtue of Cassis de Dijon 25 Years Later – It Is Not Dead. It Just Smells Funny', in K. Purnhagen and P. Rott (eds.), *Varieties of European Economic Law and Regulation: Liber Amicorum for Hans Micklitz*, pp. 315–342.
[4] Ch. Joerges, 'Die Europäisierung des Privatrechts als Rationalisierungsprozess und als Streit der Disziplinen' (1995) *Zeitschrift für Europäisches Privatrecht* 181-201, at p. 186.
[5] Weber, *Wirtschaft und Gesellschaft*, p. 503.

test is necessarily able to provide appropriate answers. The argument will be unfolded in five steps: reach, addressee, content of the argument, regulatory technique and effects.

Scope

All Member States laws and regulations, which come under the scope of the four market freedoms, such as labour or consumer law, have to pass the rationality test. The *Cassis de Dijon* logic is grounded in the initial construction of the European Union and its strong market bias, which has neither been changed by Single European Act nor by the Treaty of Lisbon through the insertion of social market economy. Secondary EU law and the Charter of Fundamental Rights enable corrections without, however, fully addressing the market bias. An endless chain of judgments demonstrates the pressure the ECJ puts on national non-economic policy areas: *Viking* and *Laval* in labour law[6] and *Cassis de Dijon* and *German Beer* in consumer law.[7] The leitbild of the consumer and the worker in EU law, the famous responsible and circumspect consumer or worker, serves to question a potentially more protective outlook.[8] The rationality test does not rule out different national *Leitbilder*, neither within the scope of application of the EU law nor outside its scope of application. However, these restrictions can only pass the rationality test, if there are non-arbitary reasons given. *Alsthom Atlantique* and *CMC Motorradcenter*[9] exempt the traditional private law orders as such from the rationality test. Collective agreements, however, come under the scope of the four freedoms. They have to pass the rationality test.

The scope and reach of the *Cassis de Dijon* logic is not limited to the four economic freedoms. The rationality test applies within secondary law-making too.[10] The *Cassis de Dijon* logic is 'the' driving force behind

---

[6] Case C-438/05, *The International Transport Workers' Federation and The Finnish Seamen's Union*; Case 341/05, *Laval un Partneri*.
[7] Case 120/78, *Rewe-Zentral AG v Bundesmonopolverwaltung für Branntwein*; Case178/84 *Commission v Germany*.
[8] On this concept in private law with regard to consumer protection issues, T. Wilhelmsson, *Critical Studies in Private Law* (Dordrecht: Kluwer Academic Publishers, 1992) and Ayres, 'Fair Driving', who demonstrates that retail car dealership systematically offered substantially better prices to white men than they did to black people and women.
[9] Case C-339/89, *Alsthom Atlantique*, para. 16; Case C-93/92, *CMC Motorradcenter v. Baskiciogullari*, paras. 10-13, where the ECJ exempted traditional private law rules from the scope of Art. 30 TFEU.
[10] Micklitz, 'Some Considerations on Cassis de Dijon and the Control of Unfair Contract Terms in Consumer Contracts' (2008), p. 37.

the overall integration process; it links market freedoms and restrictions of the market freedoms inherently together. It is a double-sided principle covering freedom *and* restrictions rather than a single-sided one meant to test restrictions against freedoms only. In this way, the *Cassis de Dijon* logic reaches beyond Weber and beyond the reading giving to it by Joerges. The extension of the *Cassis de Dijon* logic follows from the legal basis used. Art. 114 TFEU (formerly Art. 100 a, Art. 95) is the Trojan horse which introduces the rationality doctrine into secondary EU law. In *Laval* and *Gysbrechts*,[11] the ECJ extended the rationality doctrine to secondary EU law, namely the posting worker and distant selling directive. Member States are only allowed to go beyond the minimum level of harmonisation provided they respect the proportionality principle.

Rational Arguments

The key point then is what counts as *rational arguments*. Weber binds rationality to the formality of law and the doctrine that shields the formal character of the law. The ECJ uses Art. 36 TFEU as a benchmark for the rationality test, and it proceeds via policies. In line with the analysis of the successes and failures of national labour and consumer laws, the rationality test can be broken down into economic (distributive) effectiveness, societal effectiveness and economic efficiency.[12] One might understand the rationality test as a catalyst and as a tool, to examine the distributive effects and the societal impact of social regulation. *Cassis de Dijon* was decided in 1979. This was exactly the time when the national welfare state rhetoric began to crumble. The coincidence highlights the interconnectivity between the decline of the welfare state and the rise of the European social. They follow the same logic, which is enshrined in the rationality test. *Cassis de Dijon* imposed the rationality test on the Member States' social laws, not only within the ambit of EU law but, in line with the Zeitgeist, also on the Member States' social regulations. Indirectly, it reached national social regulation. The rationality test forms an integral part of Europe's intellectual history and Europe's legal consciousness. It might reach its limits when faced with the national 'identity' defence. Member States might argue that their national legal orders and their concepts of justice belongs to their 'national identity', which is protected by the treaty. National

---

[11] Case C-205/07, *Gysbrechts and Santurel Inter*.
[12] Part II. 2.

identity may be turned into a rational argument.[13] It unfolds its normative power within the limits of the subsidiarity principle and minimum harmonisation.

The *addressee* of the *Cassis de Dijon* logic is the EU as the law-maker, Member States who implement the EU directives and the private parties involved in law-making.[14] Along the lines of the proposed threefold set of criteria, this leads to far-reaching consequences. The whole body of secondary EU law is to be evaluated, with obvious and highly problematic results. The strong language the European Commission uses in its evaluation of the Member States' legislation can be turned against the EU as the instigator and against the European Parliament and the Council as the legislative organs of the EU. The European Commission, then, has to demonstrate in each and every proposal the potential economic distributive efficiency, the potential societal effectiveness and the impact of measures on culture and identity. Legally speaking, there is uncertainty as to what extent the rules of the treaty and the case law of the ECJ apply to the EU itself.[15]

The European Commission has indirectly accepted the rationality test. It has set up two mechanisms that come close to what a rationality test requires. The first is the impact assessment introduced in 2002. Modernised and adapted to the needs of the rationality test, a revised impact assessment can contribute to discover inefficient, ineffective legislative measures and to evaluate the potential effects on society as a whole. The European Commission has submitted consumer law directives to a fitness check. The design of the fitness check as well as the results probably do not meet the standards of the rationality test, despite the 3,500 pages which have been produced by the research group.[16] Full harmonisation is still the agenda that drives the project. This excludes the search for alternatives and for experiments as well as a serious evaluation of the kind of justice which has been achieved.[17]

---

[13] G. Comparato, *Nationalism and Private Law in Europe* (Oxford: Hart Publishing, 2014), in particular Chapter 3, p. 131.

[14] The *Cassis de Dijon* logic cannot be applied to national law outside the treaty or to private parties not involved in EU law- and rule-making.

[15] On the applicability of the EU law to the EU, M. Javis, '4 Scope Persons Bound' in P. Oliver (ed.), *Free Movement of Goods in the European Union* (Oxford: Oxford University Press, Fifth Edition, 2010), pp. 60–66.

[16] More information can be found on the website of DG Just, in particular the information available at: http://ec.europa.eu/newsroom/just/item-detail.cfm?item_id=59332.

[17] Twigg-Flesner, 'From REFIT to a Rethink', 185; H.-W. Micklitz, 'Eine merkwürdige Welt – Beobachtungen zur sog. Verbraucherforschung der Europäischen Kommission' (2016) *Verbraucher und Recht* 321–322.

The second mechanism is the requirement to check the compatibility of each and every piece of secondary EU law with the Charter of Fundamental Rights. The results so far show the potential of the compatibility test, but a lot needs to be done to make it a serious instrument for ensuring compliance.[18] In consumer law, the relationship between Charter of Fundamental Rights and secondary EU law is not an easy one. The key problem is that consumer protection shows up in the Charter but only as a principle that has to be observed and not as an individual right. That is why consumer interests can only be integrated into the Charter via the backdoor of more express rights. This is very different with regard to labour law and non-discrimination law, where the Charter is much more outspoken.

The much more difficult question is whether business has to pass the rationality test too in employment and consumer relations, let alone the question of horizontal direct effect of primary and secondary EU law. This would mean that within EU harmonised legal fields, business in making use of *autonomie de la volonté* (autonomy of the will), of *Privatautonomie* (private autonomy) or freedom of contract would have to provide rational arguments for any restriction of the autonomy of the worker or consumer. Is this a revolution? Already in 1942, F. Kessler[19] wrote his pivotal article on 'contrats d'adhésion' where he diagnosed a 'radical change' in the way contracts were used through parties with superior power, stressing the need to understand freedom and coercion as Siamese twins. 'Power' is a difficult category for lawyers.[20] Superior power can be exercised in private relations collectively via standardised terms or standardised marketing practices or individually outside any form of collective agreements. The legislatures around the world have extensively dealt with the regulation of standard terms and marketing practices, quite often drawing a careful line between collective and individual forms of restrictions. Under existing EU law, a distinction has to be drawn between collective agreements and collective practices. The former involve organisations and associations, the latter refer to single companies using standardised/collectivised practices. The reversal of the freedom/coercion metaphor with regard to collective agreements may be backed through the established case law of the ECJ. What is new is the extension to

---

[18] V. Kosta, *Fundamental Rights in EU Internal Market Legislation* (Oxford: Hart Publishing, 2015).
[19] F. Kessler, 'Contracts of Adhesion. Some Thoughts about Freedom of Contract' (1943) 43 *Columbia Law Review* 629–642.
[20] F. Möslein (ed.), *Private Macht* (Tübingen: Mohr Siebeck, 2016).

collective practices. Here, we are in uncharted legal territory just as in any other field of European labour, non-discrimination and consumer law, where it comes to the assessment of individual employment or consumer contracts. However, the ongoing constitutionalisation of private law moves exactly in that direction.[21]

Regulatory Technique

The regulatory technique, whether directive or regulation, whether full harmonisation or minimum harmonisation, matters with regard to the reach of the reversal of the freedom versus restriction paradigm. The rather superficial and crude distinction between full and minimum harmonisation does not do justice to the ever more sophisticated forms of harmonisation.[22] The European Commission will not give up on full harmonisation, as REFIT demonstrates. A new strategy, however, seems to avoid clear statements on the level of harmonisation, which might in turn encourage the ECJ to opt for full harmonisation.[23] Provided full harmonisation is realised, the same discourse on market freedoms and social values, on rules and exceptions, on what is agreed upon at the EU level and where there is remaining leeway for the Member States continues under the doctrine of preclusion.[24] The degree of harmonisation does not matter at least not as long as business practices come under the scope of secondary EU law. The 'fuller' the harmonisation and the more 'far reaching' the restrictions introduced under EU secondary law, the 'more extensive' is the pressure on business to rationalise the claim for freedom of contract. That is why the impact of the *Cassis de Dijon* doctrine and the rationality test in

---

[21] M. Safjan, 'The Horizontal Effect of Fundamental Rights in Private Law – On Actors, Vectors and Factors of Influence', in K. Purnhagen and P. Rott (eds.), *Varieties of European Economic Law and Regulation. Liber Amicorum for Hans Micklitz*, pp. 123–152.

[22] With regard to European private law: N. Reich, 'Von der Minimal- zur Voll- zur Halbharmonisierung – Ein europäisches Privatrechtsdrama in fünf Akten' (2010) *Zeitschrift für Europäisches Privatrecht* 7–39, shorter English version, 'From minimal to full to 'half' harmonization', in J. Devenney and M. Kenny (eds.), *European Consumer Protection. Theory and Practice* (Cambridge: Cambridge University Press, 2012), pp. 3–5; more generally on harmonization techniques, L. Azoulai, 'The Complex Weave of Harmonisation', in A. Arnull and D. Chalmers (eds.), *The Oxford Handbook of European Union Law* (Oxford: Oxford University Press, 2015), Chapter 23, pp. 589–611.

[23] Case C-183/00 *González Sánchez*, where the Court to the surprise of the Member States and most of the academia found the product liability directive to provide for full harmonisation, with highly problematic effects for the potential liability of dealers.

[24] For an attempt to categorise the various forms in fully harmonised secondary EU law, though using pre-emption (primary EU law) instead of preclusion (secondary EU law), Micklitz, 'The Targeted Full Harmonisation Approach'.

secondary EU law would be even greater the fuller the harmonisation is. Is this not exactly the *Polanyian* re-embedding of market integration through social regulation?[25] It all boils down to the question of the appropriate level. The Treaty sets clear red lines: maximum harmonisation is not in line with the treaty.

Effect

The rationality doctrine, as we have argued, has a double face. In primary EU law, the *Cassis de Dijon* logic puts Member States in a defensive position. They have to legitimise protective measures under Art. 36 TFEU and they have to provide rational arguments and evidence for economic (distributive) efficiency and societal effectiveness. The rationality test allows the disclosure of symbolic action, where the effectiveness of the rule is highly doubtful already when it is adopted. In secondary EU law, it offers new opportunities for efficient (in the meaning of redistribution) and effective (in the meaning of societal impact) legislative means in labour, non-discrimination and consumer law. First and foremost, however, it allows for the reversal of the priority between freedom and restrictions. Not only do restrictions have to be justified, but so too do freedoms. This is the double-sided effect of the generalisation of the rationality test beyond the scope of primary EU law.

One difficulty remains: how to deal with arguments that are neither related to economic distributive efficiency nor to societal effectiveness? Member States and business may escape or circumvent efficiency and effectiveness, if they refer to the different *political* and the different *cultural* background of *social justice* in their countries and to different national legal consciousness (*Rechtsbewußtsein*). One way to turn the different patterns of social justice in the three countries into a legal argument would be to raise the 'identity defence'. Then, the ECJ would have to keep the Social (societal effectiveness) separate from the economic (distributive efficiency), as well as embark on the validity of rational arguments based on culture, tradition, history, and identity. 'Culture' and 'identity' can be turned into an argument before the ECJ.[26] Europe should be

---

[25] Höpner and Schäfer, 'Embeddedness and Regional Integration', associating the EU with Hayekian liberal federalism rather than with Polanyi.

[26] Case C-208/09, *Sayn-Wittgenstein*, paras. 88, 92; Case C-391/09, *Runevič-Vardyn und Wardyn*; Case C-202/11, *Las* [2013]; on culture there is some case law in the field of commercial practices, Howells, Micklitz and Wilhelmsson, *European Fair Trading Law*, p. 83.

'united in diversity'.[27] So far, it is a formula. Provided the EU moves back into more diversity, and provided culture and identity turn into legal arguments against legislative or adjudicative intrusions, does this exclude a common European legal culture, as the 'grand seigneur' of European private law as Ole Lando[28] underlined? This is provided we can agree on an understanding of what is meant by European legal culture.[29] It would be wrong to play off national legal culture and national legal consciousness against European legal culture and European legal consciousness. Both exist together; the result is hybrid consciousness.[30] This is the consequence of the subsidiarity principle and minimum harmonisation. More politics is needed in light of the difficulties to draw a demarcation line between efficiency, effectiveness and culture/identity. The academic world is divided on whether politicisation is the cure.[31]

4.2 Shared Public-Private Competences and Shared Public-Private Responsibilities

In my understanding, the competences in law-making and in enforcement remain shared between the Member States and the EU. There is no place for exclusive powers of the EU via full harmonisation. Business comes in more indirectly through the New Approach and its followers. Sharing competences has a double face: it might mean sharing between the EU and the Member States, but it might also mean sharing between the EU/Member States on one side, and the EU on the other. Responsibilities allude to the moral and the legal implications the

---

[27] C. van Dam, 'Who is Afraid of Diversity? Cultural Diversity, European Co-operation, and European Tort Law' (2009) 20 *King's Law Journal* 281-308 and T. Wilhelmsson, 'Private Law in the EU: Harmonised or Fragmented Europeanisation?' (2002) 10 *European Review of Private Law* 77-94.

[28] C. Mak, 'Judges in Utopia: Fundamental Rights as Constitutive Elements of a European Private Legal Culture', in G. Helleringer and K. Purnhagen (eds.), *Towards a European Legal Culture* (München; Oxford; Baden-Baden: Beck; Hart; Nomos, 2014), pp. 375-395 and S. Weatherill's review (2014) 51 *Common Market Law Review* 1851-1852.

[29] H. Dedek, 'When Law Became Cultivated: 'European Legal Culture' between Kultur and Civilization', in G. Helleringer and K. Purnhagen (eds.), *Towards a European Legal Culture* (München; Oxford; Baden-Baden: Beck; Hart; Nomos, 2014), pp. 351-374; H. Collins in his book review wonders to what extent that book contributed to clarify legal culture.

[30] Conclusions under Part II. 3.

[31] Menéndez, 'Whose Justice? Which Europe?', pp. 145-146, argues under reference to Plato, Hobbes and Carl Schmitt that justice could serve as a means to set politics aside, advocating political justice which cannot be achieved without democratic politics.

competence shift invokes. Today's shared public-private competences and shared public-private responsibilities are the result of an enmeshment of the Member States with the EU and of the EU/Member States with the business sector. The outcome is a melange where it is hard to assign competences and responsibilities to the different public and private actors. Academic focus is placed on the competence grabbing of the EU, the European Commission and the ECJ, and their impact on the nation-states sovereignty and their societies. The ambiguous role of the Member States in the competence transfer and the implications of the involvement of business remain underexposed.

The Role of the Member States

By and large Member States are abiding by the rules set in the treaty and given shape in *van Gend & Loos*, *Costa Enel* and the *Cassis de Dijon* doctrine. They confirmed the existence of a genuine legal order submitted whenever they had to justify national social policy restrictions in consumer, non-discrimination and labour law before the ECJ. In the 1980s until the Sunday trading cases, Member States did not seem unhappy when Luxembourg eliminated national legislative barriers to trade.[32] Member States voluntarily and unanimously amended the treaty in 1986 (SEA), 1992 (Maastricht), 1999 (Amsterdam), 2001 (Nizza) and 2007 (Lisbon) with full knowledge of the political and legal consequences – certainly not in every detail, but in substance[33] – of delegating ever more social law-making powers in labour and consumer law away from the Member States to the EU. They adopted the Charter of Fundamental Rights in 2000, and integrated the Charter into the Treaty of Lisbon in 2007. In the new millennium, they *unanimously* passed a whole series of directives on non-discrimination laws reaching beyond the national level of protection.[34]

---

[32] With regard to Art. 30 TFEU the ECJ has delegated much of the power it had obtained after Cassis back to the Member States' courts, J. Zglinski, *Europe's Passive Virtues: The Margin of Appreciation in EU Free Movement Law*, PhD thesis, European University Institute (2016).

[33] P. Craig, 'Competence and Member State Autonomy: Causality, Consequence and Legitimacy', in H.-W. Micklitz and B. de Witte (eds.), *The European Court of Justice and the Autonomy of the Member States* (Cambridge; Antwerp: Intersentia, 2012), pp. 11–34, has forcefully described and analysed the different rounds of competence transfer through the various treaty amendments.

[34] Hepple, 'Equality at Work', p. 161; Bell, *Anti-Discrimination Law and the European Union*, Chapter 6, 'Reconciling Diverse Legal Traditions: Anti-Discrimination Law in the Member States', p. 145.

The way forward was bumpy, the two referenda in France and the Netherlands against the European Constitution and now Brexit standing out as lighthouses, shattering the very raison d'être of the EU. The people are protesting against their governments, ever since the Eurozone Crisis against the Troika and Germany. If any, it is the ECJ whose decisions reached the headlines of newspapers and raised political attention in governments, in national parliaments, in civil society and in academia: in labour law, *Viking, Laval,* and *AGET Iraklis*; in non-discrimination law, *Mangold* and *Test Achats;* and in consumer law, *Sanchez* (full harmonisation in the product liability directive), *Heininger* (doorstep selling of credit financed investments) and *Mohamed Aziz* (evictions of house owners unable to pay their mortgages). Much could be said on the pros and cons of the judgments depending on the perspective taken. It would be far too simplistic to explain these decisions as European civil society against European business, or the EU against Member States, or the ECJ against the national courts and so on. The ECJ is criticised for having gone too far or for not having gone far enough. Member States prevented the European Commission from using *Viking and Laval* as a trigger for developing a European law on the right to strike.[35] They unanimously adopted a Council Resolution against the Court's interpretation in *Sanchez,* but did nothing to amend the Product Liability Directive. They stopped the 2008 proposal to extend the non-discrimination directives beyond the labour market. However, they remained silent on the rather consumer-friendly decisions in the *Heininger* saga and the *Mohamed Aziz* saga. Social conflicts in Member States, between Member States or between the Member States and the EU are increasingly ending up in Luxembourg. The ECJ has turned into a major battlefield on how to shape and design the Social, obviously producing mixed results.

Taking treaties, secondary EU law and its interpretation by the ECJ together, it seems as if there was (is?) silent political support in the Member States governments, perhaps no longer in civil society, for the EU to take the lead in transforming the national welfare state. Two possible explanations occur, namely an economic and a political one that might make the move understandable. Member States realised that they were not able to manage the oil crisis in the 1970s whilst, at the

---

[35] Two Commission proposals: on how to strike the balance between workers' right to strike and companies' right to freedom of movement of services (COM(2012) 130 final, 21.3.2012) and how the Member States are to apply the Posting of Workers Directive (COM(2012) 131 final, 21.3.2012).

same time, maintaining the national social welfare systems. The hard conflicts the Thatcher government had to overcome in its efforts to reform the UK labour market, might even have enhanced the preparedness of the Member States to rethink the functional separation of economic powers and social powers in the Single European Act of 1986. Over time, Member States started to appreciate the benefits of letting Brussels decide via majority voting.

Delegating social conflicts away from the national political fora to the bureaucratic environment in Brussels underpins N. Komesar's theory of institutional choice.[36] In Brussels, the Member States could pool their different understandings of social justice in consumer, non-discrimination and labour law. The EU functioned like a catalyst, like the OECD of the time. The mainstream legal consciousness throughout Europe is heavily influenced by a political game that is inherently linked to the introduction of majority voting in the SEA. Member States' governments, however, played both sides of the fence.[37] Provided the voting in the Council complied with the prevailing national prerogatives, the legislative measures were sold to the national public as a success ('we' manage to convince the others to follow our proposal). However, when the outcome met resistance in the Member States, 'Brussels' was blamed for the uncomfortable results ('we' did our best but Brussels (not this and that Member State) obstructed a better solution). The widespread rhetoric was not necessarily the position national governments had taken in the Council behind closed doors.

The Role of the EU and the European Commission

The reorganisation of competences together with majority voting enhanced, at least until the Euro crisis, the position of the European Commission. The European Commission took the lead in initiating legislative action. The Member States had given away the prerogative of legislative and regulatory action, not only in the field of exclusive, but also in the field of shared, competences. This was politically intended. Majority voting strengthened the position of the European Commission to the detriment of the Member States. The constant enlargement of the EU through the inclusion of the 'new' Member States in 2004, 2006 and

---

[36] N. Komesar, *Imperfect Alternatives. Choosing Institutions in Law, Economics, and Public Policy* (Chicago: University of Chicago Press, 1994).

[37] R. D. Putnam, 'Diplomacy and domestic politics: the logic of two-level games' (1988) 42 *International Organization* 427–460; G. Tsebelis, *Nested Games. Rational Choice in Comparative Politics* (Berkeley; Los Angeles: University of California Press, 1990).

2015 blew away the careful balance between the EU legal order and governmental supranationalism.[38] The European Commission keenly made use of its newly accredited powers. It initiated extensive regulatory activities in the field of labour law and consumer law. The integration process unleashed a self-propelled dynamic, which was less controllable by the Member States. The Member States were not necessarily ready to have all these EU directives adopted, but some way or another the European Commission managed to iron out the conflicts between the Member States in the Council and to gain support in the European Parliament.

The treaty does not provide the EU with exclusive competence for the Social. The competence remains shared between the EU and the Member States. The Member States rather delegated competence through the SEA, but they also dispensed with responsibilities for the Social. However, EU competence grabbing triggered EU responsibilities for the Social and for labour, non-discrimination and consumer law. In making use of their *competences*, the EU accepted *responsibility* for giving the EU legal a social outlook. The EU turned into a political actor with regard to the shaping of the Social, however instrumentalised by the Member States for their own purposes.[39] Today shared competences and shared responsibilities are closely intertwined. EU critical legal scholarship blames and shames the EU for dismantling the social welfare state – as if the Member States, their governments, their parliaments and even their citizens have no responsibility for the EU-driven transformation of the Social. The current situation is curious: Member States appear as the potential savers of the Social, while the EU is blamed as its destroyer. Historically, this is not correct.

The Role of Business

The 1985 New Approach constitutes the turning point for the role business is playing in standardisation. What started smoothly with standardised consumer products gained a pole position in the service sector. Standards below the level of formal law play a key role in regulated markets, in telecom, in energy, in financial services, and now in the Banking Union. Business behaved the same way the European Commission did. Business seized the opportunity to develop

---

[38] J. H. H. Weiler, 'The Community System: the Dual Character of Supranationalism' (1981) 1 *Yearbook of European Law* 267–306; Weiler, 'The Transformation of Europe'.
[39] Kochenov, 'The Ought of Justice', p. 26 'the EU is a justice actor'.

European standards for the Internal Market. Since *Frabo, Elliot,* and *Tüv Germany*,[40] business is facing responsibilisation. The ECJ is not yet clear on which direction it will develop. The ECJ held that the standardisation procedure and the standards fall under its jurisdiction. Here is the bridge to the double-faceted ECJ case law in *Viking* and *Laval*. The flip side of the responsibilisation of trade unions is making business responsible and liable, at least under certain conditions.

Under the New Approach civil society, though involved in the standardisation process, remains outside responsabilisation. Their role is more symbolic than real. This might change provided civil society organisations are granted legal standing similar to the one business gained in the New Approach. What is legally and politically missing is a concept that allows for attributing responsibilities to the different actors. It constitutes one of the major challenges for the development of the post-classical legal order (Part III).

4.3 Fragmented Status, Fragmented Justice and Legal Consciousness

If we set the SEA as the benchmark, EU social regulation is 30 years old. In fact, it is 10 years older, as social regulation started in the mid 1970s with Directive 75/117 on equal pay for men and women. When the EU legislative machinery was set into motion, the economy was in good shape. After it had recovered from the oil price shock, the legal order was clearly organised – on the one hand, the employer/supplier and, on the other, the worker/consumer. Almost 40 years of EU social regulation to complete the Internal Market, to fine tune the European Constitution and, more concretely, to adopt secondary EU rules on labour, non-discrimination and consumer policy have left deep traces not only in the substance but also and in particular with regard to the legal status of the worker and the consumer. The founding years demonstrate a rather simplistic approach – the addressee of EU social regulation is the worker, the consumer, the woman. The EU focused on the front stage of market regulation, at opening up markets and offering equal opportunities for all EU workers, for all consumers, for EU citizens. After decades of regulatory measures to establish a market for winners, the losers are gaining more attention. Ironically, the scene was set in the Lisbon Agenda 2000. The impact of the financial

---

[40] Case C-171/11, *Fra.bo*; Case C-613/14, *James Elliott Construction*; Case C-219/15, *Schmitt* [2017] ECR I-000.

and the Euro crisis after 2008 has deepened the gulf between the winners and in the losers within countries and between countries thereby considerably raising political awareness. The EU responded to the transformations in the economy and society with a more sophisticated approach. The addressees became more targeted, in effect ever more fragmented. The 'class' of the workers and the 'class' of the consumers fell apart and with it, a coherent understanding of the level of justice enshrined in EU social regulation.

The Fragmentation of the Worker, the Discriminated and the Consumer

In labour law, regulatory challenges result from the increase in precarious working relations and from the tension between those workers who are fit to use the European labour market and those who are being left behind. The former are the active, mobile workers. On the other side are the passive workers, who are not mobile and who seek employment in the local environment, in which they grew up, and are socially anchored. The directives on part-time workers, on pregnant workers, on young people attempt to make this latter group fit for the labour market. It is not so much the protective, but the instrumental device that dominates.[41] The deeper conflicts in status-related protection turn around the *Laval* or *Viking* type of litigation, where the conflict is one between the resident workers who defend via their trade unions their achieved legal status and the non-resident workers from the new Member States who try to get access to the labour market via their employers or as self-employed workers.

Is the worker in the old Member States who is defending his or her privileges in need of protection, or is it the worker in the new Member States, who travels Europe in search of a job, not so much because he or she wants to but because he or she has no real choice? The whole debate triggered through the two judgments could be read as a fight over the correct level of protection that balances out the economic and social differences between the old and the new Member States. Thirty years ago, the Western world dumped their dangerous products on the third world.[42] The revised posted worker Directive will correct the blamed effects of *Laval*. Who is protected through the revision? The revision may be read as a universalist approach that overcomes fragmentation.

---

[41] Reich, *General Principles of EU Civil Law*, Chapter 2, p. 41.
[42] On dumping of dangerous products, H.-W. Micklitz, *Internationales Produktsicherheitsrecht. Zur Begründung einer Rechtsverfassung für den Handel mit risikobehafteten Produkten* (Baden-Baden: Nomos, 1995).

The long-term effects of the revised directive may demonstrate a different and more problematic result.

Drawing distinctions between the degree of discrimination sounds bizarre. However, this exactly happens when the different groups which suffer from discrimination are ranked and are then forced to fight over access to the higher level of protection. H. Collins demonstrated that there might be a tension between equal treatment and social inclusion.[43] Social inclusion widens the perspective, as now the decision as to whether somebody suffers from discrimination and needs protection is made contingent on the possible impact of the equal treatment on third groups, which have to pay the costs for the benefit granted to the discriminated person. 'Social inclusion permits unequal treatment if that measure favours an excluded group'.[44] Combining the application of non-discrimination rules to the principle of social inclusion requires more than a formalistic comparison, it requires a definition of who is 'most' in need of protection, which comes near to the distinction between average and vulnerable consumer in consumer law. The key word here is intersectionality.

Just as in labour law, consumer law demonstrates how the status of the consumer gradually erodes. The consumer within the European legal system was designed in a uniform way. The ECJ understands the consumer as a moral person, not a legal one.[45] She is somebody who makes decisions on her private consumption patterns, not somebody who is about to build a business.[46] Given the huge diversity in the legal orders of the Member States, a narrow construction might have been the only way to define a kind of a personal nucleus for consumer law. However, the unity of the consumer image fell apart in Directive 2005/29 on unfair commercial practices. In line with the Lisbon Agenda, the European Commission succeeded in achieving full harmonisation. In exchange, the European Commission had to swallow the formal recognition of the vulnerable consumer as a legal category. From there the

---

[43] H. Collins, 'Discrimination, Equality and Social Inclusion'.

[44] H. Collins, 'Discrimination, Equality and Social Inclusion', 36 under reference to *James v. Eastleigh Borough Council* (1990) 2 AC 751 HL. 'The respective Council operated a rule that persons of state pensionable ages would be admitted for free to the Council's swimming pool. At that time the pensionable age was 60 for woman and 65 for men.' This is violating the principle of equal treatment. But the equal treatment affects the costs and might yield negative impact on other groups which should equally benefit from access to the swimming pool.

[45] Case C-541/99, *Cape und Idealservice MN RE* [2001] ECR I-9094.

[46] Case C-269/95, *Benincasa v. Dentalkit* [1997] ECR I-3767.

distinction between the average and the vulnerable consumer made its way into the first generation of consumer law.[47] The second generation of consumer law, the EU rules on regulated markets, did not only elaborate on the concept of vulnerability, the directives introduced a new category – the consumer-customer.[48] Here the European legislator tied the fragmented legal status to a distinct set of contractual rights.

Legal Consciousness

It is hard to fix the exact moment at which the grumbling in the Member States and their civil societies turned into latent and then open resistance. National and European legal consciousness conflict and pit the winners against the losers across countries. 'United in diversity' looks different. Timing depends on where one looks. ECJ judgments are more often the response to societal change than their trigger. *Sanchez* in 2002, *Mangold* in 2005 and *Viking* and *Laval* in 2007 stand out. *Sanchez* shed light on the impact of full harmonisation, *Mangold* on a general principle of non-discrimination and *Viking-Laval* on the impact of the economic freedoms of workers' rights. The Lisbon Agenda 2000 unfolded its reach when the European Commission started to turn minimum harmonisation into maximum harmonisation and to fight social and financial exclusion.[49] Many of these developments remained for a long time only discussed in the realms of the European legal community. This is particularly true for the changing spirit in the European Commission triggered by the Lisbon Agenda, the 'most competitive economy of the world' rhetoric, the rise of efficiency and the ongoing move towards full harmonisation.

It seems resistance developed bottom-up in the Member States societies. The Eurobarometer shows 2004 as benchmark.[50] The list of citizen concerns is topped by 'transfers of jobs to other Member countries which lower production costs'. Between 2006 and 2009 most respondents had a rather positive perception of EU employment and social policies, although these responses show great variation among countries and demographics. This overall political climate has to be read in connection with the perceived broken promises.[51] The transfer of social

---

[47] Part III 2.1, 3.1.
[48] Reich and Micklitz, 'Economic Law, Consumer Interests and EU Integration', p. 52.
[49] Part II. 1.4.1.
[50] Diez-Sanchez, 'Justice Index' Eurobarometer and the Issue of Justice', p. 53 with regard to 2004 as benchmark, pp. 64–68 and 142 with regard to unemployment.
[51] Part I. 2.2–2.4 of the Member States.

powers to the EU from 1986 on raised expectations that the EU would continue and take over the national social welfare policies. Gradually, however, civil society realised that the EU cannot meet these expectations. Things got worse when the EU started to dismantle the national levels of protection, in labour law via the ECJ in *Viking* and *Laval*. The two judgments coincide with expressed anxieties in the Eurobarometer surveys. Consumer protection and consumer law seems different. The Eurobarometer does not demonstrate similar fears and expectations. Overall, it shows a progressive improvement of self-perceptions of Europeans in consumer confidence, consumer knowledge, consumer protection and justice. Again, this varies by demographics.[52] Full harmonisation is too specific in order to trigger reactions in the Barometer. Full harmonisation seems to be of concern for the elite of national lawyers, for NGOs directly involved in Brussels and for some Member States. The fragmentation of the legal status is nevertheless key. Before 2000 the status of the worker and the consumer as the weaker party stood firm. With the ongoing fragmentation of the legal status, the societal implications are brought to the limelight, though not necessarily in consumer law. The society in the Member States became legally divided – through EU law. EU law, the European Council, the European Commission and the ECJ exacerbated the divide between those who are 'in' and those who are 'out'.

The Member States' governments and the Member States' parliaments remained by and large loyal to the EU, perhaps until the Eurozone crisis. They resisted *Sanchez* and further attempts of the EU to Europeanise the right to strike. But the Member States did not revoke the full harmonisation objective, enshrined in the Lisbon Agenda. All that they did was to block the European Commission in its efforts to push the Common European Sales Law through, not via a democratic vote in national parliaments that met the quorum of the Lisbon Treaty, but by political intervention before the European Commission. After 30 years of explicit or implicit support, open resistance in the three areas under scrutiny could disclose the rather ambiguous role the Member States had in the 'nested games'. It would require what the Member States had so far avoided: an open democratic discourse on the role and function of the EU competence order in social regulation, on the subsidiarity principle and on their own responsibility and those of business.

---

[52] Diez-Sanchez, 'Justice Index' Eurobarometer and the Issue of Justice', pp. 117, 121.

The European private law academia plays a rather opaque role. European and national labour and consumer lawyers are divided. They are partly joining the forceful critique of trade unions and civil society organisations,[53] partly taking a more distanced stance.[54] Traditional civil lawyers and consumer lawyers who participated in the Study Group and the Acquis group got trapped by the political mandate of the European Commission. With the exception of consumer law and (to a limited extent) non-discrimination law, the two groups did not deal with EU law that forms the core of this book, neither with the relationship between primary EU law and private law, nor with labour law, nor with the law of regulated markets. The handling of the law on service contracts is paradigmatic. The laudable attempts of the Study Group to formulate the bottom line of a European law on the contract for services excluded most of the regulated markets.[55] Academic efforts for the modelling of a law on services are rare. At best they touch on the private law dimension of services, or building on the old distinction between obligation de résultat and obligation de moyen.[56] Mainstream academic research, as valuable as it is in deepening our understanding of national private laws, blinds us to what is urgently needed, namely the study of the transformations of the state, private law and justice, in the aftermath of European integration.

---

[53] Contributions in Kochenov, de Búrca and Williams (eds.), *Europe's Justice Deficit?*; Micklitz and Reich, 'Crónica de una muerte anunciada'.
[54] Deakin and Wilkinson, *The Law of the Labour Market*.
[55] J. M. Barendrecht, C. E. C. Jansen, M. B. M. Loos, A. P. Pinna, R. M. Cascao and S. van Gulijk, *Principles of European Law: Service Contracts* (München: Sellier, European Law Publishers, 2007).
[56] In a comparative perspective, but focusing on the traditional distinction, R. Zimmermann (ed.), *Service Contracts* (Tübingen: Mohr Siebeck, 2010).

5 Summary: Social, Access and Societal Justice

This book has taken us on a long road to explain and to analyse the socioeconomic background of social justice in the EU and its transformation. The political decision of the Member States to give the EU a social outlook in the SEA gradually eroded the common heritage that laid the foundations for the first 30 years of the European integration process. The mimicking of social regulation along the lines of national welfare state thinking would have required a rethinking of the common legal cultural heritage and its adjustment to the tectonic shift resulting from the move from a mere common market (1957–1986) to an Internal Market with a social outlook. Instead, the EU embarked on an uncharted journey. The turning point from which the EU developed its own path and its own understanding of the Social in a transnational economic, political and legal environment can be pinned down in three constitutive documents: the Lisbon Agenda 2000, the Charter of Fundamental Rights 2000 and the White Paper on Governance 2002. The triad of economic efficiency and international competitiveness, counterbalanced through fundamental rights and social inclusion, managed through public and private governance, left deep traces on the Social in European private law. They mark the break-even point, the break with national social justice and the rise of genuine EU justice.

The Social belongs to the heritage of Western European democracies. However, I have not reconstructed the rise of the Social in any of the former Communist countries. It is plain that the Western Social developed in contrast to, but also under pressure from, the socialist regimes on the other side of the iron curtain. What is lacking is the *commonality* of the Social that unites the Member States. The differences in the three countries under scrutiny demonstrate path dependence resulting from national economic, political, social and intellectual particularities, crystallised in different legal consciousnesses. Broadening the analysis of particular Member States would in all probability strengthen the importance of path dependencies. Broadening would add a new and important layer to, but not challenge, the overall argument of the book. There is a direct link between the lack of commonality on the Social at the national level and the rise of European experimentalism through treaty amendments, through new forms of law-making and law enforcement to give shape to the Social. The reconstruction of European labour, non-discrimination law and consumer law demonstrates uncertainties and irritations. Once the EU obtained the competence, majority voting paved the way for the adoption of a staggering number of directives and regulations on labour, non-discrimination and consumer law. The first tranche of EU law resembles national social regulation on contractual relations. The regulatory techniques are the same. Mandatory rules outweigh the imbalances between the parties to a contract. This looks very much like *social justice* through private law. Looking back, the 1990s appear like a golden age, full of hope that the EU could manage to take over the Social and establish social European private law.

The second tranche adopted after 2000 in light of the triad of economic efficiency, fundamental rights and governance, lacks such a coherent vision. It provides a messy picture where experimentalism abounds. Nevertheless, there is a success story to tell. The EU focused on non-discrimination as the leading value cutting across all fields of private law. The initial doctrine of equal pay, enshrined in the Treaty of Rome, provided the EU with the legitimacy to transform not only labour and consumer markets, but also national societies. This has provoked a boomerang effect – Brexit. The Charter on Fundamental rights provided an additional layer, which might have facilited unanimity in the Council on adopting far-reaching transformative legislative measures. Combatting economic discrimination constitutes the second limb of the post-millennium strategy. Already in the 1990s, the EU had started to dismantle former public services, whose role and function for the economy and society needed to be redefined. The liberalisation and privatisation of regulated markets could not have been achieved without guaranteeing that customers have access to what was then named universal services. The Lisbon Agenda legitimated the fight for social and financial inclusion. Both forms of discrimination are at the core of a new form of social justice: *access justice*, a materialised version of equal opportunities.

Access justice enshrines and documents the level of justice a supranational entity like the EU is able to deliver. It unfolds in a broadened legal environment which not only looks at the substance of a contract but combines materialised access with the procedural dimension on law enforcement and the institutional dimension on rule production through new forms of public-private modes of governance. Perhaps unwittingly, EU social regulation overstepped the boundaries of the market and intervened in national societies. The broadening in perspective not only results from a particular theoretical understanding of private law as economic law, but it is the result of transformations beyond the nation-state, through a market-driven regulatory push that opens towards society. Paradoxically enough, the lack of EU competences in private law facilitated the move to regulate private law relations indirectly through the economic and social environment. What looks like a disadvantage turned into a forceful tool of transformation that disentangles private law from mere bilateral or trilateral relations and opens the regulatory dimension towards legislative, excutive and judicial experimentalism beyond the market.

The current political and academic debate centers around social justice and the degree to which the EU is downgrading national social justice to European mere 'market justice'. I have tried to demonstrate that such an equation does not consider the achievements of social regulation beyond the nation-states, enshrined in access justice. What goes entirely unnoticed in the ideologically loaded debate, however, is that in the shadow of social justice versus market justice/access justice, the EU yields a third variation of justice – *societal* justice. This form of justice results from the transformation of national social labour and consumer law into European law on the labour and consumer market *society*. European social regulation overarches the boundaries of the Internal Market and interferes in the national societies. The deeper reason is to be found in the private law beyond the nation-state, where the boundaries between the economy and the society are becoming blurred. It will have to be shown how the three forms of justice leave their footprint on the post-classical tripartite European private law.

Before doing so, a word of caution is needed. The EU, mainly the European Commission, though legitimated through the Lisbon Agenda, is fighting for full harmonisation. Whilst full harmonisation in private law is ultra vires, full harmonisation would endanger the achievements of European integration. It is the political attempt to replace national patters of justice through one single form of European access justice. At least this is the argument that I advance throughout the book. Full harmonisation would not only put severe pressure on national variations of social justice top down via Brussels, it would also set an end to European experimentalism in law-making and in enforcement.

Part III

Considerations on the Post-Classical Private Law

Independent of their legal tradition and cultural background, all lawyers share the conviction that the law needs a kind of structure, no matter which form will be attributed to it. The following is an imperfect attempt to translate the transformations into a private law 'order' beyond the nation-state. The stumbling block for such an analysis is the fragmentation of legal status, the differentiation between the vulnerable, the weak/confident and the responsible market citizen.[1] To each status, a particular legal regime can be associated: to the vulnerable, the law on universal services; to the weak/confident, the law of the labour and consumer market society; and to the responsible market citizen, the new political private law. Each level can be linked to a particular form of justice: the vulnerable with access justice, the weak with social justice and the responsible market citizen with societal justice. Looking at the three levels separately, they resemble to a greater extent the legal regimes on particular logics in EU law that correspond to different areas of law. Bringing the three levels together, however, broadens the perspective beyond a mere regime and justifies understanding the EU private law as a legal order. The elaboration of the basic elements builds on previous research, on 'European civil law principles'[2] and on 'constitutionalised

---

[1] M. Everson, 'The Legacy of the Market Citizen', in J. Shaw and G. More (eds.), *New Legal Dynamics of European Union* (Oxford: Clarendon Press, 1995), pp. 73–90. Market citizenship in general is said to be inherently limited. In contrast, N. N. Shuibhne, 'The Resilience of EU Market Citizenship' (2010) 47 *Common Market Law Review* 1597–1628, believes that market citizenship may offer more than we presume.

[2] Micklitz, 'The Visible Hand of European Regulatory Private Law'; Reich, *General Principles of EU Civil Law*.

European private law concepts'.³ What is left out is the relationship between the EU private law order and national private law. This exercise forms part of a different book project.⁴

I start from the premise that the tripartite private law is composed of five basic elements which can be deduced from the existing body of law: (1) addressees, (2) access and substance, (3) rights, remedies, procedures, (4) balancing, and (5) competences and responsibilities. These five basic elements are to be analysed in their relationship with the legal status and the form of justice provided through EU law. The second and much more comprehensive step is to elaborate the basic elements⁵ with regard to the three levels of the EU legal order: universal services, the law on the labour and consumer market society and the new societal private law. All this serves the purpose of demonstrating the kind of justice the respective layer of European private law offers. The analysis concludes by briefly retracing the steps in the argument. While this chapter will show the conceptual outline of the emerging European private law, it sacrifices detailed analysis and tricky doctrinal issues (e.g. horizontal direct effect of directives) in places so that the larger transformations do not disappear amongst the thicket. For a fully fledged perspective, an entire monograph is required along the lines of C. Barnard's comprehensive *EU Employment Law*. Such an exercise allows to integrate more recent attempts such as S. Weatherill's *Contract Law of the Internal Market* and G. Howells, C. Twigg-Flesner, and T. Wilhelmsson's *Rethinking EU Consumer Law*. However, I leave this undertaking for another day.

---

[3] Based on an analysis of the ECJ, H.-W. Micklitz and C. Sieburgh, 'Primary EU Law and Private Law Concepts', in Micklitz and Sieburgh (eds.), *Primary EU Law and Private Law Concepts* (Cambridge; Antwerp: Intersentia, 2017), pp. 1–46.

[4] G. Comparato, H.-W. Micklitz and Y. Svetiev, *The Four Parameters of Interaction between European Private Law and National Private Law* (2019, forthcoming); for a preliminary account, see contributions in H.-W. Micklitz, Y. Svetiev and G. Comparato (eds.), 'European Regulatory Private Law – The Paradigm Tested' (2014) *EUI-ERC Working Paper* No. 4.

[5] Critical about generalisations, Collins, 'The Alchemy of Deriving General Principles of Contract Law from European Legislation', 220; Wilhelmsson, 'The Contract Law Acquis'.

1 The Basic Elements of the Tripartite Private Law Order

Table 8 has to be read first horizontally from the left to the right and then vertically downwards and upwards to review the five basic elements. The status determines the perspective and the type of justice provided, and the rules which can be associated to the respective three levels. Reading the chart vertically allows us to identify the differences and also the tensions that such fragmentation will bring about. The EU, this is the overall message, is transforming private law rules from autonomy to functionalism in competition and regulation.

Addressee

Structuring the new law around different categories mirrors the realities of the third globalisation that cuts across all fields of law. There is no legal person anymore in the third globalisation, but where individual rights turn into identity-based rights, which can be only shaped along the lines of groups to which the individual belongs.[1] The vulnerable, the weak/confident and the responsible consumer are difficult and, to some extent, overlapping categories. The differentiation is the consequence of the rise of the Social, which constantly postulated the need for drawing a distinction according to the contextualised role(s) in the market and in society.

---

[1] Micklitz, 'The Legal Subject, Social Class and Identity Based Rights'; Schiek, *Differenzierte Gerechtigkeit*.

Table 8

Tripartite Order	Addressee	Access + substance	Rights, remedies, procedures	Balancing	Competence + Responsibilities	Patterns of justice
Universal service obligations	The economically vulnerable	Access Affordability Continuity Non-discrimination	Obligation to contract ADR + civil society associations	No balancing on access but on residence	Shared responsibilities Shift from vertical to horizontal	Access justice
Law on the consumer and labour market	The weak The confident The vulnerable	Imbalance of power Mandatory rules	Nullity Action for injunction Ex officio Erga omnes	Balancing of legitimate expectations, inclusion of third parties	Social inclusion Tripartite responsibility EU-MS-private parties Social dialogue	Access justice/ social justice
The societal private law	The self- and societally responsible	Long-term obligations Networks Supply chains	Janecek dialogue Integrated approach	Balancing social inclusion-exclusion beyond the EU	Responsibilities of private parties and civil associations Contractual solidarity Network liability	Societal justice

Access and substance

Access to the market and to society is an economic pre-condition for participating and, societally, for securing a sense of belonging. The European legal order is committed to making sure that the economically or societally excluded is included. Once access is ensured, the question is what kind of requirements EU law guarantees. EU law does not only guarantee access but qualifies the substance of the contract. Usually, these are mandatory rules that set minimum standards or, more problematically, fully harmonised maximum standards, but they do not allow for social experimentalism. The requirements might differ and will have to differ according to the relevant addressees. The less vulnerable the addressees, the more space there is for self-responsibility in elaborating the requirements laid down in a contract or standards that affect the contract. Unfair terms may come close to barring access. This is particularly true with regard to forms of social discrimination.[2] Here fair access and fair substance intermingle. Unfair terms may result in unfair access.

Rights, Remedies and Procedures

Through the ECJ, individuals have been granted identity-based rights that allow them to challenge Member States' coercive power in limiting the availability of goods and services. This objective, what Floris de Witte[3] calls the 'good life', is at the heart of the free movement rights. It explains the key role of law and the centrality of identity-based rights in the integration process.[4] Rights without remedies and procedural safeguards are dead letter. W. v. Gerven has explained the doctrine of *ubi ius ibi remedium*.[5] However, the doctrine shows deficiencies as it focuses too much on courts. Non-discrimination law and the law on regulated markets amply demonstrate that a new actor has entered the scene, increasingly forcefully: regulatory agencies that enforce regulatory private law and that challenge legal systems that rely on private law enforcement alone, such as Germany and, to a lesser extent,

---

[2] Schiek, *Differenzierte Gerechtigkeit*, § 2 II, pp. 26–36.
[3] F. de Witte, *Justice in the EU*, pp. 55, 59, under chapter 1 'The Place of Justice', p. 15.
[4] J. H. H. Weiler, 'Van Gend en Loos: The Individual as Subject and Object and the Dilemma of European Legitimacy' (2014) 12 *International Journal of Constitutional Law* 94–103, following Weiler, F. de Witte, *Justice in the EU*, p. 169.
[5] W. van Gerven, 'Of Rights, Remedies and Procedures' (2000) 37 *Common Market Law Review* 501–536.

France.⁶ The de-privatisation and the de-judicialisation of enforcement goes hand in hand with the increasing importance of ADR mechanisms, in particular for those who have no access to courts. What both enforcement mechanisms have in common is that the 'law' and legal certainty vanish away as the 'decisions' or 'settlements' or 'recommendations' are not, or are only incompletely, publicly available. The weaker the position of the party, the more important collective means of redress are. All that the EU offers is the action for injunction as the minimum standard and the instrumentalisation of the preliminary reference procedure as a form of public interest litigation that enhances access *to* justice.⁷

Balancing

Balancing of rights is the paradigm which characterizes European constitutional law and which has left deep traces in European private law. Balancing of rights substitutes clear conceptual ideas of what the law is and of the rule of law. It is replaced through rights that have to be weighed against each other.⁸ Balancing finds its early expression in the notion of legitimate expectations that the EU legislator introduced first into product safety regulation and then into secondary EU consumer and non-discrimination law.⁹ EU law grants both parties rights to a contract, but it also creates social expectations. The vulnerable, the weak or the responsible consumer cannot expect that his or her rights and expectations will automatically be recognised via the EU legal order and the ECJ. They are only protected as long as they are 'legitimate'. Whether they are legitimate has to be tested *in concreto* through

---

[6] Like here, F. Wilman, *Private Enforcement of EU Law before National Courts. The EU Legislative Framework* (Cheltenham: Edward Elgar Publishing, 2015), p. 189 under 5.43 and p. 492 under 11.28; for a court-centred view, see v. Bar, Clive, Schulte-Nölke, Beale, Herre, Huet, Storme, Swann, Varul, Veneziano and Zoll (eds.), *Principles, Definitions and Model Rules of European Private Law (DCFR)*.

[7] In a broader perspective, Kelemen, *Eurolegalism*; L. Gormley, 'Access to Justice and Public Interest Litigation: Getting Nowhere Quickly?' in K. Purnhagen/P. Rott (eds.), *Varieties of European Economic Law and Regulation: Liber Amicorum for Hans Micklitz*, pp. 793–822.

[8] Reich, *General Principles of EU Civil Law*, chapter 5, p. 132. The chapter is based on Reich's contribution 'Balancing in Private Law and the Imperatives of the Public Interest', and in context Kennedy, 'A Transnational Genealogy of Proportionality in Private Law'.

[9] H.-W. Micklitz, 'Legitime Erwartungen als Gerechtigkeitsprinzip des europäischen Privatrechts', in L. Krämer, H.-W. Micklitz and K. Tonner (eds.), *Law and Diffuse Interests in the European Legal Order / Recht und diffuse Interessen in der Europäischen Rechtsordnung. Liber amicorum Norbert Reich* (Baden-Baden: Nomos, 1997), pp. 245–277; for a more elaborated version, H.-W. Micklitz, 'Principles of Social Justice in European Private Law'.

a balancing exercise. Enforceability of rights and expectations is linked to context. Contextualisation is key to understanding how EU law operates.

Competences and Responsibilities

The order of competence analyses the responsibilities that are assigned to the Member States and the EU in a multi-governance design. Most of the debate on multi-level governance focuses on public law and the division of responsibilities between the EU and the Member States. R. Breton[10] has shown that each level of governance must be relevant to the individual, otherwise there is no accountability. This implies that the different addressees can identify the responsible actor, which is rarely the case so far. Governance, however, is deeply anchored in contractual relations, in particular in long-term relations.[11] The order of competence reaches beyond the EU and Member States. It involves the responsibilities of private parties, not only of business but also of the responsible worker and consumer, of what has been called the market citizen. *Viking* and *Laval* could and should be read as laying down the responsibilities of private actors for public goods.[12] But also workers and consumers may bear responsibilities. This is the direct consequence of the status of the citizen worker and the citizen-consumer, from the role both play and have to play in an economic and political order beyond the nation-state. When it comes to collective involvement in developing, monitoring and supervising long-term consumer contracts, reference must and should be made to the role the labour movement played in managing employment contracts.

---

[10] R. Breton, 'Identification in Transnational Political Communities', in K. Knop, S. Ostry, R. Simeon, and K. Swinton (eds.), *Rethinking Federalism. Citizens, Markets, and Governments in a Changing World* (Vancouver: University of British Columbia Press, 1995), pp. 40–58, at p. 42; F. de Witte, *Justice in the EU*, p. 171.
[11] Cafaggi and Muir-Watt (eds.), *Making European Private Law* and *The Regulatory Function of European Private Law*; on contract governance, S. Grundmann, F. Möslein and K. Riesenhuber (eds.), *Contract Governance. Dimensions in Law and Interdisciplinary Research* (Oxford: Oxford University Press, 2015); concrete proposals on enhancing accountability of the ESAs, R. v. Gestel and T. v. Golen, 'Enforcement by the New Supervisory Agencies: Quis Custodiet Ipsos Custodes?' in K. Purnhagen and P. Rott (eds.), *Varieties of European Economic Law and Regulation: Liber Amicorum for Hans Micklitz*, pp. 757–780.
[12] Azoulai, 'The Court of Justice and the Social Market Economy'.

2 Universal Service Obligations (USOs)

To understand the role and function of universal services obligations, one has to retrace their origins to the law on regulated markets – the liberalisation and privatisation policy of former public services after 1986 – inspired by developments in the United States and in the United Kingdom. What regulated markets have in common is that consumers, customers or private end users were not yet in the limelight when the liberalisation and privatisation process started. Politicians focused on how, and by what means, markets could be established and opened towards competition. This kind of thinking is equally true for financial services, although, strictly speaking, there was no public monopoly that had to be dismantled, but there were strict public controls of capital flows pre-1970s. Increasing liberalisation and the need to secure access to energy, to telecom, to postal services, to transport and to financial services went hand in hand.

Under EU law, the concept of universal services is connected to services of general interest, services of economic interest, services of non-economic interest and social services of general interest which can be economic or non-economic.[1] The following analysis is based on the development of EU law in the field of labour, non-discrimination and consumer law. It focuses on, in essence, regulated markets. That is why there is no need to engage in the debate on where to draw the line between services of general, economic and non-economic interest.[2] Indeed, to understand the key role of universal services and its potential

---

[1] For a helpful resource, see the website of the European Commission on the services of general interests, available at: https://ec.europa.eu/info/topics/single-market/services-general-interest_en.

[2] Sauter, *Public Services in EU Law*; H.-W. Micklitz, 'Universal Services: Nucleus for a Social European Private Law', in M. Cremona (ed.), *Market Integration and Public Services in the European Union* (Oxford: Oxford University Press, 2011), pp. 63–102; N. Reich, 'Vulnerable Consumers in EU Law', in D. Leczykiewicz and S. Weatherill (eds.), *The Images of the Consumer in EU Law. Legislation, Free Movement and Competition Law* (Oxford: Hart Publishing, 2016), pp. 139–158.

future trajectory, it is necessary to link EU rules on free movement and residence, on the one hand, and the law on the regulated markets, on the other. Universal service obligations stand on the edge between free movement rights and the effects of the liberalisation and privatisation of former public services.

The extension of free movement of workers, first by broadening the concept of a 'worker' and then after the Maastricht Treaty through European citizenship, which was forcefully and actively promoted by the ECJ, loosened the ties between employment and residence. Sixty years of EU integration have left deep traces in society. Workers stayed, married and had children. Their children married other nationals, went to school, studied, made friends and sought employment in their preferred country. E. Sharpston has expressed the social implications wonderfully in *Zambrano*.[3] F. de Witte argues that the first dominant feature of European citizenship was economic engagement alone, then co-presence in the society rather than nationality and economic engagement, whereas today being 'subject to EU law' turns into the sole parameter rather than nationality, co-presence or economic engagement.[4] The EU is still struggling with the second stage – those migrants who fall in between states, as it were, who live in the host country but who do not work, or are unemployed or pensioners. Residence is bound to expectations to be treated like nationals. *Legally*, residents must have a right to minimum subsistence benefits.[5]

During the era of state monopolies, migrants with residence permits could largely rely on their host state and the respective incumbent to be supplied with water, energy and a telephone. In Germany, there was an obligation to contract. The incumbent had no right to reject a request. In cases where the recipients could not pay, it was extremely difficult for the incumbent to terminate her contract, in particular when a person was in an economically weak position. Usually, statutory social aid took over the costs. Similar mechanisms existed in France and in

---

[3] Opinion of Advocate General Sharpston delivered on 30 September 2010 – Case C-34/09, *Ruiz Zambrano* [2011] ECR I-1177, para. 128 ('[W]hen citizens move, they do so as human beings, not as robots. They fall in love, marry and have families. The family unit, depending on circumstances, may be composed solely of EU citizens, or of EU citizens and third country nationals, closely linked to one another. If family members are not treated in the same way as the EU citizen exercising rights of free movement, the concept of freedom of movement becomes devoid of any real meaning.').
[4] F. de Witte, *Justice in the EU*, p. 209.
[5] F. de Witte, *Justice in the EU*, under Chapter 4.1.3; the rights to minimum subsistence benefits, p. 153.

Italy. With the liberalisation and the privatisation of public services, incumbents turned into companies, public relationships into private ones and recipients of statutory benefits into customers. Dramatic cases in which customers' electricity is disconnected emanate from the United Kingdom and from the new Member States. These cases prompted the need to react politically. The EU legislator introduced universal service obligations in the telecom sector in the Directive of 2002.[6] One year later, similar rules were introduced in the energy sector using the same language. The original design of the eligible customer and the reference to Art. 90 ET (now Art. 106 TFEU) in Directive 98/30 turned out to be insufficient.[7] In the last few years, liberalisation and privatisation came to a halt. Currently, there is no political willingness to further liberalise public transport (beyond railways), healthcare or education. However, after more than three decades of political discussion in the Member States,[8] the EU introduced a right to a bank account.

Three phenomena matter: first and foremost, all those who have a right of access under EU law to universal services need resources to pay for the now liberalised and privatised services. It is here that we find the connection between USOs and free movement. The 'who is entitled' includes the question of whether non-nationals are included and, if they are included, under what conditions may they request subsistence benefits from the host state. Secondly, these subsistence benefits are not exportable. The migrant who receives financial support from the German government cannot take the money and move to a country where the living costs are lower. This is equally prohibited for German nationals. Thirdly, the principle of universal services is generalisable, in particular with regard to those entitled to

---

[6] Directive 97/33/EC of the European Parliament and of the Council of 30 June 1997 on interconnection in Telecommunications with regard to ensuring universal service and interoperability through application of the principles of Open Network Provision (ONP) OJ No. L 199, 26.07.1997, p. 2, amended by Directive 98/61/EC of the European Parliament and of the Council of 24 September 1968, OJ No. L 268, 3.10.1998, p. 37.

[7] Directive 98/30/EC of the European Parliament and of the Council of 22 June 1998 concerning common rules for the internal market in natural gas, OJ No. L 204, 21.7.1998, p. 1; De Almeida, *Integration through Self-Standing European Private Law: Insights from the Internal Point of View to Harmonization in Energy Market*, p. 237.

[8] In Germany, it was a big topic in the late 1970s, in connection with totally overpriced credit agreements, U. Reifner and M. Volkmer, *Ratenkredite an Konsumenten: Rechtsprobleme, Hintergründe und Strategien zum Verbraucherschutz gegnüber Banken* (Hamburg: Verbraucher-Zentrale, 1984); Reifner and Volkmer, *Neue Formen der der Verbraucherrechtsberatung*; U. Reifner, 'Das Recht auf ein Girokonto' (1995) 7 *Zeitschrift für Bankrecht und Bankwirtschaft* 243–260.

subsistence benefits. What kind of services are essential in a market society to have a decent life? Do they include shelter and a warm home; access to water, healthcare, and primary education for children; and enough money to pay for these services and for nutrition? It does not suffice, however, to look exclusively at the economic dimension. These people are citizens equally, and they need to participate in society. Today, this means access to a bank account, access to the internet, access to a telephone, and access to the broadcast media. Without such services, persons are not only economically excluded but also societally excluded. There are good reasons to understand the right to a bank account and the right to have access to the internet, telephone and the broadcast media as a universal service.[9] One may go further and ask whether access to consumer credit is essential for people who use credit to extend their future investments. This would then require a right to credit[10] or more generally a right to basic financial services as universal services.[11] There is ample evidence that the vulnerable are excluded from the credit market. Scoring plays a crucial role.[12] While the debate rages over what should be regarded as 'universal services' or as 'essential services', in the end access in a market society turns on a simple need: the availability of financial resources.

2.1 The Vulnerable

It might not necessarily be the strongest form of discrimination, but having no financial resources turns private freedoms into an empty shell. A. Sen stressed the two sides of freedom as opportunity and

---

[9] T. Wilhelmsson, 'Services of General Interests and European Private Law', in C. E. F. Rickett and T. G. W. Telfer (eds.), *International Perspectives on Consumers' Access to Justice* (Cambridge: Cambridge University Press, 2003), pp. 149–166; Reich with regard to broadcasting, *General Principles of EU Civil Law*, under reference to Art. 15 (1) and (6) of the Audiovisual Media Services Directive 2010/13/EU 'access on a fair, reasonable and non-discriminatory basis to events of high interest to the public' and ECJ in Case C-283/11, *Sky Österreich* [2013] ECR I-000, p. 66.
[10] Comparato, *The Financialisation of the Citizen*.
[11] I. Domurath, 'The Case for Vulnerability as the Normative Standard in European Consumer Credit and Mortgage Law – An Inquiry into the Paradigms of Consumer Law' (2013) 2 *Journal of European Consumer and Market Law* 124–137; now the same, *Consumer Vulnerability and Welfare in Mortgage Contracts* (Oxford: Hart Publishing, 2017) throughout.
[12] For an early analysis of the credit scores as a form of discrimination, Schiek, *Differenzierte Gerechtigkeit*, p. 270.

process.[13] Economic discrimination is most visible in cases where non-EU citizens claim subsistence benefits from their host states. They want to be treated like all the other nationals who enjoy such a right, provided they fall under the existential minimum. Their vulnerability is of an economic nature. Provided they get subsistence benefits, they have at least the chance to lead a decent life, depending on how 'minimum' subsistence is delimited. Whether or not a non-EU citizen has such a right depends on residence. A residence permit is the path to subsistence benefits. There is abundant ECJ case law on the degree to which Member States may tie residence to employment, or at least to employment seekers. Overall, the ECJ has lowered the threshold and gradually weakened the ties between employment and civil status. 'Welfare tourism' is the key marker on the political battlefield traversing free movement for EU citizens. This denotes a stigmatised category of persons who do not necessarily leave their home country to seek employment.[14]

F. de Witte claims that the right to minimum subsistence benefits 'must be extended to *all* legally resident Union citizens who fall below the level of resources set by the applicable national legislation'.[15] However, he recognises that it is legitimate for host states to set boundaries depending on the degree of social integration. This is what he develops using the notion of aspirational solidarity – the shared political commitment between the Member States and their citizens. He argues in favour of a relational concept, that is neither abstract universalism nor identity-based communitarianism, but a dynamic construction that respects particularities.[16] Whilst *Ibrahim*[17] and *Teixera*[18] nourished this line of argument, *Dano*[19] stands for a much more restrictive interpretation. Economically inactive migrants need to meet the requirements in Art. 7 (1) Directive 2004/38, the need to have sufficient resources for themselves and family members in order not to become a burden on the host state. The Court is quite outspoken:[20] Member

---

[13] A. Sen, *Rationality and Freedom* (Cambridge, MA: Harvard University Press, 2002), p. 585; Sen, *The Idea of Justice*, in particular Part III, 'The Material of Justice', p. 225.

[14] There seems to be no reliable data, but nevertheless useful: http://ec.europa.eu/social/main.jsp?catId=738&langId=de&pubId=7981&furtherPubs=yes

[15] F. de Witte, *Justice in the EU*, p. 151.

[16] F. de Witte, *Justice in the EU*, pp. 48 and 169.

[17] Case C-310/08, *Ibrahim und Secretary of State for the Home Department* [2010] ECR I-1065, at paras. 48, 56–58.

[18] Case C-480/08, *Teixeira* [2010] ECR I-1107, para. 59.

[19] Case C-333/13, *Dano* [2014] ECR I-000, para. 69.

[20] Case C-333/13, *Dano*, para. 78.

States 'must therefore have the possibility ... of refusing to grant social benefits to economically inactive citizens who exercise their right to freedom of movement solely in order to obtain social assistance although they do not have sufficient resources to claim a right to residence'. Whatever interpretation one might want to give to the ECJ's reasoning, the judgment highlights not only the difficulties associated with recognising an unconditional right to claim subsistence benefits from a host state for all European citizens, but more emphatically the economic vulnerability of inactive, non-national European citizens.

The concept of economic vulnerability is implicit in two areas where the idea of universal services is most developed – telecommunication and energy. Directive 2002/22 determines the potential addressees only indirectly, via the concept of *affordable price* (Art. 1 (2)) and via *special social needs* (Art. 9 (2)). The amendments which have been introduced through Directive 2009/136 did not change the concept of universal service nor did they change the addressees, but they did introduce disabled end-users (Art. 7). However, there are adjustments. Recital 26 refers to 'the availability of easy-to-use and configurable software or software options allowing protection for children or vulnerable persons' and Art. 1 (3) requires that 'National measures ... shall respect the fundamental rights and freedoms of natural persons.' Broadband has not yet been included as part of the universal services. Although the ECJ has acknowledged internet subscription at a fixed location as part of the universal service, it has left behind mobile communications and internet access via mobile communications services.[21]

In 2003, Directive 2003/54 and Directive 2003/55 on energy supply followed suit.[22] Universal services and public services are used interchangeably and with the same definition. The beneficiary is the economically vulnerable customer, who is secured access at reasonable or fair prices, not affordable prices (Art. 3 (7)). The vulnerable customer includes small- and medium-sized enterprises, without any explanation as to where the similarities and differences are (Art. 3 (5) Directive 2003/

---

[21] Case C-1/14, *Base Company und Mobistar* [2015] ECR I-000.
[22] Directive 2003/54/EC of the European Parliament and of the Council of 26 June 2003 concerning common rules for the internal market in electricity and repealing Directive 96/92/EC, OJ No. L 176, 15.7.2003, p. 37; Directive 2003/55/EC of the European Parliament and of the Council of 26 June 2003 concerning common rules for the internal market in natural gas and repealing Directive 98/30/EC, OJ No. L 176, 15.7.2003, p. 57.

54 and Art. 3 (3) 2003/55).[23] Only six years later, the EU legislator had to adjust the design of the electricity and gas markets to a new phenomenon. The external effects of the liberalisation of the energy market led to energy poverty. In line with this new strand of argument, Directive 2009/72 refers to social security systems that are supposed to guarantee access to energy. Member States' obligations per Recital 45 are formulated so that '... Such measures may differ according to the particular circumstances in the Member States in question and may include specific measures relating to the payment of electricity bills, or more general measures taken in the social security system'. Even more outspoken is Recital 53:

> Energy poverty is a growing problem in the Community. Member States ... should ... develop national action plans or other appropriate frameworks to tackle energy poverty, aiming at decreasing the number of people suffering such situation ... In doing so, an integrated approach, such as in the framework of social policy, could be used and measures could include social policies or energy efficiency improvements for housing.

The new policy is condensed and laid down in clear words in the revised version of Arts. 3 (7) and 3 (8) Directive 2009/72 and Arts. 3 (3) and (4) Directive 2009/73.

The Energy Directives, just as the Universal Service Directive on Telecom (also referred to as 'USD'), aim at the protection of the *economically vulnerable*, namely those who cannot pay their energy bill and need subsistence benefits from the state.[24] Prices should be 'reasonable' and 'fair'. Member States may fix a price via statutory law or leave the price-fixing to the company charged with providing the universal services.[25] Member States have the choice to subsidise the universal service providers or the citizen-consumer. If Member States choose the first option, they must observe EC rules on state aids. The second option is exempted from EC state aid law.[26] Member States must define the economic threshold from which citizens (and residents) may claim financial

---

[23] Also Recital 24 of Directive 2003/54.
[24] However, there is leeway for the Member States. Art. 3(7) Directive 2009/72 requires that 'each member state shall define the concept of vulnerable consumers which may refer to energy poverty'. In other words, EU energy law defines 'vulnerable consumers' as 'economically vulnerable'.
[25] Case C-265/08, *Federutility and Others* [2010] ECR I-3377, subject to three conditions: 1) reasonable level, 2) limited in time and 3) transparent, as concretised in Case C-36/14, *Commission v. Poland* [2015] ECR I-000, and Case C-121/15, *ANODE* [2016] ECR I-000.
[26] Article 107(2)(a) TFEU.

support, independent of the mode of payment. There are no Europe-wide standards, not even on the criteria to be applied for the calculation of the minimum subsistence, e.g. the percentage of income, which can be devoted to the rent of an apartment, for telephone bills, for health care, for food, etc. EU law simply imposes an obligation on the Member States to put in place necessary safeguards. No word is uttered, not even in recommendations under the definition of the TFEU, on the link between energy poverty and migrants who have settled or are seeking domicile in a host state. All that remains are references in policy documents.[27] However, having gained the status of a 'vulnerable' customer implies the right of access to services and the right to minimum quality standards.

2.2 Access and Substance

Access to universal services is paramount. Such a right cannot be deduced directly from primary EU law or from the Charter of Fundamental Rights (CFR). The joint reading of primary and secondary EU law, however, justifies the existence of an enforceable right. There is a difference between telecommunication and energy. Art. 1 (2) USD uses strong language that might directly lead to the existence of a right to access. Directive 2009/72 on energy is less outspoken. Art. 3 (3) ties the granting of the right to the responsibility of the Member States. In *Sabatauskas*,[28] the ECJ confirmed such a reading; however, only with regard to third-party access of the eligible customer and not with regard to universal services. The advocate general and the ECJ seemed inclined to go further if the access right of the citizen-consumer is at stake.[29]

---

[27] European Commission, London Forum, 'Vulnerable Consumers Working Group Guidance Documents on Vulnerable Consumers, November 2013,' available at: http://ec.europa.eu/energy/sites/ener/files/documents/20140106_vulnerable_consumer_report_0.pdf.

[28] On the right to access under Art. 20 of Directive 2003/54 in particular with regard to the right of access to universal services, see ECJ, Case C-239/07, *Sabatauskas and Others* [2008] ECR I-7523, para. 47 and the Opinion of Advocate General Kokott delivered on 12 June 2008, paras. 35 and 38; R. Pirstner-Ebner, 'Kein Recht zum Anschluss an das Übertragungsnetz' (2009) *Europäische Zeitschrift für Wirtschaftsrecht* 15–16, at 15, 16 under 4.

[29] P. Rott, 'A New Social Contract Law for Public Services? – Consequences from Regulation of Services of General Economic Interests in the EC' (2005) 3 *European Review of Contract Law* 323–345, at 342; for more details on the importance of the judgment with regard to the regulation of supply agreements, De Almeida, *Integration through Self-*

That is why a detour via the protocol to Art. 16 ET on Services of General Economic Interests (SGEIs)[30] and Art. 36 of the Charter on Fundamental Rights is needed. Both directives refer to human rights, in particular to the ECHR. As the Lisbon Treaty had not yet entered into force when the two directives were adopted, there was no opportunity to refer to the Charter and, in particular, to Art. 36. The introductory sentence to the protocol underlines the shared values of the Union. SGEI's are upgraded from a mere defence in Art. 107 (2)(a) TFEU to a value, which binds Member States and the EU together. The introductory sentence and the first two bullet points refer to SGEI's; the third explicitly mentions universal services. Telecom and energy fall under the scope of SGEIs.

The *first* bullet point of Art. 16 ET refers to the 'needs of the consumers'.[31] One of the cornerstones of the debate had been the over-indebtedness of consumers and the possible remedies aimed at bringing the over-indebted consumer back into business and back into social life.[32] This submits financial services under the scope of the protocol. The *second* bullet point confirms the case law of the ECJ with regard to cultural and social requirements.[33] *Geographical* particularities refer to the differences between rural areas and densely populated big-city agglomerates, and also differences between flat lands near to the sea and mountains. Geographical particularities are related to the accessibility of services. The *third* bullet point goes even further in that it refers to 'principles' which govern universal services. There is a link between the needs of the citizen-consumers and the principles set out in the third bullet point. Citizen consumers *need* services at *affordable* prices. Taking citizen-consumer needs into consideration sheds light on a new understanding of the principle of equal treatment. Affordability and equal treatment combined turn economic resources into a criterion for interpreting existing EC law.

Art. 36 of the Charter on Fundamental Rights proclaims under the heading of solidarity, 'The Union recognises and respects *access to services*

Standing European Private Law: Insights from the Internal Point of View to Harmonization in Energy Market, p. 237.

[30] Protocol (No 26) on services of general interest, OJ No. C 115, 9.5.2008, p. 308
[31] Wilhelmsson, *Critical Studies in Private Law*, p. 146.
[32] E.g. U. Reifner, 'Renting a Slave—European Contract Law in the Credit Society', in T. Wilhelmsson, E. Paunio and A. Pohjolainen (eds.), *Private Law and the Many Cultures of Europe* (Alphen aan den Rijn: Kluwer Law International, 2007), pp. 325–364.
[33] Case C-220/98, *Estée Lauder* [2000] ECR I-117, at para. 29: 'social, cultural or linguistic factors'.

of general economic interests as provided for in national laws and practices ... in order to promote the *social and territorial cohesion* of the Union [emphasis added]'. Art. 36 does not grant directly enforceable rights.[34] Access under Art. 36 contains a threefold dimension: technical, economic and social. The technical side is enshrined in the geographical dimension. Access remains an empty tool if those who should have access are barred from requesting the respective universal services due to lack of resources. According to this rationale, Art. 36 CFR backs the obligation of the Member States to provide for adequate social security. The social element refers to those citizen-consumer groups which suffer from social exclusion. Art. 36 CFR the protocol and the respective rules in secondary EU law, read together, constitute subjective enforceable rights.

The next obvious candidate for universal service obligations is financial services. So far, the EU law underpinning for such an understanding is fragmented. For P. Rott,[35] only the Directive on Payment Accounts comes close to a universal service obligation. Art. 18 guarantees an unconditional right to a bank account at a 'reasonable price', which includes non-EU citizens even if they have no residence permit.[36] The directive goes beyond what F. de Witte is asking for with regard to the right to subsistence benefits. Since *Mohamed Aziz*,[37] it is possible to speak of a right not to be evicted from one's home. This right was conceived by the ECJ in the aftermath of the economic crisis, provided the loan agreement contained unfair contract terms. It presupposes that the buyer at one point in life was solvent enough to get the necessary mortgage credits. The extensive case law cannot be turned into a right

---

[34] Regarding the interpretation of this provision and its doctrinal qualification, J. Baquero Cruz, 'Beyond Competition: Services of General Interest and European Community Law', in G. de Búrca (ed.), *EU Law and the Welfare State. In Search of Solidarity* (Oxford: Oxford University Press, 2005), pp. 169–212, at p. 178.

[35] P. Rott, 'The Low-Income Consumer in European Private Law', in K. Purnhagen and P. Rott (eds.), *Varieties of European Economic Law and Regulation: Liber Amicorum for Hans Micklitz* (New York: Springer International Publishing, 2014), pp. 675–692.

[36] Art. 16 (2) of Directive 2014/92/EU requires that 'Member States shall ensure that consumers legally resident in the Union, including consumers with no fixed address and asylum seekers, and consumers who are not granted a residence permit but whose expulsion is impossible for legal or factual reasons, have the right to open and use a payment account with basic features with credit institutions located in their territory. Such a right shall apply irrespective of the consumer's place of residence. Member States may, in full respect of the fundamental freedoms guaranteed by the Treaties, require consumers who wish to open a payment account with basic features in their territory to show a genuine interest in doing so.'

[37] Case C-415/11, *Aziz*, and Joined Cases C-154/15, C-307/15 and C-308/15, *Gutiérrez Naranjo*.

to request the necessary funds from the state to buy a home. Access to credit is limited, and there is no indication for introducing a universal right to credit. Art. 16 (4) Directive on Payments Account even prohibits overdrafts.[38] Reading the different rules together, it is hard to deduce a kind of universal services obligations composed of access to a bank account, access to credit and access to justice. However, the EU rules invite us to think about such an obligation.

Substance: The status bestowed on the vulnerable consumer is bound to a set of mandatory rights which lay down minimum conditions with regard to the respective service. Member States may go beyond the minimum, but should they do so, universal service providers cannot be compensated. In this sense, this is a true minimum. The services that fall under the universal service concept are not identical to those that do not. Quality under universal service ('specified quality') does not have to be necessarily the same as quality under Article 22 USD.

Universal services are tied together via a whole set of principles:[39] transparent price, affordability (of the price), non-discrimination, continuity of service, non-discrimination (geographic accessibility) and specified quality requirements. The *BUPA* judgment of the General Court (GC) provided the opportunity to think about minimum requirements for services of universal importance more generally.[40] *BUPA* dealt with the question whether private health insurers, which are the major competitors to the public healthcare regime, may be requested to contribute to a national risk compensation fund. The GC identified the following constitutive criteria for USOs: (1) Their *mandatory* character, i.e. the obligation to conclude a contract as the demarcation line between universal services and normal contracts; (2) the distinction between exclusive rights and the obligation to provide the service without taking costs into consideration and situations where such a privileged status is missing; (3) the limitation of universal services to

---

[38] Case C-618/10, *Banco Español de Crédito* [2012] ECR I-000.
[39] P. Larouche, *Competition Law and Regulation in European Telecommunications* (Oxford: Hart Publishing, 2000), p. 32; Rott, 'A New Social Contract Law for Public Services?'; P. Rott, 'Consumers and Services of General Interest: Is EC Consumer Law the Future?' (2007) 30 *Journal of Consumer Policy* 49–60; P. Rott, 'Services of General Interest, Contract Law and the Welfare State', in J. Rutgers (ed.), *European Contract Law and the Welfare State* (Groningen: Europa Law Publishers, 2012), pp. 79–103; N. Reich, '"I Want My Money Back": Problems, Successes and Failures in the Price Regulation of the Gas Supply Market by Civil Law Remedies in Germany' (2015) *EUI-ERC Working Paper* No. 5.
[40] Case T-289/03, *BUPA and Others v. Commission* [2008] ECR II-81, Micklitz, 'Universal Services: Nucleus for a Social European Private Law', p. 89.

minimum quality standards and (4) the link between affordability and the anti-discrimination issue. On top of the overarching general criteria, there are sector-specific quality requirements that increasingly end up in long lists of the services that have to be supplied. This is true with regard to energy,[41] to telecom[42] and to payment accounts.[43]

The language used throughout the different directives is extremely unclear: price must be 'affordable', sometimes 'reasonable', sometimes 'fair'. The common denominator of all the rhetoric is that the price to be paid must be set in relation to the overall 'income' of the customer. Affordability is a relative category that has to be concretised by Member States, not only with regard to the overall average costs of living, but also with regard to the particularities of the country. The European Commission has made various efforts to clarify the meaning.[44] In the South, heating is less important than in the North. Recital 10 of the USD provides some guidance: 'Affordable price means a price defined by Member States at national level in the light of specific national conditions, and may involve setting common tariffs irrespective of location or special tariff options to deal with the needs of low-income users. Affordability for individual consumers is related to their ability to monitor and control their expenditure'. Affordability is a European term and it remains for the ECJ to decide what it means. The ECJ held that universal services obligations do not exclude 'reasonable' profit.[45] This puts additional pressure on the calculation of the subsistence benefits. The ECJ is keen to promote competitiveness in the telecom market, thereby outsourcing the costs to national social budgets. In theory, the ECJ is free to

---

[41] Annex I to Directive 2009/72 on electricity and Directive 2009/73 on energy.
[42] According to Article 3(1) and Recital 7 of the USD, Member States should ensure that Universal Services are made available with the quality specified to all end-users in their territory. Pursuant to the amendment of the USD by Directive 2009/136/EC (OJ No. L 337, 18.12.2009, pp. 11; Recital 34), '[a] competitive market should ensure that end-users enjoy the quality of service they require, but in particular cases may be necessary to ensure that public communication networks attain minimum quality levels so as to prevent degradation of service, the blocking of access and the slowing of traffic over networks.' According to Recital 4, to this end, national regulatory authorities may require that designated operators with universal service obligations provide the services under certain performance targets. According to Article 11(4) USD, national regulators must also monitor quality standards compliance. With regard to Article 11(5) (6), quality parameters at the European level are established by the European Telecommunications Standards Institute (ETSI).
[43] Art. 17 (2) of Directive 2014/92.
[44] S. Pront-van Bommel, 'A Reasonable Price for Electricity' (2016) 39 *Journal of Consumer Policy* 141–158.
[45] Case C-508/14, *T-Mobile Czech Republic and Vodafone Czech Republic* [2015] ECR I-000.

develop denominators that have to be taken into account when it comes to the calculation of 'affordability' and 'social needs'.

The possible impact of a verdict of discrimination on universal services is more concrete. First of all, the provider is not allowed to differentiate between end users. All vulnerable customers should be granted the affordable price. The USD in telecom refers in Art. 1 (2) to 'all end-users'; the Energy Directives in Recital 50 (electricity) and Recital 47 (gas) to the 'citizens of the EU'; and the Postal Services Directive[46] ensures the permanent provision of postal services 'for all users' in Art. 3 (1).[47] Geographical barriers do not matter. The customers should not be disadvantaged because of their remote residence. A word of caution is needed. The 'household customers', those who are economically vulnerable (Art. 3(5) Directive 2009/72), could be charged different prices if the difference is justified by national law meant to protect the economically vulnerable.[48] The EU legislator leaves the Member States with different options: price regulation, setting price ceilings, or not intervening into the price-fixing and instead subsidising the customer. If the state does not fix a determined price but leaves leeway to the universal service provider, the burden falls on the national regulatory authorities who have to make sure that consumers receive the service at an affordable, non-discriminatory price. In this respect, the rationale of the EU rules on affordability and non-discrimination reaches beyond access justice and provides for a form of social justice. However, the non-discrimination principle yields counterintuitive effects. The costs of roaming are borne by the home provider. This might entail the increase of domestic tariffs, which might disproportionately affect vulnerable customers who are not mobile.[49]

---

[46] Directive 97/67/EC of the European Parliament and of the Council of 15 December 1997 on common rules for the development of the internal market of Community postal services and the improvement of quality of service, OJ No. L 15, 21.1.1998, p. 14

[47] Deutscher, 'The Principle of Non-Discrimination in EU Economic Law', under reference to O. Batura, *Universal Service in WTO and EU Law: Liberalisation and Social Regulation in Telecommunications* (The Hague: T. M. C. Asser Press, 2015).

[48] H. Kruimer, 'Non-Discriminatory Energy System Operation: What Does It Mean?' (2011) 12 *Competition and Regulation in Network Industries* 260–286, uses the term 'legalised discrimination' to describe the provisions that oblige network operators to discriminate electricity producers in case of grid congestion (B2B). However, this distinction is confusing with regard to B2C.

[49] Deutscher, 'The Principle of Non-Discrimination in EU Economic Law', p. 45, even more dramatic are the consequences of the OTT (over-the-top) providers such as Google, YouTube or Netflix who are considered as end users and benefit from the equal treatment obligation, p. 49; M. Armstrong, 'The Theory of Access Pricing and

When the price is the same for everybody, there is no room for price discrimination based on gender, race, age, disability and religion. However, there are forms of discrimination that are not related to price but that concern the circumstances under which the supply of the service is guaranteed. A well-known example is the discrimination of Roma in the urban districts in Bulgaria who were unable to monitor their energy consumption.[50] The relevant EU directives, which deal with universal services, touch upon issues of social discrimination in a very different way. There is no reference to forms of social discrimination in the Energy Directives 2009/72 and 73 or in Directives 2002/22 as amended through 2009/136 on telecom, but there is an outspoken prohibition in Art. 5 Directive 97/67 as amended through 2008/6 on postal services. Universal service provisions 'shall be made available without any form of discrimination whatsoever, especially discrimination from political, religious or ideological considerations'. Art. 15 of the Directive 2014/92 on Payment Accounts states that 'the conditions applicable to holding a payment account with basic features shall be in no way discriminatory'.

After the EU signed the UN Convention on the Rights of Persons with Disability, the EU legislator began adjusting its rules to the particular requirements of persons with disabilities. There are references to disability in the rules on telecom, postal services, payment accounts and the four EU regulations on public transport.[51] The confusing terminological differences in the EU rules on universal services do not really matter. What matters is that they have to be interpreted in light of CFR and the Convention of Human Rights.

What remains to be discussed is the issue of continuity. The disconnection in the three fields of universal services – energy, telecom and bank accounts – produces very different effects. Cutting a customer off from energy supply might endanger her life. After spectacular and tragic events, Directive 2009/72 (electricity) and Regulation 994/201(Gas) prohibit the disconnection of customers during winter times,

---

Interconnection', in M. E. Cave, S. K. Majumdar and I. Vogelsang (eds.), *Handbook of Telecommunications Economics*, Vol. I (Amsterdam; Boston: Elsevier, 2002), pp. 297–386.

[50] Case C-83/14, *CHEZ Razpredelenie Bulgaria* [2015] ECR I-000 and Case C-394/11, *Belov* [2013] ECR I-000. The latter has been rejected by the ECJ for reasons of inadmissibility.

[51] For a deeper analysis of the common denominator, Reich, 'Vulnerable Consumers in EU Law', pp. 139–143.

even in case of a supply crisis.[52] Telephone and internet disconnection might equally lead to serious risks when a customer living in a remote area falls ill. Equally important are its social implications. Having no access equates to social and societal exclusion. Interestingly, access to the bank account is unconditional and cannot be removed. EU law does not prohibit 'disconnection' *per se* but proceduralises the requirements. This reduces the possibility of simply disconnecting the vulnerable citizen-consumer from the internet if he or she has not paid the bill.[53] It seems, however, that even more guidance is required. In Germany alone each year 800,000 customers are temporarily disconnected, without adequate monitoring and surveillance of the possible consequences.[54]

2.3 Rights, Remedies and Procedures

The vulnerable consumer might have the right to claim a residence permit, the right to ask for subsistence benefits and the right to get access to universal services. If he or she goes to court because the universal service is denied, he or she might have a right to legal aid – though not under EU law, as Directive 2002/8 applies only to *cross-border* litigation in civil and commercial matters.[55] Art. 1 makes clear that the party who is applying for legal aid is domiciled or habitually resident in a Member State other than the Member State where the court is sitting or where the decision is to be enforced. Residence refers to Art. 59 of Reg. 44/2001.[56] Also, non-EU citizens have the right to apply per Art. 4.

---

[52] De Almeida, *Integration through Self-Standing European Private Law: Insights from the Internal Point of View to Harmonization in Energy Market*, p. 247. On the tragic death of an old couple in the United Kingdom and situation in the new Member States, Bartl, 'The Affordability of Energy'.

[53] Directive 2002/22 as amended through Directive 2009/136 Annex I e): 'Member States are to authorise specified measures, which are to be proportionate, non-discriminatory and published, to cover non-payment of telephone bills issued by undertakings. These measures are to ensure that due warning of any consequent service interruption or disconnection is given to the subscriber beforehand. Except in cases of fraud, persistent late payment or non-payment, these measures are to ensure, as far as is technically feasible that any service interruption is confined to the service concerned. Disconnection for non-payment of bills should take place only after due warning is given to the subscriber. Member States may allow a period of limited service prior to complete disconnection, during which only calls that do not incur a charge to the subscriber (e.g. '112' calls) are permitted.'

[54] Rott, 'The Low-Income Consumer in European Private Law', p. 681.

[55] OJ L No. L 26, 31.1.2003, pp. 41.

[56] Council Regulation (EC) No 44/2001 of 22 December 2000 on jurisdiction and the recognition and enforcement of judgments in civil and commercial matters, OJ No.

Thus, in theory, a possible conflict between a vulnerable customer seeking access to universal services and a company, which is providing the universal service, falls under the scope of the directive, if (!) there is a cross-border issue at stake, which is usually not the case. Cross-border means conflicts within the EU and not a conflict between the EU and non-EU countries. Those who have no stable residence permit are excluded.

The vulnerable consumer, who faces access problems at one or all three levels has to fight with a highly complex set of legal rules, which varies from Member State to Member State. The focus is on the enforceability of the right to obtain access to the relevant universal services. However, the previous analysis has made it clear that each and every applicant finds himself or herself in a vicious circle. What to do first? Residence permit, subsistence benefits or universal services? What can legally be kept separated forms, in reality (and for the non-lawyer), an inseparable conglomerate. Does the triad of rights, remedies and procedures, which quite necessarily leads to courts as the forum of litigation, fit?

The most vulnerable in society face the greatest barriers in accessing justice. Courts may serve as a forum only, this is what socio-legal research tells us, if the litigation is supported by a civil society association or by a public body with a social mandate. The alternative is dispute settlement bodies, which provide easy, simple, fast and low-cost procedures. The EU law on universal services has introduced dispute settlement procedures, sector by sector. In the energy sector, 'all citizens ... that enjoy the economic benefits of the internal market should also be able to enjoy high levels of consumer protection'.[57] One might therefore argue that access to dispute settlement procedures forms an integral part of the 'high level of consumer protection'. Whilst the directive discusses B2B settlement mechanisms in much more detail and puts regulatory agencies in a prominent position, the rules on B2C settlement are much less developed. They do not distinguish according to the status of the consumer, as long as the litigation comes under the scope of application of the relevant directive.

A clear statement is found in Art. 3 (7) and in Annex 1 (f) Directive 2009/72. The procedure is open to all users, including vulnerable

---

L 012, 16.01.2001, p. 1, there is abundant case law of the ECJ on the consumer's domicile, Reich, Micklitz, Rott and Tonner (eds.), *European Consumer Law*, p. 322.

[57] Recital 42 of Directive 2009/72.

consumers, as long as they are 'householders'. Therefore, granting access to ADR for non-householders is a political decision left to the Member State. The 4th Package proposes to extend the ADRs system to all end users. However, the USD on telecom 2002/22 as amended through 2009/136 is much more specific. Art. 34 (1) lays down concrete requirements.[58] The regulation on postal services in Art. 19 Directive 2008/6 resembles the rather unspecific rules in energy. Until the ADR Directive 2013/11,[59] the two Recommendations 98/257[60] and 2001/310[61] served as the benchmark, albeit in different forms, for the Universal Service Directive 2002/22/EC (Recital 47), MiFID 2004/39/EC (Recital 61), Electricity Directive 2009/72/EC (Annex I (1) f), Natural Gas Directive 2009/73/EC (Annex I (1) f) and in the 3rd Postal Service Directive 2008/06/EC (Recital 24). All other sector-specific directives contain references to the design of the schemes which correspond to the seven guiding principles of Recommendation 98/257/EC. The recommendation provides clarification and guidance due to its quasi-binding nature as held by the ECJ in *Alassini*.[62] Directive 2013/11 has transformed the recommendations into binding law. The sector-related directives have not been amended. So far, the EU legislator has shied away from taking a clear position on the relationship between the ADR directive and sector specific rules. Art. 3 states that in case of 'conflicts with a provision laid down in another legal act and relating to out for court redress procedures initiated by a consumer against a trader, the provisions of the Consumer ADR Directive shall prevail'. The consequences are far from being clear.[63]

---

[58] M. Cantero Gamito, 'Dispute Resolution in Telecommunications: A Commitment to Out-of-Court' (2017) 25 *European Review of Private Law* 387–422.

[59] Directive 2013/11/EU of the European Parliament and of the Council of 21 May 2013 on alternative dispute resolution for consumer disputes, OJ No. L 165, 18.6.2013, p. 63.

[60] Commission Recommendation 98/257/EC of 30 March 1998 on the principles applicable to the bodies responsible for out-of-court settlement of consumer disputes, OJ No. L 115, 17.4.1998, p. 31.

[61] Commission Recommendation of 4 April 2001 on the principles for out-of-court bodies involved in the consensual resolution of consumer disputes, OJ No. L 109, 19.04.2001, p. 56.

[62] Case C-317/08, *Alassini and Others* [2010] ECR I-2213.

[63] For an attempt to compare the procedural rules in Art. 34 (1) Directive 2002/22 as amended by Directive 2009/136 and the ADR Directive 2013/11, Cantero Gamito, 'Dispute Resolution in Telecommunications'. The new proposal for an Electronic Communications Code maintains sector-specific ADR and expands it to other end users, in particular micro and small enterprises. It proposes that Member States 'should enable the national regulatory authority to act as dispute settlement entity, through a separate body within that authority which should not be subject to any instructions'

Directive 2014/92 provides for quasi-universal services with regard to bank accounts. The directive explicitly mentions the need to extend dispute settlement to the pre-contractual phase, first in Recital 52, then in Art. 14. It thereby closes a gap that results from the scope of application of Directive 2013/11, which is limited to dispute settlement for existing contracts. The sector-related directives should be read so as to include the pre-contractual stage.[64] Otherwise, the inclusive rhetoric in the shape of the guidelines and the lack of distinction with regard to normal services and universal services would not make sense.[65] It is one thing to lay down EU law requirements and another to determine what Member States make of it.[66]

The problem remains that many of those who may have a right under the universal service directives do not make use of the possibility of launching a complaint to the company that should provide access and that has disconnected the consumer from the net.[67] The estimated number of unknown cases is high. There are no useful statistics available on the situation in the EU as a whole. While dispute settlement certainly provides for an alternative to courts if it works, the obvious deficiencies in implementing and enforcing the European legal requirements require collective action. *Belov* and *Nikolova*[68] represent a form of

---

(Recital 69 of the EC Code, recast). But the proposal establishes that for disputes involving consumers, the quality requirements set out in Directive 2013/11/EU (Chapter II) apply. There would be two types of procedural rules applicable to dispute resolution: (1) Consumer disputes: ADR Directive (Directive 2013/11/EU (Chapter II)) and (2) Telecom specific disputes, Article 25 proposal – Other end-users (i.e. non-consumers): sector-specific rules.

[64] Art. 34 (1) USD formulates the following: 'relating to the contractual conditions and/or performance of contracts concerning the supply of those networks and/or services'. Contractual conditions leave some room for interpretation.

[65] However, it might make sense in relation to the distinction end-users consumers v. end-users non-consumers, i.e. SMEs; Recital 49 of Directive 2002/22 and Recital 21 of Directive 2009/136.

[66] There might be a tendency to maintain and to defend particular national patterns of consumer protection in universal services; with regard to how the United Kingdom is not implementing consumer law, thereby defending the primary interests of the business sector, C. Willett, 'Contra Emptor Interpretation-Protecting Service Providers from EU Law', in K. Purnhagen and P. Rott (eds.), *Varieties of European Economic Law and Regulation: Liber Amicorum for Hans Micklitz* (New York: Springer International Publishing, 2014), pp. 709–732, with regard to Italy making out-of-court settlement mandatory, Case C-317/08, *Alassini and Others* and Case C-75/16, *Menini and Rampanelli* [2017] ECR I-000.

[67] Rott, 'The Low-Income Consumer in European Private Law', p. 681 and Bartl, 'The Affordability of Energy', in particular on Eastern Europe.

[68] Case C-83/14, *CHEZ Razpredelenie Bulgaria* and Case C-394/11, *Belov*.

public interest litigation. It is hard to imagine that individual Roma fight through all the judicial instances up to the ECJ and take the risk of paying lawyers' fees and court fees, let alone possess the expertise needed to bring the case to the ECJ. There must be civil society organisations behind these claims to back the litigation and provide the necessary resources. These were test cases, relevant not only for the applicant, but for a whole population of discriminated consumers. The question remains open as to whether the litigation has improved access to monitor energy consumption for all Roma who are victims of discriminatory practices.

In theory, the implementation and the enforcement of the universal service directives would be a perfect scenario for the open method of coordination (OMC). This was proposed years ago by U. Neergard.[69] OMC presupposes that Member States and their regulatory agencies collect the necessary information on all issues relevant for universal services recipients: the conditions under which they can gain access, the problems they face, the criteria on affordability applied in the Member States and the techniques and the success and failure rates on the surveillance and monitoring of those who are cut off from the net. None of the directives at issue point to the OMC as a method of collaborative exchange on the key issues of access, disconnection and poverty, in order to define best practices for calculating minimum subsistence benefits or for managing disconnections. In both sectors, the EU legislature granted the European Agencies ACER (Agency for the Coordination of Energy Regulation) and BEREC, a mandate for coordination.[70] There are no specific requirements on information

---

[69] U. Neergaard, 'Services of General (Economic) Interest and the Services Directive – What Is Left Out, Why and Where to Go?', in U. Neergaard, R. Nielsen, L. M. Roseberry (eds.), *The Services Directive. Consequences for the Welfare State and the European Social Model* (Copenhagen: Djøf Publishing, 2008), pp. 65–120.

[70] With regard to energy, Article 11 (1) of the ACER Regulation 713/2009 (OJ No. L 211, 14.8.2009, pp. 1) states, '1. The Agency, in close cooperation with the Commission, the Member States and the relevant national authorities including the national regulatory authorities and without prejudice to the competences of competition authorities, shall monitor the internal markets in electricity and natural gas, in particular the retail prices of electricity and natural gas, access to the network including access of electricity produced from renewable energy sources, and compliance with the consumer rights laid down in Directive 2009/72/EC and Directive 2009/73/EC'. There is no equivalent rule in telecom. BEREC's survey on the implementation and application of the universal service provisions – a synthesis of the results, BoR (17) 41, available at: http://berec.europa.eu/eng/document_register/subject_matter/berec/others/6973-berec-update-survey-on-ms-recent-experience-in-terms-of-universal-service.

duties related to universal services, only with regard to customers-consumers.[71] This information forms the basis for 'coordination'. A more OMC-like exchange occurs through the Citizen's Energy Forum.[72] What exactly happens within the different fora can only be uncovered through empirical research. These procedures, insofar as they exist, do not take a holistic perspective that takes the three dimensions of the precarious status of the vulnerable consumer (access, residence and subsistence) into account.

2.4 Balancing of USOs and Residence Rights

Access to universal services is non-negotiable. That is why there is no balancing at that stage. Their *mandatory* character, i.e. the obligation to conclude a contract on request, is said to be constitutive for the existence of universal services. Universal services limit the freedom of the service provider to conclude a contract. This is what the ECJ decided with regard to an interconnection contract.[73] There is no comparable judgment in the field of USO. Strictly speaking, the legal obligation to secure access rests with the Member States.[74] Under national law such an obligation existed as long as the service provider was the statutory incumbent. Now at times of EU-induced liberalisation and privatisation, the obligation shifts from the public sector to the private universal service provider, provided the designated universal service provider is a private company. Whoever fulfils this role, denoting a service as 'universal' precludes the possibility for the universal service provider to reject a request. The company cannot select and must enter a contract with the consumer, including the obligation to manage the risk of non-payment of bills, even if it is compensated directly through the state for

---

[71] Energy: Art. 37 (1) of Directive 2009/72 requires 'reporting annually on its activity and the fulfilment of its duties to the relevant authorities of the Member States, the Agency and the Commission. Such reports shall cover the steps taken and the results obtained as regards each of the tasks listed in this Article'. Art. 37 (1) (n) includes information duties on Annex I, which covers universal service obligations. Telecom: Art. 20 of Directive 2009/140 does not distinguish between the different potential addressees.
[72] There is no direct counterpart in the telecom sector that focuses on universal services. The only forum which comes close is the BEREC Stakeholder Forum; see 4.2. below.
[73] With regard to an interconnection contract with another operator Case C-64/06, *Telefónica O2 Czech Republic* [2007] ECR I-4887, at para. 28 and Art 3 (5)(9) Directive 2009/72.
[74] Admittedly an obligation to contract comes close to horizontal direct effect. In Case C-64/06, *Telefónica O2 Czech Republic* the ECJ had to decide whether the Czech authority is enabled (not obliged) under EU law to impose such an obligation.

having taken on the obligation. This obligation is not particularly novel, although the obligation to contract is 'constitutionally' upgraded, so to speak.

In *BUPA*,[75] the CFI undermined the overwhelming importance of that rule for the existence of universal services:

> (186) ... the concept of universal service, within the meaning of Community law, does not mean that the service in question must respond to a need common to the whole population or be supplied throughout a territory (see, in that regard, *Ahmed Saeed Flugreisen*, paragraph 181 above, paragraph 55; *Corsica Ferries France*, paragraph 97 above, paragraph 45; and *Olsen v. Commission*, paragraph 166 above, paragraph 186 et seq.) ... although those characteristics correspond to the classical type of SGEI, and the one most widely encountered in Member States, that does not preclude the existence of other, equally lawful, types of SGEIs which the Member States may validly choose to create in the exercise of their discretion.
>
> (187) Accordingly, the fact that the SGEI obligations in question have only a limited territorial or material application or that the services concerned are enjoyed by only a relatively limited group of users does not necessarily call in question the universal nature of an SGEI mission within the meaning of Community law ...

The CFI extends the concept of universal services beyond those where the EU legislator has taken regulatory action. Following this line of argument, one might consider an obligation to contract not only for telecom, energy, postal and payment services, but *by analogy* to access credit. Balancing comes in when the consumer does not pay and when the company considers disconnecting him or her. Then, the right of the company to be paid for a service delivered and the right of the consumer to rely on service continuity, even in case of non-payment, have to be balanced against each other, not only to enter the contract but also during the duration of the contract. So far, the ECJ has had no occasion to approve or reject such reasoning.[76]

Access is much more dramatic for migrants who suffer from an unstable residence status. The universal services directives do not contain rules similar to Art. 16 Directive 2014/92 on payment accounts. Both leave the complex relationship between the civil status (residence), access to universal services and access to subsistence benefits

---

[75] Case T-289/03, *BUPA and Others v. Commission* [2008] ECR II-81.
[76] Opinion of Advocate General *Bot* delivered on 12 June 2014 – Case C-222/13, *TDC* [2014] ECR I-000, at para. 106, with regard to additional mandatory services in the meaning of Art. 32 USD.

aside. The right to access universal services and the right to subsistence benefit depend rather on their residence status. At least, this seemed to be the legal positions prior to *Dano*.[77] Since *Dano*, Member States are entitled to deny subsistence benefits for 'economically inactive Union citizens'. The situation is even more complicated for non-Union citizens and asylum seekers. At the very minimum a holistic perspective is needed. The different rights of the parties have to be balanced, the rights of non-EU citizens who need access to universal services in order to survive and the right of the universal service provider who will deny the obligation to conclude a contract unless it receives the necessary financial guarantees from the host state.

Balancing provides a way out of the dilemma, as it allows courts to take a holistic perspective, which can take account of the law on universal services, the law on subsistence benefits or the law on free movement. The ECJ, in this respect, faced the potential excluding effects of national employment policies that aim at freeing jobs for the younger generation to the detriment of the older one. In numerous judgments, the ECJ not only examined whether there is discrimination or not, but also integrated into its judgments the potential effects of exclusion from the labour market. What does the economic and social situation of the elderly person who has to free his job for a younger one look like? Is she entitled to a pension that allows her a decent life? The same kind of enlarged balancing can be traced in precarious work relations.[78] Let us assume that the ECJ has to deal with a case where the claimant requests access to a universal service obligation which was rejected, because the private universal service provider is uncertain as to who will pay for the service or because the public universal service provider claims that the applicant has not yet obtained a residence permit. The ECJ would have to bring together what properly belongs together: the three areas of the law that merge in the question of access to universal services.

Such a holistic perspective would have to be taken at the national level, too, by the respective competent authorities and by national

---

[77] Case C-333/13, *Dano*.
[78] With regard to age, F. de Witte, *Justice in the EU*, pp. 179–180; S. Peers, 'Equal Treatment of Atypical Workers: A New Frontier for EU Law' (2013) 32 *Yearbook of European Law* 30–56, contributions of J. Prasse and M. Risak, D. du Toit, I. v. Hiel, J. Unterschütz, E. Eichenhofer, in Chapter II 'Precarious Work – The New Normative Model', in K. Ahlberg/N. Bruun (eds.), *The New Foundations of Labour Law* (Frankfurt a. Main: Peter Lang 2017), pp. 97–214.

courts. In the Member States, the executive competence is spread over different authorities, and the jurisdiction for the three fields is often divided. The alternative, however, is that those who are most in need conceal their vulnerability and apply for a 'normal' contract on the market, usually at higher prices. The iron rule of Western capitalism seems to work: 'the poor pay more'.[79]

2.5 Order of Competence and Responsibilities

The implications of the order of competence[80] for universal services has to respect that the addressees are the poorest of the poor, those who are suffering from all sorts of discrimination, not only economic exclusion. We are at a level where the European legal order is claimed to be at its weakest, to the detriment of those who are the worse off and where the justice deficit is the greatest. Implicit to this kind of argument is the assumption that the vulnerable were better off in the area of public services – that is to say, before liberalisation and privatisation. There are no empirical studies that have compared the economic and social situation of the vulnerable before and after European-driven liberalisation and privatisation of telecom, postal services, energy and transport. Financial services could easily be added despite the officially missing label. The assumption is that the situation is different with regard to the type of services. Nobody would like to have the old telephone services back, but people might complain that energy poverty was not a problem (was it?) prior to liberalisation and privatisation of former incumbents or that public transport is the better alternative. The oft-heard argument that the vulnerable were better protected in socialist times is bittersweet, as the energy was supplied quasi-free of charge by the Soviet Union.[81] All those who travelled to the East after the fall of the wall might well remember the waste of energy, overheated rooms and offices that could only be cooled down by opening a window. Can energy poverty be outweighed through open democratic society?

---

[79] Caplovitz, *The Poor Pay More*.
[80] L. Azoulai, 'On the Concepts of Competence and Federal Order of Competences in the EU Legal Order', in L. Azoulai (ed.), *The Question of Competence in the European Union* (Oxford: Oxford University Press, 2014), pp. 1–15.
[81] S. Buzar, *Energy Poverty in Eastern Europe. Hidden Geographies of Deprivation* (Aldershot: Ashgate, 2007), Chapter 2, 'Gaps in Theory and Policy: Tracing the Roots of Energy Poverty', pp. 17–44.

In the light of the foregoing, three different levels are to be distinguished: (1) the political order of competence, (2) the legal order of competence and (3) the enforcement order of competence, always having in mind the plea that each level of governance must be visible and accountable to the EU citizen and that there should be no 'blame culture' in a European society of shared responsibilities. The political order of competence is meant to address the question of statutory responsibilities to the Social of the EU and Member States. It is called 'political', as the borderline between a mere political and a legal, but non-enforceable obligation, is hard to draw. The legal order of competence refers to the EU constitutional level that is now concretised in the treaties. However, here, the focus is on the character of minimum standards and what it implies. The enforcement order of competence deserves to be separated because of the rather opaque division of competences.

The existing *political order of universal services* is the result of a political programme that started in the aftermath of the Single European Market but whose ideology dates back to the Treaty of Rome. The European Commission and EU Member States jointly promoted liberalisation of public services, though it was not necessarily connected with the privatisation of the former incumbent. There is a political commitment on both sides. The result is shared responsibility. Shared responsibility, however, does not mean that the old distinction of the Treaty of Rome remains – that is, the market for the EU and the Social for Member States. The visible expression of the 'commonality' is the introduction of USOs. Through USOs, the EU and Member States express their readiness to jointly realise the objective of establishing a competitive market without setting aside the interests of those who cannot handle the new freedom, as they do not enjoy the necessary financial resources. There is a *quid pro quo* – no competitive markets on former public services without USOs, and no EU responsibility for the market without USO responsibility on Member States.[82] Responsibilities towards the market and the Social exist on both sides.

Already in the 1980s, the Court of Justice started to *oblige* national courts and national administrations to enforce community law.[83]

---

[82] For telecoms, K. A. Eliassen and J. From, 'Deregulation, Privatisation and Public Service Delivery: Universal Service in Telecommunications in Europe' (2009) 27 *Policy and Society* 239–248.

[83] Regarding the national administration, Case 103/88, *Fratelli Costanzo v Comune di Milano* [1989] ECR I-1839; regarding the national courts, Case 14/83, *Von Colson and Kamann v Land Nordrhein-Westfalen* [1984] ECR I-1891.

Member States could not hide behind the division between law-making for the EU and law enforcement for Member States. The political order of competence established in the Lisbon Treaty allows for a much more nuanced and much more powerful reading of the reach of Member States' responsibilities. What was incrementally enshrined in the case law of Art. 36 TFEU can now be turned into a rule. The Lisbon Treaty imposed obligations and responsibilities on the Member States to look after the social dimension, not only of the Internal Market project, but also of European integration per se. This is the true potential which lies in combining the objectives of the Lisbon Treaty with 'justice, 'social market economy' and 'fundamental rights'. Each of them has its ambiguities. Justice is not, strictly speaking, a founding value, but it 'is central to the wider social environment that gives rise to these values'.[84] The 'social market economy' is not spelled out in the treaty, and its meaning contradicts with the protocol and the case law of the ECJ. The Charter is part of the European legal order, but the attempt to connect the EU legal order to the ECHR failed.[85]

The ECJ is far less clear and far less outspoken when it comes to deciding whether the EU is bound by the standards the Member States have to obey.[86] However, even if the EU is not built on justice, the EU is built at least on respect for human dignity and human rights.[87] The respective directives contain a reference to the European Convention on Human Rights. The more powerful argument follows from a bottom-up perspective. The development of the law on regulated markets demonstrates the power shift away from the Member States and their regulatory agencies to the European agencies and the European Commission. Via delegated powers under the comitology procedure, via supervisory powers granted to the European agencies[88] or via recommendations and guidelines, the EU has taken over and was keen to take ever more responsibilities. This goes along with the

---

[84] D. Chalmers, 'Foreword', in F. de Witte, *Justice in the EU. The Emergence of Transnational Solidarity* (Oxford: Oxford University Press, 2015), vii.

[85] ECJ Opinion 2/13, *Adhésion de l'Union à la CEDH*, ECLI:EU:C:2014:2454.

[86] M. Jarvis, in P. Oliver (ed.), *Free Movement of Goods in the European Union*, pp. 60–66.

[87] As to the question whether human rights are a substitute, see Wilkinson, 'Politicising Europe's Justice Deficit' and Somek, 'The Preoccupation with Rights and the Embrace of Inclusion'.

[88] Energy: Under Regulation 713/2009, Article 4 the Agency (ACER) shall (d) take individual decisions in the specific cases referred to in Articles 7, 8 and 9; and (e) submit to the Commission non-binding framework guidelines (framework guidelines) in accordance with Article 6 of Regulation (EC) No 714/2009 and Article 6 of Regulation (EC) No 715/2009.

reading of the GCC.[89] These responsibilities have a clear legal basis in the treaty and in the sector-specific directives but not necessarily on the same body.[90] Once having taken over these responsibilities, the EU via the Commission or via its agencies is legally obliged to take the social dimension into account. The deeper problem is whether the EU has taken over more responsibilities than conducive with regard to its legitimacy.[91] Universal services look more like a residual category that had to be somehow squeezed into the regulatory framework.[92] This is particularly true for energy, postal services and also for financial services. It is hard to understand why there is a directive on universal services in telecom but no equivalent in energy, where the problems seem to be even more pressing.

The political bargain is reflected in the *legal order of competence for universal services*. The EU legislator has laid down minimum standards for universal services. The minimum is mandatory. Users must have a right to access, and once they obtain access they have the right to certain minimum quality standards. Already, in the definition of the minimum level, the EU legislator and Member States accept shared responsibility, be it for the field as a whole – *the quid pro quo*, or be it for the level enshrined as a minimum. The minimum can be raised by the Member States if they so decide. The minimum can turn into an option when it comes to the universal service provider. As privatisation of the former incumbent is not mandatory, they can choose between nominating the public incumbent and the competitor, the private

---

[89] German Constitutional Court, 2 BvE 2/08, 30.6.2009, the judgment is available in English at: www.bundesverfassungsgericht.de/SharedDocs/Entscheidungen/EN/2009/06/es20090630_2bve000208en.html, at para 258: ' . . . pursuant to Article 23.1 first sentence of the Basic Law, Germany's participation in the process of integration depends, inter alia, on the European Union's commitment to social principles.'

[90] For instance, the powers of the commission and their increasing role derives from the Framework Directive rather than the USD. Directive 2002/21/EC of the European Parliament and of the Council of 7 March 2002 on a common regulatory framework for electronic communications networks and services, OJ No. L 108, 24.4.2002, p. 33, amended in 2009.

[91] This is undoubtedly the dark side of the competence grabbing, which was made possible through the Member States, but which was not accompanied by an adjustment of the political order.

[92] Initially K. A. Eliassen and M. Sjovaag (eds.), *European Telecommunications Liberalisation* (London; New York: Routledge, 1999); now K. A. Eliassen and J. From (eds.), *The Privatisation of European Telecommunications* (Aldershot: Ashgate, 2007), in particular from the editors Chapter 1, 'Introduction: Company Transformation, Corporatisation, Privatisation and Company Behaviour', p. 1 and Chapter 14 'Conclusion: Incumbent Company Transformation – How Far and Why', p. 257.

company, as the universal services provider. This is not a free choice, it is a 'framed choice': Member States have to respect the requirements set out in the directive when making their choice. This is a dramatic change with regard to universal services. Private companies provide former public services. The shift from public to private does not alter the character of the public service. Otherwise there would be no reason to compensate the company for servicing the vulnerable consumer, whether through direct compensation payments or indirectly through subsidies to the vulnerable.[93] However, even the private universal service provider is bound by standards on access and principled minimum substance. We are no longer dealing with a bilateral concept of shared competences and shared responsibilities but with a trilateral one – the EU, Member States and private companies. All three stand on an equal footing. There is no hierarchy and no primary or secondary or tertiary responsibility.

The intermingling of responsibilities becomes even more obvious in the *order of enforcement*. The legal and practical reality in regulated markets in general and in universal services in particular is miles away from the original distinction between law-making to establish the Common Market and enforcement of these rules through the Member States. At a superficial level, it appears that the basic distinction is still in place. National authorities are in charge of enforcing the universal service obligation, while national courts decide on access to the market, on subsistence benefits and on resident permits. National ADR provide an alternative to the national court as a low-cost, easily accessible option. However, the EU and the Member States agreed to establish not only national regulatory agencies but European agencies though with no, or limited, regulatory power. The European Court of Justice interprets EU law but sometimes goes far in instructing national courts what to do.[94] ADR bodies are surveyed and monitored by national regulatory agencies. All the information strands coalesce in the European Commission. Underneath the formal division of competence through hard legal rules, there is a dense network of soft obligations, beginning with inconspicuous information exchange and cooperation, and ending in guidelines and recommendations of the European

---

[93] Economists favour direct subsidies to the vulnerable because competition would not be distorted if no competitor could gain a competitive advantage. However, one might argue that the companies chosen benefit indirectly from the subsidies due to more favourable prices; Deutscher, *The Principle of Non-Discrimination in EU Economic Law*.

[94] Case C-317/08, *Alassini and Others*.

Commission that may gain a quasi-legal status, replacing cooperation and coordination through instruction. Taking a step back, this is the result of a European legal order, which is constantly in the making, which has limited fixed contours and where the legal frame is wide enough to allow for experimentalism.

Indeed, there are intermingling competences everywhere in the making and in the enforcement of the law. In a federation, the constitution would lay down the division of competences. The competence rules in the Lisbon Treaty do not really address the competence divide, due to the 'underworld' of delegated powers and new modes of public and private governance. The consequence is ironic. Turning the EU into a full federation would allow for clearer structures. The existing jumble of primary rules – the CFR, secondary EU law, and not to forget the soft law (technical standards, guidelines and recommendations) – could be abolished. Reality is different. The responsibilities are hard to separate, with one crucial exception – money. Member States have to pay for subsistence benefits, this means the taxpayers of the host country. If we take the plea for granted, that each level of governance must be visible and accountable to the citizens, what does visibility look like with regards to universal services? There are two extreme options: demonstrating joint responsibility or splitting the responsibilities generally or with regard to particular elements of the order of competence.[95] As there is no way back to the good old days of the sovereign nation-states, it is much more promising to reflect on how one might make this co-responsibility visible and accountable to citizens.

---

[95] It is not my intention to engage in theories on federalism at point.

3 The Law of the Labour and Consumer Market Society

The second layer is composed of four different sources: the law of the labour market society, the consumer law of the first generation – mainly and implicitly referring to consumer sales as a model, the consumer law of the second generation – the law on regulated markets and, last but not least, non-discrimination law. The focus is on the consequences of the move from sales to services, from the integrated market for products to fragmented regulated markets and how the non-discrimination principle cuts across both the old and the new consumer law. The reference to 'market society' shall indicate that the law reaches beyond the market.

The perspective is taken from the consumer, a lucent legal figure, who can change its image like a chameleon: vulnerable, confident or responsible.[1] However there is more to the concept of the consumer: the consumer in his or her role in completing the Internal Market and building the European society. There is an *institutional* concern in an open market society that the consumer behaves in a way that promotes market integration and increases economic efficiency, and that in the overall political aim of the EU, nobody gets lost. This is what is behind 'social inclusion'. The Lisbon Agenda 2000 highlights this interrelationship. Not only the functioning of the market but also its legitimacy depends on the integration of all those who are threatened with exclusion from the market, because they are the weaker party. Throughout the design of the law of the consumer and labour market society, the

---

[1] M. Dani, 'Assembling the fractured European Consumer' (2011) *LSE 'Europe in Question' Discussion Paper Series (LEQS Paper)* No. 29; Th. Roethe, *Der Verbraucher. Rechtssoziologische Betrachtungen* (Baden-Baden: Nomos, 2014); H.-W. Micklitz, 'The Consumer – Marketised, Fragmentised and Constitutionalised', in D. Leczykiewicz and S. Weatherill (eds.), *The Images of the Consumer in EU Law: Legislation, Free Movement and Competition Law* (Oxford: Hart Publishing, 2016), pp. 21–42.

individual and the institutional perspective have to be kept analytically separated. Social inclusion has a double face: it directs attention to the losers of the market agenda, in the sense that it addresses and faces the person who stands behind the deprivation or the discrimination. At the other end, social inclusion looks at all the weak and the socially discriminated as a group or different groups that are deprived of their identity. It is here that the group and the group identity matters.[2] Those who insist on the institutional dimension of social inclusion, the functionality of social inclusion for the achievement of the most competitive market society, overlook the individual dimension – the human face – that is enshrined in the concept of social inclusion.

The dialects of individual versus institutional are a direct heritage of the twentieth century. The rise of the Social is inherently connected to a collective perspective. First, this was the working class, i.e. workers not only as a group but as a 'class'. Consumer law gave rise to ideas and models building the consumer along the line of labour law as a 'class'.[3] Each and every attempt to legitimate protective legislative action through the structural imbalance of power has to approach the 'weak' and the 'discriminated' as collective identities that need to be anchored in the legal system. Focusing on the individual alone is a deeply liberal position. The relationship between the welfare state and the market state, social justice and access justice is manifested in the *Mohamed Aziz* case.[4] One way to look at the judgment of the ECJ is that it was ready to strengthen the legal position of home owners who are at risk to be evicted. Another way, certainly more cynical but equally right, is the institutional side. Household debts had reached a dimension where they tend to jeopardize the economy, if not the national budget. The Spanish Supreme Court limited the effects of nullity in unfair mortgages clauses ('floor clauses'), to avoid serious economic repercussions. The CJEU considered such limitation incompatible with Article 6(1) of the Unfair Terms Directive 93/13 (hereafter also referred to as

---

[2] Schiek, *Differenzierte Gerechtigkeit*, p. 60, arguing that a group identity cannot and may not exclude individual rights.
[3] U. Reifner, 'Der Schutzbereich eines Verbraucherschutzgesetzes und die Schutzwürdigkeit des Verbrauchers' (1978) 2 *Zeitschrift für Verbraucherpolitik* 203-213.
[4] In the aftermath of C-415/11, *Aziz* we started a comparative socio-legal project and looked into the impact of the crisis in six Member States. The full material can be found in H.-W. Micklitz, I. Domurath and G. Comparato (eds.), 'The over-indebtedness of European Consumers: A view from six Countries' (2014) *EUI Working Paper EUI-ERC* No. 10, the shortened version is published in Micklitz and Domurath (eds.), *Consumer Debt and Social Exclusion in Europe*.

'UCTD').[5] Collective measures have to be taken to save the market economy and they have to be taken out of general taxation.[6] The *Mohamed Azizs* of this world stand out as representatives for the evicted *qua* group. They need to be included back into the economy and society, otherwise the institutional balance is endangered.

3.1 The Vulnerable, the Weak and the Confident

The addressee of the law on the consumer and labour market is not clearly defined. EU law uses very different labels, 'weak', 'confident', 'average', 'vulnerable', 'discriminated', 'women', 'children', 'elderly', 'handicapped', the 'full-time' worker, the 'part-time worker' etc. 'Weak' seems to be an umbrella category, whereas vulnerable seems to be more than 'weak', particularly weak, whereas the confident consumer is tougher than the weak consumer. This at least follows from the semantics. The conceptual problem is that universal services address the vulnerable consumer alone, whereas the law on labour and consumer market addresses the two – the vulnerable and the weak. A twofold distinction is urgently needed. Vulnerability in universal services results from being cut off because the citizen has not enough economic resources. She is dependent on subsistence. Vulnerability in the law of the labour market may result from three different circumstances: physical, intellectual and economic (above subsistence) disability.[7] The second distinction concerns the delimitation between vulnerability and weakness. The first step is to document the confusion, the second is to explain and justify the twofold distinction.

Descriptive account

The concept of the vulnerable consumer shows up first in the context of universal services. Directive 2003/54 on electricity, enacted in reaction to energy poverty, referred to vulnerability. The 2002 Universal Service Directive on telecom does not mention vulnerability, but the Directive intends to ensure according to Recital 7 the '*same conditions [of] access, in*

---

[5] Spanish Supreme Court, Judgment No 241/2013 of 9 May 2013 (ES:TS:2013:1916) and Judgment No 139/2015 of 25 March 2015 (ES:TS:2015:1280) vs. Joined cases C-154/15, C-307/15 and C-308/15, *Gutiérrez Naranjo*.
[6] Mian and Sufi, *House of Debt*, dealing with the way household debt deepened the economic crisis in America.
[7] Reich, 'Vulnerable Consumers in EU Law', p. 139.

particular for the elderly, the disabled and for people with special social needs,' as amended by recital 23a of Directive 2009/136/EC of 25 November 2009.⁸

From there vulnerability found its way into Art. 5 (3) of Directive 2005/29 on unfair commercial practice (hereafter also referred to as 'UCPD') and was turned into a normative category.⁹ Vulnerable is group-based (clearly identifiable group) *mental* or *physical infirmity, age or credulity.* The forceful critique from the Nordic countries was directed against the attempts of the European Commission to codify the average consumer test as the benchmark in blatant neglect of their long-standing tradition to shield particularly vulnerable groups against targeted marketing strategies.¹⁰ Directive 2011/83 on consumer rights, the residuum of the once ambitious project to revise the consumer acquis, introduced vulnerability in Recital 34 very much along the line of Directive 2005/29.¹¹ The wording was taken over in the most recently revised package tour Directive 2015/2302 in Recitals 25.¹² However, there are no rules on vulnerability in consumer credit, in time share and in the injunction directive. Directive 2014/17 on mortgage stresses financial inclusion in Recitals 6 and 17,¹³ whereas Directive 2014/92 on payment accounts explicitly refers to the vulnerable, the consumer without a bank

---

⁸ For an evaluation see A. Nijenhuis, 'Electronic communications and the EU consumer', in F. S. Benyon (ed.), *Services and the EU citizen* (Oxford: Hart Publishing, 2013), pp. 47–74, at p. 56.

⁹ 'Commercial practices which are likely to materially distort the economic behaviour only of a *clearly identifiable group* of consumers who are particularly vulnerable to the practice or the underlying product because of their *mental* or *physical infirmity, age or credulity* in a way which the trader could reasonably be expected to foresee, shall be assessed from the perspective of the average member of that group. This is without prejudice to the common and legitimate advertising practice of making exaggerated statements or statements which are not meant to be taken literally' (emphasis added by H.M.W.).

¹⁰ Howells, Micklitz and Wilhelmsson, *European Fair Trading Law*, p. 111.

¹¹ Vulnerable consumers are defined as those made so 'because of their mental, physical or psychological infirmity, age or credulity in a way which the trader could reasonably be expected to foresee.'

¹² 'The traveller should receive all necessary information before purchasing a package, whether it is sold through means of distance communication, over the counter or through other types of distribution. In providing that information, the trader should take into account the specific needs of travellers who are particularly vulnerable because of their age or physical infirmity, which the trader could reasonably foresee'.

¹³ According to Recital 6, the Directive should 'develop a more transparent, efficient and competitive market, through consistent, flexible and fair credit agreements relating to immovable property, while promoting sustainable lending and borrowing and financial inclusion, and hence providing for a high level of consumer protection.'

account, who needs to be socially and financially included.[14] That is why one might argue that the vulnerable consumer is established in USO, in financial services, but not in traditional consumer contract law. It remains to be seen what future revisions of Directive 93/13 on unfair terms or Directive 99/44 on consumer sales will bring.

The four directives on non-discrimination do not take the category of the vulnerable or the weak consumer as a starting point. There is a lot of rhetoric on the need for 'protection', which implies a degree of weakness and vulnerability. This is even the case in the most promising candidate due to its obvious link to private law, Directive 2004/113 on products and services, which must be made available to the public without discrimination between men and women. Overall, target groups are built around the type of discrimination engaged, namely gender, race, disability age, religion. This regulatory approach has two implications. First, there is a need to define each group identity. The difficulties that the ECJ had to face in dealing with transsexuals and homosexuals, speaks volumes. The same holds true with regard to defining 'disabled', 'age' and 'children'. The UN Convention on the Rights of Persons with Disabilities provides assistance. As the EU and Member States are members of the Convention, the Convention binds the EU.[15] It provides for a broad definition which provokes delimitation problems.[16] Outside and beyond the problem of 'clearly identifying the group of discriminated' (to paraphrase the wording in Art. 5 (3) of the UCPD), the various categories are ranked according to the scope of application and the degree to which exceptions are possible and

---

[14] The vulnerable, unbanked, mobile consumers is defined in relation to a socially inclusive economy and the financial inclusion of vulnerable members of society, Recitals 3, 46, 54, Articles 17, 18(4), 28(1).

[15] Joined Cases C-335/11 and C-337/11, *HK Danmark* [2013] I-000, paras. 28–30,
L. Waddington, 'HK Danmark (Ring and Skouboe Werge). Interpreting EU equality law in the light of the UN Convention on the rights of persons with disabilities' (2013) *European Anti-Discrimination Law Review* 11–22, at 13; L. Waddington, 'The European Union and the United Nations Convention on the rights of persons with disabilities: A story of exclusive and shared competences' (2011) 18 *Maastricht Journal of European and Comparative Law* 431–453; Kelemen, *Eurolegalism*, p. 202; M. Finck and B. Kas, 'Surrogacy leave as a matter of EU law: CD and Z' (2015) 52 *Common Market Law Review* 281–298, at pp. 295–297.

[16] According to Article 2 of the UN Convention, '"Discrimination on the basis of disability" means any distinction, exclusion or restriction on the basis of disability which has the purpose or effect of impairing or nullifying the recognition, enjoyment or exercise, on an equal basis with others, of all human rights and fundamental freedoms in the political, economic, social, cultural, civil or any other field. It includes all forms of discrimination, including denial of reasonable accommodation.'

legitimate. The difference matters on the interface between non-discrimination law and private law. Providers of goods and services offered to the public may not discriminate because of gender, but they may do so because of race, age, disability and religion. In resisting the extension of Directive 2004/113 Member States invited parties to refer to human rights and fundamental rights, to the ECHR and the CFR, to fight for their rights before the European Courts.

Who is the addressee of all these duties? Is it suppliers, employers and landlords? The EU legislator does not differentiate in labour law, or in consumer law or anti-discrimination law between the formal size and the economic strength of the supplier, employer or the landlord.[17] This is all the more surprising as the EU is differentiating between 'normal' companies and SMEs (small- and medium-sized enterprises). The most common definition is the one in Article 2 of the Annex Recommendation 2003/361/EC.[18] The Draft Proposal for a European Sales Law[19] took it over. In private law, such a broad definition is not really helpful. The most concrete ideas to take regulatory action in order to protect 'weak business' against 'big business' are presented in the 'Green Paper on Unfair Trading Practices in Supply Chains'.[20] Through comparative studies, the European Commission seeks evidence for the economic 'inferiority' of small business.[21] It seems as if the project is somewhat at an impasse, not least due to the complexity of the field

---

[17] The two directives which N. Reich uses to underpin the principle of the weaker party do not make any distinction. The Directive on paid leave even emphasises that it is applicable independent of the type of the contract (open-ended, fixed-term, part-time or temporary), Reich, *General Principles of EU Civil Law*, p. 41.

[18] Commission Recommendation of 6 May 2003 concerning the definition of micro, small and medium-sized enterprises, OJ No. L 124, 20.5.2003, p. 36, Art. 2 of the Annex says:
  1. The category of micro, small and medium-sized enterprises (SMEs) is made up of enterprises which employ fewer than 250 persons and which have an annual turnover not exceeding EUR 50 million, and/or an annual balance sheet total not exceeding EUR 43 million.
  2. Within the SME category, a small enterprise is defined as an enterprise which employs fewer than 50 persons and whose annual turnover and/or annual balance sheet total does not exceed EUR 10 million.
  3. Within the SME category, a microenterprise is defined as an enterprise which employs fewer than 10 persons and whose annual turnover and/or annual balance sheet total does not exceed EUR 2 million.

[19] COM (2011) 635 final, 11.10.2011.

[20] COM (2013) 37 final, 31.1.2013.

[21] Study on the Legal Framework Covering Business-to-Business Unfair Trading Practices in the Retail Supply Chain, Final Report 26 February 2014, prepared for the European Commission, DG Internal Market DG MARKT/2012/049/E. Core research Team Andrea Renda (Project Coordinator), Fabrizio Cafaggi, Jacques Pelkmans, Paola Iamiceli,

where competition law, unfair commercial practices, unfair terms legislation and general civil law come together. Whether or not there is a need for rules to protect small business more generally and, indeed, to what extent small business could and should be treated as consumers is subject to controversy.[22] In the third globalisation, everyone is invited to present himself or herself as weak and in need of protection. There are no limits to the potential addressees. In this perspective, big companies may present themselves as weak, as was demonstrated in the conflict between VW and its suppliers in the summer of 2016.[23]

Normative Account: Physical and Intellectual Vulnerability

Vulnerability requires a clearly targeted group, and in this sense the UCPD is right. Vulnerability should remain a residual category, a safety net, narrowly defined and limited to particular groups, otherwise not only the private law system but the whole society would be thrown into turmoil. The distinction between physical and intellectual disability needs to be elaborated.

Discrimination because of *physical* disability is peremptorily forbidden. There is no room for any reasons to justify discrimination. However, the current EU contract law rules do not show a consistent picture. Sometimes directives refer to disability, and sometimes they do not. The law is most advanced in the four regulations on air passengers, sea passengers, railway passengers and bus passengers.[24] In light of the

---

Anabela Correia de Brito, Federica Mustilli and Luana Bebber, available at: http://ec.europa.eu/internal_market/retail/docs/140711-study-utp-legal-framework_en.pdf. However, the whole tender was methodologically flawed. Everybody working in the field knows that these kinds of conflicts are usually settled and do not reach the public. So, looking for cases and not putting enough pressure on empirical research led to the expected result – little or no evidence in *courts*. This does not come through in the report of the Commission COM (2016) 32 final, 29.1.2016, on unfair business-to-business practices in food supply chains.

[22] In favour, see M. W. Hesselink, 'SMEs in European Contract Law', in K. Boele-Woelki and F. W. Grosheide (eds.), *The Future of European Contract Law* (The Hague: Kluwer Law International, 2007), pp. 349–372; for criticism, see J. Stuyck, 'Do We Need Consumer Protection for Small Businesses at the EU level?', in K. Purnhagen and P. Rott (eds.), *Varieties of European Economic Law and Regulation: Liber Amicorum for Hans Micklitz* (New York: Springer International Publishing, 2014), pp. 359–370.

[23] 'Volkswagen Settles Supplier Dispute That Brought Factories to a Halt', *The Telegraph*, 23 August 2016, available at: www.telegraph.co.uk/business/2016/08/23/volkswagen-settles-supplier-dispute-that-brought-factories-to-a/.

[24] Regulation 261/2004 on air passenger rights refers to special care for passengers with disability or reduced mobility (Recital 19, Arts. 2 (i), 9 (3) and Art. 11). Regulation 261/2004 is complemented by Regulation 1107/2006 on rights of disabled persons and persons with reduced mobility when travelling by air (OJ No. L 204, 26.7.2006, p. 1).

references in the consumer law directives to the ECHR and/or to CFR and the UN Convention, such a principle and its application in private law seems justifiable. There is no other ground of discrimination that could be put on an equal footing with physical disability. Women, the elderly, ethnic groups are not *per definitionem* vulnerable. They may be situationally weak.

The second category covers a broad range of non-physical, intellectual disabilities. The private law systems rely on legal capacity to deal with children and more generally with mental disability, whether it results from age or mental illnesses. Age discrimination as such is not dealt with in the private law orders. Here we are back to *Mangold* and the ECJ case law on age discrimination, whether it is a general principle or not, and whether and to what extent it can be applied horizontally in private law relations and under what circumstances. N. Reich refers to Lynden Griggs, who uses social psychology, in order to define as 'intellectually disabled persons those who have limited rights and resources to engage in the choices possible in the relevant consumer market place'.[25] Her concept of 'transactional responsibility' comes close to the one applied by the ECJ and by national courts in consumer law.[26] It leaves leeway to the concrete circumstances of the case. Behavioural science intermingles three different legal issues: economic vulnerability, intellectual disability and the diffuse category of weakness that is not separated from vulnerability.[27]

Regulation 1371/2007 on the rights and obligations of rail passengers refers to the right to comparable travel opportunities, information, access and progressive elimination of physical obstacles for passengers with disabilities (Recitals 10, 11, 25, Art. 3 (15) and Chapter 5 (Arts. 19-25)). Also Regulation 1177/2010 on the rights of sea passengers refers to comparable travel opportunities, information, access, progressive elimination of physical obstacles (Recitals 4, 6, 7, 8, 9, 10, 11, 21, Art. 3 (a), Chapter 2 (Arts. 7-15)). The same observation applies to Regulation 181/2011 on the rights of bus passengers (Recitals 7-14, Chapter 3 (Arts. 9-18)).

[25] Reich, 'Vulnerable Consumers in EU Law', p. 142 under reference to L. Griggs, 'The Consumer with an Intellectual Disability – Do We Respond, If So, How?' (2013) 21 *Competition and Consumer Law Journal* 146-164, at 149, 163 with reference to a study by A. McClimens and M. Hyde, 'Intellectual Disability, Consumerism and Identity: To Have and Have Not?' (2012) 16 *Journal of Intellectual Disabilities* 135-144, at 137, 141.

[26] With regard of the extent to which vulnerability plays a role in the case law of the ECJ Reich, 'Vulnerable Consumers in EU Law', p. 136 and the degree to which vulnerability is relevant before national courts, study of London Economics, VVA Consulting and IPSOS, 'Consumer Vulnerability Across Key Markets in the European Union – Final Report' (European Commission, 2016), with regard to courts executive summary and p. 22, available at: http://ec.europa.eu/consumers/consumer_evidence/market_studies/docs/vulnerable_consumers_approved_27_01_2016_en.pdf

[27] The study of London Economics, VVA Consulting and IPSOS, 'Consumer Vulnerability Across Key Markets in the European Union – Final report' (European Commission,

Normative Account: The Weaker Party

The major category for social market law is the 'weaker' party, with all the uncertainties it implies. Reich's statement stands out: 'In my opinion, "vulnerability" needs to be distinguished from "weakness" in a contractual situation which is more or less typical in consumer transactions'. It also needs to be distinguished in employment.[28]

Weakness is not a status per se: weakness is relational in that it is bound to contractual relations.[29] Structural weakness can be presumed, but whether or not the weakness materialises in an economic disadvantage depends on the contractual situation. The EU legislator has never tried to define 'weakness'. The status of the employee and the status of the consumer in the 'floor rules' – the EU minimum standards – provides legitimacy to take regulatory action in order to protect him or her. This kind of social welfare thinking has penetrated European labour and European consumer law. It underpins thirty years of rule-making. The ECJ followed suit. The floor rules in labour and consumer law aim at the protection of the weaker party. The diffuse concept of weakness implies that weakness is relative.

The EU legislator and the ECJ relate weakness to imbalance of power. In *Pfeiffer* the ECJ had to decide whether the upper limit of the working time directive could be extended via collective agreements. The court rejected that possibility and held:[30]

> Any derogation from those minimum requirements must therefore be accompanied by all the safeguards necessary to ensure that, if the worker concerned is encouraged to relinquish a social right which has been directly conferred on him by the directive, he must do so freely and with full knowledge of all the facts. Those requirements are all the more important given that the *worker must*

2016), p. xx defines the vulnerable consumer as the following: 'The consumer who, as a result of socio-demographic characteristics, behavioural characteristics, personal situation, or market environment: Is at higher risk of experiencing negative outcomes in the market; Has limited ability to maximise their well-being; Has difficulty in obtaining or assimilating information; Is less able to buy, choose or access suitable products; or Is more susceptible to certain marketing practices'.

[28] Reich, 'Vulnerable Consumers in EU Law', p. 136; Reich, *General Principles of EU Civil Law*, Chapter II; E. Hondius, 'The Protection of the Weak Party in a Harmonised European Contract Law: A Synthesis' (2004) 27 *Journal of Consumer Policy* 245–251.

[29] For a different understanding, see A. Butenko and K. Cseres, 'The Regulatory Consumer: Prosumer-Driven Local Energy Production Initiatives' (2015) *Amsterdam Law School Legal Studies Research Paper* Nr. 31, at 24, argue that the second generation of electricity and the gas directives have replaced the weak consumer with the 'circumspect consumer'.

[30] Emphasis added. Joined cases C-397/01 to C-403/01, *Pfeiffer and Other* [2004] ECR I-8835, para. 82.

be regarded as the weaker party to the employment contract and it is therefore necessary to prevent the employer being in a position to disregard the intentions of the other party to the contract or to impose on that party a restriction of his rights without him having expressly given his consent in that regard.

Océano[31] clarified and confirmed the concept of the "consumer as the weaker party":

> ... it should be noted that the system of protection introduced by the Directive is based on the idea that the consumer *is in a weak position vis-à-vis the seller or supplier, as regards both his bargaining power and his level of knowledge.* This leads to the consumer agreeing to terms drawn up in advance by the seller or supplier without being able to influence the content of the terms. ... the system of protection laid down by the Directive is based on the notion that the imbalance between the consumer and the seller or supplier may only be corrected by positive action unconnected with the actual parties to the contract.

The court is materialising the autonomy of the worker and the consumer. Formal freedom is not enough. This freedom needs to be safeguarded through a balancing exercise that ensures that the worker or the consumer does not agree to detrimental contractual conditions under pressure that results from superior power. Materialised individual autonomy prevails over the collective autonomy of trade unions. This is in line with the individualisation of the worker substituting collective agreements through individual rights.[32] The parallel to *Walrave, Bosman, Angonese, Viking, Laval* and *Olympique Lyonnais* is obvious. The ECJ uses the freedom of establishment and the freedom of services to strike down collective agreements. It seems as if the ECJ is somewhat suspicious of collective power wherever it originates from. On the other hand, the ECJ has transformed rights into identity-based rights.

3.2 Access and Substance

Three different aspects will be analysed: fair and discrimination-free access, substance and imbalance of power, and good faith.

---

[31] Emphasis added. Case C-240/98, *Océano Grupo Editorial und Salvat Editore*, paras. 25, 27.
[32] With regard to *Pfeiffer*, see the critical analysis of H. Collins, 'Social Dumping, Multi-level Governance and Private Law in Employment Relationships', in D. Leczykiewicz and S. Weatherill (eds.), *The Involvement of EU Law in Private Law Relationships* (Oxford: Hart Publishing, 2013), pp. 223–253, at p. 239.

Fair and Discrimination Free Access

Access to the contract, the substance of the contract and the termination of the contract are to be regarded as a continuum. This early observation of Reich[33] is paradigmatic for the holistic perspective of the European regulatory private law. In the law of the labour and consumer market, access and substance are strongly interlinked. The interrelationship between access and standardisation of products adds another yet underexplored layer.[34] The EU rules on employment contracts, on consumer contracts and on non-discrimination should be understood as a means to guarantee the weaker party fair and non-discriminatory access to the market and to society. Emphasis has to be put on 'fair' and 'non-discriminatory'. These two elements underpin the whole field under investigation.

The set of four directives adopted in the aftermath of the Treaty of Amsterdam on the basis of Art. 13 (Art. 19 TFEU) and Art. 141 (3) (Art. 157 (3) TFEU) extend the EU non-discrimination rules beyond equal pay and equal access to employment, to race and ethnic origin, and they establish non-discrimination rules which are applicable outside the labour market in private law relations. What kind of justice do the non-discrimination rules stand for? The insertion of the non-discrimination principle into the ACQP and the DCFR, but not in CESL, fired the debate.[35]

Private lawyers attempt to shield the purity of the system against intrusion of the non-discrimination principle. The introduction of the non-discrimination principle into the DCFR was the boldest and most far-reaching move in the design of European Civil Code. Basedow[36] stands for the opposite position. He concludes his analysis of EU law with the following verdict: 'there are only limited and selective prohibitions of discrimination usually aimed at creating balance in situations of power and not a general prohibition of discrimination in the

---

[33] On the distant selling directive, N. Reich, 'Die neue Richtlinie 97/7/EG über den Verbraucherschutz bei Vertragsabschlüssen im Fernabsatz' (1997) *Europäische Zeitschrift für Wirtschaftsrecht* 581–589.

[34] H.-P. Schwintowski, 'Standardisation Prior to or Instead of Information – A Fundamental Criticism of the (European) Information Model for Financial and Insurance Products', in K. Purnhagen/P. Rott (eds.), *Varieties of European Economic Law and Regulation: Liber Amicorum for Hans Micklitz* (New York: Springer International Publishing, 2014), pp. 549–567.

[35] Art. 3:101 to 3:103 ACQP and II.-2:101 to II.-2:103 DCFR.

[36] Basedow, 'Grundsatz der Nichtdiskriminierung im europäischen Privatrecht', p. 250.

conclusion of contracts'.[37] In line with D. Schiek,[38] the EU non-discrimination rules may be regarded as part of the identity of the person (*askriptive Persönlichkeitsmerkmale*). Nationality, gender, ethnic origin, and age then replace the legal person as the pivotal point of private law. Via such a conceptual model, personal elements become an integral part of the 'person' who concludes a contract or whose request or wish is rejected. The private law system is thereby extending its boundaries and encompasses the pre-contractual stage.

Whilst employment is still the focal point of EU non-discrimination law, the prohibition is gradually approaching the core of private law. Directive 2000/43 extends, in Art. 3 (1) (h), the prohibition of discrimination on grounds of race or ethnical belonging to the supply of goods and services which are available to the public, including housing. Directive 2004/113 requires in Art. 5 (1) that the use of sex as a 'factor in the calculation of premiums and benefits for the purposes of insurance and related financial services shall not result in differences in individuals' premiums and benefits'. Under Art. 11 (1) (f) Directive 2003/109,[39] third-country nationals who are long-term residents enjoy equal treatment with nationals as regards 'access to goods and services and the supply of goods and services made available to the public and to procedures for obtaining housing.' The focus lies on goods and services 'offered to the public'. Housing is explicitly mentioned but with regard to third-country nationals the discrimination is limited to 'the procedures'. Non-discrimination rules may also be found in company law.[40]

There is not much case law available. In *Belov*, Kokott[41] regarded the supply of energy and the provision of meters as services offered to the public within Directive 2000/43, although she seems to accept the measure as justifiable. However, it was in *Nikolova* that the Court followed the logic of her argument.[42] *Test Achats* produced a long-lasting

---

[37] Translation provided by Reich, *General Principles of EU Civil Law*, p. 62.
[38] Schiek, *Differenzierte Gerechtigkeit*, p. 27.
[39] Council Directive 2003/109/EC of 25 November 2003 concerning the status of third-country nationals who are long-term residents, OJ No. L 16, 23.1.2004, p. 44
[40] Prohibiting the unequal treatment of national and foreign companies, Directive 2000/12/EEC (OJ No. L 126, 26.5.2000, p. 1), Regulation 3921/91 (OJ No. L 373, 31.12.1991, p. 1) and Regulation 3118/93 (OJ No. L 279, 12.11.1993, p. 1), replaced by Regulation 1072/2009 (OJ No. L 300, 14.11.2009, p. 72).
[41] Opinion of Advocate General Kokott delivered on 20 September 2012 – Case C-394/11, *Belov*, paras. 65, 100–123. The CJEU, however, did not regard the reference as admissible.
[42] Case C-83/14, *CHEZ Razpredelenie Bulgaria*.

outcry.[43] The ECJ set aside Art. 5 (2) Directive 2004/113, which provided the Member States with a 'délai de grâce' to adjust their insurance tariffs to the equal treatment of men and women requirement. The non-discrimination rule became unconditional and the Court had to engage in a complicated balancing of rights.[44] *Test Achats*, like *Barber*[45] and *Smith v. Avdel*,[46] demonstrates that equal treatment comes at a price. Women are worse off after the judgment. There are many more forms of indirect discriminatory strategies that could potentially be regarded as coming under the notion of 'being offered to the public'. The German legislator translated the language of the directive into *Massengeschäfte* ('mass transactions'),[47] which could be submitted to a discrimination test prior to the conclusion of the contract. This is particularly true with regard to tenant contracts and financial services. Credit scoring is an old issue, not so much with gender anymore but due to other grounds of potential discrimination, e.g. place of residence. The growing importance of algorithms in the digital economy and society has attracted political awareness.[48]

Feryn[49] was the first case to be decided under Directive 2000/43. There were no goods or services offered to the public. The incriminated practice was 'public', an advertisement of a Belgian seller of door fitters which offered a job, but not to 'immigrants', as the clients were supposed to fear that their work might endanger the security of the property. *Feryn* demonstrates how the EU non-discrimination law and the EU law on unfair commercial practices interfere in the pre-contractual stage. Instead of carefully looking at how to separate contract law from commercial practices, EU law requires a holistic perspective.

---

[43] Case C-236/09, *Association Belge des Consommateurs Test-Achats and Others*. Helpful with regard to the background of the reference of the Belgian Constitutional Court, H. Cousy, 'Discrimination in Insurance Law', in R. Schulze (ed.), *Non-Discrimination in European Private Law* (Tübingen: Mohr Siebeck, 2011), pp. 81–108.

[44] Part III. 3.3.

[45] Case C-262/88, *Barber v Guardian Royal Exchange Assurance Group*.

[46] Case C-408/92, *Smith and Others v Avdel Systems*.

[47] M. Schreier, 'Das Allgemeine Gleichbehandlungsgesetz – wirklich ein Eingriff in die Vertragsfreiheit?' (2007) *Kritische Justiz* 278–286, at 285, criticising the distinction; K. Riesenhuber, 'Das Verbot der Diskriminierung aufgrund der Rasse und der ethnischen Herkunft sowie aufgrund des Geschlechts beim Zugang zu und der Versorgung mit Gütern und Dienstleistungen', in S. Leible and M. Schlachter (eds.), *Diskriminierungsschutz durch Privatrecht* (München: Sellier, 2006), pp. 123–140.

[48] M. S. Gal and N. Elkin-Koren, 'Algorithmic Consumers' (2017) 30 *Harvard Journal of Law and Technology* 309–353.

[49] Case C-54/07, *Feryn* [2008] ECR I-5187.

The most obvious candidate is Art. 7 UCPD, which prohibits misleading consumers through omissions and the running together of the control of unfair terms and unfair commercial practices.[50] Linked to non-discrimination, new perspectives are opened up on how to perceive geo-blocking.[51] Are contractual terms and property rights that manage to limit the accessibility of goods and services all over the EU and the Internal Market not 'essential' in the meaning of Art. 7 Directive 2005/29? A holistic perspective oversteps the borders between non-discrimination, commercial practices and contract law. The general verdict on open discrimination of commercial activities in public must be read as a concretisation of the EU requirement on fair and discrimination free access.[52]

Substance and Imbalance of Power

The reference point for regulating substance differs. In first-generation consumer law, weakness implies that there is a stronger party on the other side. Usually, the EU legislature and the ECJ put emphasis on the weakness of the consumer and rarely used explicit language referring to power. In second-generation consumer law, sectorial rationality governs regulation not only with regard to market regulation, but also with regard to private law relationships. Non-discrimination law has different origins from outside the market, from the role and position of women, ethnic minorities or people with disabiities in society. Market regulation (consumer) and social regulation (non-discrimination) coalesce when it comes to economic transactions of members of discriminated groups.

Power is a difficult legal concept, if a legal concept at all. It is only in competition law that Art. 102 TFEU provides for safe ground. In the law on regulated markets, the EU legislature has introduced 'significant

---

[50] According to Art. 3 (2) UCPD, the 'Directive is without prejudice to contract law and, in particular, to the rules on the validity, formation or effect of a contract.' Analysing the interaction: M. Durovic, *European Law on Unfair Commercial Practices and Contract Law* (Oxford: Hart Publishing, 2016); H.-W. Micklitz, 'A Common Approach to the Enforcement of Unfair Commercial Practices and Unfair Contract Terms', in W. van Boom, O. Akseli and A. Garde (eds.), *The European Unfair Commercial Practices Directive. Impact, Enforcement Strategies and National Legal Systems* (Farnham: Ashgate, 2014), pp. 173–202.

[51] Proposal for a Regulation of the European Parliament and of the Council on addressing geo-blocking and other forms of discrimination based on customers' nationality, place of residence or place of establishment within the internal market and amending Regulation (EC) No 2006/2004 and Directive 2009/22/EC, COM/2016/0289 final, 25.5.2016.

[52] Schiek, *Differenzierte Gerechtigkeit*, p. 284 was exactly claiming this in 2000.

market power', which is certainly less than a dominant position. Commitment decisions provide the Commission with considerable leeway to put the party who has 'significant market power' under pressure to open markets and even to renegotiate existing contractual engagements.[53] In employment and in consumer law, the Court refers to imbalance of power. Outstanding examples are *Pfeiffer* and *Océano*. However, no threshold is defined. The ECJ starts from the presumption that the worker and the consumer are 'weaker', which releases the Court from needing to define 'power'. It is striking to see how the court shifts the discourse from imbalance of power to discrimination depending on the circumstances. In *Feryn* and *Test Achats*, the ECJ does not spend a single word on the possible or envisaged contractual relationship. The Court is exclusively concerned with whether there is direct or indirect discrimination. While both *Belov* and *Nikolova* deal with the accessibility of the metering system, comparing them is telling. In *Nikolova*, the original plaintiff is the sole trader in a district who runs a grocer's shop. The court found discriminatory practices, but did not mention a possible imbalance of power. This was entirely different in *Belov*, where the plaintiff was a normal customer, in concreto the beneficiary of universal services. Advocate General Kokott used strong language to link imbalance of power to discrimination:[54]

In legal relationships like that at issue, between *consumers and providers of services of general interest*, the principle of equal treatment is particularly important. In the same way as an employment relationship, such legal relationships are characterised by a *structural imbalance between the parties*.

From the case law on the impact of collective agreements on private law relationships – *Walrave, Bosman, Angonese, Viking, Laval, Olympique Lyonnais, Fra.bo*,[55] only *Bosman* and *Olympique Lyonnais* underpin the final judgment with references to the negotiating power. In *Bosman*, Advocate General Lenz stressed the imbalance between wealthy and less wealthy football clubs, in *Olympique Lyonnais*, Advocate General

---

[53] It is the combination of significant market power and commitment decisions in sectorial markets which matters, below the threshold of a dominant position, Y. Svetiev, 'Settling or Learning: Commitment Decisions as a Competition Enforcement Paradigm' (2014) 33 *Yearbook of European Law* 466–500, at 486.

[54] Emphasis added. Opinion of Advocate General Kokott – Case C-394/11, *Belov*, para. 81.

[55] Case 36/74, *Walrave and Koch v. Association Union Cycliste Internationale and Others*; Case C-415/93, *Union royale belge des sociétés de football association and Others v Bosman and Others*; Case C-281/98, *Angonese*; Case C-438/05, *The International Transport Workers' Federation und The Finnish Seamen's Union*; Case C-341/05, *Laval un Partneri*; Case C-171/11, *Fra.bo*.

Sharpston refers to the intention to protect the 'joueur d'espoir' against undue restrictions of his professional career.[56] *Courage* belongs to the few cases in which the ECJ was ready to engage into discussing power relations. The plaintiff brought an action for the recovery of unpaid deliveries of beer from Mr Crehan. Mr Crehan contested the action on its merits, contending that the beer tie (the standard form lease agreement) was contrary to Article 101 TFEU. He also counter-claimed for damages. The ECJ had to decide on the admissibility of the counterclaim in light of the difference in bargaining power between the brewery and the pub owner:[57]

In particular, it is for the national court to ascertain whether the party who claims to have suffered loss through concluding a contract that is liable to restrict or distort competition found himself in a *markedly weaker position than the other party, such as seriously to compromise or even eliminate his freedom to negotiate the terms of the contract* and his capacity to avoid the loss or reduce its extent, in particular by availing himself in good time of all the legal remedies available to him.

Power relations matter in legal practice. Independent of the difficulty to define the concept of individual and collective power, the 'significant' imbalance of rights and duties provides the deeper legitimacy to intervene into the contractual rules through the need to protect the weaker party. The ECJ would need more cases in order to engage in a more nuanced approach on how imbalance of power and discrimination are interlinked.

Good Faith

The opportunity to go beyond access justice is laid out in the increasing importance of good faith, which would and could encompass consumer, non-discrimination and employment law. Good faith forms an integral part of the Directive 93/13 on unfair contract terms. The directive covers goods and services, including financial services, provided the consumer is the addressee. After initial irritations and uncertainties, the ECJ has taken a rather strong hand on the control of standard terms. In *Mohamed Aziz,* the Court gave the good faith principle

---

[56] Opinion of Advocate General Lenz delivered on 20 September 1995 – Case C-415/93, *Union royale belge des sociétés de football association and Others v Bosman and Others*; at 268; Opinion AG Sharpston delivered on 16 July 2009 – Case C-325/08 Olympique Lyonnais [2010] ECR I-02177 throughout the text.
[57] Emphasis added. Case C-453/99, *Courage und Crehan* [2001] ECR I-06297, para. 33.

an interpretative direction, which even made it into the operative part of the judgment:[58]

> With regard to the question of the circumstances in which such an imbalance arises 'contrary to the requirement of good faith', having regard to the sixteenth recital in the preamble to the directive and as stated in essence by the Advocate General in point 74 of her Opinion, the national court must assess for those purposes whether the seller or supplier, dealing fairly and equitably with the consumer, *could reasonably assume that the consumer would have agreed to such a term in individual contract negotiation.*

This is quite a high benchmark that puts a lot of responsibility on the supplier. The wave of references that flooded the Court did not lead to a change of position. The Court stood firm in its commitment to the protection of the economically and societally weaker party. This does not mean that good faith has been recognised in general or specific consumer law directives. The lack of the reference to good faith in financial services is striking. The Consumer Credit Directive 2008/48 downgraded responsible lending to a mere information requirement. On the other hand, the economic crisis and its dramatic impact on household over-indebtedness led to the anchoring of responsible lending in the Mortgage Directive 2014/17. The ideological and theoretical link to good faith is obvious.

There is some movement in the regulation of investment services. Art. 106 (2) UCITS IV[59] explicitly refers to good faith, MiFiD I and II,[60] CRD IV[61], to honesty instead of good faith. Art. 19 of MiFiD I lays down standards on the conduct of business. It could be read as guiding all investment services. Arts. 25 (1) MiFiD II specified the requirements.[62]

---

[58] Emphasis added. Case C-415/11, *Aziz*, para. 69.

[59] Directive 2009/65/EC of the European Parliament and of the Council of 13 July 2009 on the coordination of laws, regulations and administrative provisions relating to undertakings for collective investment in transferable securities (UCITS), OJ No. L 302, 17.11.2009, pp. 32.

[60] MIFID I in Art. 55 (2) good faith. MIFID II in Art. 77(2) good faith; a search of the word 'honesty', however, results also in various provisions, but maybe other contexts.

[61] Directive 2013/36/EU of the European Parliament and of the Council of 26 June 2013 on access to the activity of credit institutions and the prudential supervision of credit institutions and investment firms, amending Directive 2002/87/EC and repealing Directives 2006/48/EC and 2006/49/EC, OJ No. L 176, 27.6.2013, p. 33

[62] According to Article 25(1) of MiFiD II, 'Member States shall require investment firms to ensure and demonstrate to competent authorities on request that natural persons giving investment advice or information about financial instruments, investment services or ancillary services to clients on behalf of the investment firm possess the necessary knowledge and competence to fulfil their obligations under Article 24 and

There is little case law so far. In *Bankinter*,⁶³ the Court held that it is for each Member State to determine the contractual consequences, without engaging further into what it implies and whether the general clause would have to play a role in contract law. In *Himmofinanz*,⁶⁴ without quoting *Bankinter*, the ECJ considered whether the private law remedies for prospectus liability are compatible with EU law. Notably, the ECJ quoted *Manfredi*,⁶⁵ as relevant precedence, and that the civil liability remedy laid down by Austrian Law is an appropriate remedy.

The withdrawal of CESL has led to a backlash in efforts to re-conceptualise the relationship between good faith in consumer law and the non-discrimination principle. D. Schiek demonstrated that the existing scope of the good faith clause in standard terms legislation could be extended to a principle that embraces consumer and non-discrimination law. One might seriously consider such an extension, in particular with regard to what is today called geo-blocking.⁶⁶ Business uses standard terms in order to limit services to the territory where the consumer is resident. 'Nationality' in terms of national territory turns into a condition of access. The customer is not allowed to take the services with her. The same is true when the legislator limits insurance for medical devices to the residents in the respective Member State. This was what happened in *PIP*.⁶⁷ French law makes the insurance against medical devices obligatory, contrary to most other Member States. *Allianz* limited its obligation to the French territory, thereby excluding all women who were not living in France from compensation. Behind this is the long-debated question of whether the non-discrimination principle has direct horizontal effect in private law

---

this Article. Member States shall publish the criteria to be used for assessing such knowledge and competence.'

⁶³ Case C-604/11, *Genil 48 und Comercial Hostelera de Grandes Vinos* [2013] ECR I-000, with a note from St. Grundmann, 'The Bankinter Case on MIFID Regulation and Contract Law' (2013) 9 *European Review of Contract Law* 267–280.
⁶⁴ Case C-174/12, *Hirmann* [2013] ECR I-000.
⁶⁵ Case-295/04, *Manfredi* [2006] ECR I-06619.
⁶⁶ Proposal for a Regulation of the European Parliament and of the Council on addressing geo-blocking and other forms of discrimination based on customers' nationality, place of residence or place of establishment within the internal market. The Commission Staff Working Document (SWD (2012) 146 final, 8.6.2012, p. 9) enlists the following proxies' tantamount to nationality or residence such as the country of the driving licence, of credit card issuance, place of delivery, IP addresses or lack of credit history; Deutscher, *The Principle of Non-Discrimination in EU Economic Law*.
⁶⁷ Special issue *Revue Internationale de Droit Economique*, L'indemnisation des victimes de produits de santé défectueux en Europe – L'affaire PIP, 2015 Numéro 1, 5–122.

relations.[68] The French courts refrained from referring the 'territoriality' clause in the insurance conditions of Allianz to Luxemburg. It seems as if the EU legislature is in a double bind: the 2008 proposal has been withdrawn and the DCFR is dead. Not only is the regulation of goods and services offered to the public at stake, but so is the extension of the control of standard terms to all forms of unjustified discrimination.

In 2014, Reich wrote with regard to the possibility of good faith becoming a general principle that covers B2C and B2B relations:[69] 'Whether the good faith principle is 'on the move' to becoming a general principle of EU civil law depends on further legislation by the Union and on the case law of the ECJ. In my opinion, such a trend can be observed, making it possible to speak of 'half a general principle'.

3.3 Rights, Remedies and Procedures

The dominating European Leitbild is the individual consumer and worker who goes to court and fights for his or her rights. The same is true for transborder litigation, where a complex set of regulations on jurisdiction and enforcement on the applicable law in contract and in non-contractual relations provides for a solid and safe framework. They designate the competent court, determine the applicable law and enforce the judgment of the country of residence in the country of the supplier. The court-centred Leitbild includes collective entities. For decades, the political debate focuses on the question of standing and the type of available remedies. Courts are again centre stage. The ADR Directive[70] and the ODR

---

[68] Special issue *Revue internationale de droit économique* (2015) I-II. Norbert Reich and I have argued that such an extension of the non-discrimination principle is justifiable within and under the case law of the ECJ; see H.-W. Micklitz, N. Reich and L. Boucon, 'L'Action de la victime contre l'assureur du producteur' (2015) *Revue internationale de droit économique* 37–68.

[69] Reich, *General Principles of EU Civil Law*, p. 212; in the same direction the contributions of S. Weatherill, S. Vogenauer, P. Weingerl; H. L. MacQueen and S. Bogle; D. Kimel, F. Gómez and M. Artigot, D. Carusio in 'Part III, Private Autonomy and Protection of the Weaker Party', S. Vogenauer and S. Weatherill (eds.), *General Principles of Law. European and Comparative Perspectives* (Oxford: Hart Publishing, 2017), pp. 255–354.

[70] Directive 2013/11/EU of the European Parliament and of the Council of 21 May 2013 on alternative dispute resolution for consumer disputes and amending Regulation (EC) No 2006/2004 and Directive 2009/22/EC (Directive on consumer ADR), OJ No. L 165, 18.6.2013, p. 63.

Regulation[71] have added a new layer to dispute resolution. ADR could become a convincing alternative to going to court, but only for individuals.[72] Here it is the 'true' individual and not the one who defends identity-based rights in the interest of the group he or she is representing.

Whilst there is academic debate on if ADR is a useful method for ventilating collective claims, there are no particular mechanisms designed for that purpose, at least not at the EU level.[73] In the law of the regulated markets, the newly introduced layer of conflict resolution is heavily promoted as a Leitbild. The shift from courts to ADR frees space for sector-related regulatory agencies that manage ADR and collective conflicts. The European Commission pushes public agencies not only into regulated markets but also in transborder conflicts in the law of the labour and consumer market as a whole.

The EU is moving towards a tripartite approach, with courts, ADR and regulatory agencies standing side by side. Each of the three has its particular function with regard to rights, remedies and procedures of the vulnerable and the weak. Each of the three requires a particular variant of rights, remedies and procedures. Overall and in the long run, there might be a shift away from courts towards semi-legal conflict management of individual claims through ADR and semi-legal conflict management of collective interests (not necessarily collective claims) through administrative bodies.[74] The role and function of ADR uniting the rights, the remedies and the procedure to the benefit of the socially vulnerable and the more or less weak party is similar to ADR in universal services.[75] In non-discrimination law, the policy of the European Union is more reluctant, less specific and less detailed. Under Directives 2000/43, Directive 2000/78 and 2004/113 Member States 'may establish conciliation bodies' 'where they deem it appropriate'. Directive 2006/54

---

[71] Regulation (EU) No 524/2013 of the European Parliament and of the Council of 21 May 2013 on online dispute resolution for consumer disputes and amending Regulation (EC) No 2006/2004 and Directive 2009/22/EC, OJ No. L 165, 18.6.2013, p. 1.

[72] Diez-Sanchez, 'Justice Index' Eurobarometer and the Issue of Justice', shows asymmetric knowledge about ADR among consumers; yet those who know it are willing to use it for lower amounts than for courts (meaning if the claim is worth €100, consumers are more willing to take the case to ADR than to courts, because of the lower cost of the former).

[73] E. Braun, *Collective Alternative Dispute Resolution (ADR) for the Private Enforcement of EU Competition Law*, LLM thesis, European University Institute (2016).

[74] Proposal for a Regulation of the European Parliament and of the Council on cooperation between national authorities responsible for the enforcement of consumer protection laws, COM (2016) 283 final, 25.5.2016.

[75] Part III. 2.5.

clarifies that conciliation precedes litigation in courts. It seems as if the conciliation procedure is regarded as an equivalent to administrative procedures that meet the same purpose.[76]

Rights

In European regulatory private law, the addressee of the law is not the legal subject in the meaning given to it by the French Code Civil and the German BGB. The legal subject is replaced by functional roles to which particular rights are associated. Rights are dependent on the degree of 'weakness'. Whilst this is rather obvious in employment law and consumer law, the situation is less clear in non-discrimination law. Non-discrimination law seems to connect legal status to the identity of the person (*askriptive Perönlichkeitsmerkmale*). The analysis of the directives and the cases of the court follow closely the identity-based (grounds for discrimination) rights.[77] Difficulties result from intersectionality.

The definition of legally defined collective identities yields largely unsolved problems. In consumer law, representation is bound to demonstrating a legitimate engagement in the collective interest of consumers. Starting with Directive 84/450 on advertising and Directive 93/13 on unfair contract terms, European regulatory private law grants standing to consumer and/or business organisations. Directive 98/27, today 2009/22,[78] clarified that only those organisations that are registered at the European Commission have standing. Whilst this requirement is mandatory with regard to cross-border litigation, most Member States extended the registration mechanism to the national legal system. EU law provides for minimum requirements,

---

[76] The wording in Art. 7 (1) Directive 2000/43, Art. 9 (1) Directive 2000/78, Art. 8 (1) Directive 2004/113: 'Member States shall ensure that judicial and/or administrative procedures, including where they deem it appropriate conciliation procedures, for the enforcement of obligations under this Directive are available to all persons who consider themselves wronged by failure to apply the principle of equal treatment to them, even after the relationship in which the discrimination is alleged to have occurred has ended.' According to Art. 17 (1) Directive 2006/54: 'Member States shall ensure that, *after possible recourse to other competent authorities including where they deem it appropriate conciliation procedures, judicial procedures for the enforcement of obligations* ... ' (emphasis added); Barnard, *EU Employment Law*, puts emphasis on judicial process without discussing conciliation procedures, p. 329.

[77] Barnard, *EU Employment Law*, p. 346, is distinguishing the personal and the material scope; Reich, *General Principles of EU Civil Law*, pp. 80–81, structures the analysis along the lines of the grounds of discrimination thereby taking a holistic perspective, overstepping the boundaries between personal and material scope.

[78] Directive 2009/22/EC of the European Parliament and of the Council of 23 April 2009 on injunctions for the protection of consumers' interests, OJ No. L 110, 1.5.2009, p. 30.

such as a stable organisational structure, a minimum size, a definition of the field of activity, and that these organisations are free from trade representatives.[79]

In European labour law, there are no rules on the standing of trade unions. This is entirely left to Member States. The different directives on non-discrimination entitle 'associations, organisations and other legal entities' which have a legitimate interest 'to engage on behalf or in support of the complainant'. This resembles first-generation consumer law directives. There is no registration mechanism foreseen and there is no attempt to specify what the associations, organisation or legal entity is meant to do. Obviously, women's organisations, equal opportunity commissions and trade unions come under this umbrella. However, the differentiation in the type of discrimination is reflected in civil society. This begs the question as to which association can legitimately defend whose interests.

Remedies

European law has introduced *new* individual and, to a lesser extent, *new* collective remedies into the national legal system. This does not mean that these remedies are unknown to the national legal systems. It seems as if consumer remedies are more developed than those in employment and non-discrimination law. A holistic perspective could lead to mutual enrichment *de lege lata*. The focus is on remedies that may potentially cut across the three areas under research.[80]

What is the effect of contracts containing illegal contract terms? In consumer law, standard terms that are supposed to be unfair are '*not binding*', Art. 6 (1) Directive 93/13. Non-binding has no clear equivalent in the Member States laws on standard terms legislation. In unfair terms law, the ECJ has transformed non-binding gradually into 'null and void'.[81] In competition law, the ECJ deduced out of Art. 101 (2) TFEU the right to claim compensation for antitrust injuries, which finally led to the adoption of Directive 2014/104.[82] Linking voidness to available sanctions

---

[79] H.-W. Micklitz and M. Namyslowska, 'Artikel 11 Richtlinie 2005/29/EC', in *Münchener Kommentar zum UWG*, 3rd ed. (München: C. H. Beck, 2018), nos. (numbers) 32–34.
[80] With regard to Directive 1999/44, Case C-65/09, *Gebr. Weber und Putz* [2011] ECR I-5257 and Case C-497/13, *Faber* [2015] ECR I-000, more generally, G. Wagner, 'Der Verbrauchsgüterkauf in den Händen des EuGH: Überzogener Verbraucherschutz oder ökonomische Rationalität?' (2016) *Zeitschrift für europäisches Privatrecht* 87–120.
[81] References in Micklitz and Reich, 'The Court and Sleeping Beauty'.
[82] Directive 2014/104/EU of the European Parliament and of the Council of 26 November 2014 on certain rules governing actions for damages under national law

demonstrates the potential to develop out of Art. 6 (1) the right to be compensated for the losses that result from unfair contract terms.[83] Such a remedy would increase the effectiveness of the unfair terms legislation and would help to do away with the well-known problem of ill-gotten gains.[84] The consumer is usually better off without the incriminated term. Therefore, the ECJ does not allow for adjusting the incriminated term to the legal requirements, what is called in Germany 'geltungserhaltende Reduktion'.[85] Even if the overall contract is null and void, because the contract cannot be 'continued' without the void term, the consumer will usually find another supplier who offers better conditions.

The situation of the socially discriminated is different. Declaring an incriminated term void might invalidate the whole contract as a necessary consequence. However, those who are socially discriminated against may have simply no alternative, as she or he has no real choice. The discriminatory practices might be a common practice. Annulling the contract deprives the discriminated of the opportunity to contract at all.[86] From such a perspective, the sole way out is to eliminate the discriminatory elements of the contract, but to keep the contract intact. This is just the opposite of the ECJ's approach in consumer transactions. Indeed, the four non-discrimination directives underline this point. Art. 14 (b) Directive 2000/43 and Art. 16 (b) Directive 2000/78 are literally identical.[87] Art. 13 (b) Directive 2004/

---

for infringements of the competition law provisions of the Member States and of the European Union, OJ No. L 349, 5.12.2014, p. 1.

[83] C. Cauffmann, 'The Impact of Article 101(2) TFEU Nullity on Private Law', 'The Impact of Article 101(2) TFEU Nullity on Private Law', in H.-W. Micklitz and C. Sieburgh (eds.), *Primary EU law and Private Law Concepts* (Cambridge; Antwerp: Intersentia, 2017), pp. 165–206, draws the parallel to Art. 6 (2) Directive 93/13 at p. 176.

[84] E. Hondius and A. Janssen (eds.), *Disgorgement of Profits: Gain-Based Remedies throughout the World* (Cham; Heidelberg: Springer, 2015).

[85] Case C-618/10, *Banco Español de Crédito*, para. 69 and Micklitz and Reich, 'The Court and Sleeping Beauty', p. 792.

[86] Schiek, *Differenzierte Gerechtigkeit*, pp. 372, 394.

[87] According to Art. 14 (b) Directive 2000/43 Member States shall take measures to ensure that 'any provisions contrary to the principle of equal treatment which are included in individual or collective contracts or agreements, internal rules of undertakings, rules governing profit-making or non-profit-making associations, and rules governing the independent professions and workers' and employers' organisations, are or may be declared, null and void or are amended'. Regarding Art. 16 (b) Directive 2000/78, Member States shall ensure that 'any provisions contrary to the principle of equal treatment which are included in contracts or collective agreements, internal rules of undertakings or rules governing the independent occupations and professions and workers' and employers' organisations are, or may be, declared null and void or are amended'.

113 and Art. 23 (2) Directive 2006/54 are slightly different but contain the same message.[88] Member States shall take measures to ensure that contractual provisions are or may be declared null and void. The language is even clearer than in Art. 6 (2) Directive 93/13. However, nullity must not be the consequence. The directives are silent on what '*may*' means, in particular whether adjustment to legality through a court in an individual litigation could be a solution. There is no case law of the ECJ that explicitly refers to the difference between 'are/shall' and 'may' in the four directives.

What differs are the type of contracts – individual 2004/113, respectively individual contractual provisions and collective agreements in 2000/43, 2000/78 and 2006/54. The directives focus on the incriminated contract terms. They do not directly address individual suppliers/employers; instead, they are directed at employers, workers and non-profit organisations (together with worker/employer associations 2000/43 and in 2004/113 as the only addressees) and associations.[89]

European consumer law has introduced the injunction action as the minimum standard. It is well established in commercial practices per Directive 2005/29 and standard terms legislation per Directive 93/13. In transborder conflicts, the European Commission initially relied on consumer organisations, in particular to strike down unfair commercial practices and standard terms per Directive 98/27 on injunctions. However, through Regulation 2006/2004, the EU shifted from court-based transborder enforcement and promoted conflict resolution to administrative cooperation between public authorities. The regulation obliges Member States to establish consumer agencies with regard to transborder conflicts. Since then, the action for injunction serves as a means of last resort only, although in theory the two mechanisms – court-based solution via action for injunction and agency-based solution through coordination and cooperation – stand side by side.

---

[88] According to Art. 13 (b) Directive 2004/113 Member States shall ensure that 'any contractual provisions, internal rules of undertakings, and rules governing profit-making or non-profit-making associations contrary to the principle of equal treatment are, or may be, declared null and void or are amended'. Regarding Art. 23 (b) Directive 2006/54, Member States shall ensure that 'provisions contrary to the principle of equal treatment in individual or collective contracts or agreements, internal rules of undertakings or rules governing the independent occupations and professions and workers' and employers' organisations or any other arrangements shall be, or may be, declared null and void or are amended'.

[89] As the purpose is to structure the field, I am not engaging in the long-lasting debate on the horizontal direct effect of directives.

Employment law and non-discrimination law lag behind. The four non-discrimination directives aim at the pre-contractual stage, at goods and services offered to the public. They intrude into the contract itself when terms are to be declared null and void. Despite the proximity to market behaviour as enshrined in Directives 2005/29 and 93/13, the four directives do not deal with injunctions as a potential means to eliminate discriminatory practices. It remained for the ECJ to 'invent' in *Feryn* an action for injunction, but left it for the Member States to decide over standing. The ECJ held that the concept of discrimination in Directive 2004/113 does not depend 'on the identification of a complainant who claims to have been the victim'.[90] This statement could easily be extended to the other three non-discrimination directives where the overall purpose is to eliminate discriminatory practices that bar access to the employment market and limits to the consumer market. The four directives address, in particular, collective agreements of worker and employer's organisations, non-profit organisations and internal rules of undertakings, prior to their application in a concrete case.

When it comes to remedies beyond injunctions, the Member States resist any attempt of the European Commission to establish EU-wide rules on collective compensation claims. The rather meagre outcome of a decade-long debate is Recommendation 2013/396.[91] Besides injunction and skimming off procedures, the recommendation favours opt-in compensation claims over the American opt-out procedure. The proposal for a revision of Regulation 2006/2004 intended to grant national authorities and, within limits, the commission the power to take regulatory action so as to provide collective damages. However, this remarkable proposed extension did not survive the legislative procedure.[92] It seems, again, as if the ECJ is ahead of national political developments. The case law of the ECJ contains potential to develop

---

[90] Case C-54/07, *Feryn*, para. 25.
[91] Commission Recommendation of 11 June 2013 on common principles for injunctive and compensatory collective redress mechanisms in the Member States concerning violations of rights granted under Union Law, OJ No. L 201, 26.7.2013, p. 60. On the recommendation, C. Hodges, 'Collective Redress: A Breakthrough or a Damp Squib?' (2014) 34 *Journal of Consumer Policy* 67–89.
[92] Art. 12 of the Proposal for a Regulation of the European Parliament and of the Council on cooperation between national authorities responsible for the enforcement of consumer protection laws, COM (2016) 283 final, new announcement regarding the current status available at: www.europarl.europa.eu/news/en/press-room/20171110IPR87814/buying-online-parliament-beefs-up-protection-against-fraudsters

a collective compensation claim.[93] It would remain for consumer organisations to test that avenue.

Procedure

Of utmost interest are the judicial innovations that provide potential for generalisation, the *ex officio* doctrine, the extension of legal effects to third parties and the opportunity to link substantive and procedural rules of law enforcement. Read together they look like an emergent European procedural consumer law.

Ex Officio

Relying on its rulings in *Cofidis*[94] and *Mostaza Claro*,[95] the ECJ established in *Pannon*[96] the duty of national courts to examine *ex officio* the unfairness of a term in a B2C contract. The ECJ went further than in *Océano*,[97] in which it merely confirmed the possibility of the national court to determine the unfairness of a term *ex officio*. In a whole series of follow-up references, *Pannon*,[98] *Asturcom*,[99] *Pénzügyi*,[100] *Pohotovosť*,[101] *Invitel*,[102] *Banco Español*,[103] and *Banif*,[104] the ECJ developed more and more sophisticated criteria for the new procedural remedy. The common ground is identifiable. A consumer cannot be protected through the *ex officio* doctrine against his will. There must be minimal 'contradictory proceedings' to be arranged by the national court allowing a consumer to oppose the non-application of the incriminated clause. In *Invitel*, the ECJ extended the *ex officio* doctrine to collective proceedings.[105]

Martín[106] confirmed the applicability of the *ex officio* doctrine to doorstep selling, *Rampion*[107] to consumer credit and *Duarte Hueros* (AG

---

[93] Micklitz and Reich, 'The Court and Sleeping Beauty', 771; N. Reich, 'Product Liability and Beyond: An Exercise in 'Gap-Filling'' (2016) 24 *European Review of Private Law* 619–644.
[94] Case C-473/00, *Cofidis* [2002] ERC I-10875.
[95] Case C-168/05, *Mostaza Claro* [2006] ECR I-10421.
[96] Case C-243/08, *Pannon GSM* [2009] ECR I-04713.
[97] Case C-240/98, *Océano Grupo Editorial und Salvat Editore*.
[98] Case C-243/08, *Pannon GSM*.
[99] Case C-40/08, *Asturcom Telecomunicaciones* [2009] ECR I-9579.
[100] Case C-137/08, *VB Pénzügyi Lízing* [2010] ECR I-10847.
[101] Case C-76/10, *Pohotovosť* [2010] ECR I-11557.
[102] Case C-472/10, *Invitel* [2012] ECR I-000.
[103] Case C-618/10, *Banco Español de Crédito*.
[104] Case C-472/11, *Banif Plus Bank* [2013] ECR I-000.
[105] Case C-472/10, *Invitel*, para. 43.
[106] Case C-227/08, *Martín Martín* [2009] ECR I-11939.
[107] Case C-429/05, *Rampion und Godard* [2007] ECR I-8017.

Kokott[108]) to consumer sales. In the area of consumer law, it seems fair to speak of a comprehensive encompassing procedural remedy. What remains to be decided is the degree to which the *ex officio* doctrine can be extended beyond the scope of the Unfair Contract Terms Directive to all EU rules which provide for a mandatory level of protection, not only in consumer law, but in labour law and anti-discrimination law, in short, wherever the EU sets binding standards. The strong language on compliance in Art. 7 (1) Directive 2000/43, Art. 9 (1) Directive 2000/78, Art. 8 (1) 2004/113 and Art. 17 (1) Directive 2006/54 allows the *ex officio* doctrine to extend to non-discrimination law.

Erga Omnes

When it comes to the *erga omnes* doctrine, most contract lawyers might consider the answer as well known. Judgments are binding *inter partes* only. In *Invitel*,[109] a consumer agency and the user are the relevant parties. Advocate General Trstenjak, treating the impact of the collection action on individual contracts containing the same incriminated term, puts the matter as follows: 'These terms are therefore intended for use in a large number of consumer contracts. They can therefore be combated effectively only if the decision of the national court finding a particular term to be unfair is accorded fairly wide applicability'.[110] And the ECJ further clarified:[111] 'These terms ... are not binding on either the consumers who are parties to the actions for an injunction or on those who have concluded with that seller or supplier a contract to which the same GBC apply'.

Whereas the advocate general explicitly excludes third parties not involved in the proceedings,[112] since their right to be heard has not been respected, the ECJ limits the effects to 'those who have concluded with that seller or supplier a contract'.[113] The addressee of the extension of *res judicata* is the same user of the term; it does not concern the term itself, which has been declared illegal, even though the contract is applied identically by another businessman.

---

[108] Opinion of Advocate General Kokott delivered on 28 February 2013 – Case C-32/12, *Duarte Hueros* [2013] ECR I-000, para. 52.
[109] Case C-472/10, *Invitel*, para. 38; Opinion of Advocate General Trstenjak delivered on 6 December 2011 – Case C-472/10, *Invitel*, para. 51.
[110] Opinion of Advocate General Trstenjak – Case C-472/10, *Invitel*, para. 51.
[111] Case C-472/10, *Invitel*, para. 38.
[112] Opinion of Advocate General Trstenjak – Case C-472/10, *Invitel*, paras. 59, 60.
[113] Case C-472/10, *Invitel*, para. 38.

The ECJ's formulation leaves room for interpretation.[114] It is suggested to extend the *effet utile* to the term, regardless of the original user; for instance, if a Member State wants to make use of an '*ex parte*' court order so that each and every trader must abstain from using the banned terms on penalty of fines or other sanctions. It is hard to envisage what kind of legitimate interest a trader using the same term might have.

Member States are obliged to introduce *erga omnes* effect to actions for injunctions declaring a contract term to be unfair. In two follow-on judgments, the ECJ framed the *erga omnes* effects in *Sales Sinués*[115] and *Biuro podróży Partner*.[116] The bottom line of the two judgments complies with the limits of the *ex officio* doctrine. A consumer cannot be tied to the result of the collective action and the trader must be able to contradict to the *erga omnes* effect if he is confronted with the claim of a consumer who was not part of the collective litigation. Such a restriction would make sense if the legal effects are tied to the term as such and free from the 'user' connection.

Interim Relief

The amazing development of the case law of the ECJ on the control of standard terms has led to 'proceduralisation'[117] of unfair terms. Whilst the directive is, at a first glance, concerned with substance – the good faith and significant imbalance requirement – the ECJ has interpreted the respective EU directive rules as a way to review national law enforcement. The culmination of this approach is *Mohamed Aziz*. The advocate general deduced from the principle of effectiveness the need to grant *interim relief* to protect the rights of over-indebted consumers against the disastrous effects of the separation of declaratory and enforcement proceedings. The ECJ confirmed this requirement by reference to *Unibet*.[118] The ECJ 'invented' a new procedural remedy, more or less in passing, that links enforcement proceedings and declaratory

---

[114] Case C-472/10, *Invitel*, para. 40: 'The application of a penalty of invalidity of an unfair term with regard to all consumers who have concluded a consumer contract to which the same GBC apply ensures that those consumers will not be bound by that term, but does not exclude the application of other types of adequate and effective penalties provided for by national legislation'.
[115] Joined Cases C-381/14 and C-385/14, *Sales Sinués* [2016] ECR I-000, para. 41.
[116] Case C-119/15, *Biuro podróży Partner* [2016] ECR I-000.
[117] Della Negra, 'The Uncertain Development of the Case Law on Consumer Protection in Mortgage Enforcement Proceedings'.
[118] Case C-415/11, *Aziz*, para. 59; Case C-432/05, *Unibet* [2007] ECR I-2271, para. 77.

proceedings. The procedural autonomy of Spain did not meet the effectiveness test. However, this is not a stand-alone test. Advocate General Kokott built a bridge between the rights granted under Directive 93/13/EEC and the need to provide for appropriate protection within national procedural law.[119]

The new remedy is linked to declaratory and enforcement procedures. Generalised interim relief must be granted whenever the gap between European *substantive* and national *procedural* law endangers the effective and equivalent protection of substantive EU law. Substantive EU contract law therefore shapes national procedural law. Such an extensive reading of EU law erodes the much-debated procedural autonomy of Member States.[120] One might even raise the question of whether and to what extent the procedural turn of the ECJ allows for the introduction of a European skimming-off procedure *ex lege*. To date, the users of unfair contract terms or unfair commercial practices whose terms and practices infringe EU law can keep their ill-gotten gains. This undermines the effectiveness of the action for an injunction and, more importantly, the *acquis* of the Directive 93/13/EC on unfair contract terms.[121] Such court-driven improvement of procedural remedies would close an important gap in the protection of the collective rights of consumers where no agreement between Member States on a European solution seems possible in the near future. If one links interim relief to the *ex officio* doctrine, it seems that the ECJ has started to lay the foundations for an autonomous European procedural consumer law.

3.4 Balancing of Rights, Expectations and Needs

Contrary to universal services, where there is, in principle, no balancing on the basic requirements of access and substance, balancing in the law

---

[119] Opinion of Advocate General Kokott delivered on 8 November 2012 – Case C-415/11, *Aziz*, para. 46.
[120] M. Bobek, 'Why There is No Principle of "Procedural Autonomy" of the Member States', in H.-W. Micklitz and B. de Witte (eds.), *The European Court of Justice and the Autonomy of the Member States* (Cambridge; Antwerp: Intersentia, 2012), pp. 305–324; H. Schebesta, 'Procedural Theory in EU Law', in K. Purnhagen and P. Rott (eds.), *Varieties of European Economic Law and Regulation: Liber Amicorum for Hans Micklitz*, pp. 851–862.
[121] Case C-92/11, *RWE Vertrieb* [2013] ECR I-000; for the story of the 5000 consumers behind RWE H.-W. Micklitz and N. Reich, 'Luxemburg ante portas – jetzt auch im deutschen „runderneuerten" AGB-Recht?', in P. Mankowski and W. Wurmnest (eds.), *Festschrift für Ulrich Magnus zum 70. Geburtstag* (München: Sellier European Law Publishers, 2014), pp. 631–654.

on the labour and consumer market is absolutely crucial. Vulnerability and weakness are context-dependent. Balancing is the decisive moment for deciding how far protection under EU law reaches. In European private law, balancing reaches beyond 'constitutionalised' rights of workers and consumers. The focal point is legitimate or reasonable *expectations* anchored in the directives and regulations under scrutiny and since the Lisbon Agenda that strive for social inclusion, particularly visible in financial services. Therefore, the weighing process covers, though to a different degree, *rights, expectations* and *needs*. Balancing is equally not bound to particular parties, as it opens up space for the integration of third parties. The rationality doctrine structures the difficult task of balancing. Those who restrict the rights, expectations and needs of the vulnerable and the weak find themselves under a constant obligation to provide substantial reasons, not only for legislative or regulatory action, but also for private regulation.

Rights, Expectations and Needs

The rules in the treaty and secondary EU law, which refer to the Social (labour, non-discrimination and consumer), shape the balancing process. They provide guidance on the social model of the EU,[122] in that they allow for the integration of the genuinely European 'social' values into the weighing process in all its complexity and diversity in the various fields of law under scrutiny. The formula that enshrines the balancing process needs a reference point. This is the expectation of the parties, not necessarily the parties to the contract alone, but also third parties. Expectations are not to be equated with individually enforceable rights. Expectations include what the parties to the contract expect from the political objectives enshrined in the treaty and secondary EU law. In this respect, expectations range from individually enforceable rights to mere policy objectives in the treaty, in the Charter of Fundamental Rights and in secondary EU law. The Lisbon Agenda, which inserted social inclusion as a policy objective, is simply a variation on the theme of establishing and creating expectations. Social inclusion triggers the hope of economic and societal inclusion including financial support through the EU, through Member States, through business or through society. It stretches balancing far beyond 'rights' and 'expectations' towards social needs – although not without differences.

---

[122] For an overview and a critical account, see Rödl, 'Labour Constitution', p. 627.

There is a correlation between the breadth and reach of expectations and the degree to which they are legalised. Individually enforceable rights are the strongest form of generating expectation. This is particularly true when rights are granted unconditionally through rules that have no exceptions. The weaker the legal right and/or remedy, the stronger the political promises. There is *no* individually enforceable right to social inclusion, but there is *an* individually enforceable right not to be discriminated against as a woman. Expectations can easily be created and they are difficult to satisfy. The bombastic language of the EU and the European Commission, their grand words all too often without concrete deeds, testifies to the ambivalent results of inserting policy objectives into private law relations. If policies are referenced, the language remains vague with regard to whether the addressees have rights or may only enjoy expectations. The bright side of the vague formula of expectations is that it allows courts to go beyond individually enforceable rights and to include softer and less concretised expectations, including social needs that have nevertheless found their way into the law and that broaden the balancing beyond the parties of a contract.[123]

Expectations cannot be easily ranked, certainly not without difficulty by courts, although with greater success before ADR bodies, which are inclined to find a less adversarial trade off. Each party to a contract and maybe even a third party might invoke a 'right'. If the right is individually enforceable, the position is strong; if the legal qualification of the right is unclear, the position is weaker. What matters, however, is that rights and expectations in the law of the labour and consumer market society are not unlimited. They need a corrective, contrary to the beneficiaries of universal services. The balancing exercise is bound to weigh the *legitimacy* of the expectations, social rights against economic rights, economic rights against social objectives and so on.[124] The weighing process has found its way into the EU private law. It is not by coincidence that the concept of legitimate expectations is well established in administrative law, but not in national private law. In national private law, it is either good faith or equity that fulfils the task. This is due to the regulatory character of European private law. The expectations are all

---

[123] B. van Leeuwen, 'The Impact of Intellectual Property Law and the Charter on Private Law Concepts', in H.-W. Micklitz and C. Sieburgh (eds.), *Primary EU law and Private Law Concepts* (Cambridge; Antwerp: Intersentia, 2017), pp. 241–269, at p. 248.
[124] Reich, *General Principles of EU Civil Law*, enshrines the limits in the formula of over- and underprotection, p. 141.

too often not created by the parties themselves, but by and through the political and social environment in which the parties operate. They can only be taken into consideration if they have made their way into the primary and or secondary EU law rules.

Legitimate (Reasonable) Expectations and Social Inclusion

The formula was developed during extensive discussions about Directive 85/374/EEC on product liability. The terminology has been taken over in Directive 92/59/EEC on product safety, which later became Directive 2001/95/EC. From product safety, the formula found its way into consumer contract law. Directive 99/44/EC still relies on the concept of legitimate expectation, though not as the only criterion to define the conformity of the goods with the contract.[125] The history of Directive 99/44/EC reveals how strongly the Directive is connected to the principle of legitimate expectations.[126] Art. 2 (h) Directive 2005/29 defines professional diligence as a standard of care which a trader 'must reasonably be expected to exercise'. The draft proposal on consumer rights,[127] which was never translated into binding law, deserves to be reiterated, as it foreshadows almost exactly the formula the ECJ uses in *Mohamed Aziz* to concretise good faith[128]:

> When making an assessment of good faith, particular regard should be made to the strength of the bargaining positions of the parties, whether the consumer was induced to accept the term and whether the goods or services were sold or supplied on the special order of the consumer. The requirement of good faith may be satisfied by the trader where he deals fairly and equitably with the other party whose *legitimate interests* he should take into account.

The ACQP understands legitimate expectations as a guiding rule in pre-contractual duties, Art. 2:102, and in the performance of the contract, 7:101 (2). The DCFR follows the same spirit though using reasonable instead of legitimate expectations as a yardstick in pre-contractual

---

[125] H.-W. Micklitz, 'Die Verbrauchsgüterkauf-Richtlinie' (1999) *Europäische Zeitschrift für Wirtschaftsrecht* 485–493; Art. 2 (2) (d) of Directive 99/44 runs as follows: 'Consumer goods are presumed to be in conformity with the contract if: (d) they show the quality and performance which are normal in goods of the same type and which the consumer can reasonably expect'.

[126] H. Collins, 'Good Faith in European Contract Law' (1994) 14 *Oxford Journal of Legal Studies* 229–254, at 236–238, deduces in general terms that EC policy implements a principle of fulfilment of legitimate expectations.

[127] Proposal for a Directive of the European Parliament and of the Council on consumer rights, COM (2008) 614 final, Recital 48.

[128] Emphasis added. Case C-415/11, *Aziz*, para. 69.

duties (per Art. II, 3:101), and good faith and fair dealing in the performance of contracts (III, 1:103). In the first-generation consumer law, which focuses directly or indirectly on consumer sales law, the principle of legitimate expectations seems well settled. In contractual relations, it means the consumer is granted the *'right to a contract at fair conditions with enforceable remedies'*. This right to a fair contract has to be balanced against the supplier's freedom of contract and his freedom to do business.

The second generation, the law on the regulated markets, looks different. Browsing through the different directives on energy, telecom and on financial markets shows that there is no explicit reference to 'legitimate' or to 'expectations' as a kind of a floor rule. If a formula that comes close to legitimate expectations shows up, it is with regard to sector-related particularities, like the protection of public security,[129] or particular rules on unsolicited communication,[130] or to early repayments and false expectations through advertising.[131] The dominating reference in financial services is to 'honesty'[132] and 'reasonableness',[133] though usually with regard to very particular rights and obligations. The same is true with regard to the fee for the calculation of a mortgage[134] or the price of a bank account.[135] Social inclusion appears

---

[129] Art. 11 (9) Directive 2009/72.

[130] Art. 13 (6) Directive 2009/136.

[131] Recitals 63, 68 and Art. 10 Directive 2014/17.

[132] Art. 19, 25 (MIFID I); Recital 86, Arts. 24(1), (9), 30(1), 63(1) (MIFID II); Arts. 14(1)(a), 14(2)(a) (UCITS IV); Art. 91(8) (CRD IV).

[133] Arts. 13, 18, 21, 22 (3), 27 (3), 30 (1), 31 (1), 44 (1), 45 (1) (MIFID I); Recital 59, 71, 143, Arts. 16 (4), (5), 23 (2), 24 (2), (5), 28 (3), 49 (2), 65 (1), (2), 90 (3) (MIFID II); Recital 36, Arts. 5, 9 (2), 17 (6), 18 (1), 56 (2), 62 (1), 64 (2) (PSD I); Recital 53, 71, 76, 88, Arts. 5, 10 (2), 20 (1), 28 (2), 40 (3), 73 (1), 76 (1), 79 (1), 88 (3) (PSD II); Arts. 78 (2), 101(8) (CRD IV); Recital 53, 72, Arts. 6 (2), 18 (1), 23, 32 (1), 38 (3), 44 (3), 47 (4), 66 (2), 67 (1) (BRRD).

[134] The expectations, calculations and assumptions on the consumer's financial situation shall be reasonable: Recital 54 on the calculation of the APCR, Article 7 on advisory services and Art. 25(4) on early repayments.

[135] Several references to the obligation of Member States to ensure that accounts with basic features are offered free of charge or at a reasonable fee, in particular, those accompanied by references to vulnerable consumers, Recital 46 Directive 2014/92/EU: 'In order to ensure that payment accounts with basic features are available to the widest possible range of consumers, they should be offered free of charge or for a reasonable fee. To encourage unbanked vulnerable consumers to participate in the retail banking market, Member States should be able to provide that payment accounts with basic features are to be offered to those consumers on particularly advantageous terms, such as free of charge. Member States should be free to define the mechanism to identify those consumers that can benefit from payment accounts with basic features on more advantageous terms, provided that the mechanism ensures that vulnerable consumers can access a payment account with basic features'.

in the Recital 7 of the Payment Service Directive 2015/2366,[136] in Recital 26 Directive 2014/49 on Deposit Guarantee Schemes,[137] in Recitals 6 and 17 Mortgage Directive 2014/47[138] and in Recital 3, 54, Arts. 18 (4) and 28 (1) (j) Directive 2014/92 on Payment Accounts.[139] This patchwork uncovers the tendency to grant 'expectations in whatever form' a normative dimension. However, the only EU legislation that holds all the service-related rules together is Directive 93/13 on unfair terms. There the principle of legitimate expectations is established. The ECJ is ready to engage in a balancing test that goes along with *Aziz*. The key case is certainly *RWE*.[140]

EU labour law directives do not use legitimate or reasonable expectations as a reference point for measuring the standards of access justice. This results from the fact that they do not directly regulate the employment contract but, instead, the conditions under which the worker obtains access to an employment relation. The Working Time Directive aims at the protection of the health and safety of workers.

According to Article 18(1), Member States shall ensure that the services referred to in Article 17 (basic features) are offered by credit institutions free of charge or for a reasonable fee.

[136] Accordingly, 'Payment services are essential for the functioning of vital economic and social activities'.

[137] Accordingly, 'Member States should ensure that the protection of deposits resulting from certain transactions, or serving certain social or other purposes, is higher than EUR 100 000 for a given period.'

[138] The emphasis is put on financial inclusion and access to finance: Recital 6 (promoting sustainable lending and borrowing and financial inclusion, hence providing a high level of consumer protection) and Recital 17 (ensuring that policy objectives relating to financial stability and the internal market can be met without impeding financial inclusion and access to credit).

[139] The emphasis is put on financial and social inclusion in connection to the concept of vulnerable consumer: Recital 3 (socially inclusive economy ... that takes into account the needs of more vulnerable consumers) and Recital 54 (increase financial inclusion and to assist vulnerable members of society in relation to over-indebtedness).
According to Article 18(4) on associated fees: 'Without prejudice to the right referred to in Article 16 (2) and the obligation contained in paragraph 1 of this Article, Member States may require credit institutions to implement various pricing schemes depending on the level of banking inclusion of the consumer, allowing for, in particular, more advantageous conditions for unbanked vulnerable consumers. In such cases, Member States shall ensure that consumers are provided with guidance, as well as adequate information, on the available options'. Regarding Article 28 (1) on the future review of the directive, '(j) an assessment of the effectiveness of existing measures and the need for additional measures to increase financial inclusion and to assist vulnerable members of society in relation to over-indebtedness; (k) examples of best practices among Member States for reducing consumer exclusion from access to payment services'.

[140] Case C-92/11, *RWE Vertrieb*, under the aspect of balancing Reich, *General Principles of EU Civil Law*, Chapter 5.8, p. 138.

It is based on Art. 137 (the former Art. 118 a) EC, now Art. 153 TFEU). The directive defines minimum standards on daily rests, weekly rests, maximum working time per week, etc. The Court has put particular emphasis on the right to paid annual leave. There is an obvious link to the product liability directive and the consumer safety directive, the sources of the principle of legitimate expectations. The directive sets out clear rights for workers, which have become subject to extensive litigation before the Court. The language of the Court, the emphasis on the weaker party, who needs to be protected even against collective agreements of trade unions, brings the directive close to the principle of legitimate expectations. The widely discussed circumvention strategies[141] indicate the limits of a bilateral balancing process and demonstrate the need to go beyond the parties and to involve the trade unions and business organisations. European labour and employment law is composed of bits and pieces. However, the reference to the working time directive might suffice to demonstrate that the European floor rules on labour, the second wave (F. de Witte), is guided and driven by considerations of legitimate expectations.

Non-discrimination law is different. All four directives refer continuously to legitimate reasons or legitimate exceptions or legitimate aims, or simply whether a measure is legitimate with regard to a particular type of discrimination.[142] The very same philosophy can be found in Art. 3:103 ACQP and Art. II, 2:103 DCFR. However, the logic works in reverse. The regulatory technique of the four directives starts from *the right not to be discriminated against* on grounds of nationality, gender, sexual orientation, race, age, disability or religion. The references to legitimate aims and reasons are meant to justify exceptions from the prohibition – provided they are 'legitimate', are justified by objective reasons, meet a societal need, have nothing do with the incriminated ground of differentiation, respect proportionality criteria and are proven by the defendant. The addressee of the exceptions are Member States, which are entitled to regulate the conditions under which the right to non-discrimination is outweighed by objective reasons. An employer has to translate these requirements into contractual

---

[141] Collins, 'Social Dumping, Multi-level Governance and Private Law in Employment Relationships', p. 223; and Barnard, *EU Employment Law*, p. 558.

[142] Directive 2000/43: Recital 18 and Arts. 2 (2) (b) and 7; Directive 2000/78: Recitals 18, 23, 25 and Art. 5; Directive 2002/73: Recital 11, Arts. 2 (2) and (6), 6 (3), 8 (c); Directive 2004/113: Recitals 16, 24, 25 and Arts. 2 (b), 4 (5), 8 (3) and Art. 11; Directive 2006/54: Recital 19 and Arts. 2 (b), 14 (2), 17 and 22.

practice. Provided an employer is a statutory body or a subsidiary of the state, the highly contested issue of the horizontal effects of the directives is of limited relevance. Art. 11 Directive 2004/113 explicitly addresses private employers and employees:

> With a view to promoting the principle of equal treatment, Member States shall encourage dialogue with relevant stakeholders which have, in accordance with national law and practice, a legitimate interest in contributing to the fight against discrimination on grounds of sex in the area of access to and supply of goods and services.

The tone is very different, which might be due to the relevant subject matter. Art. 11 handles the difficult issue of access to goods and services offered to the public.

Direct discrimination is prohibited, subject to legitimate exceptions depending on the ground of discrimination. The standard example is age, where an unconditional rule might lead to tensions between the older and the younger generation in the labour market. Indirect discrimination is subject to extensive balancing where employers may bring forward objective reasons.[143] There is much debate on what counts as good reasons and, in particular, whether the reasons must be objective or whether they can be subjective. The underlying conflict is one on the interrelationship between discrimination law and contract law. Defending the distinction means defending the borderline between 'objective' non-discrimination law and 'subjective' contract law.[144] A contextual approach combines objective and subjective elements with the economic and social realities and with the holistic perspective of the European regulatory private law. This goes along with the balancing test that the Court should have applied in *Test Achats*. A more flexible solution would have left women in a more favorable situation.[145]

The Importance of the Rationality Test

Whilst consumer law uses legitimate expectations as a positive concept, non-discrimination law starts from the opposite perspective. In the end, both sets of rules aim at protecting social expectations though not in an unlimited way.[146] Whilst legitimate expectations could be turned into

---

[143] Reich, *General Principles of EU Civil Law*, p. 87.
[144] K. Riesenhuber, *European employment law* (Cambridge: Intersentia, 2012), p. 251.
[145] Reich, *General Principles of EU Civil Law*, pp. 80–81.
[146] Schiek, *Differenzierte Gerechtigkeit*, p. 463.

an emergent general rule to guide the balancing process, there are opposing effects in consumer law and non-discrimination law. In consumer law, it is for the consumer to demonstrate that she has a right to a contract on fair conditions. She is in a position of defence and has to fight against the dominance placed on freedom of contract. In non-discrimination law, the burden of demonstrating that there are legitimate reasons is with the employer or supplier. These differences could only be equalised if one accepts that the rationalisation test turns the relationship between the consumer and the supplier upside down.[147] Pushed to its logical conclusion, this approach would result in employers and suppliers being burdened with the task of demonstrating that the restrictions which bar access to a contract, determine the substance of a contract or terminate the contract fulfil a rationality test. However, the rationality test, if any, is limited to the scope and reach of European law.[148]

3.5 Order of Competence and Responsibilities

The law on the labour and consumer market society goes to the heart of social welfare thinking and of relating the responsibility for taking action to the 'state'. People expect 'to be protected' beyond the minimum enshrined in the universal service obligations. Protection does not only mean being shielded against hardship but being guaranteed 'a good life'[149] and a society where wealth is not too unevenly redistributed. The Eurobarometer demonstrates that social welfare thinking, at least when it comes to protection via labour and consumer law, is not necessarily related to the nation-state of origin. At least in the past, consumers perceived differences between the Nordic way of guaranteeing protection of consumers and the Greek way. The analysis of the Eurobarometer over time demonstrates that citizens are retreating away from the perspectives of the common and internal market, and going back to 'their' nation-state.[150] Such sentiments are even more distinct after *Viking* and *Laval*, although the perception and the impact of

---

[147] Micklitz, 'Some Considerations on Cassis de Dijon and the Control of Unfair Contract Terms in Consumer Contracts'.
[148] Part II. 4.
[149] F. de Witte, *Justice in the EU*, p. 61.
[150] Diez-Sanchez, 'Justice Index' Eurobarometer and the Issue of Justice'. However, whilst there are data on consumer protection and poverty relief, the positions vary considerably with regard to the countries.

the two judgments on the legal systems have been smoothed over by national courts. There seems to be a considerable reality gap between national law as it stands after *Viking* and *Laval* and the way it is perceived.

Non-discrimination does not seem to fit so well into such a picture. First and foremost, non-discrimination policy is much more political. Equal treatment of people on the basis of gender, sexuality, gender identity, ethnic origin, disability, age and religion not only affects the society, but it transforms society. Whilst the Member States *unanimously* agreed to take the necessary legislative steps, they have not reckoned with the long-term reactions of their citizens. There are certainly differences in the reactions and the countries depending on the ground of discrimination.[151] Overall, non-discrimination policy, so strongly advocated worldwide politically, highlights the difficulties, which result from political decisions that are imposed from outside (the EU) on national societies.

The *political order of social market law* is stamped by the move of the Single European Act to the Lisbon Agenda 2000. The twin objectives – 'the most competitive economy of the world' on the one side and 'social inclusion, gender equality and quality health care'[152] on the other – have tilted the balance of political responsibilities even further towards the EU. It is no longer the Common Market, or the Internal Market, but the efficient and highly competitive market that guides and legitimates European law-making initiatives. The building blocks of the new political order of the social market are full harmonisation and 'agentification'. Efficiency does not allow for deviating national standards of protection. The Single European Act initiated the floor thinking, the idea of European minimum standards, which guarantee all citizens the identical platform of protection. The European Commission could search for best practices and could maximise the different national models and even establish as a minimum a high level of protection so long as the Member States were left leeway to deviate from the minimum. Maximum harmonisation is politically much more sensitive. That is why maximum harmonisation requires deep-going compromises that are to the detriment of the vulnerable and the weak, the ones in whose names all these measures are taken. Full harmonisation takes responsibilities away from Member States and makes the EU and the European Commission responsible for their standard of living.

---

[151] Diez-Sanchez, 'Justice Index' Eurobarometer and the Issue of Justice'.
[152] This is the language of the Lisbon Strategy of 2000.

Social inclusion covers gender equality and health care quality. In the national context, social inclusion is guaranteed through common origin, tradition and the nation-state, which makes the necessary resources available. In an EU context, social inclusion gains a different connotation. The heads of the states who adopted the Lisbon Agenda rely on cooperation between the EU and Member States.[153] There is no definition given on what social inclusion means or which areas are affected. Social inclusion seems to cover the employment market, education and training, health and housing policies, specific target groups (e.g. minorities, children, the elderly and the disabled). Women, ethnic minorities or migrants are not mentioned.[154] Social inclusion is a political aim that has to be achieved through a joint effort, not only from the EU and the Member States, but from private parties and through public-private partnership. The Union's role is to act as a 'catalyst'.[155]

---

[153] According to para. 31: 'The European social model, with its developed systems of social protection, must underpin the transformation to the knowledge economy. However, these systems need to be adapted as part of an active welfare state to ensure that work pays, to secure their long-term sustainability in the face of an ageing population, to promote social inclusion and gender equality, and to provide quality health services. Conscious that the challenge can be better addressed as part of a cooperative effort, the European Council invites the Council to: – strengthen cooperation between Member States by exchanging experiences and best practice on the basis of improved information networks which are the basic tools in this field; – mandate the High Level Working Party on Social Protection, taking into consideration the work being done by the Economic Policy Committee, to support this cooperation and, as its first priority, to prepare, on the basis of a Commission communication, a study on the future evolution of social protection from a long-term point of view, giving particular attention to the sustainability of pensions systems in different time frameworks up to 2020 and beyond, where necessary. A progress report should be available by December 2000'.

[154] As set out in para. 33: 'In particular, the European Council invites the Council and the Commission to: – promote a better understanding of social exclusion through *continued dialogue* and exchanges of information and *best practice*, on the basis of commonly agreed indicators; the High Level Working Party on Social Protection will be involved in establishing these indicators; – mainstream the promotion of inclusion in Member States' employment, education and training, health and housing policies, this being complemented at Community level by action under the Structural Funds within the present budgetary framework; – develop priority actions addressed to specific target groups (for example minority groups, children, the elderly and the disabled), with Member States choosing amongst those actions according to their particular situations and reporting subsequently on their implementation'.

[155] Para. 41 states, 'Achieving the new strategic goal will rely primarily on the private sector, as well as on public-private partnerships. It will depend on mobilising the resources available on the markets, as well as on efforts by Member States. The Union's role is to act as a catalyst in this process, by establishing an effective framework for mobilising all available resources for the transition to the knowledge-based economy

The Lisbon Agenda does not address the increasing importance of private parties in a transnational environment. The Lisbon Agenda recognises that the ambitious agenda requires the full support of business. However, it is more a commitment of private parties to join the fight against unemployment and discrimination. The three regulated markets on telecom, energy and finance cannot be construed as European markets and European regulatory space without taking into account the need to make the European sectorial markets compatible with the international markets. Transnational private regulation has made an outstanding career in the last twenty years.[156] It is here that private parties, whether individually or collectively, appear as regulators. The EU serves indeed as a catalyst as either an exporter or importer of transnational rules.

The Lisbon Agenda pushes the *European legal order of competences* for the social market law towards full harmonisation. The drivers are the European Commission and the ECJ. Whilst the European Commission has suffered from a defeat in the fight over the Consumer Rights Directive, it has not given up its overall objective as can be clearly demonstrated openly via the relentless efforts to regulate sales transactions. The second, more hidden strategy can be found in the regulation on financial services and other regulated markets, where the Commission avoids taking a clear stand on the degree of harmonisation of secondary EU law. The ECJ has twice, in a very outspoken and highly contested way, read full harmonisation into directives, in *Sanchez* into the Product Liability Directive and in *Laval* into the posting worker directives. Full harmonisation transfers the competence to the EU, more concretely to the European Commission, which has a monopoly to initiate change or not. It is hard to understand the reasons why the Court initiated a competence shift through such an imperfect setting of rules. *Viking* and *Laval* brought social dumping to the political forum. However, after six years of discussion a political solution seems under way. The revised directive establishes the principle of 'equal pay for equal work'.[157]

---

and by adding its own contribution to this effort under existing Community policies while respecting Agenda 2000'.

[156] F. Cafaggi, 'New Foundations of Transnational Private Regulation' (2011) 38 *Journal of Law and Society* 20–49 and 'Does Private Regulation Foster European Legal Integration', in K. Purnhagen and P. Rott (eds.), *Varieties of European Economic Law and Regulation. Liber Amicorum for Hans Micklitz* (New York: Springer International Publishing, 2014), pp. 259–283.

[157] Council of the European Union, Interinstitutional File: 2016/0070 (COD), Brussels, 24 October 2017 (OR. en) 13612/17 SOC 677 EMPL 518 COMPET 698 MI 744 CODEC 1668 JUSTCIV 252.

Perhaps a much more dramatic competence shift results from harmonisation through 'standardisation'. Technical standards stand as a placeholder for collective private regulation without which regulated markets cannot operate. Technical standards are the backbone of telecom, energy, transport and financial services. The 'law on standards' entered the academic debate, but still awaits its contours. EU legislation relies more and more on a chain of delegation downwards from the Parliament via the European Commission towards standard setting bodies. Formally, technical standards are not 'law', although the ECJ has accepted jurisdiction.[158] However, technical standard transport values and even rights and duties. The responsibility lies with the standard bodies. Civil organisations which participate in standard-making are meant to provide legitimacy. In the EU, ANEC has no legal status, but is involved in standard-making, in the making of service standards under Directive 2006/123[159] and also in the making of energy and telecom standards, but not in financial services. Directive 2009/72 refers to representation. Household customers can get together to strengthen their market power.[160]

The European legal order of competence provides space for bottom-up initiatives, not only for social dialogue, but also for rule-making in the field of labour law. H. Collins[161] demonstrated its potential. However, there is a lack of preparedness on the side of business and civil society organisations to engage in a dialogue and to accept responsibility for its outcome. In consumer law, civil society organisations understand themselves as more than watchdogs and controllers, rather as partners in a joint undertaking, namely the production of private

---

[158] Case C-613/14, *James Elliott Construction*.

[159] Directive 2006/123/EC of the European Parliament and of the Council of 12 December 2006 on services in the internal market, OJ No. L 376, 27.12.2006, p. 36, v. Leeuwen, *European Standardisation of Services and its Impact on Private Law*; H.-W. Micklitz, 'Services Standards: Defining the Core Elements and Their Minimum Requirements', Study commissioned by ANEC, the European Voice in Standardization, 2007, available at: www.anec.eu/attachments/ANEC-R&T-2006-SERV-004final.pdf.

[160] Art. 3 (3), last sentence, Directive 2009/72 provides: 'Nothing in this Directive shall prevent Member States from strengthening the market position of the household, small and medium-sized consumers by promoting the possibilities of voluntary aggregation of representation for that class of consumers.' It might be reinforcing the freedom of association for household customers, which could be expanded to SMEs. What could be questioned is the absence of a similar statement in the Third Gas Directive.

[161] H. Collins, 'Conformity of Goods, the Network Society and the Ethical Consumer', in D. Leczykiewicz and S. Weatherill (eds.), *The Images of the Consumer in EU Law. Legislation, Free Movement and Competition Law* (Oxford: Hart Publishing, 2016), pp. 305–324.

regulation. The dialogic relationship that the second consumer policy programme from 1981 had in mind still awaits implementation.

The *enforcement order* is composed of three major actors, courts, regulatory agencies and ADR bodies. The ECJ has been in the limelight many times. Civil organisations, trade unions, women's organisations and consumer organisations have discovered the Court in Luxemburg as the instance of last resort. Under Thatcher, UK trade unions and the Equal Opportunity Commission instrumentalised the preliminary reference procedure to fight against 'neo-liberal policies' in the United Kingdom and to implant European social standards. In consumer law, the breakthrough came with the *Heininger* Saga.[162] The twenty-billion-dollar problem behind *Heininger* led to a series of references with ambiguous results. *Mohamed Aziz* opened the floodgates, causing the ECJ to engage in unjustified evictions of house owners or debtors, who are no longer able to pay back credit on loans. The fight of women's organisations and the trade union in the United Kingdom ended in disappointment, as did *Heininger*. One might fear that the *Mohamed Aziz* saga will share the fate of its predecessors, but through national law rather than the ECJ.[163] The ECJ cannot decide cases, or may paddle back after some bold step forwards, in particular when the economic dimension of the public interest litigation becomes clear. National courts might not be ready to decide the cases to the benefit of the consumers or workers for the same reasons.

The increasing role and function of regulatory agencies and ADR bodies has attracted less attention. Regulatory agencies have no European competences to interfere in private relations. Legally, the vertical relationship between the regulatory agency and the regulatee and the relationship between the regulatee (the supplier) and the consumer has to be kept separated. Responsibilities are intransparent, not least due to the fact that the rules are made at an EU level, but that the national agencies are the ones to take action and to show up as responsible. The reporting duties towards the public and the accountability of regulatory agencies are highly underdeveloped. The same is true with regard to the ADR bodies.

---

[162] Case C-481/99, *Heininger* [2001] I-9945.
[163] Against the opinion of Advocate General Mengozzi delivered on 13 July 2016 – Joined cases C-154/15, C-307/15 and C-308/15, *Gutiérrez Naranjo*, the ECJ upheld its strong *pro-consumer* position. However, the Spanish government did not give up its attempts to make the execution of consumer rights overtly difficult.

4 The 'Societal' Private Law

The addressee in the last layer is not the circumspect and omnipotent worker and consumer in the caricature of the ECJ, but the self- and societally responsible worker-citizen and consumer-citizen in the private legal order beyond the nation-state. If separated clearly from the weak and the vulnerable, the responsible consumer opens the door to an entirely new perspective. N. Shuibhne[1] gives an ambitious understanding of market citizenship, which will be developed below.

Tentatively, I will call the third layer the 'societal' private law. A couple of years ago, *Harvard Law Review* published a series of papers under the umbrella of the 'new' private law.[2] The branding led some continental lawyers to believe or to hope that the United States and the continental European private law are coming closer together, united in the revival of doctrinalism.[3] The emphasis is put on 'new' and 'societal'. At the third level, private law plays an eminently societal role in the building of a legal order and a civil society beyond the nation-state. In this sense, the last layer reaches beyond access justice in the first layer and access justice or social justice in the second layer, and targets 'societal' justice.[4] A modest interpretation of the new societal private

---

[1] Shuibhne, 'The Resilience of EU Market Citizenship'.
[2] Symposium 'The New Private Law' (2012) 125 *Harvard Law Review* with contributions from J. Goldberg, 'Introduction: Pragmatism and Private Law', 1640-1663; S. Balganesh, 'The Obligatory Structure of Copyright Law: Unbundling the Wrong of Copying', 1664-1690; H. E. Smith, 'Property as the Law of Things', 1691-1726; S. Smith, 'Duties, Liabilities, and Damages', 1727-1756; B. C. Zipursky, 'Palsgraf, Punitive Damages and Preemption', 1757-1797.
[3] E. G. Hosemann, '"The New Private Law": Die neue amerikanische Privatrechtswissenschaft in historischer und vergleichender Perspektive' (2014) 78 *Rabels Zeitschrift für ausländisches und internationales Privatrecht* 37-70.
[4] Contributions in Chapter III from J. Priban, 'The Evolving Idea of Political Justice in the EU: From Substantive Deficits to the Systematic Contingency of European Society', pp. 193-211; Neyer, 'Justice and the Right to Justification: Conceptual Reflections'; Forst, 'Justice, Democracy and the Right to Justification: Reflections on Jürgen Neyer's Normative Theory of the European Union'; S. Tsakyrakis, 'Disproportionate Individualism', pp. 235-246; N. Walker, 'Justice in and of the European Union',

law to the debate on transnational constitutionalism and democracy would be to understand the third layer as an emerging, upcoming legal order that contributes to the private law beyond statist discourses. A more ambitious understanding suggests that the new private law is the laboratory that is about to contribute to European society building.

The most innovative approach towards a new European private law has been presented by Reich in his book *General Principles of EU Civil Law*. EU civil law is understood as mandatory European regulatory private law that aims at specific objectives written into the treaty. The seven principles are identified bottom-up in the 'judicial discovery procedure,[5] theoretically deduced from Josef Esser and Ronald Dworkin, and methodologically borrowed from T. Tridimas.[6] The general principles of EU civil law are (1) Framed autonomy, (2) protection of the weaker party, (3) non-discrimination, (4) effectiveness, (5) balancing, (6) proportionality and (7) good faith (as an emerging principle).[7] In line with A. Hartkamp, the proposed seven EU civil law principles serve gap-filling and interpretative purposes.[8] They should neither be used for further competence creep nor to legitimise ECJ judicial activism. These general principles are not meant to present a theory of private law. The concept is methodologically ambitious, focusing on the judiciary, taking a holistic perspective on primary and secondary EU law and combining substance (weaker party, non-discrimination) with procedure (balancing, effectiveness and proportionality). Why is Reich's book 'outstanding' and truly 'ground breaking' as S. Weatherill writes?[9] First and foremost, it outflanks the rather artificial top-down exercises on drafting a European civil code without taking the existing primary and secondary EU law fully into account. It equally outflanks scholarly research on the EU's social justice deficit, which excludes private law from their focus and comes to debatable conclusions on EU law and the kind of justice that the ECJ has already established over the last decades. Secondly, the general principles

---

pp. 247–258; and Davies, 'Social Legitimacy and Purposive Power', in Kochenov, de Búrca and Williams (eds.), *Europe's Justice Deficit*.

[5] C. Joerges, 'Zur Legitimität der Europäisierung des Privatrechts. Überlegungen zu einem Rechts-Fertigungs-Recht für das Mehrebenensystem der EU', in C. Joerges and G. Teubner (eds.), Rechtsverfassungsrecht – Recht-Fertigung zwischen Privatrechtsdogmatik und Gesellschaftstheorie, *Internationale Studien zur Privatrechtstheorie* vol. 4 (Baden-Baden: Nomos, 2003), pp. 183–212.
[6] Reich, *General Principles of EU Civil Law*, pp. 3–5.
[7] Reich, *General Principles of EU Civil Law*, p. 16.
[8] The assessment is taken from the introduction, in particular 0.4, 0.5, 0.9.
[9] On the backside of the book cover.

translate the debate on the constitutionalisation of private law in a holistic perspective on the intermingling of primary (constitutional) EU law and secondary EU law allows.

There are two reservations, though. The seven principles focus on the judiciary and do not take administrative practice into account. As has been amply demonstrated, regulatory agencies have a key role to play, not only in the making of private law rules, but in particular in the administrative enforcement of private law. So too do ADR bodies, to which more and more consumer complaints are wilfully delegated. Are the seven principles applied through the regulatory agencies and ADR bodies? This is largely an empirical question. The answer matters in a 'European civil law' (Reich) that deals not only with horizontal but also with vertical regulated markets. The second reservation has to do with the function of the general principles themselves. Gap-filling and interpretative purposes sound benign. The very same Josef Esser[10] has equally made clear that there is no clear line between interpretation and law-making. Therefore, the general principles should be understood as a safety net, when the dispersed rules on European private law do not contain an answer.

4.1 The Self and the Societally Responsible

In the world beyond the nation-state, the worker and the consumer do not only enjoy new rights and opportunities of a 'good life', they also benefit – or suffer – from new responsibilities. The ECJ has used the concept of the circumspect and responsible worker and consumer for EU market-building purposes, if we mainly follow Johnston and Unberath[11] in the four market freedoms. The transfer of the responsible to secondary EU law is criticised as a means to downgrade the level of protection and to replace social justice with market justice. If, however, kept separated from the vulnerable and the weak, the idea of the responsible worker and consumer bears a potential that points beyond market building, not necessarily to building a new political order, but at the very least as a contribution to European society building.[12]

---

[10] J. Esser, *Vorverständnis und Methodenwahl in der Rechtsfindung* (Frankfurt a. M.: Athenäum, 1970).

[11] Unberath and Johnston, 'The Double-Headed Approach of the ECJ Concerning Consumer Protection'.

[12] G. Comandé, 'The Fifth European Union Freedom. Aggregating Citizenship ... around Private Law', in H.-W. Micklitz (ed.), *Constitutionalization of European Private Law* (Oxford: Oxford University Press, 2014), pp. 61–101; and K. Carr, 'Regulating the Periphery –

The European Commission has used the suspicious language of the worker-citizen and the consumer-citizen for at least ten years. The European Commission 'invented' the term in the context of the liberalisation and privatisation of former public services. However, the term never made it into a EU legal document. In ordo-liberal theory, the market citizen alludes to private autonomy, to self-responsible decision-making and to civil law society (*Privatrechtsgesellschaft*). The growing mainstream critique against the EU seems to start from the premise that European ordo-liberalism paved the way for European neoliberalism after the fall of the wall.[13] Whereas ordo-liberalism provided for a firm competition order to domesticize power within which the private law society could unfold, neoliberalism is said to free the force of the market subject to rather limited restrictions (*freies Spiel der Kräfte*). In such a crude understanding, the market citizen can only appear as the one who is left ever more alone with her personal needs and societal disadvantages.[14]

In ordo-liberal thinking the two, the market and the political order, are connected. The market is compared to democratic processes, where the consumer votes via their choices.[15] M. Everson[16] distinguishes the 'market citizen' and the 'Union citizen'. Market citizenship is claimed to be inherently limited. She locates the market citizen '*in the national setting [as] a subsidiary role which citizens proper were expected to play*'. N. Shuibhne has pointed to the weakness of the argument. The reference point for the EU market citizen is not the national market or the national legal order, but the European Market which provides potential: 'drawing from both the nature of the EU as a polity and the substance of EU citizenship as it has actually developed within the paradigm of EU law, it argues that both the reality – and scope – of transnational market citizenship may offer more than we tend to

---

Shaking the Core European Identity Building through the Lens of Contract Law' (2015) *EUI Working Paper EUI-ERC* No. 40.

[13] G. Davies, 'Democracy and Legitimacy in the Shadow of Purposive Competence' (2015) 21 *European Law Journal* 2–22; Tuori, *European Constitutionalism*, p. 127.

[14] On the relationship between ordo-liberalism and neoliberalism, T. Biebricher, 'Ordoliberalism as a Variety of Neoliberalism', in J. Hien and C. Joerges (eds.), *Ordoliberalism, Law and the Rule of Economics*, (Oxford: Hart Publishing 2017), pp. 000 (book not yet available).

[15] S. Grundmann, 'Gesellschaftsordnung und Privatrecht', in S. Grundmann, H.-W. Micklitz and M. Renner (eds.), *Privatrechtstheorie*, Band 1 (Tübingen: Mohr Siebeck, 2015), Kapitel 6, pp. 405–535.

[16] Everson, 'The Legacy of the Market Citizen'.

presume.'[17] F. de Witte has convincingly demonstrated how breaking down barriers to the EU market through the market freedoms offers opportunities for a 'good life'.[18] I will not insinuate that it is possible to build a political order out of the market order, even if the market order is understood as part of the political order. The market citizen, even the one who engages into transborder transactions, can do no more than contributing to the civil order, or in more ambitious language to the building of the European society. It is not possible to build political institutions out of rights. W. v. Gerven tried to establish a fourth level of the proportionality principle, one that would lead as the very last consequence to institution building.[19] However, this line of argument never gained ground in the ECJ. The market citizen should be understood as an opportunity to think about the private law order beyond the nation-state, where the market-citizen is involved via the judiciary and via the regulatory agencies in the process of European society building.

The responsible market citizen has a double meaning. First and foremost, the responsible market citizen is neither vulnerable nor weak, but is able to make independent self-reliant decisions. But there is more to the notion of the responsible market citizen. The responsible market citizen is not only responsible for him- or herself. The responsible market citizen is societally responsible: he or she bears responsibility for society in and beyond the nation-state. The very beginning can be traced back to T. Wilhelmsson[20] who mentions as the last and most developed form of national welfarism 'public value welfarism', the type of welfarism that he alludes to as sustainable consumption. Wilhelmsson's categorisation enables the development of a flexible system of consumer rights and remedies built along the distinction between vulnerable, confident and responsible consumer-citizens. The responsible consumer-citizen could and should make responsible decisions that promote sustainable consumption.[21]

The theoretical debate is gaining pace, though under the notion of ethical consumption and the ethical consumer.[22] Ethical consumption is

---

[17] Shuibhne, 'The Resilience of EU Market Citizenship', pp. 1598, 1599.
[18] F. de Witte, *Justice in the EU*, p. 61.
[19] v. Gerven, 'Needed: A Method of Convergence for Private Law'; Micklitz, *The Politics of Judicial Co-operation in the EU*, p. 118.
[20] Wilhelmsson, 'Varieties of Welfarism in European Contract Law', p. 731.
[21] Micklitz, 'Do Consumers and Businesses need a New Architecture of Consumer Law?'
[22] H. Collins, 'Conformity of Goods, the Network Society and the Ethical Consumer', in D. Leczykiewicz and S. Weatherill (eds.), *The Images of the Consumer in EU Law. Legislation, Free Movement and Competition Law* (Oxford: Hart Publishing, 2016), pp. 305–324, who is

a difficult category and so is the ethical consumer. L. Miller writes:[23] 'Surrounded by organic, non-GMO, fair trade, low carbon footprint, dolphin friendly, energy efficient product messages, our purchasing choices have become morally and ethically complex'. Joe Shaw concurs:[24] 'individual moral virtues in the marketplace is an extremely difficult notion to construct, since the primary moral of the market should be to promote rational, self-interest behaviour.' The perspective is not so much to provide values to the internal market, but to highlight the *political* dimension which is enshrined in the combination of markets and ethics. Ethical consumption goes along with the de-individualisation of the consumer, as a legal figure embedded in the social, environmental, cultural environment. The concern is the combination between ethics and politics that lies behind the notion of the consumer citizen and that has been stressed by all those who have gone deeper into the link between markets, ethics and citizenship.[25] L. Miller draws a note of caution before making too much out of the connection, but she insists that despite all difficulties the 'notion of the consumer-citizen ... invites reflections on the more expansive, outward, or public-regarding aspect of consumption and forces consumption out of its individualistic straightjacket.'[26]

What is missing in the debate is the post-nation-state dimension that is enshrined in the European integration project. Most of the time, more implicitly than explicitly, the benchmark for measuring the EU is an idealised version of the old national welfare state. In the transnational society beyond the nation-state, the responsible consumer-citizen has more freedom but also more responsibilities towards society. The market citizen provides for an opportunity to bring to bear the societal dimension of the responsible consumer. This is indeed *responsibilisation*[27] of consumers. However, in the transnational society

---

not really developing the ethical dimension beyond the implicit plea that consumers should not buy products for which child labour has been used; for a much deeper analyis, see L. Miller, 'Ethical Consumption and the Internal Market' in the same volume at pp. 279–303.

[23] Miller, 'Ethical Consumption and the Internal Market', p. 279.
[24] J. Shaw, 'Citizenship of the Union: Towards Post-National Membership?' (1997) *Harvard Jean Monnet Working Paper* No. 6, 288.
[25] M. Everson and Ch. Joerges, 'Consumer Citizenship in Postnational Constellations?' (2006) *EUI Working Paper LAW* No. 47, 7; F. Trentmann, 'Knowing Consumers – Histories, Identities, Practices: An Introduction', in F. Trentmann (ed.), *The Making of the Consumer: Knowledge, Power and Identity in the Modern World* (Oxford: Berg, 2006), pp. 1–27.
[26] Miller, 'Ethical Consumption and the Internal Market', p. 291.
[27] Miller, 'Ethical Consumption and the Internal Market', p. 302, under reference to C. Barnett, P. Cafaro and T. Newholm, 'Philosophy and Ethical Consumption', in

there is no alternative. The state is weaker, the freedom and the responsibilities for the individual are greater. That is where the political responsibility of the societally responsible market citizen stems from.

Reshaping responsibility has two implications. It releases the market citizen from victimhood. This new responsibility is a collective responsibility and it can only be exercised collectively. The responsible individual should not be understood as the one on whom the burden lies. The responsible is first and foremost a collective entity, representing the weak, the vulnerable or the discriminated.[28] The collectivity may emerge ad hoc or may take the form of a stable organisation, if not a legal association. This collectivity is to be understood as a political actor in the post-national social environment.

4.2 Substance Shaping

The responsible market citizen and the responsible market citizen associations may and should play a more active role in using the potential of the EU regulatory private law to implement European social standards in current commercial and contractual practice. There is a huge unexploited potential of the European regulatory private law, highlighted throughout the analysis of the first and the second layers. With regard to substance, it is certainly the interplay between non-discrimination law and consumer law that deserves attention or the case law of the ECJ on discriminatory collective agreements, which could be tested with regards to collective private regulation. However, the more interesting question is why market citizens and their associations are making so little use out of the potential. One reason is the division of the legal community. The vast majority of lawyers think in national categories. They look at the European legal order as a toolbox from which bits and pieces can be taken to check the compatibility of national rules. There is only a small minority that is familiar with the respective national legal system and the European legal order as a whole. It suffices to contrast Reich's small book on the general principles with the six volumes and two books of the Study Group on a European Civil Code and the Research Group on EC Private Law

---

R. Harrison, T. Newholm and D. Shaw (eds.), *The Ethical Consumer* (London; Sage Publications, 2005), pp. 11–24, at p. 14; however, they rely on the government as the counterpart.

[28] With regard to the double collectivisation of private law H.-W. Micklitz, *Der Reparaturvertrag* (München: Schweitzer, 1984), Chapter I.

(Acquis Group), let alone the vast amount of publications surrounding their work. Private lawyers feel more tempted to write commentaries on the DCFR than to study the impact of European law on private law. The situation within civil society associations mirrors that gulf, although, contrary to the academic community, civil society associations lack the necessary knowledge base, expertise and manpower that are needed to cover the two levels in full.

The more forward-looking perspective of the responsible market citizen and responsible market citizen association shifts the focus from the application of the European regulatory private law to existing transactional and behavioural practices towards the making and the shaping of codes, guidelines, recommendations that could influence future practice. This sounds even more ambitious. However, private law beyond the nation-state requires market citizens and market citizen associations who are ready to engage in this forward-looking exercise. The transnational contractual practice is characterised by three new phenomena: long-term contracts, supply chains and networks. All three of them are current practice, but they are neither regulated within the national private law orders nor through European regulatory private law. These three demonstrate the potential role civil society associations could and should play in the shaping of model rules or codes or whatever the language might be.

It has already been highlighted that consumer transactions are increasingly transforming into long-term relations. Long-term contracts are a well-established, recognised category in business relations since S. Macauley's groundbreaking work on relational contracts in 1959.[29] The European Social Contracts Group (EuSoCo), founded by a group of academics in 2005, studies three types of long-term relations, namely consumer credit, tenant law and labour law. The first results of the working group have been presented in 2014.[30] Very much inspired by previous research of U. Reifner,[31] EuSoCo introduces lifetime contracts as 'social long-term relations that, with regard to certain periods of the lifetime of individuals, provide essential goods, services, labour and income opportunities for self-realisation and participation'. The initiative is directed against the Study Group, the Acquis Group, the DCFR and CESL, which

---

[29] S. Macaulay, 'Non-Contractual Relations in Business: A Preliminary Study' (1963) 28 *American Sociological Review* 55–67.
[30] L. Nogler and U. Reifner (eds.), *Life Time Contracts. Social Long-term Contracts in Labour, Tenancy and Consumer Credit Law* (The Hague: Eleven International Publishing, 2014).
[31] U. Reifner, 'Renting a Slave—European Contract Law in the Credit Society'.

are claimed to have neglected the category of lifetime contracts in B2C relations. It is not clear where exactly 'lifetime contracts' have to be located in between the triangle of relational contracts, organisational or network contracts and supply chains[32] and how lifetime contracts have to be delimitated from universal service obligations. The reference to essential goods seems to point in that direction. If this is so, however, it is hard to understand why other universal services like energy, water supply, telecommunication, Internet, are not examined.

Energy, telecom, Internet or financial services contracts are prime candidates for the urgent need to develop a kind of model contract, which follows the rationalities of the different sectors. Along the line of the advocated shift in responsibilities, civil society organisations should engage with business in a bottom-up rule-making exercise. In the early millennium, the European Commission had been advocating the development of standard contract terms, inter alia, for package tours. This was linked to the revision of the package tour Directive 90/314. Under the auspices of the European Commission both stakeholders met a few times in Brussels. However, the initiative ended in a deadlock. Despite this discouraging experience, the European Commission undertook a new effort in the field of energy. The trigger point is the rather diffuse Art. 3 (3) Directive 2009/72, which provides in the last sentence:

> Nothing in this Directive shall prevent Member States from strengthening the market position of the household, small and medium-sized consumers by promoting the possibilities of voluntary aggregation of representation for that class of consumers.

The Commission Working Staff Document and CEER Advisors (Council of European Energy Regulation, being a network of national regulators) mention consumer representation in the rule-making process, without referring to Article 3(3). The Commission makes references to consumer representation in Session 3 of the Working Staff Document, which is entitled 'Platforms for Exchange of *Best Practices* and Development of *Codes of Conduct*'. The platform is the Citizens' Energy Forum and the consumers are represented by the ECCG (European Consumer

---

[32] Book review by C. Mak, 'Life Time Contracts: Social Long-Term Contracts in Labour, Tenancy and Consumer Credit Law, edited by L. Nogler and U. Reifner' (2015) 2 *European Journal of Comparative Law and Governance* 379–382; S. Grundmann, F. Cafaggi, and G. Vettori (eds.), *The Organisational Contract: From Exchange to Long-Term Network Cooperation in European Contract Law* (Abingdon, Oxon: Routledge, 2013).

Consultative Group).³³ In the ECCG, there is one seat for the representative of national consumer organisations per Member State besides European Consumer Organizations (BEUC or ANEC). The CEER document is explicit about the role of representation in norm-making and monitoring compliance: A competent representation of consumers in the energy policy area is a further safeguard for better policy-making and of identification and exchange of best national practices.³⁴

Let us disentangle the complex design. CEER has shown a serious interest in involving consumer organisations at both ends, in law-making and in monitoring. The Citizens' Energy Forum is 'an annual event designed to explore consumers' views and their role in a competitive, 'smart' energy efficient and fair EU energy retail market.'³⁵ The ECCG is the Commission's main forum to consult national and European consumer organisations. Discussions turn around problems relating to consumer interests. ECCG gives an opinion on community matters affecting the protection of consumer interests; advises and guides the Commission when it outlines policies and activities having an effect on consumers; informs the Commission of developments in consumer policy in the Member States; acts as a source of information and soundboard on community action for the other national organisations.³⁶ The consumers are represented through BEUC and ANEC. All this sounds very much like a forum of exchange, but is still far away from law-making. There is no counterpart to the ECCG in telecom. Consumer protection issues are discussed in the BEREC Stakeholder Forum. The BEREC Stakeholder Forum is the materialisation of the consultation obligation of Article 17

---

[33] For more information on the European Consumer Consultative Group (ECCG), see the website of the European Commission at: http://ec.europa.eu/consumers/eu_consumer_policy/consumer_consultative_group/eccg/index_en.htm.

[34] Commission Staff Working Document, An Energy Policy for Consumers, SEC(2010) 1407 final, 11.11.2010, p. 9, available at: https://ec.europa.eu/energy/sites/ener/files/documents/sec(2010)1407.pdf; also CEER Advice on how to involve and engage consumer organisation in the regulatory process, Ref: C14-CEM-74-07, 12.3.2015, (which was endorsed by BEUC), available at: www.ceer.eu/portal/page/portal/EER_HOME/EER_PUBLICATIONS/CEER_PAPERS/Customers/2015/C14-CEM-74-07_ConsOrg%20Involvement_Advice_March%202015_0.pdf

[35] On the Citizens' Energy Forum, see the website of the European Commission at: https://ec.europa.eu/energy/en/news/citizens-energy-forum-consumers-heart-energy-union.

[36] The ECCG is composed of: one representative of national consumer organisations per country; one member from each European consumer organisation (i.e. BEUC and ANEC); two associate members (i.e. EUROCOOP and COFACE); two EEA observers (i.e. Iceland and Norway). The ECCG meets three times a year in Brussels. It has been created by Commission Decision 2003/709/EC (OJ No. L 258, 10.10.2003, p. 35), which has been repealed by Commission Decision 2009/705/EC (OJ No. L 244, 16.9.2009, p. 21).

of the BEREC Regulation (Regulation (EC) No 1211/2009). BEUC actively contributes to the Stakeholder Forum but does not enjoy a formal status.[37]

4.3 Rights, Remedies and Procedures

The triad of rights, remedies and procedures implies a court-based and court-focused perspective. In the new post-classical world, there are four actors that stand side by side and that have their role to play, namely courts, regulatory agencies, ADR bodies and self-regulatory bodies. ADR bodies are under public supervision. They are created through law, they are embedded in a legal framework and they are accountable to the public through law. Self-regulatory bodies that are involved in law enforcement, however, may result from pure business initiatives, like in the field of advertising or technical standards (standards and certification bodies).[38] The new catchword is 'compliance' management that starts within business, but may be outsourced to self-standing regulatory bodies.[39]

Through the lenses of the responsible market citizen, this array of opportunities allows and requires strategic action planning. Which kind of conflict is best located where and what measures should to be taken with regard to which entity? What is equally crucial is to maintain a holistic perspective; the four entities belong together and they need to be interlinked. It is one of the major weaknesses in European private law that new actors emerge and are promoted strongly by the EU legislature, like regulatory agencies or ADRs, but that they are in no way interlinked. Consumer organisations have written an action plan for the type of actions that could be initiated.[40] Here the objective is

---

[37] Contribution by BEUC to the BEREC public consultation (1) on the draft BEREC Report on Monitoring quality of Internet access services in the context of net neutrality, BoR PC01 (16) 019, BoR PC02 (14) 21; (2) on BEREC Guidelines on the Implementation by National Regulators of European Net Neutrality Rules; (3) on draft BEREC Report on OTT services, BoR PC06 (15) 16; (4) on the draft BEREC report on best practices to facilitate switching, BoR PC03 (10) 02.

[38] P. Verbruggen, *Enforcing Transnational Private Regulation: A Comparative Analysis of Advertising and Food Safety* (Cheltenham: Edward Elgar, 2014).

[39] M. Namyslowska, 'Monitoring Compliance with Contracts and Regulations: between Private and Public Law', in R. Brownsword, R. van Gestel and H.-W. Micklitz (eds.), *Contract and Regulation. A Handbook on New Methods of Law Making in Private Law* (Cheltenham: Elgar Publishing, 2017), pp. 259–283.

[40] Reports from the Consumer Law Enforcement Forum CLEF and from COJEF I and II (Consumer Justice Enforcement Forum), e.g., 2016 report on 'Enforcement of Consumer Rights, Strategies and Recommendations', available at: www.cojef-project.eu/Final-report-Enforcement-of.

different. The societal private law provides a large set of tools that indicate the direction in which the development is moving or should move. The responsible market citizens and the civil associations behind them are the actors that have the opportunity and the responsibility to make use of the existing tools and to develop them further.

Again, the ECJ is at the forefront of the analysis. *Scarlet*[41] should be read so as to link business responsibilities towards third parties to judicial review as a means of last resort. The most developed remedy that demonstrates the need of a holistic perspective is *Janecek*, where the ECJ invented the 'individual' right of a citizen to provide the public with an action plan on how to reduce air pollution according to European air quality standards.[42] *Janecek* could serve as the model example for public interest litigation. The plaintiff was a member of the Green Party in Germany, the litigation by an environmental NGO closely linked to the party. The facts of the case are the following:[43]

Mr Janecek lives on the Landshuter Allee on Munich's central ring road, approximately 900 metres north of an air quality measuring station. Measurements taken at that station have shown that, in 2005 and 2006, the limit value fixed for emissions of particulate matter PM_{10} was exceeded much more than 35 times, even though that is the maximum number of instances permitted under the Federal Law on combating pollution. The legal question was whether he is directly concerned what the German court denied but referred to the ECJ.

The ECJ held[44]

... Article 7(3) of Directive 96/62 must be interpreted as meaning that, where there is a risk that the limit values or alert thresholds may be exceeded, persons directly concerned must be in a position to require the competent national authorities to draw up an action plan, even though, under national law, those persons may have other courses of action available to them for requiring those authorities to take measures to combat atmospheric pollution.

Janecek is crucial for two reasons: the remedy is generalisable and the remedy shows that the right granted can only be implemented if the judiciary, the public administrations and civil organisations cooperate. EU law imposes the obligation on national regulatory agencies to

---

[41] Case C-70/10, *Scarlet Extended*.
[42] Case C-237/07, *Janecek* [2008] I-06221. In what follows I rely on the research undertaken by B. Kas, 'Hybrid' Collective Remedies in the EU Social Legal Order, PhD thesis, European University Institute (2017), Chapter 2, p. 25.
[43] Case C-237/07, *Janecek*, paras. 13–15.
[44] Case C-237/07, *Janecek*, para. 47.

develop and provide strategic action plans for the monitoring and surveillance of market practices. A prominent example is financial services, where the European demand to monitor the collective interests of private consumers/investors has become ever stronger.[45] The right to an action plan is directed against the national supervision authorities. They are responsible for the daily enforcement, not the European agencies. *Janecek* demonstrates that the difficulty begins after the judgment. The Munich court, which was in charge to implement the decision of the ECJ, struggled to define the kind of measures it could impose on the environmental authorities. An action plan is a procedural instrument. It cannot be enforced like a pecuniary debt. Courts, administrative authorities and civil organisations have to engage in mutual exchange of information and have to cooperate in order to break the action plan down into steps and to make it subject to constant public scrutiny. The public authorities remain the key actors. They have the regulatory power. Civil organisations are the watchdogs that constantly examine whether public authorities take the necessary steps. The courts are supervising the actors and are managing the whole procedure through the power of judicial review.

As long as there is a regulatory agency, the addressee of the right can be identified, provided there is a subjective right that meets the standards the ECJ has set in *Francovich*.[46] The crucial question is whether private companies or private collective entities may become the addressees of a *Janecek* type of action. Here we are back to the bright side of *Viking* and *Laval*, though in secondary EU law where the intricacies of horizontal direct effect have to be clarified in the long run. Labour lawyers focus their critique on trade unions being treated like 'public' actors, who similar to governments or governmental entities have to respect the market freedoms. However, when powerful collective civil society actors are treated like public bodies, then *argumentum a maiore ad minus* collective entities of the business sector bear the same obligations. This comes through in the established case law of collective – private – entities that have to respect the market freedoms.

---

[45] K. Purnhagen and P. Verbruggen, 'Europäische Gemeinschaft', in J. Keßler, H.-W. Micklitz and N. Reich (eds.), *Institutionelle Finanzmarktaufsicht und Verbraucherschutz. Eine rechtsvergleichende Untersuchung der Regelungssysteme in Deutschland, Italien, Schweden, dem Vereinigten Königreich und der Europäischen Gemeinschaft* (Baden-Baden: Nomos, 2010), pp. 175–242, at p. 235, where the applicability of the Janecek doctrine to financial services is discussed.

[46] Joined cases C-6/90 and C-9/90, *Francovich and Bonifaci v Italy* [1991] ECR I-5357.

The question remains whether the responsibilities reach beyond the market into society. In other words, does the proportionality principle require taking the impact of a strike on the society into account? L. Azoulai[47] gave *Viking* and *Laval* the decisive twist, in that he answered the question in the affirmative. This allows him, along the line of the case law of the ECJ on collective agreements, to discuss the social responsibility of private entities that exercise 'public power'. Thinking through the implications would mean that private parties that are exercising public power may be sued by responsible market citizens to set up an action plan on how they intend to implement their promises enshrined in codes of conduct and in CSR on health and safety at work, non-discrimination and consumer protection.[48]

The essential role of courts in the interaction between the three entities remains crucial. However, there is a need for the responsible market citizen to make regulatory agencies, ADR bodies and self-regulatory bodies accountable for their activities. The EU legislator has woven a dense net of reporting duties. In regulated markets, the addressee of the reporting duty is the respective agency that has to report to the European Commission respectively to the European agencies. With regard to ADR bodies, the situation is somewhat different. Here Member States are obliged under EU law to monitor and survey the ADR bodies. The ADR bodies have to report to the national designated authority. Self-regulatory bodies are under no statutory obligation. They may make reports on their activities available to the public along the line with their business policy to demonstrate public accountability. Three major problems can be identified. There is no obligation to make the reports available to the public, not even in a condensed form. Reports of regulatory agencies, if they are made public, are not standardised. Thereby accessibility and accountability is considerably reduced. The third and, in the long run, the most far-reaching problem results from the black box effects. Nobody knows what kind of law regulatory agencies, ADR bodies and self-regulatory bodies apply where their decisions, settlements, and recommendations are not made public and are not verifiable. The regulatory device that is gaining ground to overcome the accountability deficit is peer review. It seems, however, that peer review does not include civil society organisations as watchdogs. This would mean that peer review

---

[47] Azoulai, 'The Court of Justice and the Social Market Economy'.
[48] Beckers, 'The Regulation of Market Communication and Market Behaviour'.

establishes a kind of enlarged surveillance community, which is accountable to each other, but not the public.[49]

RRP – the rights, remedies and procedures – takes a very different form when it comes to enforcement via regulatory agencies and ADR bodies. The most basic right in order to exercise control over the black box activities is gaining access to the information that is stored within the various regulatory agencies, administrative bodies, and formal and informal committees in charge. Contrary to the United States, there is no comprehensive EU legislation on freedom for information. Access of individuals and civil society organisations to administrative information varies tremendously throughout the European Union.[50] In the 1980s and 1990s, environmental organisations in Europe used the US Freedom of Information Act to claim information from the US Environmental Protection Agency, which was used for political purposes in Europe.[51] A similar strategy would be needed to make the *Janecek* doctrine work. Access to information in the Nordic countries is much easier to get than in continental Europe or in the United Kingdom.[52]

The implications of the shift from judicial to non-judicial, administrative enforcement and compliance strategies are obvious. However, this is not yet all. An integrated approach requires to combine the strength and the weaknesses of the four avenues, in order to be able to achieve the best possible results to the benefits of the citizens. Responsible market citizens and their civil organisations have to face

---

[49] Y. Svetiev, 'Controlling the Transnational Expertocracy?', Lecture, 17.2.2017, EUI, provides for the following definition: While its operational forms differ, peer review typically involves policy-making by one state being reviewed by a committee of 'peers' from other states, who can be policy-makers, regulatory agency officials or academic experts. As such, if peer review is to be based on expertise, and conducted as review by similarly placed 'peers', it would mean that the watchdog communities are excluded. However, peer review occurs in so many different settings, for different purposes and takes different forms. Svetiev, however, asks whether other types of communities are allowed or may find some way to influence the peer review process.

[50] Access to consumer information, H.-W. Micklitz (ed.), *Informationszugang für Verbraucher in Europa und den USA. Recht und Praxis* (Baden-Baden: Nomos, 2009).

[51] I refer to my own experience in the years between 1985–1990 when I was working for what is today Consumers International, OECD and UNEP.

[52] The Aarhus Convention has not been fully implemented in the EU, on the link between Aarhus and the EU law, H.-W. Micklitz, 'Collective Action of Non-Governmental Organizations in European Consumer and European Environmental Law – A Mutual Learning Process', in R. Macrory (ed.), *Reflections on 30 Years of EU Environmental Law: A High Level of Protection* (Groningen: European Law Publishing, 2005), pp. 451–473.

a major challenge. In a way, they have to close the gap that results from withdrawal of the national state in the age of the third globalisation.

4.4 Balancing of Legitimate Expectations beyond the State

Balancing of legitimate expectations beyond the state requires turning away from privity of contract and from the national private law order, in order to open the balancing process for third parties interests and for ethical expectations on the production process. These two aspects will be analysed one by one.

The instrumentalisation of private law for building and completing the Internal Market has not only a dark side – the dominance of the market rationale – but also a bright side. Private law relationships have to be opened beyond privity so as to allow for taking the potential effect of the contract on the market into account. This requires the integration of the third party. In *Scarlet*,[53] the ECJ had to deal with the triangular relationship of a service provider, Scarlet, the Belgian associations, SABAM whose aim is to protect the property rights of its members and the users who were supposed to infringe the copy rights through peer-to-peer networks without permission of SABAM. SABAM asked for an injunction to stop the 'illegal' practice. The ECJ engaged in a balancing process, where it investigated the rights under the CFR of the three parties, including the users. Scarlet and SABAM were asked to engage in re-negotiating their contractual relation, taking due account of the Charter rights of the users per Arts. 8 and 11.[54]

This is an amazing judgment. The vehement debate over the horizontal effects of fundamental rights in contractual relationships is solved by the ECJ through the means of interpretation.[55] More generally, it means that the parties to a contract have to take the *fundamental* rights of third parties into account when concluding a contract. The ECJ even introduced a procedure that reserves for the Court the right to review the outcome of the negotiation. The balancing and weighing is clearly bound to fundamental rights and cannot be stretched towards mere expectations.

---

[53] Case C-70/10, *Scarlet Extended* [2011] ERC I-11959.
[54] For a careful analysis of *Scarlet*, see v. Leeuwen, 'The Impact of Intellectual Property Law and the Charter on Private Law Concepts', pp. 248–251.
[55] Case C-12/11, *McDonagh* [2013] ECR I-000, at para. 63 where the court refers to Art. 16 and 17 of the Charter to justify restrictions of the airline's freedom of contract.

This new line of case law opens up perspectives for integrating into triangular relations non-discrimination (Arts. 21 and 23 CFR) and consumer protection (Art. 36 CFR). Arts. 21 and 23 contain a mixture of rights and principles, Art. 36 lays down a principle only.[56] The only constitutional right that can be deduced from the EU legal order is the 'right to information' under Art. 12 TFEU. Principles enshrined in the Charter can turn into 'rights' only if there is secondary legislation that concretises the principles and upgrades them to 'rights'. The degree to which Arts. 21 and 23 provide for a 'right' depends to a large extent of the way in which the various forms of discrimination have been concretised in the four directives. With regard to consumer law, Reich argues that the 'other elements of consumer law like protection of health and safety, fairness in bargaining situations and access to law left to secondary legislation ... have evolved into a genuine principle of effective legal protection'.[57] Via this line of argument, the core of secondary EU law is upgraded to a general principle, which in Reich's argument benefits from 'constitutional standing'. Outside and beyond the constitutionalisation of private law relations, the concretised fundamental rights under Articles 21, 23 and 36 read together with *Scarlet* shatter the foundations of freedom of contract in bilateral relations. The *parties* to a contract *have* to take *third-party fundamental rights* into consideration, when they negotiate a contract that affects others. The question remains how close the relationship of the third party to the two contractual partners must be. Here we are in the middle of the debate on networks and the degree to which network relations can be handled within contract law or should be dealt with through tort law.[58]

The tripartite balancing works as long as the three parties come under EU law and as long as the third party enjoys a fundamental right, even if only concretised via secondary EU law, but upgraded to the constitutional level. This does not exclude referring to 'expectations' and 'needs', which do not enjoy a rights status.[59] However, the legal position of the third party is much weaker. If one of the three parties' residence is outside the EU, difficult questions on jurisdiction and the applicable

---

[56] Reich, *General Principles of EU Civil Law*, p. 81; with regard to non-discrimination law and with regard to consumer protection, p. 31
[57] Reich, *General Principles of EU Civil Law*, p. 39.
[58] Condon, *Tort law beyond the Reasonable Man*; M. Amstutz and G. Teubner, *Networks: Legal Issues of Multilateral Co-operation* (Oxford: Hart Publishing, 2009).
[59] Part III. 3.4.

law arise. In *Ingmar*,[60] the ECJ went far in extending the mandatory rules enshrined in Directive 86/653[61] on commercial agents beyond the borders of the EU to a US-based company. However, whilst the case triggered a debate on the degree to which mandatory rules of European private law are to be regarded as being part of the European ordre public, there have been no follow-on cases, at least not with regard to employment, non-discrimination and consumer law.[62]

The second enlargement of balancing refers to the link between consumption and production, between consumer law and labour law.[63] Consumption and production, consumer law and labour law are regarded as two separated fields standing side by side. The outsourcing of the production of consumer goods into third world countries has raised public awareness of the production conditions. The two separate worlds, production and consumption, are coming together. The UN Conventions on Child Labour define a minimum age distinguishing between the first and the third world on the one hand and the type of work to be executed.[64] Art. 32 CFR is even stricter. The Social Manifesto suggests that products made using child labour should not be placed on the market or at least consumers should have the right to rescind the purchase of such incriminated products.[65] The ILO Conventions on Child Labour impose mandatory standards on health and safety at work. Art. 31 turns health and safety at work into a fundamental right. The proposal of the Social Manifesto could easily be extended to health and safety at work. The trigger point for a possible

---

[60] Case C-381/98, *Ingmar GB* [2000] ECR I-9305, in line with that judgment the German Supreme Court struck down choice of court agreement prorogating courts of Virginia, BGH, 05.09.2012 – VII ZR 25/12, available at: http://juris.bundesgerichtshof.de/cgi-bin/rechtsprechung/document.py?Gericht=bgh&Art=en&az=VII%20ZR%2025/12&nr=61762, with comments of L. Eckhoff, 'Gerichtsstandsvereinbarung, die zum Ausschluss des Handelsvertreterausgleichsanspruchs führt, ist unwirksam' (2012) *Gesellschafts- und Wirtschaftsrecht* 486 and P. Ayad and S. Schnell 'Zuständigkeit nationaler Gerichte bei der Durchsetzung international zwingender Regeln' (2012) *Betriebsberater* 3103.
[61] Council Directive 86/653/EEC of 18 December 1986 on the coordination of the laws of the Member States relating to self-employed commercial agents, OJ No. L 382, 31.12.1986, p. 17
[62] Contributions in M. Cremona and H.-W. Micklitz (eds.), *Private Law in the External Relations of the EU* (Oxford: Oxford University Press, 2016).
[63] Collins, 'Conformity of Goods, the Network Society and the Ethical Consumer', p. 305.
[64] Case note 'German Supreme Court strikes down choice of court agreement prorogating courts of Virginia', on the blog 'Transnational Notes', available at: http://blogs.law.nyu.edu/transnational/2013/04/german-supreme-court-strikes-down-choice-of-court-agreement-prorogating-courts-of-virginia/.
[65] Study Group on Social Justice in European Private Law, 'Social Justice in European Contract Law', 668.

link between consumption and production is the reasonable expectations of the consumer enshrined in Directive 99/44.[66] Art. 2 (d) defines the expectations that the consumer might have with regard to the conformity of the product in the following words:

(d) show the quality and performance which are normal in goods of the same type and which the consumer can reasonably expect, given the nature of the goods and taking into account any public statements on the specific characteristics of the goods made about them by the seller, the producer or his representative, particularly in advertising or on labelling.

Is seems justifiable to build a link between the 'specific characteristics of the product', the 'public statements' and what the 'consumer can reasonably expect'. There is no case law, neither at the EU level nor at the national level. Rott and Glinski[67] and Collins tend to answer the question in the affirmative. The same is true with regard to the other eye-catching phenomena such as animal welfare, depletion of natural resources or genetically modified products. Provided the public statement of a producer like Apple or Nike is clear enough so as to justify the consumer's legitimate expectations, the product maybe regarded as being defective. There is certainly agreement that issues of health and safety are non-negotiable. However, the handling of child labour is more delicate. What happens when children are the breadwinners of the family? Does the Western consumer 'help' to implement the verdict on child labour, if he or she does not buy such an incriminated product? What if countries like Bolivia explicitly legalise child labour?[68]

Closely related, though legally different, are commercial practices or codes of conduct that deal with the production conditions, in terms of health and safety at work and/or environmental protection. In 2010, the regional German Consumer Advice Centre in Hamburg filed an action for injunction against Lidl for misleading advertising with respect for fair working conditions in Bangladesh.[69] This is what Lidl had been saying publicly

---

[66] Part III. 3.4.
[67] For an early attempt, see C. Glinski, P. Rott, 'Umweltfreundliches und ethisches Konsumverhalten im harmonisierten Kaufrecht', *Europäische Zeitschrift für Wirtschaftsrecht* 2003, 649–654
[68] Newspaper article entitled 'Bolivia becomes first nation to legalise child labour', in *The Independent*, 19.7.2014, available at: www.independent.co.uk/news/world/americas/bolivia-becomes-first-nation-to-legalise-child-labour-9616682.html.
[69] For background information on the case, website of the Hamburg Consumer Advice Centre at: www.vzhh.de/recht/30346/lidl.aspx.

Lidl setzt sich weltweit für faire Arbeitsbedingungen ein. Wir bei Lidl vergeben deshalb unsere Non-Food-Aufträge nur an ausgewählte Lieferanten und Produzenten, die bereit sind und nachweisen können, soziale Verantwortung aktiv zu übernehmen. [Lidl engages worldwide in fair employment conditions. We at Lidl mandate only selected suppliers and producers who are ready to provide evidence that they actively accept social responsibility.]

The consumer organisation relied on evidence brought up by two NGOs, Campaign for Clean Clothes (CCC) and the European Center for Constitutional and Human Rights (ECCHR), which had investigated working conditions in Bangladesh. When it became clear that Lidl would lose the case, Lidl settled and withdrew the advertisement. The difficulty is how to find evidence on possible infringements of self-set commitments. Self-assessments and self-produced reports on compliance are certainly not enough. There are huge problems in monitoring and surveying this kind of commitments. The German consumer organisation was just 'lucky' to have found NGOs, which engaged in monitoring. On the other hand, it is equally amazing that the court in Hamburg was ready to rely on NGOs and not on Lidl.

Dieselgate is on the edge between consumer sales law and the law on unfair commercial practices. Volkswagen advertised based on how environmental friendly diesel is, and referred to its corporate social responsibility commitment enshrined in a code of conduct. There are a number of cases in Europe pending on whether the advert should be regarded as misleading (Art. 7 (d) Directive 2005/29) and whether individual consumers may claim that their car is defective (Art. 2 (2) (d) Directive 99/44).[70]

4.5 Order of Competence and Responsibilities

The design of the order of competences focuses on the responsible market citizen, individually and collectively. Major changes are taking place in the political order of competence. Two of them will be highlighted, firstly the role and function of the responsible market citizen in what could be called civil society building through the preliminary reference procedure and secondly the joint responsibility of the market citizen and business. Both are ambitious and both deeply affect the political order of competences.

---

[70] With regard to misleading practices, Beckers, 'The Regulation of Market Communication and Market Behaviour', the *same* with regard to a potential defect under Directive 1999/44, *European Review of Contract Law*, ERCL 2018; 14(2): 1–33.

The rise of the Social in EU regulatory private law from the mid-1980s onwards, and the use of the preliminary reference procedure by citizen groups – trade unions, equal opportunity commissions, human rights groups and consumer organisations – coincide. Technically, this is done through the choice of the correct plaintiff, the one who enjoys enforceable subjective rights under EU law and through sponsoring litigation until the bitter end. Civil society associations may initiate proceedings or they may free ride on innovative lawyers, who were trying to help their clients. About 67.92 per cent out of all litigation before the ECJ results from preliminary reference procedures, out of which the vast majority comes from business.[71] Only a small minority, which nobody ever tried to quantify, comes under the scope of public interest litigation. Despite their limited number, regulatory private law is full of examples. In employment and non-discrimination law, outstanding examples include *Christel Schmidt, Mangold*, in consumer law, *Heininger, Quelle, Putz/Weber, Mohamed Aziz, Amazon, TÜV Germany*.[72] Academic research which goes beyond case studies and provides for a systematic account of public interest litigation under the preliminary reference procedure in the three areas is scarce.[73]

The preliminary reference procedure is designed to clarify the meaning of EU law which interferes into national litigation. References to the ECJ bear a particular national undertone. The conflict behind the chosen plaintiff is embedded in the national context. It may have a genuine political dimension like the fight of trade unions and women organisations against the anti-social policy of the Thatcher regime, or it may be targeted at solving a specific problem that has reached a collective dimension like in *Heininger*, or it may be focused on the availability of a particular remedy which is perceived as a lacuna in the national legal system, e.g., *Quelle* or *Putz/Weber*. By and large, civil society organisations use the Court in Luxemburg to solve a national conflict.

---

[71] About 67.92 per cent of new cases before the CJEU in the period between 2012 and 2016 stem from preliminary references (p. 88). 64.35 per cent of the completed cases in the period between 2012 and 2016 have been references for preliminary ruling (p. 91), Court of Justice of the European Union, Annual Report of 2016 on Judicial Activity, available at: https://curia.europa.eu/jcms/upload/docs/application/pdf/2017-03/ra_jur_2016_en_web.pdf.

[72] Case C-392/92, *Schmidt v. Spar- und Leihkasse der früheren Ämter Bordesholm, Kiel und Cronshagen*; Case C-144/04, *Mangold*; Case C-481/99, *Heininger* [2001] I-9945; C-404/06, *Quelle* [2008] ECR I-02685; Case C-65/09, *Gebr. Weber und Putz*; Case C-415/11, *Aziz*; C-191/15, *Verein für Konsumenteninformation* [2016] ECR I-000; C-219/15, *Schmitt*.

[73] Kelemen, *Eurolegalism*.

European society building via public interest litigation looks different. Three forms can be distinguished. The most ambitious would be that civil society associations engage in joint cross-border action. This needs organisational input from one national association or from an umbrella association at the European level, the European association of workers (EUTC) or the European associations of consumers (BEUC). Under EU law they have no standing. They may only coordinate the activities, organise the information exchange and provide resources, if they are available. Such litigation has never been launched in the EU. Somewhat less ambitious are coordinated actions, where a common problem is identified and where the national civil associations launch parallel action in their home states. Again, an organisational input from the umbrella organisations is needed. The so-called Apple Case stands for this type of coordinated action.[74] The third and the weakest is follow-on litigation. Here, a particular consumer issue, sponsored by a national civil association, is decided in Luxemburg in favour of the claimant. The successful procedure triggers follow-on procedures from a number of Member States courts, more or less supported by civil society associations. Outstanding examples are the litigation on the Working Time Directive[75] or on the impact of the economic crisis on household debts.[76]

The second major change, the *responsibilisation* of the market citizen and business, started already in the 1960s. Business led the way in striking down national statutory rules that hinder the market freedoms, while market citizens were supposed to make use of the increased choice. Trade bans were replaced via information requirements. Co-responsibility follows from the rise of social regulation in the EU, the way in which it developed and mutated after the Lisbon Agenda through the legislature, the ECJ and the regulatory agencies. The first step is the *responsibilisation* of business. Social regulation initiated expectations not only against the state but also against business. This is more developed in non-discrimination law and consumer law. However, if one is ready to understand *Viking* and *Laval* as an avenue that allows and requires business to be held responsible for the Social, European labour law appears in a different light. The last step is the concept of the

---

[74] M. Durovic, 'The Apple Case Today: Factual and Legal Assessment' (2016) *EUI Working Paper EUI-ERC* No. 3.
[75] Reich, *General Principles of EU Civil Law*, Chapter 2, at p. 41.
[76] Micklitz, Domurath and Comparato (eds.), 'The Over-Indebtedness of European Consumers'.

responsible market citizen, who is not only responsible for himself or herself, but who bears a societal responsibility.

Collective labour law is governed by, and through, co-responsibility. This was particularly clear when collective labour law remained outside the statutory sphere. When collective labour law came under the auspices of statutory legislation, the state took over a kind of subsidiary responsibility. The European Union tried to build and enhance a European-triggered social dialogue. The results, however, remain rather meagre. More promising, are the efforts in consumer law. Co-responsibility is enshrined in the emerging principle of good faith. Reich speaks of a duty to 'loyal co-operation as part of the general good faith obligation, creating obligations not only for business but also (to a limited extent) for the consumer'.[77] He refers to the Court and Advocate General Trstenjak in *Pereničová*.[78] Bits and pieces of such a duty to loyal cooperation can be found in Directive 99/44, which is understood by B. Lurger as an instrument of 'contractual solidarity'.[79] More outspoken are references in secondary EU law that impose behavioural obligations on the consumer.[80] The same kind of thinking can be found in *Brasserie, Danske Slagterier* and *Courage*.[81]

Co-responsibility in the making of rules, model contracts, codes, and technical standards presupposes loyal cooperation, otherwise the expected (negative) outcome might be predicable. Whilst co-responsibility is well known to the business sector due to the experience in collective labour law for nearly a century, co-responsibility is rather new for consumer and civil society organisations and sometimes regarded with suspicion.

The *legal order of competence* might change too, in that EU law does not prohibit the parties from engaging in collective agreements provided they do not restrict competition. The key case until today is *Albany*.[82]

---

[77] Reich, *General Principles of EU Civil Law*, p. 200.
[78] Case C-453/10, *Pereničová und Pereničˇ* [2012] ECR I-000, paras. 32–33; Opinion of Advocate General Trstenjak delivered on 29 November 2011 – Case C-453/10, *Pereničová und Pereničˇ*, para 67.
[79] B. Lurger, *Vertragliche Solidarität. Entwicklungschance für das allgemeine Vertragsrecht in Österreich und in der Europäischen Union* (Baden-Baden: Nomos, 1998).
[80] Art. 8 (2) Directive 85/374 on product liability, Art. 5 (4) Package Tour Directive 90/314, now Art. Art. 13 (2) Directive 2015/2302.
[81] Joined cases C-46/93 and C-48/93, *Brasserie du pêcheur v Bundesrepublik Deutschland and The Queen / Secretary of State for Transport, ex parte Factortame and Others* [1996] ECR I-1029, paras. 84, 87; Case C-445/06, *Danske Slagterier* [2009] ECR I-2119, para. 69; Case C-453/99, *Courage und Crehan*, paras. 31–32.
[82] Case C-67/96, *Albany* [1999] ECR I-5751.

Advocate General Jacobs set requirements that need to be met in order to exempt private parties from competition law: (1) representativity on both sides, (2) it is not a hard-core cartel, (3) subject matter is core collective bargaining matters, (4) no direct effect on third parties (i.e., it does not affect employers' relations with suppliers, competing employers, customers or consumers).[83] The ECJ was less outspoken:[84]

> It is beyond question that certain restrictions of competition are inherent in collective agreements between organisations representing employers and workers. However, the social policy objectives pursued by such agreements would be seriously undermined if management and labour were subject to Article 85(1) of the Treaty when seeking jointly to adopt measures to improve conditions of work and employment. (60) It therefore follows from an interpretation of the provisions of the Treaty as a whole which is both effective and consistent that agreements concluded in the context of collective negotiations between management and labour in pursuit of such objectives must, by virtue of their nature and purpose, be regarded as falling outside the scope of Article 85(1) of the Treaty.

The same logic applies *cum grano salis* to collective agreements between business and consumers. However, the requirements defined by Advocate General Jacobs set narrow boundaries. Representativity is an extremely difficult criterion to handle in the consumer environment. National consumer organisations would have difficulties to accept the European umbrella organisation as representing national organisations. The subject matter could and would be rules for which no, or very limited, guidance exists in the European (and national) private law. The major difficulty arises from the fourth criterion as an agreement would necessarily affect third parties, e.g., in the supply chain or in contractual networks. The later judgment of the ECJ in *Scarlet* helps to overcome the hurdle.[85] The two parties have to take third-party implications into consideration, in particular when they enjoy a fundamental right status. The ECJ does not yet explicitly claim that the third parties need a right to be heard. However, *Sales Sinués* and *Biuro podróży Partner* come close.[86]

The *enforcement order of competences* suffers from an increasing degree of complexity. Whilst the four actors stand side by side there is a kind of

---

[83] Opinion of Advocate General Jacobs delivered on 28 January 1999 – Case C-67/96, *Albany*, paras. 169, 186–194, summary as of Reich, *General Principles of EU Civil Law*, p. 33.
[84] Case C-67/96, *Albany*, para. 59.
[85] Case C-70/10, *Scarlet Extended*.
[86] Joined Cases C-381/14 and C-385/14, *Sales Sinués*; Case C-119/15, *Biuro podróży Partner*.

competition between enforcement orders, horizontally but also diagonally.[87] The neat interaction and fine-tuning of competences between the different actors function nicely on paper only. Compliance operates on a voluntary basis, ADR precedes court action, regulatory action is submitted to judicial review. However, no single event runs through the four different levels. Most of the infringements come to an end before the forum to which they are brought. It might help to draw a distinction between major and minor infringements and to link the respective enforcement bodies to the type of infringement.[88] This leaves self-regulatory bodies and ADRs with minor infringements, and courts and regulatory agencies with major infringements. The latter two should be released from pursuing minor infringements. Such a redistribution of responsibilities, however, is possible only if the four branches are closely interconnected.

---

[87] H.-W. Micklitz, 'The Transformation of Private Law through Competition' (2016) 22 *European Law Journal* 627–643.
[88] H.-W. Micklitz, 'Administrative Enforcement of European Private Law'.

5 Summary

First layer: The EU legal order on universal services guarantees a materialised (Weber) access to the market and to society. Universal services cover telecommunication, energy and, within limits, financial services. The addressee is the economically vulnerable, mainly the EU national but, within limits, also the non-national. There are deficiencies and deficits in how the EU law on universal services is construed. The biggest one is certainly the lack of a general rule that grants all people who are legally resident in the EU a right to subsistence. Only such an *un*conditional support would allow everybody to pay for the universal services. A second deficit is the lack of clear guidance on the price that the customer has to pay for the universal services. A third deficit is the scattered jurisdiction not only between courts and ADR but also between the different branches of the court

Despite all these difficulties, the social component in universal services is undeniable. There is one proviso: one has to accept that the liberalisation and perhaps even the privatisation of former public services provides potential for the addressees to improve their living conditions. Access to universal services must be understood as a form of justice. It is not only access to the market, as access to universal services is contingent upon participation in society. Where access rules are tied to economic non-discrimination, universal services even reach beyond access and provide for basic social justice.

Second layer: The law on labour and consumer market society provides for access justice and here and there even social justice, depending on the context. The major deficits result from the lack of a clear division of competences and responsibilities on the law-making but also on the law enforcement side. The EU has no competence to turn minimum harmonisation into full harmonisation. The clock has to be turned back. Only such a clear division allows for shaping responsibilities. The EU and the Member States accept responsibility for the minimum; it is for the

Member States to decide whether they go beyond this minimum. If they do so, they accept an additional responsibility.

The current messiness of law enforcement can only be overcome through legislative intervention, if not through amendments of the Treaty. Seen through the eyes of the worker and the consumer, judicial redress should be possible against those who ultimately bear responsibility. These are not only Member States and their agencies, but also the EU and, in particular, European agencies.

No amendments are needed with regard to the responsibility of private regulators. The existing rules suffice to justify a direct responsibility and liability of private regulators in the field of labour and consumer law. Civil society organisations, however, are neither making full use of the preliminary reference procedure, nor of the legal space which the EU legal order opens up for joint bottom-up rule-making together with business.

Third layer: The new societal private law requires a deep change in the understanding of private law. The addressee is the self- and societally responsible market citizen, including civil society organisations standing behind him or her. Societal responsibility in the EU context requires going beyond the national context in which the conflict arises. Civil society building can only be achieved if the responsible actors take a genuine European perspective. This implies a very different use of the preliminary reference procedure as a genuine form of European public interest litigation. It equally requires understanding the different avenues of enforcement not as parallels but as belonging together, aiming all at the same objective.

The responsibilisation of the market citizen finds its counterpart in business that equally bears responsibility for the implementation of the Social. Public interest litigation might support European society building, provided it overcomes the national perspective. However, more is needed. Civil society organisations and business have to make use of the freedom beyond the nation-state and to engage much more actively in developing collective rules under the auspices of EU and national surveillance. There is much that can be done bottom-up, through cooperation in the rule-making. Civil society building provides for societal justice in the supranational entity called the European Union.

Conclusions and Outlook

The phenomenon is well known to the reader: After years of research, I have collected many new ideas that would allow me to write another book. The point then is how to meet the expectations of the reader who might want to have a summary of the present volume and the intentions of the author to outline, at the very end, where future research will lead – whether it is the author's own or the task of someone else. I am joining all those who opt for the in-between way: a summary combined with new ideas and ideas that are hidden in the text but are not sufficiently developed.

The politics of justice in private law is embraced in the move from the classical private law order to the post-classical. The focus is placed on the EU and its role in the transformation process of social justice. The story is one of success, quite contrary to the seemingly dominating justice deficit discourse in EU legal scholarship. The EU has managed to develop a genuine concept of justice beyond the nation-state – access justice that has found its way into both legal consciousness and intellectual thought. The post-classical private law order is characterised by national and European patterns of justice that stand side by side, by a hybrid legal consciousness, by identity-based rights linked to different degrees of vulnerability or the lack thereof, and by responsibilities, which are shared between the EU and the Member States but which involve private parties, business and even citizens. The post-classical private law order is no longer to be understood as a coherent and closed normative system, but as a flexible, experimental multi-level legal order.

I have built the conclusion around four themes: the grand narratives, the great achievements, the transformations and the issues left open. There are three *grand narratives* to highlight which are constitutive of the emergent concept of European access justice – national and European legal consciousness and, as a consequence, hybridisation of consciousness. Without delving deeply into national legal consciousness and intellectual history, the variations of national justice cannot be understood, nor can the difficulties that the post-classical concept of access justice produces for established patterns of national justice be identified (Sections 1 to 3 of the conclusions). There are equally three *great EU achievements* to be reported from the European experiment: first and foremost, the shaping of access justice and, gradually, even *societal* justice; the development of a tripartite European private law order of the labour and consumer market society (emphasis on market *society* and not market alone), and a tripartite legal order that corresponds to the shared responsibilities of the EU, the Member States and private parties (Sections 4 to 6 of the conclusions). The grand narratives and the great achievements are the result of major economic and social forces that drive the *threefold transformation* – of the state, of labour and consumer law and of justice. The EU is to be regarded, moreover, much more as a catalyst than an autonomous actor. The transformations find their visible expression in a redesigned rationality doctrine which addresses not only the EU but also the Member States and even private parties and which underpins the experimental nature of the EU legal order (Sections 7 to 9 of the conclusions).

Last but not least, I will not hide but highlight *three imponderables* which still have to be tied up. These include, the impact of Brexit on European legal consciousness, the relationship between the tripartite European legal order and the national private law orders most prominently, and the suggested impact of the move from the *lex geometrica* to the *lex relativa* on the understanding of the role and function of the nation-state and its governing constitution (Sections 10 to 12 of the conclusions). Inclined readers will certainly identify more deficits, such as the Western European bias which has forcefully been brought to the limelight by Krastev in *After Europe*.[1]

Three Grand Narratives

1 Path Dependency of National (Social) Legal Consciousness

Legal consciousness is the mode of thinking that typifies the social psychology of a particular society and is predominantly shaped by the

---

[1] I. Krastev, *After Europe* (Philadelphia: University of Pennsylvania Press, 2017).

understandings of the societies' most influential philosophers. Legal consciousness is inherently linked to intellectual history, the historiography of ideas and thinkers.

The three countries under scrutiny are characterised by their particular patterns of justice and consciousness. They are rooted in their different intellectual history. Wieacker identified three key parameters which shaped the common legal culture of Europe – personalism, intellectualism and legalism – that made their way into legal consciousness. While all are axiomatic in the three countries, they vary in the degree to which they are reflected in the legal consciousness, the legal culture and values enshrined in the different private legal orders. The English private legal order is dominated by personalism combined with pragmatism, and so is English society. This explains the strong emphasis on individual freedom and the willingness to accept statutory intervention to the benefit of weaker parties only if needed in reaction to clearly demonstrated evidence. French intellectualism promotes and underpins social private law as part of a more just society for which France stands as the paradigm. Therefore, social justice is a genuinely political project ever since the French revolution. The social model provides for a highly innovative potential that might clash, however, with hard economic realities. In Germany, legalism is the dominating paradigm that overshadows personalism and intellectualism. German society bestows the highest importance upon legalism. German thinkers constantly search for the perfect legal solution that overcomes the tension between classical legal thought, as enshrined in formal law, and the realisation of the Social through the materialisation of private law. This results in an over-estimation of what the law is able to achieve.

All three countries followed their own path through the twentieth century. The intellectual mindset of the three societies and their most influential thinkers remained amazingly stable despite two world wars and despite various economic and social disruptions in the second half of the twentieth century. Each of the three had to face the same transformative powers of the state, of private law and of justice. Whilst there is a common move towards the Social at least until the late 1970s, each realised their own version of the Social reflected in national conceptions of labour and consumer laws: English personalism and pragmatism; French intellectualism and politics; and German legalism and paternalism.

2 European (Social) Legal Consciousness

Law plays a crucial role in bringing Europe to the people as enshrined in the 'integration through law' paradigm.[2] The common European heritage is foundational to the developing of European legal consciousness, first tied to the Internal Market alone and then, since the adoption of the Single European Act in 1986, to a European market with a social face. European legal consciousness has been created and promoted by a European elite of academics, public officials and politicians. It yielded expectations, in the benefits of a European Common, then Internal Market, later in a 'European Social'.

The starting conditions for the development of a European Social were not easy. Through the Single European Act, the EU is granted competence at a time when the high expectations created by the national social welfare state were being shattered. The European Social underwent two different stages. In the first stage, the European Commission 'copy-pasted' the Member States' social approach to labour and consumer law. Social *minimum* standards were quite successfully realised in European consumer law but failed to embed in labour law, not least due to the resistance of the United Kingdom. Minimum standards left leeway for the Member States to maintain and develop their national understanding of the Social in and through private law. The common heritage held the European Social together. In a second stage, the EU began to develop its own concept of the Social. Labour, non-discrimination and consumer law changed from social protection law to the law of the labour and consumer market society. The transformations the United Kingdom underwent during the Thatcher government reached the EU and, via EU legislation and ECJ judgments, also the consciousness of the people. Legal thinkers and legal theories gradually changed sides. They questioned the ongoing integration through law and warned against the impotence of national democracies to keep the achievements of the national welfare state in place. At the same time, the European legislative and adjudicative machinery went on and on. The common heritage that nourished the first thirty to forty years of European integration did not suffice

---

[2] R. Byberg, 'The History of the Integration Through Law Project: Creating the Academic Expression of a Constitutional Legal Vision for Europe' (2017) 18 *German Law Journal* 1531–1556; A. Vauchez, *Brokering Europe. Euro-Lawyers and the Making of a Transnational Polity* (Cambridge: Cambridge University Press, 2015), in particular chapters 5 and 6.

to guide the European experiment through the troubling waters after *Lehman* and the Euro crisis.[3]

Despite all the drawbacks and barriers, the EU created expectations not only in the three countries but overall in the EU. From 1986 on, European citizens expected more than just the Internal Market. Gradually the EU became perceived as the addressee of social responsibilities. As long as the EU copy-pasted the welfare state ideology, the relationship between the EU, the Member States and the citizens remained rather harmonious. The difficulties began with the second stage, with the turn away from social regulation to social market regulation, from social justice to access justice and from minimum to maximum harmonisation. In countries with high social standards like France and Germany, the EU was regarded as undermining national standards of social protection. European legal consciousness gained negative permutations. The achievements of European social regulation fell by the wayside. The change in perception was facilitated by the Member States playing nested games, claiming successes in social regulation for themselves, whilst blaming the EU for their failures. The co-responsibility of the Member States in the transformation of the Social through Europeanisation did not, or only to a limited extent, make their way into legal consciousness. Brexit tells a strange story whereby the British want to keep higher EU social standards, but want to leave the EU. Brexit demonstrates how the EU has created expectations and changed the mindset of the people. However, these social expectations are not necessarily attributed to the EU, even though they are the creations of EU law.

3 Hybridisation of Legal Consciousness

The European version of the Social enshrined in the concept of access justice is not meant to replace national patterns of social justice. All Member States, including those under scrutiny, may keep their national patterns of social justice as long as they are ready and willing to engage in redistributive taxation. 'Social' legal consciousness became divided between the EU and the Member States and divided in the minds of the people. The result is hybrid legal consciousness.

Hybrid legal consciousness results from shared competences which are anchored in the treaty and which restrain the EU from taking over

---

[3] See the contributions in M. Maduro and M. Wind (eds.), *The Transformation of Europe. Twenty-Five Years On* (Cambridge: Cambridge University Press, 2017).

the Social. Even if the EU had the power to substitute the national paradigm of the Social for a European Social, the implications of such a takeover on the legal consciousness are far from clear. It might very well be that the particular variant of national legal consciousness survives despite European legal consciousness. Hybrid legal consciousness mirrors the tricky relationship between being a citizen of a particular Member State and being a European citizen. It is hard to imagine that there is a way back to link the Social to the respective Member State alone. This is true for the United Kingdom even after Brexit.

The EU regulations and EU standards which frame private transactions are the result of transnational negotiations. The EU plays a major role in vertical (regulated markets) or horizontal (across markets) standardisation, as an exporter of European standards and as an importer of foreign transnational standards.[4] Transnational rule-making and -shaping might not be really new, but what is new is that transnationalisation reaches each and every legal order and each and every citizen whether citizens are cognizant of transnationalism or not. Many do not realise that the standards and norms which govern their lives are the result of a transnational agreement. One might therefore speak of the hidden hybridity of private transnationalism. The EU serves as a laboratory that prepares Europeans for a market society where the Social cannot be pinned down to one single addressee, where responsibilities are divided, legally between the EU and the Member States and maybe also with private actors operating beyond the nation-state.

Three Great Achievements

4 European Access Justice and European Societal Justice

European *access justice* is descriptive and normative. Access justice is meant to capture and to embrace the transformation of values. Access justice is normative in that it prescribes what is to be expected from the EU as a kind of minimum standard. European access justice stands side by side with national patterns of social justice. It does not aim to replace national patterns of justice. European *societal* justice reaches beyond access justice, beyond the market and into a European *society*. The EU

---

[4] For an exporter, see A. Bradford, 'The Brussels Effect' (2012) 107 *Northwestern University Law Review* 1–68; more generally on the role of the EU in private law relations, see Cremona and Micklitz (eds.), *Private Law in the External Relations of the EU*.

demonstrates the feasibility of establishing justice beyond the nation-state and beyond the market. Access and societal justice are the result of a dynamic interactive process where the Member States, the EU and private parties are involved.

In a normative understanding, *access justice* is bound to the completion of three requirements: *first*, breaking down barriers which limit participation and access; *second*, strengthening the position of workers and consumers to enforce their rights in a multi-governance legal order and, *third*, establishing an institutional design which can cope with the move from social protection laws to the laws on the labour and consumer market. With regard to the *first* category, access justice requires that all market participants, including consumers, must have a fair and realistic chance of entering the market, availing themselves of its products and services, as well as of partaking in the benefits of the market. Access justice in the *second* sense relates to the degree of justice the individual might gain, after he or she has been granted access. Rights are useless if they cannot be enforced, not only between the parties but also against the Member States and the EU. The *third* component of access justice requires an institutional design that involves trade unions, consumer associations and more broadly civil society in the making of the rules that underpin modern private law relations and their enforcement. Access justice reaches beyond market justice as it ties access to substantive, procedural and institutional conditions. However, the stock-taking of the existing EU rules on labour, non-discrimination and consumer law demonstrates that whilst the EU legal corpus is evolving, it does not yet meet the threefold requirements.

European *societal justice* is meant to express that European justice is not limited to a kind of *materialised* access to the market. The existing body of European regulatory private law shows that an overarching element in the EU legal order reaches beyond the market. This overarching element can already be found in ECJ judgments dealing with hard-core market freedom. The common denominator of these judgments is the opening of bilateral private law relations towards third parties affected by interpersonal agreements.[5] This process continues in the regulation of labour, non-discrimination and consumer law. EU law is opening the market towards society beyond the nation-state. Private

---

[5] With regard to property rights, Case C-70/10, *Scarlet Extended*; with regard to the impact of collective agreements, C-45/09, *Rosenbladt* para 73, ECJ Case C- 143/83 *Commission v. Kingdom of Denmark* [1985] ECR 427, para 9–10.

law beyond the nation-state leaves space for private actors not only for market building but also for society building. Justice in private law beyond the nation-state gains a particular *relational* dimension. It interconnects the people, the workers, the consumers, the employers and the suppliers in a European society. Whilst this society is market biased, it cannot be reduced to the market. European society building is legally framed. Under the auspices of the EU private law relations are to be associated with a *societal* private law order. I termed this form of transnational justice *societal* justice as it relates to the people within the developing European society. Societal justice finds its visible expression in societal European private law, which is still in its infant stage. It is feasible, however, to deduce its constitutive elements from the existing body of European rules on labour, non-discrimination and consumer law.

5 The Tripartite European Private Legal Order

The three forms of justice – access justice, social justice and societal justice – correspond to the tripartite European legal order. The law on universal services is to be associated with access justice enshrined in vulnerability, the law on the labour and consumer market society with social justice enshrined in weakness and confidence and the law on societal private relations with societal justice, enshrined in the worker and the consumer citizen. The differentiation between the three levels along the line of the vulnerable, the weak/confident and the responsible market citizen is key to understanding the highly fragmented European private law. Looking at the three 'levels' separately, they resemble legal regimes on particular logics in EU law which correspond to different areas of law. Bringing the three together justify comprehending European private law as a legal order.

The differentiation results from the European integration process in the aftermath of the Single European Act, from the moment when the EU got involved in social regulation onwards. National social labour law, national social consumer law and national non-discrimination law differentiate in two directions. The nucleus remains in social labour and consumer law. However, the EU is turning social labour and social consumer law first into the law of the labour and the consumer market and then gradually into the law of the labour and consumer market *society*. This move triggered hard ideological battles on the decline of social justice and on abolishing the protection of the weaker party. It is largely a battlefield over whether EU minimum standard can and should be topped by higher national standards of social protection. In the EU workers and consumers have to fight for their rights, maybe even harder than within an exclusively national context.

Additionally, the EU introduced two new layers, universal services as the bottom line for the protection of the vulnerable and a new 'societal private law' that imposes responsibilities on the market citizen, on civil society organisations and companies in building a market and a society beyond the nation-state. EU law guarantees access to the addressees of the law on universal services. Access is unconditional. The innovative potential leads to promising results or contains at least the kernel for promising development. The new societal private law is still in a nascent state. The EU rules that can be associated to this level are underdeveloped. Its furtherance requires trade unions, consumer associations and civil society groups ready to engage in public interest litigation. They have got a European mandate to actively promote the new societal private law not only through courts and administrative agencies. There is space for new forms of contract and administrative governance which unite business, market citizens and public authorities.

The tripartite European private law order requires a holistic perspective that cuts across the boundaries of well-established legal categories, public and private, substantive and procedural, law-making and law enforcement, national and European, hard and soft. EU law is regulatory in nature and instrumental in its focus on Internal Market building and in limits to European society building. However, EU law is not bound and tied to thinking and operating in legal boxes. The irritation with preconceived categories that this provokes should be understood as an opportunity to rethink national legal categories, concepts, and divisions rather than as a threat to their integrity. In breaking boxes, EU law unfolds its innovative character. It is here that the European laboratory is in full display to the dismay of legal thinkers who confine themselves to defending the barricades of the classical understanding of private law.

6 Shared Competences, Shared Responsibilities of the EU, MS and PPs

Shared competences and shared responsibilities for social minimum standards document a milestone in the European Social. Not only do the nation-state and the EU bear responsibilities, but private parties do as well. The corollary of the greater freedoms that the EU facilitates is social responsibility. Indeed, shared responsibility means co-responsibility of the Member States and the EU for the minimum level. The EU has first and foremost a moral responsibility. Legal responsibility, however, is lurking behind the moral responsibility, though not yet fully recognised, at least not for the Social. Beyond the minimum, Member States retain sole responsibility for the Social.

Full harmonisation looks like collusion between the Member States and the EU to the detriment of the European citizens. The European Commission is keen to receive additional competence, whereas the Member States are trying to transfer their responsibility for the Social to the EU. The result is a kind of stalemate where the EU might gain the competence to realise fully harmonised piecemeal social regulation, but lacks the powers of a sovereign state to take over the Social in all its consequences to the benefit of European citizens. The Member States lose their competence in fully harmonised areas, but remain in charge not only for the enforcement but also for all social implications that are not directly covered in fully harmonised areas. Full harmonisation leads to an opaque division of competences and responsibilities between the Member States and the EU which is nearly impossible to disentangle. Full harmonisation is a misconception, for which European citizens are paying the bill.

The move towards governance two years after the Lisbon Agenda reinforces the opaqueness both at the law-making level and at the enforcement level. The promising side of administrative governance is its experimental character, which allows new modes of rule-making and rule enforcement under conditions of uncertainty to be tested. The dark side of administrative governance is competence creep, clearly favoured by the European Commission. The rise of (experimental) governance is not limited to the three constitutional powers, the European legislature, the European executive and even the European judiciary. New modes of governance can equally be found in the mainland of private law, in contract law through the elaboration of the Common Frame of Reference, in regulatory private law through the increase of standardisation as a new form of harmonisation below the radar of formal law-making. Governance is needed and could be promoted provided it is possible to assign clear responsibilities to all parties involved.

Private law beyond the nation-state is bringing a third actor gradually into the limelight – private parties who are involved in the rule production and the rule enforcement, quite often under the umbrella of EU framework regulation. These private parties suffer the same fate as the EU. They accepted the delegation of power from the statutory to the private level. Through their active involvement they gradually become addressees of responsibility claims. This is most obvious on the business side, where the ECJ confirmed jurisdiction over technical standards and seems even ready to seriously consider the liability of private business parties, individually and collectively. Non-governmental organisations, civil society groups in whatever form, will have to face a similar challenge. The active involvement goes hand in hand first with moral responsibilities and later on with private liabilities. The legal technicalities, the reach of the famous horizontal direct effect, the where, when and under what conditions private parties of whatever 'colour' may be held legally responsible reaches beyond the purpose of the book.[6]

Three Great Transformations

7 Drivers behind the Transformations

The European debate over the claimed justice deficit overshadows that the EU is not the cause of the transformation process and that its role and function needs a more sophisticated understanding.[7] The EU jumped on the bandwagon of what is affectively called European neoliberalism.

At the *surface* level, it seems as if the European Commission is sitting in the driver's seat. It seized the opportunity provided by the Lisbon Agenda and 'New Governance' not only to expand its powers in and outside the formal competence structure but also to transform the value structure of the Social. Legitimised through the full harmonisation mandate, the European Commission submits secondary EU law to an efficiency and effectiveness test.[8] Opponents would argue that the European Commission is guided by a neoliberal philosophy, by mere market justice that undermines higher national standards of social protection, national sovereignty and national democracy. In such a perspective, the European social is seen as an imperfect shadow for national patterns of Social justice. This picture needs to be corrected.

---

[6] Condon, *Tort Law beyond the Reasonable Man*.
[7] Svetiev, 'The EU's Private Law in the Regulated Sectors', 679–680; see also in more detail Part II. 4.2.
[8] H. McColm, 'Smart Regulation: The European Commission's Updated Strategy' (2011) 2 *European Journal of Risk Regulation* 9–11; L. Allio, 'On the Smartness of Smart Regulation – A Brief Comment on the Future Reform Agenda' (2011) 2 *European Journal of Risk Regulation* 19–20.

What might be true for the Eurozone crisis and its management through the Troika does not do justice to EU labour, non-discrimination and consumer law. It would be simplistic to argue that the EU is pursuing a neoliberal approach that deregulates social regulation. In fact the EU managed to establish its own pattern of justice. In that sense, the EU might be regarded as a driver, a driver towards the formulation of justice beyond the nation-state.

At the *foundational* level, the EU and the Member States are subject to identical transformations resulting from the globalisation of the economy, from the changing society and – what is less on the agenda of this book – from the digitisation of the economy and the society.[9] The 'globalisation of the economy' is reflected in the Lisbon Agenda, in the intention of the Member States to make the EU 'the most competitive economy of the world'. The direct outcome is the move to efficiency and to full harmonisation. Both the move and the change in regulatory technique should be understood as a reaction to transformative forces from outside the EU. This does not mean that full harmonisation was a necessary and conditional political reaction. Even if the EU had maintained the minimum harmonisation approach, however, the EU and the Member States would remain under pressure from international competitiveness and from the challenge of economic efficiency. The changing society is reflected in the rise and importance of the non-discrimination doctrine that gained ground beyond employment relations within the public sphere of economic transactions. It is at the heart of the current migration crisis. The Lisbon Agenda introduced the inclusion/exclusion rhetoric into the political agenda which forms the core of the current political conflict, as enshrined in legal conflicts on access to universal services.

8 Rationality Test

If the information society is an external catalyst of change, the internal face of change is the rationality test. The rationality test could be understood as the main driver in the transformation of labour, non-discrimination and consumer law and of the Social. The rationality test is well anchored in primary EU law. In my understanding, the rationality test can be and should be extended to secondary EU law and applied to private parties. In this broadened understanding, the

---

[9] For preliminary thoughts, see Micklitz and Svetiev, 'The Transformation(s) of Private Law'.

rationality test unfolds its potential to test not only statutory restrictions to economic freedoms but also private regulatory restrictions to individual autonomy.

The rationality test has its origin in the *Cassis-de Dijon* doctrine. The test contributed considerably to striking down national statutory regulations that hampered freedom of trade. *Cassis de Dijon* stands as a synonym for a 'good life', a life where choice between an incredible number of products from all over the EU becomes the dominant paradigm. *Cassis-de Dijon* stands behind freedom of services, freedom of capital and, for workers and consumers of utmost importance, freedom of establishment. *Cassis de Dijon* helped to promote the evolution of the consumer society, not only through buying goods and services, but through increased mobility. The broad understanding of 'worker' paved the way not only for those who were keen or forced to earn their living outside their home country, but also for students and to some extent for non-EU nationals to benefit from the unfolding Internal Market.

In line with leading ECJ judgments,[10] the rationality test is to be extended to secondary EU labour, non-discrimination and consumer law. The question then is what counts as rationality. Max Weber binds rationality to legal formalism as a doctrine that shields the formal character of the law from politics. However, rationality should and must be tied to the materiality of the law, to what has been termed in line with Weber's materialisation of the law. Most if not all secondary EU law is materialising private law relations through the insertion of statutory mandatory requirements that the parties have to respect. EU regulations bind the parties directly, EU directives have to be implemented. The extension of rationality from formal to material allows for submitting national and EU social regulation to a test, where the economic distributive effectiveness, the societal effectiveness and economic efficiency of social regulation can be investigated. Through copy-pasting the European version of the Social, the EU transferred problems of effectiveness and efficiency to the European level. In the gradual elaboration of a genuine European Social, the EU via the European Commission accepted de facto the political need of a materialised rationality test, through impact assessment and through a compatibility test with fundamental rights. Whilst much of the current practice looks rather symbolic, it contains the potential for a serious test that meets the threefold criteria (economic distributive

---

[10] Case C-341/05 *Laval un Partneri* and Case C-205/07 *Gysbrechts and Santurel Inter*.

effectiveness, societal effectiveness and economic efficiency). One may wonder whether and to what extent the materialised rationality test can itself be submitted to judicial review.

In harmonised EU legal fields business will have to provide rational arguments for any restriction of the autonomy of the worker and the consumer. The reversal of the freedom/coercion paradigm can be backed through established case law of the ECJ, at least with regard to collective agreements. It seems as if the ECJ is suspicious towards collective power, even if it does not use the term. There is no comparable case law with regard to collective practices and there is uncertainty with regard to individual relations, not least due to the tricky issues revolving around horizontal direct effect. The 'power' argument, however, matters. Whenever the ECJ argues that the worker and the consumer is in a weaker position, it implicitly concedes that there is a party on the other side who is 'stronger'. It is premature to assume that the materialised rationality test has found its way into testing 'power', whether exercised collectively or individually. However, EU law moves towards testing power below the threshold of a dominant position.[11]

9 European Laboratory

The existence of a European laboratory depends on a stable/unstable constitutional infrastructure, which allows for permanent experimentalism in law-making and in law enforcement by the European legislature, the European executive and the European judiciary in order to achieve an objective that can never be achieved. It might be feasible not only to strive for the completion of the Internal Market but to realise it. However, each and every measure that reaches beyond the market, in particular the management of the European Social and its implications for the European society and the European identity, remain open ended as long as there is no clear political goal in sight. And even if there would be such a political goal, the project would be so unique that it might necessarily require constant adjustments and adaptations. Speculating on Europe's future after Brexit seems premature. For the time being and for the years to come, the EU will remain a laboratory.

There is a deep tension in the legal practice of four key European institutions, the Council, the European Parliament, the European

---

[11] Reich, *General Principles of EU Civil Law*, 'Chapter 2: The Principle of Protection of the Weaker Party', pp. 37–58

Commission, the European Court of Justice. On the *one hand*, all four are engaged in experimentalism, in seeking new forms and modes of law-making, to promote the development of a European private law order and ever-new forms and modes of enforcement to ensure that the European private law reaches European citizens. The result is a substantive body of private law rules which is constantly on the move. The ECJ has to decide cases for which the legal framework has already been overhauled. Member States are implementing European directives which are already subject to revision. The diversification of justice in private law could equally be understood as a matter of experimentalism. On the *other hand*, all four institutions are constantly trying to streamline the existing body of law, to trim it and to make it fit for purpose, for market and society building. The move from minimum to full harmonisation after Lisbon is paradigmatic. As long as minimum harmonisation prevailed, the EU legislature could engage in exchange with Member States innovations so as to improve the European body of law. In the enforcement of fully harmonised vague formulas the European Commission tries to steer the process in one particular direction, in particular through guidelines and recommendations that impose pressure on national regulatory agencies responsible for sectorial markets. Full harmonisation and even more uniformity in enforcement endanger the European experiment. In this sense, the critique against the EU is justified.[12]

The European laboratory leaves traces in legal consciousness beyond hybridity. Hybrid legal consciousness seems to end up in divided societies and divided legal communities. Personalism, intellectualism, legalism continue to dominate national private laws and the respective legal communities which are shielded and shield themselves against the influence and impact of the European integration process. It is here that we find hidden hybridity. There are European legal communities built around European labour law, European non-discrimination law and European consumer law. Personalism is shattered through identity-based rights, intellectualism through expertocracy, legalism through governance. Legal consciousness mulls over these new innovations, and these transformations are to be studied in a spirit of curiosity. Whether and how these different legal communities with their divided legal consciousnesses can be held together is one of the key

---

[12] A. Jakab and D. Kochenov (eds.), *Enforcement of EU Law and Values* (Oxford: Oxford University Press, 2017).

issues for the future of the EU as a supranational entity and for nation-state democracies.[13]

Three Open Questions

10 Brexit, the Social and European Legal Consciousness

What will Europe lose once the United Kingdom has left the EU? How will the lack of English personalism and English pragmatism impact European legal consciousness? How will the Social develop in the EU itself after the United Kingdom has left? Will European labour law, non-discrimination law and consumer law become more 'social'? There are many 'ifs' and many 'hows' on the future of Europe, on the future of the EU/UK relations and on how this uncertain future will affect peoples' mindsets and their legal consciousness. Whilst much remains a matter of speculation, it seems possible to connect the United Kingdom after Brexit with the growing scepticism of the new Member States towards the EU.

If the EU collapses, traditionalists might argue that the Member States fall back into their former status of a sovereign state and that the EU experiment is no more than an episode in the deeper strata of legal consciousness. This comes close to Krastev's *After Europe* in drawing a line between the collapse of the Austrian Empire, the collapse of the Soviet Union and the potential collapse of the EU. The Eastern Europeans, this is one lesson to learn, have a different view on the European experiment than their Western counterparts. They saw the Soviet Union vanish overnight and they might be less concerned about the collapse of the EU. If this is correct, legal consciousness might also be divided between West and East. It is certainly a weakness of the book that I have not studied the intellectual history of one of the Eastern European Member States in the same way I studied England, France and Germany. This would have allowed me to study the impact of communism on private law and on the legal mindset of the people more systematically. Overall, it seems as if the new Member States have to handle three layers of private law, the private law prior to Communism, which was reinvigorated after the collapse of Communism, the private law of Communist times that survived to some extent, and European private

---

[13] E. Flaig, *Die Niederlage der politischen Vernunft. Wie wir die Errungenschaften der Aufklärung verspielen* (Springe: zu Klampen, 2017).

law – the famous 80,000 pages that the new Member States had to transpose (often undigested) in order to join the EU. The hybridity in legal consciousness is a threefold one: pre-communist private law, communist private law, post-communist European private law.

What can be learnt from the former communist countries is equally true for the United Kingdom after Brexit. Fifty years of influence on the legal system, on the legal minds, on legal consciousness cannot be eradicated easily, even if politics so decides. Communism has left traces in the mindset of the people and their social expectations.[14] Exactly this experience suggests that the transformations of the nation-state, the social law and justice through the EU experiment will sustain, perhaps not forever but for the years to come. The United Kingdom cannot cleanse its private law from all the European rules on labour, non-discrimination and consumer law and nor is it even clear that this is the United Kingdom's aim. The United Kingdom cannot eradicate the 'European Social that has found its way into legal consciousness. To be sure, there are differences between the three fields,[15] but it seems equally true that the United Kingdom has become 'a little bit better, a little bit more committed to social justice' through European social regulation, as Mark Feedland put it.[16] The rise of the Social after the Internal Market has created expectations in the British State that governments of all colours have to meet. In that sense, legal consciousness will remain hybrid for a while. However, only informed lawyers will be able to trace back the social achievements in the United Kingdom to their European origin.

What is the future of European legal consciousness without the United Kingdom? Over decades the United Kingdom was a strong voice in the European integration process, promoting open markets

---

[14] C. Milosz, *The Captive Mind* (Penguin Books, Modern Classics, 2001).
[15] Symposium Issue 'EU Law with the UK, EU Law without the UK' of the (2017) 40 *Fordham International Law Journal*, in particular the contributions of N. Moloney, "Bending to Uniformity': EU Financial Regulation With and Without the UK', 1335–1372; S. Block-Lieb, 'The UK and EU Cross-Border Insolvency Recognition: From Empire to Europe to "Going It Alone"', 1373–1412; M. Gelter and A. M. Reif, 'What is Dead May Never Die: The UK's Influence on EU Company Law', 1413–1442; G. Monti, 'The United Kingdom's Contribution to European Union Competition Law', 1443–1474; S. Augenhofer, 'Brexit – Marriage 'With' Divorce? – The Legal Consequences for Consumer Law', 1475–1504; F. G. Nicola, 'Luxembourg Judicial Style With or Without the UK', 1505–1534; J. C. Suk, 'Equality After Brexit: Evaluating British Contributions to EU Antidiscrimination Law', 1535–1552; K. Wimmer and H. Jones, 'Brexit and Implications for Privacy', 1553–1564.
[16] Personal note to the author on 11.8.2016.

and open societies guided by the typical English combination of personalism and pragmatism in seeking manageable and feasible solutions. The UK position was consistent with the striving for and the defense of a liberal market economy. The EU after Brexit leaves more room for French intellectualism and German legalism. It might enhance and strengthen what has been termed – in contrast to LMEs – the Co-ordinated Market Economy (CME). What will be the outcome of a possible French-German project on the European Social without English personalism/pragmatism and how will this affect legal consciousness? In his speech at the Sorbonne on 26 September 2017, French President Macron advocated the 're-foundation' of Europe.[17] Put into historical perspective, this is French intellectual leadership at its best. Germany under whatever government will certainly promote legalism, but what about German idealism? Will German idealism join forces with French intellectualism? Who is responsible for pragmatism – the feasibility and manageability of such a project in 2017 – at times that are in no way comparable to the post-war period? What role can there be for the European Social between the Eurozone crisis and the migration crisis? There are strong voices, political parties and civil society organisations, not only in France and Germany, who expect the EU to become more 'social' after the United Kingdom has left. In the eyes of the promoters of a stronger social Europe, the United Kingdom appears as the 'brakeman' for the realisation of a social union. I. Goffman taught that social processes need 'bad guys' so as to stabilise societal relationships.[18] A word of caution is needed. France and Germany have many more problems to solve in the EU after Brexit than promoting the Social. Even if they do so, the new French/German European Social could look like 'idealistic-intellectualist', without the necessary dose of British pragmatism that ultimately facilitates the realisation of transnational political claims.

11 Interaction between European and National Private Law

This book focuses on how national patterns of social justice are transformed through the European integration process. The result is the European tripartite legal order. The book does not discuss the interaction

---

[17] 'Initiative pour l'Europe – Discours d'Emmanuel Macron pour une Europe souveraine, unie, démocratique', available at: www.elysee.fr/declarations/article/initiative-pour-l-europe-discours-d-emmanuel-macron-pour-une-europe-souveraine-unie-democratique/.

[18] E. Goffman, *Stigma: Notes on the Management of Spoiled Identity* (Englewood Cliffs, NJ: Prentice-Hall, 1963).

between the European private law and national private law. Guido Comparato, Yane Svetiev and myself have studied the interaction over the last five years in the ERC project on 'European Regulatory Private Law'.[19] The plan is to write a joint monograph that is built around four *normative* models of interaction: conflict and resistance, intrusion and substitution, hybridisation and convergence. The four normative models can be linked to particular types of institutions: conflict and resistance to differing orders of values, intrusion and substitution to regulated markets, hybridisation to remedies and convergence to co-/self-regulation. We have initiated PhDs and organised more than 20 conferences that provide the material on which our analysis will be based.

Conflict and resistance is suggested as one possible reaction of the Member States. Member States do not give way to the intruding European regulatory private law. Instead, they provoke a clash between the European regulatory private law and the national law and set limits to where the intruding law ends and where the national laws begin. The *Politics of Justice in European Private Law* fits in 'conflicts and resistance', as matters of justice unite and divide the Member States. However, in this book I do not discuss how the three forms of justice in the three different regimes can be made compatible with national private laws.

Intrusion and substitution suggest that EU law-making and law enforcement strategies aim at replacing national private laws in regulated markets. The result would be a self-sufficient order composed of three major elements: (1) the horizontal and vertical sectoral rules; (2) the general principles enshrined in the horizontal and vertical sectoral rules; (3) the general principles of civil law. Three PhD projects provide the ground for a deeper and more systematic analysis cutting across regulated markets, Lucila de Almeida on energy law and private law, M. Cantero Gamito on telecommunication and private law and F. della Negra on financial regulation and private law.[20] They are complemented by the monographs of

---

[19] H.-W. Micklitz and Y. Svetiev (eds.), 'A Self-sufficient European Private Law – A Viable Concept?' (2012) *EUI-ERC Working Paper* No. 31; H.-W. Micklitz, Y. Svetiev and G. Comparato (eds.), 'European Regulatory Private Law – The Paradigm Tested' (2014) *EUI-ERC Working Paper* No. 4.

[20] L. de Almeida, *Integration through Self-Standing European Private Law: Insights from the Internal Point of View to Harmonization in Energy Market*; M. Cantero Gamito, *The Private Law Dimension of the EU Regulatory Framework for Electronic Communications: Evidence of the Self-Sufficiency of European Regulatory Private Law*; F. della Negra, *Private Law and Private Enforcement in the Post-Crisis EU Retail Financial Regulation*.

G. Comparato on the financialisation of the citizen[21] and Y. Svetiev on experimentalist market regulation.[22]

Hybridisation is suggested to be an overall normative model of a composite legal order, within which the European and the national legal orders both play their part in some sort of a merged European-national private legal order. Hybridisation means that the legal character of the respective rule is neither European nor national.[23] It bears elements of both legal orders and is therefore supposed to be hybrid. Two PhD projects are studying hybridisation in more detail, B. Kas with regard to remedies and R. Condon with regard to tort law.[24]

Convergence is suggested to be a process of mutual approximation of the two different legal orders. They are not merged like in the concept of hybridisation; they still exist side by side, but they are drawing nearer to each other. Convergence is not bound to mandatory standards and default rules. It instead enshrines the new modes of governance, co-regulation and self-regulation, which are enhanced by limited and limiting state powers. Convergence is studied in the dissertation of B. van Leeuwen on services regulation and private law.[25]

12 'Geometric' and 'Relative' State

The diversification and transformation of justice hinges upon the role and the function of the nation-state, of the EU as a blueprint for studying the post-nation-state and their joint regulatory capacities. Put this way, the role and function of the state remains somewhat undertheorised. I am taking for granted that the state is transforming and that the state loses regulatory powers in a globalised economy and society. This is at least true with regard to economic regulation and partly to social regulation; not least because the survival of the welfare state depends in the end on a political decision and the preparedness of the citizens to pay for solidarity. Implicit to the transformation of the

---

[21] G. Comparato, *The Financialisation of the Citizen* (Oxford: Hart Publishing, forthcoming 2018).
[22] Y. Svetiev, *Experimentalism and Competition Law in EU Market Regulation* (Oxford: Hart Publishing, forthcoming 2018).
[23] On the idea of hybridisation platforms, see Y. Svetiev, 'European Regulatory Private Law: From Conflicts to Platforms', in K. Purnhagen and P. Rott (eds.), *Varieties of European Economic Law and Regulation: Liber Amicorum for Hans Micklitz* (New York: Springer International Publishing, 2014), pp. 153–177; Svetiev, 'The EU's Private Law in the Regulated Sectors'.
[24] Kas, 'Hybrid' Collective Remedies in the EU Social Legal Order; Condon, *Tort Law beyond the Reasonable Man: Re-Thinking Tort Law beyond the State*.
[25] v. Leeuwen, *European Standardisation of Services and Its Impact on Private Law*.

state is the decline of the Westphalian state and the decline of the *lex geometrica* that shaped our understanding of a systematic, coherent, consistent and logical legal order that holds the state and its functions together. The Westphalian State and the *lex geometrica* stands behind classical legal though and classical private law. The Westphalian state and the idea of a national private law belong to the established intellectual history of Europe. The assumed transformation of the state forms part of mainstream thinking. But what it exactly means and how much leeway there will be for the nation-state in regulating the economy and society requires a deeper analysis at the practical and the theoretical level.

Throughout the book I have argued that there is a move from classical to post-classical private law, from the nation-state to the post-nation-state and that the European experiment is key to understanding how the move is reflected in the post-classical European private law. But this reasoning does not connect the transformation of the state to deeper changes in the intellectual foundations of the state and of private law. My tentative hypothesis is that the move towards the post-classical might be linked to an intellectual current, which is much younger than the Westphalian State and the *lex geometrica*: the ground-breaking shattering of national science and (legal) philosophy in the early twentieth century. Einstein questioned Newton's world of a logical and coherent natural science, and philosophers started to question the philosophical justification of the (nation) state and the understanding of law as a system. One may wonder to what extent – although submerged – this constitutes another strand of European commonality. This strand could help to explain the post-national European consciousness and the deeper intellectual foundations of the post-nation-state and the post-nation-state private (legal) order. In natural sciences the two worlds stand side-by side. In the regulation of financial markets the two strands of natural science have left deep traces in economic theories of financialisation, but not yet in the legal systems.[26] The same might be true for the nation-state, where the old Westphalian state and the new post-nation-state co-exist.

---

[26] J. Vogl, *The Specter of Capital* (Stanford: Stanford University Press, 2015), in particular in contrasting Black-Scholes with Mandelbrot, p. 73; 'new oikodicy' on p. 78 versus 'confused empiricism' on p. 105; and overall the last chapter 'fault zone' on p. 103.

Bibliography

Adams, A., Freedland, M. and Prassl, J. 'The "Zero-Hours Contract": Regulating Casual Work, or Legitimating Precarity?' (2015) *European Labour Law Network Working Paper* No. 5, *Oxford Legal Studies Research Paper* No. 11.

Adams, J. N. and Brownsword, R. 'The Ideologies of Contract' (1987) 7 *Legal Studies* 205–223.

Adams, J. N. and Brownsword, R. *Understanding Contract Law*, 5th edition (London: Sweet & Maxwell, 2007).

Adomeit, K. 'Die gestörte Vertragsparität – ein Trugbild' (1994) 47 *Neue Juristische Wochenschrift* 2467–2469.

Adomeit, K. 'Herbert Marcuse, der Verbraucherschutz und das BGB' (2004) 57 *Neue Juristische Wochenschrift* 579–582.

Ahlberg, K. and N. Bruun (eds.), *The New Foundations of Labour Law* (Frankfurt am Main: Peter Lang 2017)

Alemanno, A. and Sibony, A. -L. (eds.), *Nudge and the Law* (Oxford: Hart Publishing, 2015).

Alexander, C. *Schadensersatz und Abschöpfung im Lauterkeits- und Kartellrecht* (Tübingen: Mohr Siebeck, 2010).

Allio, L. 'On the Smartness of Smart Regulation – A Brief Comment on the Future Reform Agenda' (2011) 2 *European Journal of Risk Regulation* 19–20.

de Almeida, L. 'Integration through Self-Standing European Private Law: Insights from the Internal Point of View to Harmonization in Energy Market', PhD thesis, European University Institute (2017).

Amstutz, M. and Teubner, G. *Networks. Legal Issues of Multilateral Co-operation* (Oxford: Hart Publishing, 2009).

Amtenbrink, F. *The Democratic Accountability of Central Banks: A Comparative Study of the European Central Bank* (Oxford: Hart Publishing, 1999).

Arendt, H. *On Revolution* (New York: Viking Press, 1963).

Aristotle, *The Nicomachean Ethics*, translated and introduced by D. Ross (Oxford: Oxford University Press, 1980).

Armstrong, K. A. 'Civil Society and the White Paper – Bridging or Jumping the Gaps?', in C. Joerges, Y. Mény and J. H. H. Weiler (eds.), 'Mountain or Molehill?

A Critical Appraisal of the Commission White Paper on Governance' (2001) *Jean Monnet Working Paper* No. 6, 119–126.
Armstrong, M. 'The Theory of Access Pricing and Interconnection', in M. E. Cave, S. K. Majumdar and I. Vogelsang (eds.), *Handbook of Telecommunications Economics*, Vol. I (Amsterdam; Boston: Elsevier, 2002), pp. 297–386.
Assmann, H. D., Brüggemeier, G., Hart, D. and Joerges, C. (eds.), *Wirtschaftsrecht als Kritik des Privatrechts* (Königstein, TS: Athenäum, 1980).
Aubin, G. and Bouveresse, J. *Introduction historique au droit du travail* (Paris: Presses Universitaires de France, 1995).
Augenhofer, S. 'Brexit – Marriage 'With' Divorce? – The Legal Consequences for Consumer Law', in Symposium Issue 'EU Law with the UK, EU Law without the UK' (2017) 40 *Fordham International Law Journal*, 1475–1504.
Augenstein, D. (guest editor), Special Issue: 'European Integration in the Shadow of The "Darker Legacies of Law in Europe" Europe's Darker Pasts Revisited' (2006) 7 *German Law Journal* 71–256.
Austin, J. *The Province of Jurisprudence Determined* (London: J. Murray, 1832).
Ayad, P. and Schnell, S. 'Zuständigkeit nationaler Gerichte bei der Durchsetzung international zwingender Regeln' (2012) 39 *Betriebsberater* 3103.
Ayres, I. 'Fair Driving: Gender and Race Discrimination in Retail Car Negotiations' (1991) 104 *Harvard Law Review* 817–872.
Ayres, I. and Schwartz, A. 'The No-Reading Problem in Consumer Contract Law' (2014) 66 *Stanford Law Review* 545–610.
Azoulai, L. 'On the Concepts of Competence and Federal Order of Competences in the EU Legal Order', in L. Azoulai (ed.), *The Question of Competence in the European Union* (Oxford: Oxford University Press, 2014), pp. 1–15.
Azoulai, L. 'The Complex Weave of Harmonisation', in A. Arnull and D. Chalmers (eds.), *The Oxford Handbook of European Union Law* (Oxford: Oxford University Press, 2015), pp. 589–611.
Azoulai, L. 'The Court of Justice and the Social Market Economy: The Emergence of an Ideal and the Conditions for Its Realisation' (2008) 45 *Common Market Law Review* 1335–1355.Backhaus, J. G. and Stephen, F. H. 'The Code of Napoleon after 200 Years' (2002) 14 *European Journal of Law and Economics* 191–192.
Bakardjieva Engelbrekt, A. *Fair Trading Law in Flux? National Legacies and Institutional Choice and the Process of Europeanisation*, PhD thesis, Stockholm University (2003).
Bakos, Y., Marotta-Wurgler, F. and Trossen, D. R. 'Does Anyone Read the Fine Print? Consumer Attention to Standard Form Contracts' (2014) *New York University Law and Economics Research Paper* No. 195.
Baldwin, J. *Small Claims in the County Courts in England and Wales: The Bargain Basement of Civil Justice* (Oxford: Clarendon Press, 1997).
Baldwin, R. and Black, J. 'Really Responsive Regulation' (2007) *LSE Law. Society and Economy Working Paper* No. 15.
Balganesh, S. 'The Obligatory Structure of Copyright Law: Unbundling the Wrong of Copying', Symposium 'The New Private Law', (2012) 125 *Harvard Law Review* 1664–1690.

Baquero Cruz, J. 'Beyond Competition: Services of General Interest and European Community Law', in G. de Búrca (ed.), *EU Law and the Welfare State: In Search of Solidarity* (Oxford: Oxford University Press, 2005), pp. 169-212.

Von Bar, C., Clive, E., Schulte-Nölke, H., Beale, H., Herre, J., Huet, J., Storme, M., Swann, St., Varul, P., Veneziano, A. and Zoll, F. (eds.), *Principles, Definitions and Model Rules of European Private Law. Draft Common Frame of Reference (DCFR)*, prepared by the Study Group on a European Civil Code and the Research Group on EC Private Law (Acquis Group), based in part on a revised version of the Principles of European Contract Law (München: Sellier European Law Publishers, 2009).

Barendrecht, J. M., Jansen, C. E. C., Loos, M. B. M., Pinna, A. P., Cascao, R. M. and van Gulijk, S., *Principles of European law. Service Contracts* (München: Sellier European Law Publishers, 2007).

Barnard, C. *EU Employment Law*, 4th edition (Oxford; New York: Oxford University Press, 2012).

Barnett, C., Cafaro, P. and Newholm, T. 'Philosophy and Ethical Consumption', in R. Harrison, T. Newholm and D. Shaw (eds.), *The Ethical Consumer* (London: Sage Publications, 2005), pp. 11-24.

Bartl, M. 'Internal Market Rationality, Private Law and the Direction of the Union: Resuscitating the Market as the Object of the Political' (2015) 21 *European Law Journal* 572-598.

Bartl, M. 'The Affordability of Energy: How Much Protection for the Vulnerable Consumer?' (2010) 33 *Journal of Consumer Policy* 225-245. Bartolini, S. *The Political*, (London; New York: ECPR Press; Rowman & Littefield, 2018).

Basedow, J. 'Grundsatz der Nichtdiskriminierung im europäischen Privatrecht' (2008) *Zeitschrift für Europäisches Privatrecht* 230-251.

Batura, O. *Universal Service in WTO and EU Law. Liberalisation and Social Regulation in Telecommunications* (The Hague: T.M.C. Asser Press, 2016).

Beck, U. *German Europe* (Cambridge: Polity Press, 2013).

Beckers, A. 'The Regulation of Market Communication and Market Behaviour: Corporate Social Responsibility and the Directives on Unfair Commercial Practices and Unfair Contract Terms' (2017) 54 *Common Market Law Review* 475-515.

Bell, J. D. M. 'Trade Unions', in A. Flanders and H. A. Clegg (eds.), *The System of Industrial Relations in Great Britain: Its History, Law and Institutions* (Oxford: Basil Blackwell, 1954), pp. 128-196.

Bell, M. *Anti-Discrimination Law and the European Union* (Oxford; New York: Oxford University Press, 2002).

Bell, M. 'Constitutionalization and EU Employment Law', in H.-W. Micklitz (ed.), *Constitutionalization of European Private Law* (Oxford: Oxford University Press, 2014), pp. 137-169.

Bell, M. 'The Principle of Equal Treatment: Widening and Deepening', in G. de Búrca and P. Craig (eds.), *The Evolution of EU Law*, 2nd edition (Oxford: Oxford University Press, 2011), pp. 611-639.

Ben-Shahar, O. 'The Myth of the 'Opportunity to Read' in Contract Law' (2009) 5 *European Review of Contract Law* 1–28.

Ben-Shahar, O. 'The Paradox of Access Justice, and Its Application to Mandatory Arbitration' (2016) 83 *The University of Chicago Law Review* 1755–1817.

Bentham, J. *An Introduction to the Principles of Morals and Legislation* (Oxford: Clarendon Press, 1907).

Bercusson, B. *European Labour Law*, 2nd edition (Cambridge: Cambridge University Press, 2009).

Berlin, I. 'Herder and the Enlightenment' in H. Hardy (ed.) *Three Critics of Enlightenment: Vico, Hamann & Herder* (Princeton: Princeton University Press, 2013) pp. 208–300.

Berman, H. J. *Recht und Revolution: Die Bildung der westlichen Rechtstradition*, translated by H. Vetter (Frankfurt: Suhrkamp, 1991).

Bhuta, N. (ed.), *The Frontiers of Human Rights: Extraterritoriality and Its Challenges* (Oxford: Oxford University Press 2016).

Blankenburg, E. and Reifner, U. *Rechtsberatung: Soziale Definition von Rechtsproblemen durch Rechtsberatungsangebote* (Neuwied; Darmstadt: Luchterhand, 1982).

Bloch, E. *Naturrecht und menschliche Würde* (Frankfurt: Suhrkamp, 1961).

Block-Lieb, S. 'The UK and EU Cross-Border Insolvency Recognition: From Empire to Europe to "Going It Alone"', in Symposium Issue 'EU Law with the UK, EU Law without the UK' (2017) 40 *Fordham International Law Journal*, 1373–1412.

Bobbitt, P. *The Shield of Achilles: War, Peace, and the Course of History* (New York: Anchor Books, 2003).

Bobek, M. 'Why There is No Principle of "Procedural Autonomy" of the Member States', in H.-W. Micklitz and B. de Witte (eds.), *The European Court of Justice and the Autonomy of the Member States* (Cambridge; Antwerp: Intersentia, 2012), pp. 305–324.

Bogg, A., Costello, C. and Davies, A. C. L. (eds.), *Research Handbook on EU Labour Law* (Cheltenham: Edward Elgar, 2016).

Bogg, A., Costello, C., Davies, A. C. L. and Prassl, J. (eds.), *The Autonomy of Labour Law* (Oxford: Hart Publishing, 2015).

Bourgoignie, T. *Eléments pour une théorie du droit de la consommation* (Bruxelles: E. Story-Scientia, 1988).

Boysen, U. and Plett, K. *Bauschlichtung in der Praxis* (Düsseldorf: Werner, 2000).

Braun, E. *Collective Alternative Dispute Resolution (ADR) for the Private Enforcement of EU Competition Law*, LLM thesis, European University Institute (2016).

Breton, R. 'Identification in Transnational Political Communities', in K. Knop, S. Ostry, R. Simeon, and K. Swinton (eds.), *Rethinking Federalism. Citizens, Markets, and Governments in a Changing World* (Vancouver: University of British Columbia Press, 1995), pp. 40–58.

Bridenthal, R. 'Beyond Kinder, Küche, Kirche: Weimar Women at Work' (1973) 6 *Central European History* 148–166.

Brönneke, T., Rott, P., Tamm, M. and Tonner, K. (eds.), *Verbraucher und Recht (VuR) – Sonderheft zur Einführung des VSBG* (2016).

Brüggemeier, G. *Entwicklung des Rechts im organisierten Kapitalismus: Band 1. Von der Gründerzeit bis zur Weimarer Republik* (Frankfurt: Syndikat, 1977).
Brüggemeier, G. *Entwicklung des Rechts im organisierten Kapitalismus: Band 2. Vom Faschismus bis zur Gegenwart* (Frankfurt: Syndikat, 1979).
Buddeberg, K. T. 'Descartes und der politische Absolutismus' (1936/37) 30 *Archiv für Rechts- und Sozialphilosophie* 541–560.
de Búrca, G. 'The Trajectories of European and American Antidiscrimination Law' (2012) 60 *American Journal of Comparative Law* 1–22.
Bussière, E., Dumoulin, M. and Schirmann, S. 'The Development of Economic Integration', in W. Loth (ed.), *Experiencing Europe: 50 Years of European Construction 1957–2007* (Baden-Baden: Nomos, 2009), pp. 45–102.
Butenko, A. and Cseres, K. 'The Regulatory Consumer: Prosumer-Driven Local Energy Production Initiatives' (2015) *Amsterdam Law School Legal Studies Research Paper* Nr. 31.
Buzar, S. *Energy Poverty in Eastern Europe: Hidden Geographies of Deprivation* (Aldershot: Ashgate, 2007).
Byberg, R. 'The History of the Integration Through Law Project: Creating the Academic Expression of a Constitutional Legal Vision for Europe' (2017) 18 *German Law Journal* 1531–1556.
Bydlinski, P. 'Die geplante Modernisierung des Verjährungsrechts', in R. Schulze and H. Schulte-Nölke (eds.), *Die Schuldrechtsreform vor dem Hintergrund des Gemeinschaftsrechts* (Tübingen: Mohr Siebeck, 2001), pp. 381–404.
Cafaggi, F. 'Rethinking Private Regulation in the European Regulatory Space', in F. Cafaggi (ed.), *Reframing Self-Regulation in European Private Law* (Alphen aan den Rijn: Kluwer Law International, 2006), pp. 3–75.
Cafaggi, F. 'New Foundations of Transnational Private Regulation' (2011) 38 *Journal of Law and Society* 20–49.
Cafaggi, F. 'Les nouveaux fondements de la régulation transnationale privée' (2013) *Revue Internationale de Droit Economique* 129–161.
Cafaggi, F. 'Does Private Regulation Foster European Legal Integration?', in K. Purnhagen and P. Rott (eds.), *Varieties of European Economic Law and Regulation: Liber Amicorum for Hans Micklitz* (New York: Springer International Publishing, 2014), pp. 259–283.
Cafaggi, F. and Micklitz, H.-W. (eds.), *New Frontiers of Consumer Protection: The Interplay between Private and Public Enforcement* (Antwerp: Intersentia, 2009).
Cafaggi, F. and Muir-Watt, H. (eds.), *Making European Private Law: Governance Design* (Cheltenham: Edward Elgar, 2008).
Cafaggi, F. and Muir-Watt, H. (eds.), *The Regulatory Function of European Private Law* (Cheltenham: Edward Elgar, 2009).
Cairney, P. *The Politics of Evidence-Based Policy Making* (Basingstoke: Palgrave MacMillan, 2017)
Calais-Auloy, J. 'Collectively Negotiated Agreements: Proposed Reforms in France' (1984) 7 *Journal of Consumer Policy* 115–123.

Calais-Auloy, J., Calais-Auloy, M.-T., Maury, J., Bricks, H., Temple, H. and Steinmetz, F. *Consumer Legislation in France* (Wokingham, Berkshire: Van Nostrand Reinhold, 1981).

Calais-Auloy, J. and Temple, H. *Droit de la Consommation*, 9th edition (Paris: Dalloz, 2015).

Calliess, G.-P. *Grenzüberschreitende Verbraucherverträge. Rechtssicherheit und Gerechtigkeit auf dem elektronischen Weltmarktplatz* (Tübingen: Mohr Siebeck, 2006).

Calliess, G.-P. 'Nach der Schuldrechtsreform: Perspektiven des deutschen, europäischen und internationalen Verbrauchervertragsrechts' (2003) 203 *Archiv für die civilistische Praxis* 575–602.

Calliess, G.-P. and Renner, M. 'Between Law and Social Norms: The Evolution of Global Governance' (2009) 22 *Ratio Juris* 260–280.

Calliess, G.-P. and Zumbansen, P., *Rough Consensus and Running Code. A Theory of Transnational Private Law* (Oxford: Hart Publishing, 2010).

Canaris, C.-W. 'Wandlungen des Schuldvertragsrechts – Tendenzen zu seiner „Materialisierung"' (2000) 200 *Archiv für die civilistische Praxis* 273–364.

Canivet, G. and Muir-Watt, H. 'Européanisation du droit privé et justice sociale' (2005) 13 *Zeitschrift für Europäisches Privatrecht* 517–522.

Cantero Gamito, M. 'EU Soft-Law, Internal Market and Private Relationships: The Rise of Executive Power in the EU and the Implementation of the EU Regulatory Framework for Electronic Communications as a Paradigm', in H.-W. Micklitz, Y. Svetiev and G. Comparato (eds.), 'European Regulatory Private Law – The Paradigm Tested' (2014) *EUI-ERC Working Paper* Nr. 4, 41–56.

Cantero Gamito, M. *The Private Law Dimension of the EU Regulatory Framework for Electronic Communications: Evidence of the Self-Sufficiency of European Regulatory Private Law*, PhD thesis, European University Institute (2015).

Cantero Gamito, M. 'Dispute Resolution in Telecommunications: A Commitment to Out-of-Court' (2017) 25 *European Review of Private Law* 387–422.

Caplovitz, D. *The Poor Pay More: Consumer practices of Low Income Families* (New York: The Free Press, 1967).

Cappelletti, M., Seccombe, M. and Weiler, J. H. H. 'Integration Through Law: Europe and the American Federal Experience', in M. Cappelletti, M. Seccombe and J. H. H. Weiler (eds.), *Integration Through Law*, Vol. 1, Book 1 (Berlin: de Gruyter, 1986), pp. 4–68.

Carr, K. 'Regulating the Periphery – Shaking the Core European Identity Building through the Lens of Contract Law' (2015) *EUI Working Paper Law* No. 40.

Cartwright, J., Vogenauer, S., and Whittaker, S. (eds.), *Reforming the French Law of Obligations: Comparative Reflections on the Avant-projet de réforme du droit des obligations et de la prescription ('the Avant-projet Catala')* (Oxford: Hart Publishing, 2009).

Caruso, D. 'Fairness at a Time of Perplexity: The Civil Law Principle of Fairness in the Court of Justice of the European Union', in S. Vogenauer and S. Weatherill (eds.), *General Principles of Law. European and Comparative Perspectives* (Oxford: Hart Publishing, 2017), pp. 329-354.

Caufmann, C. 'The Impact of Article 101 (2)TFEU Nullity on Private Law', in H.-W. Micklitz and C. Sieburgh (eds.), *Primary EU Law and Private Law Concepts* (Cambridge; Antwerp: Intersentia, 2017), pp. 165-206.

Chalmers, D. and Barroso, L. 'What Van Gend en Loos Stands For' (2014) 12 *International Journal of Constitutional Law* 105-134.

Chalmers, D., Jachtenfuchs, M., and Joerges, C. (eds.), *The End of the Eurocrats' Dream: Adjusting to European Diversity* (Cambridge: Cambridge University Press, 2016).

Chalmers, D. and Trotter, S. 'Fundamental Rights and Legal Wrongs: The Two Sides of the Same EU Coin' (2016) 22 *European Law Journal* 9-39.

Cherednychenko, O. O. *Fundamental Rights, Contract Law and the Protection of the Weaker Party: A Comparative Analysis of the Constitutionalisation of the Contract Law, with Emphasis on Risky Financial Transactions* (München: Sellier European Law Publishers, 2007).

Ciacchi, A. C., Brüggemeier, G. and Comandé, G. (eds.), *Fundamental Rights and Private Law in the European Union*, Vol. I and II (Cambridge: Cambridge University Press, 2010).

Clegg, H. A., *The System of Industrial Relations in Great Britain.* (Oxford: Basil Blackwell, 1972)

Clive, E. 'Proposal for a Common European Sales Law Withdrawn' European Private Law News Blog, 7 January 2015, available at: http://www.epln.law.ed.ac.uk/2015/01/07/proposal-for-a-common-european-sales-law-withdrawn/.

Coase, R. 'Discussion' (1964) 54 *American Economic Review* 195-197.

Cohen, G. A. 'Complete Bullshit', in G. A. Cohen (ed.), *Finding Oneself in the Other* (Princeton: Princeton University Press, 2012), pp. 94-114.

Cohen, L. *A Consumers' Republic: The Politics of Mass Consumption in Postwar America* (New York: Knopf, 2003).

Collins, H. 'Against Abstentionism in Labour Law', in J. Eekelaar and J. Bell (eds.), *Oxford Essays in Jurisprudence* (Oxford: Oxford University Press, 1987), pp. 79-101.

Collins, H. 'Book Review: G. Hellringer and K. Purnhagen (eds.), Towards a European Legal Culture (C. H. Beck/Hart/Nomos, 2014)' (2016) 12 *European Review of Contract Law* 72-76.

Collins, H. 'Conformity of Goods, the Network Society and the Ethical Consumer', in D. Leczykiewicz and S. Weatherill (eds.), *The Images of the Consumer in EU Law. Legislation, Free Movement and Competition Law* (Oxford: Hart Publishing, 2016), pp. 305-324.

Collins, H. 'Discrimination, Equality and Social Inclusion' (2003) 66 *The Modern Law Review* 16-43.

Collins, H. *Employment Law*, 2nd edition (Oxford: Oxford University Press, 2010).

Collins, H. 'Good Faith in European Contract Law' (1994) 14 *Oxford Journal of Legal Studies* 229-254.

Collins, H. 'Lord Hoffmann and the Common Law of Contract' (2009) 5 *European Review of Contract Law* 474–484.
Collins, H. *Regulating Contracts* (Oxford; New York: Oxford University Press, 1999).
Collins, H. 'Regulating the Employment Relation for Competitiveness' (2001) 30 *Industrial Law Journal* 17–48.
Collins, H. 'Social Dumping, Multi-level Governance and Private Law in Employment Relationships', in D. Leczykiewicz and S. Weatherill (eds.), *The Involvement of EU Law in Private Law Relationships* (Oxford: Hart Publishing, 2013), pp. 223–253.
Collins, H. (ed.), *Standard Contract Terms in Europe: A Basis for and a Challenge to European Contract Law* (Alphen aan den Rijn: Kluwer Law International, 2008).
Collins, H. 'The Alchemy of Deriving General Principles of Contract Law from European Legislation: In Search of the Philosopher's Stone' (2006) 2 *European Review of Contract Law* 213–226.
Collins, H. 'The Constitutionalization of European Private Law as a Path to Social Justice', in H.-W. Micklitz (ed.), *The Many Concepts of Social Justice in European Private Law* (Cheltenham: Edward Elgar, 2011), pp. 133–166.
Collins, H. 'The Revolutionary Trajectory of EU Contract Law towards Post-national Law', in S. Worthington, A. Robertson and G. Virgo (eds.), *Revolution and Evolution in Private Law* (Oxford: Hart Publishing 2017), pp. 315–336.
Comandé, G. 'The Fifth European Union Freedom. Aggregating Citizenship ... around Private Law', in H.-W. Micklitz (ed.), *Constitutionalization of European Private Law* (Oxford: Oxford University Press, 2014), pp. 61–101.
Comparato, G. *Nationalism and Private Law in Europe* (Oxford: Hart Publishing, 2014).
Comparato, G. 'Public Policy through Private Law: Introduction to a Debate on European Regulatory Private Law' (2016) 22 *European Law Journal* 621–626.
Comparato, G. *The Financialisation of the Citizen: Social and Financial Inclusion through European Private Law* (Oxford: Hart Publishing, 2018).
Comparato, G. and Micklitz, H.-W., Regulated Autonomy between Market Freedoms and Fundamental Rights in the Case Law of the CJEU, in U. Bernitz, X. Groussot and F. Schulyok (eds.), *General Principles of EU Law and European Private Law* (Aldershot: Ashgate 2013), pp. 121–154
Condon, R. *Tort Law beyond the Reasonable Man: Re-Thinking Tort Law beyond the State*, PhD thesis, European University Institute (2017).
Conrad, S. and Randeria, S. 'Geteilte Geschichten: Europa in einer postkolonialen Welt', in S. Conrad and S. Randeria (eds.), *Jenseits des Eurozentrismus: Postkoloniale Perspektiven in den Geschichts- und Kulturwissenschaften* (Frankfurt: Campus Verlag), pp. 9–49.
Constant, B. 'De la Liberté des brochures, des pamphlets et des journaux', in Alfred Roulin (ed.), *Œuvres* (Paris: Gallimard, 1957), pp. 1219–1243.
Countouris, N. 'European Social Law as an Autonomous Legal Discipline' (2009) 28 *Yearbook of European Law* 95–122.

Cousy, H. 'Discrimination in Insurance Law', in R. Schulze (ed.), *Non-Discrimination in European Private Law* (Tübingen: Mohr Siebeck, 2011), pp. 81–108.

Craig, L., Bolster, T. and Chhokar, G. 'Living Up to Expectations? The Consumer Rights Act 2015, a Year On' (2017) 31 *Global Competition Litigation Review* 1–9.

Craig, P. 'Competence and Member State Autonomy: Causality, Consequence and Legitimacy', in H.-W. Micklitz and B. de Witte (eds.), *The European Court of Justice and the Autonomy of the Member States* (Cambridge; Antwerp: Intersentia, 2012), pp. 11–34.

Cremona, M. (ed.), *Market Integration and Public Services in the European Union* (Oxford: Oxford University Press, 2011).

Cremona, M. and Micklitz, H.-W. (eds.), *Private Law in the External Relations of the EU* (Oxford: Oxford University Press, 2016).

Crouch, C. *Can Neoliberalism Be Saved from Itself?* (Social Europe Edition, 2017).

Crouch, C. *The Strange Non-Death of Neo-Liberalism* (Cambridge: Polity Press, 2011).

Cseres, K. J. *Competition Law and Consumer Protection* (The Hague: Kluwer Law International, 2005).

Culver, K. and Giudice, M. 'Not a System but an Order: An Inter-Institutional View of European Union Law', in J. Dickson and P. Eleftheriadis (eds.), *Philosophical Foundations of European Union Law* (Oxford: Oxford University Press, 2012), pp. 54–76.

Dagan, H. 'Between Regulatory and Autonomy-Based Private Law' (2016) 22 *European Law Journal* 644–658.

Dagan, H. and Heller, M. *The Choice Theory of Contracts* (Cambridge; New York: Cambridge University Press, 2017).

v. Dam, C. 'Who Is Afraid of Diversity? Cultural Diversity, European Co-operation, and European Tort Law' (2009) 20 *King's Law Journal* 281–308.

Damaška, M. *The Faces of Justice and State Authority: A Comparative Approach to the Legal Process* (New Haven: Yale University Press, 1986).

Damjanovic, D. and de Witte, B. 'Welfare Integration through EU Law: The Overall Picture in the Light of the Lisbon Treaty', in U. Neergaard, R. Nielsen, L. M. Roseberry (eds.), *Integrating Welfare Functions into EU Law: From Rome to Lisbon* (Copenhagen: Djøf Publishing, 2009), pp. 53–96.

Dani, M. 'Assembling the Fractured European Consumer' (2011) *LSE 'Europe in Question' Discussion Paper Series* (*LEQS Paper*) No. 29.

Darwin, J. *The Empire Project: The Rise and Fall of the British World-System, 1830–1970* (Cambridge; New York: Cambridge University Press, 2009).

Davies, G. 'Freedom of Contract and the Horizontal Effect of Free Movement Law', in D. Leczykiewicz and S. Weatherill (eds.), *The Involvement of EU Law in Private Law Relationships* (Oxford: Hart Publishing, 2013), pp. 53–70.

Davies, G. 'Democracy and Legitimacy in the Shadow of Purposive Competence' (2015) 21 *European Law Journal* 2–22.

Davies, G. 'Social Legitimacy and Purposive Power: The End, the Means and the Consent of the People', in D. Kochenov, G. de Búrca and A. Williams (eds.), *Europe's Justice Deficit?* (Oxford: Hart Publishing, 2015), pp. 259–276.

Davies, J. *The European Consumer Citizen in Law and Policy* (Basingstoke: Palgrave Macmillan, 2011).
Davies, J. 'Consumer Protection in a Normative Context: The Building Blocks of a Consumer Citizenship Practice', in J. Devenney and M. Kenny (eds.), *European Consumer Protection: Theory and Practice* (Cambridge: Cambridge University Press, 2012), pp. 354–377.
Davies, P. and Freedland, M. (eds.), *Kahn-Freund's Labour and the Law*, 3rd edition (London: Stevens, 1983).
Davies, P. and Freedland, M. *Labour Legislation and Public Policy* (Oxford: Clarendon Press, 1993).
Davies, P. and Freedland, M. *Towards a Flexible Labour Market: Labour Legislation and Regulation since the 1990s* (Oxford: Oxford University Press, 2007).
Dawson, M. *New Governance and the Transformation of European Law: Coordinating EU Social Law and Policy* (Cambridge: Cambridge University Press, 2011).
Deakin, S. 'Regulatory Competition after Laval' (2008) 10 *Cambridge Yearbook of European Legal Studies* 581–609.
Deakin, S. and Pistor, K. (eds.), *Legal Origin Theory* (Cheltenham: Edward Elgar, 2012).
Deakin, S. and Wilkinson, F. *The Law of the Labour Market: Industrialization, Employment and Legal Evolution* (Oxford: Oxford University Press, 2005).
Dedek, H. 'When Law Became Cultivated: 'European Legal Culture' between Kultur and Civilization', in G. Helleringer and K. Purnhagen (eds.), *Towards a European Legal Culture* (München; Oxford; Baden-Baden: Beck; Hart; Nomos, 2014), pp. 351–374.
Derleder, P. and Winter, G. 'Die Entschädigung für Contergan' (1976) *Demokratie und Recht* 260–304.
Desautels-Stein, J. and Kennedy, D. 'Foreword: Theorizing Contemporary Legal Thought' (2015) 78 *Law and Contemporary Problems*, i–x.
Deutscher, E. *The Principle of Non-Discrimination in EU Economic Law*, manuscript 2017 on file with author.
Dickie, J. 'Article 7 of the Unfair Terms in Consumer Contracts Directive' (1996) 4 *Consumer Law Journal* 112–117.
Dickson, J. 'Towards a Theory of European Union Legal Systems', in J. Dickson and P. Eleftheriadis (eds.), *Philosophical Foundations of European Union Law* (Oxford: Oxford University Press, 2012), pp. 25–53.
Diez-Sanchez, L. *Justice Index' Eurobarometer and the Issue of Justice. 1990 – 2015*, manuscript 2017, on file with the author.
Domurath, I. 'The Case for Vulnerability as the Normative Standard in European Consumer Credit and Mortgage Law: An Inquiry into the Paradigms of Consumer Law' (2013) 2 *Journal of European Consumer and Market Law* 124–137.
Domurath, I. *Consumer Vulnerability and Welfare in Mortgage Contracts* (Oxford: Hart Publishing, 2017).
Dougan, M. 'Minimum Harmonisation after Tobacco Advertising and Laval Un Partneri', in M. Bulterman, L. Hancher, A. McDonnell and H. Sevenster (eds.),

Views of European Law from the Mountain: Liber Amicorum Piet Jan Slot (The Hague: Kluwer Law International, 2009), pp. 3-18.

Douglas-Scott, S. 'Justice, Injustice and the Rule of Law in the EU', in D. Kochenov, G. de Búrca and A. Williams (eds.), *Europe's Justice Deficit?* (Oxford: Hart Publishing, 2015), pp. 51-66.

Drechsler, W. 'On the Viability of the Concept of Staatswissenschaften' (2001) 12 *European Journal of Law and Economics* 105-111.

Drexl, J. 'Wettbewerbsverfassung', in A. v. Bogdandy and J. Bast (eds.), *Europäisches Verfassungsrecht*, 2nd edition (Berlin: Springer, 2009), pp. 905-960.

Drexl, J. 'La Constitution économique européenne—L'actualité du modèle ordolibéral' (2011) *Revue internationale de droit économique* 419-454.

Duguit, L. *La Transformation Générales du Droit Privé depuis le Code Napoléon* (Paris: Alcan, 1912).

Dukes, R. *The Labour Constitution: The Enduring Idea of Labour Law* (Oxford: Oxford University Press, 2014).

Dupont-White, C. *L'individu et l'État* (Paris: Guillaumin, 1865).

Durovic, M. *European Law on Unfair Commercial Practices and Contract Law* (Oxford: Hart Publishing, 2016).

Durovic, M. 'The Apple Case Today: Factual and Legal Assessment' (2016) *EUI Working Paper EUI-ERC* No. 3.

Dürr, H.-P. (ed.), *Physik und Transzendenz. Die Großen Physiker unserer Zeit über ihre Begegnung mit dem Wunderbaren* (Bern et al.: Scherz, 1986) (Bad Essen: Driediger, 2010).

Dworkin, R. *Law's Empire* (Cambridge, MA: Harvard University Press, 1986).

Eckhoff, L. 'Gerichtsstandsvereinbarung, die zum Ausschluss des Handelsvertreterausgleichsanspruchs führt, ist unwirksam' (2012) *Gesellschafts- und Wirtschaftsrecht* 486.

Eichengreen, B. *The European Economy since 1945: Coordinated Capitalism and Beyond* (Princeton: Princeton University Press, 2008).

Eidenmüller, H. 'Ökonomik der Verjährungsregeln', in R. Schulze and H. Schulte-Nölke (eds.), *Die Schuldrechtsreform vor dem Hintergrund des Gemeinschaftsrechts* (Tübingen: Mohr Siebeck, 2001), pp. 405-415.

Eidenmüller, H., Faust, F., Grigoleit, H. C., Jansen, N., Wagner, G. and Zimmermann, R. 'The Common Frame of Reference for European Private Law – Policy Choices and Codification Problems' (2008) 28 *Oxford Journal of Legal Studies* 659-708.

Eidmann, D. *Schlichtung:s Zur Logik außergerichtlicher Konfliktregelung* (Baden-Baden: Nomos, 1994).

Eliassen, K. A. and From, J. (eds.), *The Privatisation of European Telecommunications* (Aldershot: Ashgate, 2007).

Eliassen, K. A. and From, J. 'Deregulation, Privatisation and Public Service Delivery: Universal Service in Telecommunications in Europe' (2009) 27 *Policy and Society* 239-248.

Eliassen, K. A. and Sjovaag, M. (eds.), *European Telecommunications Liberalisation* (London; New York: Routledge, 1999).

Esser, J. *Vorverständnis und Methodenwahl in der Rechtsfindung* (Frankfurt: Athenäum, 1970).
Everson, M. 'The Legacy of the Market Citizen', in J. Shaw and G. More (eds.), *New Legal Dynamics of European Union* (Oxford: Clarendon Press, 1995), pp. 73–90.
Everson, M. and Joerges, C. 'Consumer Citizenship in Postnational Constellations?' (2006) *EUI Working Paper Law* No. 47.
Ewald, F. *L'Etat providence* (Paris: Grasset, 1986).
Fabre-Magnan, M. 'What Is a Modern Law of Contracts? Elements for a New Manifesto for Social Justice in European Contract Law', (2017), 15 *European Review of Contract Law*, pp. 376–388.
Fauvarque-Cosson, B. 'Faut-il un code civil européen?' (2002) *Revue Trimestrielle De Droit Civil* 463–480.
Fauvarque-Cosson, B. 'Droit européen des contrats: première réaction au plan d'action de la Commission' (2003) *Recueil Le Dalloz* 1171–1173.
Fauvarque-Cosson, B. and Kerhuel, A.-J. 'Is Law an Economic Contest? French Reactions to the Doing Business World Bank Reports and Economic Analysis of the Law' (2009) 57 *American Journal of Comparative Law* 811–830.
Fauvarque-Cosson, B. and Mazeaud, D. (eds.), *European Contract Law: Materials for a Common Frame of Reference: Terminology, Guiding Principles, Model Rules* (München: Sellier European Law Publishers, 2008).
Fehrenbach, E. 'Der Einfluß des Code Napoléon auf das Rechtsbewußtsein in den Ländern des rheinischen Rechts', in J. Jurt, G. Krumeich and T. Würtenberger (eds.), *Wandel von Recht und Rechtsbewußtsein in Frankreich und Deutschland* (Berlin: Berlin-Verlag Spitz, 1999), pp. 133–142.
Feld, L. P., Fuest, C., Haucap, J., Schweitzer, H., Wieland, V. and Wigger, B. U. (Kronberger Kreis), 'Das entgrenzte Mandat der EZB. Das OMT-Urteil des EuGH und seine Folgen' (2016) 61 *Stiftung Marktwirtschaft*.
Finck, M. and Kas, B. 'Surrogacy Leave as a Matter of EU Law: CD and Z' (2015) 52 *Common Market Law Review* 281–298.
Flaig, E. *Die Niederlage der politischen Vernunft: Wie wir die Errungenschaften der Aufklärung verspielen* (Springe: zu Klampen, 2017).
Flanders, A. and Clegg, H. A. (eds.), *The System of Industrial Relations in Great Britain: Its History, Law and Institutions* (Oxford: Basil Blackwell, 1954).
Flume, W. 'Vom Beruf unserer Zeit für die Gesetzgebung' (2000) *Zeitschrift für Wirtschaftsrecht* 1427–1430.
Forst, R. 'Justice, Democracy and the Right to Justification: Reflections on Jürgen Neyer's Normative Theory of the European Union', in D. Kochenov, G. de Búrca and A. Williams (eds.), *Europe's Justice Deficit?* (Oxford: Hart Publishing, 2015), pp. 227–234.
Fraenkel, E. *Zur Soziologie der Klassenjustiz* (Berlin: E. Laub, 1927).
Frank, R. *La hantise du déclin: La France de 1914 à 2014* (Paris: Belin, 2014).
Freedland, M. 'Otto Kahn-Freund, the Contract of Employment and the Autonomy of Labour Law', in A. Bogg, C. Costello, A. C. L. Davies and J. Prassl (eds.), *The Autonomy of Labour Law* (Oxford: Hart Publishing, 2015), pp. 29–44.

Freedland, M. and Prassl, J. (eds.), *Viking, Laval and Beyond* (Oxford: Hart Publishing, 2014).
Frerichs, S. *Judicial Governance in der Europäischen Rechtsgemeinschaft* (Baden-Baden: Nomos, 2008).
Fuller, L. L. *The Morality of the Law* (New Haven: Yale University Press, 1964).
Gal, M. S. and Elkin-Koren, N. 'Algorithmic Consumers' (2017) 30 *Harvard Journal of Law and Technology* 309–353.
Galanter, M. 'Why the Haves Come out Ahead: Speculations on the Limits of Legal Change' (1974) 9 *Law and Society Review* 95–160, reprinted (with corrections) in R. Cotterrell (ed.), *Law and Society* (Aldershot: Dartmouth, 1994), pp. 165–230.
Galbraith, J. K. *The Affluent Society* (London: Hamish Hamilton, 1958).
Gaudemet, E. *L'interprétation du code civil en France depuis 1804* (Bâle: Helbing et Lichtenhahn; Paris: Sirey, 1935).
Gelter, M. and Reif, A. M. 'What is Dead May Never Die: The UK's Influence on EU Company Law', in Symposium Issue 'EU Law with the UK, EU Law without the UK' (2017) 40 *Fordham International Law Journal*, 1413–1442.
Gény, F. *Méthode d'Interprétation et Sources en Droit Privé Positif*, 2nd edition (Paris: Librairie générale de droit et de jurisprudence, 1919).
Gerber, D. 'Constitutionalizing the Economy: German Neo-Liberalism, Competition Law and the 'New' Europe' (1994) 42 *American Journal of Comparative Law* 25–84.
Gerstenberg, O. 'The Question of Standards for the EU: From 'Democratic Deficit' to 'Justice Deficit?'', in D. Kochenov, G. de Búrca and A. Williams (eds.), *Europe's Justice Deficit?* (Oxford: Hart Publishing, 2015), pp. 67–78.
v. Gerven, W. 'Of Rights, Remedies and Procedures' (2000) 37 *Common Market Law Review* 501–536.
v. Gerven, W. 'Needed: A Method of Convergence for Private Law', in A. Furrer (ed.), *Europäisches Privatrecht im wissenschaftlichen Diskurs* (Bern: Stämpfli, 2006), pp. 437–460.
v. Gestel, R. and v. Golen, Th. 'Enforcement by the New Supervisory Agencies: Quis Custodiet Ipsos Custodes?' in K. Purnhagen/P. Rott (eds.), *Varieties of European Economic Law and Regulation: Liber Amicorum for Hans Micklitz*, (New York: Springer International Publishing, 2014), pp. 757–780.
v. Gestel, R. and Micklitz, H.-W. 'Why Methods Matter in European Legal Scholarship' (2014) 20 *European Law Journal* 292–316.
v. Gierke, O. *Die soziale Aufgabe des Privatrechts: Vortrag gehalten am 5. April 1889 in der juristischen Gesellschaft zu Wien* (Berlin: Springer, 1889).
Glinki, C., and Joerges, C. 'European Unity in Diversity?! A Conflicts-Law Reconstruction of Controversial Current Developments', in K. Purnhagen/ P. Rott (eds.), *Varieties of European Economic Law and Regulation: Liber Amicorum for Hans Micklitz* (New York: Springer International Publishing, 2014), pp. 285–314.

Glinski, C., and Rott, P. 'Umweltfreundliches und ethisches Konsumverhalten im harmonisierten Kaufrecht' (2003) *Europäische Zeitschrift für Wirtschaftsrecht* 649–654.

Lord Goff, 'The Future of the Common Law' (1997) 46 *International and Comparative Law Quarterly* 745–761.

Goldberg, J. 'Introduction: Pragmatism and Private Law' (2012) 125 *Harvard Law Review* 1640–1663.

Goode, R. 'Insularity or Leadership? The Role of the United Kingdom in the Harmonisation of Commercial Law' (2001) 50 *International and Comparative Law Quarterly* 751–765.

Gormley, L. 'Access to Justice and Public Interest Litigation: Getting Nowhere Quickly?' in K. Purnhagen and P. Rott (eds.), *Varieties of European Economic Law and Regulation: Liber Amicorum for Hans Micklitz*, (New York: Springer International Publishing, 2014), pp. 793–822.

Greenberg, U. *The Weimar Century: German Émigrés and the Ideological Foundations of the Cold War* (Princeton: Princeton University Press, 2014).

Griggs, L. 'The Consumer with an Intellectual Disability – Do We Respond, If So, How?' (2013) 21 *Competition and Consumer Law Journal* 146–164.

Grimm, D. *Solidarität als Rechtsprinzip* (Frankfurt: Athenäum-Verlag, 1973).

Grossmann-Doerth, H. *Selbstgeschaffenes Recht der Wirtschaft und staatliches Recht* (Freiburg: Wagner'sche Univ. Buchh., 1933).

Grundmann, S. 'The Bankinter Case on MIFID Regulation and Contract Law' (2013) 9 *European Review of Contract Law* 267–280.

Grundmann, S. 'Europäisches Wirtschaftsrecht im Wandel – von der Wettbewerbsunion zur Finanzunion', in B. Limperg, J. Bormann, A. C. Filges, M. L. Graf-Schlicker and H. Prütting (eds.), *Recht im Wandel deutscher und europäischer Rechtspolitik: Festschrift 200 Jahre Carl Heymanns Verlag* (Köln: Carl Heymanns Verlag, 2015), pp. 193–209.

Grundmann, S., Cafaggi, F. and Vettori, G. (eds.), *The Organisational Contract: From Exchange to Long-Term Network Cooperation in European Contract Law* (Abingdon, Oxon: Routledge, 2013).

Grundmann, S., Micklitz, H.-W. and Renner, M. (eds.), *Privatrechtstheorie*, Vol. I and II (Tübingen: Mohr Siebeck, 2015).

Grundmann, S., Möslein, F. and Riesenhuber, K. (eds.), *Contract Governance: Dimensions in Law and Interdisciplinary Research* (Oxford: Oxford University Press, 2015).

Gutman, K. 'The Commission's 2010 Green Paper on European Contract Law: Reflections on Union Competence in Light of the Proposed Options' (2011) 7 *European Review of Contract Law* 151–172.

Haar, B. P. T. and Copeland, P. 'What Are the Future Prospects for the European Social Model? An Analysis of EU Equal Opportunities and Employment Policy' (2010) 16 *European Law Journal* 273–291.

Habermas, J. *Faktizität und Geltung* (Frankfurt: Suhrkamp, 1992).

Habermas, J. 'Staatsbürgerschaft und nationale Identität', in J. Habermas, *Faktizität und Geltung* (Frankfurt: Suhrkamp, 1992), pp. 632–660.

Habermas, J. *The Lure of Technocracy* (Cambridge: Polity Press, 2015).
Halfmeier, A. *Popularklagen im Privatrecht* (Tübingen: Mohr Siebeck, 2006).
Hallstein, W. *Der unvollendete Bundesstaat* (Düsseldorf; Wien: ECON, 1969).
Hallstein, W. *Europe in the Making*, translated by C. Roetter (London: George Allen & Unwin Ltd, 1972).
Hancock, A.-M. *Intersectionality: An Intellectual History* (New York: Oxford University Press, 2016).
Hart, D. *Allgemeine Geschäftsbedingungen und Justizsystem* (Kronberg: Scriptor-Verlag, 1975).
Hart, D. 'Substantive and Reflective Elements in Modern Contract Law', in T. Bourgoignie (ed.), *Unfair Terms in Consumer Contracts* (Louvain-la-Neuve; Brussels: Cabay; Brulant: 1983), 3-32.
Haselbach, D. *Autoritärer Liberalismus und Soziale Marktwirtschaft: Gesellschaft und Politik im Ordoliberalismus* (Baden-Baden: Nomos, 1991).
Haupt, H.-G. *Sozialgeschichte Frankreichs seit 1789* (Frankfurt: Suhrkamp, 1989).
Haupt, H.-G. 'Sozialpolitik und ihre gesellschaftlichen Grenzen in Frankreich vor 1914', in *Jahrbuch für Wirtschaftsgeschichte* (Berlin: Akademie Verlag, 1995), pp. 171-192.
Haupt, H.-G. and Torp, Co. (eds.), *Die Konsumgesellschaft in Deutschland 1890-1990: Ein Handbuch* (Frankfurt; New York: Campus Verlag, 2009).
Hazareesingh, S. *How the French Think: An Affectionate Portrait of an Intellectual People*. (London: Allen Lane, Penguin Random House, 2015).
Hedemann, J.-W. *Die Fortschritte des Zivilrechts im XIX. Jahrhundert: Ein Überblick über die Entfaltung des Privatrechts in Deutschland, Österreich, Frankreich und der Schweiz. Erster Teil. Die Neuordnung des Verkehrslebens*, Vol. I (Berlin: Heymann, 1910).
Heiderhoff, B. *Europäisches Privatrecht* (Heidelberg: C. F. Müller, 2004).
Heiderhoff, B. *Grundstrukturen des nationalen und europäischen Verbrauchervertragsrechts: insbesondere zur Reichweite europäischer Auslegung* (München: Sellier European Law Publishers, 2004).
v. d. Heijden, P. 'Post-Industrial Labour Law and Industrial Relations in The Netherlands', in Lord Wedderburn, M. Rood, G. Lyon-Caen, W. Däubler and P. van der Heijden (eds.), *Labour Law in the Post-industrial Era: Essays in honour of Hugo Sinzheimer* (Aldershot: Dartmouth, 1994), pp. 133-148.
Heinig, H. M. *Der Sozialstaat im Dienst der Freiheit* (Tübingen: Mohr Siebeck, 2008).
Helleringer, G. and Purnhagen, K. (eds.), *Towards a European Legal Culture* (München; Oxford; Baden-Baden: Beck; Hart; Nomos, 2014).
Hepple, B. (ed.), *The Making of Labour Law in Europe: A Comparative Study of Nine Countries up to 1945* (London: Mansell Publishing, 1986).
Hepple, B. 'Introduction', in B. Hepple (ed.), *The Making of Labour Law in Europe: A Comparative Study of Nine Countries up to 1945* (London: Mansell Publishing, 1986), pp. 1-30.
Hepple, B. 'Welfare Legislation and Wage-Labour', in B. Hepple (ed.), *The Making of Labour Law in Europe: A Comparative Study of Nine Countries up to 1945* (London: Mansell Publishing, 1986), pp. 114-153.

Hepple, B. and Veneziani, B. (eds.), *The Transformation of Labour Law in Europe: A Comparative Study of 15 Countries 1945–2004* (Oxford: Hart Publishing, 2009).
Hepple, B. and Veneziani, B. 'Introduction', in B. Hepple and B. Veneziani (eds.), *The Transformation of Labour Law in Europe: A Comparative Study of 15 Countries 1945–2004* (Oxford: Hart Publishing, 2009), pp. 1–29.
Hepple, B. 'Equality at Work', in B. Hepple and B. Veneziani (eds.), *The Transformation of Labour Law in Europe*: *A Comparative Study of 15 Countries 1945–2004* (Oxford: Hart Publishing, 2009), pp. 129–164.
Héritier, A. 'Market Integration and Social Cohesion: The Politics of Public Services in European Regulation' (2001) 8 *Journal of European Public Policy* 825–852.
Herzog, R. and Gerken, L. 'Stop the European Court of Justice', *euobserver*, 10. 9.2008, available at: https://euobserver.com/opinion/26714, the same 'Stoppt den Europäischen Gerichtshof', *Frankfurter Allgemeine Zeitung*, 8. 9.2008, p. 8.
Hesselink, M. W. 'The Politics of a European Civil Code' (2004) 10 *European Law Journal* 675–697.
Hesselink, M. W. 'SMEs in European Contract Law', in K. Boele-Woelki and F. W. Grosheide (eds.), *The Future of European Contract Law* (The Hague: Kluwer Law International, 2007), pp. 349–372.
Hesselink, M. W. *CFR & Social Justice: A Short Study for the European Parliament on the Values Underlying the Draft Common Frame of Reference for European Private Law: What Roles for Fairness and Social Justice?* (München: Sellier European Law Publishers, 2008).
Hesselink, M. W. 'Pluralism in a New Key – Between Plurality and Normativity', in L. Niglia (ed.), *Pluralism and European Private Law* (Oxford: Hart Publishing, 2013), pp. 249–260.
Hesselink, M. W. 'Post-Private Law?', in K. Purnhagen and P. Rott (eds.), *Varieties of European Economic Law and Regulation: Liber Amicorum for Hans Micklitz* (New York: Springer International Publishing, 2014), pp. 31–42.
Hesselink, M. W. 'Private Law, Regulation and Justice' (2016) 22 *European Law Journal* 681–695.
Hesselink, M. W. 'Unjust Conduct in the Internal Market: On the Role of European Private Law in the Division of Moral Responsibility between the EU, Its Member States and their Citizens' (2016) 35 *Yearbook of European Law* 410–452.
Heut, J. 'Nous faut-il un 'euro' droit civil?' (2002) *Receuil Le Dalloz* 2611–2614.
Heywood, C. *The Development of the French Economy, 1750–1914* (Cambridge: Cambridge University Press, 1995).
Hinterhuber, E. M. and Vasterling, V. 'Gender and Diversity Studies in European Perspectives: International conference, 8–10 January 2015, Rhine-Waal University of Applied Sciences, Kleve' (2015) 7 *Gender: Zeitschrift für Geschlecht, Kultur und Gesellschaft* 136–142.
v. Hippel, E. *Verbraucherschutz*, 3rd edition (Tübingen: Mohr, 1986).
Hodges, C. *The Reform of Class and Representative Actions in European Legal Systems: A New Framework for Collective Redress in Europe* (Oxford: Hart Publishing, 2008).

Hodges, C., Benöhr, I. and Creutzfeldt, N. *Consumer ADR in Europe* (Oxford: Hart Publishing, 2012)

Hodges, C. 'Collective Redress: A Breakthrough or a Damp Squib?' (2014) 34 *Journal of Consumer Policy* 67–89.

Höffe, O. *Gerechtigkeit: Eine philosophische Einführung* (München: C.H. Beck, 2001).

Höffe, O. 'Soziale Gerechtigkeit: Über die Bedingungen realer Freiheit' (2005) *Neue Zürcher Zeitung* 67.

Lord Hoffmann, 'The Universality of Human Rights', Judicial Studies Board Annual Lecture 19 March 2009, available at: https://www.judiciary.gov.uk/announcements/speech-by-lord-hoffmann-the-universality-of-human-rights/.

Hoffmann, S. 'Paradoxes of the French Political Community', in S. Hoffmann, C. P. Kindleberger, L. W. Wylie, J. R. Pitts, J.-B. Duroselle and F. Goguel (eds.), *In Search of France* (Cambridge, MA: Harvard University Press, 1963), pp. 1–117.

Hondius, E. 'The Protection of the Weak Party in a Harmonised European Contract Law: A Synthesis' (2004) 27 *Journal of Consumer Policy* 245–251.

Hondius, E. 'Against a New Architecture of Consumer Law – A Traditional View', in K. Purnhagen and P. Rott (eds.), *Varieties of European Economic Law and Regulation: Liber Amicorum for Hans Micklitz* (New York: Springer International Publishing, 2014), pp. 599–610.

Hondius, E. and Janssen, A. (eds.), *Disgorgement of Profits: Gain-Based Remedies throughout the World* (Cham: Springer, 2015).

Honsell, H. 'Die Erosion des Privatrechts durch das Europarecht' (2008) *Zeitschrift für Wirtschaftsrecht (ZIP)* 621–630.

Höpner, M. and Schäfer, A. 'Embeddedness and Regional Integration: Waiting for Polanyi in a Hayekian Setting' (2012) 66 *International Organization* 429–455.

Horwitz, M. J. 'Republicanism and Liberalism in American Constitutional Thought' (1987) 29 *William & Mary Law Review* 57–74.

Hosemann, E. G. '"The New Private Law": Die neue amerikanische Privatrechtswissenschaft in historischer und vergleichender Perspektive' (2014) 78 *Rabels Zeitschrift für ausländisches und internationales Privatrecht* 37–70.

Howells, G., Micklitz, H.-W. and Wilhelmsson, T. *European Fair Trading Law: The Unfair Commercial Practices Directive* (Aldershot: Ashgate, 2006).

Howells, G. and Schulze, R. (eds.), *Modernising and Harmonising Consumer Contract Law* (München: Sellier European law Publishers, 2009).

Howells, G., Twigg-Flesner, C. and Wilhelmsson, T. *Rethinking European Consumer Law* (Abingdon: Routledge, 2017).

Howells, G. and Weatherill, S. *Consumer Protection Law* (Aldershot: Ashgate, 2005).

Jäckel, E. *Das deutsche Jahrhundert: Eine historische Bilanz* (Stuttgart: Deutsche Verlags-Anstalt, 1996).

Jacobs, A. 'Collective Self-Regulation', in B. Hepple (ed.), *The Making of Labour Law in Europe: A Comparative Study of Nine Countries up to 1945* (London: Mansell Publishing, 1986), pp. 193–240.

Jaggi, S. *The 1989 Revolution in East Germany and Its Impact on Unified Germany's Constitutional Law: The Forgotten Revolution?* (Baden-Baden: Nomos, 2016).

Jagielska, M. and Jagielski, M. 'Are Consumer Rights Human Rights?', in J. Devenney and M. Kenny (eds.), *European Consumer Protection: Theory and Practice* (Cambridge: Cambridge University Press, 2012), pp. 336–353.

Jakab, A. and Kochenov, D. (eds.), *Enforcement of EU Law and Values* (Oxford: Oxford University Press, 2017).

James, H. *A German Identity 1770–1990* (New York: Routledge, 1989); (Frankfurt: Campus-Verlag, 1991).

James, H. 'Monetary and Fiscal Unification in Nineteenth-Century Germany: What Can Kohl Learn from Bismarck?' (1997) *Princeton Essays in International Finance* 2–38.

James, L. *The Rise and Fall of the British Empire* (London: Little Brown, 1994).

Jansen, N. 'Klauselkontrolle im Europäischen Privatrecht' (2010) *Zeitschrift für europäisches Privatrecht* 69–106.

Jansen, N. *The Making of Legal Authority: Non-Legislative Codifications in Historical and Comparative Perspective* (Oxford: Oxford University Press, 2010).

Jasper, G. 'Improvisierte Demokratie? Die Entstehung der Weimarer Verfassung', in T. Stammen (ed.), *Die Weimarer Republik. Band I – 1918-23: Das schwere Erbe* (München: Bayerische Landeszentrale für Politische Bildungsarbeit, 1992), pp. 117–146.

Jestaedt, M. 'Phänomen Bundesverfassungsgericht: Was das Gericht zu dem macht, was es ist', in M. Jestaedt, O. Lepsius, C. Möllers and C. Schönberger, *Das entgrenzte Gericht: Eine kritische Bilanz nach sechzig Jahren Bundesverfassungsgericht* (Berlin: Suhrkamp, 2011), pp. 77–158.

Jestaedt, M., Lepsius, O., Möllers, C. and Schönberger, C. *Das entgrenzte Gericht: Eine kritische Bilanz nach sechzig Jahren Bundesverfassungsgericht* (Berlin: Suhrkamp, 2011).

Joerges, C. *Verbraucherschutz als Rechtsproblem* (Heidelberg: Verlagsgesellschaft Recht und Wirtschaft, 1981).

Joerges, C. 'Die Europäisierung des Privatrechts als Rationalisierungsprozess und als Streit der Disziplinen' (1995) *Zeitschrift für Europäisches Privatrecht* 181–201.

Joerges, C. 'On the Legitimacy of Europeanising Private Law: Considerations on a Law of Justi(ce)-fication (Justum Facere) for the EU Multi-Level System', in A. Hartkamp, M. W. Hesselink, E. Hondius, C. Joustra, E. du Perron and M. Veldman (eds.), *Towards a European Civil Code*, 3rd edition (Alphen aan den Rijn: Kluwer Law International; Nijmegen: Ars Aequi Libri, 2004), pp. 159–190.

Joerges, C. 'Der Europäisierungsprozess als Herausforderung des Privatrechts: Plädoyer für eine neue Rechtsdisziplin', in A. Furrer (ed.), *Europäisches Privatrecht im wissenschaftlichen Diskurs* (Bern: Stämpfli, 2006), pp. 133–188.

Joerges, C. 'Integration through De-Legalisation? An Irritated Heckler' (2007) *European Governance Papers (EUROGOV)* No. N-07-03.

Joerges, C. 'A Renaissance of the European Economic Constitution', in U. Neergaard, R. Nielsen, L. M. Roseberry (eds.), *Integrating Welfare Functions into EU Law: From Rome to Lisbon* (Copenhagen: Djøf Publishing, 2009), pp. 42–52.

Joerges, C., Falke, J., Micklitz, H.-W. and Brüggemeier, G. *Die Sicherheit von Konsumgütern und die Entwicklung der Europäischen Gemeinschaft* (Baden-Baden: Nomos, 1988).

Joerges, C., Falke, J., Micklitz, H.-W. and Brüggemeier, G. 'European Product Safety, Internal Market Policy and the New Approach to Technical Harmonisation and Standards' (1991) *EUI Working Paper Law* No. 10-14; (2010) 6 *Hanse Law Review* 109.

Joerges, C. and Ghaleigh, N. S. (eds.) *Darker Legacies of Law in Europe: The Shadow of National Socialism and Fascism over Europe and its Legal Traditions* (Oxford: Hart Publishing, 2003).

Joerges, C., Mény, Y. and Weiler, J. H. H. (eds.), 'Mountain or Molehill? A Critical Appraisal of the Commission White Paper on Governance' (2001) *Jean Monnet Working Paper* No. 6.

Joerges, C. and Ralli, T. (eds.), 'European Constitutionalism without Private Law – Private Law without Democracy' (2011) *RECON Report* No. 14, *ARENA Report* No. 3.

Joerges, C. and Rödl, F. 'À propos de l'évolution fonctionnelle du droit des conflits de lois II: une constitution légitime pour la constellation post-nationale' (2013) *Revue Internationale de Droit Economique* 79-93.

Joerges, C. and Teubner, G. (eds.), *Rechtsverfassungsrecht – Recht-Fertigung zwischen Privatrechtsdogmatik und Gesellschaftstheorie* (Baden-Baden: Nomos, 2003).

Johnston, A. 'Seeking the EU 'Consumer' in Services of General Economic Interest', in D. Leczykiewicz and S. Weatherill (eds.), *The Images of the Consumer in EU Law: Legislation, Free Movement and Competition Law* (Oxford: Hart Publishing, 2016), pp. 93-138.

Josserand, L. 'L'évolution de la responsabilité (conférence donnée aux Facultés de Droit de Lisbonne, de Coimbre, de Belgrade, de Bucarest, d'Orades, de Bruxells, à l'institut français de Madrid, aux centres juridiques de L'Institut des Hautes Études marocaines à Rabat et á Casablanca)', in L. Josserand (ed.), *Évolutions et Actualités. Conférences de Droit Civil* (Paris: Recueil Sirey, 1936), chapter 29, section 5.

Jurt, J. 'Die Rolle der Nationalsymbole in Deutschland und Frankreich', in J. Jurt, G. Krumeich and T. Würtenberger (eds.), *Wandel von Recht und Rechtsbewußtsein in Frankreich und Deutschland* (Berlin: Berlin-Verlag Spitz, 1999), pp. 67-90.

Kahn-Freund, O. 'Legal Framework', in A. Flanders and H. A. Clegg (eds.), *The System of Industrial Relations in Great Britain: Its History, Law and Institutions* (Oxford: Basil Blackwell, 1954), pp. 42-127.

Karanikic, M., Micklitz, H.-W. and Reich, N. (eds.), *Modernising Consumer Law: The Experience of the Western Balkan* (Baden-Baden: Nomos, 2012).

Kas, B. *'Hybrid' Collective Remedies in the EU Social Legal Order*, PhD thesis, European University Institute (2017).

Kelemen, D. *Eurolegalism: The Transformation of Law and Regulation in the European Union* (Cambridge, MA: Harvard University Press, 2011).

Kennedy, D. 'Two Globalizations of Law & Legal Thought: 1850-1968' (2003) 36 *Suffolk University Law Review* 631-679.

Kennedy, D. 'The Rule of Law, Political Choices and Developing Common Sense', in D. M. Trubek and A. Santos (eds.), *The New Law and Economic Development: A Critical Appraisal* (Cambridge; New York: Cambridge University Press, 2006), pp. 95-173.

Kennedy, D. 'Thoughts on Coherence, Social Values and National Traditions in Private Law', in M. W. Hesselink (ed.), *The Politics of a European Civil Code* (The Hague: Kluwer, 2006), pp. 9-31.

Kennedy, D. 'Three Globalizations of Law and Legal Thought: 1850-2000', in D. M. Trubek and A. Santos (eds.), *The New Law and Economic Development: A Critical Appraisal* (Cambridge; New York: Cambridge University Press, 2006), pp. 19-73.

Kennedy, D. 'A Transnational Genealogy of Proportionality in Private Law', in R. Brownsword, H.-W. Micklitz, L. Niglia and S. Weatherill (eds.), *The Foundations of European Private Law* (Oxford: Hart Publishing, 2011), pp. 185-220.

Kessler, F. 'Contracts of Adhesion: Some Thoughts about Freedom of Contract' (1943) 43 *Columbia Law Review* 629-642.

Keßler, J. and Micklitz, H.-W. *Kundenschutz auf liberalisierten Märkten. Energie. Vergleich der Konzepte, Maßnahmen und Wirkungen in Europa* (Baden-Baden: Nomos, 2008).

Keßler, J. and Micklitz, H.-W. *Kundenschutz auf liberalisierten Märkten. Personenverkehr/Eisenbahn. Vergleich der Konzepte, Maßnahmen und Wirkungen in Europa* (Baden-Baden: Nomos, 2008).

Keßler, J. and Micklitz, H.-W. *Kundenschutz auf liberalisierten Märkten. Telekommunikation. Vergleich der Konzepte, Maßnahmen und Wirkungen in Europa* (Baden-Baden: Nomos, 2008).

Kiesow, R. M. 'Rechtswissenschaft – was ist das?' (2010) 65 *JuristenZeitung* 586-591.

Kingsbury, B., Krisch, N. and Stewart, R. B. 'L'émergence du droit administratif global' (2013) *Revue Internationale de Droit Economique* 37-58.

Kochenov, D. 'The Ought of Justice', in D. Kochenov, G. de Búrca and A. Williams (eds.), *Europe's Justice Deficit?* (Oxford: Hart Publishing, 2015), pp. 21-33.

Kochenov, D., de Búrca, G. and Williams, A. (eds.), *Europe's Justice Deficit?* (Oxford: Hart Publishing, 2015).

Kocher, E. *Funktionen der Rechtsprechung: Konfliktlösung im deutschen und englischen Verbraucherprozessrecht* (Tübingen: Mohr Siebeck, 2007).

Kolba, P. *David gegen Goliath: Der VW Skandal und die Möglichkeit von Sammelklagen* (Wien; Berlin: Mandelbaum, 2017).

Komesar, N. *Imperfect Alternatives: Choosing Institutions in Law, Economics, and Public Policy* (Chicago: University of Chicago Press, 1994).

Koopmans, T. 'The Birth of European Law at the Crossroads of Legal Traditions' (1991) 39 *The American Journal of Comparative Law* 493-507.

Kosta, V. 'Internal Market Legislation and the Private Law of the Member States – The Impact of Fundamental Rights' (2010) 6 *European Review of Contract Law* 409-436.

Kosta, V. *Fundamental Rights in EU Internal Market Legislation* (Oxford: Hart Publishing, 2015).
Krämer, L. *EWG-Verbraucherrecht* (Baden-Baden: Nomos, 1985).
Krämer, L., Micklitz, H.-W. and Tonner, K. (eds.), *Law and Diffuse Interests in the European Legal Order / Recht und diffuse Interessen in der Europäischen Rechtsordnung: Liber amicorum Norbert Reich* (Baden-Baden: Nomos, 1997).
Krastev, I. *After Europe* (Philadelphia: University of Pennsylvania Press, 2017).
Kruimer, H. 'Non-Discriminatory Energy System Operation: What Does It Mean?' (2011) 12 *Competition and Regulation in Network Industries* 260–286.
Kukovec, D. 'Law and the Periphery' (2015) 21 *European Law Journal* 406–428.
Kumm, M. 'The Moral Point of Constitutional Pluralism: Defining the Domain of Legitimate Institutional Civil Disobedience and Conscientious Objection', in J. Dickson and P. Eleftheriadis (eds.), *Philosophical Foundations of European Union Law* (Oxford: Oxford University Press, 2012), pp. 216–246.
Lacroix, M. *Éloge du patriotisme: Petite philosophie du sentiment national* (Paris: Robert Laffont, 2011).
Ladeur, K.-H. 'Globalization and Public Governance – a Contradiction?', in K.-H. Ladeur (ed.), *Public Governance in the Age of Globalization* (Aldershot: Ashgate, 2004), pp. 1–24.
Ladeur, K.-H. 'The Evolution of General Administrative Law and the Emergence of Postmodern Administrative Law' (2011) *Comparative Research in Law & Political Economy. Research Paper* No. 16.
Laffont, J.-J. and Tirole, J. 'The Politics of Government Decision-Making: A Theory of Regulatory Capture' (1991) 106 *Quarterly Journal of Economics* 1089–1127.
Lando, O. 'The Structure and the Legal Values of the Common Frame of Reference (CFR)' (2007) 3 *European Review of Contract Law* 245–256.
Lang, A. T. F. 'The Legal Construction of Economic Rationalities?' (2013) 40 *Journal of Law and Society* 155–171.
Largeaud, J.-M. *Napoléon et Waterloo. La défaite glorieuses. De 1815 à nos jours* (Paris: La Boutique de l'Histoire, 2006).
Larouche, P. *Competition Law and Regulation in European Telecommunications* (Oxford: Hart Publishing, 2000).
Lasser, M. de S.-O.-l'E., 'Judical (Self-) Portraits: Judicial Discourse in the French Legal System', (1995) 104 *The Yale Law Journal*, 1325–1410.
v. Leeuwen, B. *European Standardisation of Services and Its Impact on Private Law* (Oxford: Hart Publishing, 2017).
v. Leeuwen, B. 'The Impact of Intellectual Property Law and the Charter on Private Law Concepts', in H.-W. Micklitz and C. Sieburgh (eds.), *Primary EU Law and Private Law Concepts* (Cambridge; Antwerp: Intersentia, 2017), pp. 241–269.
Legrand, P. 'European Legal Systems Are Not Converging' (1996) 45 *International and Comparative Law Quarterly* 52–81.
Lepsius, O. 'Die maßstabsetzende Gewalt', in M. Jestaedt, O. Lepsius, Ch. Möllers and Ch. Schönberger, *Das entgrenzte Gericht. Eine kritische Bilanz nach sechzig Jahren Bundesverfassungsgericht* (Berlin: Suhrkamp, 2011), pp. 159–280.

Lequette, Y. 'Quelques remarques à propos du projet de code civil européen de Monsieur von Bar' (2002) *Recueil Le Dalloz* 2202–2214.
Lorenz, St. 'Fünf Jahre „neues" Schuldrecht im Spiegel der Rechtsprechung' (2007) *Neue Juristische Wochenschrift* 1–8.
Loth, W. (ed.), *Experiencing Europe: 50 Years of European Construction 1957–2007* (Baden-Baden: Nomos, 2009).
Luhmann, N. 'Die Rückgabe des zwölften Kamels: Zum Sinn einer soziologischen Analyse des Rechts (1985)', in G. Teubner (ed.), *Die Rückgabe des zwölften Kamels: Niklas Luhmann in der Diskussion über Gerechtigkeit* (Stuttgart: Lucius & Lucius, 2000), pp. 3–60.
Luhmann, N. *Soziale Systeme: Grundriss einer allgemeinen Theorie* (Frankfurt: Suhrkamp, 1984).
Lurger, B. *Vertragliche Solidarität: Entwicklungschance für das allgemeine Vertragsrecht in Österreich und in der Europäischen Union* (Baden-Baden: Nomos, 1998).
Luth, H. *Behavioural Economics in Consumer Policy: The Economic Analysis of Standard Terms in Consumer Contracts Revisited* (Antwerp: Intersentia, 2010).
Macaulay, S. 'Non-Contractual Relations in Business: A Preliminary Study' (1963) 28 *American Sociological Review* 55–67.
Maduro, M. and Wind, M. (eds.), *The Transformation of Europe: Twenty-Five Years On* (Cambridge: Cambridge University Press, 2017).
Magnus, U. and Micklitz, H.-W. *Liability for the Safety of Services* (Baden-Baden: Nomos, 2006).
Maine, H. *Ancient Law: Its Connection with the Early History of Society, and Its Relation to Modern Ideas*, edited by J. H. Morgan (London: J. M. Dent & Sons Ltd., 1917).
Mak, C. *Fundamental Rights in European Contract Law: A Comparison of the Impact of Fundamental Rights on Contractual Relationships in Germany, the Netherlands, Italy and England* (Alphen aan den Rijn: Kluwer Law International, 2008).
Mak, C. 'Judges in Utopia: Fundamental Rights as Constitutive Elements of a European Private Legal Culture', in G. Helleringer and K. Purnhagen (eds.), *Towards a European Legal Culture* (München; Oxford; Baden-Baden: Beck; Hart; Nomos, 2014), pp. 375–395.
Mak, C. 'Life Time Contracts: Social Long-Term Contracts in Labour, Tenancy and Consumer Credit Law, edited by L. Nogler and U. Reifner' (2015) 2 *European Journal of Comparative Law and Governance* 379–382.
Mak, V. 'Full Harmonization in European Private Law: A Two-Track Concept' (2012) 20 *European Review of Private Law* 213–235.
Malinvaud, P. 'Réponse – hors délai – à la Commission européenne: à propos d'un code européen des contracts' (2002) *Recueil Le Dalloz* 2542–2551.
Marella, M. R. 'The Old and the New Limits to Freedom of Contract in Europe' (2006) 2 *European Review of Contract Law* 257–274.
Markesinis, B. S. 'Learning from Europe and Learning in Europe', in B. S. Markesinis (ed.), *The Gradual Convergence: Foreign Ideas, Foreign Influences and English Law on the Eve of the 21st Century* (Oxford: Clarendon Press, 1994), pp. 1–32.

Marx, K. *Die deutsche Ideologie, Band I. Kapitel I. Feuerbach. Gegensatz von materialistischer und idealistischer Anschauung* (Dietz Verlag: Berlin, 1972).

Marx, K. 'On the Jewish Question', in J. O'Malley and R. A. Davies (eds.), *Marx: Early Political Writings* (Cambridge: Cambridge University Press, 1994), pp. 28–56.

Mascini, P. *Law and Behavioral Sciences. Why We Need Less Purity Rather than More, Erasmus Law Lectures 41* (The Hague: Eleven International Publishing, 2016).

Mathias, P. and Polland, S. (eds.), *The Cambridge Economic History of Europe*, Volume VIII (Cambridge: Cambridge University Press, 1989).

Mattei, U. and di Robilant, A. 'The Art and Science of Critical Scholarship: Post-Modernism and International Style in the Legal Architecture of Europe' (2002) 10 *European Review of Private Law* 29–59.

Mattei, U. and Nicola, F. 'A 'Social Dimension' in European Private Law? The Call for Setting a Progressive Agenda, (2006) 41 *New England Law Review*, pp. 1–65.

Maugeri, M. R. 'Abuse of Dominant Position: A System of Undistorted Competition or Social Protection?' (2006) 2 *European Review of Contract Law* 250–256.

Mayer, J. *Dark Money: The Hidden History of the Billionaires Behind the Rises of the Radical Right* (New York: Doubleday, 2016).

McClimens, A. and Hyde, M. 'Intellectual Disability, Consumerism and Identity: To Have and Have Not?' (2012) 16 *Journal of Intellectual Disabilities* 135–144.

McColm, H. 'Smart Regulation: The European Commission's Updated Strategy' (2011) 2 *European Journal of Risk Regulation* 9–11.

Meli, M. 'Social Justice, Constitutional Principles and Protection of the Weaker Party' (2006) 2 *European Review of Contract Law* 159–166.

Menéndez, A. J. 'European Citizenship after Martínez Sala and Baumbast: Has European Law Become More Human But Less Social?', in M. Maduro and L. Azoulai (eds.), *The Past and the Future of EU Law: The Classics of EU Law Revisited on the 50th Anniversary of the Rome Treaty* (Oxford: Hart Publishing, 2010), pp. 363–393.

Menéndez, A. J. 'Whose Justice? Which Europe?', in D. Kochenov, G. de Búrca and A. Williams (eds.), *Europe's Justice Deficit?* (Oxford: Hart Publishing, 2015), pp. 137–152.

Menger, A. *Das Bürgerliche Recht und die besitzlosen Volksklassen: Eine Kritik des Entwurfs eines Bürgerlichen Gesetzbuches für das Deutsche Reich* (Tübingen: Laupp, 1890).

Mestmäcker, E.-J. 'Auf dem Wege zu einer Ordnungspolitik für Europa', in E.-J. Mestmäcker, H. Möller, H. P. Schwartz (eds.), *Eine Ordnungspolitik für Europa: Festschrift für Hans von der Groeben* (Baden-Baden: Nomos, 1987), pp. 9–49.

Mestmäcker, E.-J. *Wirtschaft und Verfassung in der Europäischen Union: Beiträge zu Recht, Theorie und Politik der Europäischen Integration*, 2nd ed. (Baden-Baden: Nomos, 2006).

Metz, R. 'Credit Scoring: Will Our Digital Identity Replace the Real Person?', in K. Purnhagen and P. Rott (eds.), *Varieties of European Economic Law and Regulation:*

Liber Amicorum for Hans Micklitz (New York: Springer International Publishing, 2014), pp. 635–650.

Mian, A. and Sufi, A. *House of Debt: How They (and You) Caused the Great Recession, and How We Can Prevent It from Happening Again* (Chicago: Chicago University Press, 2014).

Micklitz, H.-W. 'Produktsicherheit und technische Normung in der Europäischen Gemeinschaft – Zu den Leistungsmöglichkeiten und -grenzen des Selbstregulierungsmodells als Mittel des Verbraucherschutzes', in H. Paetow and K. Tonner (eds.), *Staatliche Wirtschaftsregulierung in der Krise* (Opladen: Westdeutscher Verlag, 1986), pp. 109–126.

Micklitz, H.-W. (ed.), *Post Market Control of Consumer Goods* (Baden-Baden: Nomos, 1990).

Micklitz, H.-W. 'The Maastricht Treaty, the Principle of Subsidiarity and the Theory of Integration' (1993) 4 *LAKIMIES Special Issue on European Integration* (periodical of the Association of Finnish lawyers) 508–539.

Micklitz, H.-W. 'Divergente Ausgansbedingungen des Verbraucherrechts in Ost und West', in H.-W. Micklitz (ed.), *Rechtseinheit oder Rechtsvielfalt in Europa? Rolle und Funktion des Verbraucherrechts in der EG und MOE-Staaten* (Baden-Baden: Nomos, 1996), pp. 3–22.

Micklitz, H.-W. 'Legitime Erwartungen als Gerechtigkeitsprinzip des europäischen Privatrechts', in L. Krämer, H.-W. Micklitz and K. Tonner (eds.), *Law and Diffuse Interests in the European Legal Order / Recht und diffuse Interessen in der Europäischen Rechtsordnung: Liber amicorum Norbert Reich* (Baden-Baden: Nomos, 1997), pp. 245–277.

Micklitz, H.-W. 'Die Verbrauchsgüterkauf-Richtlinie' (1999) *Europäische Zeitschrift für Wirtschaftsrecht* 485–493.

Micklitz, H.-W. 'Principles of Social Justice in European Private Law' (1999) 19 *Yearbook of European Law* 167–204.

Micklitz, H.-W. '... und die USA?', Kolloquium zur Zukunft der Produkthaftung aus Anlaß des 70. Geburtstages von Prof. Dr. Hans-Claudius Taschner, (2002) *Zeitschrift für europarechtliche Studien* 75–102.

Micklitz, H.-W. 'The Principles of European Contract Law and the Protection of the Weaker Party' (2004) 27 *Journal of Consumer Policy* 339–356.

Micklitz, H.-W. 'Collective Action of Non-Governmental Organizations in European Consumer and European Environmental Law – A Mutual Learning Process', in R. Macrory (ed.), *Reflections on 30 Years of EU Environmental Law: A High Level of Protection* (Groningen: European Law Publishing, 2005), pp. 451–473.

Micklitz, H.-W. 'Concept of Competitive Contract Law' (2005) 23 *Penn State International Law Review* 549–585.

Micklitz, H.-W. *The Politics of Judicial Co-operation in the EU: Sunday Trading, Equal Treatment, and Good Faith* (Cambridge: Cambridge University Press, 2005).

Micklitz, H.-W. 'House of Lords – Fair Trading v National Bank' (2006) 2 *European Review of Contract Law* 471–480.

Micklitz, H.-W. 'The Relationship between National and European Consumer Policy – Challenges and Perspectives', in C. Twigg-Flesner, D. Parry, G. Howells and A. Nordhausen (eds.), *The Yearbook of Consumer Law 2008* (Aldershot: Ashgate, 2007), pp. 35–66.

Micklitz, H.-W. 'Review of Academic Approaches to the European Contract Law Codification Project', in M. Andenas, S. Diaz Alabart, B. Markesinis, H.-W. Micklitz and N. Pasquino, *Liber Amicorum Guido Alpa: Private Law Beyond the National Systems* (London: British Institute of International and Comparative Law, 2007), pp. 699–728.

Micklitz, H.-W. 'Some Considerations on Cassis de Dijon and the Control of Unfair Contract Terms in Consumer Contracts', in K. Boele-Woelki and F. W. Grosheide (eds.), *The Future of European Contract Law* (The Hague: Kluwer Law International, 2007), pp. 387–410, reprinted in H. Collins (ed.), *Standard Contract Terms in Europe. A Basis for and a Challenge to European Contract Law* (Alphen aan den Rijn: Kluwer Law International, 2008), pp. 19–42.

Micklitz, H.-W. 'Jack Is out of the Box: The Efficient Consumer-Shopper' (2009) *Tidskrift Utgiven av Juridiska Föreningen i Finland* 417–436.

Micklitz, H.-W. 'The Targeted Full Harmonisation Approach: Looking behind The Curtain', in G. Howells and R. Schulze (eds.), *Modernising and Harmonising Consumer Contract Law* (München: Sellier European Law Publishers, 2009), pp. 47–86.

Micklitz, H.-W. 'The Visible Hand of European Regulatory Private Law: The Transformation of European Private Law from Autonomy to Functionalism in Competition and Regulation' (2009) 28 *Yearbook of European Law* 3–59.

Micklitz, H.-W. (ed.), *Informationszugang für Verbraucher in Europa und den USA: Recht und Praxis* (Baden-Baden: Nomos, 2009).

Micklitz, H.-W. 'Failures or Ideological Preconceptions? Thoughts on Two Grand Projects: The European Constitution and the European Civil Code', in K. Tuori and S. Sankari (eds.), *The Many Constitutions of Europe* (Farnham: Ashgate, 2010), pp. 109–142.

Micklitz, H.-W. 'Administrative Enforcement of European Private Law', in R. Brownsword, H.-W. Micklitz, L. Niglia and S. Weatherill (eds.), *The Foundations of European Private Law* (Oxford: Hart Publishing, 2011), pp. 563–592.

Micklitz, H.-W. 'German Constitutional Court (Bundesverfassungsgericht BVerfG) 2 BvE 2/08, 30. 6.2009—Organstreitproceedings between members of the German Parliament and the Federal Government' (2011) 7 *European Review of Contract Law* 528–546.

Micklitz, H.-W. 'Universal Services: Nucleus for a Social European Private Law', in M. Cremona (ed.), *Market Integration and Public Services in the European Union* (Oxford: Oxford University Press, 2011), pp. 63–102.

Micklitz, H.-W. (ed.), *The Many Concepts of Social Justice in European Private Law* (Cheltenham: Edward Elgar, 2011).

Micklitz, H.-W. 'The Expulsion of the Concept of Protection from the Consumer Law and the Return of Social Elements in the Civil Law: A Bittersweet Polemic' (2012) 35 *Journal of Consumer Policy* 283-296.

Micklitz, H.-W. 'Three Questions to the Opponents of the Viking and Laval Judgments' (2012) OSE (Observatoire Social Européen) Opinion Paper No. 8.

Micklitz, H.-W. 'Do Consumers and Businesses Need a New Architecture for Consumer Law? A Thought Provoking Impulse' (2013) 32 *Yearbook of European Law* 266-367.

Micklitz, H.-W. 'Philosophical Foundations of European Union Law by Julie Dickson and Pavlos Eleftheriadis (eds)' (2013) 32 *Yearbook of European Law* 538-554.

Micklitz, H.-W. 'A Common Approach to the Enforcement of Unfair Commercial Practices and Unfair Contract Terms', in W. van Boom, O. Akseli and A. Garde (eds.), *The European Unfair Commercial Practices Directive. Impact, Enforcement Strategies and National Legal Systems* (Farnham: Ashgate, 2014), pp. 173-202.

Micklitz, H.-W. 'The Public and the Private – European Regulatory Private Law and Financial Services' (2014) 10 *European Review of Contract law* 473-475.

Micklitz, H.-W. 'The EU as a Federal Order of Competences and the Private Law', in L. Azoulai (ed.), *The Question of Competence in the European Union* (Oxford: Oxford University Press, 2014), pp. 125-152.

Micklitz, H.-W. 'The (Un)-Systematics of (Private) Law as an Element of European Culture', in G. Helleringer and K. Purnhagen (eds.), *Towards a European Legal Culture* (München; Oxford; Baden-Baden: C. H. Beck; Hart Publishing; Nomos, 2014), pp. 81-115.

Micklitz, H.-W. 'On the Intellectual History of Freedom of Contract and Regulation' (2015) 4 *Penn State Journal of Law & International Affairs* 1-32.

Micklitz, H.-W. 'A European Advantage in Legal Scholarship?', in R. van Gestel, H.-W. Micklitz and E. L. Rubin (eds.), *Rethinking Legal Scholarship: A Transatlantic Dialogue* (New York: Cambridge University Press, 2016), pp. 262-309.

Micklitz, H.-W. 'An Essay on the Bifurcation of Legal Education – National vs Transnational', in C. Gane and R. Hui Huang (eds.), *Legal Education in the Global Contex. Opportunities and Challenges* (Abingdon; New York: Routledge, 2016), pp. 43-60.

Micklitz, H.-W. 'Eine merkwürdige Welt – Beobachtungen zur sog. Verbraucherforschung der Europäischen Kommission' (2016) *Verbraucher und Recht* 321-322.

Micklitz, H.-W. 'The Consumer – Marketised, Fragmentised and Constitutionalised', in D. Leczykiewicz and T. Weatherill (eds.), *The Images of the Consumer in EU Law: Legislation, Free Movement and Competition Law* (Oxford: Hart Publishing, 2016), pp. 21-42.

Micklitz, H.-W. 'The Legal Subject, Social Class and Identity Based Rights', in L. Azoulai, S. Barbou des Places and E. Pataut (eds.), *Constructing the Person in EU Law: Rights, Roles, Identities* (Oxford: Hart Publishing, 2016), pp. 285-310.

Micklitz, H.-W. 'The Transformation of Private Law through Competition' (2016) 22 *European Law Journal* 627–643.

Micklitz, H.-W. 'The Constitutional Transformation of Private Law Pillars through the CJEU', in H. Collins (ed.), *European Contract Law and the EU Charter of Fundamental Rights* (Cambridge; Antwerp; Portland: Intersentia, 2017), pp. 49–91.

Micklitz, H.-W. 'The Internal Market and the Banking Union', in S. Grundmann and H.-W. Micklitz (eds.), *The European Banking Union and Constitution: Beacon for Advanced Integration or Death-Knell for Democracy* (Oxford: Hart Publishing, 2018 forthcoming).

Micklitz, H.-W. and Cafaggi, F. (eds.), *European Private Law after the Common Frame of References* (Cheltenham; Northampton, Mass.: Edward Elgar, 2010).

Micklitz, H.-W. and Domurath, I. (eds.), *Consumer Debt and Social Exclusion in Europe* (Farnham; Burlington: Ashgate, 2015).

Micklitz, H.-W., Domurath, I. and Comparato, G. (eds.), 'The Over-Indebtedness of European Consumers: A View from Six Countries' (2014) *EUI Working Paper EUI-ERC* No. 10.

Micklitz, H.-W. and Patterson, D. 'From the Nation State to the Market: The Evolution of EU Private Law as Regulation of the Economy beyond the Boundaries of the Union?', in B. van Vooren, S. Blockmans and J. Wouters (eds.), *The EU's Role in Global Governance. The Legal Dimension* (Oxford: Oxford University Press, 2013), pp. 59–78.

Micklitz, H.-W. and Radeideh, M. 'CLAB-Europe – The European database on unfair terms in consumer contracts' (2005) 28 *Journal of Consumer Policy* 325–360.

Micklitz, H.-W. and Reich, N. 'Verbraucherschutz im Vertrag über die Europäische Union. Perspektiven für 1993' (1992) *Europäische Zeitschrift für Wirtschaftsrecht* 593–598.

Micklitz, H.-W. and Reich, N. 'Crónica de una muerte anunciada: The Commission Proposal for a 'Directive on Consumer Rights" (2009) 46 *Common Market Law Review* 471–519.

Micklitz, H.-W. and Reich, N. 'Luxemburg ante portas – jetzt auch im deutschen "runderneuerten" AGB-Recht?', in P. Mankowski and W. Wurmnest (eds.), *Festschrift für Ulrich Magnus zum 70. Geburtstag* (München: Sellier European Law Publishers, 2014), pp. 631–654.

Micklitz, H.-W. and Reich, N. 'The Court and Sleeping Beauty: The Revival of the Unfair Contract Terms Directive (UCTD)' (2014) 51 *Common Market Law Review* 771–808.

Micklitz, H.-W., Reich, N. and Boucon, L. 'L'Action de la victime contre l'assureur du producteur' (2015) *Revue internationale de droit économique* 37–68.

Micklitz, H.-W., Reich, N. and Weatherill, S. 'EU Treaty Revision and Consumer Protection' (2004) 27 *Journal of Consumer Policy* 367–399.

Micklitz, H.-W. and Roethe, T. *Produktsicherheit und Marktüberwachung im Ostseeraum: Rechtsrahmen und Vollzugspraxis* (Baden-Baden: Nomos, 2008).

Micklitz, H.-W., Roethe, T. and Weatherill, S. (eds.), *Federalism and Responsibility: A Study on Product Safety Law and Practice in the European Community* (London: Graham & Trotmann, 1994).
Micklitz, H.-W., Sibony, A.- L. and Esposito, F. (eds.), *Research Methods in Law and in Consumer Research*, 2018 forthcoming.
Micklitz, H.-W. and Sieburgh, C. (eds.), *Primary EU law and Private Law Concepts* (Cambridge; Antwerp: Intersentia, 2017).
Micklitz, H.-W., Stuyck J. and Terryn. E. (eds.), *Cases, Materials and Text on Consumer Law* (Oxford: Hart Publishing, 2010).
Micklitz, H.-W. and Svetiev, Y. (eds.), 'A Self-sufficient European Private Law – A Viable Concept?' (2012) *EUI-ERC Working Paper* No. 31.
Micklitz, H.-W., Svetiev, Y. and Comparato, G. (eds.), 'European Regulatory Private Law – The Paradigm Tested' (2014) *EUI-ERC Working Paper* No. 4.
Micklitz, H.-W. and Weatherill, S. 'Consumer Policy in the European Community: Before and after Maastricht' (1993) 16 *Journal of Consumer Policy* 285–321.
Micklitz, H.-W. and Wechsler, A. (eds.) *The Transformation of Enforcement: European Economic Law in a Global Perspective* (Oxford: Hart Publishing, 2016).
Micklitz, H.-W. and de Witte, B. (eds.), *The European Court of Justice and the Autonomy of the Member States* (Cambridge; Antwerp: Intersentia, 2012).
Miller, L. 'Ethical Consumption and the Internal Market', in D. Leczykiewicz and S. Weatherill (eds.), *The Images of the Consumer in EU Law: Legislation, Free Movement and Competition Law* (Oxford: Hart Publishing, 2016), pp. 279–303.
Milosz, C. *The Captive Mind*, (London: Penguin Books, 2001).
Moloney, N. 'Bending to Uniformity': EU Financial Regulation With and Without the UK', in Symposium Issue 'EU Law with the UK, EU Law without the UK' (2017) 40 *Fordham International Law Journal*, 1335–1372.
Monti, G. 'The United Kingdom's Contribution to European Union Competition Law', in Symposium Issue 'EU Law with the UK, EU Law without the UK' (2017) 40 *Fordham International Law Journal*, 1443–1474.
Möslein, F. (ed.), *Private Macht* (Tübingen: Mohr Siebeck, 2016).
Motte, O. 'Duguit, Léon', in M. Stolleis (ed.), *Juristen. Ein biographisches Lexikon: Von der Antike bis zum 20. Jahrhundert*, 2nd edition (München: C. H. Beck, 2001), pp. 187–188.
Mückenberger, U. 'Workers' Representation at the Plant and Enterprise Level', in B. Hepple and B. Veneziani (eds.), *The Transformation of Labour Law in Europe: A Comparative Study of 15 Countries 1945–2004* (Oxford: Hart Publishing, 2009), pp. 233–262.
Muir-Watt, H. 'Concurrence ou confluence? Droit international privé et droits fondamentaux dans la gouvernance globale' (2013) *Revue Internationale de Droit Economique* 59–78.
Müller-Graff, Ch. *Privatrecht und Europäisches Gemeinschaftsrecht. Gemeinschaftsprivatrecht* (Baden-Baden: Nomos, 1989).
Münch, R. 'Constructing a European Society by Jurisdiction' (2008) 14 *European Law Journal* 519–541.

Münch, R. *Die Konstruktion der Europäischen Gesellschaft. Zur Dialektik von transnationaler Integration und nationaler Desintegration* (Frankfurt: Campus Verlag, 2008).

Münch, R. *European Governmentality: The Liberal Drift of Multilevel Governance* (London; New York: Routledge, 2010).

Namyslowska, M. 'Monitoring Compliance with Contracts and Regulations: Between Private and Public Law', in R. Brownsword, R. van Gestel and H.-W. Micklitz (eds.), *Contract and Regulation: A Handbook on New Methods of Law Making in Private Law* (Cheltenham: Elgar Publishing, 2017), pp. 259-283.

Nannery, A. *The 'conscience of Europe' in the European sovereign debt crisis: an analysis of the judgments of the European Court of Human Rights and the European Committee of Social Rights on austerity measures*, LLM thesis, European University Institute (2015).

Naphtali, F. *Wirtschaftsdemokratie: Ihr Wesen, Weg und Ziel* (Berlin: Verlagsgesellschaft des Allgemeinen Deutschen Gewerkschaftsbundes, 1928).

Neergaard, U. 'Services of General (Economic) Interest and the Services Directive – What Is Left Out, Why and Where to Go?', in U. Neergaard, R. Nielsen, L. M. Roseberry (eds.), *The Services Directive: Consequences for the Welfare State and the European Social Model* (Copenhagen: Djøf Publishing, 2008), pp. 65-120.

Neergaard, U., Szyszczak, E., v. de Gronden, J. W. and Krajewski, M. (eds.), *Social Services of General Interest in the EU* (The Hague: T.M.C. Asser Press, 2013).

Della Negra, F. *Private Law and Private Enforcement in the post-crisis EU retail financial regulation*, PhD thesis, European University Institute (2017).

Della Negra, F. 'The Uncertain Development of the Case Law on Consumer Protection in Mortgage Enforcement Proceedings: Sánchez Morcillo and Kušionová' (2015) 52 *Common Market Law Review* 1009-1032.

Neyer, J. 'Justice and the Right to Justification: Conceptual Reflections', in D. Kochenov, G. de Búrca and A. Williams (eds.), *Europe's Justice Deficit?* (Oxford: Hart Publishing, 2015), pp. 211-226.

Nicola, F. G. 'Luxembourg Judicial Style With or Without the UK', in Symposium Issue 'EU Law with the UK, EU Law without the UK' (2017) 40 *Fordham International Law Journal*, 1505-1534.

Niglia, L. (ed.), *Pluralism and European Private Law* (Oxford: Hart Publishing, 2013).

Niglia, L. 'The Double Life of Pluralism in Europe', in L. Niglia (ed.), *Pluralism and European Private Law* (Oxford: Hart Publishing, 2013), pp. 13-28.

Niglia, L. 'Law or Economics – Some Thoughts on Transnational Private Law', in K. Purnhagen/P. Rott (eds.), *Varieties of European Economic Law and Regulation: Liber Amicorum for Hans Micklitz*, (New York: Springer International Publishing, 2014), pp. 93-104

Nijenhuis, A. 'Electronic Communications and the EU Consumer', in F. S. Benyon (ed.), *Services and the EU citizen* (Oxford: Hart Publishing, 2013), pp. 47-74.

Nogler, L. and Reifner, U. (eds.), *Life Time Contracts: Social Long-term Contracts in Labour, Tenancy and Consumer Credit Law* (The Hague: Eleven International Publishing, 2014).

Nörr, K. W. *Die Republik der Wirtschaft, Part I and II* (Tübingen: Mohr Siebeck, 1999 and 2007).

Offe, C. 'The European Model of "Social" Capitalism: Can It Survive European Integration?' (2003) 11 *The Journal of Political Philosophy* 437–469.

Oliver, P. *Free Movement of Goods in the European Union*, 5th Edition (Oxford: Oxford University Press, 2010)

Olsen, N. 'From Choice To Welfare: The Concept of the Consumer in the Chicago School of Economics' (2017) 14 *Modern Intellectual History* 507–535.

Osterhammel, J. *Die Verwandlung der Welt. Eine Geschichte des 19: Jahrhunderts* (München: C. H. Beck, 2011).

Packard, V. *The Hidden Persuaders* (Harmondsworth: Penguin, 1957).

Paletschek, S. 'Kinder, Küche, Kirche', in É. François and H. Schulze (eds.), *Deutsche Erinnerungsorte*, Vol. 2 (München: C. H. Beck, 2001), pp. 419–433.

Paschukanis, E. *Allgemeine Rechtslehre und Marxismus*, 3rd edition (Frankfurt: Verlag Neue Kritik, 1970).

Patterson, D. and Afilalo, A. *The New Global Trading Order: The Evolving State and the Future of Trade* (Cambridge; New York: Cambridge University Press, 2008).

Peers, S. 'Equal Treatment of Atypical Workers: A New Frontier for EU Law' (2013) 32 *Yearbook of European Law* 30–56.

Pernice, I. and Hindelang, S. 'Potenziale europäischer Politik nach Lissabon – Europapolitische Perspektiven für Deutschland, seine Institutionen, seine Wirtschaft und seine Bürger nach dem Inkrafttreten des Vertrags von Lissabon' (2010) 21 *Europäische Zeitschrift für Wirtschaftsrecht* 407–413.

Pescatore, P. *The Law of Integration: Emergence of New Phenomenon in International Relations, Based on Experience of the European Communities* (Leiden: Sijthoff, 1974).

Phelan, W. 'The Revolutionary Doctrines of European Law and the Legal Philosophy of Robert Lecourt' (2016) *EUI Working Paper Law* Nr. 18.

Pirstner-Ebner, R. 'Kein Recht zum Anschluss an das Übertragungsnetz' (2009) *Europäische Zeitschrift für Wirtschaftsrecht* 15–16.

Pistor, K. 'Legal Ground Rules in Coordinated and Liberal Market Economies', in K. J. Hopt, E. Wymeersch, H. Kanada and H. Baum (eds.), *Corporate Governance in Context: Corporations, States, and Markets in Europe, Japan and the US* (Oxford: Oxford University Press, 2005), pp. 249–280.

Pistor, K. 'Contesting Property Rights: Towards an Integrated Theory of Institutional and System Change' (2011) 11 *Global Jurist (Frontiers)*, Article 6, 1–26.

La Porta, R., Lopez-de-Silanes, F. and Shleifer, A. 'The Economic Consequences of Legal Origins' (2008) 46 *Journal of Economic Literature* 285–332.

La Porta, R., Lopez-de-Silanes, F., Shleifer, A. and Vishny, R. W. 'Law and Finance' (1998) 106 *The Journal of Political Economy* 1113–1155.

Pound, R. *The Spirit of the Common Law*, College of Law, Faculty Publications (Francestown, NH: Marshall Jones Company, 1921).

Priban, J. 'The Evolving Idea of Political Justice in the EU: From Substantive Deficits to the Systematic Contingency of European Society', in D. Kochenov, G. de Búrca and A. Williams (eds.), *Europe's Justice Deficit?* (Oxford: Hart Publishing, 2015), pp. 193-211.

Prien, T. 'Under the Spell of Society. System Theoretical Perspective of Justice', in W. Matiaske, S. Costa and H. Brunkhorst (eds.), *Contemporary Perspectives on Justice* (München: Rainer Hampp Verlag, 2010), pp. 41-68.

Pront-van Bommel, S. 'A Reasonable Price for Electricity' (2016) 39 *Journal of Consumer Policy* 141-158.

Purnhagen, K. 'The Virtue of Cassis de Dijon 25 Years Later – It Is Not Dead. It Just Smells Funny', in K. Purnhagen and P. Rott (eds.), *Varieties of European Economic Law and Regulation: Liber Amicorum for Hans Micklitz*, (New York: Springer International Publishing, 2014), pp. 315-342

Purnhagen, K. and Rott, P. (eds.), *Varieties of European Economic Law and Regulation: Liber Amicorum for Hans Micklitz* (New York: Springer International Publishing, 2014).

Purnhagen, K. and Verbruggen, P. 'Europäische Gemeinschaft', in J. Keßler, H.-W. Micklitz and N. Reich (eds.), *Institutionelle Finanzmarktaufsicht und Verbraucherschutz: Eine rechtsvergleichende Untersuchung der Regelungssysteme in Deutschland, Italien, Schweden, dem Vereinigten Königreich und der Europäischen Gemeinschaft* (Baden-Baden: Nomos, 2010), pp. 175-242.

Purnhagen, K. and Wahlen, S. 'Der Verbraucherbegriff, § 13 BGB und die Sharing Economy', in H.-W. Micklitz, L. Reisch, G. Joost, H. Zander-Hayat (eds.), *Verbraucherrecht 2.0 – Verbraucher in der digitalen Welt* (Baden-Baden: Nomos, 2017), pp. 185-220.

Putnam, R. D. 'Diplomacy and Domestic Politics: The Logic of Two-Level Games' (1988) 42 *International Organization* 427-460.

Radeideh, M., *Fair Trading in EC Law: Information and Consumer Choice in the Internal Market* (Groningen: Europa Law Publishing, 2005).

Raiser, L. *Das Recht der Allgemeinen Geschäftsbedingungen* (Hamburg: Hanseat. Verl. Anst., 1935).

Ramm, T. 'Epilogue: The New Ordering of Labour Law 1918-45', in B. Hepple (ed.), *The Making of Labour Law in Europe: A Comparative Study of Nine Countries up to 1945* (London; New York: Mansell, 1986), pp. 277-300.

Ramm, T. 'Pluralismus ohne Kodifikation: Die Arbeitsrechtswissenschaft nach 1945', in D. Simon (ed.), *Rechtswissenschaft in der Bonner Republik: Studien zur Wissenschaftsgeschichte der Jurisprudenz* (Frankfurt: Suhrkamp, 1994), pp. 449-528.

Rasehorn, T. *Recht und Klassen: Zur Klassenjustiz in der Bundesrepublik* (Darmstadt; Neuwied: Luchterhand, 1974).

Raulff, U. (ed.), *Mentalitäten-Geschichte: Zur Historischen Rekonstruktion geistiger Prozesse* (Berlin: Wagenbach, 1987).

Rawls, J. *The Law of Peoples* (Cambridge, MA: Harvard University Press, 1999).

Rawls, J. *A Theory of Justice* (Cambridge, MA: Harvard University Press 1971).

Rawls, J. and Van Parijs, P. 'Three Letters on The Law of Peoples and the European Union' (2003) 4 *Revue de philosophie économique* 7–20.
Redding, P. 'German Idealism', in G. Klosko (ed.), *The Oxford Handbook of the History of Political Philosophy* (Oxford: Oxford University Press, 2011), pp. 348–368.
Reich, N. 'Verbraucherpolitische Probleme bei der Anwendung des Gesetzes zur Regelung des Rechts der Allgemeinen Geschäftsbedingungen (AGBG)' (1978) 2 *Zeitschrift für Verbraucherpolitik* 236–248.
Reich, N. 'The Regulatory Crisis: Does It Exist and Can It Be Solved? Some Comparative Remarks on the Situation of Social Regulation in the USA and the EEC' (1984) 2 *Environment and Planning C: Government and Policy* 177–197.
Reich, N. 'Die neue Richtlinie 97/7/EG über den Verbraucherschutz bei Vertragsabschlüssen im Fernabsatz' (1997) *Europäische Zeitschrift für Wirtschaftsrecht* 581–589.
Reich, N. *Bürgerrechte in der Europäischen Union* (Baden-Baden: Nomos, 1999).
Reich, N. 'A European Contract Law, or an EU Contract Regulation for Consumers?' (2005) 28 *Journal of Consumer Policy* 383–407.
Reich, N. 'Protection of Consumers' Economic Interests by EC Contract Law – Some Follow-up Remarks' (2006) 28 *Sydney Law Review* 37–62.
Reich, N. 'The Interrelation between Rights and Duties in EU Law: Reflections on the State of Liability Law in the Multilevel Governance System of the Union: Is There a Need for a More Coherent Approach in European Private Law?' (2010) 29 *Yearbook of European Law* 112–163.
Reich, N. 'The Public/Private Divide in European law', in H.-W. Micklitz and F. Cafaggi (eds.), *European Private Law after the Common Frame of Reference* (Cheltenham: Elgar, 2010), pp. 56–89.
Reich, N. 'Balancing in Private Law and the Imperatives of the Public Interest: National Experiences and (Missed?) European Opportunities', in R. Brownsword, H.-W. Micklitz, L. Niglia and S. Weatherill (eds.), *The Foundations of European Private Law* (Oxford: Hart Publishing, 2011), pp. 221–248.
Reich, N. 'From Minimal to Full to 'Half' Harmonization', in J. Devenney and M. Kenny (eds.), *European Consumer Protection: Theory and Practice* (Cambridge: Cambridge University Press, 2012), pp. 3–5.
Reich, N. 'Book Review: The Many Concepts of Social Justice in European Private Law', edited by Hans W. Micklitz. (Cheltenham: Edward Elgar, 2011)' (2013) 50 *Common Market Law Review* 1523–1525.
Reich, N. *General Principles of EU Civil Law* (Cambridge: Intersentia, 2014).
Reich, N. "'Reflexive Contract Governance in the EU': David Trubek's Contribution to a More Focused Approach to EU Contract Legislation', in G. de Búrca, C. Kilpatrick and J. Scott (eds.), *Critical Legal Perspectives On Global Governance: Liber amicorum David M. Trubek* (Oxford: Hart Publishing, 2014), pp. 273–294.
Reich, N. '"I Want My Money Back": Problems, Successes and Failures in the Price Regulation of the Gas Supply Market by Civil Law Remedies in Germany' (2015) EUI-ERC Working Paper No. 5.

Reich, N. 'Product Liability and Beyond: An Exercise in 'Gap-Filling" (2016) 24 *European Review of Private Law* 619–644.
Reich, N. 'Vulnerable Consumers in EU Law', in D. Leczykiewicz and S. Weatherill (eds.), *The Images of the Consumer in EU Law: Legislation, Free Movement and Competition Law* (Oxford: Hart Publishing, 2016), pp. 139–158.
Reich, N. and Micklitz, H.-W. *Consumer Legislation in the EC Countries: A Comparative Analysis* (New York: Van Nostrand Reinhold, 1980).
Reich, N. and Micklitz, H.-W. *Europäisches Verbraucherrecht*, 4th edition (Baden-Baden, Nomos, 2003).
Reich, N. and Micklitz, H.-W. 'Vollharmonisierung durch die Hintertür? – Zur Kritik der Schlussanträge der Generalanwältin Trstenjak in der Rs. Gysbrechts, C-205/07, v. 17. 7.2008' (2008) 23 *Verbraucher und Recht* 349–351.
Reich, N., Micklitz, H.-W., Rott, P. and Tonner, K. (eds.), *European Consumer Law*, 2nd edition (Antwerp: Intersentia, 2014).
Reich, N., Tonner, K. and Wegener, H. *Verbraucher und Recht* (Göttingen: Schwartz, 1976).
Reifner, U. 'Der Schutzbereich eines Verbraucherschutzgesetzes und die Schutzwürdigkeit des Verbrauchers' (1978) 2 *Zeitschrift für Verbraucherpolitik* 203–213.
Reifner, U. 'Das Recht auf ein Girokonto' (1995) 7 *Zeitschrift für Bankrecht und Bankwirtschaft* 243–260.
Reifner, U. 'Renting a Slave—European Contract Law in the Credit Society', in T. Wilhelmsson, E. Paunio and A. Pohjolainen (eds.), *Private Law and the Many Cultures of Europe* (Alphen aan den Rijn: Kluwer Law International, 2007), pp. 325–364.
Reifner, U. and Volkmer, M. *Ratenkredite an Konsumenten: Rechtsprobleme, Hintergründe und Strategien zum Verbraucherschutz gegnüber Banken* (Hamburg: Verbraucher-Zentrale, 1984).
Reifner, U. and Volkmer, M. *Neue Formen der Verbraucherrechtsberatung* (Frankfurt: Campus Verlag, 1988).
Reimann, M. 'The American Advantage in Global Lawyering' (2014) 78 *Rabels Zeitschrift für ausländisches und internationales Privatrecht* 1–36.
Renner, M. 'Formalisierung, Materialisierung, Prozeduralisierung', in S. Grundmann, H.-W. Micklitz and M. Renner (eds.), *Privatrechtstheorie*, Band 1 (Tübingen: Mohr Siebeck, 2015), Kapitel 10, pp. 821–873.
Research Group on EC Private Law (Acquis Group), *Principles of the Existing EC Contract Law (Acquis Principles): Contract I. Precontractual Obligations, Conclusion of Contract, Unfair Terms* (München: Sellier European law Publishers, 2007).
Research Group on EC Private Law (Acquis Group), *Principles of the Existing EC Contract Law (Acquis Principles): Contract II. General Provisions, Delivery of Goods, Package Travel and Payment Services* (München: Sellier European Law Publishers, 2009).
Riesenhuber, K. 'Das Verbot der Diskriminierung aufgrund der Rasse und der ethnischen Herkunft sowie aufgrund des Geschlechts beim Zugang zu und der Versorgung mit Gütern und Dienstleistungen', in S. Leible and

M. Schlachter (eds.), *Diskriminierungsschutz durch Privatrecht* (München: Sellier European Law Publishers, 2006), pp. 123–140.

Riesenhuber, K. *European Employment Law* (Cambridge: Intersentia, 2012).

Ripert, G. *Le Régime démocratique et le droit civil moderne*, 2nd edition (Paris: Librairie générale de droit et de jurisprudence, 1948).

Roberts, E. *Which? 25: Consumers Association, 1957–82* (London: Consumers Association, 1982).

Rödl, F. 'Labour Constitution', in A. v. Bogdandy and J. Bast (eds.), *Principles of European Constitutional Law*, 2nd edition (Oxford: Hart Publishing, 2009), pp. 623–658.

Roethe, T. 'Zum Konsumentenschutz in den MOE-Staaten – Transition und Rechtsvielfalt", in H.-W. Micklitz (ed.), *Rechtseinheit oder Rechtsvielfalt in Europa? Rolle und Funktion des Verbraucherrechts in der EG und MOE-Staaten* (Baden-Baden: Nomos, 1996), pp. 205–240.

Roethe, T. *Arbeiten wie bei Honecker, leben wie bei Kohl: Ein Plädoyer für das Ende der Schonzeit* (Frankfurt: Eichborn, 1999).

Roethe, T. *Der Verbraucher: Rechtssoziologische Betrachtungen* (Baden-Baden: Nomos, 2014).

Rösler, H. *Europäisches Konsumentenvertragsrecht: Grundkonzeption, Prinzipien und Fortentwicklung* (München: C. H. Beck, 2004).

Rösler, H. 'Harmonizing the German Civil Code of the Nineteenth Century with a Modern Constitution: The Lüth Revolution 50 Years Ago in Comparative Perspective' (2008) 23 *Tulane European and Civil Law Forum* 1–36.

Rott, P. 'A New Social Contract Law for Public Services? Consequences from Regulation of Services of General Economic Interests in the EC' (2005) 3 *European Review of Contract Law* 323–345.

Rott, P. 'Consumers and Services of General Interest: Is EC Consumer Law the Future?' (2007) 30 *Journal of Consumer Policy* 49–60.

Rott, P. 'Services of General Interest, Contract Law and the Welfare State', in J. Rutgers (ed.), *European Contract Law and the Welfare State* (Groningen: Europa Law Publishing, 2012), pp. 79–103.

Rott, P. 'The Low-Income Consumer in European Private Law', in K. Purnhagen and P. Rott (eds.), *Varieties of European Economic Law and Regulation: Liber Amicorum for Hans Micklitz* (New York: Springer International Publishing, 2014), pp. 675–692.

Rott, P. 'Der "Durchschnittsverbraucher" – ein Auslaufmodell angesichts personalisierten Marketings?' (2015) *Verbraucher und Recht* 163–167.

Rouvière, F. 'Les valeurs économiques de la réforme du droit des contrats' (2016) *Revue des contrats* 600–607.

Rühl, G. 'Extending Ingmar to Jurisdiction and Arbitration Clauses: The End of Party Autonomy in Contracts with Commercial Agents?' (2007) 15 *European Review of Private Law* 891–903.

Rühl, G. 'Party Autonomy in the Private International Law of Contracts: Transatlantic Convergence and Economic Efficiency', in E. Gottschalk,

R. Michaels, G. Rühl and J. von Hein (eds.), *Conflict of Laws in a Globalized World* (Cambridge: Cambridge University Press, 2007), pp. 153-183.

Russell, B. *A History of Western Philosophy* (Sydney: Unwin Hyman Paperbacks, 1979).

Rust, U. and Falke, J. (eds.), *AGG. Allgemeines Gleichbehandlungsgesetz mit weiterführenden Vorschriften: Kommentar* (Berlin: Erich Schmidt Verlag, 2007).

Rüthers, B. *Die unbegrenzte Auslegung: Zum Wandel der Privatrechtsordnung im Nationalsozialismus*, 8th edition (Tübingen: Mohr Siebeck, 2017).

Sabel, C. F. and Gerstenberg, O. 'Constitutionalising an Overlapping Consensus: The ECJ and the Emergence of a Coordinate Constitutional Order' (2010) 16 *European Law Journal* 511-550.

Sabel, C. F. and Zeitlin, J. 'Learning from Difference: The New Architecture of Experimentalist Governance in the EU' (2008) 14 *European Law Journal* 271-327.

Sabel, C. F. and Zeitlin, J. 'Experimentalism in the EU: Common Ground and Persistent Differences' (2012) 6 *Regulation & Governance* 410-426.

Säcker, F. J. 'Vertragsfreiheit und Schutz vor Diskriminierung' (2006) 14 *Zeitschrift für Europäisches Privatrecht* 1-6.

Safjan, M. The Horizontal Effect of Fundamental Rights in Private Law – On Actors, Vectors and Factors of influence, in K. Purnhagen and P. Rott (eds.), *Varieties of European Economic Law and Regulation: Liber Amicorum for Hans Micklitz*, (New York: Springer International Publishing, 2014), pp. 123-152

Safjan, M. and Düsterhaus, D. 'A Union of Effective Judicial Protection: Addressing a Multi-level Challenge through the Lens of Art 47 CFREU' (2014) 33 *Yearbook of European Law* 3-40.

Safranski, R. *Schiller oder die Erfindung des deutschen Idealismus* (München: Carl Hanser Verlag, 2004).

Safranski, R. *Romantik: Eine deutsche Affäre* (München: Carl Hanser Verlag, 2007).

Sagnac, P. *La législation civile de la révolution française (1789-1804): Essai d'histoire sociale* (Paris: Hachette, 1898).

Saleilles, R. *Les accidents de travail et la responsabilité civile: Essai d'une théorie objective de la responsabilité délictuelle* (Paris: A. Rousseau, 1897).

v. Salomon, E. *Der Tote Preusse: Roman einer Staatsidee* (Frankfurt; Berlin: Ullstein, 1988).

Sangiovanni, A. 'Solidarity in the European Union: Problems and Prospects', in J. Dickson and P. Eleftheriadis (eds.), *Philosophical Foundations of European Union Law* (Oxford: Oxford University Press, 2012), pp. 384-411.

Sauter, W. *Public Services in EU Law* (Cambridge: Cambridge University Press, 2015).

Saydé, A. 'Defining the Concept of Abuse of Union Law' (2014) 33 *Yearbook of European Law* 138-162.

Scharpf, F. W. *Crisis and Choice in European Social Democracy* (Ithaca, NY: Cornell University Press: 1991).

Scharpf, F. W. *Governing in Europe: Effective and Democratic?* (Oxford; New York: Oxford University Press, 1999).

Scharpf, F. W. 'Monetary Union, Fiscal Crisis and the Pre-Emption of Democracy' (2011) 9 *Zeitschrift für Staats- und Europawissenschaften / Journal for Comparative Government and European Policy* 163–198.
Schebesta, H. 'Procedural Theory in EU Law', in K. Purnhagen and P. Rott (eds.), *Varieties of European Economic Law and Regulation: Liber Amicorum for Hans Micklitz* (New York: Springer International Publishing, 2014), pp. 851–862
Schepel, H. 'Professorenrecht? The Field of European Private Law', in H. Schepel and A. Jettinghoff (eds.), *Lawyers' Circles: Lawyers and European Legal Integration* (The Hague: Elsevier Reed, 2004), pp. 115–124.
Schepel, H. *The Constitution of Private Governance* (Oxford: Hart Publishing, 2005).
Schepel, H. 'The European Brotherhood of Lawyers: The Reinvention of Legal Science in the Making of European Private Law' (2007) 32 *Law & Social Inquiry* 183–199.
Schiek, D. *Differenzierte Gerechtigkeit: Diskriminierungsschutz und Vertragsrecht* (Baden-Baden: Nomos, 2000).
Schiek, D. 'Zwischenruf: Den Pudding an die Wand nageln? Überlegungen zu einer progressiven Agenda für das EU-Anti-Diskriminierungsrecht' (2014) 47 *Kritische Justiz* 396–402.
Schiek, D., Waddington, L. and Bell, M. (eds.), *Cases, Materials and Text on National, Supranational and International Non-Discrimination Law* (Oxford: Hart Publishing, 2007).
Schiemann, K. 'Europe—Our Common Legal Principles' (1999) 19 (1) *Yearbook of European Law* 205–216.
Schirmbacher, M. *Verbrauchervertriebsrecht: Die Vereinheitlichung der Vorschriften über Haustürgeschäfte, Fernabsatzverträge und Verträge im elektronischen Geschäftsverkehr* (Baden-Baden: Nomos, 2005).
Schmidt, K. I. 'Henry Maine's "Modern Law": From Status to Contract and Back Again?' (2017) 65 *The American Journal of Comparative Law* 145–186.
Schmitt, C. *Politische Theologie* (München; Leipzig: Duncker & Humblot, 1922).
Scholten, M. and v. Rijsbergen, M. 'The Limits of Agencification in the European Union' (2014) 15 *German Law Journal* 1223–1256.
Schreier, M. 'Das Allgemeine Gleichbehandlungsgesetz – wirklich ein Eingriff in die Vertragsfreiheit?' (2007) *Kritische Justiz* 278–286.
Schuck, G. *Rheinbundpatriotismus und politische Öffentlichkeit zwischen Aufklärung und Frühliberalismus: Kontinuitätsdenken und Diskontinuitätserfahrung in den Staatsrechts- und Verfassungsdebatten der Rheinbundpublizistik* (Stuttgart: Steiner, 1994).
Schulin, E. *Handelsstaat England. Das politische Interesse der Nation im Außenhandel vom 16. bis ins frühe 18. Jahrhundert* (Wiesbaden: F. Steiner, 1969).
Schulte-Nölke, H. and Bundesministerium der Justiz und für Verbraucherschutz (eds.), *Neue Wege zur Durchsetzung des Verbraucherrechts* (Berlin: Springer, 2017).
Schulze, H. 'Mentalitätsgeschichte – Chancen und Grenzen eines Paradigmas der französischen Geschichtswissenschaft' (1985) 36 *Geschichte in Wissenschaft und Unterricht* 247–270.
Schulze, H. 'German Identity' (1989) 32 *The Historical Journal* 1005–1011.

Schulze, R. 'Französisches Recht und Europäische Rechtsgeschichte im 19. Jahrhundert', in R. Schulze (ed.), *Französisches Zivilrecht in Europa während des 19: Jahrhunderts* (Berlin: Duncker und Humblot, 1994), pp. 9-36.

Schwarzkopf, S. 'The Consumer as "Voter", "Judge" and "Jury": Historical Origins and Political Consequences of a Marketing Myth' (2011) 31 *Journal of Macromarketing* 8-18.

Schwintowski, H.-P. *Recht und Gerechtigkeit: Eine Einführung in Grundfragen des Rechts* (Berlin: Springer, 1996).

Schwintowski, H.-P. 'Standardisation *Prior to or Instead of* Information – A Fundamental Criticism of the (European) Information Model for Financial and Insurance Products', in K. Purnhagen and P. Rott (eds.), *Varieties of European Economic Law and Regulation: Liber Amicorum for Hans Micklitz* (New York: Springer International Publishing, 2014), pp. 549-567.

Scotland, N. 'Methodism and the English Labour Movement 1800-1906' (1997) 14 *Anvil* 36-48.

Sefton-Green, R. 'Social Justice and European Identity in European Contract Law' (2006) 2 *European Review of Contract Law* 275-286.

Sen, A. *Development as Freedom* (Oxford: Oxford University Press, 1999).

Sen, A. *Rationality and Freedom* (Cambridge, MA: Harvard University Press, 2002).

Sen, A. *The idea of justice* (Cambridge, MA: Harvard University Press, 2009).

Shaw, J. 'Citizenship of the Union: Towards Post-National Membership?' (1997) *Harvard Jean Monnet Working Paper* No. 6.

Shuibhne, N. N. 'The Resilience of EU Market Citizenship' (2010) 47 *Common Market Law Review* 1597-1628.

Simon, D. (ed.), *Rechtswissenschaft in der Bonner Republik: Studien zur Wissenschaftsgeschichte der Jurisprudenz* (Frankfurt: Suhrkamp, 1994).

Sinzheimer, H. 'Die Fortentwicklung des Arbeitsrechts und die Aufgabe der Rechtslehre' (1910-1911) 20 *Soziale Praxis* 1203.

Sinzheimer, H. *Ein Arbeitstarifgesetz: Die Idee der sozialen Selbstbestimmung im Recht* (München; Leipzig: Duncker & Humblot, 1916).

Sinzheimer, H. *Grundzüge des Arbeitsrechts* (Jena: G. Fischer, 1921).

Skinner, Q. 'Thomas Hobbes and His Disciples in France and England' (1966) 8 *Comparative Studies in Society and History* 153-167.

Sloterdijk, P. *Die schrecklichen Kinder der Neuzeit* (Berlin: Suhrkamp Verlag, 2014).

Smismans, S. 'From Harmonization to Co-ordination? EU Law in the Lisbon Governance Architecture' (2011) 18 *Journal of European Public Policy* 504-524.

Smith, H. E. 'Property as the Law of Things', Symposium 'The New Private Law', (2012) 125 *Harvard Law Review* 1691-1726.

Smith, S. 'Duties, Liabilities, and Damages', Symposium 'The New Private Law', (2012) 125 *Harvard Law Review* 1727-1756.

Smith, T. B. *France in Crisis: Welfare, Inequality, and Globalization since 1980* (Cambridge; New York: Cambridge University Press, 2004).

Smith, T. B. *La France injuste, 1975-2006: Pourquoi le modèle social français ne fonctionne plus* (Paris: Autrement, 2006).

Smits, J. 'Who Does What? On The Distribution of Competences Among the European Union and the Member States', in K. Purnhagen/P. Rott (eds.), *Varieties of European Economic Law and Regulation: Liber Amicorum for Hans Micklitz*, (New York: Springer International Publishing, 2014), pp. 343–357.
Somek, A. *Engineering Equality: An Essay on European Anti-Discrimination Law* (Oxford: Oxford University Press, 2011).
Somek, A. *The Cosmopolitan Constitution* (Oxford: Oxford University Press, 2014).
Somek, A. 'The Darling Dogma of Bourgeois Europeanists' (2014) 20 *European Law Journal* 688–712.
Somek, A. 'The Preoccupation with Rights and the Embrace of Inclusion: A Critique', in D. Kochenov, G. de Búrca and A. Williams (eds.), *Europe's Justice Deficit?* (Oxford: Hart Publishing, 2015), pp. 295–310.
Somek, A. 'Zwei Welten der Rechtslehre und der Philosophie des Rechts' (2016) 71 *Juristen Zeitung* 481–486.
Somek, A. *Rechtstheorie zur Einführung* (Hamburg: Junius, 2017).
Somma, A. 'Social Justice and the Market in European Contract Law' (2006) 2 *European Review of Contract Law* 181–198.
Soper, K. and Trentmann, F. (eds.), *Citizenship and Consumption* (Basingstoke, England; New York: Palgrave Macmillan, 2008).
de Sousa Santos, B. 'Law: A Map of Misreading: Toward a Postmodern Conception of Law' (1987) 14 *Journal of Law and Society* 279–302.
Southern, R. W. *The Making of the Middle Ages* (New Haven: Yale University Press, 1953).
Stein, E. 'Lawyers, Judges and the Making of a Transnational Constitution' (1981) 75 *American Journal of International Law* 1–27.
Steindorff, E. *EG-Vertrag und Privatrecht* (Baden-Baden: Nomos, 1996).
Steinmo, S. *The Evolution of Modern States: Sweden, Japan, and the United States* (New York: Cambridge University Press, 2010).
Stigler, G. *The Theory of Competitive Price* (New York: Macmillan, 1942).
Stoffels, M. *AGB-Recht* (München: C. H. Beck, 2003).
Stolleis, M. 'Prologue: Reluctance to Glance in the Mirror: The Changing Face of German Jurisprudence after 1933 and post-1945', in C. Joerges and N. S. Ghaleigh, *Darker Legacies of Law in Europe: The Shadow of National Socialism and Fascism over Europe and its Legal Traditions* (Oxford: Hart Publishing, 2003), pp. 1–18.
Straumann, B. *Roman Law in the State of Nature: The Classical Foundations of Hugo Grotius' Natural Law* (Cambridge: Cambridge University Press, 2015).
Streeck, W. *How Will Capitalism End?* (London: Verso, 2016).
Streeck, W. 'Scenario for a Wonderful Tomorrow', Book Review of Europe's Orphan: The Future of the Euro and the Politics of Debt by Martin Sandbu (Princeton: Princeton University Press 2015)', (2016) 38 *London Review of Books* 7–10.
Study Group on Social Justice in European Private Law, 'Social Justice in European Contract Law: A Manifesto' (2004) 10 *European Law Journal* 653–674.

Stuyck, J. 'Patterns of Justice in the European Constitutional Charter: Minimum Harmonisation in the Field of Consumer Law', in L. Krämer, H.-W. Micklitz and K. Tonner (eds.), *Law and Diffuse Interests in the European Legal Order / Recht und diffuse Interessen in der Europäischen Rechtsordnung: Liber amicorum Norbert Reich* (Baden-Baden: Nomos, 1997), pp. 279-289.

Stuyck, J. 'Do We Need Consumer Protection' for Small Businesses at the EU level?', in K. Purnhagen and P. Rott (eds.), *Varieties of European Economic Law and Regulation: Liber Amicorum for Hans Micklitz* (New York: Springer International Publishing, 2014), pp. 359-370.

Stuyck, J. 'The Court of Justice and the Unfair Commercial Practices Directive' (2015) 52 *Common Market Law Review* 721-752.

Suk, J. C. 'Equality After Brexit: Evaluating British Contributions to EU Antidiscrimination Law', in Symposium Issue 'EU Law with the UK, EU Law without the UK' (2017) 40 *Fordham International Law Journal*, 1535-1552.

Sunstein, C. R. and Thaler, R. H. 'Libertarian Paternalism Is Not an Oxymoron' (2003) 70 *The University of Chicago Law Review* 1159-1202.

Svetiev, Y. 'Settling or Learning: Commitment Decisions as a Competition Enforcement Paradigm' (2014) 33 *Yearbook of European Law* 466-500.

Svetiev, Y. 'European Regulatory Private Law: From Conflicts to Platforms', in K. Purnhagen and P. Rott (eds.), *Varieties of European Economic Law and Regulation: Liber Amicorum for Hans Micklitz* (New York: Springer International Publishing, 2014), pp. 153-177.

Svetiev, Y. 'The EU's Private Law in the Regulated Sectors: Competitive Market Handmaiden or Institutional Platform?' (2016) 22 *European Law Journal* 659-680.

Lord Sweyn, 'The Role of Good Faith and Fair Dealing in Contract Law: A Hair-Shirt Philosophy?' (1991) 6 *The Denning Law Journal* 131-141.

Szyszczak, E., Davies, J., Andenas, M. and Bekkedal, T. (eds.), *Developments in Services of General Interest* (The Hague: T. M. C. Asser Press, 2011).

Tenreiro, M. 'The Community Directive on Unfair Terms and National Legal Systems: The Principle of Good Faith and Remedies for Unfair Terms' (1995) 3 *European Review of Private Law* 273-284.

Teubner, G. *Law as an Autopoietic System* (Oxford: Blackwell, 1993).

Teubner, G. 'Legal Irritants: Good Faith in British Law or How Unifying Law Ends up in New Divergences' (1998) 61 *Modern Law Review* 11-32.

Teubner, G. 'Ein Fall von struktureller Korruption? Die Familienbürgschaft in der Kollision unverträglicher Handlungslogiken' (2000) 83 *Kritische Vierteljahresschrift für Gesetzgebung und Rechtswissenschaft* 388-404.

Thaler, R. H. and Sunstein, C. R. *Nudge: Improving Decisions about Health, Wealth and Happiness* (New Haven: Yale University Press, 2008).

Thibaut, A. F. J. and v. Savigny, F. C., *Thibaut und Savigny: Ihre programmatischen Schriften. Mit einer Einführung von Hans Hattenhauer* (München: Franz Vahlen, 1973).

Thomson, D. *Europe Since Napoleon*, rev. edition (Harmondsworth: Penguin, 1966).

Thornhill, C. 'The Constitutionalization of Labour Law and the Crisis of National Democracy', in P. F. Kjaer and N. Olsen (eds.), *Critical Theories of Crisis in Europe: From Weimar to the Euro* (London: Rowman & Littlefield, 2016), pp. 89–105.
de Tocqueville, A. *The Old Regime and the French Revolution* (New York: Anchor Books, 1955).
Tonner, K., Willingmann, A., and Tamm, M. *Vertragsrecht: Kommentar* (Köln: Luchterhand Verlag, 2010).
Torp, C. *Konsum und Politik in der Weimarer Republik* (Göttingen: Vandenhoeck & Ruprecht, 2011).
Torp, C. *Wachstum, Sicherheit, Moral: Politische Legitimationen des Konsums im 20. Jahrhundert* (Göttingen: Wallstein-Verlag, 2012).
Trentmann, F. 'Knowing Consumers – Histories, Identities, Practices: An Introduction', in F. Trentmann (ed.), *The Making of the Consumer: Knowledge, Power and Identity in the Modern World* (Oxford: Berg, 2006), pp. 1–27.
Trentmann, F. *Empire of Things: How We Became a World of Consumers, from the Fifteenth Century to the Twenty-First* (London: Penguin Books, 2016).
Triana, P. 'Debt That Costs Less Than Nothing: Greece's Unique Opportunity' (2017), available at: https://papers.ssrn.com/sol3/papers.cfm?abstract_id=2941023.
Tridimas, T. 'Precedent and the Court of Justice: A Jurisprudence of Doubt?', in J. Dickson and P. Eleftheriadis (eds.), *Philosophical Foundations of European Union Law* (Oxford: Oxford University Press, 2012), pp. 307–330.
Trubek, D. M. and Trubek, L. G. 'Hard and Soft Law in the Construction of Social Europe: The Role of the Open Method of Co-ordination' (2005) *European Law Journal* 343–364.
Trumbull, G. *Consumer Lending in France and America: Credit and Welfare* (Cambridge: Cambridge University Press, 2014).
Tsakyrakis, S. 'Disproportionate Individualism', in D. Kochenov, G. de Búrca and A. Williams (eds.), *Europe's Justice Deficit?* (Oxford: Hart Publishing, 2015), pp. 235–246.
Tsebelis, G. *Nested Games. Rational Choice in Comparative Politics* (Berkeley; Los Angeles: University of California Press, 1990).
Tuori, K. 'Vers une théorie du droit transnational' (2013) *Revue Internationale de Droit Economique* 9–36.
Tuori, K. 'European Social Constitution: Between Solidarity and Access Justice', in K. Purnhagen and P. Rott (eds.), *Varieties of European Economic Law and Regulation: Liber Amicorum for Hans Micklitz*, (New York: Springer International Publishing, 2014), pp. 371–400.
Tuori, K. *European Constitutionalism* (Cambridge: Cambridge University Press, 2015).
Twigg-Flesner, C. 'From REFIT to a Rethink: Time for Fundamental EU Consumer Law Reform?' (2017) 6 *Journal of European Consumer and Market Law* 185–189.
Ulmer, P. 'Schutz vor unbilligen Allgemeinen Geschäftsbedingungen als Aufgabe eines speziellen Verbraucherrechts oder des allgemeinen Zivilrechts? Zu Reichs Beitrag' (1978) 2 *Zeitschrift für Verbraucherpolitik* 248–252.

Unberath, H. and Johnston, A. 'The Double-Headed Approach of the ECJ concerning Consumer Protection' (2007) 44 *Common Market Law Review* 1237–1284.

Vandenberghe, A.-S. 'The Economics of the Non-Discrimination Principle in General Contract Law' (2007) 3 *European Review of Contract Law* 410–431.

Varsori, A. 'Development of European Social Policy', in W. Loth (ed.), *Experiencing Europe: 50 Years of European Construction 1957–2007* (Baden-Baden: Nomos 2009), pp. 169–192.

Vauchez, A. *Brokering Europe: Euro-Lawyers and the Making of a Transnational Polity* (Cambridge: Cambridge University Press, 2015).

Verbruggen, P. *Enforcing Transnational Private Regulation: A Comparative Analysis of Advertising and Food Safety* (Cheltenham: Edward Elgar, 2014).

Viehoff, J. and Nikolaïdis, K. 'Social Justice and the European Union: The Puzzles of Solidarity, Reciprocity and Choice', in D. Kochenov, G. de Búrca and A. Williams (eds.), *Europe's Justice Deficit?* (Oxford: Hart Publishing, 2015), pp. 277–294.

Vogenauer, St. and Weatherill, S. (eds.), *General Principles of Law: European and Comparative Perspectives* (Oxford: Hart Publishing, 2017).

Vogl, J. *The Specter of Capital* (Stanford: Stanford University Press, 2015).

Waddington, L. 'The European Union and the United Nations Convention on the Rights of Persons with Disabilities: A Story of Exclusive and Shared Competences' (2011) 18 *Maastricht Journal of European and Comparative Law* 431–453.

Waddington, L. 'HK Danmark (Ring and Skouboe Werge): Interpreting EU equality law in the light of the UN Convention on the rights of persons with disabilities' (2013) *European Anti-Discrimination Law Review* 11–22.

Wagner, G. 'Zwingendes Privatrecht – Eine Analyse anhand des Vorschlags einer Richtlinie über Rechte der Verbraucher' (2010) *Zeitschrift für europäisches Privatrecht* 243–278.

Wagner, G. 'Der Verbrauchsgüterkauf in den Händen des EuGH: Überzogener Verbraucherschutz oder ökonomische Rationalität?' (2016) *Zeitschrift für europäisches Privatrecht* 87–120.

Walker, N. 'Europe's Constitutional Momentum and the Search for Polity Legitimacy' (2005) 3 *International Journal of Constitutional Law* 211–238.

Walker, N. 'Legal Theory and the European Union: A 25th Anniversary Essay' (2005) 25 *Oxford Journal of Legal Studies* 581–601.

Walker, N. 'Big 'C' or Small 'c'' (2006) 12 *European Law Journal* 12–14.

Walker, N. 'Justice in and of the European Union', in D. Kochenov, G. de Búrca and A. Williams (eds.), *Europe's Justice Deficit?* (Oxford: Hart Publishing, 2015), pp. 247–258.

Wassermann, R. (ed.), *Kommentar zum BGB (Reihe Alternativkommentare)*, multiple volumes (Neuwied: Luchterhand, 1980–1990).

Weatherill, S. 'The Evolution of European Consumer Law and Policy: From Well Informed Consumer to Confident Consumer', in H.-W. Micklitz (ed.),

Rechtseinheit oder Rechtsvielfalt in Europa? Rolle und Funktion des Verbraucherrechts in der EG und MOE-Staaten (Baden-Baden: Nomos, 1996), pp. 423–468.

Weatherill, S. 'Justifying Limits to Party Autonomy in the Internal Market – EC Legislation in the Field of Consumer Protection', in S. Grundmann, W. Kerber and S. Weatherill, *Party Autonomy and the Role of Information in the Internal Market* (Berlin: Walter de Gruyter, 2001), pp. 173–196.

Weatherill, S. *EU Consumer Law and Policy*, 2nd edition (Cheltenham: Edward Elgar, 2005).

Weatherill, S. 'Minimum Harmonisation as Oxymoron? The Case of Consumer Law', in H.-W. Micklitz (ed.), *Verbraucherrecht in Deutschland – Stand und Perspektiven* (Baden-Baden: Nomos, 2005), pp. 15–36.

Weatherill, S. 'Who Is the 'Average Consumer'?', in S. Weatherill and U. Bernitz (eds.), *The Regulation of Unfair Commercial Practices under EC Directive 2005/29: New Rules and new Techniques* (Oxford: Hart Publishing, 2007), pp. 115–138.

Weatherill, S. 'Competence and Legitimacy', in C. Barnard and O. Odudu (eds.), *The Outer Limits of European Union Law* (Oxford: Hart Publishing, 2009), pp. 17–34.

Weatherill, S. 'The Consumer Rights Directive: How and Why a Quest for "Coherence" Has (Largely) Failed' (2012) 49 *Common Market Law Review* 1279–1317.

Weatherill, S. 'Why There Is No 'Principle of Mutual Recognition in EU Law (and Why that Matters to Consumer Lawyers), in K. Purnhagen and P. Rott (eds.), *Varieties of European Economic Law and Regulation: Liber Amicorum for Hans Micklitz*, (New York: Springer International Publishing, 2014), pp. 401–418

Weatherill, S. 'Book Review: Towards a European Legal Culture, edited by Geneviève Helleringer and Kai Purnhagen. (Baden-Baden/Munich/Portland: Nomos/C.H. Beck/Hart Publishing, 2014)' (2014) 51 *Common Market Law Review*, 1851–1852.

Weatherill, S. *Contract Law of the Internal Market* (Cambridge: Intersentia, 2016).

Weatherill, S. 'Empowerment Is Not the Only Fruit', in D. Leczykiewicz and S. Weatherill (eds.), *The Images of the Consumer in EU Law: Legislation, Free Movement and Competition Law* (Oxford: Hart Publishing, 2016), pp. 203–222.

Weber, M. *Wirtschaft und Gesellschaft*, 5th rev. reprint (Tübingen: J. C. B. Mohr Siebeck, 1972).

Weiler, J. H. H. 'The Community System: The Dual Character of Supranationalism' (1981) 1 *Yearbook of European Law* 267–306.

Weiler, J. H. H. 'The Transformation of Europe' (1991) 100 *The Yale Law Journal* 2403–2483.

Weiler, J. H. H. 'Epilogue', in Ch. Joerges and N. S. Ghaleigh, *Darker Legacies of Law in Europe: The Shadow of National Socialism and Fascism over Europe and Its Legal Traditions* (Oxford: Hart Publishing, 2003), pp. 389–402.

Weiler, J. H. H. 'Deciphering the Political and Legal DNA of European Integration: An Exploratory Essay', in J. Dickson and P. Eleftheriadis (eds.), *Philosophical Foundations of European Union Law* (Oxford: Oxford University Press, 2012), pp. 137–158.

Weiler, J. H. H. 'Van Gend en Loos: The Individual as Subject and Object and the Dilemma of European Legitimacy' (2014) 12 *International Journal of Constitutional Law* 94–103.

Wendehorst, C. and Zöchling-Jud, B. (eds.), *Ein Neues Vertragsrecht für den digitalen Binnenmarkt?* (Wien: Manz, 2016).

Wesel, U. *Geschichte des Rechts: Von den Frühformen bis zur Gegenwart*, 2nd edition (München: C. H. Beck, 2001).

Whincup, M. *Consumer Legislation in the United Kingdom and the Republic of Ireland: A Study Prepared for the EC Commission* (London: Van Nostrand Reinhold, 1980).

Whitman, J. Q. *The legacy of Roman Law in the German Romantic Era: Historical Vision and Legal Change* (Princeton: Princeton University Press, 2014).

Wieacker, F. *Das Sozialmodell der klassischen Privatrechtsgesetzbücher und die Entwicklung der modernen Gesellschaft* (Karlsruhe: C. F. Müller, 1953).

Wieacker, F. 'Foundations of European Legal Culture' (1990) 38 *American Journal of Comparative Law* 1–29.

Wieacker, F. *A History of Private Law in Europe*, translated by T. Weir (Oxford: Clarendon Press, 1995).

Wieland, R. *Ich schlage vor, dass wir uns küssen* (München: Kunstmann, 2009).

Wilhelmsson, T. *Critical Studies in Private Law: A Treatise on Need-Rational Principles in Modern Law* (Dordrecht: Kluwer Academic Publishers, 1992).

Wilhelmsson, T. 'Private Law in the EU: Harmonised or Fragmented Europeanisation?' (2002) 10 *European Review of Private Law* 77–94.

Wilhelmsson, T. 'Services of General Interests and European Private Law', in C. E. F. Rickett and T. G. W. Telfer (eds.), *International Perspectives on Consumers' Access to Justice* (Cambridge: Cambridge University Press, 2003), pp. 149–166.

Wilhelmsson, T. 'The Abuse of the "Confident Consumer" as a Justification for EC Consumer Law' (2004) 27 *Journal of Consumer Policy* 317–337.

Wilhelmsson, T. 'Varieties of Welfarism in European Contract Law' (2004) 10 *European Law Journal* 712–733.

Wilhelmsson, T. 'European Consumer Law: Theses on the Task of the Member States', in H.-W. Micklitz (ed.), *Verbraucherrecht in Deutschland – Stand und Perspektiven* (Baden-Baden: Nomos, 2005), pp. 37–63.

Wilhelmsson, T. 'The Contract Law Acquis: Towards more Coherence through Generalisations?', *in 4. Europäischer Juristentag* (Wien: Manz, 2008), pp. 111–145.

Wilhelmsson, T., Paunio, E. and Pohjolainen, A. (eds.), *Private Law and the Many Cultures of Europe* (Alphen aan den Rijn: Kluwer Law International, 2007).

Wilkinson, M. A. 'Politicising Europe's Justice Deficit: Some Preliminaries', in D. Kochenov, G. de Búrca and A. Williams (eds.), *Europe's Justice Deficit?* (Oxford: Hart Publishing, 2015), pp. 111–136.

Willet, C. 'General Clauses on Fairness and the Promotion of Values Important in Services of General Interest', in C. Twigg-Flesner, D. Parry, G. Howells and A. Nordhausen, *The Yearbook of Consumer Law 2008* (Aldershot: Ashgate, 2007), pp. 67–106.

Willett, C. 'Contra Emptor Interpretation-Protecting Service Providers from EU Law', in K. Purnhagen and P. Rott (eds.), *Varieties of European Economic Law and Regulation: Liber Amicorum for Hans Micklitz* (New York: Springer International Publishing, 2014), pp. 709–732.

Williams, A. 'A Reply to Somek', in D. Kochenov, G. de Búrca and A. Williams (eds.), *Europe's Justice Deficit?* (Oxford: Hart Publishing, 2015), pp. 311–318.

Williams, A. 'The Problem(s) of Justice in the European Union', in D. Kochenov, G. de Búrca and A. Williams (eds.), *Europe's Justice Deficit?* (Oxford: Hart Publishing, 2015), pp. 33–50.

Wilman, F. *Private Enforcement of EU Law Before National Courts: The EU Legislative Framework* (Cheltenham: Edward Elgar Publishing, 2015).

Wimmer, K. and Jones, H. 'Brexit and Implications for Privacy', in Symposium Issue 'EU Law with the UK, EU Law without the UK' (2017) 40 *Fordham International Law Journal*, 1553–1564.

de Witte, B. 'New Institutions for Promoting Equality in Europe: Legal Transfers, National Bricolage and European Governance' (2012) 60 *American Journal of Comparative Law* 49–74.

de Witte, F. *Justice in the EU: The Emergence of Transnational Solidarity* (Oxford: Oxford University Press, 2015).

Wunder, A. *The Usage of Solidarity in the Jurisdiction of the ECJ: Symbolism or a European Legal Concept?*, LLM thesis, European University Institute (2015).

Wurmnest, W. 'Common Core, Grundregeln, Kodifikationsentwürfe, Acquis-Grundsätze – Ansätze internationaler Wissenschaftlergruppen zur Privatrechtsvereinheitlichung in Europa' (2003) *Zeitschrift für Europäisches Privatrecht* 714–744.

Würtenberger, T. 'Zeitgeist-Metaphorik und Recht in Frankreich und in Deutschland im ausgehenden 18. und beginnenden 19. Jahrhundert', in J. Jurt, G. Krumeich and T. Würtenberger (eds.), *Wandel von Recht und Rechtsbewußtsein in Frankreich und Deutschland* (Berlin: Berlin-Verlag Spitz, 1999), pp. 91–106.

Xenidis, R. 'Shaking the Normative Foundations of EU Equality Law: Evolution and Hierarchy between Market Integration and Human Rights Rationales' (2017) *EUI-ERC Working Paper* No. 4.

Zeitlin, J. and Venhercke, B. *Socialising the European Semester? Economic Governance and Social Policy Considerations in Europe 2020*, Swedish Institute for European Policy Studies 2014:7

Zglinski, J. *Europe's Passive Virtues: The Margin of Appreciation in EU Free Movement Law*, PhD thesis, European University Institute (2016).

Zimmermann, R. 'Heard Melodies Are Sweet, But Those Unheard Are Sweeter...': Condicio tacita, Implied Condition und die Fortbildung des europäischen Vertragsrechts' (1993) 193 *Archiv für die civilistische Praxis* 121–173.

Zimmermann, R. 'Savigny's Legacy: Legal History, Comparative Law, and the Emergence of a European Science' (1996) 112 *Law Quarterly Review* 576–605, in French 'L'héritage de Savigny. Histoire du droit, droit comparé, et émergence d'une science juridique européenne' (2013) *Revue Internationale de Droit Economique* 95–127.

Zimmermann, R. 'Consumer Contract Law and General Contract Law: The German Experience' (2005) 58 *Current Legal Problems* 415–489.

Zimmermann, R. (ed.), *Service Contracts* (Tübingen: Mohr Siebeck, 2010).

Zimmermann, R. and MacPherson, A. 'The Clapham Omnibus – Revisited' (2015) 23 *Zeitschrift für Europäisches Privatrecht* 685–688.

Zipursky, B. C. 'Palsgraf, Punitive Damages and Preemption', Symposium 'The New Private Law', (2012) 125 *Harvard Law Review* 1757–1797.

Index

abstract universalism, 292
access in tripartite private law, 285
access justice. *see* European access justice
Acquis Group, 83-88, 248, 275, 364-365
Acquis Principles (ACQP), 178, 215, 248, 326, 347
acquisitive individualism, 216
Act on Work Councils (Betriebsrätegesetz) (1922), 102
addressee in tripartite private law, 283
ADR bodies, 368
affordability of social justice, 119-124
age of reform, 57
agentification, 67, 244, 353
air pollution action plan, 369-371
allocative libertarian justice, 18-24
American Law Institute, 150
anti-discrimination, 10, 252
antitrust injuries, 337
Aquinas, Thomas, 53
Arbeiterbildungsvereine, 100
Aristotle (Greek philosopher), 53
Aron, Raymond, 193-194
Association Henri Capitant des Amis de La Culture Juridique Française, 88
Austrian Empire, 400
authoritarianism, 32, 100-103, 112, 115
autonomie de la volonté, 262
autonomy
  collective autonomy, 32, 59, 60, 61, 62, 81, 325
  of consumer, 325
  of decision, 170
  individual autonomy, 24, 26, 325, 397
  market citizen, 361
  private autonomy, 22, 361
  regulated autonomy, 22
  role for private law, 204
axiomatic role of law, 92-97

Bacon, Francis, 55, 56, 73
Bakardjieva-Engelbrekt, 108
balancing of rights in tripartite private law, 286-287, 374-375
Banking Union, 153, 189, 247
barrier-free conditions, 219
Basic Law *(Grundgesetz)*, 144
behavioural law and economics (BLE), 149
Bentham, Jeremy, 58
Bercusson, Brian, 157
BEREC Stakeholder Forum, 367
bilateral concept of shared competences/responsibilities, 314
bottom-up rule making, 366
Brandt, Willy, 105
breadwinner model, 158, 376
Breton, R., 287
Brexit, 43, 153-154, 252, 267, 277, 386, 398, 400-402
British empiricism. *see* empiricism
BUPA judgment, 298-299, 308

Calais-Auloy, Jean, 68, 87
Campaign for Clean Clothes (CCC), 377
Canon law, 54
Cappelletti, Mauro, 163-164
Cartesian philosophy, 74, 75
Cassis de Dijon doctrine, 16, 25-26, 162, 225, 226, 257-259, 260-263, 397
Catholic Church, 13, 47, 74
CEER Advisors (Council of European Energy Regulation), 366, 367
CGPF employers trade union confederation (Confédération Générale de la Production Française), 82
CGT trade union (Confédération Générale du Travail), 82
Charter of Fundamental Rights, 6, 24, 164, 181, 185-186, 215, 217, 262, 266, 276, 345

452 INDEX

Chicago School of Economics, 148, 149
child labour, 376
Christian social ethics, 13
Citizens' Energy Forum, 307, 367
civil law, 88, 110
civil society organisations, 372
Civil War, 57, 58
Classical Legal Thought, 3
Co-ordinated Market Economy (CME), 402
co-responsibility, 380
codes of conduct, 366, 377
codetermination
    (Mitbestimmungsgesetz), 102
codification, 58, 91
Cohen, G.A., 71
collective agreements, 17-18, 82, 101, 141, 204, 219, 259, 262, 324, 325, 330, 364
collective autonomy, 32, 59, 60, 61, 62, 81, 325
collective bargaining, 8, 61, 62-63, 381
collective claims, 66, 335
collective control, 130-134
Collective Labour Law, 380
collective laissez faire system, 59
collective private regulation, 219, 242
Collins, Hugh, 129-130, 272
Commission des Clauses Abusives, 133, 143
Committee on Women's Rights and Equal Opportunities at the Parliament, 206
Common Agricultural Policy (CAP), 167
Common European Sales Law (CESL), 178, 179, 202, 274, 326, 333, 365
common heritage, 168-172, 176-180
Common Market, 6
communism, 125, 400
communitarianism, 292
competencies
    bilateral concept of, 314
    enforcement order of, 245, 381
    European private law, 393-395
    European Union (EU) law, 393-395
    Internal Market-building, 175
    legal order of, 313, 380
    Order of Competence, 27, 352-357
Competition and Markets Authority (CMA), 65, 133
competition law
    antitrust injuries, 337
    economic inferiority, 321-322
    European legal order, 22-23
    European Union and, 166, 248
    exemptions from, 380-381
    Federal Trade Commission, 148
    power and, 329
compliance management, 368
Conseil de Prud'hommes, 142

Conseil National de la Consommation (CNC), 85
Constitutional Charter (2000), 180
constitutionalisation, 33, 123, 173, 186, 250-251
constitutionalism, 68, 359
consumer challenges, 271-273
consumer-citizen, 361
consumer contract law, 234-235
Consumer Credit Act (1974), 64
consumer individualisation, 138
consumer law
    access justice as paradigm shift, 184
    Basic Law *(Grundgesetz)*, 144
    constitutionalisation of, 186
    consumer protection paradigm, 225-228, 232, 233-238, 239-241
    development of, 49
    European Union (EU) law, 222-225, 228-233
    German, 107, 108, 110
    governing of, 192
    impact of EU law, 196-245
    introduction to, 15, 16, 87
    irritations at surface level, 156-159
    national consumer law, 9, 232
    politicalisation of, 84
    post-classical consumer law, 239-245
    rise of, 140
    social effectiveness vs. economic efficiency, 146
    social justice in, 64-67, 162
    social welfare thinking, 324
    substance shaping, 364-368
    Sutherland report, 229
consumer market society, 352-357, 377-382
    access and substance, 325-334
    addressee of the law on consumer, 318-325
    balancing of rights, expectations and needs, 344-347
    descriptive account, 318-322
    erga omnes doctrine, 342-343
    ex officio doctrine, 341-342
    fair and discrimination free access, 326-329
    good faith, 331-334
    importance of rationality test, 351-352
    interim relief, 343-344
    introduction to, 7-10, 316-318
    legitimate expectations, 347-351, 373-377
    order of competence and responsibilities, 352-357, 377-382
    physical/intellectual vulnerability, 322-323

INDEX   453

rights, remedies and procedures, 334-344, 368-373
the self and societal responsibility, 360-364
substance and imbalance of power, 329-331
substance shaping, 364-368
summary of, 383-384, 386
weaker party in, 324-325
consumer protection paradigm, 225-228, 232, 233-238, 239-241
consumer society, 5, 64, 83, 85, 107, 139, 172, 239
consumer vs. customer differentiation, 243-244
consumer-worker-citizens, 147
contractualisation of labour relations, 63
convergence process, 403, 404
Corporate Social Responsibility, 377
corporative *(ständische)* barriers to private law, 5
court-based litigation, 244
credit scoring, 328
Cromwell, Oliver, 47
cross-border litigation, 302

Davies, Paul, 59, 61, 62, 101-102
de Búrca, G., 222
de-judicialisation of enforcement, 286
de-privatisation of enforcement, 286
de-regulation of labour market, 61
de Villepin, Dominique, 69
de Witte, Floris, 285, 289, 292, 362
democracy, 58, 71, 75, 90, 93, 103, 148, 168-169, 359, 395
Deposit Guarantee Schemes, 349
Descartes, René, 74-75
descriptive model of access justice, 24-25
desireability of social justice, 119-124
DG Justice, 238
Dickson, J., 193
Direction génerale de la concurrence, de la consommation et de la répression des fraudes (DGCCRF), 143
Directive 75/129/EEC, 205
Directive 76/207/EEC, 205, 214
Directive 77/187/EEC, 205
Directive 80/987/EEC, 205, 207
Directive 84/450/EEC, 336
Directive 85/374/EEC, 224, 235-236, 267, 347
Directive 85/577/EEC, 227, 234
Directive 86/378/EEC, 206
Directive 87/102/EEC, 227
Directive 90/314/EEC, 229-230, 366
Directive 91/533/EEC, 207
Directive 92/59/EEC, 86, 224, 347

Directive 93/13/EEC, 65, 130, 142, 229-230, 234, 317, 319-320, 331, 336, 340, 344
Directive 94/19/EEC, 240
Directive 94/47/EEC, 233-234
Directive 97/7/EEC, 109, 229-230, 234
Directive 98/30/EEC, 290
Directive 99/44/EEC, 235-236, 347, 380
Directive 2000/43/EEC, 327, 328, 335, 338-339
Directive 2000/78/EEC, 335, 338-339
Directive 2001/95/EEC, 347
Directive 2002/8/EEC, 302
Directive 2002/22/EEC, 293
Directive 2003/54/EEC, 293-294, 318-319
Directive 2003/55/EEC, 293-294
Directive 2004/113/EEC, 320, 321, 335, 338-339, 340
Directive 2005/29/EEC, 319, 329, 340
Directive 2006/54/EEC, 338-339
Directive 2008/48/EEC, 332
Directive 2009/22/EEC, 336
Directive 2009/72/EEC, 294, 301, 366
Directive 2009/136/EEC, 293, 318-319, 356
Directive 2011/83/EEC, 319
Directive 2014/17/EEC, 319-320, 332
Directive 2014/92/EEC, 319-320
Directive 2015/2302/EEC, 319
Directive on Payment Accounts, 297
discovery procedure, 36
discrimination concerns, 10, 20, 241, 252, 271-273, 291-295, 326-329. *see also* non-discrimination law
discriminatory collective agreements, 364
dispute settlement procedures, 303
distributional (justice) concerns, 149
distributive (collective) effectiveness of private law, 124-134
Draft Common Frame of Reference (DCFR), 99, 179, 202, 252, 326, 347-348, 365

Ebert, Friedrich, 93
economic discrimination, 20, 241, 291-295
economic efficiency, 14, 41, 54, 121, 145-151, 181-186, 260, 276, 277, 316
economic interests, 223, 225, 239, 288, 296
economic success, 57-58
effectiveness of social justice, 119-124
effet utile, 343
efficiency of social justice, 119-124
Ehrlich, Eugen, 98
Eigentumsordnung (private property), 99
Eleftheriadis, P., 193
empiricism, 50, 53, 55, 70, 91
energy poverty, 310
enforcement competences, 245, 381
enforcement experimentalism, 254-255

INDEX

enforcement order, 357
English empiricism, 91, 97
English law (common law), 54
English model of social justice
  common heritage, 168–172, 176–180
  common intellectual history, 166–172
  constitutional standstill, 186–191
  consumer law, 64–67
  impact of EU law, 196–245
  introduction to, 47–48, 50
  labour law, 58–63
  Lisbon Council, 23, 180, 181–186
  overview of, 50–67
  post-classical foundations, 191–195
  post-classical move in European integration, 180–195
  pragmatism and personalism, 50–54
  societal continuity and economic success, 57–58
  utilitarian thinking, 54–56
English pragmatism, 50–54, 56, 75, 97–100, 122, 137, 152, 153–156, 402
English utilitarian thinking, 54–56, 66, 72, 112, 163
Equal Opportunities Action Programme, 206
Equal Opportunities Commission, 141, 142, 206
Equal Opportunities Unit, 206
equal opportunity access justice, 24–27
erga omnes doctrine, 342–343
erosion of welfare state, 7
essential goods, 365, 366
Esser, Josef, 360
ethical consumption, 362–363
ethnic group vulnerability, 323
Eurocrisis management, 1, 26
European access justice
  allocative libertarian justice, 18–24
  defined, 2
  equal opportunity and market justice, 24–27
  measuring standards of, 349
  overview of, 12–18, 216
  as paradigm shift, 184, 202
  social distributive justice, 18–24
  social justice and, 27–30
  summary of, 277, 386, 390–392
  theoretical localization of, 18–30
European Agencies ACER (Agency for the Co-ordination of Energy Regulation), 306
European and Common Law, 112
European association of workers (EUTC), 379
European associations of consumers (BEUC), 379
European Center for Constitutional and Human Rights (ECCHR), 377
European Civil Code, 28, 155, 161, 164, 173, 176, 184, 241, 326
European Code on Civil Law, 88
European Commission (EC)
  collective control mechanism, 132
  enforcement competencies, 245
  influences on, 86
  introduction to, 21, 67
  liberalising of public services, 143
  Lisbon Council, 23, 180, 181–186, 273
  non-tariff barriers to trade, 224
  Open Method of Coordination, 187–188, 213
  role of, 268–269
  social policy programme, 167
  universal service obligations, 299
European constitution, 161, 164, 173, 176, 178, 186–191
European consumer law. *see* consumer law
European Consumer Organizations, 367
European Consumer Policy, 230
European Convention of Human Rights, 216
European Cooperative Society (SCE), 28
European Court of Human Rights (ECHR), 212, 323
European Court of Justice (ECJ)
  air pollution action plan, 369–371
  competition law, 381
  consumer contract law, 234–235
  consumer protection paradigm, 225–228, 232, 233–238
  discriminatory collective agreements, 364
  European integration and, 167
  European law interpretation, 314
  free movement of workers, 205
  judicial activism, 60, 156, 359
  private law relations, 189
  rationality test, 397
  residence rights, 309
  support for Member States, 267
European Economic Community, 6, 72, 167
European Economic Constitution, 166
European Employment Strategy (EES), 213
European Governance (2002), 180
European integration
  non-binding documents, 192
  overview of, 177
  post-classical move in, 180–195
  process of, 3, 11, 41, 222, 231
European laboratory, 253, 398–400
European legal (social) consciousness
  Brexit and, 400–402
  hybridization of, 42, 386, 389–390, 403, 404

introduction to, 38–41
overview of, 164, 388–389
post-classical European private law, 273–275
pre-conceptions and methodology, 38–41
private law justice, 337, 386–387
Single European Act (SEA), 388
European legal order, 22–23
European Monetary Union, 174–175
European Parliament, 177
European private law. *see also* post-classical European private law; tripartite private law
access to justice, 140–145
argument for, 2–3
collective control of standard contracts, 130–134
communist impact on, 400
consumer law and, 222–225, 228–233
consumer protection paradigm, 225–228
determinants of, 201–222
distributive (collective) effectiveness of, 124–134
European access justice, 12–18
expert statements, 128–130
fair access to, 20
free movement of workers, 203–207
in Germany, 110
hidden mode, 211–215
imbalance of power, 135–137
impact of, 196–245
introduction to, 1–2, 3–4, 196
labour and consumer market society, 7–10
materialisation of, 33, 125, 250
nation state and, 10–12
national consumer law, 9
national legal consciousness, 337, 386–387
national private law, 402–404
national social justice, 12–18
new societal private law, 393
non-discrimination law, 15, 17, 215–222
overview of, 41–43, 119–124, 196–201, 200t
path dependency, 152–159
post-classical consumer law, 239–245
post-classical European private law, 246–256
powers of, 32
pre-communist private law, 401
relaxed attention, 146–148
role of, 268–269
shared competencies and responsibilities, 393–395

social (individual) effectiveness of, 134–145
social effectiveness *vs.* economic efficiency, 145–151
social Europe, 207–211
social justice and, 119
as social law, 83–88
societal private law, 42, 161–162
status and, 137–140
summary of, 385
transformation of, 4–7
treaty amendments, 7, 9
European regulatory private law, 326
European Review of Contract law, 128
European Sales Law, 28
European Social Contracts Group (EuSoCo), 365
European Social Model, 6
European societal justice, 161–162, 163–165, 165t, 390–392,
Everson, M., 361
evidence-based policy, 125
ex officio doctrine, 341–342
experimentalism, 252–254, 315, 398, 399
expert statements, 128–130

fair access to private law justice, 20
'Fairness at Work' doctrine, 62
family law, 79
Federal Republic of Germany, 95, 102, 144
feudal barriers to private law, 5
FIN-USE annual report (2007/2008), 190–191
Financial Services Action Plan, 190
Financial Services Authority (FSA), 66
financialisation, 123
framed choice, 314
France in Crisis (Smith), 126
Franco-Prussian War 1870/71, 78
Frank, R., 154–155
Frankfurt Constitution (1848), 90
free movement of workers, 203–207, 219, 289, 292–293
Freedland, Mark, 59, 61, 62, 101–102
freedom/coercion metaphor, 262
freedom of will, 170
Freeland, Mark, 401
French Academic Group, 88
French Civil Code, 67, 68, 70, 71, 76–79, 98, 155, 336
French Code du Travail, 80
French Constitution, 47, 67, 71, 76–79
French existentialism, 73
French intellectualism, 152, 153–156, 163

French model of social justice
  Constitution and Civil Code beyond national boundaries, 76-79
  intellectual and political conception, 73-76
  intellectualism, 68-73
  introduction to, 67-68
  overview of, 67-88
  private law as social law, 83-88
  self- and state-help, 79-83
French Rationalism, 54, 71, 97, 114, 115, 126
French Revolution, 47, 50, 83, 90, 387
Fritz W. Scharpf, 26
full harmonisation, 261, 263-264, 274, 278-279, 353, 394, 396, 399
Fundamental Rights Agency, 21, 221, 255
fundamental rights of third parties, 373

Galanter, M., 135
geltungserhaltende Reduktion, 338
geometric state, 404-405
German Automobile Club (ADAC), 145
German Basic Law, 94, 155-156, 336
German Civil Code (GCC), 89, 97, 98-100, 106-111, 313
German Confederation (Deutscher Bund), 89, 90
German Constitutional Court, 65, 95, 136, 144, 217
German Consumer Advice Centre, 376
German contract law *(Schuldrechts-Modernisierungsgesetz)*, 110
German Democratic Republic, 95
German idealism, 54, 94, 96-98, 116, 137, 152, 153-156
German legal naturalism, 91
German legalism, 38-39, 163, 169, 387
German Ministry of Justice, 254
German model of social justice
  authoritarianism to ordo-liberalism, 100-103
  axiomatic role of law, 92-97
  introduction to, 89-92
  market pragmatism and idealistic societal visions, 97-100
  overview of, 89-111
  Sonderprivatrecht, 106-111
  turmoil and continuity, 103-106
German national anthem, 92
German Reichsgericht, 95
German Reichstag, 100, 101
German social policy, 157
German Unfair Terms Act (AGBG), 131
German Verfassungspatriotismus (constitutional patriotism), 95
German welfare state, 23

Globalisation of Legal Thought, 3
globalization, 152, 396
Goffman, I., 402
good faith in consumer market society, 331-334, 347
Greek philosophers, 53
Green Paper on Unfair Trading Practices in Supply Chains, 321
Green Party, 94, 369
Gregory VII, Pope, 47
Griggs, Lynden, 323
Grossi, Paolo, 168-169
group-based identities, 215-216

Habermas, Jürgen, 250
Hallstein, Walter, 163
harmonisation, 28, 257
  full harmonisation, 261, 263-264, 274, 278-279, 353, 394, 396, 399
  maximum harmonisation, 224, 233, 234, 264, 273, 353, 389
  minimum harmonisation, 242-243, 261, 389, 399
Harvard Law Review, 358
Haupt, H.-G., 77
Heiderhoff, Bettina, 146
Helsinki Council (HC), 182
Henry IV, Emperor, 47
Heuss, Theodor, 94
Hobbes, Thomas, 56, 74-75
Hoffman von Fallersleben, Heinrich, 92, 93
human rights aversion, 54-55
humanism, 69
hybridization of consciousness, 42, 386, 389-390, 403

idealistic societal visions, 97-100
ideological criticism, 31-35
ILO Conventions on Child Labour, 375
imbalance of power, 135-137, 329-331
incriminated contract terms, 339
individual autonomy, 24, 26, 32, 325, 397
individual in competitive market, 317-318
individual laissez faire system, 59
individualization, 63, 123, 138, 325
individually enforceable right, 346
industrial evolution, 57
industrial relations, 8, 59, 102, 124, 202
Industrial Relations Act (1971), 62
industrialization, 57, 84, 91
inequality compensation, 9
institutional (constitutional) experimentalism, 251-252
institutional choice theory, 268
institutional concern in open market society, 316
institutional for law enforcement, 2

instrumentalisation of private law, 373
insurance law, 237
intellectual history, 38–41, 193
intellectual property rights, 20
intellectual vulnerability in consumer market society, 322–323
intellectualism, 68–73, 169, 177, 399
interim relief in consumer market society, 343–344
Internal Market-building
  Banking Union and, 153
  competence rules, 175
  completion of, 231
  European social consciousness, 164, 388
  minimum standards for workers, 174
  overview, 9, 20, 22, 30
  private law objective, 254
  rise of, 227, 240
  summary of, 276
  Sutherland report, 229
International Labour Organisation (ILO), 13
International Olympic Committee, 94
Internet of Things, 159
intrusion in EU law-making, 403–404
Iraklis, Aget, 212

Joerges, Christian, 258
Johnston, Angus, 247
Judeo-Christian tradition, 169
judicial activism, 359
judicial experimentalism, 36, 253
justice. *see also* European access justice; European private law; European societal justice; French model of social justice; German model of social justice; post-classical European private law; social justice
  access to, 140–145
  deficit of, 8, 12
  market justice, 4, 19, 24–27, 278, 360, 391, 395
  national social justice, 12–18, 392
  pure market justice, 4
  social distributive justice, 18–24, 189
  universal justice, 54–55

Kahn-Freund, Otto, 101–102, 108
Kant, Immanuel, 96
Kennedy, D., 137, 191, 243
Kennedy, John F., 135–136
Kennedy declaration (1962), 64, 105
Kessler, F., 262
Keynesianism, 60, 121
Klassengesellschaft, defined, 77
Komesar, N., 268
kundenfeindlichste Auslegung, 131

labour law
  access justice as paradigm shift, 184
  administrative enforcement, 221
  constitutionalisation of, 186
  consumer market society, 156–159
  consumer society, 139
  development of, 49
  French, 82
  German, 107, 108
  impact of EU law, 196–245
  introduction to, 14, 16, 18
  irritations at surface level, 156–159
  master-servant relationship, 137
  rise of, 140
  social effectiveness *vs.* economic efficiency, 146
  social justice in, 58–63
  social welfare thinking, 324
labour market society, 7–10, 207, 316
Lacroix, Michel, 70
Lamfalussy procedure, 37, 252
land law, 14, 58, 79–80
law making, 252–254
legal consciousness. *see* European legal (social) consciousness
legal naturalism, 91, 96–97, 98, 107, 109
legal order of competence, 313, 380
Legal Origin Theory (LOT), 112
legal sociology *(Rechtssoziologie)*, 98
legalism, 169, 170–171, 177, 387
legitimate expectations, 347–351, 373–377
lex geometrica, 164, 405
liberal market economies, 129, 402
liberal utilitarian thinking, 112
liberalisation, 236, 244, 288, 290, 310
liberalism, 100–103, 170, 361, 395
libertarian paternalism, 114
Lisbon Agenda, 164, 181–182, 183, 224, 233, 270, 273, 276, 316, 345, 353, 355, 394, 395–396
Lisbon Council, 23, 180, 181–186
Lisbon Treaty. *see* Treaty of Lisbon
Locke, John, 52, 56, 75
Luger, B., 380

Maastricht Treaty, 230, 231, 240
mandatory contract law, 150
Marella, M., 139–140
market behaviour law, 232
market citizen, 361, 365
market justice, 4, 19, 24–27, 278, 360, 391, 395
market pragmatism, 97–100
market-rational welfarism, 129
market regulation, 329
Marx, Karl, 156
Marxist theories, 12

master-servant relationship, 137
materialisation of private law, 33, 125, 250
Matignon Agreements, 82
maximum harmonisation, 224, 233, 234, 264, 273, 353, 389
Meli, Marisa, 129
Member States, role of, 266–268
Merkel, Angela, 155–156
migrant residence rights, 307–310
Miller, L., 363
minimum harmonisation, 242–243, 261, 389, 399
minimum protections to workers, 207
minimum wages, 8
modernisation, 7, 63
Molony Report, 64
Monetary Union, 1
More, Thomas, 54
mortgage calculations, 348
mutual enrichment *de lege lata*, 337

Naranjo, Gutiérrez, 189
national consumer law, 9, 232
national consumer organisations, 381
national legal consciousness, 38–41, 337, 386–387
national private law. *see* European private law
national social justice, 12–18, 392
National Supervisory Authorities, 237
national welfare state, 2, 4, 7
naturalism, 80, 98
Naturrechtslehre, 55
Nazi-Regime, 103
Neergard, U., 306
neoformalism, 3, 152, 191–192
New Deal, 148
new procedural remedy, 343
new societal private law, 393
Newton, Isaac, 195
nominalism, 50, 53, 54, 55
non-contractual relations, 334
non-discrimination law
  access justice as paradigm shift, 184, 202
  administrative enforcement, 221
  assessment of, 248
  concerns over, 188
  constitutionalisation of, 186
  consumer market society, 350–351
  European Union (EU) law, 215–222
  governing of, 192
  impact of EU law, 196–245
  introduction to, 10
  social justice and, 162
  substance shaping, 364–368
  trade unions and, 141
  as unconditional, 328

non-discrimination principle, 15, 17, 34, 42
non-economic interests, 288
non-tariff barriers to trade, 224
normative model of access justice, 24–25
Notablengesellschaft, defined, 77

Ockham's razor, 55
Office of Fair Trading, 133
open market society, 316
Open Method of Coordination (OMC), 20–21, 184–185, 213, 221, 306
Order of Competence, 27, 352–357
ordo-liberalism, 100–103, 361

Paris Summit (1990), 230
parliamentarian system, 50
paternalistic market design. *see* German model of social justice
path dependency, xv, xvi, 3, 31, 42, 46, 61, 152–159
personalism, 50–54, 169, 177, 399, 402
phantom control, 131
physical vulnerability in consumer market society, 322–323
Plato (Greek philosopher), 53
political background of social justice, 47–48, 163–164
political order of social market law, 353
political order of universal services, 311
political thinking, 112
politics of justice in private law. *see* European private law; post-classical European private law; tripartite private law
post-classical consumer law, 239–245
post-classical European private law
  business, role of, 269–270
  conflicts over, 271–273
  considerations on, 281–282
  enforcement experimentalism, 254–255
  EU, role of, 268–269
  European Commission, role of, 268–269
  European Union (EU) law, 246–256
  future of, 257–258
  general features, 246–256
  institutional (constitutional) experimentalism, 251–252
  introduction to, 246
  law making/interpreting experimentalism, 252–254
  legal consciousness, 273–275
  Member States, role of, 266–268
  nature of, 249–251
  public-private competences/ responsibilities, 265–270
  quantity of rules, 246–247
  rational arguments, 260–263

rationality in, 247-249
rationality test, 258-265
regulatory technique, 263-264
summary of, 276-279, 385
post-classical labour, 162, 196
post-classical move, 35-38
post-national private law, 4
pragmatism. *see* English pragmatism
pre-communist private law, 401
pre-conceptions and methodology
  ideological criticism, 31-35
  intellectual history, 38-41
  introduction to, 30-31
  legal consciousness, 38-41
  post-classical move, 35-38
premarket activation, 211
'Presidential Conclusions' of the European Council in Lisbon (2000), 180
private autonomy, 22, 361
private law. *see* European private law
private legal order making, 67
privatisation, 236, 244, 288, 290, 310
procedural law, 344
procedural requirements for law enforcement, 2
proceduralisation, 34, 36, 120, 213, 343
procedures in tripartite private law, 285-286
protective legislation, 10, 101
protective welfare state, 5, 81, 82
Prussian Regime, 100
public-private competences/responsibilities, 265-270
puritan faith, 57

quality under universal service, 298

radical subjectivism, 74
Raiser, Ludwig, 105-106
Ramm, Thilo, 58-59
rationalism, 112, 193, 260-263
rationality in post-classical European private law, 247-249
rationality test, 258-265, 351-352, 396-398
realistic opportunity for law enforcement, 2
Rechtssubjekt, 99
Rechtstatsachenforschung, 98
recommendations to universal service obligations, 304
redistribution of wealth, 5, 11, 32, 127, 129
Referendariat, defined, 68
regulated autonomy, 22
regulatory powers, 8, 263-264
regulatory welfare state, 5
Reich, N., 216, 323, 324, 364-365, 374, 380
Reifner, U., 365

relative state, 404-405
relaxed attention, 146-148
remedies in tripartite private law, 285-286
republicanism, 170
Rerum Novarum (New Things, 1891), 13
res judicata, 342
residence permits for migrants, 289, 292
residence rights and universal service obligations, 307-310
responsibilisation, 363, 379
responsibilities
  bilateral concept, 314
  co-responsibility, 380
  consumer market society, 352-357, 377-382
  Corporate Social Responsibility, 377
  European private law, 393-395
  European Union (EU) law, 393-395
  post-classical European private law, 265-270
  the self and, 360-364
  societal responsibility, 360-364
  transactional responsibility, 323
  tripartite private law, 287
  universal service obligations, 310-315
right of access, 290, 291
right to information, 374
rights in tripartite private law, 285-286
Rome Treaty. *see* Treaty of Rome
Rott, P., 297
Rousseau, Jean-Jacques, 75, 115

SABAM (Belgian associations), 373
Savigny, Friedrich Carl von, 96, 97-98
Schepel, H., 250
scholasticism, 50, 53, 54, 90
scope of rationality test, 259-260
Seccombe, Monica, 163-164
secondary law making, 259, 345
the self and consumer market society, 360-364
self-help principle, 58-59, 141
self-referential system, 132
self-regulatory bodies, 371
self-standing principles, 8, 216
semi-legal conflict management, 335
Sharpson, E., 289
Shaw, Joe, 363
Shuibhne, N., 361-362
single currency, 212
Single European Act (SEA)
  access justice and, 173
  constitutionalisation in, 123
  enlarged competencies, 174
  European social consciousness, 388
  foreshadowing of, 201
  health and safety at work, 202

Single European Act (SEA) (cont.)
  introduction to, 6, 16, 42
  political order of social market law, 353
  scope of rationality test, 259
  separation of economic and social powers, 268
  Social European Model, 203
  Sutherland report, 229
Single Market project, 45
Sinzheimer, Hugo, 97, 101, 135
situational weakness, 323
Small Claims Court, 141
SMEs (Small and Medium Sized Companies), 321
Smith, Timothy B., 126, 135
Smth v. Advel, 220
social (individual) effectiveness of private law, 134-145
social contract law, 80
social deficit, 6, 8
social democrats, 41, 100
social discrimination, 17, 20, 21, 191, 248, 285, 301
social distributive justice, 18-24, 189
social effectiveness, 145-151
social embeddedness of the capitalist market, 174
Social European Model, 203, 207-211
social exclusion, 182-183
social inclusion, 24, 182, 317, 347-351, 354
social justice. *see also* European societal justice; French model of social justice; German model of social justice
  access justice and, 27-30
  conceptions in comparison, 111
  in consumer law, 64-67
  cultural background of, 264
  English model, 50-67
  French model, 67-88
  German model, 89-111
  identification of deficit, 257
  introduction to, 5, 45-46
  in labour law, 58-63
  market order and society, 115-117, 117t
  national social justice, 12-18, 392
  orientation chart, 48-50, 49t
  overview of, 119-124
  perceived patterns of, 111-113, 112t
  private law and, 119
  role of law in remedying deficits, 113-115, 115t
  societal private law, 42, 161-162
  socio-economic/political background of, 47-48
  state *vs.* individual, 198.30 t, 117-118
  transformation of, 12-18
Social Justice Group, 128
social law as private law, 83-88
Social Legal Thought, 3
Social Manifesto, 375
social market economy, 29, 104, 187, 259, 312
social market law, 42, 324, 353, 355
Social Policy Agreement, 174
social protective welfare state, 57
social rights, 7, 26, 101, 157, 170, 175, 210, 212, 222, 241, 346
social security, 8, 82, 101, 127
social welfare state, 5, 10, 324
socialist theories, 12
societal continuity, 57-58
societal differentiation process, 14
societal efficiency paradigm, 148-151
societal experimentalism, 36, 37
societal private law, 42, 161-162
societal responsibility, 360-364
Société de Législation Comparée, 88
socio-economic background of social justice, 47-48, 163-164
Sonderprivatrecht, 106-111
Soviet Union, 310, 400
Soziale Marktwirtschaft, 104
Spanish Supreme Court, 317
spectateurs engages, 154
standard contract terms, 130-134
state-help principle, 58-59, 81, 100
status and private law, 137-140
statutory paternalism, 114
Stern, Fritz, 193-194
substance in tripartite private law, 285
substance shaping, 364-368
substantive law, 344
substitution in EU law-making, 403-404
sustainable consumption, 362
Sutherland report, 229

technical standards, 249
technolaw, 250, 253
Tenancy (land) Law, 99
Thatcherism, 60, 388
theoretical chance for law enforcement, 2
Thibaut, Anton Friedrich Justus, 97-98
third party fundamental rights, 374
trade unions
  CGPF employers trade union confederation, 82
  CGT trade union, 82
  collective autonomy of, 325
  consumer law and, 64
  in Germany, 105
  growth of, 81
  non-discrimination law and, 141

INDEX   461

transactional responsibility, 323
transformation process
  drivers behind, 395-396
  geometric and relative states, 404-405
  private law justice, 4-7
  rationality test, 258-265, 351-352, 396-398
  social justice, 12-18
transnationalism, 12, 390
treaty amendments, 7, 9
Treaty of Amsterdam, 201, 205, 213, 230, 326
Treaty of Lisbon, 6, 28, 178, 180, 216, 266, 312
Treaty of Maastricht. *see* Maastricht Treaty
Treaty of Nice, 186
Treaty of Rome, 9, 168-169, 177, 180, 201, 203, 213, 222-223, 311
Treaty of Versailles (1919), 13
triangular relations non-discrimination, 374
tripartite balancing, 374
tripartite private law. *see also* European private law
  access and substance, 285
  addressee, 283
  balancing of rights, 286-287
  basic elements, 283-287, 284t
  competencies and responsibilities, 287
  introduction to, 10
  overview, 282
  rights, remedies and procedures, 285-286
  summary of, 386, 392-393
Tuori, K., 192

ubi ius ibi remedium doctrine, 285
UK Labour Law, 141
UK Office of Fair Trading, 65
UK Supreme Court, 136
UN Convention of Human Rights, 301
UN Convention on the Rights of Persons with Disability, 301, 320
unemployment policy, 8
Unfair Contract Terms Act (1977), 64
Unfair Dismissal Act (1972), 60
Unfair Terms Law, 337
universal justice, 54-55

Universal Service Directive (USD) on Telecom, 294
universal service obligations (USOs)
  access and substance, 295-302
  introduction to, 288-291
  order of competence and responsibilities, 310-315
  residence rights and, 307-310
  rights, remedies and procedures, 302-307
  vulnerable persons, 291-295
universalism, 42, 68, 69, 193
universality of social rights, 157
US Environmental Protection Agency, 372
utilitarian pragmatism, 72, 153-156
utilitarianism, 53, 55, 56

van Gerven, Walter, 185, 362
van Lando, Ole, 265
Vienna Congress (1814-1815), 89
Voltaire, 75
vulnerable persons, 291-295, 318

Wasserman, R., 107
Weber, Max, 98, 250, 258, 260, 397
Weiler, Joseph H.H., 163-164, 171
Weimar Constitution, 102, 144
Weimar Republic, 101, 102, 104, 105-106
welfare tourism, 292
welfarism contract law, 129
White Paper on European Governance (2001), 21, 164
White Paper on European Governance (2002), 176, 181, 184, 276
White Paper on the Completion of the Internal Market, 10, 229
White Paper on the Completion of the Single European Market, 8
Wieacker, Franz, 163, 168-169, 194
Wilhelmsson, Th., 362
Wirtschaftsprivatrecht (economic law), 108
women and politics, 14-15
worker-citizen, 361
worker fragmentation, 271-273
World War II Germany, 84

Zimmermann, R., 194
Zugangsgerechtigkeit, 23